FUNDAMENTALS HANDBOOK OF ELECTRICAL AND COMPUTER ENGINEERING

VOLUME III
Computer Hardware, Software, and Applications

Edited by

SHELDON S. L. CHANG, *Fellow, I.E.E.E.*
Department of Electrical Engineering
State University of New York at Stony Brook

A Wiley-Interscience Publication

JOHN WILEY & SONS

New York · Chichester · Brisbane · Toronto · Singapore

Library of Congress Cataloging in Publication Data:

Main entry under title:
Fundamentals handbook of electrical and computer
engineering.

    "A Wiley-Interscience publication."
    Includes index.
    Contents: v. 1. Circuits, fields, and electronics—
v. 2. Communication, control, devices, and systems—
v. 3. Computer hardware, software, and applications.
    1. Electric engineering—Handbooks, manuals, etc.
2. Computer engineering—Handbooks, manuals, etc.
I. Chang, Sheldon S. L.
TK151.F86   621.3   82-4872
ISBN 0-471-86215-0 (v. 1)
ISBN 0-471-86213-4 (v. 2)
ISBN 0-471-86214-2 (v. 3)

Printed in the United States of America

10 9 8 7 6 5 4 3 2 1

To

Bridget

Andrew, Edward, and Ingrid

CONTRIBUTORS

Nikitas A. Alexandridis
Chair of Digital Systems and
  Computer
National Technical University of
  Athens
Athens, Greece

Harold A. Anderson, Jr.
IBM Thomas J. Watson Research
  Center
Yorktown Heights, New York

Gregory R. Andrews
Department of Computer Science
University of Arizona
Tucson, Arizona

David F. Bantz
IBM Thomas J. Watson Research
  Center
Yorktown Heights, New York

G. Campbell
Applied Mathematics Department
Brookhaven National Laboratory
Upton, New York

William C. Carter
IBM Thomas J. Watson Research
  Center
Yorktown Heights, New York

J. Cherniavsky
Computer Science Section
National Science Foundation
Washington, D.C.

K. Ekanadham
IBM Thomas J. Watson Research
  Center
Yorktown Heights, New York

Philip H. Enslow, Jr.
School of Information and Computer
  Science
Georgia Institute of Technology
Atlanta, Georgia

George C. Feth
IBM Thomas J. Watson Research
  Center
Yorktown Heights, New York

Harry C. Forsdick
Bolt, Beranek and Newman, Inc.
Cambridge, Massachusetts

I. Hajj
Department of Electrical Engineering
University of Illinois
Urbana, Illinois

J. Heller
Department of Computer Science
State University of New York
  at Stony Brook

P. Henderson
Department of Computer Science
State University of New York
  at Stony Brook

M. Hofri
Department of Computer Science
Technion, IIT
Haifa, Israel

Yih-chyun Jenq
Bell Telephone Laboratories
Holmdel, New Jersey

Walter J. Kleinfelder
Data Systems Division
IBM Corporation
Poughkeepsie, New York

Gary D. Knott
National Institutes of Health
Division of Computer Research and
    Technology
Bethesda, Maryland

D. Maier
Department of Computer Science and
    Engineering
Oregon Graduate Center
Beaverton, Oregon

Dennis J. McBride
IBM Thomas J. Watson Research
    Center
Yorktown Heights, New York

Charles R. Minter
Interactive Systems, Inc.
Santa Monica, California

Stephen S. Rappaport
Department of Electrical Engineering
State University of New York
    at Stony Brook

Daniel J. Rosenkrantz
Department of Computer Science
State University of New York
    at Albany

Manfred Ruschitzka
Department of Electrical and
    Computer Engineering
University of California
Davis, California

S. Salveter
Mathematics Department
Boston University
Boston, Massachusetts

Richard Schantz
Bolt, Beranek & Newman, Inc.
Cambridge, Massachusetts

F. Schneider
Department of Computer Science
Cornell University
Ithaca, New York

Dominic Seraphin
Computing Center
State University of New York
    at Stony Brook

Arie Shoshani
Lawrence Berkeley Laboratory
Computer Science and Mathematics
    Department
Berkeley, California

Paul Siegel
Paul Siegel Computer Enterprises, Inc.
Hauppauge, New York

Stephen Sussman-Fort
Department of Electrical Engineering
State University of New York
    at Stony Brook

Earl E. Swartzlander, Jr.
TRW Defense Systems Group
Redondo Beach, California

Charles P. Thacker
Xerox Palo Alto Research Center
Palo Alto, California

James E. Thornton
Network Systems Corp.
Brooklyn Park, Minnesota

Kenneth T. Thurber
Architecture Technology Corporation
Minneapolis, Minnesota

Kishor S. Trivedi
Department of Computer Science
Duke University
Durham, North Carolina

Daniel H. Tycko
Technicon Instruments Corp.
Tarrytown, New York

Walter V. Vilkelis
Data Systems Division
IBM Corporation
Poughkeepsie, New York

S. Wecker
Technology Concepts
Sudbury, Massachusetts

PREFACE

The three volumes of this "fundamentals handbook" are designed to meet a need frequently felt by engineers: the need to broaden themselves and to keep up with technological developments so that they can do a better job. In an environment of rapid technological and scientific advance, the importance of keeping up-to-date is self-evident. The importance of not overspecializing is less recognized, but it is there. A versatile engineer is a tremendous asset to an employer in meeting today's changing needs, ways, and means.

These three volumes constitute a coherent, concise treatise of the core areas of electrical and computer engineering with emphasis on system, device, and circuit design. While a handbook of this type is not new in other disciplines—consider *The Handbook of Physics*, for example—it is the first of its kind in electrical engineering. Each volume of *The Handbook of Physics* is devoted to a significant area of research, and a similar handbook of electrical engineering at the same level would be enormous. However, the engineer's job, unlike the phycisist's, is not to search for new engineering principles but to apply existing principles to design and develop new products. The level of these three volumes was determined with this objective in mind.

Volume III gives an integrated treatment of computer hardware and software and two major areas of applications: computer graphics, and computer-aided circuit analysis and design. A dividing line between hardware and software is the instruction set. It defines a computer architecture that can be realized by hardware in many ways with varying cost, speed, and reliability. On the other hand, software packages are designed from the instruction set up. However, a competent designer in either hardware or software must know some aspects of both. The same basic software design principles and techniques are used in computer graphics and computer-aided design. Thus to learn the whole subject takes far less effort than to learn all the subjects separately.

Section 1, computer hardware, covers the full range of computer system capabilities from microprocessors to large mainframe computers. The system structure principles, components, and concepts presented are applicable to both. With the advancement of integrated circuits technology, microprocessors are expanding into system functions that used to be the exclusive domain of large computers. Thus an integrated treatment, as is presented here, is the only forward-looking solution. The section starts with a discussion of aspects of computer architecture. Programming basics are presented to provide motivation for the various instructions that constitute an architecture. Hardware components are then treated individually: the arithmetic logic unit; main memory and high-speed storage; control, timing, and system signals, including microgram control; input/output devices; interfacing; and busing. Engineering topics include logic system realization; reliability, availability, and serviceability; computer power supply; and designing with microprocessors. A glossary is also included. Most of the contributors are from IBM's Thomas J. Watson Research Center, and the section is closely organized.

Section 2 presents software design information that is most useful to electrical and computer engineers: data structures, basic support software and techniques, operating systems, network software, and algorithms. The data structures include array, pointer, stack, linked list, hash tables, symbol tables, tree, and files. Basic operations for each structure type are described. Support software and techniques include languages at various levels, linking and loading, assemblers, compilers, and interpreters. Emphasis is placed on mechanisms basic to all languages and certain common programming techniques. The material on operating systems includes widely used algorithms and techniques as well as newer developments, in particular, kernel systems, hierarchical architectures, and high-level languages—all of which will be keys to future developments with the accelerated use of microprocessors. Central to computer networks is the issue of protocols: the agreements between entities on how communication between them is to take place. Network design considerations, communication, routing, and various protocols are discussed.

Section 3 gives an introduction to computer-aided circuit analysis and design. No attempt is made to provide the details of any particular circuit analysis program. Rather, the basic structure and algorithms common to all analysis and design packages are presented. Topics include input/output specifications, device circuit models and library, circuit equations formulation and solution, sparse matrix techniques, d.c. and transient analysis, sensitivity analysis with Tellegen's theorem, and numerical optimization methods.

Section 4 covers both the hardware and the software aspects of an interactive graphical system. Topics include graphical input/output devices, display controllers, geometric transforms, graphics packages, application programs, and three actual examples of graphics facilities. The material is concisely and clearly presented and has been carefully selected to suit the needs of an electrical engineer who may be designing graphics equipment or using computer graphics to improve circuit and device design.

I am very grateful to Drs. J. G. Truxal, R. W. Lucky, R. E. Miller, and S. S. Director for their many helpful suggestions, to Da Zhong Zheng, Dao Rung Hsu, and Wen Min Pan, Visiting Scholars from the People's Republic of China, for their help and helpful suggestions in the final preparation of the manuscript, and to the section editors and contributors for their help. Many section editors and contributors are leaders in their respective areas of specialization, and their reputations extend far beyond the scope of these three volumes. They contributed because they share a common goal: to help our fellow engineers help themselves, and to share American know-how with the rest of the world in a most effective way.

SHELDON S. L. CHANG

Stony Brook, New York
November 1982

CONTENTS

FUNDAMENTALS HANDBOOK OF ELECTRICAL AND COMPUTER ENGINEERING

SECTION 1

COMPUTER ORGANIZATION AND ARCHITECTURE AND MICROPROCESSOR SYSTEM ENGINEERING

JACK L. ROSENFELD, EDITOR
Computer Sciences Department
IBM Thomas J. Watson Research Center
Yorktown Heights, New York

JAMES E. THORNTON
Network Systems Corp.
Brooklyn Park, Minnisota

DENNIS J. MCBRIDE
Applied Research Department
IBM Thomas J. Watson Research Center
Yorktown Heights, New York

EARL E. SWARTZLANDER, JR.
TRW Defense and Space Systems Group
1 Space Park
Redondo Beach, California

GEORGE C. FETH
IBM Thomas J. Watson Research Center
Yorktown Heights, New York

KISHOR S. TRIVEDI
Department of Computer Science
Duke University
Durham, North Carolina

NIKITAS A. ALEXANDRIDIS
Department of Digital Systems and Computers
National Technical University of Athens
Athens, Greece

DAVID F. BANTZ
Computer Sciences Department
IBM Thomas J. Watson Research Center
Yorktown Heights, New York

KENNETH J. THURBER
Architecture Technology Corp.
Minneapolis, Minnisota

WALTER J. KLEINFELDER
IBM Data Systems Division
Poughkeepsie, New York

WALTER V. VILKELIS
IBM Data Systems Division
Poughkeepsie, New York

WILLIAM C. CARTER
Computer Sciences Department
IBM Thomas J. Watson Research Center
Yorktown Heights, New York

PHILIP H. ENSLOW, JR.
School of Information and Computer Science
Georgia Institute of Technology at Atlanta

This section includes 18 articles on computer technology, design, and use. It is planned to serve those who (1) use computers to solve engineering problems, (2) design interfaces between computers and laboratory equipment or other devices, (3) design computers or parts of computers, (4) apply aspects of computer design to other engineering design problems, or (5) need to expand their knowledge of this important engineering discipline. We hope it will prove to be an indispensable reference for all such engineers, as well as students of computer engineering and computer science.

The full range of computer system capability is covered here, from functional units of microprocessors to collections of large mainframe computers. Stress is placed on microprocessors, in the belief that this handbook will be used most widely by engineers of microprocessor-based systems.

Conventional Computer Organization

Before proceeding to summarize the articles in this section, we pause for a brief discussion of computer organization. The conventional computer organization shown in Fig. 1 is the starting point for most analyses of computers. There are three major blocks: the central processing unit (CPU), main memory, and input-output (I/O). The CPU performs the data processing. It controls the entire computer system. Main memory retains data that have been or will be processed. In all conventional computers, main memory also holds instructions to the CPU: codes that describe the operations to be performed on the data. The input component brings data from devices such as teletypewriter consoles and magnetic tape drives into main memory to be processed; the output component moves results from main memory to devices such as printers and transducers. The instructions are also brought from input devices to main memory. Some devices are used to store data rather than to serve as source input or sink output. These storage devices also transmit data to and from memory via the input/output control component.

The CPU comprises a control unit, an arithmetic-logic unit (ALU), and a number of registers. The control unit generates signals that control the operation of the entire system. The sequence of signals generated depends on what instruction is being executed. The registers are collections of flip-flops that hold control information or data. The ALU performs arithmetic—both for data processing requirements and for determining where required data and instructions can be found.

Memory is organized into words, each with the same number of bits of information and each with its own address. Consecutively executed instructions are normally fetched from consecutive addresses. This normal sequence may be modified by branches in the program. The capability to branch according to observed conditions gives the CPU the ability to do more than simply execute a fixed sequence of instructions. The instructions themselves specify where in memory or registers the operands are to be found. The control unit fetches the operands from their designated locations and stores the results appropriately.

Figure 1 shows paths of data flow and control signals. Data and instructions move from input devices, through input control, and into main memory, all under the direction of the control unit in the CPU. Data words are moved from memory to registers. From there, they may make one or more passes through the ALU and back to the registers before being written back in memory. Results are moved from main memory to output devices. Instructions are brought from main memory into a register before being moved to the control unit for interpretation. The paths drawn with dashed lines in Fig. 1 represent alternative paths found in some computers.

Summary of Articles in This Section

The first articles, on architecture (Secs. 1.1 to 1.3), present a complete discussion of computer architecture—the functional description of a computer's operation—from the point of view of the programmer. A single architecture can be implemented in many ways,

4

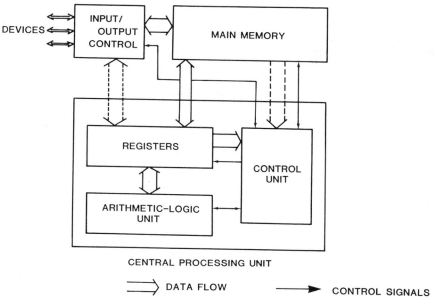

CENTRAL PROCESSING UNIT

DATA FLOW   CONTROL SIGNALS

Fig. 1   Conventional computer organization.

using different technologies. The IBM System/370 is an example of a single architecture that has been implemented in many embodiments. These appear virtually identical to the programmer but have different costs and speeds. The articles discuss how registers and main memory can be addressed, how the instructions manipulate the information in the registers and main memory, how the computer's "interrupt" system permits it to interact with external signals that signify the occurrence of events to which the computer must respond, and how bit-slice organization provides a way to design, from off-the-shelf components, small, high-performance CPUs that are optimum for special applications.

Section 1.4 discusses the preparation of sequences of CPU instructions to carry out specified functions. This article on computer programming is included in this section on computer design because it is important that the hardware designer understand how the computer instructions are used. Section 1.5 describes the design of arithmetic-logic units and how they perform complex operations (e.g., floating-point multiplication) by executing series of simple operations such as addition, under the management of the control unit. Sections 1.6 to 1.8 present the electronic technologies and physical structures used to embody main memory, describe how main memory and attached storage devices are organized and how they can present the user with a "virtual memory" that is larger than the available main memory, and explore the concerns specific to microprocessor systems. A microprocessor is a CPU on a silicon chip. Some require more than one chip, and some include memory and I/O control on the chip. Section 1.9 contains an extensive analysis of control units. A frequently used control unit design uses very regular structures called "microprograms." (These must not be confused with programs for microprocessors, which are almost identical to programs for larger CPUs.)

Sections 1.10 to 1.12 include a general systems description of I/O: the interface among devices, controller, main memory, and CPU, and the interchange of control signals that takes place during an I/O operation. The technology of attached storage devices and techniques used for I/O in microprocessor systems are also analyzed. Section 1.13 describes buses, cables carrying data and control signals between (and within) components of a computer. Alternative busing strategies are analyzed in this article. Section 1.14 views the problems faced by logic designers (e.g., partitioning, packaging, and testing). Section 1.15 presents methods for introducing improved RAS (reliability, availability, and serviceability) and fault tolerance into computer systems. Special architectures that differ from the conventional computer organization are analyzed in Sec. 1.16. Section 1.17 deals with powering computer systems, and Sec. 1.18 discusses techniques for designing microprocessor-based systems and the tools available for developing them.

A glossary and section on sources of information follow.

1.1   ARCHITECTURE: REGISTERS, ADDRESSING, AND INSTRUCTIONS

James E. Thornton

1.1.1   Background

A computer architecture must be defined independently of any specific implementation, since there are often several different implementations over a period of time. There are numerous ways to view an architecture, ranging from user application programs written in a high-level language to specific instruction sets, including those privileged ones used by the operating system. We choose the latter for this description. In order to provide enough understanding of how the architecture works, reference will be made to some implementation detail and occasionally to some alternative implementations.

During execution, a program views the architecture as a set of *registers*, a main memory with various *addressing modes*, and a processing unit *instruction set* (see the introduction to this section for a summary of computer organization). For very simple machines, there may be no privileged instructions or addressing modes. The machine executes a specific program for which all the resources of the machine are available (i.e., the entire main memory). For machines that are shared by many programs operating one at a time (multiprogramming), the architecture needs to provide privileged facilities for allocating and managing resources.

1.1.2   Registers and Local Memory

One distinguishing feature of a computer architecture is the register structure of the central processing unit. A register is a group of flip-flops or latches operating together to temporarily store data or control information.

All operations in a computer system result in modifications of bits in registers or main memory. An instruction may cause one or more operations to take place, generally in a specific sequence. At the completion of each instruction, the information stored in registers and main memory is available for subsequent instructions or other access.

Some processors make use of a single register for temporarily storing data. This register is typically called the *accumulator* (see Fig. 1). It operates in conjunction with the arithmetic-logic unit (ALU) component of the processing unit. The accumulator can, for example, receive a number from main memory and add it to the one already stored in it, clear its contents, and transfer its contents to main memory, among other properties. Most arithmetic operations store the results in the accumulator. In conjunction with the accumulator, an additional register is often used in order to implement multiply and divide operations. These operations usually require the additional register to hold partial results during the iterative execution of the instruction. This register has been called the Q register or the M–Q register since it holds the multiplier or quotient.

The length of the accumulator and other registers used to store data is determined by the largest number to be held or processed. Since a fraction can be infinitely long, the choice of length is arbitrary. The choice sets the maximum integer size and determines the precision of the central processing unit. (See Sec. 1.4.6 for a discussion of scaling, which enables larger integers to be represented.) The relationship of the length of the accumulator to the length of a memory word is subject to varying implementation choices. The architecture defines data types (see later discussion) which may be shorter in length than a memory word or, alternatively, may require more than one memory word. For simplicity we may think of the accumulator length and memory word length as equal, but this is not necessary. The accumulator and memory, in any event, must accommodate the data types defined by the architecture.

Other registers are also utilized to store control information in the processing unit. These are generally not "visible" to the architecture, but are described here to provide a description of execution of instructions. The implementation of these control registers may vary. The principal one is the *instruction counter* which holds the main-memory address of the current instruction being executed. To begin a program, this register is set to the location of the first instruction in the program either by an operator in a simple system or by the operating system. Subsequently, the register is incremented during the normal course of execution of each instruction and in preparation for obtaining the next instruction from main memory. Each instruction is brought from main memory into the processing unit and resides in a register (the instruction register) during the course of instruction execution.

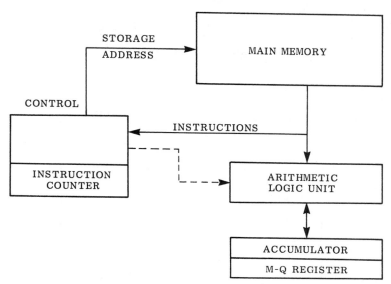

Fig. 1   Simple register configuration.

In general, an instruction set may include instructions of different lengths, for reasons to be explained later. The length in bits of an instruction is often a multiple of the length of a memory word, since efficiency in storing programs in memory is a major objective.

The execution of a single instruction (see also Sec. 1.9.1) involves a number of elementary steps, such as:

Increment instruction counter.

Read next instruction from main memory.

Interpret the instruction.

Read operand (if required).

Perform the arithmetic function.

Store result (if required). (In branch-type instructions, the result may be a modification of the contents of the instruction counter.)

The accumulator represents all that is necessary to describe the registers of a simple architecture. The instruction set for such an architecture can also be quite simple. In general, an instruction will contain the function code, identifying the function to be performed, and an address of main memory. The address may refer to data to be fetched or stored or to a new location for the next instruction.

If main-memory access time were as rapid as that of registers, there would perhaps be no need to create a more complex architecture. Instructions would then execute as rapidly with operands from main memory as they do with operands from intimately located high-speed registers. However, historically, this factor plus other ease-of-use factors have combined to generate more registers and more architectural structure.

For instance, in the matter of addressing main memory for data, it is convenient to hold an index to be added to the base address of an array of data. The index provides a means to traverse the array without modifying the base address. In this case a more complex instruction may be added to the instruction set, or a program loop using simple instructions may be used. In either case the instruction itself now must contain some reference to the index register. In Fig. 2 the instruction contains three fields: identifying the function to be executed, the register containing the base address, and the register containing the index (in general, there may be more than one).

An architecture may utilize multiple base registers and multiple index registers for program efficiency or ease of use. For example, with only one base register, this may require reloading from main memory often to deal with multiple arrays of data. While this gets back to the implementation question of why registers are required at all, the architecture has been adjusted or enlarged to accommodate implementation efficiency. At this point, it is convenient to refer to the multiple index and base registers (as well as other registers used to store data) as a *local memory*. Local memory may be any size, and a field (or fields) of some instructions is used to refer to the desired word, just as a

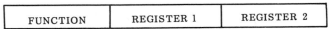

FUNCTION	REGISTER 1	REGISTER 2

Fig. 2   Instruction format.

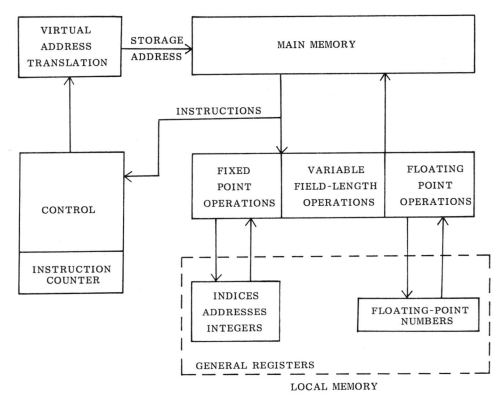

Fig. 3   General register configuration.

field in an instruction may refer to main memory. Figure 3 is descriptive of the local memory of the IBM System/370. For clarity, these registers are shown in two groups, one for indices, integers, and addresses, the other for floating-point numbers. These two groups may contain registers of different length, but this is not necessary. The arithmetic-logic unit utilizes the integer group of registers for fixed-point operations and the other register group for floating-point operations. In general, variable-field-length operations make references to main memory for data types that do not have a fixed length, such as alphanumeric text.

The registers remain an area where the user program can be entirely free of interaction with the operating system. If a user program is interrupted, the contents of these registers are stored in main memory and reloaded when the program is restarted. The operating system may be required to assist in saving the registers, although the instruction counter must be saved. Interaction with main memory, on the other hand, is subject to operating system control over the physical location and protection of a main memory word. In Fig. 3 a virtual address translation is shown as one means of accomplishing this control. This is discussed in detail in a later section.

At this point, the nature of the information being stored or processed is not being examined. This is treated in sections that follow on the instruction set and data types.

1.1.3 Addressing

Increasing complexity of the central processing unit instruction set derives in a major way from the methods employed in addressing main memory and local memory. The address may be carried directly in the instruction or may be constructed by references to local memory registers. Instructions may reference more than one address; however, we treat first the concepts of addressing memory and then the modes by which the addresses are constructed.

Main Memory

Traditional methods of addressing main memory use an address that identifies a specific word in real memory. (Reference is made to "real" memory here to differentiate from "virtual" memory, which is discussed later.) Differences in the implementation of main memory may require fetching or storing a portion of a memory word or more than one memory word, depending on the data type called for in the instruction. The architecture does not view these implementation details.

Space in main memory may be allocated by the operating system (if there is one) for the user's program. In computers that do not employ virtual addressing, the user is not allowed to make memory references outside that allocated space. Such space is usually allocated in contiguous blocks.

Multiprogramming (jobs sharing memory, executing one at a time) requires that independent blocks of addresses be allocated to each program. As this complexity has grown, the user program has deferred to the operating system to make space available and to protect it from other programs coresident in main memory. In central processing units that do not employ virtual addressing, programs that require more space may be halted until more contiguous space is available for assignment. This operation may also entail relocation of blocks to utilize "holes" left in the address space by departing programs. Much of this difficulty is removed by simply having enough real main memory. Technology has responded admirably to this need over the years. Another reduction of difficulty would be to return to "monoprogramming" in the computer and relegate the problem to secondary storage only.

Virtual Memory.* The concept of virtual memory entirely separates the real address space from the user program address space. The user program may assume that it has nearly unlimited space available, limited only by the maximum address that can be generated using the instruction set address fields and index and address registers. These fields and register lengths have expanded gradually over time, with a few architectures employing truly "single-level" storage of essentially unlimited space. These require very long addresses, one example being 48 bits. Earlier virtual storage address fields of 24 bits and even less place upper limits on the space available to the user program.

The virtual memory concept is built on a system of fixed blocks of contiguous real memory locations called *page frames*. The program or its data may be stored in main memory by assigning it a number of independent page frames. The page frames are more or less arbitrarily located, and only the locations within each page frame must be contiguous in the real address realm (see Fig. 4). Page sizes are fixed (usually ranging from 512 to 4096 8-bit bytes) and may not overlap when stored in main memory or secondary storage. Pages from virtual address space containing programs and data are loaded by the operating system by locating them in secondary storage and moving them to main memory. On initially loading a program, page frames are assigned to it by the operating system, utilizing a table of the available page frames. As the program executes and calls for virtual addresses not yet loaded, it will be halted on each such memory reference while the operating system brings the appropriate page into main memory from secondary storage. If all page frames in main memory are in use, the operating system must also remove pages to allow new ones in. For this purpose, typically the page removed is the one least recently used.

The virtual address map (or page table) is typically held in a protected area of main memory. The virtual address translation unit (Fig. 3) may also include a small associative memory which contains most recently used entries in the page table.

A virtual address is made up of a page address and a byte identifier, as shown in Fig. 4. The page address is translated to the real page address obtained from the page table (see also Sec. 1.7.1).

The effects of the translation of the virtual address to the real address are both good and bad. There is, for example, a cost in time to locate the correct map entry. This can be minimized by holding recently referenced entries in the virtual address translation unit. Following references to the same page are likely to find the entry still there. A further penalty occurs when the capacity of main memory is approached and pages must be swapped out to secondary storage. The normal swapping of pages can degenerate to a condition called "thrashing," when each independent program has been reduced to too few assigned page frames in main memory. Thus each time a program is restarted, it quickly references a page that has been swapped out. This ripples on to the next program, and so on. On the positive side, numerous benefits accrue to user programs, which need not be restricted in address space, and to the operating system, which can more effectively allocate and manage main memory as well as secondary storage. The system need not require large contiguous blocks of main memory to accommodate entire user programs. Only those pages actually needed by the program are fetched.

---

*More detailed aspects of virtual memories are presented in Sec. 1.7.1.

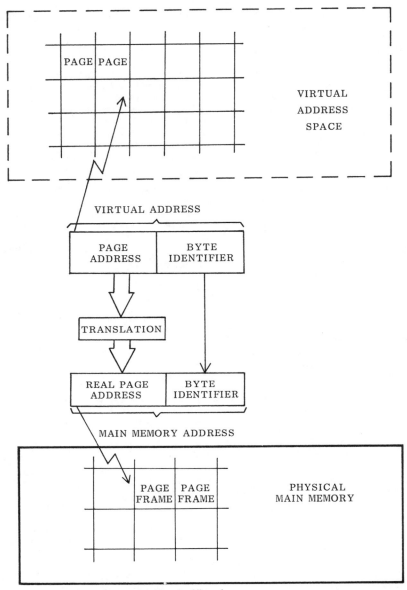

Fig. 4   Virtual memory.

Segments*

Program and data areas are generally larger than a single page. It is convenient in some systems to deal with these larger groups of stored information in an ordered way within the virtual addressing system. The reasons may derive from the way pages are stored in secondary storage (it may be convenient to transfer multiple pages) or from the usefulness of a higher-level organization of virtual address space by the user.

A *segment* is merely a collection of contiguous pages in virtual address space. The virtual address translation still deals with pages, and there is no need for the pages to occupy contiguous page frames

*See also Sec. 1.7.1.

VIRTUAL ADDRESS

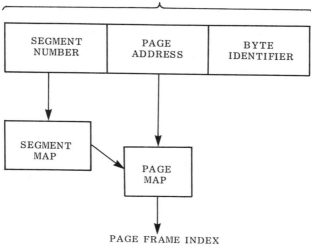

PAGE FRAME INDEX

Fig. 5 Segment addressing.

in main memory. If the virtual address is subdivided as in Fig. 5 to include a segment number, this provides a kind of two-level addressing. A segment map is searched first. On a match, the proper page map is identified for the page address search. Segmenting allows the operating system to control access to the more natural segment rather than each page, on the basis that segments are entire programs or data sets.

To summarize the virtual addressing schemes, a number of benefits accrue to the programmer and system designer. Transfers of pages between main memory and secondary storage are hidden from the application program, allowing the program to run on a variety of system configurations or utilizing a variable amount of main memory. The operating system allocates main memory space in fixed increments and overlaps transfers between storage levels.

Local Memory

Registers making up local memory are either explicitly defined, such as the accumulator, or belong to a set of general registers. Addressing these registers is accomplished by certain fields within each instruction. In instruction sets with multiple addresses per instruction, each address requires an address field. The number of registers is thus limited by the size of the address field. A 4-bit field, for example, will address 16 general registers.

The general register organization is something of a compromise between single-address instructions and multiple-address instructions with full address fields. It avoids some of the extra instructions necessary for shuffling data, inherent in a single-address organization, yet it does not take space in the instruction for a full additional main-memory address. In contrast, shorter instructions can be used in which multiple addresses need only enough address bits to reference the local memory.

Addressing Modes

There are a variety of useful ways to construct an address. These derive from the ease of use factors that have historically evolved in computer architecture. They also represent compromises in allocating fields of bits within an instruction. For example, it would be grossly inefficient to always carry full address fields, even in single-address instruction sets. Therefore, judicious use of general registers and local memory addressing to produce main memory addresses is preferable.

Base Register. Any of the general registers in local memory may be assigned as a base register. One convenient use of a base register is to point to a main-memory location representing the beginning of an array of data or a table. After initially loading the base register, subsequent instructions may construct main-memory addresses by adding a positive integer to the contents of the base register. The positive integer may be supplied directly from a field of bits in the instruction or from another local memory word. When supplied from the instruction, this mode of addressing is referred to as *base-displacement addressing.* When supplied from local memory, the positive integer is normally considered an index. Remember that the resulting address is still only the logical address (or the virtual address for architectures utilizing virtual memory). This must undergo further translation, as required by the operating system, to the real main-memory address.

Accesses to several large arrays may take significant time if the base address has to be loaded each time. Therefore, it is convenient to maintain several base registers in those cases. For example, a move of data may use a base register for the beginning address of the source and another base register for the beginning address of the destination. An alternative is a single base register and two displacements.

Indexing. A base address may be indexed by another general register in constructing the main-memory address. In the case of a data move, the index is added to the source base address to obtain the first source word. The index is then added to the destination base address to obtain the first destination word. Following these two steps, the general register containing the index is incremented by a quantity equal to the word length, and the steps are repeated until the index reaches the length of the data field to be moved. This indexing operation would normally be executed in a program loop containing explicit instructions for constructing the memory addresses, reading, storing, incrementing the index, and either returning to the beginning or terminating the loop. As discussed in Sec. 1.1.5, this may require four to eight instructions.

This illustrates the value of an index for efficiency and for ease of use. The index serves the purpose of advancing the source and destination addresses in step as well as providing a test against the desired length.

Arrays in two dimensions may be addressed in a similar manner using two independent indices. The horizontal index is incremented a word at a time, with the assumption that the second row begins immediately following the last word of the first row as far as main memory is concerned. In the vertical direction, the index is incremented by a quantity equal to the length of a row. The indexing operation terminates at the end of either the row or the column.

The use of index registers in machines with simple instruction sets permits general treatment of such data types as vectors, arrays, and strings. Computer architectures may include complex instructions that apply to operations on entire vectors or arrays. These would implement entire loops, such as those above, in a single instruction, including the indexing, incrementing, terminating, and arithmetic function on the array.

Relative Addressing. Another form of constructing a main-memory address is relative addressing. This has some similarity to the base-displacement method. A positive or negative integer is carried in the instruction identifying a memory location in relation to the location of the current instruction. The integer is similar to the displacement field, except that it can be positive or negative. Rather than a general register for the base, the instruction counter is used. Thus an address can be calculated relative to the current instruction's address in main memory. This type of addressing generally does not count forward or backward by instruction but rather by memory word.

The principal value of relative addressing is for small displacement fields in the instruction, to conserve wasted instruction space. This makes it useful only in limited ranges of addresses. It is also complicated for hand assembly and debugging.

Indirect Addressing. In indirect addressing, the main-memory address is first calculated using any of the methods previously described. Under control of a single bit carried in the instruction, this address is used to read another address from main memory. This new address is the "indirect" address actually used by the instruction. Each time an indirect address step is taken, it requires an additional main-memory reference.

Through indirect addressing under the control of a single bit in the instruction, a larger block of seldom used base addresses can be kept in main memory, for example. Other innovative uses can be made, including some schemes that allow multiple levels of indirection. In these cases, a bit is carried in the main memory word, together with the address it contains, identifying whether another level exists. One can construct decision trees in this manner.

Stack. A contrasting method of addressing main memory or local memory, especially for inter-mediate results, is the use of a *pushdown stack.** These are generally employed instead of general registers and local memory. The stack operates as a last-in-first-out storage. A program may place intermediate results or input data into the stack without regard to the number of operands. They are simply pushed down as needed. Arithmetic operations may be executed on the last value in the stack (the top of the stack), with the intermediate result left there or removed to an explicit address in main memory.

---

*The use of a pushdown stack to save status upon interruption or subroutine entry is discussed in Sec. 1.4.8.

A stack is a useful concept for computing expressions with variable numbers of operands and operators. This is quite different from the general register approach, in which the general registers are explicitly addressed by the instruction. Methods are available by which the correct intermediate result will arrive at the top of the stack in the correct order for solving the expression. The competitive issue between a stack architecture and a general register architecture reduces to the relative difficulty of managing the assignment of general registers versus the difficulty of maintaining the proper order of operands in the stack. Most user programs depend on the compiler to handle these problems.

Protection / Relocation

In a multiprogramming environment, there is a need to prevent one program from making references to main memory at addresses assigned to another program. The means to accomplish this are not visible to the user program but are under the control of the operating system. A primitive and inefficient means would be to carry a protection bit with each word in main storage. This permits two independent programs or groups of programs to be protected from each other.

A more general means to provide protection is to control access to entire program segments and data areas on a program-by-program basis. In an architecture that does not employ virtual storage addressing, this protection is generally applied to blocks of contiguous main-memory addresses. A user program requests a block of addresses from the operating system. In loading a user program, the operating system uses two control registers: a relocation register and a protection register. The contents of these registers represent the boundary addresses for the contiguous space assigned to the program. The registers are loaded by the operating system whenever the program is to be activated.

The user program is written as though its origin were location 0. The relocation register specifies the actual location of the user, and the protection register specifies the number of words allowed or the upper boundary address. To accomplish this, all storage addresses for main memory will be added to the contents of the relocation register and tested against the protection register. This function takes the same position in the central processing unit as the virtual translation unit does in a machine with virtual memory.

For an architecture employing virtual storage addressing, the relocation and protection function applies to pages rather than entire program segments and data fields. Each page is relocated independently, and each page may be protected independently. The relocation occurs simply by the translation from virtual to real address, as explained earlier. The virtual map containing the virtual address and its current real address may also be used to provide protection. To do this, each virtual map entry also contains a field of bits defined as a *lock*. In loading a page into main memory, the operating system assigns the lock bits. Thereafter, each program is provided with a key or set of keys which are loaded into a control register by the operating system in preparation for the program to be activated. One key must match the lock for every storage address being translated; otherwise, an abort occurs. An abort of this kind returns control to the operating system for action to be taken following an attempted unauthorized access. Each key may also be assigned a particular form of restriction; for example:

1. No restriction.
2. Read only as data.
3. Read only as program.
4. Write.

This fairly elegant type of protection allows many user programs to access main memory in a well-protected but flexible way. The operating system would, of course, be provided with a master key and would have a special key controlling its main memory usage. For architectures that do not employ virtual addressing, the entire contiguous block of addresses can be protected implicitly by not allowing accesses beyond the upper boundary.

1.1.4   Data Representations

An architecture must generally deal with a variety of data types, including numeric and nonnumeric data. The range of possible data types includes:

Bit	Integer
Bit string	Multiple-precision integer
Byte	Floating-point number
Byte string	Single precision
Character	Double Precision
Character string	Vector
Decimal digit	Array
Decimal number	

The bit and bit string data types are identified with control and decision functions and may not be directly viewed by the architecture. However, the instruction set may have the capability to directly address to the bit level and may contain bit processing instructions, or it may require manipulation, such as shifting a data word left or right to bring a specific bit or bit string into alignment for processing.

The byte and character types are related in that they are interchangeable in some architectures. A byte is usually 8 bits in length and contains alphanumeric data, one symbol per byte. Characters have generally been in 6-bit lengths. Since characters may be stored or transmitted in 6-, 7-, or 8-bit formats, there is some variety to deal with. In general, a character set is intended to represent all of the symbols used to display, print, read, or store words or numbers, plus a collection of control characters used to control a variety of functions related to the human–machine interface. This printed page, for example, can be represented by a long string of characters which, if the page were printed by an automatic typewriter, would include characters for the spaces between words and carriage returns where needed. It should be noted that the 8-bit character representation allows more symbols to be added to the character set to account for advancing technology in the display and printing area. Two standards exist for interchange codes and specify the byte or character code representation: the ASCII (American Standard Code for Information Interchange) and EBCDIC (Extended Binary Coded Decimal Interchange Code).

Decimal numbers are a subset of the full character set, as represented in the 8-bit coded format. However, they may also be packed two to an 8-bit byte and treated separately from the character-handling logic. Decimal numbers are represented as sign-magnitude, as seen in the example in Fig. 6. Other representations are possible; this one is in use in the IBM System/370. The 4-bit sign representation is in the rightmost 4 bits of the rightmost byte of the field. The leftmost 4 bits of the rightmost byte contain the least significant digit of the number. This is convenient in implementations that execute decimal arithmetic a byte at a time. The sign is delivered to the ALU first, followed by the least significant digit, and so on.

Integers are stored as a sign bit and n bits of integer, generally limited to the length of a general register. There are three common methods of representing integers: the 1's- and 2's-complement notations and the sign-magnitude notation (see Sec. 1.5.4 for definitions of these notations). Integers are normally treated as fixed-point quantities with the radix point assumed just to the right of the least significant digit. In decimal arithmetic, the radix point is the decimal point.

Floating-point numbers take the form of a signed mantissa and a signed exponent, as in Fig. 7. Not all architectures handle floating-point numbers, just as some do not directly handle decimal numbers, character strings, and so on. For a fixed word size, machines have a much wider range of representable numbers using floating-point representation than fixed point unless the numbers are scaled using a scaling algorithm, which effectively moves the radix point. A floating-point number can be expressed as mr^e, where m is the mantissa, r the radix, and e the exponent. Normally, the radix of the exponent is 2; however, some representations (IBM/370) use a higher radix in order to extend the number range. The mantissa is normally represented as a fraction with the radix point at the left end. Conversion from floating-point to integer form therefore requires realignment of the mantissa to shift the radix point to the right of the least significant digit.

Single-precision floating-point representations occupy one word in most common practice. Since floating-point operations generate results exceeding a single word size, the mantissa is generally normalized for single-precision computation. This means that the mantissa is shifted to the left as far as possible, eliminating any leading zeros, with an appropriate reduction in the value of the exponent. Any remaining bits of the mantissa to the right of the word are lost. In some "overflow" cases, a right

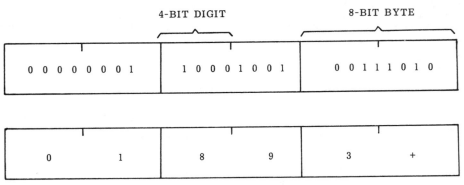

Fig. 6   Packed decimal format.

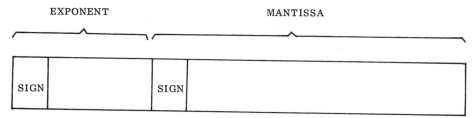

Fig. 7   Floating-point number.

shift is required. In multiple-precision computation, extra words are used to capture more significant bits of the results of floating-point operations. The representation of such numbers includes a signed exponent and signed mantissa for the word retained. Alternatively, the least significant bits of the mantissa could take up an entire word without the need for another exponent.

A *vector* is an ordered sequence of scalar numbers. Each floating-point scalar number is represented in the same manner as a floating-point number discussed above. Vectors are stored in main memory as a contiguous sequence of data words. A two-dimensional array can be represented in a linear fashion by a vector in which each row of the array follows immediately in sequence with the previous row. In accessing the array in the vertical, or column, direction the sequence of addresses is indexed by an integer equal to the length of a row. Vectors and arrays are treated in some architectures with complex instructions. In the more traditional architectures, they are handled by programs.

1.1.5   Instructions

The instruction set of the processing unit can range from very simple to very complex. Complexity is greater in architectures that are designed for greater specialization or ease of use to the programmer (or language compiler). We deal with the instruction set as viewed by the user programmer and the system programmer, although it should be understood that the two instruction sets could be grossly different. Conventional architectures add certain privileged instructions or properties to the basic set for the use of the systems programmer.

Two instruction sets are discussed here and are depicted in Figs. 8 and 9. The first is a simple instruction set used in the central processing unit of the Control Data 6600 (CYBER) [1-3]. The second is the more complex instruction set used in the IBM System/370 [4].

Formats

It is convenient to organize the instruction set into classes by format. The CYBER formats are shown in Fig. 10. Instructions are either 15 or 30 bits in length and are packed in the 60-bit main-memory word. A 30-bit instruction may not cross word boundaries. The 15-bit instructions are three-address register transfer types which identify two source registers and a destination register. There are three separate sets of general registers in this architecture. They are *address*, *integer*, and *floating-point* registers. The 30-bit format contains an 18-bit immediate field which may be a source operand, as noted in the instruction set.

The System/370 formats are shown in Fig. 11. There are six basic instruction formats which require from one to three half-words. (A half-word is 16-bits or 2 bytes.) This architecture is two-address in general. The RR format provides for register transfer instructions in local memory as well as more complex instructions which make use of additional general registers. In addressing main memory, the address is contained in a register designated by the R field in the instruction or is calculated from the following three binary numbers:

1. *Base address* is a 24-bit number contained in a general register specified by the 4-bit field, called the B field, in the instruction.
2. *Index* is a 24-bit number contained in a general register designated in a 4-bit field, called the X field, in the instruction.
3. *Displacement* is a 12-bit number contained in a field, called the D field, in the instruction.

Types (CYBER)

In the following subsections, the instruction set is classified by function as opposed to addressing method, data type, or format. The simpler CYBER instruction set is treated first, with selected

00	STOP	40	FLOATING PROD Xj × Xk → Xi
010	RETURN JUMP	41	ROUND FLT PROD Xj × Xk → Xi
011	READ ECS (Bj + K) WORDS FROM XO	42	FLT DP PROD Xj × Xk → Xi
012	WRITE ECS	43	FORM jK MASK IN Xi
02	GO TO K + Bi	44	FLT DIVIDE Xj by Xk → Xi
03	GO TO K if Xj (ZR, NZ, etc.)	45	ROUND FLT DIVIDE
04	GO TO K if Bi = Bj	46	
05	Bi ≠ Bj	47	SUM OF 1s in Xk → Xi
06	Bi ≥ Bj		
07	Bi < Bj		
10	Xj → Xi	50	Aj + K → Ai
11	Xj AND Xk → Xi	51	Bj + K → Ai
12	Xi OR Xk → Xi	52	Xj + K → Ai
13	Xi ⊕ Xk → Xi	53	Xj + Bk → Ai
14	X̄k → Xi	54	Aj + Bk → Ai
15	X̄k AND Xj → Xi	55	Aj − Bk → Ai
16	X̄k OR Xj → Xi	56	Bj + Bk → Ai
17	X̄k ⊕ Xj → Xi	57	Bj − Bk → Ai
20	SHIFT Xi L jk places → Xi	60	Aj + K → Bi
21	SHIFT Xi R jk places → Xi	61	Bj + K → Bi
22	SHIFT Xk L Bj places → Xi	62	Xj + K → Bi
23	SHIFT Xk R Bj places → Xi	63	Xj + Bk → Bi
24	NORMALIZE Xk in Xi; CT → Bj	64	Aj + Bk → Bi
25	ROUND & NORMALIZE	65	Aj − Bk → Bi
26	UNPACK Xk → Xi; EXP → Bj	66	Bj + Bk → Bi
27	PACK Xk & Bj → Xi	67	Bj − Bk → Bi
30	FLOATING ADD Xj + Xk → Xi	70	Aj + K → Xi
31	FLOATING SUBT Xj + Xk → Xi	71	Bj + K → Xi
32	FLOATING DP ADD Xj + Xk → Xi	72	Xj + K → Xi
33	FLOATING DP SUBT Xj + Xk → Xi	73	Xj + Bk → Xi
34	ROUND FLT ADD Xj + Xk → Xi	74	Aj + Bk → Xi
35	ROUND FLT SUBT Xj + Xk → Xi	75	Aj − Bk → Xi
36	INTEGER Xj + Xk → Xi	76	Bj + Bk → Xi
37	INTEGER Xj − Xk → Xi	77	Bj − Bk → Xi

Fig. 8   CYBER instruction set.

instructions from System/370. (For more comprehensive explanation, see the Principles of Operations manuals for these machines.)

Data Manipulation.   The CYBER architecture provides main memory references for *LOAD* and *STORE* through the use of specified address (A) registers as shown in Fig. 12. The eight instructions that define an A register as the destination (codes 50–57), calculate the main memory address, which, when it is entered into the A register, initiates the memory reference. Five A registers (A_1–A_5) are assigned to the LOAD function and will cause a main memory word to be loaded into the corresponding X register (X_1–X_5). Two A registers (A_6 and A_7) are assigned to the STORE function and will cause a word to be stored in main memory from the corresponding X register (X_6 and X_7). A LOAD or STORE address can thus be calculated by base-displacement methods, indexing, or direct address. (The reason for several registers is that, for some models of CYBER, a number of main memory references can be executed in parallel. An architectural benefit of retaining key addresses is also a reason.)

The CYBER architecture also contains a group of instructions (10–17) which perform *LOGICAL* manipulation of binary data. These instructions relate data in two registers on a bit-by-bit basis, transferring the result to a third register. Such operations as AND, OR, and exclusive OR are provided. These are useful for masking, merging, and selecting data contained within one 60-bit word.

In CYBER, binary arithmetic instructions on *INTEGERS* can be executed with results transferred to any of the 24 general registers. Data representation is in 1's-complement form, as described in Sec. 1.5.4. The 50 through 77 series of instructions operate on integers of 18 bits in length (sign is extended in the 60-bit X registers). Two instructions (36 and 37) provide integer add and subtract on 60-bit numbers.

STANDARD INSTRUCTION SET

ADD	MOVE
ADD LOGICAL	MOVE NUMERICS
AND	MOVE WITH OFFSET
BRANCH AND LINK	MOVE ZONES
BRANCH ON CONDITION	MULTIPLY
BRANCH ON COUNT	OR
BRANCH ON INDEX HIGH	PACK
BRANCH ON INDEX LOW OR EQUAL	SET CLOCK
CLEAR I/O	SET PROGRAM MASK
COMPARE	SET STORAGE KEY
COMPARE LOGICAL	SET SYSTEM MASK
COMPARE LOGICAL CHARACTERS	SHIFT LEFT
UNDER MASK	SHIFT LEFT LOGICAL
CONVERT TO BINARY	SHIFT RIGHT
CONVERT TO DECIMAL	SHIFT RIGHT LOGICAL
DIAGNOSE	START I/O
DIVIDE	START I/O FAST RELEASE
EXCLUSIVE OR	STORE
EXECUTE	STORE CHANNEL ID
HALT DEVICE	STORE CHARACTERS UNDER MASK
HALT I/O	STORE CLOCK
INSERT CHARACTER	STORE CONTROL
INSERT CHARACTERS UNDER MASK	STORE CPUID
INSERT STORAGE KEY	STORE MULTIPLE
LOAD	SUBTRACT
LOAD ADDRESS	SUBTRACT LOGICAL
LOAD AND TEST	SUPERVISOR CALL
LOAD COMPLEMENT	TEST AND SET
LOAD CONTROL	TEST CHANNEL
LOAD MULTIPLE	TEST I/O
LOAD NEGATIVE	TEST UNDER MASK
LOAD POSITIVE	TRANSLATE
LOAD PSW	TRANSLATE AND TEST
MONITOR CALL	UNPACK

FLOATING-POINT INSTRUCTIONS   DECIMAL-INSTRUCTIONS

ADD NORMALIZED	ADD DECIMAL
ADD UNNORMALIZED	COMPARE DECIMAL
COMPARE	DIVIDE DECIMAL
DIVIDE	EDIT
HALVE	EDIT AND MARK
LOAD	MULTIPLY DECIMAL
LOAD AND TEST	SHIFT AND ROUND DECIMAL
LOAD COMPLEMENT	SUBTRACT DECIMAL
LOAD NEGATIVE	ZERO AND ADD
LOAD POSITIVE	
MULTIPLY	
STORE	
SUBTRACT NORMALIZED	
SUBTRACT UNNORMALIZED	

Fig. 9 IBM System/370 instruction set.

Four arithmetic operations can be performed on *FLOATING-POINT* numbers with single and double precision and with results unrounded or rounded. There are floating ADD, SUBTRACT, MULTIPLY, and DIVIDE (double-precision excluded on divide). The execution of add and subtract (see Sec. 1.5.5) requires an alignment of the mantissas first. This is accomplished by comparing exponents, following which the mantissa of the operand having the smaller exponent is effectively shifted to the right the number of bits corresponding to the difference in exponents, prior to the add or subtract.

The floating-point add, subtract, and multiply instructions may produce result mantissas up to twice the length of the source operands' mantissas. This is handled in the CYBER architecture by

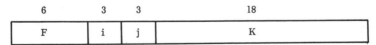

Fig. 10   CYBER instruction formats.

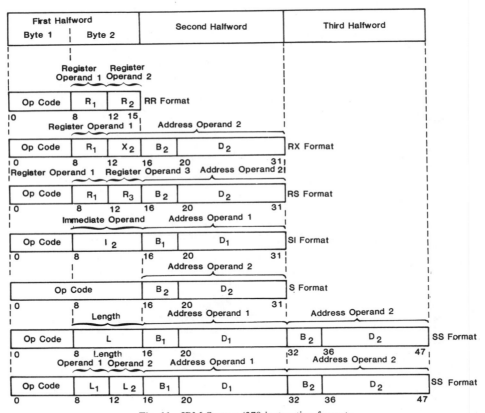

Fig. 11   IBM System/370 instruction formats.

unnormalized instructions which separately compute the two halves of the result. A normalized result is one in which the mantissa is positioned with its most significant nonzero digit shifted to the far left. In multiple-precision floating-point arithmetic, this shifting is not done, thereby retaining leading zeros and increasing precision. Single-precision floating-point instructions can optionally round the result.

Finally, the CYBER instruction set includes a set of SHIFT instructions (20–23). A 60-bit word in one of the X registers may be shifted left or right by a quantity contained in the j and k fields of the instruction. The left shift is circular with the leftmost bit returned to the rightmost bit location for each bit shifted. The right shift does not recirculate but allows the rightmost bit to be dropped for

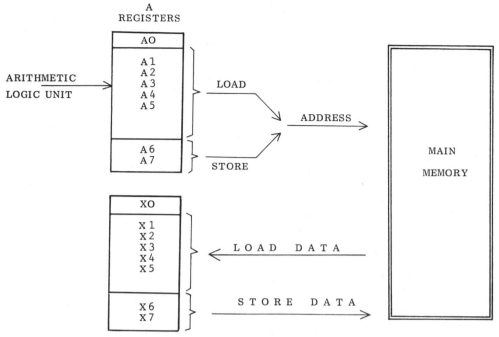

Fig. 12 CYBER load and store.

each bit shifted. Also on right shift, the sign bit is retained and also shifted right, effectively retaining the proper sign of the number being shifted. A quantity in a selected X register may also be shifted left or right by an amount contained in a B register. This is useful for scaling and for realigning unpacked floating-point numbers. The pack and unpack instructions (26 and 27) utilize an X register for mantissa and a B register for exponent with an X register for the packed floating-point number. An X register floating-point quantity may also be normalized and optionally rounded. The normalize operation shifts the mantissa left until the most significant nonzero bit is positioned to the leftmost bit location of the mantissa. Each bit shift is accompanied by a reduction of the exponent, and the count of the number of bits shifted is placed in a B register.

Although the CYBER instruction set is simpler than the IBM System/370, many of the same kinds of instructions as those described above are found in both. In Sec. 1.1.5 a set of variable-field-length instructions is described which also comes under the category of data manipulation, but these are not present in the CYBER architecture.

Instruction Sequencing.   A program proceeds in sequence until a jump is encountered or until an interrupt occurs. In the latter case, the sequence is not modified but the program will not be resumed until the interrupt is processed. Most machines allow interruptions to occur following completion of an instruction. The interrupt may be generated by an internal fault condition or an external condition requiring the operating system to respond. Control is therefore returned to a predetermined location in the operating system program. The operating system is then obliged to place the interrupted program in a state of suspension from which it can be resumed as if no interruption had occurred. In CYBER, this is significantly aided by a sequence called the EXCHANGE JUMP, which exchanges the contents of all the registers in local memory with an "exchange package" in main memory. In effect, the entire state of the central processing unit is exchanged, leaving it immediately available for the operating system program to proceed. When the suspended program is ready to be resumed, another EXCHANGE JUMP is executed, returning the CPU to the state that existed at the time of the interruption.

1.   *Branching.* The sequence of instructions may be modified by several branch instructions in the CYBER architecture. An unconditional branch (02) will cause the instruction counter to be set to a new value equal to the sum of the immediate K field (18 bits) and the quantity contained in a specified B register. This can therefore be a form of base-displacement or indexed addressing for calculating the destination of the branch.

Conditional branching can be done conditional on the quantity in an X register (03) or on comparison between quantities in two B registers (04–07). In the former, the condition may be specified as zero, nonzero, positive, negative, and so on. In the latter, the condition may be specified as equal, not equal, greater than or equal, and less than, referring to the comparison between the specified registers.

In more complex instruction sets than CYBER, other data manipulation functions can be included in the branch beyond that of the comparison and address calculation. These could include an increment or decrement of an index or other arithmetic function with branching conditional on the result. Also other architectures may branch conditional on previous results which may be stored in a control register or a normal operand location.

2. *Subroutine calls.* Subroutine or procedure calls utilize an instruction that, in addition to an unconditional branch, provides the subroutine with arguments and a way of returning to the calling program, so that the calling program can resume execution properly. A subroutine is defined as a program that is expected to be used often and which is more convenient to store in main memory once rather than repeating it "in line" with the normal program sequence. Such programs are very often written as "reentrant" subroutines, which means that neither the instructions nor the data are modified during execution of the subroutine in such a way as to prevent reuse of the subroutine. This must also hold true even if the subroutine is interrupted.

In the CYBER architecture, a subroutine is normally entered by a RETURN JUMP (010). This instruction is unconditional and causes a word to be stored in main memory at the address defined by the immediate K field in the instruction and then to branch to address K plus one. The word stored contains an unconditional jump back to an address, which is essentially the address of the next word in sequence of the originating program. This type of instruction allows the subroutine to be "called" by any program module with great flexibility. This is different from the exchange jump, which exchanges all the registers (see "Monitor Calls" below). In the return jump, the registers are left intact and by convention, some registers will represent input operands for the subroutine and others will carry the results.

3. *Monitor calls.* A user program may contain instructions to provide trace and other monitor services from an operating system utility. The monitor call is treated as if it were an INTERRUPT (see Sec. 1.2.2). The user program is halted, and control is given to the operating system. The operating system utility will maintain records of such monitor calls and provide other program debugging services. In CYBER, the exchange jump (013) is used for the monitor call.

Variable-Field-Length Operations.   There are no CYBER instructions for manipulating variable-field-length data. Such data may be strings of characters or bytes, decimal numbers, or vectors or linear arrays. Programs operating in the CYBER architectures deal with these data directly by means of sequences of instructions.

In contrast, the IBM System/370 contains a number of instructions that execute complex byte string and decimal numeric manipulation. These instructions are highlighted in this section, and the simpler instructions which are roughly comparable to CYBER are not discussed. Full treatment of all instructions in either machine may be found in their publications on principles of operations. Neither machine has instructions that directly manipulate vectors or arrays.

An example of a byte string operation is the MOVE (MVC) and MOVE LONG (MVCL). The MVC instruction uses the first 48-bit format (SS) in Fig. 11. This format contains a length field (L) and two operand address fields utilizing base-displacement addressing. The base addresses are contained in registers in local memory and specified by B1 and B2. The displacements are 12-bit immediate fields (D1 for the first operand and D2 for the second). The instruction moves the second operand into the first operand location. Each operand field is processed from left to right (i.e., from lower byte address up). When the operands overlap, the result is obtained as if the operands were processed one byte at a time and each result byte were stored immediately after the necessary operand byte is fetched. This move instruction allows up to 256 bytes to be moved.

The MOVE LONG (MVCL) instruction utilizes the 16-bit format (RR) shown in Fig. 11. The R1 and R2 fields each specify an even–odd pair of general registers in local memory and must designate an even-numbered register (see Fig. 13). The R1 register contains a 24-bit address of the first operand. The R1 + 1 register contains a 24-bit length of the first operand. These are contained in 32-bit registers with the remaining bits ignored. Similarly, R2 and R2 + 1 registers contain the address and length, respectively, of the second operand, except that the remaining 8-bit field in register R2 + 1 contains a pad byte. The second operand is placed in the first operand location, provided that overlapping does not affect the final contents of the first operand location. The remaining low-order byte positions, if any, of the first operand location are filled with the padding byte. If the length of the second operand is longer than the first, the operation is halted at the limit of the first operand length.

Since the MVCL instruction can take an extended time, it is interruptible. When an interruption occurs, the contents of registers R1 + 1 and R2 + 1 are decremented by the number of bytes moved, and the contents of registers R1 and R2 are incremented by the same number, so that the instruction when reexecuted, resumes at the point of interruption.

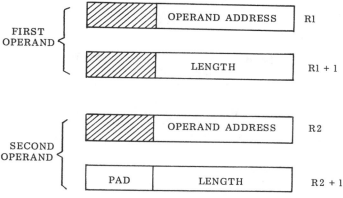

Fig. 13 Register use in MOVE LONG.

This class of variable-field-length instructions illustrates the "long" and "short" methods used in System/370. The long requires use of four registers in local memory, whereas the short requires only two base registers.

A similar pair of instructions, CLC and CLCL, are used to COMPARE LOGICAL. The first operand is compared with the second operand, and the result is indicated in the condition code (a following instruction will test the result). The COMPARE LOGICAL instruction treats all bits alike as part of an unsigned binary quantity, with all codes valid. These instructions also use formats SS and RR, respectively, and treat the two operands in a manner similar to the MOVE instructions. The "short" method (CLC) uses two base registers and can compare field lengths up to 256 bytes.

The "long" method (CLCL) uses four general registers, similar to MOVE LONG (see Fig. 13). The instruction executes until a mismatch occurs between the two operands. At this point, the contents of $R1+1$ and $R2+1$ are decremented by the number of bytes that matched and the contents of registers R_1 and R_2 are incremented by the same number. The condition code can identify operands equal, first operand low and first operand high.

Other, more complex instructions are included in System/370 which execute on variable-length fields of data. These include a number of DECIMAL instructions and text manipulation instructions, such as EDIT and TRANSLATE. See Ref. 4 for a detailed explanation.

Supervisory. Both the CYBER architecture and the System/370 architecture assume a supervisory program that coordinates the use of system resources and executes all I/O instructions, handles exceptional conditions, and supervises scheduling and execution of multiple programs. System/370 differentiates between MONITOR calls and SUPERVISOR calls, with the former being used for tracing the course of execution of a program and the latter being used for communication with the supervisory program. The CYBER architecture utilizes the CPU and other independent peripheral processing units (PPUs) to execute the supervisory program.

A supervisor call is treated as an interruption that places the CPU in the supervisory state. While in this state, certain instructions are valid that are not allowed for user programs. These generally provide a means to change the contents of control and status registers and provide relocation and protection services. These instructions are called *privileged* (see Sec. 1.2.1) and will cause an exception condition interrupt if encountered in a user program.

A supervisor call may be made to the supervisory program for execution of I/O operations and other services. Main-memory management is not normally included in this service, since a memory reference to an address out of range, or to a page not currently in main memory, is handled by exception interrupt. The supervisory program maintains time-of-day clock and other timers accounting for the CPU time of individual user programs. A user program is restarted by the supervisory program by replacing appropriate contents of the general registers and control registers such that the program will resume where it left off. In CYBER, this is accomplished in one instruction, the Exchange Jump (01).

Input/Output. Section 1.10 discusses all aspects of I/O architecture. In this section attention is restricted to the I/O channel method. The CYBER architecture utilizes a set of peripheral processing units (PPUs), each of which is a small programmable processor with private memory and access to main memory. Part of the operating system function, particularly that of I/O, is executed in the

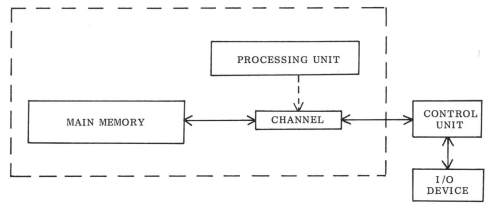

Fig. 14 Data channel.

PPUs. In fact, the CPU need not execute any I/O except to communicate with the PPUs through privileged locations in main memory.

System/370 utilizes programmable data channels for the execution of I/O operations. The data channels provide the data path and control for I/O devices as they communicate with main memory (see Fig. 14). The data channel presents a standard interface to a control unit driving the I/O device. The interface passes commands and data to the control unit and receives responses, data, and external interrupts. The commands are part of a channel program that directs the control unit operation independently of the CPU.

The CPU initiates a channel program with a privileged instruction (START I/O) which is allowable only in the supervisory mode. When initiated, the channel fetches its own control word sequence (the channel program), governs the transfer of data and control signals and counts record lengths. The channel executes the channel program and, on completion, interrupts the CPU. For this purpose, each command word contains command code, main memory address, and a length where needed. This is a single-address rudimentary program structure that can branch in a limited way to deliver commands and data to the device control unit.

Thus the principal method of operation is for the user program (or an operating system utility program) to prepare a channel program in main memory and call the operating system, which initiates the specified channel and returns control to the user program or to another user program.

More than one channel can execute concurrently, and certain types of channels can connect more than one device control unit and can multiplex channel programs on a single channel. Since the user program does not see this activity, the implementation may vary extensively and may include microprogrammed auxiliary control similar to the PPU concept. The programmable data channels each operate independently of the CPU and each other.

REFERENCES

1. C. G. BELL and A. NEWELL, "Parallel Operation in the Control Data 6600," in *Computer Structures*, McGraw-Hill, New York, 1971, pp. 470–476, 489–503.
2. J. E. THORNTON, *Design of a Computer, the Control Data 6600*, Scott, Foresman, Glenview, Ill., 1970.
3. D. J. KUCK, *The Structure of Computers and Computations*, Wiley, New York, 1978, pp. 37, 254, 284.
4. *IBM System/370 Principles of Operation*, IBM Publication GA22-7000, IBM Corporation, White Plains, N.Y.

1.2   ARCHITECTURE: INTERRUPT SYSTEMS AND SYSTEM STATES

Dennis J. McBride and Earl E. Swartzlander, Jr.

One of the most useful architectural features of a CPU is its ability to conditionally alter the instruction execution sequence. This means that conditions arising during program execution can be tested by branch instructions (see Sec. 1.1.5) and a new instruction address can be specified. Without this ability, the computer would be able to execute only a very restricted class of algorithms.

Designating the types of conditions that are tested by branch instructions is an important architectural issue.

The ability of the CPU to do useful work is usually predicated on its ability to perform various I/O tasks as well, and the I/O data transfer process is typically controlled by an interrupt system. Consequently, the interrupt system is a fundamental part of the system architecture. The CPU hardware can be designed to alter the instruction execution sequence automatically upon the occurrence of interrupts. Either external or internal CPU events can cause interrupts. The currently executing program is usually suspended, rather than abnormally terminated, so that it can resume execution once the interrupt has been serviced (by the execution of a program which takes care of the situation that created the interrupt).

Finally, some CPU control mechanisms provide the ability to declare different subsets of the full instruction set to be valid at different times, or to switch among several complete instruction sets. Specific instructions or hardware conditions cause appropriate changes from one instruction set to another. Traps (internally generated interrupts) are used to detect attempts to execute illegal instructions.

All three of these mechanisms are important architectural features. The branch conditions are essential for normal algorithmic processing. The interrupts and traps have implications at a higher architectural level. An attribute, often called the *system state*, is used to differentiate the various modes of CPU operation (i.e., normal versus interrupted, running versus stopped, etc.). Section 1.2.1 discusses the system states, and Sec. 1.2.2 discusses interrupt mechanisms.

1.2.1   System States

In the most general sense, the contents of all registers, memory locations, and other storage elements are necessary to describe an entire computer's state at any instant. The minimum information that must be retained (including next instruction address) in order to support a call–return control structure for interrupt handling, or for related activities such as subroutine nesting and multiprogramming is collectively referred to as the *processor status* or *machine status*. Even though the components of processor status may be generated in various parts of the CPU, they are often brought together in a single register to facilitate easy storage and retrieval when necessary. Typical names for this register are *status register* or *program status word* (PSW). Memory locations may be reserved for storing additional status and control information.

The term "system state" carries a particular meaning, as defined by the architectural description of a given CPU. The commonly identified states that a CPU can assume are discussed in the following paragraphs.

Supervisor or Privileged State

For the case of large mainframe computers, the base architecture is usually designed with a software operating system in mind. A set of special, or privileged, instructions is made available for the operating system programmers to use (e.g., set CPU timer, insert storage key, load PSW). In the case of IBM System/370 these instructions can execute only while the system is in the *supervisor state*. This concept also exists in other machines. In the supervisor state, all instructions are valid, although some of these instructions may be configuration, model, or timing dependent. The supervisor state is reserved for software which handles interrupts and other exception conditions at the primitive hardware level, or CPU control level. Application programs do not have access to the supervisor state, except indirectly through special calls to "utility" programs within the supervisor.

Normal or Problem State

The normal or problem state is defined for application programs and higher levels of system software in systems that have a privileged class of instructions. Only a subset of the executable instructions is allowed in this state. An attempt to execute a privileged instruction usually generates an exception condition, or trap. The application software and much of the operating system software can therefore run at minimum risk to the vital CPU control mechanisms. In other words, the system is protected against misuse of instructions or accidental errors in most programs, with respect to the vital CPU control and hardware status operations.

A less sophisticated CPU, with a less complicated operating system, might not have these two modes or states. In this case the application program must be able to handle I/O and special CPU control.

Wait State

Since a CPU may not have any instruction processing to do at a particular instant (e.g., because it might be waiting for I/O activity to execute), the system can enter the wait state, pending the arrival of an interrupt. The computer is not performing any useful work while in the wait state.

Stopped or Halted State

The stopped or halted state is normally provided as a console function, which allows the computer to be powered on but otherwise inactive. This function is desirable in the event of machine malfunction and for certain types of manual I/O operations: for the purpose of changing disks, tapes, printer paper, card decks, and so on. In large computing systems, however, much of this manual activity can be done by making an I/O device temporarily "unavailable." The system will either wait, as described above, or process other pending jobs if this kind of multitasking operation is supported by the operating system.

Other States or Modes

Other modes of operation are possible: for example, a *diagnostic* mode, which is not normally evident to application or operating system programmers. This would be used primarily by engineers and programmers who have special training for the purpose of architectural validation or hardware repair.

Another special mode of operation is *emulation*, whereby one machine type interprets instruction formats from a different machine architecture (see Sec. 1.9.6). This mode is sometimes made available to aid in conversion from one machine type to another, so that previously written programs can still be used.

Microcomputer States

The concept of changing machine state relative to software structure is not yet common in microprocessor architectures. For the microcomputers of the early 1980s the phrase "system state" is considered to be more closely related to the hardware and clock timing. State information in this context indicates whether the current activity is an instruction fetch, data fetch, wait cycle, or interrupt condition.

Interrupt State

There are I/O devices as well as internal CPU exception conditions which demand immediate attention. All interrupts cause a fundamental change in the system state, so that the interrupt state is explicitly defined in most systems. The interrupt system itself is described in the following section.

1.2.2   Interrupt Handling

A computer can be viewed as a finite-state machine that moves from one state to another via the execution of a program. Interrupt mechanisms provide a well-defined way of altering the sequence of states in response to internal traps or outside asynchronous events (interrupts). There are many ways to handle interrupts, depending on the system requirements. The choice of a particular interrupt mechanism can have a significant impact on the throughput and flexibility of a system.

Polling and Nonpolling

One of the simplest ways to handle asynchronous events is the polling method. With each possible event, there is an associated flag that can be accessed by the program, to determine if service is required. (The flag is generated within the CPU in the case of traps, and externally for interrupts.) This method trades simple hardware for software complexity. It requires program memory space and also requires time for polling the flags (whether or not service is required). The polling method has low system throughput, high overhead time, and slow response time (see also Sec. 1.10.5).

In nonpolled interrupt handling systems, the asynchronous event generates an interrupt request signal, which is passed to the processor. The processor suspends execution of the current process and starts execution of an interrupt service routine. When the interrupt routine is completed, the processor resumes execution of the suspended process. This system is called an *interrupt-driven system* because it executes interrupt service routines that are initiated by interrupt requests.

Although this method requires more hardware, it has many advantages. Because the execution of interrupt service routines is transparent to the current process, the programmer does not need to write specialized polling routines. The response time is faster because no time is spent interrogating nonactive interrupts, which also increases the system throughput. There is less time overhead and less memory space required because only the service routine exists in memory, and no polling routines are required.

Level of Interrupt Handling

There are two levels on which interrupts may be handled. The first and most common is the machine-level interrupt. In this method, the presence of interrupt requests is checked at the start of each instruction fetch cycle. This guarantees that an interrupt is detected only when a machine instruction is complete and before a new instruction starts.

The second level of handling interrupts is at the microprogram level, in which the microprogram can be interrupted at any time. This method has a faster response for servicing interrupt requests but requires that restrictions be placed on the microprogram and the hardware used to implement the interrupt mechanism.

Types of Interrupts

There are basically four types of interrupts, based on the relationship of the source of the interrupt to the processor:

1. *Intraprocessor* interrupts, or traps, are those asynchronous events that happen within the processor during the execution of a machine instruction. This group includes such things as attempting to divide by zero, overflow, accessing restricted memory, execution of a privileged instruction, and machine failure.
2. *Intrasystem* interrupts are created by system peripherals, such as disks, printers, and keyboards, that have completed operations or require service.
3. *Executive* interrupts are caused by the program that is currently executing. This provides a way for the current program to make a request of the operating system (executive). These requests include starting new tasks, allocating resources (disks, line printers, main memory), and communication with other tasks.
4. *Interprocessor* interrupts are used in multiprocessor systems as, for example, part of communication protocols.

Events for Interrupt Handling

When an interrupt occurs, a sequence of six events must take place. These events, which can be implemented in microcode or machine code, comprise, when integrated with the hardware, the interrupt mechanism. The sequence of events provides a smooth transfer from the current process environment to an interrupt servicing environment and back again. The sequence ensures that the processor status will be the same immediately after an interrupt is serviced as it was immediately before the interrupt occurred. The events may depend on the machine design and application.

1. *Interrupt recognition.* This step is the recognition by the processor of an interrupt request due to activation of an interrupt request line or an internal mechanism. In this step the processor can determine which device or CPU component made the request. The method used to determine which device to service is directly related to the interrupt structure of the machine. The different types of interrupt structures are discussed in more detail below.

2. *Save status.* The goal of this step is to make the interrupt sequence transparent to the interrupted process. Therefore, the processor saves the flags and registers that may be changed by the interrupt service routine so that they may be restored after the service routine is finished. The flags and registers that are saved automatically by the CPU are those that will be destroyed in the transfer of control from the current process to the interrupt service routine. It is then the responsibility of the service routine to save any other registers that it might change. The minimum set of flags and registers might include the instruction counter, overflow flag, sign flag, interrupt mask, and so on. The minimum set also includes any register or flag that needs to be saved but that the interrupt service routine cannot access.

3. *Interrupt masking.* This step can overlap some of the other steps. For the first few steps of the sequence, all interrupts are masked out so that no other interrupt may be processed before the processor status is saved. Usually, the mask is then set to accept interrupts of higher priority. Some machines also allow the service routine, selectively, to enable or disable interrupts. There may be other variations to this step, depending on the application.

4. *Interrupt acknowledgment.* At some point, the processor must acknowledge the interrupt being serviced, so that the interrupting device becomes free to continue its task. The processor can acknowledge in several different ways. One of the ways is to have an external signal line devoted to interrupt acknowledge. Another method relies upon the interrupting device recognizing an acknowledge when the cause of the interrupt is serviced by some CPU action. Some processor designs also use an acknowledge signal as a request for the interrupting device to place an ID on the data bus (see the following paragraph).

5. *Interrupt service routine.* At this point the processor initiates the interrupt service routine. The address of the routine can be obtained in several ways, depending on the system architecture. The simplest is found in the polling method, in which one routine polls each device to find which one interrupted. Some designs require that the interrupting device put an address on the data bus so that the processor can store it in its program counter and branch to it. Other designs use an ID number derived from the priority of the interrupt that is put through a mapping ROM or lookup table in memory in order to obtain the address of the service routine.

6. *Restore and return.* After the interrupt service routine has completed its processing, it restores all the registers it has changed, and the processor restores all the registers and flags that were saved at the initiation of the interrupt routine. If this is done correctly, the processor should have the same status as before the interrupt was recognized.

Interrupt Structures

Listed below are some of the more common interrupt structures used. As usual, there is a trade-off among hardware, software, and firmware. The particular structures vary in the way that the processor determines which device made the interrupt request.

Single Request, Multiple Poll.   In this structure there is one request line that is shared among all the interrupting devices. When the processor recognizes an interrupt request, it polls all the devices to find the interrupting device. Priority is introduced via the order in which the devices are polled and can be dynamically reallocated by changing the polling sequence, if desired.

Single Request, Daisy-Chain Acknowledge.   In this structure there is one request line, which is shared. When the processor receives an interrupt, it sends out a signal acknowledging the interrupt. The acknowledge signal is passed from I/O device to I/O device until the interrupting device receives the signal. At this point, the interrupting device identifies itself by putting an ID number on the data bus. This structure requires less software but has a static priority associated with the order of interconnection of the devices. There is also a time delay associated with the daisy-chain acknowledge structure, because the interrupt acknowledge signal has to pass through several gate delays in each device, although this is much faster than polling.

Multiple Request.   This structure features one request line (and one device) per priority level. The multiple-line structure gives the fastest response time, since the interrupting device can be identified immediately. It also results in simpler interfaces in the peripheral units—in general, a single interrupt request flip-flop. This structure often has a mask bit associated with each priority level. The limitations associated with this method are that more hardware is required in its implementation and that there is a limit of one peripheral per priority level.

Multiple Request, Daisy-Chain Acknowledge.   This structure combines the single request, daisy-chain acknowledge with the multiple-request structure. For each interrupt request line, there is an interrupt acknowledge line that is connected to a string of devices in a daisy-chain fashion. When the appropriate device receives the interrupt acknowledge, it puts an ID number on the data bus. The advantage of this structure is that many devices can be handled while maintaining short daisy chains. This gives a shorter access time than a single daisy chain, with less CPU hardware than an interrupt request line per device. The disadvantage is that each device must contain logic to pass on the acknowledge signal, which requires more hardware in each device.

Priority.   In systems with asynchronous requests, two or more requests can arrive simultaneously. In order to handle this situation, there must be a prioritization mechanism to pick which request is serviced first. The two most common priority schemes are the static and the rotating approaches. In the static scheme, all the interrupt levels are ordered, from the lowest priority to the highest priority. This can be fixed in software or hardware and is usually permanent. In the rotating structure, the possible interrupt requests are logically arranged in a circle, with a pointer indicating the lowest-priority interrupt. The priority of each interrupt increases as one travels around the circle, with the highest-priority interrupt being adjacent to the lowest-priority interrupt. As an interrupt is serviced, the pointer is changed to point to the interrupt that was just serviced. This structure is advantageous when all interrupts have similar priority and service-rate requirements.

"Nesting" allows only higher-priority interrupts to interrupt an active interrupt service routine. Nesting requires inhibiting equal and lower-level interrupts. This requires that the interrupt structure hold the priority of the interrupt being serviced. This can be implemented with a register that holds the value as a binary encoded number or as a bit associated with each interrupt. Prioritization determines which interrupt request is serviced first when several requests are pending and control returns from the interrupt service routine for a higher-priority request.

However nesting is performed, all computers must have machine-level instructions to enable and disable interrupts and set and clear mask bits. Interrupt handlers can be written using these instructions to accomplish nesting of interrupts, although it can be implemented quite efficiently with microcode and hardware. In the simplest computers, the interrupt structure only prioritizes interrupts, leaving nesting to the software interrupt handlers.

Section 1.18.3 contains a detailed description of a commercial priority interrupt chip that contains many of the features necessary to implement a priority interrupt system on a CPU with very limited interrupt-handling capabilities.

BIBLIOGRAPHY

H. S. STONE, *Introduction to Computer Organization and Data Structures*, McGraw-Hill, New York, 1972.

A. S. TANENBAUM, *Structured Computer Organization*, Prentice-Hall, Englewood Cliffs, N.J., 1976.

C. C. FOSTER, *Computer Architecture*, Van Nostrand, New York, 1970.

1.3 ARCHITECTURE: BIT-SLICE ORGANIZATION

Dennis J. McBride

Bit-slice organization is a technique for constructing a CPU from general-purpose building blocks (slices) that can be connected in a variety of ways in order to meet particular CPU design requirements. Designers can, within broad constraints, create their own CPU architecture by choosing the data path widths, the number of registers, and the interpretation of instructions residing in main memory. This flexibility is maximized when each slice is realized as a single integrated device, because the functional partitioning is both natural and modular. In this case the designer is somewhat buffered from the technology and only need satisfy the interfacing and higher-level packaging requirements. It is this realization of bit-slice devices that will be described here; it is usually classified in the spectrum of machine types as a miniprocessor (the CPU portion of a minicomputer).

The sizes of the CPU, memory, and I/O portions of a computer depend on the performance and cost objectives, and on the technology used for implementation. The technique of organizing the CPU as a parallel connection of bit slices, however, can be found across the entire spectrum of CPU designs. Bit-slice organization can be used within a single integrated device or on a large scale as part of a highly specialized CPU.

The elements of a typical CPU are the ALU, one or more accumulators, special registers, instruction-decoding logic, timing, and other control. A particular CPU can be schematically represented by connecting these pieces in block diagram form (see Fig. 1 of the introduction to Sec. 1). For the case of bit-slice organizations, CPU elements may consist of one or more interconnected slices of these specific element types (see Fig. 1).

1.3.1 Bit-Slice Realization of CPU Elements

One measure of the processing power of a CPU is the "width" of its ALU. This determines how many bits can be operated on in parallel. For optimum performance, registers should have the same width as the ALU. Multiple ALU operation cycles can be used, however, for operands that are wider than the ALU. This is essentially a multiple-precision technique. Architecture is directly affected, however, by the types of operations that can be performed by the ALU logic, by the number and types of registers, and by the decode logic which defines the machine-level instruction set. Bit-slice devices allow certain kinds of flexibility but also impose some constraints on the CPU architecture.

The width and complexity of a bit-slice component is closely related to the integration density allowed by the technology. The bit widths of components, however, are also chosen to provide modularity. This suggests widths of 2 or 4 bits for each component, so that a number of widths can be realized in the typical range of 4 to 32 bits. Although these slices can be connected in an arbitrarily wide configuration, the propagation delay of logic signals begins to limit the performance. The rather modest width and function of a single bit-slice component, combined with integrated-circuit technology, results in the use of very high speed logic circuitry to realize these single chip functions. It is this high performance, as well as architectural flexibility, which makes bit-slice organization an important approach to CPU design.

ALU Slices

The ALU slice is a very important component of the CPU, since it directly influences the kinds of instructions that can be supported efficiently. The ALU slice accepts one or two operands and

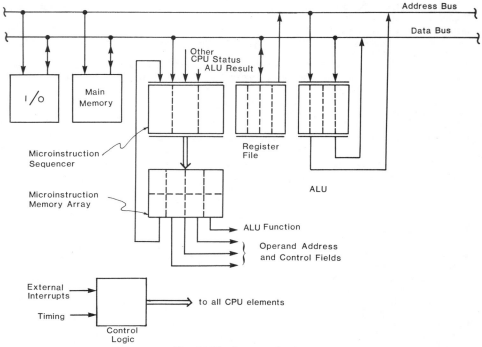

Fig. 1 Bit-slice organization.

produces a result (see Sec. 1.5). The operation is specified by an input control field which is typically 4 or 5 bits, permitting 16 or 32 arithmetic and logic functions. Each slice also requires a carry input and produces a carry output for execution of functions such as addition. Parallel connection of ALU slices is straightforward, by chaining* the carry signals, and by sending the same control signals to each slice. Carry lookahead logic is often available as a single device which is typically capable of handling up to four slices in parallel. It can significantly reduce the cycle time for ALU operations, especially for wide ALUs that use many slices.

Register Files

Some ALU slices contain only combinatorial logic. The CPU control logic, however, is clocked, which means that registers must be used to hold the ALU input operands. Registers are common items in any logic technology, so they are readily available to use with bit-slice components. Although these registers, typically 4 bits wide, can be thought of as slices, they are not dependent on each other when connected in parallel. They are simply controlled by a common clock signal. The need for specific registers depends on the internal design of the other CPU elements. Some ALU slices, for example, also contain the corresponding accumulator slice and other logic to help distribute the CPU control mechanism.

A *single-accumulator architecture* can be implemented using bit slices. This is called a single-address machine, because only one operand is addressed explicitly, and it resides in main memory. The second, or implied, operand is the accumulator contents, and the ALU result is returned to the accumulator. Many architectures, however, use multiple accumulators by means of a general-purpose register file. This type of architecture allows faster execution for those instructions that address the register file, because the path to main memory is necessarily slower. Specific nonarithmetic operations

---

*Each ALU slice must have its carry output connected to the carry input of the next-higher-order ALU slice. Carry input to the lowest-order slice can be fixed, or it can depend on the currently executing instruction type.

must be available in either of these architectures for transferring the accumulator data to and from main memory.

Register files have been implemented as bit-slice devices, typically 4 bits wide, with 16 registers on a single chip. A 4-bit-wide address is used to access one of these registers at a time. As with single registers, register files can be paralleled to match the ALU width. The register address signals and the clock or control signals are common to all slices of the register file. For maximum performance, some files provide two independent address and data paths, so that two operands can be gated to the ALU on the same clock cycle.

Another register building block is the *last-in-first-out* (LIFO) register file, usually called a stack. Register contents are accessed via *push* and *pop* operations, which means that no explicit register address is required. If the register contents are interpreted as memory addresses, the stack allows an easy call–return linkage for nesting of subroutines. It is also a useful structure to have for certain kinds of algorithmic processing of data. Since operands can be obtained from the stack and the ALU result can be pushed onto the stack, all register addresses are automatically implied. This is called a *zero address architecture*, and it can be implemented in bit-slice form. Again, data transfer (nonarithmetic) operations are used to move data on the stack to and from memory.

Instruction Decoding

The most complex element of a CPU is the control mechanism that decodes and interprets instructions residing in main memory (see Sec. 1.9). This control logic is an interface between the detailed operations required to make the CPU elements communicate with each other and the more compact representation of main-memory operation codes.

CPUs organized with bit slices are generally controlled by microprogram (see Sec. 1.9.3). Main-memory instructions are interpreted by the sequential execution of one or more "microinstructions." The control logic thus includes a microinstruction sequencer which addresses the currently executing microinstruction located in a special memory called control store. A fixed menu of the microinstructions is available for effecting the execution of machine instructions. Microinstruction width depends on the architecture, but it is generally 32 bits. High-performance read-only memories (ROMs) are used with the appropriate width and address space for control store memory.

Microinstruction sequencers (see Sec. 1.9.4) are available in bit-slice form, typically in 4-bit widths. These can be paralleled to expand microinstruction address space to 256 words, 4096 words, and so on. Although these sizes are typical, other address space sizes are also available. Proper incrementing of control store addresses requires that the carry-out of a given slice of the microinstruction address register be connected to the carry-in of the next-higher-order slice, as with the ALU. The interconnections here become more complex, though, because each control store sequencer slice may be responsible for many control fields. Fields within the microinstruction directly control the operand register address, ALU function, and so on. The next microinstruction address is also determined by a field within the current microinstruction, and is sometimes conditioned by the contents of a status register. Some control information must therefore be connected to each microsequencer slice. Some control store sequencers also allow microinstruction subroutines via an on-chip address stack.

1.3.2 Available Devices*

The bit-slice technique has been described as being most evident in miniprocessor architectures. Miniprocessors are usually realized via a technology that is higher in performance but lower in integration density than the technology used for microprocessors. Thus miniprocessors have to be partitioned across many integrated-circuit devices, whereas a microprocessor can be integrated into a single device. The partitioning between sequential and combinatorial logic is used to advantage here. It is natural to separate the control store, since it is one or more standard memory devices. The microprogram sequencer is not simply the latch for a sequential machine, but often has the architectural features found at the higher levels of interpretation in a computer. These features depend on the manufacturer's design.

A given manufacturer will usually provide a family of bit-slice components, the most important architectural element being the microprogram sequencer. The ease of interpretation of machine language instructions, sometimes called *macroinstructions*, depends directly on this underlying structure. Other bit-slice components, such as registers or even ALUs, may be acquired from other manufacturers, as long as the signal levels are compatible. This is generally not a problem, since bit-slice components for the popular high-performance technologies (TTL and ECL) are provided by many manufacturers. A hybrid CPU can be built by custom designing some of the instruction decoding and control logic and using bit-slice components for the remaining portion. Variations in

*See also Sec. 1.18.3.

performance and function do exist among manufacturers, though, because each one may optimize around a different design point. The CPU designer is usually assured maximum compatibility by staying within a given family of components.

An additional component type found in bit-slice processors (but not exclusively in these) is the bus buffer—an amplifier interposed between the CPU and the memory bus to prevent the load of the relatively long line from CPU to memory and I/O devices from degrading the bus signals. The buffers are important in the system design and realization but do not appear in the architecture.

It should also be noted that entire applications are sometimes written at the microinstruction level, with main-memory addresses used only to access I/O devices or to hold application data. The programming is more tedious at this level, but it is being traded for instruction flexibility and ultimate performance.

BIBLIOGRAPHY

N. A. ALEXANDRIDIS, "Bit-Sliced Microprocessor Architecture," *Computer*, **11**(6), 56–80 (June 1978).

AUERBACH, *Auerbach on Minicomputers*, Mason and Lipscomb, 1974.

C. WEITZMAN, *Minicomputer Systems — Structure, Implementation, and Application*, Prentice-Hall, Englewood Cliffs, N.J., 1974.

1.4 PROGRAMMING BASICS

Jack L. Rosenfeld

This article deals with techniques for programming in *machine language*—designing sequences of CPU instructions. Because an understanding of how machine instructions are used is essential for processor architects and designers, this article is included in a section otherwise devoted to computer hardware. Machine language instructions are sequences of 0 and 1 bits that are interpreted by the control unit of the CPU and executed (see Sec. 1.9). Instructions in assembly language, which is closely related to machine language, contain alphanumeric symbols (easily remembered by the programmer) for instruction operation codes, storage addresses, and occasionally the data itself. An assembler is a program that transforms a program in assembly language to its equivalent in machine language (see Sec. 2.11).

High-level languages (HLLs) such as PL/I, FORTRAN, COBOL, BASIC, and Pascal are provided for virtually all mainframes and minicomputers, and for an increasing number of microcomputers (see Sec. 2.13). The advantages of HLLs—ease of programming, of modifying, and of debugging, portability, and self-documentation—so far outweigh the disadvantages of somewhat reduced speed, increased storage occupancy, and limited flexibility that the programmer must have a compelling reason to eschew a HLL for machine language. In fact, optimizing compilers frequently produce better code than that created by average programmers in machine language.

The two most significant reasons for choosing machine language are unavailability of an appropriate HLL compiler and need to make the program being designed, or a part of it, especially efficient in its use of resources such as CPU time or storage occupied by the program or the data. If only a part of the program is critical, the remainder may well be programmed in a HLL.

The following sections deal with the basic aspects of machine instructions: accessing operands, branching, using index registers, invoking subroutines, and fixed-point arithmetic. A section on self-modifying code is included to strengthen the reader's comprehension of the concepts introduced. A brief section on "tricks of the trade" points out what facilities may be available to the alert programmer. The article concludes with a section on topics of concern to the programmer of a microprocessor system—how to cope with restrictions found in microprocessor systems—that programmers of larger systems generally may not be concerned with.

The program examples in this article are in a format resembling assembly language for many CPUs. The instruction set is chosen from a number of CPUs and is designed to be illustrative but not complete. The addresses and values selected for the examples are completely arbitrary. Numbers rather than symbols are used for addresses in order to emphasize the difference between addresses and data values.

All CPU registers are assumed to have the width of memory words, and all instructions and numbers are also assumed to be one word wide. Cases in which the assumptions are unreasonable are dealt with. The form of the instructions is meant to enhance understanding—not to resemble any specific assembly language. One can learn the details of a specific computer's instruction set from the manufacturer's manual and from texts based on the more popular computers.

1.4.1 Operands

Operands of some instructions are explicit memory locations.* For example, the instruction

LOADA 123

means load register A from memory location 123: that is, replace the current contents of A with the contents of memory at 123. It *does not* mean place the number 123 in A. In fact, LOADA has two operands: register A and memory location 123; the former is implicit, and the latter is explicit. Many other instructions also have implicit operands. For example, the instruction

CLEARA

means "clear register A," that is, replace the contents of A with the number 0. We now consider means of specifying explicit operands in memory. These are discussed in Sec. 1.1.3.

Addressing Memory Operands

A memory operand may be addressed directly, indirectly, or relatively. A *direct address* is an explicit memory address. The previous example, LOADA 123, has such a direct memory address.

In an architecture that permits *indirect addresses*, one generally finds one bit in the instruction that indicates that the operand is an indirect address. When that bit is 1, the contents of the memory location specified in the instruction are accessed; the data in that memory word are treated as an address; the contents of that indirect memory location are then used as the operand of the instruction. Let us designate an instruction with the indirect address bit equal 1 by "IND" following the operation code mnemonic, such as

LOADA IND 123

Consider the following example:

Location	Instruction or Data
	LOADA IND 123
	$\vdots$
123	257
	$\vdots$
257	142

The result of executing the instruction LOADA IND 123 is to replace the contents of register A with the number 142. First, location 123 is accessed to fetch the address (257). Then the LOADA operation is executed with the contents of address 257 as operand, which means that 142 (the contents of memory location 257) replaces the previous contents of register A.

(Before proceeding with the next example, recall that successive instructions are normally fetched from successive main-memory locations. This sequence may be modified by branching instructions, which are discussed in Sec. 1.4.2.)

Indirect addressing is useful for looking up values in a table. Consider the following example, in which codes for characters may range from 0 to 255 and must be translated to other codes (e.g., from codes for lowercase characters to uppercase codes). The program segment starts with the source code in register A and ends with the translated code in register A.

Location	Instruction or Data		Comments
	ADDA	100	Generates address
	STORA	101	in table
	LOADA IND	101	
	$\vdots$		

(*continued on p*. 32)

---

*In this article the size of memory operands is treated, in general, as a fixed number of bits. In some architectures, each instruction implies the number of bits comprising its operand(s); for some designs, operands are multiples of the basic memory word size. For example, in IBM system/370, the basic memory unit is the 8-bit "byte." Operands are denoted—byte, half-word (2 bytes), full-word (4 bytes), and double-word (8 bytes). The n-byte operand with address X comprises the bytes at locations X to $X + n - 1$.

100	389	
101	—	Receives address in table: 389+i
	⋮	
389	Code for 0	
	⋮	
644	Code for 255	

The first instruction, ADDA 100, means add the operand (contents of location 100, which equals 389) to the current contents of register A and leave the sum in register A. The second instruction means place the contents of register A in memory location 101. If one started with i in register A, then $i + 389$ would now be found at location 101. The third instruction has its indirect addressing flag equal to 1, so the contents of memory location 101 are accessed, and then the contents of location $389 + i$ are loaded into register A. So if A originally contained the code i for a lowercase letter and location $389 + i$ contained the code for the same letter in uppercase, the result in register A would be the code for the uppercase letter. Section 1.4.4 describes how the same operation can be done with the use of an index register.

Some architectures permit more than one level of indirection. There could be an indirect addressing bit in each indirectly addressed location. Depending on that bit, the word is interpreted as the address of the memory word holding either the operand or the address of the operand. Obviously, an indefinite number of levels of indirection can be achieved, if the architecture permits it.

Relative addressing in an architecture implies that the address of the operand is determined by adding the number in the instruction to the address of the instruction itself. Instructions with relative addressing generally have short address fields and occupy less storage than instructions with direct addressing. Consider this code:

Location	Instruction or Data	
100	35	
	⋮	
223	LOADA	−123

In a CPU with relative addressing, the LOADA instruction would replace the contents of register A with the number 35, since the address of the instruction operand is determined by adding −123 to 223 (the address of the instruction itself). Although relative addressing may be a nuisance to programmers, especially when they must insert or delete instructions from an existing sequence, an assembler can relieve most such problems.

An *immediate operand* is one found in the instruction itself; it is treated like data rather than the address where data can be found. For architectures permitting immediate operands, we designate an instruction with an immediate operand by "IMM" following the operation code. If the following sequence of three instructions is executed, the result in register A will be 155.

Location	Instruction or Data			Contents of Register A
	LOADA	IMM	25	25
	ADDA		25	125
	ADDA	IND	25	155
	⋮			
25	100			
	⋮			
100	30			

In some CPUs, the relative address is with respect to the address of the following instruction rather than the current instruction.

Register Operands

Registers may be explicit or implicit operands of an instruction. In all the instructions introduced so far, register A was an implicit operand; it either received data or was the source of data. Some architectures provide for a multiplicity of explicit operands in registers (also called local memory or a register file), main memory, or both: for example,

$$\text{MOVE} \quad A,B$$
$$\text{ADD} \quad C,75$$

The first instruction replaces the contents of register A with those of register B. The second instruction adds the contents of memory location 75 to the contents of register C and places the sum in C.

The following code segment places the sum of the contents of locations 300 to 305 in register A.

$$\text{LOAD} \quad A,300$$
$$\text{ADD} \quad A,301$$
$$\text{ADD} \quad A,302$$
$$\text{ADD} \quad A,303$$
$$\text{ADD} \quad A,304$$
$$\text{ADD} \quad A,305$$

There is a better way to do this, with the use of an index register and branching.

1.4.2 Branching

Unconditional branching instructions, such as

$$\text{BRA} \quad 75$$

cause the next instruction to be executed from an explicitly specified location (in this case, 75) rather than the next instruction in sequence. Conditional branching instructions specify what instruction is to be executed next if a specified condition is satisfied.

Conditions

Some of the conditions that may be tested are: arithmetic result is positive, negative, zero, overflowed, underflowed (for floating-point numbers), or generated a carry. Other conditions that can be tested include parity errors, I/O status, protection violation, machine failure, and interrupt pending. Some architectures require that a result be tested immediately after an arithmetic operation. In other architectures, certain control bits are set, depending on the instruction executed, and are not changed until another instruction that affects them is executed. For example, a "carry" bit would be set by add and subtract instructions but not by store or branch instructions. If a condition is not to affect the flow of program control until after the pertinent control bit is no longer valid, the program must save the status of the control bit (perhaps by setting a storage word to 0 or 1, depending on the control bit status) and test that saved status at the appropriate time.

Branch Instructions

Conditional branch instructions generally specify the condition(s) tested and the location of the instruction to be executed next if the condition is satisfied. In some architectures, each condition is implied by the instruction, for example,

$$\text{BRA} \quad \text{NEG} \quad 200$$

which executes the instruction at location 200 if the sign control bit is 1 (the result of the preceding arithmetic operation was negative) and the following instruction otherwise. Other general conditional branch instructions permit arbitrary combinations of the condition control bits to be tested. Some branch instructions have no explicit address, but skip the instruction after the branch instruction if the condition is satisfied or execute that instruction if it is not. There are variations to this implicit addressing mode.

At this point we have the repertoire of instructions necessary to sum a specified number of memory locations in sequence. Suppose that initially register A holds the address (ad) of the first number (N_1) in the sequence and B holds the count (ct) of numbers to be added.

Location	Instruction or Data		Comments
100	STORE	A,200	Location 200 holds the address of the next number to be added
101	CLEAR	A	Sum is 0 so far
102	STORE	B,201	Location 201 holds the count of numbers remaining

103	ADD	IND	A, 200	Add next number to sum
104	LOAD		B, 200	Increment address
105	ADD	IMM	B, 1	of next number
106	STORE		B, 200	
107	LOAD		B, 201	Decrement count of
108	SUB	IMM	B, 1	numbers remaining
109	BRA	NONZERO	102	Test count of numbers remaining
110	Next instruction			
$\vdots$				
200	—			Address of next number
201	—			Count of numbers left
				to accumulate

When the instruction at memory location 110 is executed, register A holds the sum of the ct numbers from ad to $ad + ct - 1$: $N_1 + N_2 + \cdots + N_{ct}$. The conditional branch instruction at memory location 109 tests the condition control bit set by the subtract instruction at 108. If the result of that subtraction is not zero (when fewer than ct numbers have been added), control branches back to the STORE instruction at location 102. The indirect add instruction at location 103 accesses location 200, which holds the *address* of the next number to be added, and adds the number. The STORE instruction at 106 replaces the address at 200 with the contents of register B, the incremented address. The STORE at 102 puts the decremented count at 201. Let us now satisfy ourselves that the program is correct. When the *indirect* ADD instruction at 103 is executed the first time, location 200 holds ad, 201 holds ct, and A holds 0. When the branch instruction at 109 is executed the first time, 200 holds $ad + 1$, 201 holds $ct - 1$, and A holds N_1. This table gives the contents *after* each iteration of the loop from 102 to 109:

Iteration	200	201	A
1	$ad + 1$	$ct - 1$	N_1
2	$ad + 2$	$ct - 2$	$N_1 + N_2$
$\vdots$			
ct	$ad + ct$	0	$N_1 + \cdots + N_{ct}$

In comparing this with the code sequence at the end of Sec. 1.4.1, one finds that in the former, ct instructions are executed, whereas in the program just described, the same function requires $8ct + 2$ instructions. In the former, the "program" occupies ct words of memory, and in the latter 10 words (plus two temporary storage words). The former program is dependent on the number of numbers to be added; the latter is not. The use of an index register to simplify this program is discussed in Sec. 1.4.4.

1.4.3 Self-Modifying Code

This subject is introduced to reinforce the reader's understanding of the meaning of machine instructions—not as a suggestion of acceptable programming technique. (Code that modifies itself is very risky to use, since any error can easily be responsible for the code being incorrectly modified. Furthermore, such "bugs" are especially difficult to detect. In a microprocessor system in which the code is written in read-only memory (ROM), self-modifying code is, obviously, impossible.) If, however, one uses a primitive architecture without indirect addressing or an index register, one might arrive at the following code segment to perform the operation of the code sequence in the previous example.

Location	Instruction or Data			Comments
400	ADD		A, 500	Initialize the instruction
401	STORE		A, 405	at 405
402	ADD		A, B	Initialize limit constant
403	STORE		A, 501	
404	CLEAR		A	
405	—			ADD A, $ad + i - 1$
406	LOAD		B, 405	Increment address field
407	ADD	IMM	B, 1	
408	STORE		B, 405	
409	SUB		B, 501	

```
410        BRA     NONZERO    405
            .
            .
            .
500        ADD                A,0        Constant
501         —                            ADD A, ad + ct
```

To understand this, one must recall that each instruction is a word in main memory with a bit pattern that includes a code for the operation, a code for the registers, and a code for the address. Like any data word, it can be manipulated by other instructions. Let us assume that the instruction ADD A, 100 looks something like this:

```
ADD      A       100
01011010 | 0 | 00...001100100
```

One can increment the address field by loading the instruction word itself into a register, adding 1 to it, and storing it back. That is the basic principle in the loop from 405 to 410. Here it is assumed, as before, that initially register A holds ad and B holds ct.

The first instruction creates the instruction ADD A, ad in register A, and the second instruction places it at location 405. The third instruction, ADD A, B, adds the contents of registers A and B and places the result in A. In this case, the sum is the instruction ADD A, $ad + ct$, which is placed in location 501 by the following STORE instruction. The first time the instruction at 405 is executed, the contents of memory location ad (N_1) are placed in register A. The instructions from 406 to 408 increment the address in that instruction. The instruction at 409 subtracts the bit pattern for the instruction ADD A, $ad + ct$, which has been placed in 501, from the bit pattern for ADD A, $ad + 1$, leaving $-ct + 1$ in register B.

The following table gives the contents of location 405 and the A and B registers *after* each execution of the instruction at 410.

Iteration	405		B	A
1	ADD	A, $ad + 1$	$-ct + 1$	N_1
2	ADD	A, $ad + 2$	$-ct + 2$	$N_1 + N_2$
.				
.				
ct	ADD	A, $ad + ct$	0	$N_1 + \cdots + N_{ct}$

Note that should the operation code of the ADD instruction correspond to a negative number, a subtract instruction would be used at 407, and the initializing instructions would be modified somewhat. If the address field were not in the low-order bits of the instruction, the code would have to be changed slightly.

Another example of self-modifying code is to determine the proper address for a branch to take and place the address in the branch instruction before it is executed.

1.4.4 Index Registers

An additional register can eliminate difficulties associated with addressing arrays of data, as well as general counting-type operations. Index registers, in addition to participating in some arithmetic operations, participate in the calculation of storage addresses. Most instructions that address operands in main memory can have the contents of an index register added to the address in the instruction itself, the sum specifying the main-memory location of the operand. If we denote by "X" a bit in an instruction that is 1 when such an effective address calculation is to be made, then the notation

LOAD X A, 100

means: fetch the contents of memory at location (100 + contents of index register) and place it in register A.

With such a facility, the problem of adding ct numbers starting at ad can be solved as follows. Here XR denotes the index register. Assume that ad is initially in register A and ct in B.

Location	Instruction or Data			Comments
600	MOVE		XR, A	Move ad to index register
601	CLEAR		A	
602	ADD	X	A, 0	Effective address is $ad + i - 1$
603	ADD	IMM	XR, 1	Increment index register
604	SUB	IMM	B, 1	Decrement count
605	BRA	NONZERO	602	

The first instruction copies the address from A into the index register. The ADD instruction at 602 has an effective address of $ad + 0$ (the index register contents plus 0). This is incremented by 1 in the following instruction. The next instruction at 604 decrements the count, and the branch instruction loops back until the count has been reduced to 0. This code carries out the operation with $4ct + 2$ instruction executions, considerably better than before.

In some CPUs, special instructions combine the incrementing and conditional branching operations; the IBM System/370 instruction Branch on Index High,

$$\text{BXH } R1, R2, R3, a$$

is such an instruction. The following description of BXH is somewhat simplified: the contents of register R2 are added to the contents of register R1, the sum being placed in R1; if the sum is greater than the contents of register R3, the next instruction is fetched from location a; otherwise, the instruction following the BXH is executed next. The sum of an array can be coded as follows, using this instruction:

Location	Instruction or Data			Comments
801	MOVE		C, A	Place ad in register C
802	ADD		A, B	Place $ad + ct$ in
803	MOVE		XR, A	index register
804	LOAD	IMM	B, −1	Place −1 in B
805	CLEAR		A	
806	ADD	X	A, −1	Effective address: $ad + ct - i$
807	BXH		XR, B, C, 806	

Values have been chosen to decrement the index, for the sake of illustrating a different approach. The instructions from 801 to 804 load the registers with proper initial values. Since the B register holds -1 during the loop from 806 to 807, the BXH instruction always decrements the XR by 1. The comparand in register C is the constant address ad. The register contents are as follows each time *after* the BXH is executed:

Iteration	XR	A
1	$ad + ct - 1$	N_{ct}
2	$ad + ct - 2$	$N_{ct} + N_{ct-1}$
⋮		
⋮		
ct	ad	$N_{ct} + \cdots + N_1$

The last time the ADD at 806 is executed, XR holds $ad + 1$. The effective address is ad, since the XR contents are added to the address in the instruction (-1). The BXH instruction decrements XR to ad, and the branch back to 806 is not taken, since ad is not higher than the comparand value in register C. This code has $2ct + 5$ instructions executed to accumulate the ct values.

Some architectures have several registers that can be used as index registers; a field in the instruction is used to specify which one, if any, is used. In some architectures, the effective address is calculated by summing an address field, contents of an index register, and the contents of one or more other registers. (In IBM System/370, the additional register is called a base register.) This permits a great deal of flexibility.

1.4.5 Subroutine Calls

Virtually every architecture has at least one instruction to facilitate invoking a subroutine, and often an instruction to return control to the calling program (see the section "Procedures" in Sec. 2.13.4). The primary feature for transferring control involves saving the address of the calling location. This is not essential; witness the following program, which calls a subroutine to sum an array of numbers.

Assume that before the code is executed, the array address and count are loaded at 353 and 354, respectively.

	Location	Instruction or Data		Comments
	350	LOAD	XR, 352	Place address 355 in XR
	351	BRA	798	Subroutine call
Calling sequence	352	355		Location of next instruction
	353	*ad*		Address of array
	354	*ct*		Count of numbers
	355	Next instruction		
		:		
		:		
	798	LOAD X	A, −2	*ad* into register A
	799	LOAD X	B, −1	*ct* into B
	800	STORE	XR, 901	Save return address
Subroutine	801	.		
		.		Code from previous example
	807	.		
	808	LOAD	XR, 901	Restore return address
	809	BRA X	0	
		:		
		:		
	901	—		Holds return address

The LOAD at 350 places the address 355 in the index register. (The instruction LOAD IMM 355 would also be satisfactory.) It serves as both return address and address by which arguments can be located. The subroutine itself consists of the code from the last example in Sec. 1.4.4 plus a prologue (798 to 800) and an epilogue (808 and 809). In the prologue, *ad* and *ct* are loaded into registers A and B, respectively. (The effective address of the LOAD at 798 is 355−2, the address of the location holding *ad*.) The STORE at 800 saves the return address; it is restored in the index register by the LOAD at 808 and used by the *indexed* BRA at 809 to return control to location 355.

The subroutine can be written more efficiently. Arguments can be passed in registers rather than in a list, as shown. The example should be studied more for an understanding of the techniques involved than for learning a model.

The preceding example would be slightly simpler with an instruction

BSY   a

that saves the address of the following memory word in an index register YR and branches to the subroutine:

	Location	Instruction or Data		Comments
Calling sequence	350	BSY	798	YR gets 351
	351	400		Address of argument list
	352	Next instruction		
		:		
	400	*ad*		Argument list
	401	*ct*		
		:		
	798	LOAD Y	XR, 0	XR gets argument list address
	799	LOAD X	A, 0	A gets *ad*
Subroutine	800	LOAD X	B, 1	B gets *ct*
	801	.		
		.		Code from previous example
	807	.		
	808	BRA Y	1	

(A different concept is illustrated here: an argument list separate from the calling sequence. This is preferred, since it permits calling the subroutine from the same point, at different times with different arguments, without modifying the calling sequence itself.) The indexed LOAD at 798 uses YR as an index register to load XR from memory at 351. The BRA at 808 has an effective address of 352.

Architectural features helpful for subroutine execution are an instruction that combines the saving of the return address in some accessible location with a branch to the subroutine; an instruction that returns control to the calling program; an instruction that saves the contents of registers that will be used by the subroutine; an instruction that restores those registers; and means for accessing an argument list created by the calling program. Pushdown stacks, which facilitate subroutine execution, are included in many architectures, especially those of microprocessors. They are described in Sec. 1.4.8.

1.4.6 Fixed-Point Arithmetic

Floating-point arithmetic varies so much from architecture to architecture that it is difficult to generalize. Consequently, this section deals only with fixed-point numbers and decimal arithmetic.

Addition and Subtraction

Sections 1.1 and 1.5 treat binary numbers as having a fixed binary point either just beyond the least significant bit or between the most significant bit and the second most significant bit. In the former case, all numbers are integers; in the latter, all numbers X are fractions ($-1 \leqslant X < 1$). In reality, adders (described in Sec. 1.5.3) treat all bit positions identically. The binary point is an imaginary concept helpful to the user of the CPU. The user can think of the bit pattern $b_{n-1} \cdots b_0$ in an n-bit register as representing a number $X = N \times S$, where N is the integer represented by the bits in the register ($N = \Sigma_{i=0}^{n-1} b_i 2^i$), and S is a scale factor. If $S = 1$, the number is an integer ($0 \leqslant X < 2^n$) corresponding to the binary point to the right. If $S = 2^{-n}$, the number is a fraction ($0 \leqslant X < 1$) corresponding to the binary point to the left. If $S = 2^{-n+1}$, the number ($0 \leqslant X < 2$) is less than 2. In this case, the number can also be interpreted as a fraction in 2's-complement form ($-1 \leqslant X < 1$) (see Sec. 1.5.4). Very small numbers may be handled by using $S = 2^{-a}$, very large numbers by $S = 2^a$, where a is large.

To illustrate the principle, we consider a program that adds a number of positive integers, the sum of which may exceed 2^n. It is preceded by code to initialize the index register and other registers for looping.

Location	Instruction or Data		Comments
78	CLEAR	A	A will hold scaled sum
79	CLEAR	B	B will hold overflow count
80	LOAD X	C,0	C receives N_i
			(effective address: $ad + i - 1$)
81	SHIFT RIGHT	C,B	Scale down N_i
82	ADD	A,C	A holds $N_1 + \cdots + N_i$
83	BRA NOTOVER	86	scaled down
84	SHIFT RIGHT	A,1	Scale down $N_1 + \cdots + N_i$
85	ADD IMM	B,1	Increment overflow count
86	BXH	XR,...,80	

The ADD instruction at 82 adds N_i to the sum $N_1 + \cdots + N_{i-1}$, just like the accumulating add in the previous examples. If the sum is at least 2^{n-1}, an overflow bit is set in a control register (see Sec. 1.5.5). This bit can be tested by a conditional branch instruction such as that at 83, which skips to 86 if the overflow bit is 0. When an overflow occurs, the sum is scaled down by one-half by a shift right instruction that shifts the contents of A right one position and introduces a 0 in the high-order bit. Such a SHIFT is at 84. After this has occurred, all numbers accumulated must also be scaled down by one-half before being added to the sum. If the overflow occurs a second time, the sum is scaled down by one-half again, and all numbers added in the future must be scaled down by one-fourth, and so on. The instruction at 85 increments, in register B, the count of number of times an overflow has occurred. The LOAD at 80 brings N_i into register C, and the SHIFT at 81 shifts this right the number of times specified in the B register (the overflow count). Note the difference between the two SHIFT instructions. At 81 the number of shifts of C is specified by a register contents; at 84 it is specified by an immediate operand. Other architectures may permit other shift specifications. The BXH instruction causes the loop to be executed and XR to be incremented (or decremented) an appropriate number of times. Upon completion, A holds I and B holds J, and the total is $I \times 2^J$. Of course, some precision may be lost in this process, and we have not considered rounding. Note that some shift instructions shift operands while preserving the sign of the number, some shift over two registers, and others shift in other ways.

Multiplication and Division

Fixed-point *multiplication* generally produces a product with the number of bits equal to the sum of the multiplier and multiplicand bits (e.g., two 16-bit operands result in a 32-bit product). The user must use either the entire product or the part that is known to be significant. Assume that the instruction

$$\text{MPY} \quad \text{A,a}$$

creates the product of the contents of register A and of the memory location a and places the high-order n bits of the product in register A and the low-order n bits in B.

If it is known that $\Sigma x_i y_i$ is always less than 2^{n-1}, the following program calculates that scalar product. Assume that the vector of multiplicands is located in memory from ad to $ad + ct - 1$ and the multipliers from $ad + 1000$ to $ad + 1000 + ct - 1$. The following code sequence is preceded by code to initialize the index register and other registers for looping.

Location	Instruction or Data			Comments
32	CLEAR		C	
33	LOAD	X	A,0	Multiplicand into A
				from $ad + i - 1$
34	MPY	X	A,1000	Multiplier at $ad + 1000 + i - 1$
35	ADD		C,B	Accumulate sum in C
36	BXH		XR,...,33	

The LOAD in 33 brings the multiplicand from memory location $ad + i - 1$. The MPY instruction multiplies this by the multiplier. Note that the address field is 1000, so the effective address is 1000 greater than for the preceding instruction. The lower-order half of the product is in register B and accumulated in C by the ADD at 35. The high-order half is 0. Should the high-order half be significant, instead, the ADD instruction could accumulate the products from register A. Some precision would be lost. Alternative scaling is possible.

Division often involves a double-length dividend (DD) and a single-length divisor (DR), quotient (Q), and remainder (R). They satisfy the relation

$$DD = Q \times DR + R$$

A key requirement found in many architectures is that the user must scale the dividend and divisor so that the quotient fits in a single n-bit register. Assume that

$$\text{DIV} \quad \text{AB,a}$$

divides the double-length dividend in registers A and B by the divisor at a in memory, leaving the quotient in A and the remainder in B.

Following is a program to convert from binary to decimal using the divide instruction. (The binary number is assumed less than 2^n.) This is based on the knowledge that a decimal number can be described as

$$(((\ldots)10 + d_2)10 + d_1)10 + d_0$$

where d_i are the digits, d_0 being the least significant. The following code sequence is preceded by code to initialize the index register and other registers for looping.

Location	Instruction or Data			Comments
31	LOAD		B,76	Load binary number
32	CLEAR		A	into AB
33	DIV	IMM	AB,10	Divide by 10
34	STORE	X	B,0	Remainder d_i
				stored at $ad - i$
35	MOVE		B,A	Quotient moved to B
36	BXH		XR,...,32	
	:			
	:			
76	Binary number to be converted			

The first division at 33 yields a quotient

$$((\cdots)10 + d_2)10 + d_1$$

in A and a remainder d_0 in B. Each number d_i is the binary representation of a digit from 0 to 9. d_0 is stored in the last word of an array ending at ad by the STORE instruction. The quotient is moved to the A/B register by the instructions at 35 and 32. Successive iterations store d_i at $ad - i$. This loop is repeated *ct* times, corresponding to the maximum number of decimal digits possible for an *n*-bit number. Otherwise, the iterations can be ended when the quotient is 0.

Decimal Arithmetic

Each architecture has its own means of encoding decimal numbers (strings of codes for decimal digits) as well as instructions for manipulating them. Operands are generally variable length, with the maximum allowed length specified in the instruction or elsewhere. Arithmetic instructions generally have two such operands, the result replacing one of the operands. Other operations on strings in memory are also included in some architectures.

In CPUs without decimal addition instructions, there is often a helpful "decimal adjust" instruction. This is used following a normal binary addition of two words, each containing two or more binary-coded decimal strings. It uses control bits set by internal carries to adjust the sum to represent a binary-coded decimal number.

1.4.7 Tricks of the Trade

Each instruction set has some instructions that can be used effectively in ways that are not obvious initially. For example, the IBM System/370 architecture has no CLEAR instruction; however, the subtract instruction (denoted SR) can be used to clear any register by subtracting it from itself: SR R,R.

Another example concerns a microprocessor whose index register is twice as long as its memory word length. One way to move an address from locations 100 and 101 to 200 and 202 is

```
LOAD     A,100
STORE    A,200
LOAD     A,101
STORE    A,202
```

A better way is

```
LOAD     X,100
STORE    X,200
```

if the LOAD and STORE instructions for index registers automatically handle two-word addresses. The latter method would normally be executed more rapidly than the former and occupy less memory space.

These techniques are learned from texts and manuals that discuss specific CPUs—sometimes even by experimenting with an instruction set.

1.4.8 Microprocessor Techniques

In most ways, microprocessor programs are no different from those for mainframe processors. (Incidentally, programs for microprocessors are not "microprograms"—operation sequences for CPU control units. The latter are described in Sec. 1.9.3.) On the other hand, there are certain areas in which dealing with microprocessors requires more ingenuity on the part of the programmer. This section deals with those areas.

Word Size

In general, microprocessor word sizes are smaller than mainframe or miniprocessor word sizes, and techniques to cope with these smaller sizes must be mastered. Although the word sizes of new microprocessors are increasing from year to year, there may always be a need for CPUs with small word size.

The basic approach to achieving precision with small word width is to combine a number of smaller words into a wider word. For example, if a word is *n* bits wide but the user requires *kn* bits of precision, he or she can represent numbers by *k* consecutive words of storage. The principle behind addition (and subtraction) of such numbers is to add the *k* corresponding pairs of *n*-bit words, starting with the least significant word pair, and adding the carry bit generated by the previous operation. The following example subtracts the three-word number at memory locations 200–202 from the one at 100–102 and places the difference at 300–302. The least significant words of the numbers are at 102 and 202.

LOAD		A, 102
SUB		A, 202
STORE		A, 302
LOAD		A, 101
SUB	BOR	A, 201
STORE		A, 301
LOAD		A, 100
SUB	BOR	A, 200
STORE		A, 300
BRA BORROW		1000

The "BOR" following two of the three SUB instructions means that when the second operand is subtracted from the first operand (e.g., contents of memory at 201 from the A register), the borrow bit generated by the previous operation is also subtracted. Often, the borrow and carry flags are identical. The last instruction of the sequence checks whether a borrow remains after subtraction of the most significant words. This implies a negative result, which is presumed to be handled by code at location 1000.

The subtract with borrow instructions use the borrow flag that was set by the previous SUB instruction. Should the intervening STORE and LOAD instructions affect the borrow flag, this code would not be correct. The programmer must always be aware of what instructions affect what status flags if tests are not made immediately after the execution of the instructions setting the flags.

This type of software manipulation is similar to the functions performed on strings of data by hardware, in mainframes with rich instruction sets. Multiplication and division can also be performed in microprocessor software, using similar techniques.

Addressing Modes

Consider a CPU (e.g., the Motorola M6800) with only one index register and an address field smaller than the address length. The simple task of moving a string of words from one set of locations to another is not so simple to program, in general. Although the second example in Sec. 1.4.6 illustrates how two arrays can be addressed by a single index register, that technique cannot be used in many instances. If the starting points of the arrays are w words apart, and if the address field in indexed instructions cannot accommodate numbers as large as w, a program using two index quantities must be used for the task:

Location	Instruction or Data			Comments
85	LOAD		XR, 201	Initialize pointer
86	STORE		XR, 204	to target array
87	LOAD		XR, 200	Initialize source pointer
88	LOAD	X	A, 0	Register A gets N_i
89	INCREMENT XR			
90	STORE		XR, 203	Source pointer
91	LOAD		XR, 204	Target pointer
92	STORE	X	A, 0	
93	INCREMENT XR			
94	STORE		XR, 204	
95	LOAD		XR, 203	Source pointer
96	COMPARE XR		202	
97	BRA UNEQUAL		88	
	⋮			
200	$ad1$			Address of source array
201	$ad2$			Address of target array
202	$ad1 + ct$			Upper limit of source array
203	—			$ad1 + i - 1$
204	—			$ad2 + i - 1$

The instruction

INCREMENT XR

simply adds 1 to the index register contents. The instruction

COMPARE XR a

compares the index register with memory at location a. A control bit, which can be tested by the BRA UNEQUAL instruction, is set if the contents are equal. The index register is loaded with one address for accessing the source array at instruction 88 and with another address for accessing the target array at instruction 92. The preponderance of the program updates these two addresses and moves them between the index register and memory.

Note the assumption that the address of the word beyond the end of the source array can be found at location 202. If it is necessary to calculate this and if addresses occupy two or more memory words, the addition must be performed as described in the previous section.

Stacks

Automatic pushdown stacks are used to save information when an interrupt occurs, when a subroutine is called, and when a program pushes data onto them. This stack is different from the stack described in Sec. 1.1.3. The stack described there is an integral part of the arithmetic-logic unit and participates in virtually every data manipulation instruction. In "stack" architectures, it is sometimes possible to combine into a single stack the pushdown stack that holds operands and the one that holds status.

The principle behind the pushdown stack for storing status is easy to understand. An area of main memory is reserved (generally by the programmer) to hold the stack. The number of words occupied by the stack changes size from time to time. A special register called the *stack pointer* (SP) is used to hold the address of the top of the stack, usually the next location available to receive data. When information is pushed onto the stack, either automatically or by program, the data are placed into successive memory locations at the SP address and above, and the address in the SP is decremented by the number of words pushed onto the stack. Conversely, when data are removed from the stack, the words are read from main memory at the locations below the stack pointer, placed in the designated registers, and the address in the SP is incremented appropriately. Instructions usually exist to set the SP and to manipulate its contents in other ways; these instructions vary from architecture to architecture.

In general, some CPU status (instruction counter and other register contents, and control bits) is automatically pushed onto the stack when an interrupt is accepted by the CPU, and automatically restored when an instruction to return from the interrupt handler is executed. The information stored may be only the instruction counter, or all registers and control bits, depending on the architecture. In some architectures, a separate set of registers for the interrupt level is provided, in which case no saving and restoring is necessary. Depending on the registers that the interrupt-handling program uses, some additional status information must be saved explicitly by the interrupt servicing program, usually in the stack. Prior to returning to the interrupted program, the interrupt handler must restore the information explicitly saved. A return-type instruction restores automatically what was previously saved automatically. The interrupt handler may also inspect the stack if there is a need to determine something about the CPU status when the interrupt occurred. Enough memory must be reserved for the stack. If the stack is in the same memory space as instructions and data, there may be no means of protecting the stack from programs, or vice versa. The programmer must ensure that no interference occurs.

Subroutine calls are analogous to interrupts. The subroutine call instruction pushes the instruction counter contents onto the stack, and perhaps more information. The return instruction pops (restores) all that was stored. It is up to the programmer explicitly to push anything more that he or she requires. The stack permits passing arguments to the subroutine either in the stack itself or in an argument list located at a known displacement from the instruction that passes control to the subroutine. In either case, the programmer must be aware of how much data is automatically pushed onto the stack, so that the information desired can be located.

The following two examples assume that (1) when a subroutine is called, 13 words of status are automatically saved; (2) the stack pointer is decremented by 13; (3) the return address, which is the address of the instruction following the branch to subroutine instruction, is located at the new stack pointer contents +9; (4) the index register contents are not saved automatically in the stack; and (5) two arguments must be passed to the subroutine. The following code illustrates passing the arguments in the stack.

	Location	Instruction or Data		Comments
	250	PUSH	A	First argument
Calling sequence	251	PUSH	B	Second argument
	252	BRASUB	305	
	253	POP	B	Clear stack upon
	254	POP	A	return
	.			
	.			
	.			

	305	PUSH		XR	Save index register
	306	MOVE		XR, SP	
	307	LOAD	X	B, 15	Load second argument
Subroutine	308	LOAD	X	A, 16	Load first argument
		⋮ Body of subroutine			
		POP		XR	Restore index register
		RETURN			

The two PUSH instructions at the beginning of the calling sequence push the arguments onto the stack, where the subroutine can fetch them. The BRASUB pushes CPU status onto the stack and loads the instruction counter with the subroutine address. The initial PUSH in the subroutine saves the index register contents on the stack, since the register is needed for what follows. The PUSH also decrements the stack pointer address. (Assume that the decrement is 1.) The MOVE instruction places the stack address in the index register so that it can be used to address data. The following indexed LOAD instruction addresses memory at the stack pointer plus 15 (1 for the XR, 13 for the CPU status, and 1 for the second argument pushed). The instruction at 308 has an address of 16, corresponding to the first argument, which is found below the second. After the subroutine is executed, the index register is restored, and the RETURN from subroutine instructions are executed. When control returns to 253, two POP instructions are executed to clear the arguments from the stack. Note that they are popped in the opposite order from that in which they were pushed.

Now consider passing arguments in a list in the calling sequence.

	Location	Instruction or Data			Comments
	321	BRASUB		430	
Calling sequence	322	BRA		325	Branch past arguments
	323	Argument 1			
	324	Argument 2			
	325	Next instruction			
		⋮			
		⋮			
	430	PUSH		XR	Save XR
	431	MOVE		XR, SP	
	432	LOAD	X	XR, 10	XR gets address of arg1
	433	LOAD	X	A, 1	A gets arg1
Subroutine	434	LOAD	X	B, 2	
		⋮ Body of subroutine			
		POP			Restore XR
		RETURN			

Here the indexed LOAD at 432 in the subroutine fetches the word 10 words down in the stack (1 for the index register and 9 for the known displacement of the return address). In this case the return address is 322. This address is placed in the index register by the LOAD. The following two *indexed* LOADs bring the arguments into the A and B registers. The branch instruction at 322 exists to hop over the arguments when control returns to the calling program.

Note that XR is first loaded with the stack pointer and used to calculate the effective address of the place where the return address is stored. Then it is loaded with the address pushed onto the stack and used to calculate the effective address of the arguments. This indirect addressing sequence of loading the index register with a value used to calculate the effective address for another load of the index register is a common technique with processors having few index registers.

Although the stack pointer often can be manipulated like any other register, it may not be safely used unless interrupts cannot occur—otherwise, CPU status would be written at locations to which the pointer points.

Other Concerns

There are never enough registers in any processor. This is especially true for microprocessors. Some techniques for dealing with this have been observed already (e.g., saving a register's contents in memory while another value is loaded into the register). Another useful technique is "unwinding" a loop. This means repeating the code sequence for an operation the desired number of times rather than using a register to contain a count, then decrementing and conditionally branching after each time the sequence is executed. The code sequence of LOAD and ADDs in Sec. 1.4.1 is such an unwound loop. It requires no register for indexing or counting. Unwinding is clearly impractical when the sequence is repeated many times. This approach also represents a trade-off in program design: the greater speed of the unwound loop against the larger amount of storage required for the program.

The limited instruction sets of microprocessors means that operations done by hardware in some mainframes must be done in software in microprocessors. Obvious examples are instructions for floating-point arithmetic, variable-length decimal arithmetic, and fixed-point multiplication and division. The hardware algorithms described in Sec. 1.5 can be translated into software subroutines to perform these same operations. Other limitations are apt to prove irksome. For example, in a processor where addresses are double-word size, there may be no instruction to add a single-word number to a double-length index register. If one desires to add 7 to the index register, one may do this:

Location	Instruction or Data			Comments
13	STORE		XR, 38	Assume that this stores a double-word
14	LOAD		A, 39	Low-order half of
15	ADD	IMM	A, 7	XR contents
16	STORE		A, 39	
17	CLEARA			
18	ADD	CAR	A, 38	High-order half
19	STORE		A, 38	
20	LOAD		XR, 38	
	⋮			
38	—			Hold contents of XR
39	—			and later 7 + C(XR)

The STORE at 13 places the double-word index register contents in storage at 38 and 39, so that they can be loaded into another register for addition. The ADD at 15 adds 7 to the low-order half of the index. The ADD CAR at 18 adds 0 (in register A) and the high-order half of the index and the carry from the addition of the low-order half. This is then put back to storage, from which the index register is loaded at instruction 20. Note that fewer instructions are required to increment the index register 7 times.

One major concern of the microprocessor programmer is that of handling interrupts (see Sec. 1.2). Because of the variety of architectures, it is impossible to generalize on useful programming techniques. In some systems, integral hardware exists to direct control to an interrupt handler specifically for the condition causing the interrupt. In other systems, the designer must either provide such hardware, or the program must determine the condition and transfer control accordingly. Programming for input/output is often simpler in microprocessor systems (see Sec. 1.12), since devices can be addressed like memory locations. Nonetheless, "handshaking" protocols do exist and vary from system to system.

A final mention should be made of the occasional need to assemble a microprocessor program by hand. The need may arise due to the unavailability of an assembler, or because it is faster to assemble a small program by hand. This entails assigning memory locations to all instructions and data words. Then any symbols used for addresses must be converted to numerical addresses, and the binary codes for the instructions must be looked up. Section 2.11 can provide some guidance.

1.5 ARITHMETIC-LOGIC UNIT

Earl E. Swartzlander, Jr.

The arithmetic-logic unit (ALU) is the component of a computer that performs arithmetic and logical operations. This article begins with an overview of ALU usage and then examines ALU functions, implementation, and algorithms.

1.5.1 ALU Usage

In a general-purpose computer, the ALU implements and performs all arithmetic operations as specified by the program sequence and is also used in generating memory addresses. This article briefly examines the concept of the basic stored program computer, since it provides a perspective for how the ALU is used.

At a minimum, the ALU must compute the four basic arithmetic operations (add, subtract, multiply, and divide) as well as a number of logical operations (and, or, invert, etc.). With the exception of a few operations such as logical inversion and square root, ALU operations are dyadic (i.e., performed on two operands). Since data are fetched from the memory a word at a time, some form of data storage must be provided in conjunction with the ALU. A variety of approaches have been used, including accumulators, stacks, register files, and scratch pad memories. Section 1.1 examines these approaches in greater detail.

In implementing the ALU for minicomputers and microprocessors, it would generally be too complex to provide a dedicated hardware multiplier or divider. Instead, these functions are performed in firmware with a series of add and shift operations (for multiply) or subtract and shift operations (for divide). By contrast, large scientific computers use fully parallel logical arrays to implement multiplication directly. In the large machines, division is implemented either with special-purpose hardware or with an iterative procedure based on Newton's method. A final distinction between the smaller machines and large scientific computers is that the latter generally contain a floating-point ALU which directly computes both the exponent and the mantissa (or fraction) for arithmetic operations. In smaller machines, floating-point arithmetic is often implemented via a micropro-grammed sequence of integer or fractional (micro) operations.

ALU Usage in Signal Processors

Special-purpose computers are becoming practical for applications in real-time signal processing. In this context the ALU is used strictly for data stream computation. This results in a somewhat different set of requirements for the ALU design. In basic terms, signal processing differs from general-purpose computing in that the operation sequences are usually not data dependent. Since the ALU is processing data only, higher instruction rates are achieved in signal processing.

In some signal-processing applications, it may be desirable to use an ALU with multiple data ports. This concept is shown in Fig. 1. On each memory cycle, a three-port data memory accesses two operands and stores a result. These three ports are directly connected to the inputs and output of the ALU. High ALU throughput is achieved without requiring high-speed data transfers.

1.5.2 ALU Functions

The most important characteristics of an ALU are the functional capabilities and the internal architecture. This section provides an overview of the capability and architecture of commercially available building-block ALU integrated circuits.

Arithmetic and Logic Functions

Commercial ALU circuits are an extension of standard adder/subtractor circuits, where additional arithmetic and logic functions can be performed at little increase in complexity.

The most widely used ALU is the 54181/74181, developed in 1970 in standard TTL. It has since been made in Schottky and low-power Schottky technologies, and functionally similar circuits have been made in ECL and CMOS. It is a 4-bit-wide building block that can implement arbitrary width ALUs. Inputs consist of two 4-bit operands (A_0, A_1, A_2, A_3 and B_0, B_1, B_2, B_3), a carry-in to the low-order stage, C_n, a mode control, M, and a 4-bit function select code (S_0, S_1, S_2, S_3). The outputs consist of four data lines (F_0, F_1, F_2, F_3), a flag that indicates when all outputs are zero, a carry-out signal from the high-order stage, C_{n+4}, and carry lookahead signals, P and G (see Sec. 1.5.3 for a detailed discussion of carries). Thirty-two arithmetic and logical functions are realized by the 54181/74181, including addition, subtraction, AND, OR, and so on. In most applications, only a few of the available functions are used; as a result, subsequent ALU designs have eliminated most of the

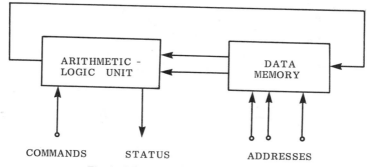

Fig. 1 Multiport memory/ALU interface.

superfluous operations. This allows the function selection to be performed with fewer lines, which saves package pins and simplifies ALU usage.

The 54181/74181 ALU is a combinational circuit (i.e., it does not have internal data registers or latches). In many applications, external storage registers are needed to buffer the ALU operands. Some of the subsequent integrated-circuit ALU designs have added internal registers. Bit-slice microprocessor designs (see Sec. 1.3) are extensions of this concept that include complete sets of working registers.

Commercial ALU Circuits

This section describes several commercial integrated-circuit ALU designs. These designs, which are all commercially available TTL circuits, serve to indicate the range of implementation options that are available to system designers.

The 54181/74181 4-bit ALU is the first commercial design implementing many rarely used functions. Figure 2 shows an 8-bit adder/subtractor built with the 54181/74181. The add/subtract command is latched into a flip-flop so that both Q and $\overline{Q}$ outputs are available to generate the necessary add and subtract commands. The Q output is used as the least significant carry input, so that a carry in is provided during subtraction. This implements 2's-complement subtraction, which is examined in greater depth in Sec. 1.5.5.

The functional block diagram of the 54281/74281 ALU/accumulator is shown in Fig. 3. Basically, it consists of an ALU with an internal register for one input and a shift matrix between the ALU output and the register. The internal register is used as an accumulator when a sum of many terms is to be computed. The shift unit allows intermediate terms to be shifted up or down, as required, for rescaling arithmetic results. Only eight arithmetic functions are generated; however, these are more useful than the larger number of 54181/74181 functions.

The 54381/74381 logic design is similar to the 54181/74181; it is a combinational circuit without storage registers. It differs by only providing three arithmetic operations, $A+B$, $A-B$, and $B-A$; three logic operations, $A \cdot B$, $A+B$, and $A \oplus B$; and the capability to preset to all 0's or all 1's. Thus only three control signals are required, and a package with fewer pins may be used.

In comparing ALU designs for a specific application, several interdependent specifications should be considered. These include operations to be performed, number of data ports, and storage (register) requirements.

The operations required for the system must be realized with the available arithmetic and logical functions of the selected ALU. There are three data ports (two inputs and one output) for the combinational ALU designs or two (one input and one output) for ALUs that include internal storage. Three-port designs are preferred for large mainframe computers, high-speed signal processors, and

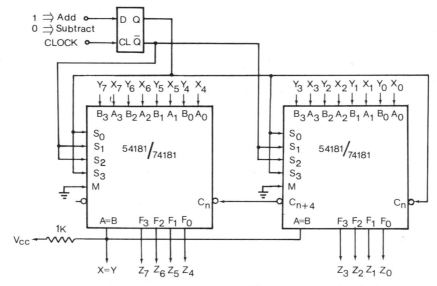

Fig. 2 8-bit adder/subtractor implemented with 54181/74181 using ripple carry.

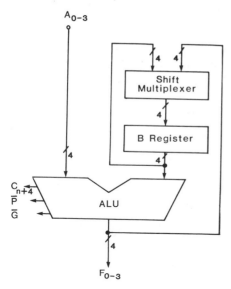

A_0-3

Shift Multiplexer

B Register

ALU

$\overline{C}_{n+4}$
$\overline{P}$
$\overline{G}$

F_0-3

Fig. 3 54281/74281 arithmetic-logic unit/accumulator.

other specialized high-speed applications where maximum speed is required; two-port architectures are well suited to general-purpose (i.e., minicomputer) applications.

Internal storage in the form of input registers, an accumulator, or register files reduces the need to access main memory, and is also useful in storing temporary variables in signal-processing applications.

1.5.3 ALU Implementation

This section examines the implementation of ALUs of arbitrary size. The basic approach involves developing a module which is a slice of a wide-word ALU. It is an extension of the use of full adders to implement wide-word addition circuits. Figure 4 shows the truth table of a "full adder" stage and the interconnection of n such stages to create a parallel adder for n-bit words. At the kth-bit position, the kth bits of the operands A_k and B_k and a carry signal from the preceding full adder are used to generate the kth bit of the sum S_k, and a carry to the $(k+1)$st full-adder stage.

The logical equations that describe the operation of the kth adder stage are

$$S_k = A_k \oplus B_k \oplus C_k \tag{1}$$

$$C'_k = A_k B_k + A_k C_k + B_k C_k \tag{2}$$

where A_k, B_k, and C_k are the inputs to the kth full-adder stage, and S_k and C'_k are the sum and carry outputs, respectively. This is called a *ripple carry adder*, since the carry signals propagate (i.e., ripple) from the least significant stage to the most significant. This rippling occurs since the carry-out from each stage depends on the carry input to that stage (i.e., the carry-out of the preceding stage). Thus if the time from carry-in to carry-out requires a single delay, an n-bit ripple carry adder may require n delays. Although analysis has shown that the average maximum carry chain length is approximately $1 + \log_2 n$, the worst-case delay of n must be allowed [1].

One approach for circumventing the long, worst-case delay is the use of adders which generate signals indicating when carry propagation is complete. This technique is not widely used, since it results in data-dependent timing, which greatly raises the system complexity.

A third adder approach is the carry lookahead adder. Here specialized carry logic determines the carry status by looking across a wide word. In each module, outputs indicate that a carry has been generated within that module, or that a lower-output carry would be propagated across that module. To understand the concept, refer to (2), which describes ripple carry operation, and define $G_k \equiv A_k B_k$ and $P_k \equiv A_k + B_k$:

$$C'_k = G_k + P_k C_k \tag{3}$$

This helps to explain the concept of carry generation and propagation: at a given stage a carry is

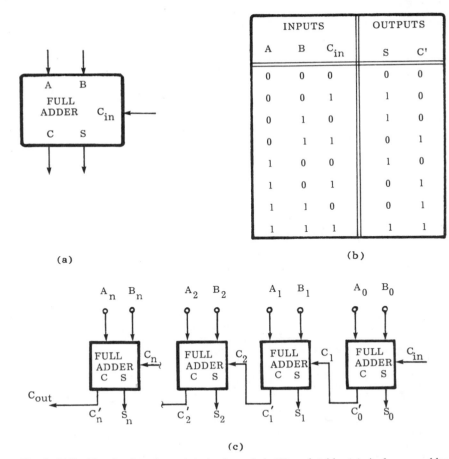

INPUTS			OUTPUTS	
A	B	C_{in}	S	C'
0	0	0	0	0
0	0	1	1	0
0	1	0	1	0
0	1	1	0	1
1	0	0	1	0
1	0	1	0	1
1	1	0	0	1
1	1	1	1	1

(a)

(b)

(c)

Fig. 4 Full-adder circuit and use: (*a*) circuit symbol; (*b*) truth table; (*c*) ripple carry adder.

generated if G_k is true (i.e., $A_k = B_k = 1$), and a stage transmits (or propagates) an input carry to its output if P_k is true (i.e., either A_k or B_k is a 1). Extending this definition to a 4-bit-wide module:

$$S_k = A_k \oplus B_k \oplus C_k \tag{4}$$

$$S_{k+1} = A_{k+1} \oplus B_{k+1} \oplus (G_k + P_k C_k) \tag{5}$$

Equation (5) results from evaluating (4) for the $(k+1)$st stage and substituting C_{k+1} ($\equiv C_k'$) from (3). Extending to subsequent stages, we obtain

$$S_{k+2} = A_{k+2} \oplus B_{k+2} \oplus (G_{k+1} + P_{k+1} G_k + P_{k+1} P_k C_k) \tag{6}$$

$$S_{k+3} = A_{k+3} \oplus B_{k+3} \oplus (G_{k+2} + P_{k+2} G_{k+1} + P_{k+2} P_{k+1} G_k + P_{k+2} P_{k+1} P_k C_k) \tag{7}$$

Recognize that a carry is emitted from stage $k+2$ if (1) a carry is generated there, (2) a carry was emitted from stage $k+1$ and propagated across stage $k+2$, (3) a carry was emitted from stage k and propagated across both stages $k+1$ and $k+2$, and so on.

$$P_{block} = P_{k+3} P_{k+2} P_{k+1} P_k \tag{8}$$

$$G_{block} = G_{k+3} + P_{k+3} G_{k+2} + P_{k+3} P_{k+2} G_{k+1} + P_{k+3} P_{k+2} P_{k+1} G_k \tag{9}$$

$$C_{k+4} = G_{block} + P_{block} C_k \tag{10}$$

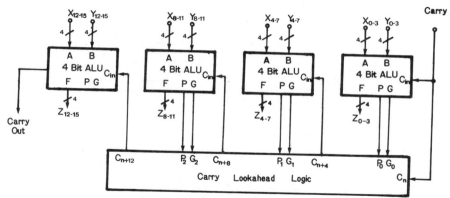

Fig. 5   16-bit carry lookahead adder.

Equation (10), which is (3) extended over the 4-bit block, shows that the carry of a 4-bit-wide block can be computed in only two gate delays [one to compute P_n and G_n for $n = k$ through $k+3$ and one to evaluate (10) using (8), (9), and the P_n and G_n values]. This compares with eight delays to compute the carry from a four-stage ripple carry adder [from equation (2) and Fig. 4].

Carry lookahead can be extended to larger blocks, but the number of inputs to the logical gates increases in direct proportion to the block size. Industry practice has standardized on 4-bit-wide blocks which: (1) can be combined to form adders for the most common word sizes (i.e., 16, 24, 32, 60, and 64 bits), (2) use a small number of package pins, and (3) are implemented with gates with at most four inputs. The various bit-slice ALU designs of Sec. 1.5.2 all provide P and G signals for carry lookahead according to these equations.

Figure 5 shows the interconnection of four 4-bit ALU circuits and a carry lookahead block to realize a 16-bit fast adder. The sequence of events that occur during an add operation is as follows: (1) apply A, B, and carry-in signals, (2) each 4-bit ALU computes P and G, (3) carry lookahead logic computes all carry outputs, and (4) each ALU computes the F outputs.

This process may be extended to larger adders by subdividing the large adder into 16-bit blocks. Each 16-bit-wide block is implemented as shown in Fig. 5. The easiest method to cascade the 16-bit block adders is with ripple carry: the carry-out of each adder is connected to the carry input of the next more significant adder. An alternative approach is to use a second level of carry lookahead, as exemplified for 64-bit word size in Fig. 6. This segments the words to be added into 16-bit blocks with carry lookahead between the carry lookahead blocks. The advantage is that with two-level carry lookahead, the delay for a 64-bit adder is only slightly greater than for the 16-bit single-level lookahead adder. With ripple carry between blocks, the delay is proportional to the number of 16-bit blocks.

The typical delay of each of these approaches is graphed in Fig. 7 for word sizes of 4 to 64 bits. At all sizes, carry lookahead produces a speed increase, but the improvement is most striking for wide-word (i.e., 32 to 64 bits wide) ALU designs. Because of the simplicity and performance gain achieved by use of carry lookahead logic, it is nearly universally accepted for ALU implementation

1.5.4   Representation of Numbers

Before considering algorithms for addition, subtraction, multiplication, and division, it is appropriate to consider the choice of number system. Fixed point and floating point are the two types in common use. Fixed-point systems use constant scaling (i.e., binary points that are fixed in a specific position) and are generally fractional systems that express numbers in the range $|X| \leqslant 1$. Integers are often used in addressing, but the arithmetic is identical for all fixed-point number systems. Floating-point numbers consist of a fixed-point exponent (used to denote a scale factor) and a fixed-point fraction (i.e., the mantissa).

Fixed-point numbers and the mantissas of floating-point numbers are usually expressed as 2's-complement numbers. This choice has prevailed over sign-magnitude and 1's-complement forms, because the 2's-complement form produces much simpler algorithms for addition and subtraction, the two most frequent arithmetic operations. Sign-magnitude produces a simpler multiplication algorithm, but the lower frequency of multiplication and the existence of satisfactory 2's-complement multiplication algorithms have resulted in nearly universal selection of the 2's-complement form. Positive 2's-

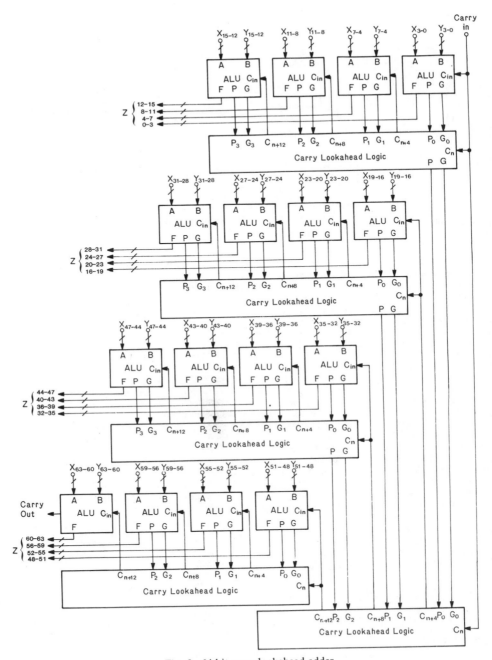

Fig. 6 64-bit carry lookahead adder.

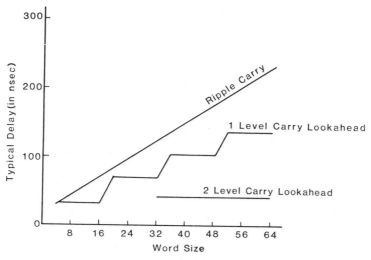

Fig. 7 ALU delay for various word sizes.

complement fractions are represented by n bits $(a_{n-1}, a_{n-2}, \ldots, a_1, a_0)$:

$$A = \sum_{i=0}^{n-2} a_i 2^{i-n+1} \tag{11}$$

for example: $1/8 \leftarrow 0.00100\ldots, 1/4 \leftarrow 0.0100\ldots$, and so on. The sign bit $a_{n-1} = 0$ (by definition), and $A < 1$. A negative 2's-complement number is represented by subtracting its absolute value from 2 (hence the name "2's complement"). Since the absolute value of the number is less than or equal to 1, the leading bit (a_{n-1}) is always 1. A single notation will suffice to express both positive and negative 2's-complement numbers:

$$A = -a_{n-1} + \sum_{i=0}^{n-2} a_i 2^{i-n+1} \tag{12}$$

Note that $-1/8 \leftarrow 1.11100\ldots, -1/4 \leftarrow 1.1100\ldots$, and so on.

The largest and smallest positive numbers are $1 - 2^{-n+1}$ and 2^{-n+1}, expressed as $0.111\ldots11$ and $0.000\ldots01$, respectively; the most negative number is -1, expressed as $1.000\ldots00$; and there is a single representation for zero, $0.000\ldots00$. The 2's complement of a number is obtained by complementing each bit and adding a one to the least significant bit of the word.

The 1's-complement representation of a number is identical to the 2's-complement form for positive numbers. The representation for negative numbers, however, is the bit-by-bit complement of the corresponding positive value. For example, $-1/8 \leftarrow 1.11011\ldots, -1/4 \leftarrow 1.1011\ldots$, and so on. The most negative number is $2^{-n+1} - 1 \leftarrow 1.00\ldots$. There are two representations for zero: $0.00\ldots$ and $1.11\ldots$ (called minus 0).

The sign-magnitude representation is the same as the 1's- and 2's-complement forms for positive numbers. The representation for negative numbers uses a sign bit of 1 followed by the representation for the corresponding positive value. For example, $-1/8 \leftarrow 1.00100\ldots, -1/4 \leftarrow 1.0100\ldots$, and so on. There are two representations for zero: $0.00\ldots$ and $1.00\ldots$ (called minus 0).

In large computers, especially, decimal and hexadecimal (i.e., base 16) arithmetic is often performed. In both cases, data are represented by 4-bit characters. In decimal implementations, special arithmetic circuits perform the arithmetic; hex implementations use 4-bit ALU modules as described in Sec. 1.5.2.

1.5.5 Arithmetic Algorithms

In this section, fixed-point algorithms for addition/subtraction, multiplication, and division are examined. An introduction to arithmetic algorithms for floating-point number systems is also provided. Further information on ALU arithmetic is available in Refs. 2 and 3.

Fixed-Point Addition/Subtraction

Two's-complement addition is performed as a normal addition of two n-bit binary numbers, including the sign bit. Subtraction is performed by summing the minuend and the 2's complement of the subtrahend.

Overflow is detected by comparing the carry signals into and out of the most significant adder stage (i.e., the stage that computes the sign bit). If the carries disagree, the arithmetic has overflowed and the result is invalid.

A circuit for a ripple-carry adder/subtractor is shown in Fig. 8. It consists of a standard ripple carry adder (as shown in Fig. 4) with exclusive-OR gates to complement operand Y when performing subtraction, and a sign comparison circuit to check for overflow. It forms either $X+Y$ or $X-Y$ with 2's-complement arithmetic. In the case of $X+Y$, the mode selector causes the exclusive-OR gates to pass operand Y directly to the ripple carry adder. The carry into the least significant adder stage is a zero, so standard addition occurs. Overflow is detected by comparing the carry into and out of the most significant adder stage; as long as these carrys agree, overflow has not occurred. Subtraction is implemented by using the exclusive-OR gates to complement the bits of Y; the 2's complement is formed by setting the carry into the least significant adder stage.

Fixed-Point Multiplication

Multiplication is generally implemented either via a sequence of addition, subtraction, and shift operations or with a specialized LSI circuit. In the latter case, which is described below, a parallel array of adders forms the product at speeds comparable to memory or ALU cycles. Booth's algorithm [4] is widely used for 2's-complement multiplication, since it is easy to implement and achieves high speed.

Booth's method for the multiplication of X and Y involves examining the ith bit of the multiplier X (x_i) starting with the least significant (i.e., $i=0$) and assuming that $x_{-1}=0$:

If $x_i=x_{i-1}$, shift the sum of partial products to the right (multiply by $\frac{1}{2}$).
If $x_i=0, x_{i-1}=1$, add Y to the existing sum of partial products and shift one place to the right.
If $x_i=1, x_{i-1}=0$, subtract Y by adding its 2's complement to the existing sum of partial products and shift one place to the right.

No shift is performed on the last stage (i.e., when $i=n-1$). All shift operations are arithmetic shifts (i.e., the sign bit is copied into the position to its right), and overflows in the addition process are ignored. Booth's multiplication algorithm is illustrated in Table 1, in which all sign combinations for the product of $\pm 5/8 \times \pm 3/4$ are computed for 4-bit operands.

An alternative approach to multiplication involves the combinational generation of all bit products and their summation with an array of full adders. Since the speed of this approach is constrained only by the delay of cascade chains of logic gates, this approach is much faster than sequential/iterative processes. In the early 1980s, single-chip multipliers will be available for input operand sizes of 8, 12,

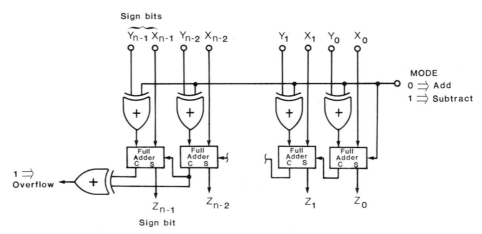

Fig. 8 Two's-complement adder/subtractor.

Table 1. Example of Booth's Algorithm

i	X_i	X_{i-1}	Sum of Partial Products		Operation	Result
$X = 5/8\ (=0.101)$					$Y = 3/4\ (=0.110)$	
0	1	0	0.000		$-Y$	1.010
1	0	1	1.1010		$+Y$	0.0110
2	1	0	0.00110		$-Y$	1.01110
3	0	1	1.101110		$+Y$	0.011110 $(=15/32)$
Thus $5/8 \times 3/4 = 15/32$						
$X = -5/8\ (=1.011)$					$Y = 3/4\ (=0.110)$	
0	1	0	0.000		$-Y$	1.010
1	1	1	1.1010		—	1.1010
2	0	1	1.11010		$+Y$	0.10010
3	1	0	0.010010		$-Y$	1.100010 $(=-15/32)$
Thus $-5/8 \times 3/4 = -15/32$						
$X = 5/8\ (=0.101)$					$Y = -3/4\ (=1.010)$	
0	1	0	0.000		$-Y$	0.110
1	0	1	0.0110		$+Y$	1.1010
2	1	0	1.11010		$-Y$	0.10010
3	0	1	0.010010		$+Y$	1.100010 $(=-15/32)$
Thus $5/8 \times -3/4 = -15/32$						
$X = -5/8(=1.011)$					$Y = -3/4\ (=1.010)$	
0	1	0	0.000		$-Y$	0.110
1	1	1	0.0110		—	0.0110
2	0	1	0.00110		$+Y$	1.01110
3	1	0	1.101110		$-Y$	0.011110 $(=15/32)$
Thus $-5/8 \times -3/4 = 15/32$						

and 16 bits. Figure 9 shows an example of the bit product terms that are summed to form the product of an n-bit number X and an m bit number Y (for arbitrary m and n). The terms that are added consist of all combinations of $x_i \cdot y_j$ for $0 \leqslant i \leqslant n-2$ and $0 \leqslant j \leqslant m-2$ and three rows of correction terms shown at the bottom of the matrix. See Ref. 5 for derivation of the correction terms.

Although much effort has been expended in the development of efficient implementations of parallel or array multipliers, the details are beyond the scope of this section. It is sufficient for the user to understand the chip interfaces and control options.

A block diagram of a typical 16-bit single chip multiplier constructed along these lines is shown in Fig. 10. It consists of an array of full adders which form and sum the bit products shown in Fig. 9 (shown as "asynchronous multiplier array"). Registers are provided for the two 16-bit operands, X and Y, and for the least significant and most significant halves of the product, LSP and MSP, respectively. Due to package pin limitations, the least significant half of the product, LSP, is output via the Y input port.

These devices perform 2's-complement arithmetic directly, with rounding (if desired), which is implemented by adding a one at the most significant bit of the LSP. This is especially useful for signal-processing applications where constant data precision is desired at all stages of the computation, and for single-precision floating-point operations.

Fixed-Point Division

Division is traditionally implemented as a shift, subtract, and compare operation, in contrast to the shift and add approach employed for multiplication. The comparison operation is significant: it results in a serial process that is not amenable to parallel implementation.

$$
\begin{array}{cccccccccc}
 & y_{m-1} & \cdots & & y_4 & y_3 & y_2 & y_1 & y_0 \\
 & & & & x_{n-1} & \cdots & x_2 & x_1 & x_0 \\[4pt]
 & & & & & & x_0y_2 & x_0y_1 & x_0y_0 \\
 & & & & & & x_1y_1 & x_1y_0 & \\
 & & & & & & x_2y_0 & & \\
 & & & & & x_1y_2 & & & \\
 & & & & & x_2y_1 & & & \\
 & & & & \vdots & & & & \\
 & & & & x_{n-2}y_0 & & & & \\
 & & x_0y_{m-2} & \cdots & x_{n-2}y_2 & x_{n-2}y_1 & & & \\
 & & & & x_{n-1}\bar{y}_2 & x_{n-1}\bar{y}_1 & x_{n-1}\bar{y}_0 & & \\
 & x_1y_{m-2} & \cdots & x_{n-1}\bar{y}_2 & & & & & \\
 & x_2y_{m-2} & & x_{n-1} & & & & & \\
 & \vdots & & & & & & & \\
 0 & x_{n-2}y_{m-2} & \cdots & x_{n-1}\bar{y}_{m-1} & & & & & \\
x_{n-1}\bar{y}_{m-2} & x_{n-1}\bar{y}_{m-3} & \bar{x}_0y_{m-1} & & & & & & \\
\bar{x}_{n-1}\bar{y}_{m-1} & \bar{x}_{n-2}y_{m-1} & & & & & & & \\
\bar{x}_{n-1}\, \bar{y}_{m-1} & & & & & & & & \\
x_{n-1}y_{m-1} & & & & & & & & \\
1 & & & & & & & & \\[4pt]
p_{n+m-1}\;\; p_{n+m-2}\;\; p_{n+m-3}\;\; p_{n+m-4} & \cdots & p_{m-1}\cdots p_{n+1} & p_n & p_{n-1} & p_{n-2}\cdots p_3 & p_2 & p_1 & p_0
\end{array}
$$

Fig. 9 Two's complement array multiplier bit product matrix.

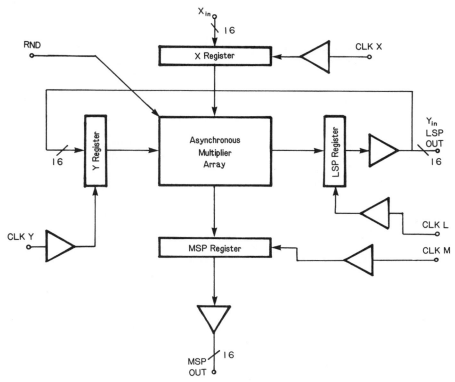

Fig. 10 Single-chip multiplier block diagram.

Traditional division is based on selecting digits of the quotient Q to satisfy the following equation:

$$R^{(i+1)} = rR^{(i)} - q_{n-j-1}D \qquad \text{for } j = 0, 1, \dots, n-1 \tag{13}$$

where D is the divisor, $R^{(0)}$ is the dividend (subject to the constraint $|R^{(0)}| < |D|$), $R^{(j)}$ is the partial remainder after selection of the jth quotient digit, r is the radix ($= 2$ for binary numbers), and q_{n-j-1} is the jth quotient digit to the right of the binary point. Nonrestoring division is the most widely used algorithm. In nonrestoring division, the quotient digits are constrained to be either $+1$ or -1. The digit selection and resulting partial remainder are given for the jth iteration by the following relations:

$$\left.\begin{array}{l} \text{If } 0 < R^{(j)} < D, \quad \text{then } q_{n-j-1} = 1, \\[4pt] \text{and } R^{(j+1)} = 2R^{(j)} - D \\[4pt] \text{If } 0 > R^{(j)} > -D, \quad \text{then } q_{n-j-1} = -1, \\[4pt] \text{and } R^{(j+1)} = 2R^{(j)} + D \end{array}\right\} \tag{14}$$

This process continues either for a set number of iterations or until the partial remainder is smaller than a specified error criterion. The quotient resulting from this procedure is a coded signed digit number (comprised of digits of ± 1). It is converted into a conventional binary number by subtracting a number formed from the -1's from the number with the $+1$'s. The algorithm is illustrated in Table 2, where $\frac{5}{16}$ is divided by $\frac{3}{8}$.

A second division technique uses a form of Newton–Raphson iteration to derive a quadratically convergent approximation to the reciprocal of the divisor, which is then multiplied by the dividend to produce the quotient. This process often operates faster than conventional division algorithms, especially in systems that include a fast multiplier. For this technique it is assumed that the divisor D is normalized (i.e., $\frac{1}{2} \leqslant D < 1$). Since $1/D$ would be larger than 1, $Y = \frac{1}{2D}$ is computed to avoid

Table 2. Example of Binary Nonrestoring Division

$R^{(0)} =$ dividend 0.0101 ($\leftarrow \frac{5}{16}$)
$D =$ divisor 0.0110 ($\leftarrow \frac{3}{8}$)

$R^{(0)} > 0 \rightarrow q_1 = 1$	$2R^{(0)} \rightarrow$	0.1010
	$-D \rightarrow$	+1.1010
	$R^{(1)} \rightarrow$	0.0100
$R^{(1)} > 0 \rightarrow q_2 = 1$	$2R^{(1)} \rightarrow$	0.1000
	$-D \rightarrow$	+1.1010
	$R^{(2)} \rightarrow$	0.0010
$R^{(2)} > 0 \rightarrow q_3 = 1$	$2R^{(2)} \rightarrow$	0.0100
	$-D \rightarrow$	+1.1010
	$R^{(3)} \rightarrow$	1.1110
$R^{(3)} < 0 \rightarrow q_4 = -1$	$2R^{(3)} \rightarrow$	1.1100
	$+D \rightarrow$	+0.0110
	$R^{(4)} \rightarrow$	0.0010

$Q = 0.\quad 1\quad 1\quad 1\quad -1$ (signed digit form)
$Q = P - N$, where $P = 0.1110$ and $N = 0.0001$

$$P \rightarrow \quad 0.1110$$
$$-N \rightarrow \quad +1.1111$$
$$Q \rightarrow \quad 0.1101 \leftarrow 13/16$$

arithmetic overflow. The algorithm consists of three basic steps:

$$Y^{(0)} = 1.457107 - D \tag{15}$$

$$Y^{(i+1)} = 2Y^{(i)}[1 - DY^{(i)}], \quad i = 0, 1, \ldots, k \tag{16}$$

$$Q = 2NY^{(k)} \tag{17}$$

where i is the iteration count and N is the numerator.

With Newton–Raphson iterative division, the error decreases quadratically, so that the number of correct bits in each approximation is roughly twice the number of correct bits in the previous iteration. Thus from a 4-bit initial approximation, two iterations produce a reciprocal estimate accurate to 16 bits, and so on.

The efficiency of this process is dependent on the availability of a fast multiplier, since each iteration of (16) requires two multiplications, a subtraction, and a doubling operation. The complete process for the initial estimate, two iterations, and the final quotient determination requires six addition operations and five multiplication operations to produce a 16-bit quotient. This is two to three times faster than a conventional nonrestoring divider if multiplication is roughly as fast as addition, a condition which is usually satisfied for systems that include single-chip parallel multipliers. Table 3 illustrates the Newton–Raphson iterative division process.

Floating-Point Arithmetic

Floating-point numbers consist of a pair of fixed-point numbers: a mantissa (or fraction) M, and an exponent (or characteristic) e. The value of a number V is given by the equation

$$V = Mr^e \tag{18}$$

Table 3. Example of Division Using Newton–Raphson Iteration

Dividend: $\frac{5}{8}$
Divisor: $\frac{3}{4}$

	Error
$Y_0 = 1.457107 - 0.75 = 0.707107$	0.040440
$Y_1 = 2 \times 0.707107(1 - 0.75 \times 0.707107) = 0.664214$	0.002453
$Y_2 = 2 \times 0.664214(1 - 0.75 \times 0.664214) = 0.666658$	0.000009
$Q = 2 \times 0.625 \times 0.666658 = 0.833323$	

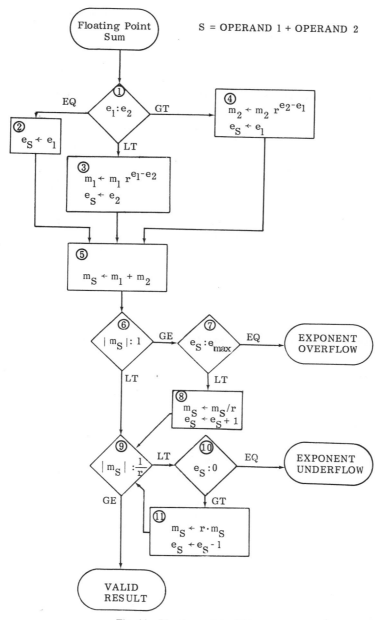

Fig. 11 Floating-point addition.

where r is the radix of the floating-point system (see Sec. 1.5.4). Many floating-point implementations are based on normalized representations of all numbers: this indicates that the most significant digit of the fraction is nonzero. A detailed analysis of the advantages and disadvantages of the use of various numbering systems is beyond the scope of this section (see Ref. 2 or 6). A typical 32-bit floating-point format has an 8-bit integer characteristic which ranges between 0 and 255. The value of the exponent is determined by subtracting the bias value from the characteristic. For this number system, a bias value of 128 would be used, so the exponent range is -128 to 127. The mantissa is a 24-bit 2's-complement fraction.

A flowchart for floating-point addition is shown in Fig. 11 (see also Sec. 1.16.5). The operands are (e_1, m_1) and (e_2, m_2), the result is (e_s, m_s). In ① the operand exponents or characteristics are compared; if they are unequal, the mantissa of the number with the smaller exponent is shifted right in ③ or ④ by the exponent difference to properly align the mantissas. For example, to add 0.367×10^5 and 0.112×10^4, the latter would be shifted right one place and 0.367 added to 0.0112 to give a sum of 0.3782×10^5. The addition is performed in ⑤. Step ⑥ tests for overflow and shifts the result right (in ⑧) unless the downshift operation would cause exponent overflow. Similarly, the loop ⑨ – ⑪ scales small values upward to normalize the result unless exponent underflow would occur as a result.

Floating-point subtraction is implemented with a similar algorithm. Many refinements are possible to improve the speed of the addition and subtraction algorithms, but floating-point addition will, in general, be much slower than fixed-point addition.

The algorithm for floating-point multiplication is simpler. In the first step, the fixed-point double-precision product of the operand mantissas is computed. The exponent of the product is formed by summing the operand characteristics and subtracting the bias (otherwise, two biased exponents have been summed, yielding a doubly biased product exponent). Next, the computed exponent is tested for overflow, and the product mantissa is tested and normalized. Only a single left shift need be performed; if the operands were normalized, this will be adequate. Then the normalized product is rounded to single precision. Finally, the product exponent is checked for underflow (i.e., a result that is smaller than the minimum representable number).

In implementing floating-point multiplication, it is possible to perform the mantissa multiplication, normalization, and rounding in a single VLSI circuit. Such circuits must provide flags to indicate when overflow has occurred and when the product is normalized. Subsequent to the generation of these flags, a shifter is provided to shift the product down one bit position (to correct for overflow) or up one position (to normalize an unnormalized output).

Floating-point division is similarly implemented. A fixed-point divider computes the quotient of the mantissas, and a subtractor forms the quotient exponent. The quotient is normalized (if possible), and overflow and underflow tests are performed.

All floating-point algorithms may require rounding to produce a result in the correct format. This may be performed by adding a 1 at the most-significant-bit position, which will be truncated. This causes a propagation of a carry into the bits which will be retained if the most significant bit of the "truncated" data is a 1. A variety of alternative rounding schemes have been developed over the years; selection should be based on both static and dynamic performance measures [7].

REFERENCES

1. G. W. REITWEISNER, "Binary Arithmetic," in *Advances in Computers*, Vol. 1, F. L. Alt (ed.), Academic Press, New York, 1960, pp. 231–308.
2. K. HWANG, *Computer Arithmetic: Principles, Architecture, and Design*, Wiley, New York, 1979.
3. E. E. SWARTZLANDER, JR., *Computer Arithmetic*, Dowden, Hutchinson & Ross, Stroudsburg, Pa., 1980.
4. A. D. BOOTH, "A Signed Binary Multiplication Technique," *Q. J. Mech. Appl. Math.*, **4**, Pt. 2, 236–240 (1951). Reprinted in Ref. 3.
5. C. R. BAUGH and B. A. WOOLEY, "A Two's Complement Parallel Array Multiplication Algorithm," *IEEE Trans. Comput.*, **C-22**, 1045–1047 (1973). Reprinted in Ref. 3.
6. J. B. GOSLING, "Design of Large High-Speed Floating-Point Arithmetic Units," *Proc. Inst. Electr. Eng. (Lond.)*, **118**, 493–498 (1971). Reprinted in Ref. 3.
7. D. J. KUCK, D. S. PARKER, JR., and A. H. SAMEH, "Analysis of Rounding Methods in Floating-Point Arithmetic," *IEEE Trans. Comput.*, **C-26**, 643–650 (1977).Reprinted in Ref. 3.

1.6   MAIN MEMORY AND HIGH-SPEED STORAGE: TECHNOLOGIES

George C. Feth

1.6.1   OVERVIEW

A memory may be characterized by the function that it performs, how it carries out the function, and the technology in which it is implemented. The basic function of memory is to retain information, as described in the introduction to Sec. 1.* Various kinds of memory and commonly used terminology follow.

*Throughout Sec. 1, *memory* is used to refer to entities that store information that is immediately accessible to the CPU; *storage* is used to refer to entities that store information in a less rapidly available way (as well as for the more inclusive function of retaining information in general).

Read–Write and Read-Only Memory.   *Read–write* (RW) memory is used to retain information that must be "stored" or "written" and later "retrieved," "fetched," or "read." *Read-only memory* (ROM; sometimes called *read-only storage*, ROS) is used to retain information that does not change, such as control programs or conversion tables. ROM has these advantages: it retains its information content when the computer is turned off, it costs less per bit than RW memory, and it is not susceptible to inadvertent changes of stored information.

There are several forms of memory in which the capability of writing is intermediate between RW and ROM. These are *programmable ROM* (PROM) or *write-once ROM* (WOROM), *erasable programmable ROM* (EPROM), and *electrically alterable ROM* (EAROM) or *read-mostly memory* (RMM). These are described in more detail, together with the technologies commonly used to implement them (primarily semiconductors), in Sec. 1.6.3.

Random-Access, Sequential-Access, and Content-Addressable Memory.   In memory, the information usually is stored as fixed-length words which have a specific address; any such address can be selected at random for either reading or writing. This is called *random-access memory* (RAM). In contrast, a memory in which the bits or words are available only one after the other in a certain time sequence is called *sequential-storage* or *a sequentially accessed* memory (e.g., a shift register or magnetic tape). Another way of accessing a memory is by way of its contents: a *content-addressable memory* (CAM) or *associative memory*. Here the contents, or a selected portion of them for each word, constitute its address, as in a directory or dictionary (see Sec. 1.7.2). An alternative means of realizing the same function is a *sequential search*, sequentially reading each word and comparing the selected portion of the contents with the desired value.

Destructive Read and Nondestructive Read.   The reading of stored information from a memory cell may cause the original storage state to be altered, depending on the technology with which the memory is implemented. If reading causes destruction of the information (e.g., as with ferrite-core memory and one-device dynamic-RAM semiconductor memory), the read operation is termed *destructive read* (DR); if the original information is reliably retained (e.g., as with static semiconductor memory), it is termed *nondestructive read* (NDR). DR memories are provided with means to rewrite or *regenerate* the information that has been read, so functionally, the data are not lost.

Static and Dynamic; Volatility.   In some memories, once the information is written, it is retained as long as the necessary power is supplied to the memory; this is termed a *static* memory. In other memories, even though the power is maintained, the physical quantity that represents the data gradually degrades unless it is refreshed periodically; such a memory is termed *dynamic*. Although the periodic refreshing does decrease the availibility of the memory for reading and writing, long retention time and simultaneous refreshing of many bits keep the refresh duty cycle small (about 10%), practically.

Memories that can retain the stored information even if power is not maintained (e.g., ferrite-core and magnetic bubbles) are termed *nonvolatile*, in contrast to *volatile* memories, which lose information when the power is removed. However, even though a memory cell may be inherently nonvolatile, loss of information may occur unless special care is taken in the design of the memory system so that no spurious writing or destructive reading can occur during transients in the powering.

Criteria of Merit

The *criteria of merit* for memories include capacity, speed, cost, reliability, volatility, life, volume, weight, and power consumption. These are interrelated, and their relative importance depends on the application. Desirable characteristics of memories in a computing system are:

Large *capacity*, ranging upward to 10^8 or 10^9 bits.

High *speed*, in order to interchange blocks of information rapidly between faster and slower memory units, between memory and attached storage, and between memory and processor, the latter in times of the order of a machine cycle. Memory access time, cycle time, and data rate are pertinent measures of performance, and may have different values for write, read, or read–modify–write cycles.

Low *cost*, specifically, the cost per bit of memory should be much less than that of a logic gate. For large-capacity stores, the cost per bit is most important; for small capacity, the cost of the minimum capacity store (i.e., the entry cost) is often more important. (Capacity, speed, and cost are usually intimately related.)

Small *volume*, *weight*, and *power* consumption, which are especially important for aerospace applications and for portable equipment; power consumption and the attendant cooling requirements must be dealt with in any design. Power requirements increase with speed, and speed is related to physical size due to the propagation delay of the signals along cables, wires, or optical paths, as limited by the speed of light.

High *reliability* and long *life*, which may be influenced by environmental factors and design. Error-detection and error-correction codes (ECC) (see Vol. 2, Sec. 2) often are included to extend the inherent device capabilities to meet the system objectives.

Nonvolatility, which is mandatory at the largest-capacity storage level of the system but is not necessary at every level. Instead, the system may be designed to transfer information from volatile memories into a nonvolatile store whenever a threat is detected.

Of course, simultaneous attainment of all these attributes in a single memory is impractical; compromises need to be made. One means of doing this is via a *storage hierarchy*, which uses several levels of storage having a range of characteristics and employs an appropriate technology for each level (see Sec. 1.7). The relatively large capacity levels, having low cost per bit but slow access, are referred to as *attached storage*. For these, *magnetic recording* is a practical technology (i.e., magnetic tape and disk files; see Sec. 1.11). At the other extreme, maximum memory speed for interaction with the CPU is obtained by supplementing the *registers*, which are part of the CPU, by a very high speed but modest-capacity *cache memory*. This complements the *main memory*, which has larger capacity and lower cost per bit but slower speed. For cache (see Sec. 1.7.1) and main memory, *semiconductor technology* provides an attractive range of speed and cost; nonvolatility is not mandatory, and ECC is available for reliability.

Between the high-speed but rather expensive memory closely associated with the CPU and the very low-cost-per-bit but slow-access attached storage, there is a large disparity in speed, cost, and capacity. This motivates hardware approaches to provide intermediate levels, sometimes referred to as *backing stores* or *file-gap fillers*, with capacity and cost intermediate between main memory and files. Such backing stores may be implemented with either RAM or sequential-storage technologies. RAM technologies are discussed in this article, attached storage in Sec. 1.11.

1.6.2 How a Memory Works

Three types of signals flow between the CPU and memory: *address*, *data*, and *control*, as indicated in Fig. 1. The address bits determine the sites in memory which are accessed, the controls effect the desired operation (e.g., write or read), and the data lines carry the information to and from the memory.

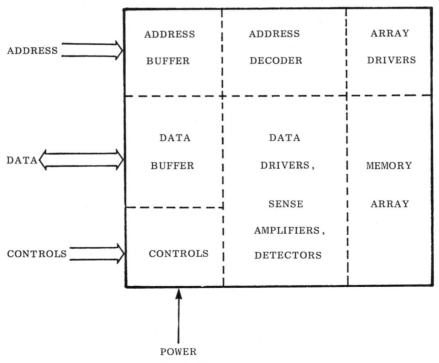

Fig. 1 Memory system.

The *memory cell* is the site where binary information is stored. These cells are arranged in two- or three-dimensional arrays, and each cell is coupled to at least two external paths, which are used for selecting the cell and for data transfer. The details of the memory cell and its external connections vary with the technology used for the cells and are covered in Sec. 1.6.3.

Memory cycles are initiated by the processor; it issues an address and also provides control signals (possibly by way of a storage-control unit). Common modes of operation are write, read, or read–modify–write. For a write operation, the data to be written are presented by way of the memory bus (see Sec. 1.13), and the address is supplied from the memory address register via the address bus. The memory address register and the memory data register may be considered to be part of either the CPU or of the memory; in some systems, additional registers or buffers for either or both may be included within the memory, as depicted in Fig. 1. The address bits are decoded in the *address decoder*, which selects the appropriate set of *array drivers* to energize the addressed memory cells for writing. However, the output of the decoder is gated by a control signal which *enables* the write operation to proceed; the design must assure that the correct address and data signals are valid when the decoder receives the enable signal. The data to be written are provided via the data drivers and data lines (also commonly called *bit-sense* lines) to the selected cells, resulting in storing this information. For a read operation, the address is similarly presented, but now the driving of the selected memory cells causes them to apply signals representing their stored information onto their respective data lines; from there, the signals propagate to the *sense amplifier* and *detector* circuits, where they are amplified and detected (sensed). Then they set the data buffer and propagate to the memory bus. (If reading is destructive, then as part of the read cycle these sense-amplifier and detector circuits will provide outputs also to the data lines to rewrite or *restore* the same data). A read–modify–write cycle combines the read cycle

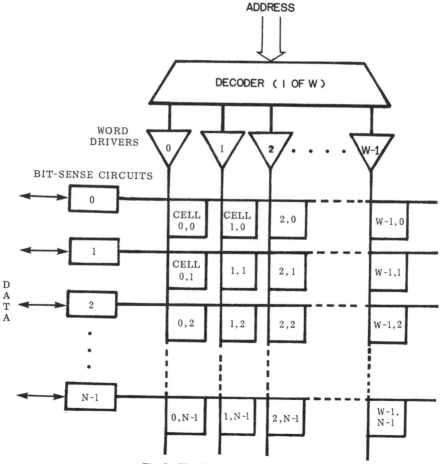

Fig. 2 Word-organized memory.

at a given address, propagation of the detected data to the memory bus, presentation of new data on the memory bus by the processor, and writing the modified data at the same address.

A basic function of the control signals is to select the desired memory mode. The controls then generate and distribute appropriate timing and other control pulses to various parts of the memory. For instance, the same lines in the memory array are used for both reading and writing a given word. However, it is the combination of appropriate polarity, magnitude, and timing of the excitation of these lines which effects the desired mode, and this is governed by the controls.

The power required to maintain stored information is much less than that needed to read or write it at the required speed; hence in many memory implementations, the supplied voltage(s) is reduced in the standby condition to a level where the data are just maintained. When a read or write operation is initiated, the full operating voltage is applied by the controls to that portion of the memory that is addressed, continuing for the duration of that memory cycle. In dynamic memories, the controls must initiate a refresh mode at intervals less than the minimum retention time. Some memory applications provide more than one port, so that data may be controlled to flow simultaneously to and from the memory via different ports.

Memories may be *organized* and *addressed* in a variety of ways. Usually, they are organized as some number of words, W, by some number of bits, N, where N may include both the data bits and bits for parity or for more sophisticated ECC. Memories are frequently composed of multiple subunits (e.g., basic storage modules, semiconductor chips, ferrite-core planes, etc.). One common memory organization is the *word-organized* memory (see Fig. 2). In such an organization, all the bits of the memory word are located along a physical *word line*, which passes through the memory array and is energized by the appropriate array drivers when that word is selected. Each bit on the word line is also associated with a *data line* or bit-sense line (which also links the other bits in the same position on other word lines in the array). When the word line is energized for writing or reading, all the memory bits on that line are written or read simultaneously, each bit storing the signal from its own data line for writing, or coupling its stored information to its data line for reading. In contrast, the memory may be organized into multiple two-dimensional arrays of memory sites, each site being linked by a pair of

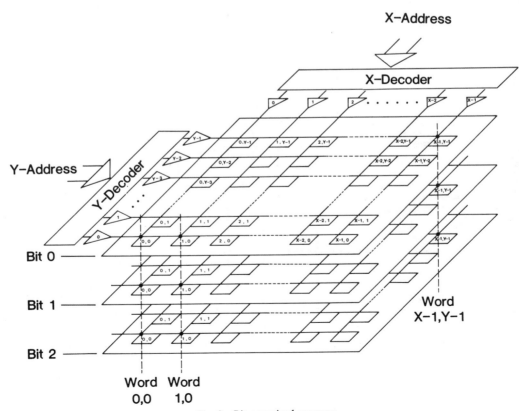

Fig. 3 Bit-organized memory.

orthogonal x and y conductors (see Fig. 3). One site in each array is selected by simultaneously energizing the appropriate x and y lines in each array. This is termed *coincident selection* (or *XY* or *two-dimensional selection* [2D]), the logical AND function of the signals on the x and y lines being performed in each memory cell. Additional lines are used to carry the signals from the cells to the sense amplifiers. In this scheme (called *bit-organized* in a ferrite-core memory or *bit per chip* in a semiconductor memory), each bit of the memory word comes from a different array. Variations of these organizations are possible; the relative advantages have to do with the number of devices and circuits required for driving and sensing and the speed of operation. Briefly, bit organization requires fewer supporting circuits (of the order of $X + Y + N$ compared to $X \cdot Y + N$ for word organization) but is slower because of the heavier loading on the bit circuitry.

1.6.3 Memory Technologies and Their Characteristics

Semiconductors are the primary technology for memory. This has come about because of the advances that have been made in silicon planar technology, making possible high levels of integration, inclusion of the decode, drive, sense, and control circuitry on the memory chip, and achieving high density, good yield, low cost, high speed, and low power. Semiconductors are superior to magnetic cores, which preceded semiconductors as the major memory technology, in essentially all aspects except nonvolatility. Josephson-junction technology appears to be the only other potentially important RAM technology in the foreseeable future, and it appears to be applicable only for the high-performance, large-system requirements [1,2].

Semiconductor Memories

There are two basic types of memory cell used in semiconductor RW memories; one uses the *flip-flop*, the other uses *charge storage* on a capacitor. The charge-storage cell can be implemented with as few as one active (switching) device plus capacitor (one-device or 1D cell); it is a dynamic cell. The flip-flop requires at least the four devices of the flip-flop; it provides a static cell. The trade-offs between the flip-flop and capacitor-switch cells involve: density (hence cost), performance, and static versus dynamic operation. The dynamic, charge-storage cells, requiring fewer devices than the static, can be laid out more densely on a chip. (Since semiconductor processing is a batch operation, the greater the density, the more bits per batch and the lower the cost per bit.) However, the signal to be sensed is just the small amount of stored charge; hence sensing is more complex and slower than for the static cells, which inherently have gain within the cell. Moreover, the charge-storage cells require periodic refresh; however, this can be done for many cells simultaneously, and uses a relatively insignificant fraction of memory time. Thus the cache and high-speed memory functions are ordinarily implemented with static memory technologies, whereas large-capacity main memories (especially when used in conjunction with a cache memory) and backing stores are usually designed using dynamic memory technologies. Semiconductor RW memories are volatile; however, at the system level they can be provided with uninterrupted power sources to maintain data during outages of utility power.

There are two major branches of semiconductor technology: *bipolar* and *metal-oxide-semiconductor* (*MOS*); each of these has further subbranches corresponding to particular device and circuit technologies. Bipolar memories are used primarily for high speed and are usually implemented with static cells. Bipolar dynamic memory is achieved by storing minority carriers in *pn* junctions; it offers lower cost and fairly high speed and is competitive with MOS memory. Flip-flops implemented in bipolar technology may use circuitry akin to emitter-coupled logic (ECL), transistor-transistor logic (T^2L), or integrated injection logic (I^2L) for the cells and support circuitry in order to achieve the desired speed–power–cost trade-off and compatibility with the logic family being used in the CPU. ECL is used for the highest-speed requirements but dissipates much power. T^2L provides somewhat lower speed but requires less power and costs less. ECL and TTL memories are usually used for cache memories to achieve high speed. On the other hand, I^2L, also known as *merged-transistor logic* (MTL) because of its suitability for very compact integration, has potential for very large scale integrated memories suitable for main memory.

Semiconductor main memory first became practical with MOS technology, as sufficient density was achieved to lower the cost to levels competitive with ferrite-core memory at comparable performance. Both static and dynamic MOS memories are practical commercial products. Increasingly large levels of integration are being achieved as lithography capabilities for fine lines over large fields are improved, as chip dimensions are increased, and as device and cell design and technology capabilities are enhanced.

A common static MOS RAM cell is implemented with six devices (6D), four for the flip-flop and two as transmission gates to connect the cell to the data lines under control of the select line (see Fig. 4a). A common dynamic MOS RAM cell is the (1D) charge-storage cell (see Fig. 4b). The single MOS transistor connects the storage capacitor to its data line; it is switched from its gate, which is connected to a select line. (In a word-organized memory, the select line is the word line, whereas in a

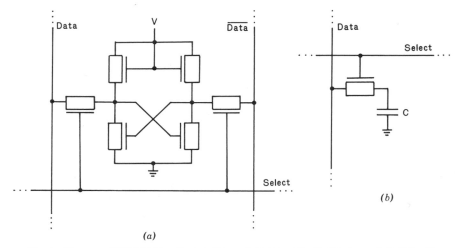

Fig. 4　Common MOS RAM cells: (*a*) 6D static RAM cell; (*b*) 1D dynamic RAM cell.

bit per chip organization, the select node itself may be driven from XY selection gates.) Sophisticated sensing techniques have been developed to detect the small stored charge of the cell when it is transferred to the capacitance of the data line. Retention times are of the order of milliseconds. (Other RAM cells have also been used [3].) The predominant technology for MOS memory is NMOS using silicon gates, since this gives the best speed–power–density tradeoffs. PMOS is still used in low-performance, low-cost applications. CMOS has very small standby power requirement and is attractive for portable or other battery-operated equipment or where cooling is a problem; however, it is more expensive than NMOS. NMOS memory cells are being combined with CMOS peripheral circuits to reduce the power required in static RAMs.

An important application of semiconductor memory is ROM. Semiconductor memory became practical just after microprogrammed control became widespread in mainframe computers; then, at the beginning of the microcomputer era, semiconductors were applied to implement ROMs. A ROM system is essentially the same as shown in Fig. 1, except that data flow only out from the memory, and no write or refresh controls or data drivers are used. The ROM cell must couple an electrical signal from the word drive line to the data line wherever a binary 1 is stored and nowhere else, and must prevent unwanted coupling or "sneak paths." This can be accomplished in any of the semiconductor technologies using a suitable diode or transistor in the memory cell to provide the coupling between word lines and data lines. Actually, the coupling device may be present in every cell, the distinction between the binary value of 1 or 0 of the stored information being determined only by whether the coupling device is electrically connected. In a ROM, this connection is preprogrammed into the mask that is used to fabricate the metal interconnections. In a PROM, a fusible link (e.g., of Nichrome or polycrystalline silicon) is included in each cell, and each cell can be selected and written once by burning out its fusible link. [This requires extra write circuitry (e.g., data drivers and higher current capability compared to a ROM) and is implemented in bipolar technology.] Such ROM and PROM memories are nonvolatile. The choice of the technology with which to implement a ROM is based on the required speed–cost–power trade-offs: bipolar for high speed, MOS for low cost, CMOS for low power.

A truly electronically alterable ROM is desirable, but of several approaches developed, none is ideal in all characteristics. One type of EPROM which is widely used employs an MOS transistor with a floating gate (so-called *floating-gate, avalanche-injection MOS* or FAMOS); it can be programmed by selectively applying a large reverse voltage to the channel-to-drain diode, causing avalanche injection, which generates hot electrons that charge the floating gate. The cell cannot be selectively rewritten, but the whole memory can be erased by x-ray or ultraviolet radiation of the chip.

One form of EAROM cell has been implemented, also using an MOS structure but with a composite gate dielectric [a thin layer of silicon dioxide and, for example, a thicker layer of silicon nitride (MNOS technology) or aluminum oxide (MAOS technology)]. Writing and erasing are accomplished by selectively applying large voltages to the device electrodes to cause electrons to tunnel through the silicon dioxide layer to or from the interface between the dielectrics, thus altering the conduction state of the channel. However, write and erase are relatively slow. The memory is essentially nonvolatile, but there is a trade-off between the write-erase speed, the retention time of the devices, and the number of write–erase cycles to which they can be subjected, due to the very high electric-field stresses used in writing. Another form of EAROM, sometimes called EE-PROM (*electrically erasable* PROM), has been developed more recently [4]. It has a floating gate and a second gate, which is driven directly. The floating gate is charged by electrons that tunnel to or from the floating gate through the thin insulation layers under the influence of electric fields produced by appropriate electrical excitation of the other electrodes of the device.

Ferrite-Core Memories

Ferrite-core memory was the mainstay of main memory until semiconductors displaced it, and in fact, the main memory of a computing system is still sometimes referred to as "core memory." Ferrite-core memory can be designed to be nonvolatile, which is its only remaining advantage over semiconductor memory for most new applications.

Toroidal ferrite cores with pronounced magnetic hysteresis (called "square-loop" cores) are the memory cells. They are arranged in *core planes*, where they are threaded by the appropriate wires used for driving and sensing. The operation of the basic memory cell depends on the magnetic hysteresis characteristics of the core (see Vol. 1, Sec. 3.7, for a more complete description). When the algebraic sum of the fields produced by the currents in all the conductors which thread a core exceeds the coercive force (H_c, a threshold magnetic field for switching), the core flux switches to its nominal value with the same sense as the applied field. When the resultant field is reversed and again exceeds H_c in the new direction, the flux reverses in sign. These two values of flux with opposite sign represent the two binary states. When the flux switches, it induces a voltage with corresponding polarity in the sense winding. When a magnetic field of given sense and exceeding H_c is applied to a core, the presence or absence of an induced voltage pulse in the sense winding indicates the previous state of the core; core memories have destructive read.

Cores are arranged in a core plane in a two-dimensional array with individual wires running parallel to the X and Y axes and threading all the cores in their paths, so that each core is threaded by one X and one Y line. If a current whose magnetic field is less than H_c is passed through a line, it is insufficient to switch the cores on the line. However, currents each providing magnetic fields just less than H_c and in the same sense in both an X and Y line will add up to exceed H_c and will switch the core at their intersection but will not switch cores elsewhere; such selective switching of a core is called *coincident selection*. The threshold properties of the cores and the appropriate excitation of orthogonal lines in arrays are used to design both word-oriented (or 2D) memories and bit-oriented (or 3D) memories. Additional conductors are used for sensing and for biasing the cores, as needed [5].

REFERENCES

1. R. E. MATICK, *Computer Storage Systems and Technology*, Wiley, New York, 1977.
2. *IBM J. Res. Dev.*, **24**(2), Mar. 1980 (Special Issue on Josephson Computer Technology).
3. E. R. HNATEK, *A User's Handbook of Semiconductor Memories*, Wiley, New York, 1977.
4. W. S. JOHNSON, G. L. KUHN, A. L. RENNINGER, and G. PERLEGOS, "16-K EE-PROM Relies on Tunneling for Byte-Erasable Program Storage," *Electronics*, Feb. 28, 1980, pp. 113–117.
5. S. MIDDELHOEK, P. K. GEORGE, and P. DEKKER, *Physics of Computer Memory Devices*, Academic Press, New York, 1976.

BIBLIOGRAPHY

W. E. PROEBSTER, (ed.), *Digital Memory and Storage*, Vieweg, Braunschweig, 1978.

G. LUECKE, J. P. MIZE, and W. N. CARR,, *Semiconductor Memory Design and Applications*, McGraw-Hill, New York, 1973.

1.7 MAIN MEMORY AND HIGH-SPEED STORAGE: ORGANIZATION

Kishor S. Trivedi

The purpose of a memory system is to hold information in a cost-effective manner. The need for a large-capacity high-speed main memory cannot usually be fulfilled at an acceptable cost with a single memory technology. To meet cost–performance goals, it becomes necessary to synthesize a memory hierarchy combining a variety of technologies with differing characteristics. The technologies are ordered into levels on the basis of speed and cost (per byte) so that most frequently used information is kept in fast but expensive memory while the less frequently used information is stored in cheaper and slower memories. A properly designed hierarchy displays the favorable features of its constituent elements and behaves like a high-speed, low-cost, large-capacity storage device.

The levels of a hierarchy may be divided into two groups by an access gap (or delay boundary), as shown in Fig. 1. The memory levels above the delay boundary are directly addressable by the CPU, whereas the information in levels below the delay boundary can be accessed only after it is moved to one of the directly addressable memories. The lower speeds of memories below the delay boundary require that a process generating a request to such a memory be suspended and the CPU context be switched to another process until the information is moved to a directly addressable memory. The alternative of waiting for the request to be satisfied is usually too wasteful of CPU time.

The study of a memory hierarchy can be divided into the design issues and the management issues. The design problem consists of determining the number of levels in the hierarchy, the technology of each level, the capacity of each level, and the topology of the hierarchy. The management problem consists of determining where information is stored, how it can be located upon request, and when it should be moved. We restrict our discussion to management issues only; a discussion of design issues may be found in Ref. 9.

The objective of a management strategy is to maintain currently used data in faster memory levels in order to minimize access time. This requires recognizing periods of inactivity of data and moving (or percolating) such data to slower and cheaper devices. The movement of data may be controlled by users by allowing them to input their knowledge of data and program usage; however, the current trend is toward automatically managed hierarchies to relieve the programmer of the burden of hierarchy management. Portions of the hierarchy may be managed completely in hardware (typically, the levels above the delay boundary), and portions may be managed by the operating system (typically, the levels below the delay boundary). Hardware control is more efficient, but it is inflexible and expensive. Software (operating system) control is flexible, but the overhead of managing the hierarchy may be large. A judicious mixture of the two techniques may be used to achieve the desired cost–performance goals.

Two techniques of managing directly addressable memories are available: centralized execution and distributed execution. In the *centralized mode* of execution, all information must be transferred into the fastest level before it can be referenced by the CPU. In the distributed mode of execution, the CPU is allowed to reference information in a slower directly addressable level without transferring it into the fastest level. The more frequently referenced information should be stored in faster levels. The *distributed mode* of execution can reduce the traffic between the levels in the hierarchy. If the access frequencies are stationary, a preallocation of information across levels may be made. More commonly, however, access patterns are time dependent, and a promotion policy is based on a trade-off between the time to move the information to a faster level and the performance penalty of executing at the slower speed. Because of the difficulties involved in implementing such a promotion policy, the centralized mode of execution is usually preferred [2, 8].

Next we consider a management strategy for the entire memory hierarchy, including the levels below the delay boundary. A staging hierarchy is a good example of an automatically managed

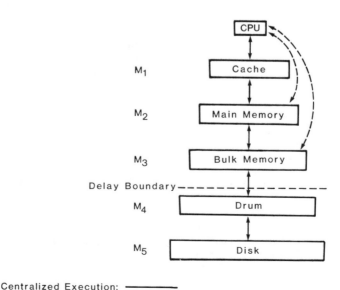

Fig. 1   Memory hierarchy. (Solid lines, centralized execution; dashed lines, distributed execution.)

hierarchy. Such a hierarchy has two or more levels of memory, denoted by $M_1, M_2, \ldots, M_H$, with capacities $C_1 \leqslant C_2 \leqslant \cdots \leqslant C_H$ (bytes), and access times $t_1 \leqslant t_2 \leqslant \cdots \leqslant t_H$. Information movement is between adjacent levels only. Movement between levels M_i and M_{i+1} occurs in blocks of size B_i (bytes), so that $B_1 \leqslant B_2 \leqslant \cdots \leqslant B_{H-1}$. Each block of size B_i is composed of an integral number of blocks of size B_{i-1}, called its *descendants*. Similarly, each block of size B_i has a unique *parent* block of size B_{i+1}. All CPU references to the hierarchy are always satisfied at the fastest level by M_1 (i.e., centralized mode of execution). Movement of information within the hierarchy obeys the staging rule: whenever a block x is moved upward into a faster level M_i, its parent block x' must have been moved into level M_{i+1} (If it was not already there). Blocks may be moved up on demand or in anticipation. The usual approach is to use demand staging. The downward movement at any level occurs as a result of the application of a replacement algorithm. The usual replacement algorithm for each level is LRU (least recently used) or an approximation to it. For further discussion of memory hierarchies, see Refs. 5 and 8.

The management of memory hierarchies is explored further in the next section. Although the discussion is based on two-level hierarchies, the concepts generalize naturally to the multilevel hierarchies. The discussion of hierarchy management will reveal the fact that associative (or content-addressable) memories are needed for efficiency in implementation. Therefore, we discuss associative memories in the last section.

1.7.1   Two-Level Hierarchies

In the early days of computing, main memory was expensive and small. This implied that programs requiring larger memories had to be divided into a number of pieces, called *overlays*. The programmer was responsible for breaking the program into pieces and issuing input/output commands to transport overlays between the main and the secondary memory. This manual overlaying process tended to consume a large fraction of total program development time. The concept of virtual memory, which provides automatic overlaying, is now commonly employed, freeing the programmer from the tedious bookkeeping task. Such two-level hierarchies consisting of the main memory and the secondary storage are discussed below.

Another type of memory hierarchy evolved from the ubiquitous speed differential between the CPU and the main memory. This speed differential gave rise to program accessible registers, instruction buffers, data buffers, and ultimately to the cache. Cache (or high-speed buffer) is a small, fast memory, typically implemented in bipolar technology, interposed between the CPU and the main memory. The most frequently used information (both instructions and data) is kept in the high-speed cache so that the slower main memory is referenced only infrequently. Cache-to-main memory hierarchies are discussed later in this section.

Cache-based systems are usually implemented in hardware for high speed, whereas virtual memory systems are implemented partly in hardware and partly in software (as part of the operating system) for flexibility. Other than these differences, the two types of hierarchies are common in concept.

Virtual Memory Systems

In order to classify various techniques of memory management, we make a distinction between the address space N of a program and the physical memory space M allocated to it. (Note that in a multiprogramming environment, the physical space M allocated to a program may be a small fraction of the total available memory space.) Since the program generates references to the address space N while the CPU can only make references to the locations in M, an address translation is required. Let f denote this address map, $f: N \to M$. We classify memory management techniques by the nature of the associated address map (see Fig. 2). The simplest scheme fixes f; hence it does not allow the program to be relocated in memory. The static relocation scheme allows the program to be relocated from one run to the next, but no relocation is allowed during a run of the program.

Schemes with static f are constraining for two reasons. In multiprogrammed systems, main memory is simultaneously shared among many programs. Programs may have to be moved around in memory to make space for other programs, or they may have to be moved in and out of memory. This implies that the program occupies different areas of main memory at different times; hence, f must be dynamic. Such a scheme is known as *dynamic relocation*. Another reason for a dynamic f occurs when the size of the address space N is larger than the size of the allocated memory space M. Different subsets of N will occupy the memory space M at different times, and we have a dynamic allocation of main memory. Such a scheme is also known as *folding*. The folding process may be carried out manually by the programmer, or it can be performed automatically by the system. Systems with automatic folding are said to provide a virtual memory that is potentially larger than the real memory space. The mapping mechanisms that implement virtual memory also provide the capability of dynamic relocation. Paging, segmentation, and a combination of the two are the three common schemes for providing a virtual memory.

Besides relieving the programmer of the difficult task of manual folding, a virtual memory system provides several other advantages. Programs are unaffected by changes in the size of main memory,

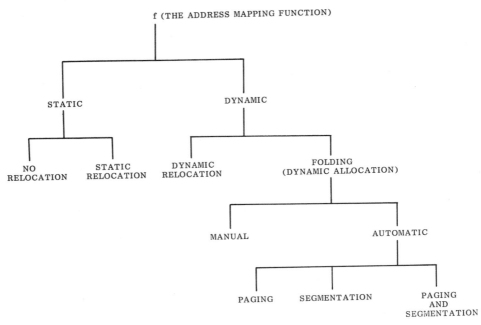

Fig. 2   Classification of memory management schemes.

which would require reprogramming in a non-virtual-memory system. In a multiprogramming system, the use of virtual memory provides flexibility in memory allocation, since programs may be provided variable amounts of memory. This flexibility in memory allocation can be used to improve system efficiency.

Paging Systems.*   In paging systems it is assumed that the entire address space N of the program resides in secondary storage. This address space is broken up into equal-size units called *pages*. Page sizes ranging from 512 to 4096 bytes are common. For our discussion, assume a page size of 2^p bytes. Main memory is broken into pieces of the same size called *page frames*. Assume that a main-memory real address is m bits long and a virtual address is n bits long. Thus the size of the address space is 2^n bytes (or 2^{n-p} pages), whereas the size of main memory is 2^m bytes (or 2^{m-p} page frames). Typically, m is much smaller than n. Therefore, all pages cannot be in memory at once. A page table is used to keep track of the pages that are currently in memory. The page table is an array with an entry for each of the 2^{n-p} pages. Each entry includes several flags and pointers (see Fig. 3).

The mapping of an n-bit virtual address to an m-bit real address is performed by a hardware-implemented address translation mechanism. The most significant $(n - p)$ bits of the virtual address represent the index of the required page, identifying a page table entry, while the least significant p bits give the byte address within the page. If the *fault* flag of the page table entry is zero, the required page is in main memory, and a field of the entry gives the index of the main memory page frame on which the page resides. The real address is then obtained by concatenating the $(m - p)$-bit page frame index with the p-bit byte address.

If the fault flag of the page table entry is equal to 1, the required page is not in memory, and a hardware interrupt known as a *missing page fault* is generated. Since address mapping takes place on every memory reference, it is implemented in hardware. A page fault is a less frequent event, however, and it triggers a complex sequence of actions. Therefore, an operating system routine called the *paging algorithm* handles the response to a page fault. The paging algorithm locates the required page on the secondary storage, using a field of the page table entry, decides where to place this page in main memory (this may require the replacement of a page currently resident in main memory), issues instructions to fetch the page from the secondary storage, and updates the page table entries as required. The program that generated the page fault is unable to execute until the page fetch is complete; therefore, the operating system schedules another program for execution, if one is available.

*See also Sec. 1.1.3.

PAGE FRAME NUMBER	SECONDARY STORAGE ADDRESS	FAULT	USAGE	DIRTY
4	4096	0	1	0
16	5192	0	0	1
-	.	1	-	-
-	.	1	-	-
8	.	0	1	1
36	.	0	1	0

2^{n-p} ENTRIES

m-p BITS

Fig. 3   Example page table.

The page tables of all active users are usually kept in main memory. The address mapping scheme described above is inefficient, since every virtual address reference requires two accesses to main memory (one to consult the page table and the other to access the required byte). To solve this problem, a small associative memory (see Sec. 1.7.2) is used to hold the page table entries for the most recently used pages. Since the associative memory is capable of fast parallel search, the penalty of consulting the memory resident page table is eliminated whenever the required entry is found in the associative memory. Experiments have indicated that an associative memory that can hold 8 to 16 page table entries provides a high probability of finding the required entry in the associative memory.

When a new page needs to be fetched and there is no available page frame, one of the pages currently resident in main memory needs to be replaced. The most common replacement policy is to replace the least recently used (LRU) page. This algorithm replaces that memory page whose last reference was longest ago. This implies that the pages in main memory have to be ordered by their most recent usage, and this list needs to be updated at the time of every reference. Therefore, the implementation of a true LRU algorithm tends to be expensive. Fortunately, however, one can make good approximations to LRU with the help of one or more usage bits associated with each page [3].

When a particular page is selected for replacement, a page-out operation will normally be required. However, if the page was not modified (or written into), no page-out operation is needed, since a valid copy exists in the secondary storage. To exploit this possibility, a flag known as the *dirty bit* is provided as part of each page table entry. Whenever the contents of a page frame are written into, this bit is set. The paging algorithm may examine appropriate dirty bits in making a replacement decision.

The complex sequence of actions triggered by a page fault usually requires the execution of several thousand instructions. This overhead can be reduced by either reducing the number of page faults or by decreasing the time to service a page fault. The latter can be achieved by a proper redesign of the paging algorithm or by increased use of hardware/firmware aids. To reduce the number of page faults, one can train programmers to produce better programs [2,3] or use automatic methods of program transformations [8]. Another way to reduce page faults is to increase the main-memory allocation of a program.

Increasing memory allocation of a program can reduce its page faults, but it may have a detrimental effect on system performance in a multiprogramming environment. For a given amount of real memory, increased allocation per program implies a reduction in the degree of multiprogramming, which in turn reduces the probability of finding a program ready to run when the current program incurs a page fault. On the other hand, a large degree of multiprogramming will reduce the memory allocation of each program and can result in an excessive number of page faults, producing very little useful activity. Such behavior of the system is called *thrashing* [2]. To avoid thrashing it is important, therefore, to make accurate estimates of memory demands of programs, and allocate main memory based on these estimates.

A practical scheme for main-memory allocation is to estimate the program's future memory requirements from the observation of its immediate past behavior. Furthermore, since we expect the memory requirements of a program to vary during execution, dynamic estimation of memory requirements is needed. Denning's working set (WS) algorithm is the most useful example of this technique [2].

Next we consider the factors that the system designer has to consider when selecting the page size. For systems that use an electromechanical secondary storage device, a major consideration in the selection of the page size is the efficiency of the page transport operation (see Sec. 1.11.2). To reduce the latency overhead per byte of accessing the device, a large page size is required. With an electronic secondary storage device, however, a small page size is feasible.

Other considerations in the selection of the page size are its effect on the page fault rate and storage fragmentation. Programs are known to be more compressible when the page size is small; that is, they will not page fault heavily with a small allotment of main memory. A small page size is, therefore, desirable in a system with small memory size. A small page size is also desirable in a time-sharing system with a small time quantum. Page fault behavior is relatively insensitive to the page size with a large allotment of main memory.

Next consider the fragmentation problem. The size of the address space of a program may not be an integral multiple of the page size. The effect of rounding, to obtain an integral number of pages, is to leave unused words in the last page. Reducing the page size reduces this internal fragmentation of storage but also implies an increase in the size of the page table. The loss of storage due to page tables is known as table fragmentation. Denning [2] derives an expression for the page size that minimizes the total fragmentation. He concludes that a page size close to 50 words is optimal. However, as pointed out earlier, such a small page size is feasible only when an electronic secondary storage device is used.

Segmentation. *   Division of the address space into equal-size pages provides an efficient technique for storage management. However, the pages are physical units having no logical significance, and the address space is a linear array devoid of any visible logical structure. As a result, sharing programs or data between several concurrently active users tends to be cumbersome. Also, if a variable-size data structure is a part of the address space, a portion of the address space large enough to hold the maximum size must be allocated in advance. Segmentation avoids some of these difficulties of a paging system.

The technique of segmentation divides the address space into user-defined, variable-size units, called *segments*. The segments can be referenced by symbolic names, and these names need not be bound to the address space until the time of first reference. The address mapping process is similar to that for paging systems.

The advantages of segmentation stem from the fact that segment boundaries are usually natural program and data boundaries. Each program module (procedure or data) can be a named segment, and it can have unique access privileges (read, write, execute, etc.). Access control to the segments is naturally exercised as part of the address mapping process. Because of their logical independence, procedure segments can be recompiled and data segments can grow (or shrink) in size without affecting other segments. A segment can be given different names in different users' address spaces, providing a convenient method of sharing segments.

We have seen that paging provides a convenient mechanism for memory management, while segmentation provides a useful logical division of the address space. It is possible to combine the advantages of the two schemes [6].

Cache - Based Systems

Until recently, the use of cache was restricted to large-scale machines. Now this concept provides a cost-effective technique for speeding up minicomputers as well.

In such systems, the cache and the main memory are divided into equal-size units called *blocks*. There is an associative memory (Sec. 1.7.2) to perform the mapping between main-memory blocks and cache blocks. When the CPU generates a reference to a main-memory block, the mapping memory is searched using the main-memory address of the block as the key. If a match occurs, the required block is in cache (this is called a *hit*), and the execution proceeds at cache speed. If there is no match (this is called a *miss*), the required block must be fetched from the main memory.

Like the page fault rate of paging systems, the performance of a cache is measured by the *miss ratio*, which is defined to be the fraction of CPU references not found in cache. As in virtual memory systems, the mapping of a main-memory address into a cache address is performed in hardware. In addition, the response to a cache miss is also handled by hardware, which constitutes the main difference between a cache-based system and a virtual memory system.

Important design parameters of such a system are the cache size, the cache organization, the block replacement algorithm, the block size, and the manner in which CPU write operations to memory are handled. We discuss each of these in the following paragraphs.

*See also Sec. 1.1.3.

Of the parameters described above, performance is most sensitive to cache size. However, cache is expensive, and cost is a major consideration. Selection of optimal cache size to meet the desired cost performance goals is an important system design problem and is discussed in Refs. 1, 8, and 9.

The cache organization providing the smallest miss ratio, known as *fully associative cache*, allows any memory block to be assigned to any cache block. To perform the mapping from a CPU-generated main-memory address into a cache address, an associative mapping memory (or index directory) is needed to indicate which block from the memory is in which block frame of the cache. Also, a list must be maintained that orders the cache blocks by their replacement priority when space is needed. For each CPU request, the entire directory must be searched associatively, and the priority list must be updated. With current technology, fully associative cache is either slow or expensive or both.

An alternative cache organization is direct addressing, where the main memory is partitioned in such a way that all blocks in one partition can reside only in a unique cache block. The required block can now be accessed by indexing (if present in cache). This eliminates a search of the mapping memory altogether, but since many main-memory blocks will compete for a single cache slot, the miss ratio is likely to be large.

An intermediate type of cache organization, called the *set associative scheme*, is known to perform well at an acceptable cost. In this scheme the cache is divided into a number of sets (or classes), each of which contains one or more blocks. Blocks within a set are searched associatively, whereas the required set is obtained by indexing. Since the replacement decision concerns the blocks in a set (which will be small), a true LRU algorithm is feasible (unlike the situation in paging systems). An important design consideration is the number of sets employed (or equivalently, the size of each set). Strecker's [1] simulation experiments show that a larger set size reduces the miss ratio, and the largest improvement occurs in going from set size of one block (i.e., direct mapping) to a set size of two blocks.

The size of a cache block is also an important factor. It has been observed that programs possess the property of sequentiality—a tendency of referencing successive addresses in the address space. A larger block size exploits the sequentiality property but requires a smaller number of blocks to be in cache at a time. Strecker found that a larger block significantly reduces the miss ratio, especially in a smaller cache. However, a large block size implies a long time to fetch a block from main memory. The block fetch time is usually reduced by employing wide data paths between the cache and main memory [5]. But this implies increased cost in bus hardware and control logic. For minicomputers, a small block size (e.g., 4 bytes) may be chosen to minimize cost. For larger systems, a block size of 32 to 64 bytes is common to provide enhanced performance.

So far, we have not made a distinction between read and write accesses to memory. When the CPU makes a write access, one strategy is to update both the main-memory location and its cache copy (if there is a hit) simultaneously. This strategy is called *write-through* (or *store-through*). Thus there is never a need to replace a block from cache; it can simply be erased without copying it into main memory. The alternative strategy is to update only the cache on a write hit. Now, when a modified cache block is replaced on a future reference, it must be recopied into main memory. This strategy is known as *write-back*. Experience suggests that only a small percentage (roughly 10%) of memory references are write accesses; hence write-through can be more efficient and is often used in practice. A related technique for speeding up cache operation is known as *load-through*. It allows portions of the block, as it is being fetched into cache, to be available to the CPU simultaneously, before the block transfer is completed [5].

As an example, we consider the cache organization of the IBM 370/155 shown in Fig. 4. The 8K cache is divided into 256 32-byte blocks. This is organized into 128 sets (or columns), each set containing two blocks. The main memory (assumed to hold 1024K bytes) is divided into 128 sets with 256 blocks per set (called rows). Blocks in set *i* of main memory may be placed only in set *i* of the cache.

A 1 million-byte main memory is addressed with a 20-bit address, whereas the 8K cache is addressed with a 13-bit address. (The associative mapping memory is also called the index directory.) The main-memory address is divided into several fields. The column field designates the mapping memory column to be used for search. Each of the two mapping memory entries indicates the main-memory row whose block contents are currently held in the corresponding cache block. The row field of the effective address is associatively compared against the two entries in the index. If a match is found, the column field is used to access the corresponding cache block. If no match occurs, the requested block must be fetched from main memory, requiring a replacement of an existing cache block. Since the choice for replacement is restricted to one of the two blocks for the set involved, the LRU algorithm is easily implemented with a single usage bit.

If a cache-based system also possesses virtual memory, the main-memory address itself is obtained after a mapping from the CPU-generated virtual address. All CPU references are directed to a unit known as the *storage control unit* [4], which contains the virtual memory address mapping hardware, the index directory of the cache, and cache hardware controls (e.g., the block replacement algorithm).

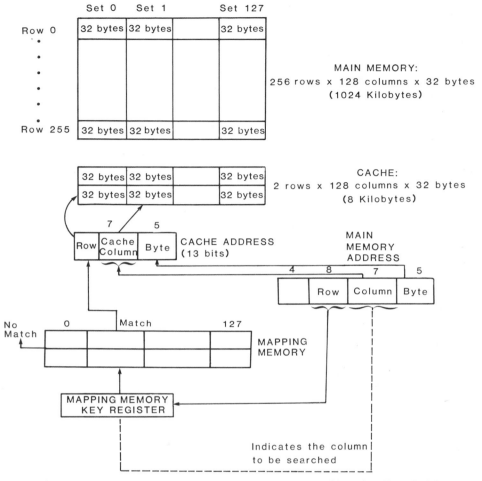

Fig. 4 Mapping process in IBM 370/155 cache main-memory hierarchy. (From Ref. 3.)

The storage control unit also handles main-memory requests generated by the cache controls and by the I/O channel controls.

1.7.2. Associative Memories*

Many computer applications require the search of items stored in a table. Searching a page table is an example discussed in sec. 1.7.1. Searching a table is a common operation in a data base system. If a conventional random-access memory is used to store the table, an access can be performed by specifying the physical address of the item desired. If the physical address of the desired item is not known, a search procedure is required. The search procedure is a strategy for choosing a sequence of addresses, reading the content of memory at each address, and comparing the data read with the item being searched. The search procedure terminates successfully if a match is found, or unsuccessfully if the entire table is searched without a match. Many techniques have been developed to minimize the number of accesses while searching for an item in a random- or sequential-access memory.

The search time can be reduced considerably by using an associative memory or content addressable memory (CAM). Such a memory can be accessed by using the contents of a subfield of the information being searched rather than by an address. The subfield chosen to address the memory is

*See also Sec. 1.16.5.

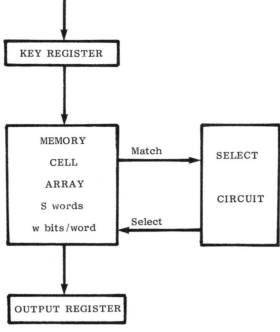

Fig. 5 Associative memory.

known as the key. Thus items stored in an associative memory may be thought of as pairs, (KEY, DATA). For example, if items of a page table are stored in such a memory, the page number (in the address space) will be the KEY, while the page frame number in which the said page is located and various flags will constitute the DATA.

An associative memory is searched in parallel for the required item. When a word is written in such a memory, no address is specified. The memory hardware is equipped to find an unused location and store the word. Upon reading, the content of the word, or a part thereof, is specified. The memory will locate all cells whose contents match the specified content and mark the cells for reading. The additional logic required for the parallel searching and matching circuits makes associative memories more complex and expensive compared to conventional memories. For this reason, the use of associative memories is limited to applications with a relatively small search space and requirements for a very short search time (e.g., address mapping hardware in virtual memory systems and cache-based systems).

Figure 5 shows the block diagram of an associative memory. In this simple example, each entry in the storage array is a fixed-length (w-bit) word. Any subfield of the word may be chosen as a search field. The desired key is specified by the key register, which is compared simultaneously with the appropriate bits of all S words. Words matching the key emit match signals, which enter a select circuit. If several words match the key, the select circuit determines which word will be read out and placed in the output register. The select circuit may also read out all matching words in some predetermined sequence. Note that all words in the memory must simultaneously compare their keys with the input key; hence each word must have its own match circuit.

In the associative mapping memory of a virtual memory system, the ($n - p$)-bit page index from the virtual address will be input to the key register. If a match occurs, the required page table entry is obtained in the output register. If no match occurs, the required page table entry must be obtained from the main-memory resident page table.

As another example, consider a set associative cache as in Fig. 4. Each column i of the index directory is an independent associative memory for mapping into set i of the cache. Thus the column field of the main-memory address indicates the specific associative memory to be used, and the row field is used as the search key. If no match occurs, the required block is not in cache. In case of a match, the cache row in which the required block resides is the output of the associative memory (no DATA field is necessary).

Since the cells of an associative memory have logical capabilities, such a memory is also referred to as a logic-in-memory device (or distributed logic memory). This can naturally be extended so that each cell may perform standard arithmetic and logic functions. In this case it is more appropriate to refer to the resulting device as an associative processor [7].

REFERENCES

1. C. G. BELL, J. C. MUDGE, and J. E. McNAMARA (eds.), *Computer Engineering*: *A DEC View of Hardware System Design*, Digital Press, Bedford, Mass., 1978, pp. 263–267.
2. P. J. DENNING, "Virtual Memory," *Comput. Surv.*, **2**(3), 153–189 (Sept. 1970).
3. H. HELLERMAN and T. E. CONROY, *Computer System Performance*, McGraw-Hill, New York, 1975.
4. IBM Corp., *IBM System /370 Model* 168 *Functional Characteristics*, IBM Publication GA22-7010, IBM Corp. Data Processing Division, White Plains, N.Y.
5. R. E. MATICK, *Computer Storage Systems and Technology*, Wiley-Interscience, New York, 1977.
6. E. I. ORGANICK, *The Multics System*: *An Examination of Its Structure*, MIT Press, Cambridge, Mass., 1972.
7. K. J. THURBER, *Large Scale Computer Architecture*, Hayden, Rochelle Park, N.J., 1976.
8. K. S. TRIVEDI, "Analytic Modeling of Computer Systems," *Computer*, **11**(10), 38–56 (Oct. 1978).
9. K. S. TRIVEDI and T. M. SIGMON, "Optimal Design of Linear Storage Hierarchies," *JACM* (Apr. 1981).

1.8   MAIN MEMORY AND HIGH-SPEED STORAGE: MICROPROCESSOR SYSTEM CONSIDERATIONS

Dennis J. McBride

The term *microcomputer* indicates a computer that is small in terms of its size, power consumption, performance, cost, and other characteristics compared with other types of general-purpose computers. Some applications can take advantage of single-chip integrated-circuit microcomputers. Otherwise, the CPU, memory, and I/O functions are spread across some small number of chips. In this article we discuss aspects of system design wherein the CPU, memory, and I/O are separate entities and therefore need to be interfaced with each other. First is a discussion of selection signals, by which one memory location is chosen for reading or writing. Also, alternative means of using memory chips (and I/O devices) to fill the required address space are presented. Finally, we discuss other concerns, such as reserving memory for interrupt handlers, stack operations, and restrictions on address decoding. For more information, see Sec. 1.18.

1.8.1   Selection Signals

Consider the microcomputer system memory as an array of N memory locations, with each location M bits wide. For ease of design the width M is usually made to match the width of the CPU internal data path. The most common widths are 4, 8, 16, and occasionally 12 bits. Although this width is a reflection of the number of bits that can be operated on in parallel, it does not preclude the use of two or more contiguous memory locations to represent a data structure or an instruction.

Address Selection

In order to specify one memory location, the CPU generates an ordered set of binary logic signals which can be thought of as representing a positive binary integer. We call the conductors on which these signals appear the address bus, and we say that the address bus holds the encoded representation of the memory location. The decoded representation appears within the memory subsystem to allow a read or write operation only to the single location that has been addressed.

EXAMPLE. Memory integrated circuits are available which contain 64K* locations, where each location is 1 bit wide. These memory devices thus require a 16-bit address bus as an input to describe a memory location uniquely. If the data path between the memory and the CPU is 8 bits wide, this

---

*We define 1K as equal 1024, so 64K is really 64×1024.

address bus must be connected to each of eight identical memory devices in order to have a total configuration that is $64K \times 8$. We also refer to the data path as a bus; in this case, each memory device is responsible for a bit on one of the eight data bus paths.

Read and Write Selection

In addition to the address signals, it is necessary to supply a control signal to designate whether the operation is read or write. This is typically implemented as a single control line, and is often labeled R/W.

The timing and control for memory and I/O operations originate within the CPU. The technical specifications of a given microprocessor include this detailed timing information (see Sec. 1.9.7 for an example). It is usually presented as a set of timing diagrams. These diagrams illustrate (1) when the CPU address to memory is valid, (2) when the CPU places data signals on the data bus for a write operation, (3) when the CPU samples the data bus for a read operation, and (4) when the states of control signals change in order to effect the given operation. A unique sequence may exist for each type of CPU/memory interaction (instruction fetch, data fetch, data store). These details become important in system design, because memory devices must be chosen that match or exceed the performance required by the microprocessor. Timing diagrams are also used to present the performance of a particular memory device. Again, different diagrams are usually required for the read and the write operations.

For whatever memory operation is required, the microprocessor presents the address first. Some systems have a control signal that explicitly declares the time period of the valid address. After the memory location is specified by the address bus, the memory data appear on the data bus. For the read, or fetch, sequence the microprocessor simply waits one or more clock cycles after presenting a valid address and then samples the data bus, storing it in an internal CPU register. In some systems, the processor requires a "ready" signal from memory to indicate when the data bus may be sampled. This permits the use of a variety of memories (or other devices) with different cycle times. If the CPU is going to write data into memory, the address is presented first, with the R/W signal in its read state. This ensures that an arbitrary memory location will not be altered while the address bus is settling into its valid state. The CPU ignores the state of the data bus. The bus must be turned around, so to speak, by now declaring a write operation. This transition on the R/W control line tells the memory devices to deactivate their driver circuits. The contents of an internal CPU register can now be presented to memory, and will be saved in the designated location as the R/W line returns to its read state. The CPU is now allowed to change the state of the address bus to initiate the next operation.

Notice that the discussion above assumes that the microprocessor and the memory are connected to a bidirectional data bus. Both sources must therefore be able to put their bus driver circuitry in a high (virtually infinite) impedance state. This is standard practice. Some memory devices, however, use separate signal paths for incoming and outgoing data. This permits faster memory performance. These devices can still be interfaced with a bidirectional bus, and bus interface devices are commonly available for this purpose.

Device Selection

The addressing range, or address space, as defined by the width of the address bus is usually not fully populated; part of the address space, perhaps even most of it, remains vacant. That is, physical memory locations do not exist for all addresses that can be generated by the CPU. There are various reasons for this. First, the majority of applications do not demand the maximum memory configuration. Second, the width of the address bus is defined by CPU architectural considerations, and not necessarily with a fully populated address space in mind. For example, some microprocessors have a 24-bit address bus, permitting a 16-megabyte address space. Only a modest proportion of large mainframe computers, or very specialized applications, can justify the associated cost of this quantity of memory. A third aspect, discussed below, is that some microprocessors do not have instructions especially for I/O or for a dedicated I/O device address space. Part of memory address space must be reserved for I/O-device addresses. Frequently, the highest-order address bit is defined by the system designer as a memory versus I/O address indicator. This cuts the memory address space in half. In view of the infrequent need to populate all of address space, however, the assignment of I/O-device addresses within memory address space is not a burden. In fact, it can be an advantage.

Memory integrated circuits are available in standard widths of 1, 4, and 8 bits. The number of locations on a single device is chosen to be an integer power of 2, with 1K, 4K, 16K, and 64K being the most popular. Clearly, the product of length times width is limited by the current state of technology. We therefore need a technique for expanding the width and length of main memory, to match our requirements, by using an array of standard memory devices.

When an array of memory devices is used to implement the memory space of a microcomputer system, means must be provided to select the appropriate one(s) of these to satisfy a specific memory access operation. Therefore, we require an additional control input to each memory integrated circuit. It is called a *device select*, or *chip enable signal*. When this is in its active state, the device can be addressed for read or write operations. Otherwise, the device virtually disappears from the data bus by assuming a high-impedance state. One can use this, for example, to provide a 2K location memory using two 1K location chips. Connect the 10 least significant bits of the address bus to both memory devices. The next-most-significant address bit is connected to the chip enable for one device, and the same address bit is inverted and then connected to the second device. Now only one device can be active at a time, so the data buses of the two devices can be common. One device populates locations 0 through 1023, and the other device occupies locations 1024 through 2047. This explicit control of the high-impedance state for memory devices gives very good expansion capability for ease of system design.

Some systems provide the minimum amount of decoding to select one of the memory devices at a time. This minimum decoding, however, causes a given actual location to be selected periodically throughout address space (e.g., in the preceding example, any memory word at address X from 0 to 2K will also be selected if the CPU generates address $X + 2nK$ for $n = 1, 2, \ldots$; however, location X is usually referred to in software only at its primary intended address). This technique of minimum decoding reduces costs for a minimum system but is otherwise not a recommended practice.

Bus Loading

We have several types of memory devices to choose from in configuring a total memory system. This means that many implementations are possible to realize a given total array size. Furthermore, the chip select technique makes practically any one of these implementations easy to carry out. We should now consider the second-order effects, however, since there may be an optimum approach. If the address bus is 16 bits wide, there are 64 regions of 1K locations each. In order to do a complete decoding for selection of 1K memory chips, we have to perform a 6 line-to-64 line decode of the 6 highest address bits. The 10 lowest-order address lines still go to all the memory devices. The extra decoding is explicitly required because there are 64 possible states that the 6 highest address bits can assume, so we use one of the 64 lines as a chip select for the lowest 1024 locations. We use a second line to select the next 1024 locations, and so on.

Let us now compare implementing a memory space with chips of 1K locations by 4 bits versus $4K \times 1$ chip organizations, for an 8-bit data bus. For the $1K \times 4$ chips, two devices must be placed in parallel, each for 4 bits of the data bus. The chip select line for each region must simultaneously activate two memory devices, and each chip sees the 10 lowest-order address lines. For modest amounts of total memory this design approach is reasonable. Now, a $4K \times 1$ device, with eight chips in parallel, needs two more address lines, but it uses three fewer data lines, per chip. It is a slightly more efficient package. Second, the remaining address lines are now only 4 in number compared to 6. Unique decoding can be accomplished via a 4-to-16 line decoder, as there are only 16 regions of 4K in the address space. This function is readily available in a single integrated-circuit package. The previous 6-to-64 line decoder borders on being unmanageable, because of chip I/O pin limitations and the relatively high cost of circuit card wiring compared to integrated device wiring. Next, eight of these memory devices must be used in parallel to have an 8-bit bus. The address bus therefore feeds eight memory chips per 4K region. This was also the case before, since the 1024×4 implementation used eight devices, stacked four high and two wide. Finally, notice that our new arrangement places only a single device load on each data bus line, whereas the previous design placed four loads on each data line. For maximum performance (highest speed) the data bus should have a minimum of loading. The general approach is therefore to use the single-bit-wide organization, with n bits in parallel for an n-bit data bus, when minimum loading is essential.

I/O Selection

The same combination of R/W and chip select signals used to select memory devices can activate a register whose width matches the data bus. This register can serve as an I/O device itself or be part of a device controller (see Sec. 1.10.6). This register can be thought of as a memory device which makes the state of each bit visible to the external environment. We now have an *output port* at a designated memory address. Similarly, the address bus can be decoded for a CPU read operation. Data from the external environment would be placed on the data bus when this location is referenced. We call this an *input port*. This technique can be used for any modest number and combination of input and output ports. The circuitry to perform unique decoding becomes a limiting factor, as does loading of the data bus by too many devices. Some of the decoding function can be implemented within each I/O peripheral unit, thus distributing the logic as well as the loading. Access timing for these I/O locations must match or exceed the performance required by the CPU. This technique is called *memory-mapped I/O*, and it generally does not interfere with the implementation of modest amounts of main memory.

The beauty of this technique from a programming point of view is that input- and output-device addresses are accessible via all the powerful addressing modes made available for memory operations. Microprocessors that do support a separate address space for I/O devices also have a weaker instruction set for accessing these locations. This is because the complexity of the instruction decode logic in the CPU is limited. The extra decoding for I/O instructions must necessarily subtract from the total function possible on a single chip. There are applications where the optimum design takes advantage of both techniques in order to minimize explicit decoding.

Refresh Control

Microcomputers that use a large array for main memory often use devices characterized as dynamic (see Sec. 1.6.3). These devices do not use bistable storage elements such as flip-flops or latches. They rely on the presence or absence of charge on a capacitor to represent each memory bit. Those bits that contain charge will eventually change state, since the charge will eventually leak away. These memory devices have a provision for comparing the state of a bit against a threshold, and then resetting the charge to maximum, or zero, but this happens only when the chip is accessed. The microcomputer system must guarantee that specific addresses will be reactivated more often than a total period which is typically 2 to 4 ms. This is much too cumbersome to implement in software, so special hardware must be designed to address specific locations of all memory devices according to the given time constraint. Devices are available that assist in this task, and some memory devices incorporate all or most of this special function. This makes them appear to be bistable when, in fact, they are dynamic. The term often applied to these devices is *quasistatic*, since most of the dynamic behavior is transparent from the system designer's point of view. In any memory that is fundamentally dynamic, though, there is a probability that memory access by the CPU will be delayed because of a concurrent refresh operation at that same address. The details of timing and performance must take into account the worst-case access situation.

1.8.2 Organizing Address Space

If we look at the address bus of a microcomputer, we may find several different devices sharing the total address space. An arbitrary memory location might be vacant, or it could be within the address space of a RAM, ROM, or PROM, or it could be a memory-mapped I/O-device address. For a discussion of ROM, see Sec. 1.6.3. The memory locations which remain vacant and those which are populated by various devices are determined by the decoding logic, which in turn is defined by the system designer. All of these devices are wired to the data bus. Only one source may be active at a time. We have to understand the microprocessor architecture, though, to guarantee that any special-purpose memory locations required for instruction execution have been implemented. This varies from one architecture to another in terms of detail, but the concepts are general in nature.

Reserved Memory Locations

Most microprocessors have one or more interrupt mechanisms, which access specific memory locations. During the interrupt process the currently active instruction sequence is suspended (see Sec. 1.3). Information pertaining to the current state is saved, typically on a push-pop stack, so that instruction processing can resume where it was stopped after the interrupt-handling program has been executed. Except for any implications that a time delay might have, the interrupted program is not aware that it was ever disturbed. Meanwhile, the address of an interrupt-handling program is placed in the instruction counter, and interrupt processing occurs.

Most microprocessor architectures define a fixed address to be loaded into the instruction counter when an interrupt occurs. Some architectures allow the interrupting device to specify part of this address field. Generally, these fixed locations should contain branch instructions to other locations in main memory where the interrupt servicing routines are found. After power is applied, and before the first interrupt is allowed to occur, these locations must be loaded (written into) with the entry addresses for interrupt processing. Frequently, two or more sequential locations are required to hold these entry addresses. These locations must therefore be populated, either with RAM or ROM, so that interrupt processing can be supported. Some microprocessors define several such sets of memory locations, one set for each distinct type of interrupt. These interrupt types might include external and internal, maskable or nonmaskable, single level or multilevel.

Next, let us consider some stack techniques (see Sec. 1.4.8). It is possible to maintain a small stack on the CPU chip itself. This type of stack is not part of main-memory address space. An arbitrarily large stack can be implemented by using an internal CPU register called the stack pointer. The address in this register is the location of the top of the stack. If the stack pointer is as wide as the address bus, any location can be the top of the stack. As interrupts occur or as explicit push instructions are executed, this register points to successively lower locations. Nesting of interrupts or push operations is thus limited according to the amount of contiguous address space that has been populated below the starting stack address.

If the stack pointer register is not as wide as the address bus, at least part of the address space that can be reached by this register must contain RAM. In some architectures, the stack register is only 8 bits wide and defines a specific region of 256 locations as the stack. It is very desirable in this case to provide RAM at all 256 of these locations.

Many microprocessors are designed to detect the initial application of power, at which time the instruction counter is reset to location zero or preset to a defined value. The instruction at this address is loaded into the instruction register, and processing begins. For ease of use, many microcomputers are designed with ROM in this part of address space. Some level of application support can thus be made immediately available, upon which higher levels of function can be loaded into RAM from magnetic tape, paper tape, diskette, and so on.

Decoding the Address Bus

The most straightforward decoding approach is to choose RAM and ROM chips with the same number of locations. They do not have to be the same width, as this is easily handled via parallel layout of the appropriate number of devices for a given width. The decoding for chip enable can now select banks of memory which all contain the same number of locations. This means that banks of memory can easily be relocated by interchanging the routing of the select lines between the decoder and the memory devices. This is very important when address space is not fully populated, especially for satisfying absolute address regions required by previously written software. Systems are often designed to have these address select lines brought out to some kind of circuit card connector and then back onto the card on their way to the memory devices. Relocation of memory addresses is particularly easy in this case, by rewiring or replacing the circuit card I/O connector. Equivalently, miniature switches can be placed directly on the circuit card, so that the absolute address of a block of memory is determined by the switch settings.

If enough address space is uncommitted, an I/O device address can be enabled with an unused memory chip enable, or bank select signal. The input or output port will be selected whenever any of the memory addresses within the decoded region are placed on the address bus. If, for example, external memory decoding has been tailored for devices with 4096 locations each, I/O selection using these same lines will cause each port to consume 4096 locations of the total address space. For this reason, a second level of address decoding is often made part of the system design, for I/O selection, to reduce the address space defined by each port. In the extreme, decoding can be used to guarantee that each port is assigned a unique address. But this requires additional circuitry, and the uniqueness must be justified.

BIBLIOGRAPHY

C. A. OGDIN, *Microcomputer Design*, Prentice-Hall, Englewood Cliffs, N.J. 1978.

J. L. HILBURN, AND P. M. JULICH, *Microcomputers/Microprocessors: Hardware, Software, and Applications*, Prentice-Hall, Englewood Cliffs, N.J., 1976.

1.9   CONTROL, TIMING, AND SYSTEM SIGNALS

Nikitas A. Alexandridis

In this article we describe the control and timing function of a digital processing system. Both intramodule and intermodule signals are analyzed. Signals required to carry out the instruction execution steps are described. We also illustrate various ways of implementing this control and timing function, all of them grouped into two major alternatives: the hardwired sequential control implementation and the microprogrammed control implementation. Other features related to the control function are also described, such as operation overlap, instruction lookahead, pipelined operation, and microprogrammable control as a tool for emulation. Finally, LSI devices incorporated in the control section of a digital system are presented.

In any digital processing system, two of its major components are the arithmetic-logic unit (ALU) and the control section. They make up what is called the central processing unit (CPU) of a computer. The ALU is composed of properly interconnected data routing switches (that establish the paths for moving data around) and a data-transformation unit (that carries out the arithmetic and logical operations). The control section directs the internal activities of the ALU and controls all modules of the system. During the system's operation, the CPU fetches machine language instructions (sometimes called "macroinstructions") from main memory. Then the operation code field of the instruction is interpreted by the circuitry in the control section (i.e., mapped into a series of control signals), and the operand(s) specified by the instruction is (are) routed to the ALU to be used in computations.

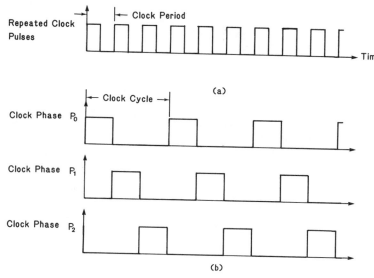

Fig. 1 Clocks: (*a*) single-phase clock; (*b*) three-phase clock.

The function of the control section is to issue properly timed signals to control the data-handling operations within the processor module (*intramodule control*), to coordinate the operations in all other modules of the system, and to synchronize the intermodule communications and data transfers (*intermodule control*). Intermodule control is discussed in Sec. 1.9.7, where we cover microprocessor system signals. Some of the activities carried out in the control section include: use the instruction counter to address the instruction, fetch this instruction, modify the instruction counter to point to the "next" instruction, decode the fetched instruction, and generate the appropriate control signals needed for its execution. To carry out its tasks properly, the control section must contain at least the following three facilities:

1. Decision logic for generating the next control state. This next-state selection is done through a proper combination of the present-state information, the CPU module's external inputs, and certain feedback lines either from within the module (e.g., flags and conditions from the ALU) or from other modules of the system (system status signals).
2. A facility to store the information that corresponds to the current control state.
3. Some means for translating this state into proper control signals to be issued either within the module or to other modules of the system.

There are differences in the requirements and characteristics between intra- and intermodule controls and their respective ways of implementing these control and timing functions.

Since almost all modern digital systems synchronize their events with single- or multiple-phase clocks, these control signals are issued in synchronism with precise clock pulses. We therefore confine our presentation to the synchronous (clocked) implementation, where it will be inferred that there exists such a timing mechanism or module to synchronize control state transitions and data-flow switching by supplying those precisely timed, properly shaped clock pulses to all parts of the system. The organization of this timing module is basically very simple, and it is discussed as an integral part of the control system.

1.9.1   Timing and Control Sequences

Timing

All actions of the logic circuits in a computer are initiated by a sequence or sequences of pulses generated by a clock. Usually, polyphase clocks are used. Figure 1 depicts the pulses of a single-phase and a three-phase clock that we use in this article. The time interval between two adjacent clock pulses of the single-phase clock is the *clock period*. In the polyphase clock, the adjacent pulses, with one pulse from each phase, form a cycle, called the *clock cycle*. Thus the clock cycle of Fig. 1*b* is composed of

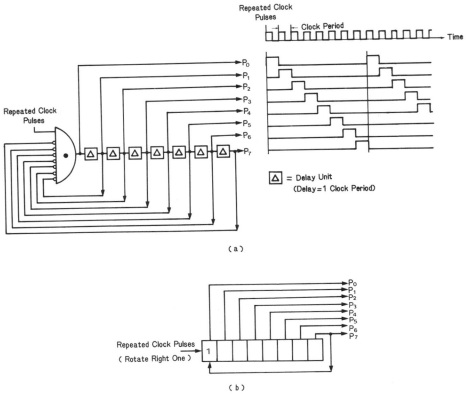

Fig. 2 Implementations for generating eight clock phases: (*a*) pulse distribution; (*b*) ring counter.

three periods. Each phase P_i occurs at the beginning of the clock period and lasts for one period. These three pulses P_0, P_1, P_2 in a clock cycle of this clock can be used to control a three-step sequence.

Various physical implementations exist for generating multiple clock phases.* Figure 2 shows three implementation examples (*c* and *d* are similar) for generating an eight-phase clock, the pulses of each phase applied to a separate wire. Figure 2*d* shows a register and decoder implementation that we use in Sec. 1.9.2 in the design of the control section. At the beginning of each clock pulse, the corresponding phase P_i will be activated, depending on the binary value contained in register C.

Microoperations

Digital systems and computers are required to perform complex operations which are effected by executing sequences of primitive operations called *microoperations*. Microoperations are carried out by properly connecting the system's basic hardware resources, such as registers, ALU components, and data links in a variety of combinations.

Microoperations may be classified into set-constant, transfer, unary, and binary microoperations. The most fundamental of them is the set-constant microoperation, which sets a register to a constant number value. The transfer microoperation transfers the contents of one or two registers to another register. In the unary and binary microoperations, the ALU receives information from one or two registers over data paths, and transforms the input into a result, which is usually gated to another register. Examples of unary microoperations include the shift, rotate, and count operations. Binary microoperations include logical (e.g., AND and OR) and arithmetic (e.g., ADD and SUBTRACT) operations.

In this article we also use complex conditional microoperations of the type IF–THEN or IF–THEN–ELSE which are carried out under certain conditions. For example, the microoperation

*N. R. SCOTT, *Analog and Digital Computer Technology*, McGraw-Hill, New York, 1960.

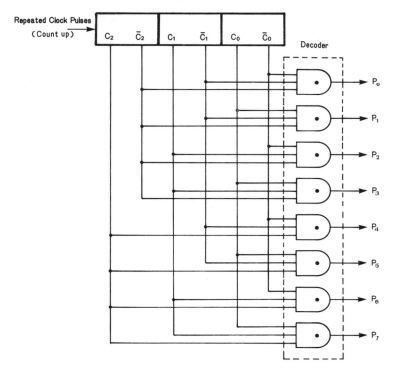

(c)

(d)

Fig. 2 (continued) (c) binary counter; (d) register and decoder combination.

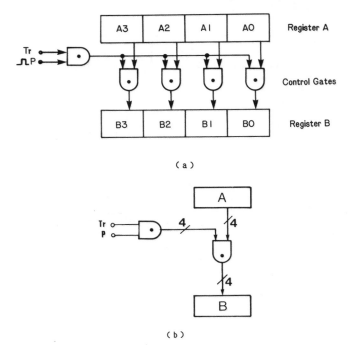

(a)

(b)

Fig. 3 Two graphic representations for the register transfer microoperation T_r and $P:B \leftarrow (A)$.

IF $(STR \neq 0)$ THEN $(IC \leftarrow (IC)+1)$ ELSE $(IC \leftarrow (IC)+2)$ indicates that the instruction counter will be incremented by one if $STR \neq 0$; otherwise, the microoperation of incrementing the instruction counter by two will be executed.

In carrying out these microoperations, proper control signals must be issued to activate data paths and to select source and destination registers, as well as a transformation unit. These control signals must be precisely timed so that all actions will take place at the appropriate instant.

Some microoperations are more complex than others. For example, a transfer microoperation is simpler than a unary or binary microoperation and requires only one control signal. Even for this simplest microoperation, however, the transfer is not done instantaneously; a finite amount of time is required. A clock period larger than this amount of time is usually chosen so that the microoperation can be completed within the clock period. Figure 3 shows graphical representations of the "transfer contents of register A to register B" microoperation. Here, two 4-bit registers are connected through a 4-bit data path containing an equal number of control gates. The duration of the clock period of P has been properly chosen to allow enough time for the execution of the microoperation. Symbolically, this transfer microoperation is expressed as*

$$T_r \text{ AND } P: B \leftarrow (A)$$

that is, the contents of register A are transferred to register B when both the command signal T_r and the pulse P of the single-phase clock are present. The logical-AND operation of T_r and P constitutes

*The following notation is used in this article:

Notation	Meaning
X	Register X
(X)	Contents of register X
M	Memory
M^x	Memory location specified by *contents* of register X; note that this is not consistent with the preceding, but it is less cumbersome than $M^{(x)}$
(M^x)	Contents of memory at location specified by contents of register X
$Y \leftarrow (X)$	Contents of Y are replaced by contents of X
$Y \leftarrow k$	Contents of Y are set to k

the *control signal* required for this microoperation. In general, such a control signal may initiate one or more microoperations. For example, the statement above should be changed to

$$T_r \text{ AND P}: B \leftarrow (A), T_r \leftarrow 0$$

if we do not want the transfer to be taking place each time a clock pulse P appears. Here the second microoperation resets the command signal T_r, and the logical value of the control signal T_r AND P is no longer 1.

Instruction Sequencing

During the normal sequencing of a stored-program digital system, the instructions are executed one after the other following the order in which they are stored in main memory. In general, each machine language instruction is carried out by executing a sequence of one or more microoperations. For each instruction, the fetch sequence is carried out first, followed by the execution sequence. During the fetch sequence, the instruction addressed by the instruction counter is fetched from main memory into the control section, the operation code (or op code) field of the instruction is decoded, the operand address is computed and transferred to the memory address register (if necessary), and the instruction counter is modified to point to the "next" instruction in memory. Then, having decoded the op code, the control section must now issue proper control signals to carry out the microoperations necessary to execute this instruction. The time taken to carry out the execution cycle of a simple instruction (e.g., ADD) corresponds to the *CPU cycle time*.

Like the CPU, the main memory also operates on a *memory cycle*. A memory cycle is used for a memory read or write operation. Each such operation is carried out as a sequence of activities as follows:

1. *For a memory read.* The address is first transferred to the memory address register (MAR); a memory read operation is initiated; the addressed word is read out of memory into the memory data register (MDR); and the word is then restored (written back) at the same location (assuming that reading is a destructive operation).

2. *For a memory write.* The address is first transferred to the MAR; a memory write operation is initiated; reading of the addressed word into the MDR is inhibited; the word in the MDR is written

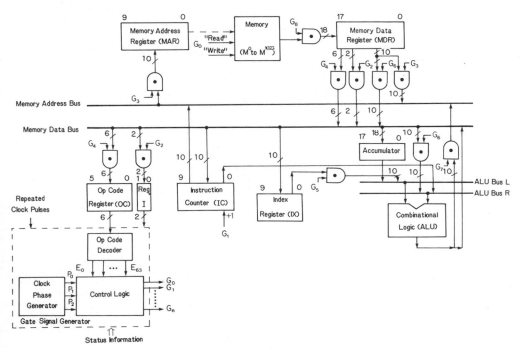

Fig. 4 Configuration of a simple, stored-program, digital system.

Table 1.   Instruction Subset

Command Signal	Mnemonic Name	Function	Execution
E_0	HLT	Halt	STR $\leftarrow$ 0 (the START flag is reset)
E_1	ADD	Addition	ACC $\leftarrow$ (ACC)+(M^{adr})
$\vdots$			
E_{10}	LDA	Load accumulator	ACC $\leftarrow$ (M^{adr})
E_{11}	STA	Store accumulator	$M^{adr} \leftarrow$ (ACC)
$\vdots$			
E_{20}	JMP	Jump (unconditional)	IC $\leftarrow$ adr
E_{21}	BAZ	$\left\{\begin{array}{l}\text{Branch if accumulator}\\ \text{zero}\end{array}\right.$	$\left\{\begin{array}{l}\text{If (ACC)}\neq 0\text{, then IC}\leftarrow\text{(IC)}+1\\ \text{If (ACC)}=0\text{, then IC}\leftarrow\text{adr}\end{array}\right.$
$\vdots$			

into the memory. The *memory access time* is that part of the memory cycle time during which the read operation is performed.

In order to be more specific in our description, we shall use the simple system shown in Fig. 4. Although the CPU cycle time is much faster than the memory cycle time, for simplicity we assume here that the memory cycle time is equal to the CPU cycle time, and that both are chosen to coincide with the clock cycle defined in Fig. 1, composed of three clock phases P_0, P_1, P_2.

This system has a memory of 1024 words by 18 bits (with a memory address register and memory data register), an ALU with an 18-bit accumulator, and a control section containing a 6-bit op code register, a 2-bit register I (for indexing and/or indirection), a 10-bit instruction counter, one 10-bit index register, and the necessary circuitry (gate signal generator) for issuing appropriate control signals to the rest of the system. The control section, the ALU, the registers, and the memory module of this system are interconnected via appropriate buses. Figure 4 also shows some interconnections and control gates which, when activated by their *control gate signals* G_i, initiate respective microoperations (discussed in detail in Sec. 1.9.2). Each instruction is composed (from left to right) of a 6-bit operation code field, an 1-bit index tag, an 1-bit indirect addressing tag, and a 10-bit address field (adr). We assume single-address instructions and no overlap between the instruction fetch and execute sequences.

Decoding of the 6-bit-wide op code may activate one of up to 64 different E_i *command signals*, each command signal initiating a different set of microoperations required to execute the instruction. Each command signal E_i remains valid for the whole duration of the respective instruction execution sequence. As we will see later, the 6-bit combination 111111 is not assigned to an instruction op code but, instead, is reserved for setting the op code register to a value that generates the special command signal E_{63}. If $E_{63}=1$, this implies that the system is in its instruction fetch sequence; if $E_{63}=0$, this implies that the system is in its instruction execution sequence. It is assumed that the command signal E_{63} also remains valid for the whole duration of the respective sequence.

The gate signal generator in Fig. 4 combines the command signals, the timing pulses from the clock, and other system state information (such as ACC = 0) and generates gate signals to initiate the respective microoperations. The details of this gate signal generator are discussed in Sec. 1.9.2. Table 1 shows a subset of the system's instructions, their mnemonic names, and the symbolic representation of their executions.

Microoperation Sequencing

The role of the control section is to provide the control signals for the rest of the system and to determine what the next control signals will be. The *next* control signals generally depend on the results of the present microoperation(s) and on the status of certain system flags which are generated.

The processing of each instruction always starts with the fetch sequence for extracting the instruction from memory. This instruction fetch sequence is the same for all instructions (i.e., it is carried out by the execution of the same sequence of microoperations). (In this section we disregard both index and indirect addressing tags. We will use these tags in Sec. 1.9.2 when we give the detailed implementation of the hardwired sequential control section.) The instruction execution sequence varies from instruction to instruction depending on the specific instruction to be executed.

For the simple system in Fig. 4, the following activities must be carried out during the instruction fetch sequence:

MAR ← (IC). The contents of the instruction counter are transferred to the memory address register.

Read ← 1. Memory fetch request is signaled.

MDR ← (M^{MAR}). The memory word located at the address in MAR is transferred to the memory data register.

IC ← (IC) + 1. The instruction counter is incremented by one to point to the next instruction.

MAR ← (MDR_{9-0}). The address part (the rightmost 10 bits) of the MDR is transferred to the MAR register.

OC ← (MDR_{17-12}). The op code part (the leftmost 6 bits) of the MDR is transferred to the op code register.

Before we continue to define the control signals required to sequence the activities outlined above, we pause momentarily to explain the control signals needed for accessing the (main) memory. Since we assumed that the memory cycle coincides with the clock cycle, and since the clock cycle is made up of three clock phases, we must allocate all memory activities (discussed earlier) into three major steps, each step controlled by one clock phase. One way of doing this for the memory read and write cycles is as follows:

1. *Memory read cycle.* The transfer of the address to the memory address register occurs at clock phase P_2 of the preceding clock cycle; the signaling to initiate a memory read operation and the reading out of the addressed word into the memory data register both occur at the same clock phase: phase P_0 of the current clock cycle. Thus we have:

$$P_2: MAR \leftarrow (IC) \text{ or } MAR \leftarrow (MDR_{9-0}) \qquad \text{Beginning of memory cycle}$$

$$P_0: MDR \leftarrow (M^{MAR}), \text{Read} \leftarrow 1$$

$$P_1: \qquad\qquad\qquad\qquad\qquad\qquad\qquad\qquad\quad \text{End of memory cycle}$$

2. *Memory write cycle.* The transfer of the address to the memory address register occurs at clock phase P_2 of the preceding clock cycle; the word to be stored in memory is placed into the memory data register at clock phase P_0 of the current clock cycle; the signaling to initiate a memory write operation and the word in the memory data register written into the memory both occur at the same clock phase P_1. Thus we have:

$$P_2: MAR \leftarrow (IC) \text{ or } MAR \leftarrow (MDR_{9-0}) \qquad \text{Beginning of memory cycle}$$

$$P_0: MDR \leftarrow (ACC)$$

$$P_1: M^{MAR} \leftarrow (MDR), \text{Write} \leftarrow 1 \qquad\qquad \text{End of memory cycle}$$

Let us now return to define the control signals required to execute the instruction fetch sequence. Again the three phases of the clock must be used, and all the activities of the fetch sequence must be grouped into three major steps. The command signal E_{63} initiates the fetch sequence. This E_{63} can be generated by putting six 1's in the op code register of Fig. 4 (i.e., OC ← 63) at the end of each instruction execution sequence. Then, assuming that MAR ← (IC) was done during clock phase P_2 of the preceding clock cycle, we have the following for the instruction fetch sequence:

$$E_{63} \text{ AND } P_0: MDR \leftarrow (M^{MAR}), \text{Read} \leftarrow 1$$

$$E_{63} \text{ AND } P_1: IC \leftarrow (IC) + 1$$

$$E_{63} \text{ AND } P_2: OC \leftarrow (MDR_{17-12}), MAR \leftarrow (MDR_{9-0})$$

It is noticed that more than one microoperation may be executed during a single clock phase, initiated by a control signal generated by the logical-AND operation of E_{63} with the respective clock phase P_i.

Also note that the operand address is placed into MAR during P_2, to be ready for the succeeding instruction execution sequence, regardless of whether the operand will be stored (or fetched) by the instruction.

The sequence chart for our simplified system is given in Fig. 5, showing the respective microoperation sequences for the instruction subset of Table 1. With the powering-on of the system, flag STR is set to zero, and the system is in the wait state, executing the wait loop at the lower left corner of Fig. 5. When the START button is pressed, flag STR is set to 1, and the computer begins execution of the fetch sequence, executing the first instruction from memory location 0. Transitions from one state to another take place at the end of every clock phase. It is observed that the fetch sequence and its microoperations are the same for each instruction and that three clock phases are required to traverse through its three states. At the end of the fetch sequence, the control section interprets the operation code field of the instruction that has arrived from main memory. This usually results in a sequence of changes of the system's state and causes stimuli to be sent to the other modules of the machine. Depending on the command signal E_i generated from decoding the instruction, a separate and unique sequence of steps will be followed during the instruction execution sequence. It has been assumed that the reading part of the memory cycle occurs during clock phase P_0 and the writing part during clock phase P_1, and that for all instructions, their execution sequence is complete at the end of clock phase P_2. For the HLT instruction, the START flag is reset to zero (STR $\leftarrow$ 0) and the system goes into the wait loop, from which it exits when the START flag is (manually) set to 1 (i.e., STR $\leftarrow$ 1).

For example, consider the execution sequence for instruction ADD, which, when decoded, generates the command signal E_1. A sequence of three control signals is required to carry out the three steps of the instruction shown in Fig. 5, as follows:

$$E_1 \text{ AND } P_0: \text{MDR} \leftarrow (\text{M}^{\text{MAR}}), \text{ Read} \leftarrow 1$$

$$E_1 \text{ AND } P_1: \text{ACC} \leftarrow (\text{ACC}) + (\text{MDR})$$

$$E_1 \text{ AND } P_2: \text{MAR} \leftarrow (\text{IC}), \text{ OC} \leftarrow 63$$

Here we assume that both simple operations (such as a register transfer) and complex operations (such as addition) are carried out within one clock phase. The microoperation OC $\leftarrow$ 63 terminates the instruction execution sequence and causes command signal E_{63} to be issued, to initiate a new fetch sequence for the next instruction.

For the execution of the conditional transfer instruction $E_{21}(=\text{BAZ})$, the following control signals are required for the two steps:

Step 1. $E_{21} \text{ AND } P_1 \text{ AND } [(\text{ACC}) = 0]: \text{IC} \leftarrow (\text{MDR}_{9-0})$
$\quad\quad\quad$ $E_{21} \text{ AND } P_1 \text{ AND } [(\text{ACC}) \neq 0]: \text{no action}$
Step 2. $E_{21} \text{ AND } P_2: \text{MAR} \leftarrow (\text{IC}), \text{ OC} \leftarrow 63$

Of course, it must be appreciated that this is an overly simplified design. Only a subset of very simple instructions has been used, and the CPU cycle time and memory cycle time were chosen to be the same and both equal the three-phase clock cycle. It has also been implied here that the control section, the ALU, and the memory module are working together synchronously. In real situations, many more complicated instructions and clocking schemes are used. Longer instructions also exist (e.g., multiply, divide) which require iterative executions of sequences of microoperations (see Sec. 1.5.5).

To summarize, the control section must contain capabilities for issuing several control signals, properly synchronized with a timing source, to ensure that the microoperations are executed at the proper times and sequence. There are two major ways of generating the control signals to activate the system's microoperations: through hardwired sequential logic implementation (discussed in Sec. 1.9.2) and through microprogrammed implementation (discussed in Sec. 1.9.3).

1.9.2 Hardwired Sequential Control

In this section we discuss the techniques and implementations for hardwired sequential control. The hardwired implementation of the control section is a complex system of discrete logic elements and sequential circuits, which are often interrelated and synchronized by an elaborate timing generator, which ensures that the microoperations required for the instruction occur at the right times in the correct sequence.

Next we present the detailed hardware implementation of the control section for the simple system of Fig. 4. We again use the instruction fetch sequence as an example, but augmented here to include the handling of indexing and indirection. We show the respective microoperations involved, and describe the control circuit that will issue the appropriate signals to sequence through this set of

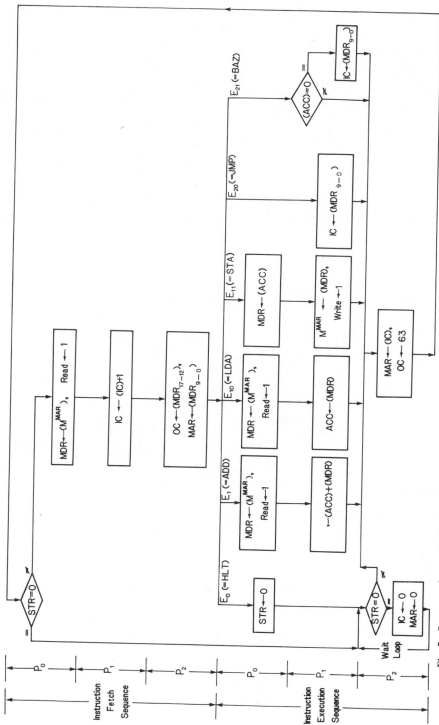

Fig. 5 Sequence chart with the respective microoperations for the instruction subset of Table 1 (no indexing, no indirect addressing).

87

microoperations. The concepts we present through this example can also be applied to implement the instruction execution sequence.

The detailed hardware configuration of the gate signal generator is given in Fig. 6a. It is designed using sequential logic, and it is composed primarily of the next-control-state generator and the control matrix. The next-control-state generator is similar to the circuit of Fig. 2d, using a combination of a 3-bit register C and a decoder. The eight outputs T_i from the decoder give eight single-step control-state signals, T_0 to T_7. Only one of the eight outputs is active at any one time, according to the value set in register C. Its signal will activate the respective microoperation(s) to be executed during that control state. Each control state signal T_i occurs at the beginning of the clock period, lasts for one period, and all microoperations activated will complete before the end of that clock period. The control matrix receives as inputs the control state signals T_0–T_7, the command signals E_0–E_{63} from the op code decoder, the index and indirect tags I_1 and I_0 from register I, and some other status information, such as $(ACC) = 0$. For each state T_i, the control matrix generates: (1) the gate signals required to initiate the corresponding microoperation(s) to be executed during this state, and (2) appropriate signals to the next-control-state generator to set register C to the proper value of the next state.

The instruction fetch sequence we discuss here is more complicated than that described in Sec. 1.9.1, since we are now also making use of the index and indirect addressing tags of the 18-bit instruction of our system. (For indirect addressing, see also the discussions in Secs. 1.1.3 and 1.4.1.) Each instruction

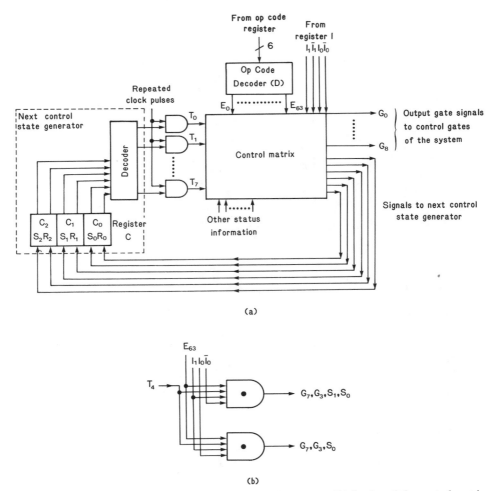

(a)

(b)

Fig. 6 (a) Hardware implementation of the gate signal generator. (b) Section of the control matrix for generating the signals needed during control state T_4 (see also Table 2).

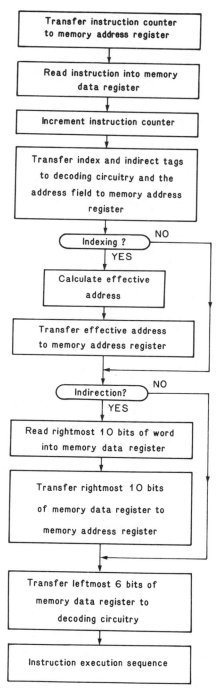

Fig. 7 Flowchart for indexing and/or indirect addressing (single level) during the instruction fetch sequence.

being fetched must now be examined further to see whether it specifies indexing and/or indirect addressing, as shown in the flowchart of Fig. 7.

Therefore, the instruction fetch sequence of Fig. 5 has now been enlarged to that given in Table 2. (For simplicity, we disregard here the examination of STR = 0.) It is noticed that eight control states T_0–T_7 are required for the instruction fetch sequence. The second and third columns in Table 2 show the control signals issued and the corresponding microoperations(s) executed during each control state T_i. The fourth and fifth columns in Table 2 signify the outputs of the control matrix of the gate signal generator. The gate signals G_i listed in the fourth column activate the respective control gates to execute the microoperations. The signals generated by the control matrix to define the next control state of the system are in the fifth column, and the next control states in the sixth column.

The operation of Table 2 is as follows. At the end of each instruction execution sequence, (1) the operation code register is set to six 1's (i.e., OC ← 63), which, when decoded, will issue command signal E_{63} to initiate the instruction fetch sequence; this E_{63} will remain on during the whole fetch sequence, and (2) register C in the next-control-state generator is set to zero (by triggering its three reset inputs) to initiate the first state T_0 of the instruction fetch sequence.

During control state T_0, the control matrix generates the gate signals G_8 and G_0 to execute the two microoperations that read the instruction out of memory into MDR. The control matrix also issues appropriate signals (here, $S_0 = 1$) to advance the next-control-state generator to the next control state T_1.

During control state T_1, the instruction counter is incremented (by opening gate G_1), and register C is set to the value 010 to advance to the next control state T_2.

During control state T_2, the index and indirect addressing tags of the instruction are examined (by opening gates G_2), the address field of the instruction is transferred to MAR (by opening gates G_3) to be ready for the instruction execution sequence in case neither indexing nor indirect addressing is specified, and the control matrix generates the inputs to register C (here, $S_0 = 1$) to advance to the next control state T_3.

If it is concluded during control state T_3 that neither indexing nor indirect addressing was specified by the instruction (i.e., $I_1 = I_0 = 0$), the system advances to the last control state T_7 of the instruction fetch sequence. If the instruction specifies either indexing only or both indexing and indirect addressing (i.e., $I_1 = 1$), the indexing operation starts by transmitting the contents of the index register and the address field of the instruction to the ALU (by opening gates G_5 and G_6) where they are added, and the system advances to the next control state T_4. If it is concluded that only indirect addressing was specified (i.e., $I_1 = 0$, $I_0 = 1$), the system goes to control state T_5 (and then to T_6) to perform the indirection.

If indexing only were specified (i.e., $I_1 = 1$ and $I_0 = 0$), then, during control state T_4, the indexed effective address is transferred from ALU (assuming intermediate latching in the ALU) to the MAR, and the system advances to the last control state T_7 of the instruction fetch sequence. If both indexing and indirect addressing were specified (i.e., $I_1 = I_0 = 1$), then, during control state T_4, the indexed effective address is again transferred to MAR, but now the system advances to the next control state T_5 (and then T_6) to perform indirect addressing. Notice that two control states are allocated here for the more complex operations (such as indexing).

The last control state of the instruction fetch sequence is T_7, during which the op code field of the instruction is transferred to the op code register to be decoded. When decoded, it will issue a command signal E_i ($E_i \neq E_{63}$) which will indicate the beginning of the instruction execution sequence. This command signal E_i will remain on during the whole instruction execution sequence and will be used by the control matrix to issue appropriate gate signals needed to execute the instruction. Also at T_7, the next-control-state generator is signaled to advance to control state T_0, the first control state of the instruction execution sequence.

Figure 6b shows, as an example, the part of the control matrix involved during control phase T_4. As noted from Table 2, depending on its inputs I_1 and I_0, the control matrix will either generate gate signals G_7 and G_3 to initiate microoperation MAR ← (ALU) and signals $S_1 = 1$ and $S_0 = 1$ to set register C to 7, or it will generate gate signals G_7 and G_3 to initiate the same microoperation and the signal $S_0 = 1$ to set register C to 5.

Of course, it must be appreciated that the above has been an oversimplified, nonoptimal, partial design. Nothing has been said about the details of the instruction execution sequence (which becomes very complicated for complex instructions such as multiply and divide), about effective address calculations through multiple index and base registers, about ways of saving return addresses for subroutine jumps, and so on. Also, no attempt was made to minimize the number of control states required or the hardware involved for the instruction fetch sequence given in Table 2.

To summarize: The instruction fetch sequencing of Table 2 (with indexing and indirection) requires eight control states T_0–T_7 used to control the execution of the 14 microoperations shown in Table 3. Each microoperation is initiated by the opening of the respective control gate in the fourth column of the table. The third column shows the test conditions examined for the execution of these microoperations. The fifth column lists the control state(s) during which each microoperation is executed. The gate signal generator of Fig. 4 makes use of sequential logic control, and its register C generates the

Table 2. Gate Signals and Inputs to the Next-Control-State Generator for an Instruction Fetch Sequence (Including Indexing and/or Indirect Addressing)

Control State	Control Signal	Microoperation	Control Gate Signal	Inputs to Register C	Next Control State	Explanation
T_0	E_{63} AND T_0:	$MDR \leftarrow (M^{MAR})$,	G_8	—		Instruction read out into MDR.
		$Read \leftarrow 1$,	G_0	—		
		$C \leftarrow (C)+1$	—	$S_0=1$	T_1	Advance to next state T_1.
T_1	E_{63} AND T_1:	$IC \leftarrow (IC)+1$,	G_1	—		Increment instruction counter and
		$C \leftarrow (C)+1$	—	$S_1=1, R_0=1$	T_2	advance to next state T_2.
T_2	E_{63} AND T_2:	$I \leftarrow (MDR_{11-10})$,	G_2	—		Index and indirect tags transferred to register I.
		$MAR \leftarrow (MDR_{9-0})$,	G_3	—		Address field of instruction (10 bits) transferred to MAR.
		$C \leftarrow (C)+1$	—	$S_0=1$	T_3	Advance to next state T_3.
T_3	E_{63} AND T_3 AND $\bar{I}_1$ AND $\bar{I}_0$:	$C \leftarrow 7$	—	$S_2=1$	T_7	Neither indexing nor indirection. Go to T_7.
	E_{63} AND T_3 AND I_1;	$ALU \leftarrow (IX)$,	G_5	—		Either indexing only, or indexing followed by indirect addressing.
		$ALU \leftarrow (MDR_{9-0})$,	G_6	—		
		$C \leftarrow (C)+1$	—	$S_2=1, R_1=1, R_0=1$	T_4	Advance to next state T_4.
	E_{63} AND T_3 AND $\bar{I}_1$ AND I_0:	$C \leftarrow 5$	—	$S_2=1, R_1=1$	T_5	Only indirection. Go to T_5.
T_4	E_{63} AND T_4 AND I_1 AND $\bar{I}_0$:	$MAR \leftarrow (ALU)$,	G_7, G_3	—		Perform indexing only. Go to T_7.
		$C \leftarrow 7$	—	$S_1=1, S_0=1$	T_7	
	E_{63} AND T_4 AND I_1 AND I_0:	$MAR \leftarrow (ALU)$,	G_7, G_3	—		After indexing go for indirect addressing. Advance to next state T_5.
		$C \leftarrow (C)+1$	—	$S_0=1$	T_5	
T_5	E_{63} AND T_5	$MDR \leftarrow (M_{9-0}^{MAR})$,	G_8^*	—		Start indirect addressing (G_8^* reads the rightmost 10 bits of the word into MDR).
		$Read \leftarrow 1$,	G_0	—		
		$C \leftarrow (C)+1$	—	$S_1=1, R_0=1$	T_6	Advance to next state T_6.
T_6	E_{63} AND T_6:	$MAR \leftarrow (MDR_{9-0})$,	G_3	—		End of indirect addressing. Advance to next state T_7.
		$C \leftarrow (C)+1$	—	$S_0=1$	T_7	
T_7	E_{63} AND T_7:	$OC \leftarrow (MDR_{17-12})$,	G_4	—		Op code field of the instruction (6 bits) is transferred to op code register to be decoded.
		$C \leftarrow 0$	—	$R_2=1, R_1=1, R_0=1$	T_0 of execute sequence	Advance to T_0, the first state of the instruction execution sequence.

Table 3. The 14 Microoperations Needed for the Instruction Fetch Sequence (with Indexing and/or Indirect Addressing)

Microoperation	Number	Test Condition	Signal to Control Gates	Control State
$MDR \leftarrow (M^{MAR})$	0		G_8	T_0
$Read \leftarrow 1$	1		G_0	T_0, T_5
$IC \leftarrow (IC)+1$	2		G_1	T_1
$I \leftarrow (MDR_{11-10})$	3		G_2	T_2
$MAR \leftarrow (MDR_{9-0})$	4		G_3	T_2, T_6
$ALU \leftarrow (IX)$	5	$I_1 = 1$	G_5	T_3
$ALU \leftarrow (MDR_{9-0})$	6	$I_1 = 1$	G_6	T_3
$MAR \leftarrow (ALU)$	7	$I_1 = 1$	G_7, G_3	T_4
$MDR \leftarrow (M_{9-0}^{MAR})$	8		G_8^*	T_5
$OC \leftarrow (MDR_{17-12})$	9		G_4	T_7
$C \leftarrow (C)+1$	10		—	T_0 to T_7
$C \leftarrow 7$	11	$I_0 = 0$	—	T_3, T_4
$C \leftarrow 5$	12	$I_1 = 0, I_0 = 1$	—	T_3
$C \leftarrow 0$	13		—	T_7

control sequence according to the inputs it receives from the control matrix. Each value of register C corresponds to one control state T_i assigned to command one or more microoperations (see Table 2).

1.9.3 Microprogrammed Control

Instead of being embodied with sequential logic, a control unit may also be realized by means of a microprogram stored in a fast memory called a control store. The functional operation of the system and the data flow within a module or between modules are usually considered to be independent of whether control is hardwired or microprogrammed.

A simple microprogrammed control section has the configuration shown in Fig. 8. It typically consists of a control store with its control store address register and microinstruction register (the equivalent of the memory data register), a control store sequencer, and some remaining circuitry such as selection and control logic, registers, and so on. The *control store* (also called microprogram control memory or microprogram memory) is generally several times faster than the system's main memory; it contains "microprograms" composed of "microinstructions" and generates control signals timed to control the rest of the system. Each *microinstruction* defines the state of the control store's output control lines, and the execution of these microinstructions specifies the steps through which the machine will sequence to exercise control over the operation of all modules. The *control store sequencer* (also called the next-control-store-address generation circuit, microprogram control unit, or microprogram sequencer) provides the machine instruction decode logic and specifies the "next microaddress" generation scheme for sequencing the execution of these microinstructions. Program instructions are fetched from the system's main memory under the direction of microinstructions read from the control store. The op code of each instruction is interpreted by the control store sequencer (i.e., mapped into a control store address), and the instruction is then executed as a *microprogram* (i.e., a sequence of microinstructions).* Each microinstruction fetched from the control store and placed into the MIR activates a number of control gates G_i. If each bit in the microinstruction is assigned to one microoperation, then, since more than one bit can be 1, more than one microoperation can occur simultaneously. Therefore, the execution of each microinstruction generates one or more control signals to discrete control gates of the system, each such signal initiating the respective microoperation. Since each microinstruction can generate a multitude of control signals, the microprogram executed generates the sequence of control signals required to execute the machine instruction. The sequencing of the microinstructions in a microprogram is established by the control store sequencer. As we see later, there are various ways of doing this; for example, by incrementing the control store address register, by transferring an address field of the microinstruction to the control store address register, or by using branch condition bits in the microinstruction to examine external conditions before generating the proper next microinstruction address. Detailed descriptions of the control store sequencer and the control store are given below.

---

*"Microprograms" should not be confused with programs for microcomputers.

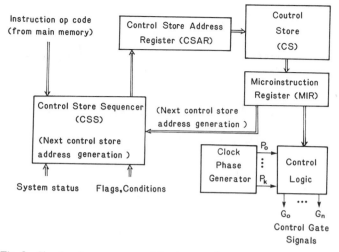

Fig. 8 Simple microprogrammed implementation of the control function.

Timing and Sequencing Considerations

Microinstruction Execution Timing Schemes. We assume that microinstructions are fetched serially from control store; the next microinstruction to be executed does not begin until the execution of the current microinstruction terminates. The control store is a read-only memory. The control store operates on a cycle time called *control store cycle time*, or *control cycle* of the microprogrammed control unit, or *microcycle*. It corresponds to the time required to transfer the next microinstruction address to CSAR plus the time required for the microinstruction to be read into the MIR (i.e., the access time). During each microcycle, a microinstruction is fetched from control store and the microoperations it specifies are then executed. Under this description then, a two-phase clock (or two-phase microcycle) would suffice for the microprogrammed control unit. During the first phase, the address of the next microinstruction is transferred to CSAR, and, at the same time, the microoperations activated by the microinstruction control bits in the MIR register are carried out. During the second phase, the next microinstruction is read out of control store into register MIR. However, some microoperations may be of the conditional type—for example for the BAZ instruction in Fig. 5, we have the conditional microoperation IF $((ACC) = 0)$ THEN $(IC \leftarrow (MDR_{9-0}))$ ELSE $(MAR \leftarrow (IC), OC \leftarrow 63)$. Since this condition may not be known until the CPU microoperations are executed, the next microinstruction address transfer to CSAR and the execution of the CPU microoperations cannot occur at the same clock phase. Therefore, a third phase is used for the microcycle. Now, during the first phase, the address of the next microinstruction is transferred to CSAR; during the second phase, the microinstruction is read into MIR; and during the third phase, the microinstruction is executed (i.e., the respective microoperations are performed). The events involved during each microcycle are shown in Fig. 9, and they are as follows:

P_2 : MIR $\leftarrow (CS^{CSAR})$ Fetch next microinstruction

P_0 :   Execute microinstruction

P_1 : CSAR $\leftarrow$ (CSS)   (Conditions have been examined)
Set next microinstruction
address into CSAR

Depending on the way the control bits of the microinstruction activate microoperations, there can be a monophase or a polyphase implementation. In the *monophase* implementation, the execution of each individual microinstruction requires only one clock phase. In other words, all the microoperations that this microinstruction initiates are completed within this clock phase duration P_0 as shown in Fig. 10a. In the *polyphase* implementation, the execution of each individual microinstruction requires

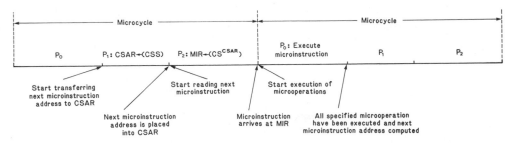

Fig. 9 Events involved during a microcycle.

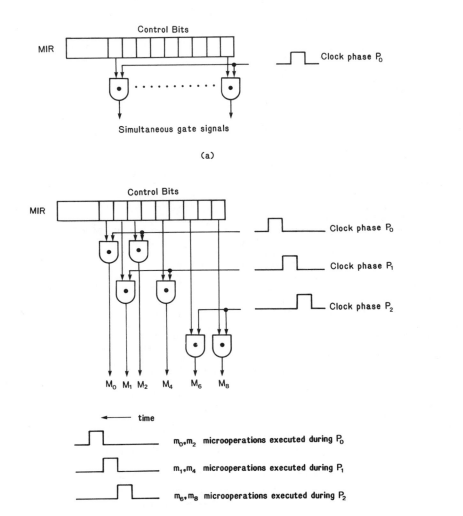

Fig. 10 (a) Monophase implementation: all microoperations initiated and completed within one clock phase P_0; (b) polyphase implementation: during every clock phase a pair of microoperations is executed, but these three pairs are executed during three different clock phases P_0, P_1, P_2.

more than a single clock phase. The control signals of a single microinstruction are issued in sequence over a number of clock phases (Fig. 10b), sequencing accordingly the respective microoperations. Furthermore, polyphase implementations are characterized as synchronous or asynchronous. In the *synchronous polyphase*, the number of clock cycles required for the microinstruction execution remains constant (i.e., same number of clock phases for every microinstruction). In the *asynchronous polyphase*, the number of clock phases required to execute a microinstruction depends on the complexity of its microoperations.

Microinstruction Sequencing. Another major consideration involves the way of sequencing (i.e., fetching and executing) these microinstructions. The two aspects of microinstruction sequencing have to do with timing of microinstruction fetches (serial or parallel, depending on the nonoverlap or complete overlap of the execution of the current microinstruction with the fetching of the next microinstruction) and with methods used to take care of conditional branch situations in the microprogram and to generate the next-control-store-address. So far we have discussed *serial* microinstruction sequencing, where the next microinstruction is not fetched from the control store before the current microinstruction has completed its execution. *Parallel* microinstruction sequencing, on the other hand, allows the next microinstruction to be fetched concurrently with the execution of the current microinstruction (Fig. 11a). This, of course, yields speed advantages, and parallel implementa-

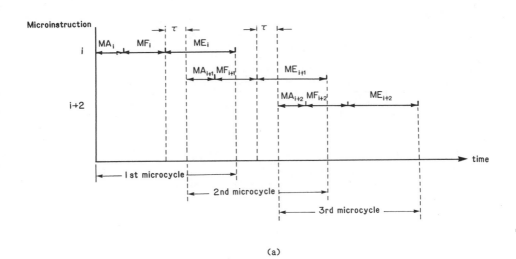

(a)

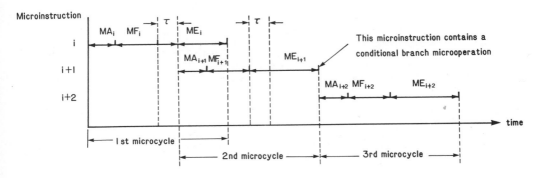

(b)

Fig. 11 (a) Parallel implementation; (b) combined serial–parallel implementation, where microinstruction i + 1 contains a conditional branch microoperation. MA, transfer microinstruction address to CSAR; MF, fetch microinstruction into MIR; ME, execute microinstruction; τ, time to decode microinstruction op code (to assure no conditional branches).

tion runs almost twice as fast as the serial implementation. The parallel case, however, presents some problems, the most important one having to do with properly treating conditional branches. The microcycle for the next microinstruction cannot start before the current microinstruction has been executed (or its op code decoded) and the correct next address has been extracted. Several techniques are available to deal with such problems. One approach to deal with conditional branches is the *serial – parallel* implementation shown in Fig. 11*b*. Here the microcycle for the next microinstruction follows the execution of the current microinstruction if the current microinstruction contains a conditional branch microoperation.

Next-Control-Store Address Generation.   As shown in Fig. 8, the logic to generate the next control address is included in the control store sequencer. This sequencing logic may be as simple as a number of logic gates or as complex as a special LSI device.

In the simplest implementation, the control store sequencer and the control store address register may be replaced by a control store address counter (Fig. 12*a*). The instruction op code from main memory goes directly into the control store address counter. The address of the next microinstruction is generated simply by incrementing the control store address counter by one at the end of each microinstruction execution. The microinstruction itself does not contain a "next address" field. This counter technique permits only sequential control; it provides no means for altering—conditionally or unconditionally—the established flow of control.

Control store sequencers can be used for sequencing with branching capabilities, if they may load a new number that is present on their data input lines. For example, for each microinstruction, the counter shown in Fig. 12*a* may be loaded with the next address from a field in the microinstruction currently executing. The microinstructions now become wider, but they offer additional capability for performing unconditional jumps in the microprogram.

In most situations, however, control store sequencers are also required to facilitate conditional branching capabilities in the microprogram. The control store sequencer will have more decision-making capability if it can examine—before branching—condition or status signals that originate from various parts within the system. There are many possible alternative implementations available. We present here only one of them, shown in Fig. 12*b*. This control store sequencer is composed of a decoder and a decision logic box. The decoder decodes the condition code field bits of the microinstruction. The decision logic combines the decoder outputs and the condition signals originating from various parts of the system and decides whether it should advance to the next microinstruction in the microprogram (i.e., it signals the $+1$ input of the control store address counter to advance by one), or whether it should branch to the address specified by the current microinstruction (by enabling the LD input of the control store address counter to parallel load the next address).

For example, if the branch condition code field of the microinstruction is 3 bits wide, the decoder specifies eight condition codes. Assume that a branch condition code field having the values of 000, 001, 010 indicates normal advancing to the next microinstruction; a branch condition code of 011 indicates branch if $(ACC) = 0$; a code of 100 indicates branch if $(IX) = 0$; a 101 indicates branch if $(IC) = 0$; and codes 110 or 111 indicate branch if ACC overflows.

Microprogrammed Control Unit

The hardwired control implementation for the configuration of Fig. 4 was realized by the sequential logic network of the type shown in Fig. 6, associated with a control register C which generated the control sequence. Each value in register C was assigned to command one or more microoperations to be executed during the same control state. For our simple system of Fig. 4, three control states would have been required, corresponding to the three clock phases used: P_0, P_1, P_2.

In the microprogrammed control implementation in the configuration of Fig. 8, the control sequence is carried out by the microprogram stored in the control store. Under such an implementation, the sequence chart of Fig. 5 will now be converted to that of Fig. 13 (where, for the sake of simplicity, we do not show the read signaling of the control store). One microinstruction is used for the instruction fetch sequence and one microinstruction for each of the execution sequences of the six instructions. We assume a polyphase timing scheme, where each microinstruction requires three clock phases, P_0, P_1, P_2, and no indexing or indirect addressing is considered. It must be noticed that microoperation $OC \leftarrow (MDR_{17-12})$ of Fig. 5 has now been modified to $CSAR \leftarrow (MDR_{17-12})$ and that two more microoperations

$$CSAR \leftarrow (CSS) \qquad \text{Set "next" microinstruction address}$$

$$MIR \leftarrow (CS^{CSAR}) \qquad \text{Fetch next microinstruction}$$

are now required due to the existence of the control store. With the power-on of the system, the STR flag is set to zero and the system is in the wait state, executing the wait loop at the lower left corner of

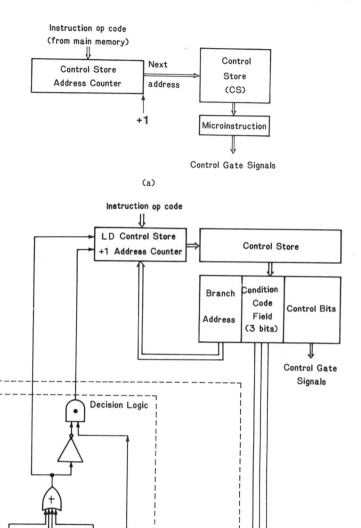

Fig. 12 Alternative implementations of control store sequencers: (*a*) using a control store address counter; (*b*) providing conditional branching capability based on external condition signals.

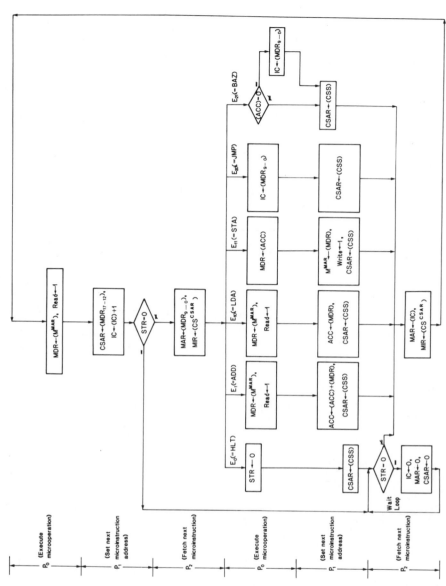

Fig. 13 Sequence chart of Fig. 5 for the microprogrammed implementation of Fig. 8 (no indexing and no indirect addressing examined).

Fig. 13. The microinstruction that corresponds to the instruction fetch sequence is assumed located in control store location zero. When the START button is pressed, the STR flag is set to 1, the first microinstruction is read out from control store location zero, and the computer operation is started.

The sequence chart of Fig. 13 for the microprogrammed control implementation involves a total of 18 microoperations listed in Table 4. If each control bit in the microinstruction is assigned to one microoperation, the microinstruction will require an 18-bit-long control field. An additional nineteenth bit will be required to indicate instruction fetch or execution sequence. Since more than one microoperation occurs simultaneously during each clock phase, more than one bit of each microinstruction will be 1.

For our specific example here, two techniques can be used to reduce the microinstruction width. For the seven microinstructions required, we can do the following:

1. We can group the microoperations that always occur at the same time under one control signal. For example, the two microoperations $MDR \leftarrow (M^{MAR})$ and $Read \leftarrow 1$ that occur at phase P_0 can be grouped under one control signal; similarly, the two microoperations $IC \leftarrow (IC)+1$ and $CSAR \leftarrow (MDR_{17-12})$ that occur at P_1, the two microoperations $M^{MAR} \leftarrow (MDR)$ and $Write \leftarrow 1$ that occur at P_1, and the two microoperations $MAR \leftarrow (IC)$ and $MIR \leftarrow (CS^{CSAR})$ that occur at P_2. It must be noted, however, that such a reduction gives up the use of each individual microoperation if such a use occurs later.

2. In addition, we can group those microoperations that can take place in the different phases of the same clock cycle under one control bit. For example, the following microoperations can be grouped under one control bit: microoperation $CSAR \leftarrow (CSS)$ at clock phase P_1 and microoperations $MAR \leftarrow (IC)$ and $MIR \leftarrow (CS^{CSAR})$ both at clock phase P_2. Again this reduction limits the future use of the individual microoperations.

Therefore, the microoperations can now be assigned to a smaller number of control bits, the bits MIR_{10} to MIR_0 of the microinstruction, as shown in Table 5.

Let us assume that the seven microinstructions are stored in control store locations 0–6. Then with the control bit assignments of Table 5, the microprogram in the control store of our simple system would be that of Fig. 14.

For example, the instruction fetch sequence executed by microinstruction FETCH in control store location 0 would be as follows:

$$FETCH \text{ AND } MIR_9 \text{ AND } P_0 : MDR \leftarrow (M^{MAR}), Read \leftarrow 1$$

$$FETCH \text{ AND } MIR_8 \text{ AND } P_1 : CSAR \leftarrow (MDR_{17-12}), IC \leftarrow (IC)+1$$

$$FETCH \text{ AND } MIR_7 \text{ AND } P_2 : IF (STR \neq 0) \text{ THEN } (MAR \leftarrow (MDR_{9-0}), MIR \leftarrow (CS^{CSAR}))$$

$$ELSE (IC \leftarrow 0, MAR \leftarrow 0, CSAR \leftarrow 0)$$

Similarly, the instruction execution sequence for instruction ADD carried out by the corresponding

Table 4. The 18 Microoperations of the Sequence Chart in Fig. 13

Microoperation	Number	Test Condition	Clock Phase
$MDR \leftarrow (M^{MAR})$	0		P_0
$Read \leftarrow 1$	1		P_0
$IC \leftarrow (IC)+1$	2		P_1
$CSAR \leftarrow (MDR_{17-12})$	3		P_1
$MAR \leftarrow (MDR_{9-0})$	4	$STR \neq 0$	P_2
$MIR \leftarrow (CS^{CSAR})$	5	$STR \neq 0$	P_2
$STR \leftarrow 0$	6		P_0
$IC \leftarrow 0$	7	$STR = 0$	P_2
$MAR \leftarrow 0$	8	$STR = 0$	P_2
$CSAR \leftarrow 0$	9	$STR = 0$	P_2
$ACC \leftarrow (ACC)+(MDR)$	10		P_1
$CSAR \leftarrow (CSS)$	11		P_1
$ACC \leftarrow (MDR)$	12		P_1
$MDR \leftarrow (ACC)$	13		P_0
$M^{MAR} \leftarrow (MDR)$	14		P_1
$Write \leftarrow 1$	15		P_1
$IC \leftarrow (MDR_{9-0})$	16	$ACC = 0$	P_0
$MAR \leftarrow (IC)$	17		P_2

Table 5. Assigning the 18 Microoperations of Table 4 to Control Bits of the Microinstruction

Control Bit	Clock Phase	Microoperation
MIR_{10}		If $MIR_{10} = 1$ then fetch sequence; otherwise execute sequence
MIR_9	P_0	$MDR \leftarrow (M^{MAR})$, Read $\leftarrow 1$
MIR_8	P_1	$CSAR \leftarrow (MDR_{17-12})$, $IC \leftarrow (IC) + 1$
MIR_7	P_2	IF $(STR \neq 0)$ THEN $(MAR \leftarrow (MDR_{9-0})$, $MIR \leftarrow (CS^{CSAR}))$
		ELSE $(IC \leftarrow 0, MAR \leftarrow 0, CSAR \leftarrow 0)$
MIR_6	P_1	$CSAR \leftarrow (CSS)$
	P_2	$MAR \leftarrow (IC)$, $MIR \leftarrow (CS^{CSAR})$
MIR_5	P_0	$STR \leftarrow 0$
MIR_4	P_1	$ACC \leftarrow (ACC) + (MDR)$
MIR_3	P_1	$ACC \leftarrow (MDR)$
MIR_2	P_0	$MDR \leftarrow (ACC)$
	P_1	$M^{MAR} \leftarrow (MDR)$, Write $\leftarrow 1$
MIR_1	P_0	$IC \leftarrow (MDR_{9-0})$
MIR_0	P_0	IF $(ACC = 0)$ THEN $(IC \leftarrow (MDR_{9-0}))$

Control Store Location

	Code	MIR_{10}	MIR_9	MIR_8	MIR_7	MIR_6	MIR_5	MIR_4	MIR_3	MIR_2	MIR_1	MIR_0
0	FETCH	1	1	1	1	0	0	0	0	0	0	0
1	HLT	0	0	0	0	1	1	0	0	0	0	0
2	ADD	0	1	0	0	1	0	1	0	0	0	0
3	LDA	0	1	0	0	1	0	0	1	0	0	0
4	STA	0	0	0	0	1	0	0	0	1	0	0
5	JMP	0	0	0	0	1	0	0	0	0	1	0
6	BAZ	0	0	0	0	1	0	0	0	0	0	1

Fig. 14 Microprogram of our simple system (with the control bit assignments of Table 5, and no indexing and no indirect addressing).

microinstruction in control store location 2 would be as follows:

$$ADD \text{ AND } MIR_9 \text{ AND } P_0 : MDR \leftarrow (M^{MAR}), \text{Read} \leftarrow 1$$

$$ADD \text{ AND } MIR_4 \text{ AND } P_1 : ACC \leftarrow (ACC) + (MDR)$$

$$ADD \text{ AND } MIR_6 \text{ AND } P_1 : CSAR \leftarrow (CSS)$$

$$ADD \text{ AND } MIR_6 \text{ AND } P_2 : MAR \leftarrow (IC), MIR \leftarrow (CS^{CSAR})$$

Microinstruction Format

Designing the microinstruction word is not a simple task. The factors affecting the number of bits and how they are arranged in a microinstruction word are: the number of different microoperations the system can perform, the desired degree of parallelism in executing these microoperations, the way of sequencing the microinstructions of the microprogram, and the flexibility to be retained.

In its simpler form, a microinstruction usually has two functional parts: (1) those bits that correspond to the control signal patterns which control the microoperations to be carried out and (2) those bits that specify the address of the next microinstruction to be executed.

Fixed and Variable Formats. The microinstruction's format may be fixed or variable. In the fixed format, each bit in the microinstruction is always interpreted the same way, whereas in the variable format, the meaning of the bits or fields changes according to certain system states. The variable format leads to shorter microinstructions. but it also requires more complex decoding logic.

Horizontal and Vertical Microinstructions. *Horizontal* microinstructions represent several microoperations that in general are executed concurrently. In the extreme, each horizontal microinstruction controls all the hardware resources of the system. Each control bit corresponds to a distinct microoperation: a 1 appearing in a bit position is used solely to activate a separate control line or point in the system, indicating that the corresponding microoperation is to be executed. This formatting was used earlier. Because these microinstructions control multiple resources simultaneously, they usually have more control bits than the other implementations we will see. Lengths of 48 bits or more are common. Such an organization has the advantage of utilizing hardware more efficiently, and it requires smaller numbers of microinstructions per microprogram. However, it is rarely used in organizing control stores, since for any reasonable size machine, the microinstruction lengths become very large. This scheme is of historical interest, since it corresponds to Wilkes' original model,* where each microoperation was the opening of a hardware gate.

The *vertical* microinstruction format resembles the classical instruction formats comprised of one microoperation code (mop code), one or more operands, and some other fields (such as a condition code field for conditional branches). Each vertical microinstruction generally represents a single microoperation (e.g., a transfer or a data transformation operation), while operands may specify the data sink and source. For example, for the simple microprogrammed implementation discussed in the preceding section, the vertical microinstructions would have a one-to-one correspondence with the microoperations shown in Table 4. Since vertical microinstructions resemble instructions in format and operation, it is easier to write vertical microprograms than their horizontal counterparts, and this ability enhances a system's microprogrammability. This scheme also requires relatively short word lengths, in the range 16 to 64 bits. On the other hand, vertical microinstructions require more complex decoding logic and do not take full advantage of parallelism in the system's microarchitecture. Microprogram execution is slower, since only one microoperation is done at a time. Vertical control store organizations are also relatively inflexible, because the addition of a new microinstruction type may require a change in the decoder logic. Two examples of computers that use vertical microinstructions are the Burroughs B1700[†] and the Microdata 1600.[‡] Since a number of simple microoperations can now be combined into one more complex microoperation, the dividing line between horizontal and vertical microinstructions is difficult to define exactly.

Reducing the Number of Control Bits. One way of reducing microinstruction length, and consequently control store width, is to group these microoperations that always occur at the same time under one control signal. Thus only one control bit is used to control several microoperations. Such a grouping was used earlier.

Another way is to group together in one encoded control field the mutually exclusive microoperations, those microoperations of which only one occurs at one time. No information is lost with such an encoding scheme. If each microoperation corresponds to the activation of a single control line and if, for example, 2^n mutually exclusive lines exist, an n-bit field in the microinstruction is required. These n bits, through a decoder, regenerate these 2^n control signals when the microinstruction is executed. Two such groups of microoperations that are not mutually exclusive must be controlled by two separate encoded fields in the microinstruction. There may be several ways of performing this microinstruction encoding, and the decision to group microoperations together in one or more separate encoded fields depends on their potential for being executed in parallel. The use of separate control fields for each independent functional unit, such as ALU, shifters, and so on, allows simultaneous use of system resources, as long as they do not conflict. Generally, for the encoded formats, a number of output decoders are required for the various fields of the microinstruction. However, since the widths of these fields are usually small, these decoders are less complex than those required for the highly encoded vertical microinstructions. Two examples of computers that use encoded microinstructions are the Varian V75[§] and the Nanodata QM-1.[¶]

In choosing the microinstruction format, the designer has the task of balancing control store size, complicated clocking schemes and speeds, branching flexibility, and the complexity of output circuitry

---

*M. V. WILKES and J. B. STRINGER, "Micro-programming and the Design of the Control Circuits in an Electronic Digital Computer," *Proc. Camb. Philos. Soc.*, **49**, 230–238 (Apr. 1953).

[†] W. T. WILNER, "Design of the Burroughs B1700," *Proc. 1972 AFIPS Fall Joint Comput. Conf.*, Part I, AFIPS Press, Montvale, N.J., pp. 489–497.

[‡] *Microprogramming Handbook*, 2nd ed., Microdata Corp., Santa Ana, Calif., 1970.

[§] *Varian Microprogramming Guide*, Varian Data Machines, Irvine, Calif., July 1975.

[¶] *QM-1 Hardware Level User's Manual*, 2nd ed., Nanodata Corp., Williamsville, N.Y., 1974.

required to handle microinstruction control bits or to decode encoded microinstruction fields. In general, microinstruction characteristics are strongly influenced by the data flow design of the processing section and by the machine language instruction set the system supports.

*Organization of the Control Store**,† [B2]

A central issue in the design of a microprogrammed control section is the organization of its control store, which contains the microinstructions that constitute the microprograms to be executed. Advances in memory technology have resulted in the availability of large, fast, inexpensive control stores and in the appearance of several types of control store structures.

Functional Characteristics.   Most microprogrammed computers have several memory facilities available: main memory, control store, and local memory, the latter consisting primarily of functional registers. The control store usually has one level, although there are machines such as the QM-1 that also contain a second level, the nanostore (see Sec. 1.16). Usually, control store is distinct from main memory, although there are exceptions to this, in which microprograms are executed from a protected section of main memory. Between the microinstructions in the control store and the control gates that they activate, there exists at least a buffer register (the microinstruction register, MIR) and there may also exist some decoding logic.

One characteristic of the control store is whether it is writeable. ROM-based nonalterable control stores are usually provided (written) by the manufacturer, are usually tailor-made, and depend on the system's architecture. On the other hand, writeable control store (WCS), realized using fast random-access memories (RAMs), has the advantage that it provides user microprogrammability, allowing a user to create the system's architecture. Advances in technology will continue to produce larger and faster RAMs, so their utilization for the implementation of control stores will allow greater freedom and flexibility in system designs. Users will then have the ability of defining the instruction set best suited to the specific application. They can also implement certain critical routines (e.g., specialized I/O and interrupt-handling procedures, floating-point routines, system tables, etc.) as microprograms, thus improving system performance for a given application. Dynamically microprogrammable systems can also be implemented with WCS, whose microprograms can be modified electronically during operation. Between these two extremes, various technologies also permit intermediate characteristics employing, for example, a facility to switch from one ROM to another.

Speed.   An important characteristic of the control store is its speed, described by its *access time*, which corresponds to the time required to read a microinstruction from the control store into the MIR. This speed is very important and is generally the limiting factor in the overall speed of the system. On the other hand, the control store should be fast enough so that the degradation it may cause (relative to hardwired control) to the system's speed will be compensated for by the advantages of microprogramming. If user microprogrammability is to be allowed, to make attractive the implementation of functions in firmware rather than in software, the ratio of main-memory cycle time to control store cycle time is usually of the order of 10 : 1.

Size.   The size of the control store may be a limiting factor to what applications can be micropro-grammed on the system. The number of microinstruction words in the control store depends primarily on the instruction repertoire. On contemporary user-microprogrammable machines, the lengths tend to vary from 256 to 4K words of 16 to 64 bits.

Control Store Organizations.   In the simplest and most common structure, there is one microin-struction in each control store location. A different structure may have two microinstructions per location, thus reducing the number of control store references. A third alternative divides the control store into blocks (sometimes called pages), and the addressing scheme used addresses either within the same block as the current microinstruction or to another block. This shortens the addresses when addressing is done within the same block. Another scheme is the split control store, which comprises two separate storage units that have different word lengths. The shorter-word-length unit contains microinstructions that move data or initiate the execution of a microinstruction that resides in the other storage unit. The longer microinstructions that reside in the other unit can exercise more direct control over machine resources. A final scheme involves structuring the control store into multilevel

*A. B. SALISBURY, "A Study of General-Purpose Microprogrammable Computer Architectures," *Tech. Report No. 59*, Digital Systems Laboratory, Stanford University, July 1973 (available through NTIS, U.S. Dept. of Commerce, No. AD-768884).
†S. DASGUPTA, "The Organization of Microprogram Stores," *Comput. Surv.*, **11**(1), 39–65 (Mar. 1979).

organizations;[*,†,‡] in the two-level case, the second level contains longer microinstructions called *nanoinstructions* and the unit that contains them is called the *nanostore*. Section 1.16.6 discusses multilevel microprogrammed control.

Hardwired versus Microprogrammed Control

The speed of operation of a hardwired control is limited by the speed of logic circuitry. The speed of operation of a microprogrammed implementation is limited by the speed of the control store. Since control stores operate more slowly than the logic circuitry, microprogram control does not give the fastest speed of operation. It is also generally agreed that for a well-defined application, the hardwired implementation approach results in a somewhat smaller control section than that of the microprogrammed approach. However, changing the visible machine and its instruction set requires rewiring, new layouts, and so on, whereas in the microprogrammed version, this involves only changes or additions to the microprogram. The microprogrammed approach also provides flexibility and coherence to the control design, and a level of diagnosability not attainable with a nonmicroprogrammed approach. Although the hardwired control can be faster, as the complexity of the system increases, it becomes more expensive, since its cost is somehow proportional to the complexity of the control. The cost of microprogrammed implementation is essentially determined by the cost of the control store, and ROMs, PLAs, and other LSI devices used today as control stores continuously show a dramatic reduction in prices. At some level, however, there is always the need for some hardwired control (e.g., in decoding the outputs of the control store, for sequencing the microprogrammed control, etc). Even with microprocessors and microcomputers, some of them have microprogrammed control and some do not.

Execution of a COMPARE Instruction in a Microprogrammed System

In order to make clearer the design requirements of a microprogrammed control unit, we now present an example of defining the microoperations and control signals involved in the execution of the following simple COMPARE instruction [§,¶] [B4]:

$$\text{IF (ACC)} = \text{(B)} \quad \text{THEN} \quad \text{IC} \leftarrow \text{(IC)} + 2$$

$$\text{ELSE} \quad \text{IC} \leftarrow \text{(IC)} + 1$$

The details of the system to be used are shown in Fig. 15. The system uses 2's-complement notation, and the parallel adder can add two operands, with input carry G_{20} being 0 or 1. The ALU section has zero detect logic that issues a 1 when the output of the adder is all zeros; otherwise, it issues a 0. A temporary register B is also used.

The necessary microoperations are grouped and coded in assigned fields of the microinstruction with one code of the field usually designating one microoperation. The leftmost 6 bits of the microinstruction are the field NMA which signifies the next microinstruction address. The next 2-bit field LIN is chosen to designate the left inputs to the adder, as shown in Table 6. This table also shows the corresponding control gate signals.

The next 2-bit field RIN is used to designate the right inputs to the adder, as shown in Table 7. (B') is the 1's complement of (B).

The next 1-bit field ADC is used to designate the microoperations of the parallel adder as follows. When ADC = 0 (i.e., $G_{20} = 0$) the addition is performed with no carry-in; if ADC = 1 (i.e., $G_{20} = 1$) the addition is performed with carry-in. (See Sec. 1.5.4 regarding 2's-complement addition.)

The 2-bit field DBIN designates connections to the data bus, as shown in Table 8.

[*]A. GRASSELLI, "The Design of Program-Modifiable Microprogrammed Control Units," *IRE Trans. Electron. Comput.*, **EC-11**(6), 334–339 (June 1962).

[†]M. TSUCHIYA and C. V. RAMAMOORTHY, "Design of a Multi-level Microprogrammable Computer and a High Level Microprogramming Language," *Tech. Report No. 135*, Electronics Research Center, University of Texas at Austin, Aug. 15, 1972.

[‡]*QM-1 Hardware Level User's Manual*, 2nd ed., Nanodata Corp., Williamsville, N.Y., 1974.

[§]N. A. ALEXANDRIDIS, "Bit-Sliced Microprocessor Architecture," *IEEE Comput.*, June 1978, pp. 56–80.

[¶]G. C. VANDING and D. E. WALDECKER, "The Microprogram Control Technique for Digital Logic Design," *Comput. Des.*, Aug. 1969, pp. 44–51.

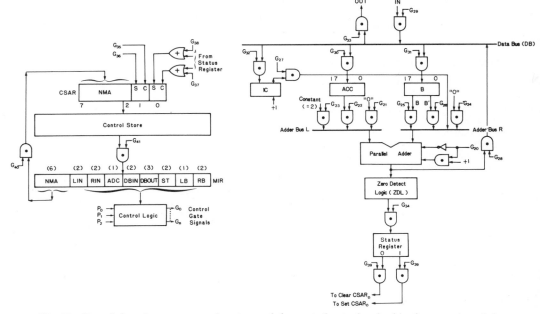

Fig. 15 Part of the microprogrammed system and the control gates involved in the execution of the COMPARE instruction.

Table 6. Field LIN

Code	Microoperation	Control Gate Signal
00	Adder ← "0"	G_{21}
01	Adder ← (ACC)	G_{22}
10	Adder ← "2"	G_{23}
11	Not used	—

Table 7. Field RIN

Code	Microoperation	Control Gate Signal
00	Adder ← "0"	G_{24}
01	Adder ← (B)	G_{25}
10	Adder ← (B')	G_{26}
11	Adder ← (IC)	G_{27}

Table 8. Field DBIN

Code	Microoperations	Control Gate Signal
00	Not used	—
01	DB ← Adder	G_{28}
10	DB ← IN	G_{29}
11	Not used	—

The next 3-bit field DBOUT designates the destination of the information on the data bus, as shown in Table 9.

Storing of the result of the zero detect logic ZDL in the 1-bit register STATUS is designated by the 1-bit field ST, as shown in Table 10.

The control store in Fig. 15 has an 8-bit control store address register (CSAR). Its six high-order bits, $CSAR_{7-2}$, are provided by the next microinstruction address field NMA of the microinstruction in MIR. The two low-order bits $CSAR_1$ and $CSAR_0$ are determined by fields LB and RB, as shown in Tables 11 and 12.

The comparison in this example is performed by subtracting the number in register B from the accumulator; then the examination of the value of the zero detection logic will determine whether IC will be incremented by one or by two.

As shown in Fig. 16, this COMPARE instruction requires three microinstructions. The first microinstruction, in location YYYYYYYY, performs the comparison noted above; the subtraction is carried out by adding the 2's-complement of the number in register B to the number in the accumulator. Either the microinstruction in location ZZZZZZ00 [i.e., $IC \leftarrow (IC)+1$] or the microinstruction in location ZZZZZZ01 [i.e., $IC \leftarrow (IC)+2$] will be executed next, depending on the result of the first microinstruction. Finally, no matter which one of the two is executed, the sequence eventually reaches the microinstruction in location ZZZZZZ11.

As before, each microinstruction in the control store is processed under the control of a three-phase clock, P_0, P_1, P_2. Assume that during the previous microcycle a control signal G is provided to start the

Table 9. Field DBOUT

Code	Microoperation	Control Gate Signal
000	Not used	—
001	$ACC \leftarrow (DB)$	G_{30}
010	$B \leftarrow (DB)$	G_{31}
011	$IC \leftarrow (DB)$	G_{32}
100	$OUT \leftarrow (DB)$	G_{33}
101 }		—
110 } Not used		—
111 }		—

Table 10. Field ST

Code	Microoperation	Control Gate Signal
0	No operation	—
1	IF $(ZDL = 0)$ THEN $(STATUS \leftarrow 0)$ ELSE $(STATUS \leftarrow 1)$	G_{34}

Table 11. Field LB

Code	Microoperation	Control Gate Signal
0	$CSAR_1 \leftarrow 0$	G_{35}
1	$CSAR_1 \leftarrow 1$	G_{36}

Table 12. Field RB

Code	Microoperation	Control Gate Signal
00	$CSAR_0 \leftarrow 0$	G_{37}
01	$CSAR_0 \leftarrow 1$	G_{38}
10	$CSAR_0 \leftarrow (STATUS)$	G_{39}
11	Not used	—

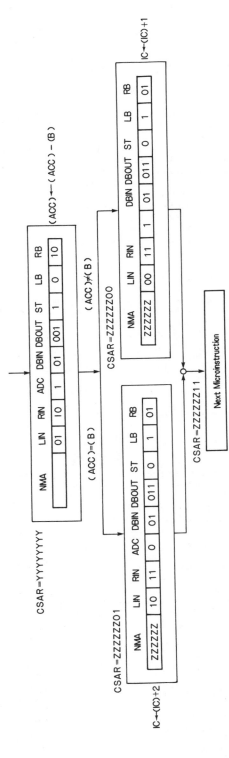

Fig. 16 Microinstruction address assignments and microinstruction structure for execution of the COMPARE instruction.

sequence with a proper address in CSAR as follows:

$$P_0 : G \leftarrow 0$$
$$\overline{G} \text{ AND } P_1 : CSAR \leftarrow YYYYYYYY, G \leftarrow 1$$
$$G \text{ AND } P_2 : MIR \leftarrow (CS^{CSAR})$$

Then, for the first microinstruction in location YYYYYYYY, which compares the contents of register B and the accumulator, the sequence of microoperations executed and the control gate signals emitted are shown in Table 13. The sequence of microoperations executed and the control gate signals emitted for the microinstruction in location ZZZZZZ00 [i.e., $IC \leftarrow (IC) + 1$] are shown in Table 14, and the microoperations executed and the control gate signals emitted for the microinstruction in location ZZZZZZ01 [i.e., $IC \leftarrow (IC) + 2$] are shown in Table 15.

Table 13. Execution Sequence for Microinstruction $ACC \leftarrow (ACC)-(B)$

Timing	Microoperation	Control Gate Signal
$(LIN = 1)$ AND P_0	$Adder \leftarrow (ACC)$	G_{22}
$(RIN = 2)$ AND P_0	$Adder \leftarrow (B')$	G_{26}
$(ADC = 1)$ AND P_0	$G_{20} \leftarrow 1$	G_{20}
$(DBIN = 1)$ AND P_0	$DB \leftarrow Adder$	G_{28}
$(DBOUT = 1)$ AND P_0	$ACC \leftarrow (DB)$	G_{30}
$(ST = 1)$ AND P_0	IF $(ZDL = 0)$ THEN $(STATUS \leftarrow 0)$ ELSE $(STATUS \leftarrow 1)$	G_{34}
$(LB = 0)$ AND P_1	$CSAR_1 \leftarrow 0$	G_{35}
$(RB = 2)$ AND P_1	$CSAR_0 \leftarrow (STATUS)$	G_{39}
G AND P_1	$CSAR_{7-2} \leftarrow (NMA)$	G_{40}
G AND P_2	$MIR \leftarrow (CS^{CSAR})$	G_{41}

Table 14. Execution Sequence for Microinstruction $IC \leftarrow (IC) + 1$

Timing	Microoperation	Control Gate Signal
$(LIN = 0)$ AND P_0	$Adder \leftarrow 0$	G_{21}
$(RIN = 3)$ AND P_0	$Adder \leftarrow (IC)$	G_{27}
$(ADC = 1)$ AND P_0	$G_{20} \leftarrow 1$	G_{20}
$(DBIN = 1)$ AND P_0	$DB \leftarrow Adder$	G_{28}
$(DBOUT = 3)$ AND P_0	$IC \leftarrow (DB)$	G_{32}
$(ST = 0)$ AND P_0	—	—
$(LB = 1)$ AND P_1	$CSAR_1 \leftarrow 1$	G_{36}
$(RB = 1)$ AND P_1	$CSAR_0 \leftarrow 1$	G_{38}
G AND P_1	$CSAR_{7-2} \leftarrow (NMA)$	G_{40}
G AND P_2	$MIR \leftarrow (CS^{CSAR})$	G_{41}

Table 15. Execution Sequence for Microinstruction $IC \leftarrow (IC) + 2$

Timing	Microoperation	Control Gate Signal
$(LIN = 2)$ AND P_0	$Adder \leftarrow 2$	G_{23}
$(RIN = 3)$ AND P_0	$Adder \leftarrow (IC)$	G_{27}
$(ADC = 0)$ AND P_0	$G_{20} \leftarrow 0$	G'_{20}
$(DBIN = 1)$ AND P_0	$DB \leftarrow Adder$	G_{28}
$(DBOUT = 3)$ AND P_0	$IC \leftarrow (DB)$	G_{32}
$(ST = 0)$ AND P_0	—	—
$(LB = 1)$ AND P_1	$CSAR_1 \leftarrow 1$	G_{36}
$(RB = 1)$ AND P_1	$CSAR_0 \leftarrow 1$	G_{38}
G AND P_1	$CSAR_{7-2} \leftarrow (NMA)$	G_{40}
G AND P_2	$MIR \leftarrow (CS^{CSAR})$	G_{41}

1.9.4 LSI Control Elements

So far, we have seen some of the hardware elements that support microprogrammed control: control stores (usually ROMs, but sometimes RAMs) to hold the microinstructions that sequence control; circuits (counters, decision logic gates, etc.) for testing conditions and status signals, extracting microinstruction fields, and generating the next microinstruction address; and various other elements, such as registers and decoders.

New developments in semiconductor technology are having a significant effect on the design and structure of microprogrammed control. In this section we discuss two of these new LSI developments in more detail—the programmable logic array (PLA) and the control store sequencer—and their use in the control function.

Programmable Logic Arrays

Principles of Operation.   The principles of PLA operation are covered in detail in Vol. 1, Sec. 7.4.2.

Simply stated, the PLA may be viewed as an LSI implementation of the classic logical sum-of-products structure. Figure 17a gives a block diagram of the PLA, and Fig. 17b presents more details of its internal structure. The first-level AND array performs the logical AND for selected combinations of the input signals. These AND gates produce logical product terms (or P-terms), $P_1, P_2, \ldots, P_m$. The second level is considered to be composed of OR gates that, by logically summing some or all of the P-terms produced by the first level, produce the final outputs (or sum terms), $F_1, F_2, \ldots, F_k$. One may go directly from the logic equations (preferably in their minimal form) to the programming of the AND and OR arrays of the PLA. Since the PLA can be programmed to handle only the useful combinations of the input variables, it is advantageous to use PLAs when there is a large number of inputs and only a small subset of the possible combinations of these inputs is required (used).

In sequential logic implementations, the PLA can be used for replacing the combinational part of the circuit. A new type of PLA, the "sequential PLA," includes latching flip-flops at its output (i.e., storage elements in the feedback path to store the state of the circuit) and can lead directly to an easier realization of clocked sequential logic or control-logic circuits.

PLAs Used in the Control Function.   In the hardwired sequential implementation of the control function discussed in Sec. 1.9.2, the PLA can be used to realize the gate signal generator (see Fig. 6). Especially the control matrix, which is of AND–OR nature, can be easily replaced by a PLA.

In the microprogrammed implementation, the PLA can be effectively used at various places in the control section:

1. The PLA can be used as an *instruction op code decoder*, to translate the instruction op code in the instruction register to the control store starting address. In simple machines, this address mapping can be done by a decoder or a ROM. But in more complex cases where the instruction is composed of a number of fields and has a variable format, PLAs can be used to interpret a large number of bits at once, ignoring or interpreting some fields based on the contents of other fields. For example, the control store address can be the output of two PLAs, one PLA used as an instruction interpreter, the second PLA used as an addressing mode interpreter.

2. Another application of the PLA is for *control store patching*. Quite often, after the final design of the control section, there may be cases where the microprogram for the system needs revisions, or faults may appear in some locations of a large, otherwise functional control store. Rather than replacing the control store with a new one, one may use a PLA. This PLA will decode the address locations the engineer wants to change or will detect attempts to access a faulty location. In such cases, it can disable the control memory and either generate new data or enable a small "backup" ROM to which it redirects addresses translated from those originally intended for the control store. Figure 18 shows such an implementation where, for example, a PLA with i inputs, j P-terms, and k outputs can detect j addresses in a 2^i control store address space, generate an enable/disable signal, and generate j addresses to a small 2^{k-1}-word backup ROM.

3.   The PLA can also be used, although not generally, *to store the microprogram instructions*.

4.   Finally, another example of applying PLAs in the microprogrammed control section is for *generating the branch addresses* for the modified counter implementation scheme. In such an implementation, the branch addresses may be encoded prior to storing the microprogram in the appropriate next address bits of the microinstructions and decoded with a PLA. If for example, there are 32 branch addresses in a control store of 1024 locations, the PLA implementation would require only 5 bits to encode the addresses; 10 bits would have been required, otherwise. This PLA would require 5 inputs, 32 P terms, and 10 outputs.

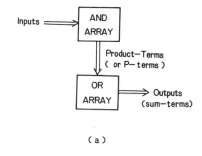

(a)

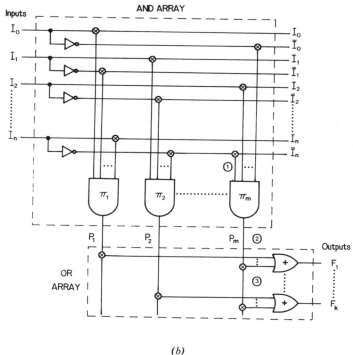

(b)

Fig. 17 PLA: (a) block diagram; (b) details of its internal structure. ① up to 2^n inputs/gate; ② P_i's are product terms; ③, up to m inputs/gate; ⊗ programmable connection.

LSI Sequencers

The main purpose of any control store sequencer is to present an address to the control store so that a microinstruction may be fetched and executed. The "next address" logic part of the sequencer determines the source of the address to be loaded into the control store address register/counter.

Today's commercial LSI control store sequencers have much more than the capabilities mentioned so far. They receive many more control signals and system status bits, and they include everything required for address-incrementing functions and complex multiway conditional microbranching. They have on-chip loop counters for repeated microprogram loops and may also include on-chip hardware stacks and pointers, a useful feature for saving the return-to addresses of nested microsubroutines. A typical block diagram of a commercial sequencer is shown in Fig. 19, where the "next address" logic is now quite complex (see also Fig. 1.18.4). The choice of the address source is guided by the next address information bits the sequencer receives; these bits can generally specify one of the following: increment, conditional skip next microinstruction, conditional branch to a microsubroutine, and others.

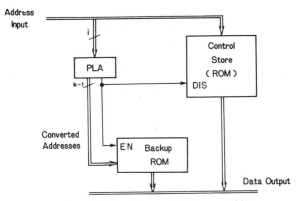

Fig. 18 PLA used for control store patching.

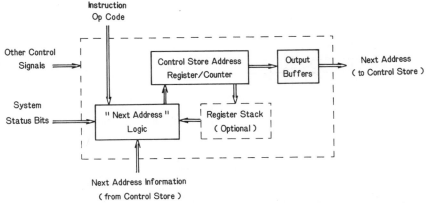

Fig. 19 General block diagram of an LSI control store sequencer.

Available LSI control store sequencers may be divided into two general categories: those with a fixed number of memory locations within their addressing capability, and those which are cascadable bit-slice devices.* (see Sec. 1.3). While bit-slice sequencers are easily expandable, the fixed-address sequencers require additional circuits and paging techniques to extend their memory-access range.

Another difference among the available sequencers is that some of them provide on-chip address-output latches, whereas others do not have such latches. The latter category allows more flexibility but requires the designer to add his own latches.

Cycle times for some of these sequencers today range from around 40 to 100 ns.

1.9.5 Lookahead and Pipelining

The concepts of operation overlap, instruction lookahead and processor pipelining are significant architectural features used to increase the average speed of the instruction set and the overall throughput rate of the system. Such concepts are found not only in larger mainframe CPUs but also in minicomputer CPUs and even in 16-bit microprocessors.

Instruction Lookahead

Through instruction *prefetching*, or *lookahead*, an effective overlap is achieved among instruction fetching, decoding, and execution (data handling and transformation) times. The delay involved

---

*J. GOLD, "Bipolar Controllers—They're Fast, Cheap and Easy to Use," *Electron. Des.*, **22**, 106–110 (Oct. 25, 1976).

between the initiation of a memory read and the arrival of the word at its destination (memory access time delay, memory busy time [servicing a higher-priority request], and delays in the word transfer path) is usually relatively long. Lookahead mechanisms that fetch a number of instructions and operands from main memory in advance of execution by the ALU section of the system can effectively reduce the average delay. This technique "looks" several instructions ahead of the one currently being executed. Buffers or scratch registers are used within the CPU as speed-matching devices (1) in the control section of the CPU to hold the instructions fetched in advance or to hold several instructions to improve performance for small loops, and (2) interposed between the ALU and memory to hold prefetched operands and to avoid storing and refetching data used by successive instructions. Through this lookahead technique, if various references are initiated early enough, the operands are usually available in the ALU buffer by the time the ALU is ready for them.

If we assume that processing for each instruction is composed of three equal subtasks:

$$F = \text{instruction fetch and decoding}$$

$$A = \text{address calculation and operand fetches}$$

$$E = \text{instruction execution}$$

the instruction lookahead is very similar to Fig. 11a, where F of one instruction, A of the prior instruction, and E of the one before that occur simultaneously, yielding a threefold improvement over serial processing.

This lookahead concept attempts to have instructions and operands arrive from memory at a rate approximately equal to the rate at which the CPU can utilize them. However, some interlock problems may arise [B3]. First, if an instruction depends on previous ALU results, it should not be started before these results are available. Second, if a conditional-branch-type instruction is encountered, and the previous instruction that sets those conditions has not been completed, the control section will not know whether to prefetch the instruction following the conditional branch or the instruction at the target of the branch. Third, problems also arise when fetching operands that have not reached storage, or when attempting to modify an instruction by a preceding store operation (i.e., treating instructions as data as in Sec. 1.4.3.).

Several techniques have been used to take care of such deadlocks [B10]:

1. There are three basic ways for handling the problem of conditional branching on ALU results:
    (a) The control section can stop the flow of instructions until the ALU has completed the preceding operation and the result is known, and then fetch the next instruction. Whether the branch is taken or not, this always causes a delay.
    (b) Based on past experience with the program, make a "guess" which way the branch is going to go before it is taken, follow this path, and continue to prepare instructions; if the guess proves later to be wrong, the prepared instructions must be discarded and the correct path taken instead.
    (c) The control section can be simultaneously fetching the instructions following the conditional branch as well as instructions at the target of the branch; when the ALU generates the condition(s), the control section can decide which of the two groups of prepared instructions to use.

2. Problems similar to that of treating instructions as data can be handled by the control section if, as soon as the instruction is loaded, the control section tests the instruction to see whether it is a *store-type* instruction, in which case the fetch sequence must wait until the effective address has been prepared to see whether it is going to modify a successive instruction.

3. The problems of fetching operands that have not reached storage yet can be handled, if the result of the ALU can return first to the operand's buffer, before being sent to storage.

Prefetching and lookahead have an impact on the control function, since it must implement this technique and take care of all deadlocks that may arise during system operation. Incorporating additional scratch registers and buffers in the system increases the number of gates requiring control. In the microprogrammed control version, this increases the number of control bits in the microinstruction, and the width and cost of the control store. It also requires proper microprograms to achieve this instruction overlap, incorporating sophisticated algorithms for determining the next step (especially in the case of conditional branches).

Pipelining

The lookahead operation we just discussed can be used for matching the speeds of the ALU and main memory by greatly reducing the time spent by the ALU waiting for an operand.

The effect of the speed of the ALU itself on overall system performance is also very important. To increase the ALU speed, an "assembly-line technique" called *pipelining* has been effectively used (see

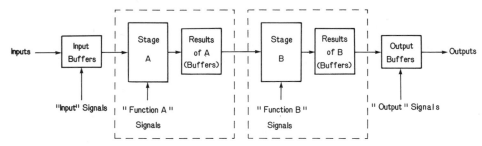

Fig. 20   Simple two-stage pipeline data flow.

	P_i	P_{i+1}	P_{i+2}	P_{i+3}	P_{i+4}	P_{i+5}	P_{i+6}	P_{i+7}	P_{i+8}
datum$_j$	Input	Function A	Function B	Output					
datum$_{j+1}$		Input	Function A	Function B	Output				
datum$_{j+2}$			Input	Function A	Function B	Output			
datum$_{j+3}$				Input	Function A	Function B	Output		
datum$_{j+4}$					Input	Function A	Function B	Output	
datum$_{j+5}$						Input	Function A	Function B	Output

Fig. 21   Timing diagram of the operations, performed by a two-stage pipeline during every clock phase P_i.

also Sec. 1.16.5). The basic philosophy is to divide a computational task into several sequential subtasks, each being handled by a separate stage or station of the ALU. All stages operate simultaneously with independent sets of data; temporary storage buffers exist between stages; individual computation advances from one stage to the next; and results are closer to completion as the end of the pipeline is approached. This pipelined ALU accepts new inputs before the previously accepted inputs have been completely processed and put out from the pipeline. When one subtask result leaves a stage, the logic associated with that stage becomes free and can accept new data (results) from the previous stage. The rate at which inputs are accepted to the ALU is chosen in relation to the time required to get through one stage, with the main goal of keeping all portions of the pipeline fully utilized. Once the pipeline is full, the output rate will match the input rate.

The pipelined ALU can be effectively used for executing complex repetitive-type instructions (such as multiply/divide) and floating-point instructions.* As far as a single individual instruction goes, the time required for its execution via a pipelined implementation may be the same or slightly longer than with a parallel ALU used iteratively. However, the fact that several steps of the instruction execution are carried out concurrently in the pipeline increases the number of instructions that may be completed per second, thus increasing significantly the overall throughput capability of the system.

Again, several requirements exist to properly control the operation of such a pipelined ALU. The control function for pipelines is considerably more complex than for more conventional structures. The control section must determine what data should be input to the pipeline, the specific operation of each stage (i.e., what inputs it should receive from the previous stage, what functions it should perform on them, what results it should pass to the next stage), and what outputs should be sequentially generated at the end of the pipeline.

For example, consider the simple two-stage pipeline of Fig. 20. Figure 21 shows the timing diagram of the operations performed by this two-stage pipeline, for every clock phase P_i. Inputs are gated to the pipeline by the "input" signals during clock phase P_i. During clock phase P_{i+1}, the "Function A" control signals are issued to select the inputs to be gated to stage A and to specify the function to be performed by state A;† at the same time, since the input buffers of the pipeline become available, the "input" signals may be issued again to fill the buffers with the next data to be fed into the pipeline. During clock phase P_{i+2}, three things happen simultaneously:

1. "Function B" control signals are issued to select which results of stage A will be gated into stage B and to specify the function to be performed by stage B.

*S. F. ANDERSON ET AL., "The IBM System/360 Model 91: Floating-Point Execution Unit," *IBM J.*, Jan. 1967, pp. 34–53.

†We assume that during one clock phase, the operation of a stage is carried out and the results are properly placed in its output buffers.

2. "Function A" control signals are issued to select the next inputs to be gated to stage A and to specify the operation to be performed by stage A.

3. "Input" signals are again issued to feed the pipeline with new data.

From that point on, during every clock phase, four types of control signals (input, Function A, Function B, and output) are simultaneously applied to the pipeline: two types of signals at the pipeline's input and output points, and one type of signal for each stage. In general, for a k-stage pipeline, $k+2$ types of control signals would be simultaneously issued during each clock phase. It is observed that inputs are gated into the pipeline during each clock phase, and similarly, during each clock phase, outputs are being produced by the pipeline. All these operations, of course, are transparent to the user and the programmer of the system.

1.9.6 Emulation

Often, a computer user may purchase a new computer and wish to convert old programs to run on the new machine. Or a user may wish to convert application programs written for one machine to run on another machine that exists in the local environment to permit the user to take advantage of all the additional features of his or her machine.

There are several approaches for performing this conversion. At the one end of the spectrum lies the reprogramming effort, where the user reprograms all problems in the new machine language. The next point in the spectrum is the recompiling process, where if the programs are all written in a high-level language, guaranteeing absolute machine independence, the task of conversion is reduced to recompiling these programs for the new system. The next approach involves substituting for each machine instruction in the source program for the old system, one or more instructions of the new machine that execute the same operation, then assembling the resulting code and executing it. This is an inefficient approach of converting one program to another and presents serious problems, since the architectures may be very different. Another approach used to perform this conversion is (software) *simulation*, through which the functioning of the one system is represented by another. Simulators usually run their programs significantly more slowly than on the original machine, and their degree of efficiency depends on the detail to which the original machine is simulated. On the other hand, simulation does not require any hardware, and it is conceptually simple to design.

The final point on the program conversion scale is *emulation*. Microprogramming techniques may be used here to accomplish this step of executing programs in the old machine language whose instructions are properly interpreted in the new system. This new physical machine, as defined by its hardware, its microinstructions, and their actions, is called the *host* machine. The old machine emulated by sets of microprogrammed routines is called the *image*, *virtual*, or *target* machine. Thus emulation is a combined hardware–software approach to simulation. It can be done by either adding hardware facilities in the host system for handling special features of the target machine or by providing these facilities through microprogramming techniques. An emulator is basically an extension of the host machine's architecture, hardware, and software, to include the microarchitecture of the target machine. It is relatively easy for a simple host system to emulate more than one target machine. Since it executes the instruction set of the target machine at the control level rather than in software, the emulator is much faster than a simulator. In general, emulators offer a one-to-one throughput compared to the target machine, while simulators are normally 5 to 10 times slower. Usually, a host machine used for emulation will have (at least) two types of microprograms: one for its own conventional machine language and one or more (called the emulators) for the target machines' languages. Means should be provided for the host to execute one such microprogram type at a time. The emulator must:

1. Map the components of the target machine (i.e., main memory, registers, I/O subsystem, and other resources that are addressable by the source program) into those of the host machine.

2. Interpret the machine language instructions of the target machine.

3. Identify the respective microroutines in the host machine that will execute the target machine instructions.

4. Provide some means for efficient linkage and interfacing between host machine mode of operation and emulation mode of operation.

All activities of the emulator are governed by an *emulator control program* discussed below.[*,†]

[*]J. C. DEMCO and T. A. MARSLAND, "An Insight into PDP-11 Emulator," *SIGMICRO Newsl.*, 7(3), 20–26 (Sept. 1976).
[†]T. D. DENNIS and O. G. JOHNSON, "Design Problems in Emulating the MIX Computer on the Microdata 1600," *SIGMICRO Newsl.*, 7(3), 27–32 (Sept. 1976).

Mapping the Components of the Target Machine to Those of the Host Machine

In general, the smaller the mismatch between the host microarchitecture and the target machine architecture, the easier the construction of an efficient emulator. When the differences are significant, they may impose real restrictions and implementation shortcomings, resulting in certain features of the target machine not being supported by the host.

When mapping the target main memory to the host memory, the following considerations must be taken into account: main-memory capacities for both the target and the host machines, addressing modes and address boundary alignments, lengths and formats of memory words, how many host bits to be used for emulating a target word or byte, and other factors. This mapping function must ensure that a minimum addressable memory cell of the target machine will be contained in the smallest possible host machine memory cell, and that address translations from target address to host address and vice versa should not be time consuming. If, after such mapping, there is still surplus host memory available, this can be effectively used to temporarily store I/O-type information (for the case where the target machine performs I/O in concurrent mode) or to keep some of the target machine's registers containing privileged data that the target machine user cannot use.

If the host machine has at least as many registers, counters, and so on, as the target machine, of equal or larger length, they can be used effectively to emulate those of the target machine. If the number of the host machine registers is less than those of the target machine to be emulated, a secondary register file might need to be created in the host's main memory. The most important and frequently used registers of the target machine (e.g., the accumulator, the instruction counter, the instruction register, etc.) can be assigned to the main registers of the host, while the rest of the target registers (e.g., index registers, overflow and indicators, etc.) can be assigned to the secondary file in host's memory. A page map mechanism (see Sec. 1.7.1) of the emulator control program can designate which target registers are in the host's register file and which are in its secondary file at any time. This, of course, introduces considerable overhead and requires some sort of scheduling to determine which register should be paged out to make room for the incoming register. It must also be noted here that mapping the condition codes generated by the host's hardware to convert them to target machine condition codes is not a trivial effort.

Mapping of I/O devices is simpler than main-memory mapping. A static one-to-one mapping of target I/O device registers into host I/O subsystem registers or host main-memory locations may be done. We shall see below how these are handled by an I/O instruction or an I/O interrupt.

Interpreting and Executing Target Instructions

Having defined the mapping of the target machine microarchitecture into the host machine, the designer must then develop the firmware for interpreting target instructions. A number of micro-routines must be written in the microprogrammable host, such as (1) a start microroutine, for initializing the emulator prior to the processing of any target instructions; (2) a fetch microroutine, for fetching the next target instruction pointed to by the instruction counter, and one or more micro-routines to perform target instruction format parsing, effective operand address computation, and op code decoding (these microroutines are repeated for every target instruction in the program to be converted, before branching off to the corresponding instruction module for executing it); and (3) the various instruction modules containing the microroutine(s) that execute the individual target instructions.

An emulator control program must also be designed to sequence the activities described above, and contain proper microroutines for handling exceptions and error situations (error handler), interrupts (interrupt handler), and I/O microroutines (I/O handler) to be used by the I/O instructions as well as the interrupt handler, as described below. The emulator control program may also perform data conversion and transmission, as well as the linkage between the CPU and I/O.

When the target instruction to be executed is an I/O instruction, control is passed to the emulator control program. The control program searches a table of address pairs to match the I/O device register address; the second address of the pair is the entry point into the I/O device handler. Also passed to the I/O device handler microroutine is a read/write flag. The device handler responds to the request by accessing the I/O devices directly. When the I/O is done in a concurrent mode, part of the host's surplus main memory may be used to store the I/O information, to be used by the I/O handler for carrying out this data transfer activity.

In an analogous fashion, the appearance of an interrupt transfers control to an interrupt handler in the emulator control program. This handler may use the I/O microroutines. It identifies the interrupt type and source, saves all pertinent information into a priority-ordered queue, and sets a flag. The interrupt-handler microroutine is executed after the execution of one instruction and prior to fetching the next instruction. When the emulator is restarted, the instruction fetch microroutine interrogates this flag, and control is conditionally passed to the next stage of processing.

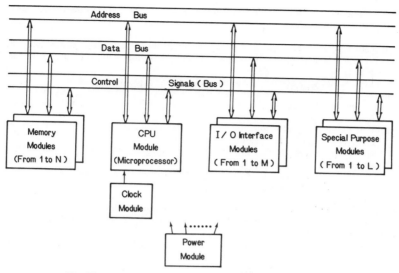

Fig. 22 Modular microprocessor-based digital system.

1.9.7 Microprocessor System Signals

So far in Sec. 1.9, we have discussed primarily intramodule control and timing signals. We have chosen as an example the most complicated module of a digital system—the CPU processor module. Therefore, the control and timing signals we mentioned corresponded mainly to those required by the ALU to carry out the instruction execution microsequences. We also mentioned signals to memory to fetch instructions and data, to move addresses, to increment counters, and so on. System-wide control and timing signals are also required to synchronize the operations of the separate and different modules and to facilitate their intercommunication activities over the buses.

As a typical modular system of today, we consider a microprocessor system whose general block diagram is given in Fig. 22. Note that we are now talking about systems controlled by a microprocessor, not about a microprogrammable control unit. Before describing the microprocessor system signals, we explain the operation of a microprocessor and the cycles it follows for fetching and executing an instruction. We then discuss the timing and synchronization requirements of a microprocessor-based system. This will help us understand better the role and function of some of the microprocessor system signals. The rest of the system signals are covered later.

Microprocessor Systems

Operation. The microprocessor of a system,* like the CPU of a general-purpose computer, communicates with the memory modules and the I/O modules by sending addresses to them and sending them data or receiving data from them (see Secs. 1.12.1 and 1.13). Thus two of the interconnecting buses shown in Fig. 22 are devoted to addresses and data. In the most straightforward design, the widths of these buses are selected to correspond to the widths of the system addresses and data. In this case, for an 8-bit data word microprocessor capable of directly addressing a 64-byte memory space, an 8-bit data bus and a 16-bit address bus would be required. Alternative design techniques may also be used, incorporating bus multiplexing (see Sec. 1.13.6). The following key questions arise with regard to the use of the buses: Which module should use a bus at any time? Should all modules attempt to use a bus, should it be allocated to the module that first requested its use? Should there be a more orderly sequence for allocating a bus to the proper module at a given time? Who will determine to which module to allocate the bus at any given time?

Since the microprocessor is the major component of such a digital system, it has been assigned this task of determining the bus allocation. Knowing the system state at all times, it provides all other modules of the system with properly timed control signals to inform them of the state of the

---

*Some microprocessors are made up of a number of chips. We discuss here the single-chip microprocessor, for reasons of simplicity.

microprocessor and what information is on the bus at all times. These signals then synchronize the rest of the system to the microprocessor.

Microprocessor Cycles. The system-wide signals issued by the microprocessor provide the following functions: synchronization, microprocessor system scheduling (interrupt and I/O), and other facilities, such as clock and reset.

We use a representative 8-bit microprocessor (Intel 8080) to discuss the microprocessor system signals shown in Fig. 23. This microprocessor chip is driven by an external two-phase clock on a separate chip (input pins ϕ_1 and ϕ_2), and all processing activities are referred to the period of this clock.

The execution time of an instruction (fetching and execution) may consist of one to five *machine cycles*, denoted $M_1, M_2, \ldots, M_5$. The beginning of every machine cycle is specified by the SYNC signal issued by the microprocessor, as explained in the next section. The 8080, like many other microprocessors, can issue only one memory address per machine cycle, each address accessing a byte. Since the instruction length may be 1, 2, or 3 bytes long, fetching an instruction may require from one (M_1) to three machine cycles (M_1, M_2, M_3). The additional number of machine cycles required to execute the instruction varies from instruction to instruction. Some instructions do not reference memory or a peripheral device (i.e., no address is issued during their execution); therefore, no additional machine cycles are required. Others may require the extra M_4 and even M_5 machine cycles, since their execution may send data to memory or to a peripheral device or receive data from them.

Each machine cycle consists of three to five clock periods, called *states*, and denoted $T_1, T_2, \ldots, T_5$. States are the smallest unit of processing activity. The clock phase ϕ_1 subdivides each machine cycle into states. A state lasts one clock period of ϕ_1 (i.e., the time between two consecutive rising edges of ϕ_1). With each clock pulse ϕ_1, a transition occurs from one state to the next.

System Timing and Synchronization

To understand better the timing and synchronization requirements of the microprocessor system, we examine in detail the fetching and execution of the single-byte instruction

$$\text{``ADD M''} : \text{ACC} \leftarrow (\text{ACC}) + (M^{H,L})$$

This instruction specifies addition between the contents of the 8-bit accumulator with the contents of a memory location (one byte) whose 16-bit address is specified by the two bytes previously loaded in registers H and L in the microprocessor. The 8-bit sum is stored in the accumulator.

Instruction Fetching. The instruction fetching is always started at state T_1 of machine cycle M_1. In this simplest case of a single-byte instruction, memory cycle M_1 consists of three states, T_1, T_2, T_3. The timing relationships for the machine cycle M_1 during which the instruction fetching is performed is given in Fig. 24.

State T_1. The microprocessor communicates with the other system modules through a 16-bit address and an 8-bit data bus. In state T_1, the rising edge of clock phase ϕ_2 initiates the SYNC signal.

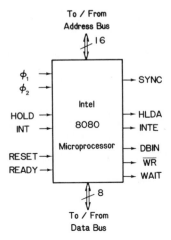

Fig. 23   Intel 8080 microprocessor system signals.

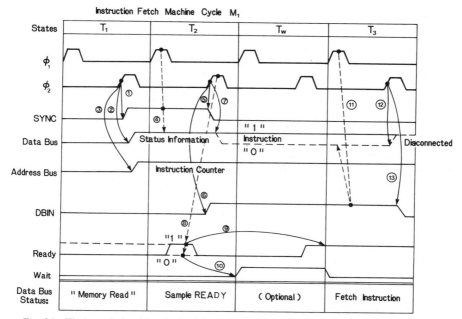

Fig. 24 Timing relationships for fetching a single-byte instruction at machine cycle M_1.

This dependency is shown in Fig. 24 with the number ① arrow from the rising edge of the ϕ_2 pulse to the SYNC signal. This SYNC signal issued by the microprocessor is used simply to inform all system modules of the first state T_1 of each machine cycle M_i. During this state T_1, the microprocessor uses the 8-bit data bus to transmit an 8-bit status word, through which it notifies all other modules of the system of the type of machine cycle (e.g., instruction fetch, memory read, memory write). The transmission of this status word on the data bus during T_1 is also initiated by the rising edge of ϕ_2 (arrow number ② in Fig. 24). Furthermore, the rising edge of ϕ_2 during T_1 causes the microprocessor to place the contents of the instruction counter on the address bus (arrow ③). The address bus lines hold their values stable until the first clock ϕ_2 after state T_3. This gives ample time for the microprocessor to read the instruction byte returning from memory.

State T_2. External logic reads and examines the status word when both ϕ_1 and SYNC are "1" (dotted time marker ④). Assume that during state T_2 the external signal READY input to the microprocessor is "1." (We shall see below what happens when READY = 0.) This means that memory had enough time to access the instruction byte, and at the same time send the signal READY = 1 to the microprocessor. The rising edge of ϕ_2 ends the SYNC signal (arrow ⑤), initiates the signal DBIN (arrow ⑥), and removes the status word from the data bus (arrow ⑦). The microprocessor issues this DBIN signal to notify the rest of the system that the data bus is in an input state and can therefore be used by memory to place information on it. Immediately thereafter, memory places the accessed instruction byte on the data bus.

State T_3. Since READY was 1, the system enters state T_3 (arrows ⑧ and ⑨). The specific operations performed during state T_3 depend on the type of machine cycle M_i. Since here it is the M_1 cycle of the instruction fetch, the microprocessor recognizes that the word found on its data bus is an instruction, and reads it during state T_3 (dotted time marker ⑪). The rising edge of ϕ_2 ends the period that the data bus carries information, and the data bus is considered now as being "disconnected" from the microprocessor (arrow ⑫). Finally, the rising edge of ϕ_2 also ends the signal DBIN (arrow ⑬).

Since the microprocessor is usually faster than most of the external memories, it can remain idle until the memory has had time to supply the instruction. If, after the microprocessor has sent an address to memory, the microprocessor receives a "1" on its READY input, it will proceed to state T_3 and read the information found on the data bus. If, however, the memory did not have enough time to access the instruction, it would not send READY = 1 to the microprocessor. In that case, instead of advancing to the next state, T_3, the microprocessor enters a "wait" state, T_w, after finishing its T_2 state. State T_w, which lies between states T_2 and T_3, starts—like all other states—with the rising edge of ϕ_1. At the same time, the microprocessor notifies the rest of the system that it is entering state T_w by issuing a "1" on its output pin WAIT (arrow ⑩). This wait period can last for an indefinite number of clock periods, as long as READY = 0. Then the microprocessor enters state T_3 with the next rising edge of clock ϕ_1. With the READY signal, the microprocessor can be delayed so that it will always stay in synchronism with other, slower modules of the system. This input pin READY can also be used to let the microprocessor execute the instructions step by step, something that is very useful for debugging purposes.

Instruction Execution. Thus the one-byte instruction "ADD M" has been fetched into the microprocessor during the first three states T_1, T_2, T_3 of the first machine cycle M_1. Since it specifies adding the contents of the ACC and the contents of a memory location, a new reference to memory is required to fetch the operand. This will be done during the first three states, T_1, T_2, T_3, of the second machine cycle M_2. The microprocessor issues the data address (the contents of its two registers H and L) to memory during T_1, the memory accesses the operand and places it on the data bus during the state T_2, and the microprocessor reads this operand byte and places it in its temporary register during T_3. The timing diagram during these three states for fetching the data is similar to that of Fig. 24. Finally, during state T_4 of machine cycle M_2, the contents of the ACC and of this temporary register are added in the ALU and the result is placed in the ACC. Thus the fetching and execution of this single-byte instruction "ADD M" requires two machine cycles and a total of seven states.

Other System Signals

We now give some of the other system signals listed in Fig. 23 that have not been discussed so far.

RESET. This input signal to the microprocessor is used to initialize the system after a power-down condition or to reinitialize the microprocessor. Usually, after the RESET signal has been applied, the instruction counter is loaded with the contents of a standard starting address.

INT. The microprocessor recognizes an interrupt request—placed on this line by an external I/O interface device—at the end of the current instruction or while halted. If the interrupt is accepted, the microprocessor sends during state T_1 the INTA (Interrupt Acknowledge) signal, a specific bit of the status word placed on the data bus lines, and enters the "interrupt cycle."

INTE. Most microprocessors have two instructions, the EI (Enable Interrupts) and DI (Disable Interrupts), that place an internal Interrupt Enable flip-flop in the state 1 or 0, respectively, and specify whether the microprocessor is allowed to accept interrupts or not. If this Interrupt Enable flip-flop is reset, the microprocessor will not honor the interrupt request. The INTE (Interrupt Enable) signal indicates the contents of this internal flip-flop. It is automatically reset (disabling further interrupts) at time T_1 of the instruction fetch cycle (M_1) when an interrupt is accepted and is also reset by the RESET signal. The INTE signal is used by the specific I/O device to decide whether it can interrupt the microprocessor (by sending a signal to its INT input) or not.

HOLD and HLDA. The HOLD input signal requests the microprocessor to enter the HOLD state. The microprocessor acknowledges being in the HOLD state by placing a signal on its HLDA (Hold Acknowledge) pin, indicating to the other modules of the system that its data bus and address bus are in their high-impedance state (i.e., "disconnected" from the microprocessor). Therefore, an external module can gain control of these buses as soon as the microprocessor has completed its use of these buses for the current machine cycle. This HOLD signal is recognized either when the microprocessor is in the HALT state or when it is in the T_2 or T_w state and the READY signal is active. The HLDA signal begins: (1) at T_3 for read memory or input operation or (2) at the clock period following T_3 for write memory or output operation. These HOLD and HLDA signals are usually used by certain I/O modules that want to perform high-speed data exchange with the system.

$\overline{WR}$. This signal is issued by the microprocessor to indicate memory write or I/O control operation. (Signals are often denoted by $\overline{X}$ rather than X.) Data to be written in memory or to be output remain stable on the data bus as long as $\overline{WR} = 0$.

  To summarize, then, in order to orchestrate and synchronize the operation of all the system modules, timing, control, and status signals are required. The timing signals input to the microprocessor (in our case clock phases ϕ_1 and ϕ_2) are generated by an external clock generator. The timing signal used by all other modules of the system is the SYNC signal issued by the microprocessor during state T_1 of each machine cycle M_i It was also mentioned that, during state T_1 of each machine cycle M_i, the information the microprocessor places on the data bus is an 8-bit status word. This status word defines the type of the machine cycle (e.g., instruction fetch, memory read, memory write, input operation, output operation, etc.). Since this status word is available on the data bus for only one ϕ_2 clock period, external latching logic must be used to store it, in order to use it appropriately during subsequent states of the machine cycle.

REFERENCES

B1. S. S. HUSSON, *Microprogramming: Principles and Practices*, Prentice-Hall, Englewood Cliffs, N.J., 1970.

B2. A. K. AGRAWALA and T. G. RAUSCHER, *Foundations of Microprogramming: Architecture, Software, and Applications*, Academic Press, New York, 1976.

B3. A. S. TANENBAUM *Structured Computer Organization*, Prentice-Hall, Englewood Cliffs, N.J., 1976.

B4. Y. CHU, *Computer Organization and Microprogramming*, Prentice-Hall, Englewood Cliffs, N.J., 1972.

B5. M. V. WILKES, "The Growth of Interest in Microprogramming: A Literature Survey," *Comput. Surv.*, **1** (3), 139–145 (Sept. 1969).

B6. M. J. FLYNN, "Microprogramming—Another Look at Internal Computer Control," *Proc. IEEE*, **63** (11), 1554–1567 (Nov. 1975).

B7. P. M. DAVIES, "Readings in Microprogramming," *IBM Syst. J.*, **11** (1), 16–40 (1972).

B8. D. R. McGLYNN, *Microprocessors*, Wiley, New York, 1976.

B9. E. E. KLINGMAN, *Microprocessor Systems Design*, Prentice-Hall, Englewood Cliffs, N.J., 1977.

B10. W. BUCHHOLZ (ed.), *Planning a Computer System*, McGraw-Hill, New York, 1962.

1.10 INPUT/OUTPUT AND DEVICES: GENERAL CONSIDERATIONS

David F. Bantz

1.10.1 Definitions

Input/output (I/O) refers to the exercise of control by a processor over its attached peripheral devices and the exchange of data between the processor and those devices. Figure 1 is a block diagram of the general form of an I/O system. Devices are attached to *device controllers*, which contain device-specific logic. Device controllers are sometimes referred to as "control units." Two forms of device controller attachment are shown in the figure: to a memory bus and to an I/O bus. The processor may allow device controller attachment directly to the memory bus or may contain a subsystem to control I/O, and an I/O interface which exchanges signals with an I/O bus.

A *unit data transfer* is that amount of data that can be transferred with one exchange of signals, either on the memory or I/O buses. The width of the buses determines how many bits of data are transferred in a unit data transfer. Typically, from 1 to 16 bits are transferred. A *block* of data consists of an integral number of units of data, requiring multiple unit data transfers.

1.10.2 Device Controller Attachment

In some I/O system designs, device controllers are attached directly to the memory bus.* Device controller A in Fig. 1 is attached to the memory bus. In these systems the processor may move data between device controller registers and processor registers using the same mechanism that the processor uses to exchange data with its own memory. Alternatively, the device controllers may access processor memory directly to retrieve or deposit data. If the device controller can move a block of data between the device and memory, it is capable of the direct memory access function, described in more detail in Sec. 1.12.1. The programming of DMA is described in Sec. 1.10.5.

The processor may communicate control information with the device controller by moving data between processor and device controller registers. Certain portions of the memory address space may be recognized as designating the control registers in the device controller. This technique is known as *memory mapping* the device controller registers (see also Sec. 1.8.1). The program in the processor first sets these registers by executing "store" instructions to the designated addresses and then initiates the data transfer with an access to a designated address. Status (see Sec. 1.10.4) can be retrieved from the

PDP/11 Interface Handbook, Digital Equipment Corp., Maynard, Mass.

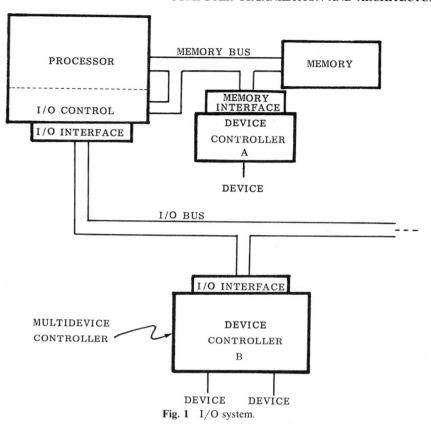

Fig. 1 I/O system.

device controller by executing a *load* instruction whose operand address is recognized by the device controller status register.

A limitation of memory-bus attachment of device controllers for large computer systems is the difficulty of satisfying simultaneously the physical and electrical requirements of an I/O interface and a memory interface. Memory-to-processor data rates are often an order of magnitude greater than I/O transfer rates, and physical distances are small. In large systems, I/O systems must allow tens or hundreds of meters between the device controllers and the processor, and widely varying device controller response times must be accommodated.

An alternative to using the memory bus for I/O is to devote some processor hardware to I/O control, which allows transfer of data between a separate I/O interface and either memory or processor registers. This allows separate optimization of the memory and I/O interfaces. The I/O interface is attached to a bus, called the *I/O bus*, which communicates signals between the processor I/O interface and the I/O interfaces of all the device controllers. Device controller B in Fig. 1 is attached to an I/O bus.

Processor hardware capable of communicating blocks of data between memory and an I/O interface is called an *I/O channel*. When I/O channels are used, the processor must have a set of special instructions to control the channel. These instructions interrogate the state of the channel, transmit parameters of an I/O transfer, and start and stop transfers. I/O channels are described further in Sec. 1.10.5. A thorough description of a rather complex I/O interface is available for the IBM System/360-370 computers.*

---

*"IBM System/360 and System/370 I/O Interface Channel to Control Unit: Original Equipment Manufacturers' Information," IBM form number GA22-6974, IBM Corp. Data Processing Division, White Plains, N.Y.

1.10.3 I/O Path Alternatives

The I/O path connects the processor I/O interface with those of the device controllers. The most common form of the I/O path is a bus, controlled by the processor I/O interface. For an example of a protocol constraining the exchange of signals on a bus, see Sec. 1.13.4. In large computer systems with many device controllers, physical cabling restrictions and cost may become limiting factors in the I/O bus design. Signal-to-noise ratios and propagation delays limit the length of a bus and the number of device controllers that can share the bus. One solution is a loop topology (see Sec. 1.16.3). A commonly adopted solution is to provide multiple I/O buses, each controlled by a separate I/O channel.

The connection of a device controller to a particular I/O bus may be static through cabling or may be dynamic. In the dynamic case, device controllers may be switched from one I/O bus to another, manually or under processor control. Often, device controllers are designed to attach to two I/O buses so that the device controller and its attached devices can be shared by two processors. Dynamic connections also allow a system to continue functioning with all its device controllers in the event of the failure of one I/O bus.

1.10.4 I/O Protocols

Communication between a processor and a device controller follows a structured form: a protocol. I/O protocols prescribe what are the permitted actions and necessary reactions while a processor and a device controller are exchanging control information and data. Protocols are effectively described by multiple interacting state diagrams and timing charts. An example of a protocol described as a timing chart is given in Fig. 2 and is described later in this section.

Sessions

A *session* is a period of time during which there is an interchange of control information and data between the processor and a device controller. Sessions do not necessarily consist of continuous signaling but are characterized by retained information (*status*) in both the processor and the device controller. For example, if a magnetic tape drive has been commanded to rewind by a processor and its device controller has accepted the command, the processor expects to be notified, sooner or later, of the completion of the rewind operation. Furthermore, once rewound, the magnetic tape drive is expected to stay at the load point; both the processor and the device controller retain this information.

Device controllers may be *off-line*, meaning that no data communication between the device controller and the processor is possible, or *on-line* and thus capable of exchanging data with the processor. Off-line device controllers are logically removed from the system, and if their design permits may be powered down or physically disconnected for maintenance or replacement. On-line device controllers are expected to be capable of entering a session with a processor.

Device Controller Selection

A processor enters a session with a device controller through the process of *selection*. In general, selection consists of the transmission of a device controller address by the processor together with a command. The device controller must respond with either a positive or diagnostic negative response to the command; if the response is positive, a session is established.

Status

Status is information retained in the device controller that characterizes the state of the device controller and its attached devices. Especially for device controllers that serve several devices (e.g., device controller B in Fig. 1), there is an important distinction between the *device* status (or the status of some portion of the device controller that is dedicated to a device) and the *controller* status. Separate status indications should be available for the controller and for each device connected to the controller. Codes for device and device controller status information are, in general, specific to a particular unit, but several general classes of status exist. Examples of controller status are "off-line," "temporarily unavailable," "busy," and "command reject." Examples of device status are "busy," "not operational," and "data error." Status must be sufficiently detailed that the processor operating system may take recovery action, but not so detailed that many processor instructions are needed to analyze the status. Different device controllers should encode status in the same way, whenever possible.

Commands

"Commands" are control information sent by the processor to a device controller to invoke a device controller function. Commands are, in general, specific to a device or device controller. However, there are several general classes of such commands. For each device and device controller, some command from the processor should cause the device controller to return status. Similarly, some command should force a device and device controller to be reset to some known state. One command should cause the device controller to disconnect from the I/O interface, to facilitate maintenance and isolate faults. Another command should cause the device controller to return an identification of the type of device controller and number and type of devices to facilitate automatic system configuration.

Commands requesting data transmission must specify the direction of that transmission but may *imply* which or how much data is to be transferred. For example, a command to read a card from an 80-column card reader implies that all 80 columns of the next card are to be read.

Data Transmission

One major variation in data transmission concerns whether the I/O bus is shared or used exclusively by a device controller during data transmission and—if used exclusively—for how much data. IBM terminology distinguishes among selector, multiplexer, and block multiplexer channels. A *selector* channel dedicates the I/O bus to a device controller for the duration of a session. A *multiplexer* channel allows sharing of the I/O bus by several sessions, switching the path for each unit data transmission. A *block multiplexer* channel allows several simultaneous sessions but dedicates the path during the transmission of a block of data.

When the I/O bus is shared, the channel must be able to resolve contention for the path, and device controllers must be able to notify the processor of a data transmission request. The channel must be able to identify which of the device controllers wishes to exchange data. One or more units of data may follow. The last unit of data may be flagged, or a count may be prefixed to the data, or the count may be implicit.

It may be necessary during a data transmission sequence for either the processor or the device controller to terminate the sequence prematurely. This is referred to as an *abort*. When the device controller aborts, the signaling of the abort can take the form of an unsolicited error status transmission by the device controller. When the processor aborts, this may take the form of a missing or negative acknowledgment to a full block of data, or a special signal to be interpreted by the device controller.

Normal termination of a data transmission sequence may be inferred or may be explicitly signaled by the processor or the device controller. One method for a device controller to terminate or acknowledge an inferred termination is to present normal status to the processor. This termination may leave either the device controller or device in a state incapable of accepting new commands, since the completion of data transmission does not necessarily imply readiness to accept a new command. For this reason, some systems signal "device controller available" status and "device available" status some time after the completion of data transmission.

Processor Interruptions

The processor program involved in I/O may continually interrogate (*poll*) a device controller for a change in status, or may prepare an interrupt-handling program to be invoked automatically when a device controller changes status. Polling is described further in Sec. 1.10.5 and interrupt system implementation in Sec. 1.2. Interrupt system programming considerations are discussed in Sec. 1.10.5. Interrupts may occur to signal a change in status of a device controller from off-line to on-line. During a session, interrupts can be used to signal the rejection of a command by a device controller, the completion of the transfer of a block of data, or an error during the I/O operation.

Example of a Session

Figure 2 describes a complete session (in simplified form) between the processor and a device controller in the form of a *timing chart*. Timing charts show the timing relationships between signals. In Fig. 2, three sets of signal lines are shown: control signals outbound from the processor, control signals inbound to the processor from the device controller, and the signals COMMAND/ DATA/STATUS and ADDRESS, which may originate at either the processor or the device controller. The direction of signal propagation on this latter set of lines is determined by the outbound and inbound control lines. For example, if the outbound COMMAND VALID line is 1, the processor has placed a command on the COMMAND/DATA/STATUS lines and the signals are outbound from the processor.

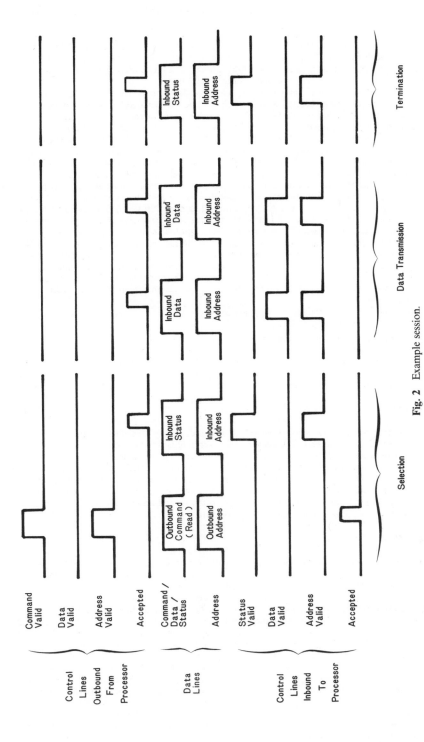

Fig. 2 Example session.

Both the outbound and inbound lines have an ACCEPTED line, driven by either the processor or the device controller, respectively. If the direction of signals on COMMAND/DATA/STATUS is outbound, the device controller signals its acceptance of those data on the inbound ACCEPTED line; if the device controller is placing signals on COMMAND/DATA/STATUS, the processor signals its acceptance of those signals on the outbound ACCEPTED line.

Figure 2 is divided into three major sections: selection, data transmission, and termination. During the selection sequence the processor sends a READ command, together with a device controller address. The device controller responds with its own address and with its current status. The purpose of the inbound device controller address is twofold: to ensure that no error in address recognition was made by the device controller, and to be compatible with the case where multiple sessions can be active at the same time ("multiplexer" channel). Once the processor has signaled its acceptance of this status, a session is established. During data transmission, the device controller sends its address and data inbound, and the processor signals its acceptance for each unit data transfer. During the termination sequence, the device controller sends completion status inbound together with the device controller address. Once the processor signals acceptance, the session is complete. The I/O channel may generate an interrupt to the processor on receipt of termination status from the device controller.

In some I/O bus designs, there are limits on the time intervals between changes in signal levels. For example, in Fig. 2 a design might require that the response to an outbound command by the device controller should occur not more than 1 μs after the fall of the inbound ACCEPTED signal. This is indicated on a timing chart by drawing an arrow from the trailing edge of the pulse on the inbound ACCEPTED line to the leading edge of the inbound status and address on COMMAND/DATA/STATUS and ADDRESS, respectively, and marking the arrow with a description of the timing constraint. Both minimum, maximum, and nominal timing requirements are found in such descriptions.

Another example of bus handshaking appears in Sec. 1.9.7.

1.10.5   Processor I/O Considerations

This section concerns the processor hardware for the I/O interface and programming considerations for I/O. Different techniques for processor I/O can be distinguished by the amount of processor intervention during an I/O transfer.

Polling I/O

When a processor performs I/O by repetitively interrogating a device controller and transferring data whenever possible, the mode of I/O is called *polling*. Polling is done to determine a change in device controller status when hardware is incapable of automatically alerting the processor to that change. Polling requires a minimum of processor hardware, but requires that the processor possibly execute many unproductive instructions, interrogating device controller status that does not change. Polling need not be continuous; a program may poll several device controllers in turn. In general, a program determines a *polling schedule* which determines how often to poll and which device controllers are to be polled. Continuous polling is known as "busy-waiting."

Interrupt-Driven I/O

If a processor can be alerted automatically to a change in device controller status, many of the instructions executed by a polling program are not needed, and the processor can perform other work during I/O. Interrupts provide a limited capability for processor alerting. Usually, the interrupt does not provide all the status change information, so the processor must subsequently read device status.

The program to perform interrupt-driven I/O must first set the address of the I/O interrupt-handling routine into a processor register or memory location, so that when an I/O interrupt occurs, the processor will automatically invoke that routine. The program can then initiate the I/O operation. When the device controller needs service by the processor, it generates an interrupt request. When the processor recognizes the interrupt, it must first save the state of the interrupted program and then begin execution of the interrupt-handling routine. This routine then determines the cause of the interrupt, usually by interrogating each device controller capable of generating the interrupt. In order that the processor not receive multiple responses to an interrogation, the processor must choose a specific device controller to respond to an interrogation request. This is done by prefixing or accompanying the interrogation request with an address—a number unique to the particular device controller. When the interrupt-handling routine finishes, the state of the interrupted program must be restored and its execution resumed.

Once the I/O initiation is complete, the initiating program continues to run (with momentary interruptions) while the I/O transfer continues. This is known as *immediate return* or *asynchronous* program execution. At some point in its execution, the initiating program should check to see whether the I/O transfer completed correctly: this can be done by "busy-waiting" on a flag set by the I/O interrupt handler, or through the facilities of a multitasking monitor. Interrupt-driven I/O still requires processor intervention for each unit of data transfer, but the processor executes interrupt-handler instructions only in response to a status change in the device controller.

Direct Memory Access I/O

In interrupt-driven I/O, a major portion of the instructions executed are for the purpose of detecting and responding to a change in device controller status, and for transferring data. Additional hardware can be provided in memory-bus I/O systems (discussed earlier) to handle data transmission without the need to execute instructions in the processor. This hardware, called *direct memory access* (DMA), enables the transmission of data between the device controller and main memory, terminating the transfer when a predetermined number of units of data have been transmitted. DMA implementation is treated in detail in Sec. 1.12.1.

DMA hardware consists of a count register which may be decremented and tested for zero, a memory address register which may be incremented, and sequencing logic to request data transfers on the memory bus. Once the I/O transfer is initiated, the DMA sequencing logic contends for the memory bus and when access is granted transmits the data between the device controller and main memory. Use of the memory bus implies that a memory address and a function (READ, WRITE) be transmitted by the DMA as well. The DMA is usually capable of generating an interrupt on completion of the I/O transfer. The sharing of the memory bus between the processor and the DMA where the DMA has priority is referred to as *cycle stealing*. The DMA logic is often implemented in the device controller. Note that I/O is asynchronous with the execution of the I/O invoking program except for memory cycles stolen by the DMA. Provided that the DMA hardware is sufficiently fast, the maximum data transfer rate of DMA I/O is limited only by the rate at which main-memory cycles are available to the DMA.

To transfer data via DMA, the processor must first prepare an interrupt-handler routine to be invoked at the completion of the data transfer. The processor must set the starting address of the I/O data buffer area of main memory into a DMA register, together with a count of the number of unit data transfers required. The processor must then enable the DMA, often by setting a register in the DMA logic.

Channel I/O

In systems with a separate I/O bus, the hardware necessary to handle the transmission of blocks of data between memory and device controllers is called a *channel* or an *input/output processor* (IOP). The purpose of a channel or IOP is to reduce to a minimum the number of instructions executed by the main processor in support of I/O. Figure 3 shows the relationships among the channel, the processor, and memory. The channel fetches *channel command words* (CCWs), which specify the address and length of I/O data buffers in main memory, from an area of memory called the *channel program*. The processor sends the address of the first CCW in the channel program to the channel at the time of initiation of an I/O transfer. Once the channel has been started, the channel uses the CCWs, one after the other, to specify the transfer of blocks of data between a device controller and the I/O data buffers. Each CCW may specify that an interrupt be generated to the processor when an I/O data buffer has been filled or emptied.

Another alternative in the design of an IOP is to provide it with a more general-purpose instruction set and with its own memory for channel programs. This allows the transfer of more complex data structures and permits "intelligent" preprocessing of I/O data.

I/O Control Software

Operating systems usually contain a component responsible for managing the I/O subsystem, recovering from errors, and providing a more convenient way for user programs to perform I/O operations. This component, the input/output control system (IOCS), can easily become the most complex and sophisticated software subsystem of the operating system. It is discussed further in Sec. 2.22.

1.10.6 Device Controller Design

The device controller serves several purposes: it must conform to the I/O interface and execute the "universal" commands discussed in Sec. 1.10.4, it must conform to the device interface, and it must control the device in response to a device-specific command. A general form of a device controller is illustrated in Fig. 4.

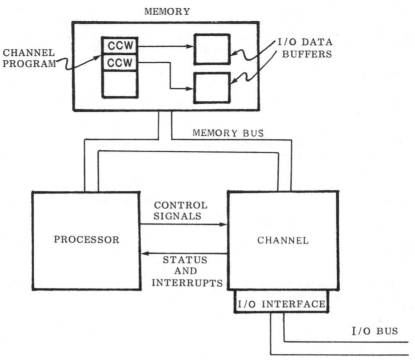

Fig. 3 Relationship of the channel to the processor and memory.

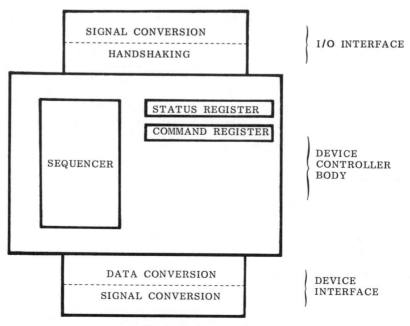

Fig. 4 Device controller.

I/O Interface

The I/O interface portion of a device controller connects to the I/O bus. In Fig. 4 the I/O interface is shown as having a signal conversion portion and a handshaking portion. The purpose of the signal conversion portion is to transmit signals to the I/O bus and to receive signals from it. This may involve driver/receiver circuits and protection from potentially dangerous transients. Logic and relays to allow orderly disconnection of the device controller from the I/O bus for maintenance also reside in this section. The handshaking portion responds to and generates the signal sequences defined for the I/O bus. If the I/O bus signaling protocol has timing restrictions, these restrictions apply to the handshaking portion. The signal conversion and handshaking portions of the I/O interface act together to exchange commands, status, and data with the I/O bus.

Device Controller Body

This section of a device controller contains a sequencer to implement the I/O protocol and registers to hold the current command and status. Some device controller designs, especially disk controllers, may contain data buffers in the device controller body. For example, one portion of the sequencer might behave as shown in Fig. 2 and described in Sec. 1.10.4. After selection, the command register would contain the command for the device controller to execute. Certain commands can be executed by the device controller body without affecting the device. For example, if the command specified that the device controller be placed off-line, the sequencer would enter a state in which no subsequent commands could be accepted and only "off-line" status returned. Other commands require interaction with the device: for example, those that specify transfer of data. The sequencer would then exchange control and data signals with the device through the device interface to perform the desired function.

If the I/O protocol is simple, the sequencer may be realized directly as a finite-state machine, but a more general and flexible implementation partitions the sequencer functions into those which are done during a unit data transfer (and must be fast) and those which are concerned with the interpretation of commands and exceptional conditions within the device. The data transfer sequencing functions are done by specialized finite-state machines, as for DMA. The more complex but less time critical sequencing is done by a small processor, typically with limited RAM to hold status and command information and with a ROM program store. For slow transfers, the data transfer sequencing can also be done by this small processor.

Device Interface

Among the devices that may be found attached to device controllers are:

Open reel and cassette magnetic tape transports
Floppy and rigid disk drives
Serial and line printers
Graphic and video display terminals
Punched card and tape readers and punches

Current, detailed information on these devices and their interfaces is available from their manufacturers and from the trade press. See Sec. 1.20 for a list of publications containing such information.

The device interface varies greatly from device to device, but the general requirement of a device controller is to conform to the electrical, mechanical, timing, and sequencing restrictions imposed by the device. In Fig. 4 the device interface is shown as having a signal conversion portion and a data conversion portion. Especially for electromechanical devices, the protection of signal lines from dangerous electrical transients by the signal conversion portion is essential, and wide variations in timing must be accommodated. The data conversion portion reformats the data transferred between the device and the device controller body. For example, for a disk device, the data will have to be serialized or deserialized. If the data are recorded in encoded form, the code conversion is done in the data conversion portion of the device interface. Some specific examples of device interfaces are given in Sec. 1.12.5.

1.11 INPUT/OUTPUT AND DEVICES: ATTACHED STORAGE DEVICES

George C. Feth

1.11.1 Overview

Attached storage is used to provide the large-capacity, nonvolatile storage that is required in computing systems. The most common attached-storage devices are magnetic tape, disk, and drum *files*; these are described in more detail later in this article. Although such files are commonly called "devices," they are really rather complex systems or subsystems. Several kinds of storage devices may be integrated into a storage hierarchy (see Sec. 1.7), to optimize the capacity–speed–cost trade-off.

In the majority of attached storage devices, the data are stored sequentially along paths in a continuous two-dimensional *storage medium*, *transducers* are used to write and read the data, and relative *mechanical motion* between medium and transducers is used to position the transducers and the storage sites. This is in contrast to random-access memory, where individual memory sites are identifiable entities, not part of a continuum, and are selected electronically without mechanical motion.

Magnetic recording continues to be the major technology for storage; however, it is not the sole possibility. *Electron-beam* or *optical* transducers can be used together with the appropriate media, and have been used in some write-once, read-only stores (WOROS). In addition, solid-state *magnetic bubbles*, *charge-coupled devices* (*CCD*), and *electron-beam accessed MOS* (*EBAM*) have been developed.

The *criteria of merit* for attached stores are primarily capacity and cost per bit. Nonvolatility is essential, at least in the largest capacity store in a system. Speed is also important, primarily in terms of the time required to transfer a block of data. In data-base-type systems with many concurrent users, an additional criterion is the access rate: the number of accesses per second that the system can provide. Cost has two components: a more-or-less fixed cost due to the controls and ancillary equipment not directly related to the capacity, and a variable cost, which increases with the storage capacity. For small systems, the cost of a minimum-capacity system, the "entry-level" cost, may be most important. To achieve the very lowest cost per bit, *off-line* storage is used; that is, the storage medium is removed from the file and stored elsewhere. For example, a tape reel is removed from a tape drive or a disk cartridge from a disk drive and stored in racks "off-line." The cost per bit of off-line storage is primarily the cost of the medium and its carrying assemblage; whereas for *on-line* storage (i.e., storage that is not removed from its file), the true cost per bit is more nearly the total cost of the file as well as its dedicated control system divided by the total storage capacity. Reliability, as well as nonvolatility, is essential to assure that data are not irretrievably lost due to malfunction. To this end, error-detection and error-correction coding (see Vol. 2, Sec. 2) is used with many storage devices so that errors due to noise or dropouts, so-called "soft" errors, can be corrected. Uncorrectable errors, or "hard" errors, must be drastically limited. Practically, hard-error rates of the order of 1 in 10^{11} or more bits can be achieved; soft-error rates may be one or two orders of magnitude larger.

1.11.2 Magnetic-Recording Storage Devices and Technology

A magnetic-recording storage device includes, in general: the storage medium; the transducers or *heads* for transferring information into and out of the storage medium; mechanisms to move the storage medium, and in some devices, to position the transducers relative to the storage medium; and electronics for reading and writing, for control and for signal and data processing. Signals representing data and control flow to and from the file (see Fig. 1). The physical distinctions between the different kinds of devices—tape, disk, and drum—have to do primarily with the forms of the storage medium

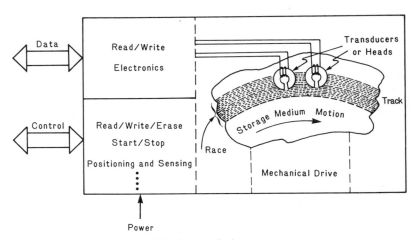

Fig. 1 Attached store.

and the mechanical aspects of the devices, which in turn affect the storage capacity, cost, and performance of the files.

In a magnetic-tape file, the medium is magnetic tape, and information is stored sequentially in records, one after the other, along the tape (see Fig. 2). The long, flexible, tape medium is stored in tape reels, cartridges, or cassettes. In a magnetic drum, the recording medium is a coating on the surface of a cylinder, the information is recorded in circular *tracks* around the cylinder and one or more read–write transducers is provided for each track (see Fig. 3). These are commonly called *head-per-track* or *fixed-head* files. In order to select the desired track, the path between the read–write amplifier and the appropriate head is switched electronically. The medium may also be in the form of a disk, rather than a drum; the tracks are recorded in a band of concentric circles, or *race*, near the outer periphery of the disk; this is called a *fixed-head disk* file. Some disk files are built so that the head can be moved radially over the disk from track to track, so that a single set of recording heads can *access* any of the recorded track positions in the race; these are referred to as *moving-head disk* files (see Fig. 4). Disks can be made to be recorded on one or both sides, and multiple disks can be mounted coaxially along the same shaft or *spindle*. One set of transducers is used for each disk *side* or *surface*, the transducers are mounted on arms that extend between the disks, and the arms are mechanically attached to the same structure, or ganged, so that they move radially together. This structure is moved by an *access mechanism* to position the heads on the desired track. One head and disk side are commonly used in a feedback-control system for positioning the heads. The set of tracks which are simultaneously beneath the transducers on the various disks is called a *cylinder*; electronic switching is used to access the single desired head within a cylinder. In disk files, the heads can be used to access the desired track location directly, and these files are commonly called *direct-access storage devices (DASD)*, in contradistinction to tape files, where the records are sequentially accessed. Disks may be flexible or rigid, and they may be designed to be removed from the spindle for storage off-line. The arms holding the heads may be designed to be retractible so that the disks can be removed, or the heads and disks may be designed into the same sealed cartridge, which is removed as a unit. More than one spindle may be driven from the same motor or disk *drive unit*. A *control unit* is

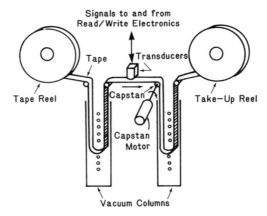

Fig. 2   Magnetic tape drive.

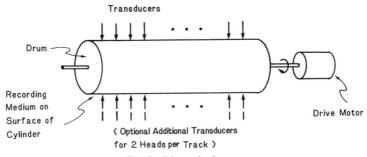

Fig. 3   Magnetic drum.

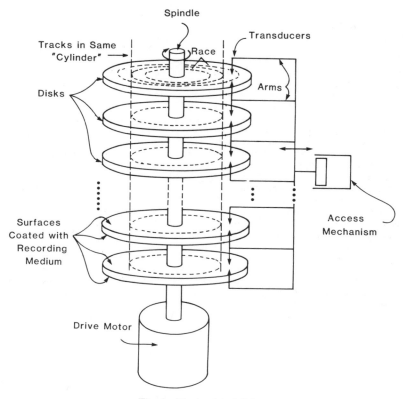

Fig. 4   Moving-head disk.

frequently designed separately from the disk or tape storage unit but for operation with that specific storage device. The control unit may be designed to handle numerous storage units, so that its cost is distributed over more storage capacity.

Magnetic-Recording Technology

The magnetic-recording medium is central to the magnetic-recording technology. Storage media consist of a layer of ferromagnetic material coated onto a supporting substrate. The information is stored in the ferromagnetic layer in the form of little magnets having magnetic flux in one of two antiparallel directions. The magnetization is fairly uniform and essentially at saturation flux density B_s, throughout the thickness of the coating, except at the transition regions, where the direction of magnetization changes spatially by180° (see Vol. 1, Sec. 3.7). In these regions, the magnetic flux leaves the medium and closes on itself through the opposite ends of the recorded magnet. It is this closure flux which is sensed in reading, so for large signals, large B_s and thick coatings would be used. However, the demagnetizing field, which is proportional to this external flux, must be less than the coercive force H_c of the ferromagnetic material. The material properties B_s and H_c, together with the coating thickness, determine the minimum allowable length of the recording magnet and hence the maximum recording density. Recording densities up to about 4K bits/cm and 200 tracks/cm are used (i.e., about 1M bits/cm^2) and further increases are anticipated.

Two types of ferromagnetic materials are commonly employed for magnetic recording: ferromagnetic oxides and plated ferromagnetic metal alloys. Among the oxides, ferric oxide and chromium dioxide are widely used, and improved characteristics may be obtained with additions of other materials. These oxides are prepared as very fine particles (of the order of 1 μm largest dimension) and are uniformly dispersed in a plastic binder as "paint." When used for magnetic tape, this "paint" material is applied uniformly to one surface of a thin (commonly 25 μm) plastic tape in a very thin layer (10 μm or less). The particles, being needle-like, may also be aligned or "oriented" by an applied magnetic field during manufacture of the tape, giving anisotropic magnetic properties which are superior for achieving higher signal-to-noise ratio in recording. The coated plastic tape is then slit to the desired width. Similar tape, but not oriented, and with one or both sides coated, serves as the flexible medium from which flexible or "floppy" disks are cut. Alternatively, the magnetic paint can be applied in even thinner layers (2 μm) to the surfaces of smooth aluminum disks to form so-called "hard" disks. In manufacturing, considerable care is given to the overall quality of the media: the smoothness of the substrate, the dispersion of the particles, the surface finish of the media, and surface lubricants to reduce wear. Electroplated metallic coatings, first used for magnetic drums, are commonly made of nickel–cobalt or nickel–cobalt–phosphorus alloys. Such coatings are submicrometer in thickness, since their flux density is large.

Magnetic-recording heads (see Fig. 1) are the transducers for changing and sensing the recorded flux. *Write heads* are used to change or write the magnetization to the intended direction corresponding to the data; *read heads* are used to sense the change of direction of magnetization; *erase heads* may be used to obliterate previously stored information by driving the magnetization to saturation in one direction throughout its depth (although erasing is not mandatory with saturation recording). A head contains a *ferromagnetic path* which is closed except for a fine *air gap* which separates the two pole pieces in the face of the head; this face, containing the pole pieces and gap, is the portion of the head that is brought into close proximity to the storage medium. A winding of one or more turns of a conductor links the ferromagnetic structure. In the write head, the current passing through the winding produces the drive field in the vicinity of the gap, and this field writes the desired magnetization state in the medium, aligning the magnetization of the medium with that of the drive field as the medium passes the gap. In the read head, the flux that enters the two pole pieces changes when the transition region of the recorded magnetization passes the gap. In an *inductive* read head the resulting change of flux linkages induces a voltage in the winding, the sense of the voltage corresponding to the sense of the flux change in the transition. Read heads can also be implemented using other magnetic effects: magnetoresistance, Hall effect, magnetooptics. For instance, in a *magnetoresistive* head the flux external to the recording medium is concentrated by a high-permeability ferromagnetic structure and is applied to a magnetoresistive element (i.e., a resistor whose value of resistance changes with the magnetic field applied to it); such change of resistance can be detected in a Wheatstone bridge circuit near its balance point. A single head, possibly with multiple windings, can be used for write and read (and erase). However, in many instances it is preferable to separate the functions. (Example are: read-after-write, to check the validity of the data just written; and write-wide/read-narrow, which assures that the track of the written data is wider than the farthest lateral excursion of the read head, thereby minimizing crosstalk with adjacent recorded tracks.) Track-to-track spacing, or track density, together with bit density determine overall magnetic-recording density. Track density is limited by signal and noise considerations. The signal magnitude is proportional to the overlap of the read head with recorded track width. Crosstalk is produced by the proximity of neighboring tracks and is affected by inaccuracies of the relative positioning of head and medium, specifically the repeatability of the positioning.

Very crucial aspects of the recording process, in addition to the magnetic properties of the medium, are the gap dimension in the head, the head-to-medium spacing, and the thickness of the medium. All three of these dimensions must be considerably smaller than the shortest magnet to be recorded. Often, on flexible media, *contact recording* is used, the head touching the medium to minimize the head-to-medium spacing; even so, there is some minimum value of effective spacing. Moreover, such a system is prone to wear and is susceptible to surface irregularities of the medium. To use a higher speed of the medium and yet maintain very small spacing from head to medium, especially in disk files, the head is designed as part of an air bearing, the other bearing surface being the medium. The spacing can be quite precisely controlled in such a *flying head* system, depending on the bearing characteristics and on the force exerted on the head toward the medium by the supporting structure. For such a system the head is fabricated in a *slider*, which provides the bearing characteristics. Hydrostatic bearings, which maintain their spacing with no relative motion between head and medium by flow of a compressed gas in the space between them, have been found to be less practical than hydrodynamic bearings, which utilize the relative motion of head and medium and the slider geometry to provide the pressurized gas flow in the separation region. Here, however, the separation, or so-called flying height, is maintained only when the motion is sustained, and contact occurs at rest and while starting and stopping.

Heads have generally been constructed using ferrite pole pieces or magnetic metal laminations, such as Permalloy, a high-permeability nickel–iron alloy, and using wire-wound coils. However, *film heads* have been developed recently using sophisticated film deposition and patterning techniques to build up the heads in a batch-fabrication process by sequentially depositing appropriate layers for Permalloy pole pieces, for insulators and gap spacers, and for conductors. Advantages of film heads are their fine dimensions, particularly for the gap, their low mass, and the possibility of integrating many heads in a single assembly, and even integrating the heads with the electronics, which may alleviate the problems associated with interconnections, electrical crosstalk, and so on. Head wear may be a more serious problem with film than with ferrite heads. Film techniques are suitable for both inductive heads and magnetoresistive read heads.

The electronic circuitry for magnetic recording is used to drive the write heads, to amplify and detect the readback data signals, and to convert between binary data and the signal waveforms involved with both writing and reading, in accord with the selected recording technique. Fairly wide bandwidth is required for the highest-performance systems to handle the bit rates in excess of 10 MHz; modestly large current and voltage levels are required for driving the inductive write heads.

Several recording techniques are in common use; they were developed to achieve high packing density, yet reliable data recovery. *Longitudinal recording* is usually used (i.e., with the recorded magnetization parallel to the direction of motion between the medium and head, in contrast to transverse recording or vertical recording). *Saturation recording* is common, driving the flux to saturation in one or the other direction, in contrast to linear recording. One such method uses a non-return-to-zero (NRZ) technique. In such a system the write head is driven with either positive or negative current to record one or the other direction of saturation magnetization in the medium. The direction of magnetization corresponds to the binary data, changes in magnetization and the corresponding induced voltage in the read head occurring only when there is a change in value of the binary data, the polarity of the sensed signal indicating whether the transition is from binary 0 to 1, or vice versa. Another recording scheme uses a change of the magnetization direction for each bit which is a 1, with no change for a 0, so-called NRZI recording. Other schemes employ a single reversal of direction of magnetization within a bit cell for one binary state, and two reversals within the same cell interval for the other state; this is effectively a frequency-modulation technique.

Actually, the signals that are recorded are not the original binary data issued by the data stream of the computer but are encoded in order to serve several special purposes (e.g., self-timing, formatting, error correction, baseline independence). The magnetic recording system, being inductively coupled, has no dc response and has a low-frequency falloff; thus, for NRZ and NRZI recording, the encoding algorithms are chosen to ensure that in a given string of data, the distance between successive recorded changes of magnetization is short enough to be within the passband of the system. Moreover, the encoding is designed to provide transitions sufficiently often that a timing signal may be generated from the data itself to synchronize a clock that corresponds to the speed of the medium at that moment, so that the data stream will be self-timed. This is done to avoid timing problems, for example, in tape systems, which have start/stop operation, or in disks, where the rotational speed may vary somewhat due to variations in the power-line frequency or voltage. The sense amplifier is designed not only to detect the data but also to process the signal to perform the clock recovery. Error-detection and error-correction features can also be included in the encoding. Such encoding and decoding require suitable circuitry for buffering the data and for the required logical manipulations and transformations.

Additional circuitry is used for controls in the storage devices. In devices with many transducers but only a single data stream, such as fixed-head files or moving-head files with more than one recording head, the transducer to be activated is switched electronically. In moving-head files, the head positioning is controlled electronically through an access mechanism; often, a feedback-control system is used to position the heads to the desired cylinder. In a tape or removable-disk file, the position of the tape and the presence or absence of the medium may be electronically sensed. In some disks and drums, there are several blocks of data, or records, per revolution of the medium, and *rotational position sensing* is included to sense what sector is approaching the transducer, so that the appropriate transducer can be selected to read or write in that sector.

The *mechanics* of a storage device basically provide the motion between the medium and the transducer. In disks and drums, electric motors are used to rotate the spindles or drums. Desirable characteristics include: relatively constant speed, low runout and vibration, and appropriate fluid dynamics for flying the heads and for circulating filtered cooling air. In addition, access mechanisms for moving-head files employ voice-coil actuators or lead screws driven by stepping motors for the required linear motion. Mechanisms are required for retracting the heads in removable media disks. In a tape system the major mechanical problems are obtaining the desired tape speed and responsiveness despite the high inertia of tape reels. The tape motion at the heads is controlled by a capstan driven by a low-inertia driving motor. Additional tape guiding mechanisms, pinch rollers, vacuum columns and vacuum pumps, and automatic threading mechanisms may be included. Rotary heads are used in some tape systems, and automated tape files include appropriate mechanisms for handling and positioning the tape cartridges.

Control Units and Data Formats

Generally, the device control unit that provides the interface between an attached storage device and the I/O bus (see Sec. 1.10.2) performs the following functions:

Converting the parallel data words from the I/O bus into a serial by bit data stream to the device, and deserializing for data flow in the opposite direction

Controlling the mechanical motion of access arms, tape-drive capstans, and so on

Selecting the proper read or write head

Monitoring the status of the device and communicating this to the processor

Keeping track of the rotational position

Formatting the data into records, blocks, sectors, and so on

Keeping count of the records read

Searching for a desired record by comparing data on the device with data in main memory

Adding error-checking and error-correcting codes (ECCs) to written data; and

Checking ECCs in data from the device

The format of the data on the device varies from device to device and from manufacturer to manufacturer. Data on tape are generally written in blocks or records with gaps between them. Special codes may be recorded to denote the end of each file or similar division. On fixed-head files and moving-head files, data are commonly divided into blocks or records which are usually shorter than a total track or revolution of the medium. Tracks may be divided further into sectors. There is generally a code to mark the start of each track or sector. Special fields within each record, perhaps written by the control unit and removed by it when data are transmitted to the processor, may be added to the data in order to identify the track and cylinder, to index the record, and to include ECC.

Moving-Head Disk Files (MHF)

MHFs are used to store large amounts of data which must be retrieved quickly. The time to access and transfer a random block of data is the sum of three components: the time required for the head to move to the specified track and settle there—*seek time*; the time for the disk to rotate so that the beginning of the block reaches the head—*latency time*; and the time for the entire block to pass beneath the head—*block-transmission* time. The time required to electronically switch between heads is negligible in comparison. High-performance drives commonly are designed with rotational speed of 60 revolutions per second, which results in an average latency time of about 8 ms; track seeking requires as little as about 10 ms for a one-track increment, or 25 ms average; and block-transmission time for a 4K-byte block recorded at 2500 bits/cm on a 35-cm-diameter disk is about 2 ms (corresponding to a data rate of about 15M bits/s or approximately 2M bytes/s. Since actual read or write time is but a small part of the overall block-acquisition time, the read–write circuitry can be used to handle several drives. This is done by maintaining a queue of requests for all the drives and setting the accessing in motion for each drive as it is freed up or as a request for that drive arrives. When the head is at the sought cylinder (and approaches the appropriate sector in a disk which has a rotational position-sensing feature), the pertinent head is selected electronically. Sometimes there is blocking due to the electronics being busy, so individual requests are delayed. The *access rate*, the number of data blocks that can be accessed in a given time, depends on the number of independent electronic channels, the number of access mechanisms, the block size, and the distribution or clustering of requests in the file.

MHFs span a large range of applications. At the one end are the small-diameter "floppy disks" with storage capacity starting in the fractional megabyte range, costing several hundred dollars, and having block-acquisition times of tenths of a second; these are commonly used with minicomputers and microcomputers. At the other extreme are the large disk systems with capacities of hundreds of megabytes per spindle, costing the order of a millicent per bit for on-line storage, and achieving block-acquisition time of the order of 30 ms. Commonly used disk sizes are 13-, 20-, and 35-cm diameters. For even lower cost per bit, removable media—disk packs or cassettes—are used to store data off-line at a small fraction of the cost of the storage system. However, for the highest density recording, of the order of 10^6 bits/cm^2, often only fixed media are available because of the sophistication required for the fine dimensions and tolerances and the required degree of cleanliness. With the development of integrated heads and electronics, it may become practical to integrate several heads per slider so that multiple cylinders are covered with a single slider position.

Drums and Fixed-Head Files (FHF)

Magnetic recording drums were the early form of fixed-head file, and FHFs are still often loosely called drums, even though disks may be used as the recording surfaces in order to increase the capacity per drive. FHFs are used for the fastest access requirements in order to eliminate the seek time encountered in MHFs, this being the largest component of their acquisition time. FHFs are often used for swapping data with main memory in multiprogrammed computers and for storage of frequently used parts of the operating system. The data are arranged in sectors, and access requests are queued for each sector in order to increase the throughput. The cost penalty for this less-than-order-of-magnitude improvement in speed over MHFs is often well over an order-of-magnitude increase in cost per bit. Some disk files are designed with the option of including fixed-head and moving-head disks on the same spindles to obtain FHF performance at a more modest cost premium. However, for the fastest access requirements, FHFs with higher rotational speeds and more than one head per track have been used to decrease the average latency time.

FHFs with lower cost, albeit lower capacity and performance, are available also for use with smaller mainframe computers and minicomputers. FHFs find application in militarized systems, where they have the advantage of being more rugged than MHFs.

Tape Files

Magnetic tape files are used for the lowest cost per bit and largest capacity read–write storage. Data are recorded sequentially on the tape and are commonly grouped in blocks called *records*. Tape drives are usually designed to reverse direction for rewinding and for backing up to preceding records; this requires start/stop capability. Gaps in the recording are left between records so that the tape motion can be brought up to speed in the interrecord gap in start/stop operation. All but the lowest-performance files record in several tracks in parallel on the tape, six and eight data tracks being common. An additional track for parity checking is often used, and additional bits may be added to the record length, as well, for error detection and correction. The bits that were written simultaneously may not all reach the read heads simultaneously, due, for example, to nonuniform stretching of the tape medium or different alignment of the heads on the writing and on the reading tape drives. This results in skew of the sensed data. De-skewing buffers are used to realign the data for reading.

In most systems, the tape is stored off-line and is accessed manually by a machine operator. However, automated tape files, in which the tape handling and storage are performed without human intervention, have been developed for mass storage, and a random-access time of the order of 10 s for storage capacity of the order of 10^{12} bits is achieved.

Tape can be fabricated in a wide range of widths and lengths. Narrow tape, 6 mm, may be used for tape-cartridge or tape-cassette systems for minicomputers. Tape drives for intermediate and large systems commonly use 12 mm tape on reels. Tape speeds range to over 250 cm/s and longitudinal bit densities to over 2500 bits/cm, with resultant data rates approaching a megabyte per second. Some automated tape files employ common tape and reel sizes. However, others are designed altogether differently, using wider tape (e.g., 5 cm) in special cartridges and using rotary recording heads which record a single bit track at a time at very high speed diagonally across the tape. As the need for higher recording densities in disk files leads to nonremovable (and more costly) media, the reliance on tape files for low-cost storage increases.

1.11.3   Other Technologies for Sequential Storage

Some regions of the two-dimensional cost–speed space are not filled by present-day magnetic-recording capabilities. One such region is in the access time–cost–capacity range intermediate between RAM and disk—the so-called access gap or file gap. Here magnetic-bubble memory (MBM; see Vol. 1, Sec. 6.10), electron-beam accessed memory (EBAM), and charge-coupled devices (CCDs) are contenders. Another such region is extremely high-density, large-capacity stores. Optical and electron-beam techniques have been proposed for this and have been used to a limited extent. Read-only storage is acceptable for some applications.

Charge-Coupled Devices (CCD)

CCDs employ charge storage in planar semiconductor structures using technology closely allied with that of 1D RAM cells (see Sec. 1.6.3) but operating like a shift register rather than a RAM. Using MOS technology with polycrystalline silicon gates, appropriate potentials applied to the gates create potential wells within the silicon. Quantities of charge are injected at one end of the CCD shift register according to the binary data to be stored, and neighboring gates are driven by multiphase voltage waveforms in such a way as to create potential wells which hold the charge and move it along the CCD shift register to the detector at the far end. CCD storage is volatile unless provided with an uninterruptible power source. Basic shift rates of several MHz are possible. Higher densities are potentially achievable by using the analog nature of the charge storage to store more than one bit per cell (or even analog information). Data rates and access time capabilities appear adequate to consider designing CCD stores for attachment to the memory bus rather than through a channel. However, advances in CCDs and RAMs are closely coupled, and the half-generation advantage of CCDs over RAMs in level of integration may not be adequate for CCDs to continue as a separate viable product.

Electron-Beam Accessed Memory (EBAM)

EBAM employs an electron beam in a cathode-ray tube for addressing storage sites on an MOS wafer used as a target. For writing or erasing, the beam impinges on an MOS structure in which the metal is biased appropriately relative to the semiconductor to cause charge either to be stored in the oxide or to be freed from it. The semiconductor contains a *pn* junction parallel to its surface. In reading, the incoming electrons in the beam each create many hole–electron pairs; for one storage state these carriers are allowed to reach the oxide semiconductor interface, where they recombine and produce no current through the junction. In the other storage state, the electrons are conducted away by the inverted semiconductor surface, and the holes diffuse to the junction region, where they are swept across the junction by the electric field in the depletion region. The resulting current is amplified and detected in a sense amplifier connected to the substrate, thereby indicating the stored binary states. Storage sites are not delimited lithographically, so storage density is limited only by the beam size, positioning accuracy, and charge spreading in the target. Two levels of deflection are used, the first to position the beam on the one lenslet of an array of lenslets, which in turn use electrostatic focusing and the second level of deflection to sweep the beam across a subfield of the target. Such storage is nonvolatile, but reading decreases the intensity of the storage somewhat, so for continuing storage the data that are read are rewritten when the signal level has decreased but is still detectable, after about 20 reads.

The data rate is of the order of 10M bits/s for each tube. Reading and writing rates may differ, corresponding to the different charge dosages or beam intensities for the different functions. Storage densities of the order of 10^7 to 10^8 bits/cm^2 have been demonstrated, and densities of two orders of magnitude greater have been projected. The cost per bit of the electronics is kept low by driving all the second-stage deflection lenslets in one tube by the same X and Y drivers, and further, systems are proposed using many such tubes in parallel, sharing the electronics cost and providing ECC which could keep the system functional even if one tube failed. The cost of even a minimum system is quite large, so EBAM is only applicable in large computing systems. Block acquisition time is the sum of terms related to the beam-positioning time, which is negligible, and the data rate. Assuming a byte-wide storage path, a 4K-byte block at 10M bytes/s would require 0.4 ms. Such performance is an order of magnitude faster than FHF and is potentially fast enough to consider designing EBAM storage to connect to the memory bus directly rather than via a channel. At the higher-density extreme, EBAM would provide storage commonly implemented by MHF but with much faster access, although probably at a somewhat higher cost per bit.

Ultra-Large-Capacity Storage

As the need for storage capacity increases, higher-density-storage approaches are sought. Optical and electron-beam (EB) techniques have appeared attractive because beams can be focused to very small dimensions. Storage systems have been built but with limited quantity production. One system used EB exposure of photographic film for writing, chemical development of the film, and optical reading. Another used a laser beam to write by ablation of a thin metallic film on a flexible tape, and reading was done optically. Both of these are write-once, read-only stores (WOROS). WOROS is suitable for some archival storage applications, especially if writing can be done at any time in previously unwritten locations in the medium, for then it is possible to rewrite modified information in a new location while flagging the old storage position as obsolete and storing the forwarding address.

The developing videodisk technology, leading to storage density of the order of 10^7 bits/cm^2, appears potentially of interest, but is limited to read-only storage. Holographic storage techniques have been proposed, but the lack of a reversible (or read–write) storage medium is a limitation.

BIBLIOGRAPHY

R. E. MATICK, *Computer Storage Systems and Technology*, Wiley, New York, 1977.

S. MIDDELHOCK, P. K. GEORGE and P. DEKKER, *Physics of Computer Memory Devices*, Academic Press, New York, 1976.

W. E. PROEBSTER, (ed.), *Digital Memory and Storage*, Vieweg, Braunschweig, 1978.

1.12 INPUT/OUTPUT AND DEVICES: MICROPROCESSOR SYSTEM I/O

David F. Bantz

Microprocessor I/O systems differ from large-and medium-scale computer I/O systems primarily in that a limited number of pins on the microprocessor package itself are available for I/O. A separate I/O interface is generally not feasible: virtually every microprocessor communicates with its I/O attachments over the same bus that is used to attach the microprocessor's memory. In some microprocessors, memory access instructions are used to set and read I/O attachment registers; in others, a special class of I/O instructions performs this function, although the path to the I/O attachment is the memory bus. Some microprocessors have a bit-serial I/O facility, intended for the attachment of slow devices.

1.12.1 Memory-Bus I/O

Microprocessors differ in whether bus cycles for I/O are distinguished from bus cycles for memory access, or not. In some microprocessors, a signal line is available to designate a particular bus cycle as having resulted from the execution of an I/O instruction.The attachments to these microprocessors can use this signal line to determine whether the address portion of the bus contains a memory address or an I/O attachment address. In microprocessors lacking such a signal line, the registers in the I/O attachment are accessed as memory locations by the microprocessor; only the contents of the address bus distinguish an I/O operation from a memory access operation. This form of memory-bus I/O is referred to as *memory-mapped* (see Sec. 1.8.1). Microprocessors using memory-mapped I/O have no explicit I/O instructions. Any processor with a memory bus can be adapted to do memory-mapped I/O.

Disadvantages of having a signal that distinguishes I/O bus cycles from memory cycles include the extra operation codes and processor circuitry and the extra package pin needed for the signal. A disadvantage of memory-mapped I/O is that a portion of the processor address space (the range of valid addresses) must be dedicated to I/O registers.

Address Decoding

Each I/O attachment must contain circuitry to recognize its address. In order to simplify address recognition circuitry, one may design circuitry to examine only a subset of the address lines. For example, the circuitry may be designed to select the register if the most significant bit of the address is true. Then for 16-bit addresses, any address in the range 8000 to FFFF (hexadecimal) will select the register. In general, if the address recognition circuitry has N gate inputs connected to the high-order bits of an address bus of M bits, a contiguous block of 2^{M-N} addresses is dedicated to the register.

Multiplexed Addressing

In some systems, a single bus is multiplexed between address and data information. The implication for I/O attachments is that the address information must be latched into a register to enable valid address recognition. Alternatively, the address may be recognized at the time it is presented by the microprocessor, and only the signal representing address recognition need be latched. This indication must be reset before the next address is presented by the microprocessor. In the Intel 8085 only the low-order address bits are multiplexed on a common bus. If high-order bits are used for register selection, no latching is required.

Data Transmission

Once the address of an I/O attachment has been recognized, the attachment must either accept or present data to the microprocessor. Some microprocessors have a bus signal which when 1 indicates that data are to be presented, and when 0 indicates that data are to be accepted. Other microprocessors use two separate lines for this purpose. Microprocessors usually generate a signal that indicates that data are valid on the data lines of the bus, or that data have been captured by the microprocessor from the data lines. Most often, this signal is a transition from logical 1 to 0, or vice versa. Thus to present data to the microprocessor, the I/O attachment must recognize its address, sense that data are to be presented, and remove the data from the data lines after detecting the signal that the data have been captured. To accept data from the microprocessor, the I/O attachment must recognize its address, sense that data are to be accepted, and capture the data when the transition occurs that signals that the data are valid on the data lines.

Example

Figure 1 details the logic necessary to connect an external register to the Intel 8085 bus, which has a signal line distinguishing bus cycles for I/O. The register is selected by the RECO output from the address recognition circuitry. This circuitry compares a prewired address with the contents of A8–A15 (high-order address bits), which contains the I/O attachment address during an I/O operation; when the comparison succeeds, when IOCYCLE designates an I/O bus cycle, and when ADDRESS LATCH ENABLE makes a positive transition, the RECO output becomes true. The next positive transition on ADDRESS LATCH ENABLE sets RECO false. If the regter is selected and NOT READ is 0, indicating a bus read operation, the OUTPUT ENABLE control input to the register is 1, causing the register to place its contents on DATA. During an I/O write, INPUT ENABLE is 1, and when STROBE makes a negative transition, the data on DATA are latched into the register. The 8085 bus timing ensures that IOCYCLE is 1, NOT WRITE is 0, and CLK makes a negative transition only while data are valid on AD0–AD7 (the multiplexed address/data bits).

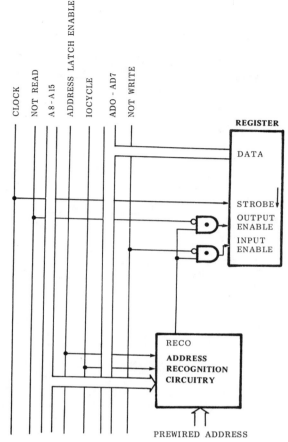

Fig. 1 Intel 8085 I/O interface.

A timing diagram for the I/O read operation is shown in Fig. 2. Note that the signal OUTPUT ENABLE can be 1 only when the signal NOT READ is 0, and when the I/O attachment has been recognized.

Direct Memory Access (DMA)

When data are transferred between the microprocessor and an I/O attachment under direct control of the microprocessor program, each byte or word of data requires the execution of several instructions to transfer. Some I/O devices require higher data transfer rates than are achievable with this technique. For these devices, the I/O attachment may use direct memory access (DMA). DMA allows the direct transfer of data between an I/O attachment and the microprocessor memory. The microprocessor first initializes the DMA controller circuitry by storing a count and a starting memory address in its registers. Once started, a DMA transfer proceeds without further microprocessor intervention, except that an interrupt (see Sec. 1.12.3) may be generated upon completion of the DMA operation.

I/O attachments using DMA (see Sec. 1.10.5) incorporate circuitry similar to that of Fig. 3. Circuitry to allow the microprocessor to set the COUNTER and ADDRESS COUNTER registers is not shown. The signal BUS CYCLE is assumed to define the interval of time during which addresses are presented and data are exchanged on the bus. The DMA controller connects to the I/O attachment with the lines TRANSMIT REQUEST and REQUEST GRANTED.

When the I/O attachment wishes to use a bus cycle, it raises the line TRANSMIT REQUEST. If the DMA count register is nonzero, the signal is placed on the BUS REQUEST line to the processor.

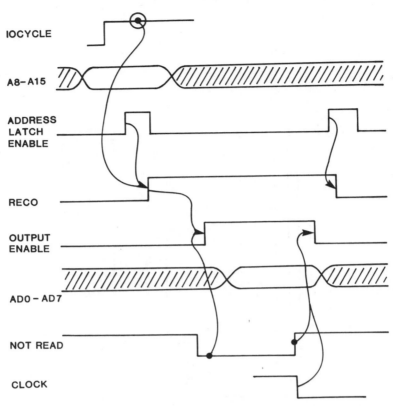

Fig. 2   Intel 8085 I/O interface timing for I/O read operation.

The processor hardware periodically examines this signal, and when it is 1 the processor waits until the end of the current bus cycle, stops, places its address and data line drivers in the high-impedance state, and raises the line BUS GRANT. The processor is effectively isolated from the bus during bus cycles granted to the DMA controller. When BUS GRANT is sensed 1 by the DMA controller, it places the contents of its ADDRESS COUNTER register on the ADDRESS lines and signals the I/O attachment on REQUEST GRANTED that it may use the current bus cycle for transmission of data. The I/O attachment itself may drive the bus lines that determine the direction of data transfer, or additional circuitry in the DMA controller may drive these lines. As long as TRANSMIT REQUEST is held at 1, consecutive bus cycles may be used by the I/O attachment.

If several I/O attachments, each with its own DMA channel, wish to use the bus simultaneously, hardware must be provided to resolve the contention among the various channels. This resolution may be either on a priority basis or may grant bus cycles to competing DMA channels on a round-robin basis.

The circuitry of Fig. 3 is capable of using successive bus cycles ("burst mode") or using bus cycles intermittently. The choice depends on the data transfer rate of the I/O attachment. Often, the microprocessor must use several bus cycles in preparation for relinquishing the bus by generating BUS GRANT, and must use several bus cycles after regaining the bus. These cycles are unproductive in that they do not contribute to instruction execution or data transfer. Therefore, DMA transfers that use consecutive bus cycles make more efficient use of the bus.

1.12.2   Non-Memory-Bus I/O

Some microprocessors have a serial I/O bus separate from their memory bus. Here, separate serial input and output channels allow transmission between an I/O attachment and the microprocessor. The I/O attachment address is signaled serially by the processor, followed by outbound or inbound data. The I/O attachment uses a separate clock line driven by the microprocessor to control the rate

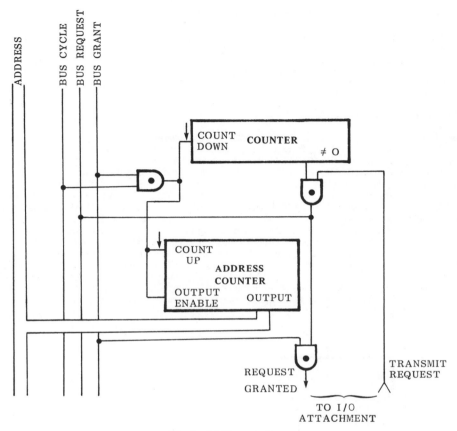

Fig. 3   DMA controller.

at which data are captured or signaled. A single instruction causes a transfer; the microprocessor cannot execute the next instruction until the transfer is complete. This serial I/O facility is usually intended for the attachment of I/O devices with low data rates.

1.12.3   Interrupts

To determine whether a particular I/O attachment requires data transmission, the microprocessor must interrogate the I/O attachment. This usually repetitive interrogation is called *polling*. The ability of an I/O attachment to interrupt the execution of a program in the microprocessor can be used to signal the requirement for data transmission more efficiently than polling.

Microprocessor interrupt systems usually depend on a logic circuit (attached to the microprocessor like an I/O attachment) devoted to controlling the interrupts on behalf of the processor. This alternative is most often chosen in preference to dedicating a pin of the microprocessor package to each interrupt level (see also Fig. 1.18.6). One pin signals the microprocessor that an interrupt has occurred; a second pin may be used for a high-priority interrupt to signal error conditions. The interrupt controller resolves contention among the individual interrupts on a priority basis, encoding the number of the highest-priority interrupt into an internal "status" register. When the "status" register is read by the microprocessor, its contents are automatically transferred to an internal "level" register. Only an interrupt whose priority exceeds the current contents of the "level" register will cause a new interrupt to the microprocessor. Finally, the interrupt controller contains a "mask" register, which can be set by the microprocessor and which is ANDed with the individual interrupts. This facility is valuable, since it allows the microprocessor program to defer the recognition of selected interrupts without masking them all.

1.12.4 General Parallel and Serial Interface Systems

Integrated-circuit manufacturers, recognizing the need to implement I/O attachments, supply a wide variety of packaged components that attach directly to microprocessor buses and present a general interface to a device. This interface may allow either serial or parallel transfer of data to the device and often provides the ability to generate an interrupt signal to the microprocessor when a transfer is complete.

Parallel Interface

This family of integrated circuits, sometimes called *parallel interface adapters* (PIAs), is designed to simplify the attachment of devices requiring parallel data transfer, or devices requiring registers containing control information set by the microprocessor. An example of such a parallel interface device is shown in Fig. 4. The signals between the parallel interface and the microprocessor, on the memory bus, are the data, address, and control signals required for any I/O attachment. The signals between the parallel interface and the device carry data (DATA IN, DATA OUT) and control (OUTPUT READY, OUTPUT CAPTURED, INPUT READY, and INPUT CAPTURED). The control signals are sometimes called *handshaking* signals. For example, when the microprocessor sets data into the OUT DATA REGISTER, the handshaking line OUTPUT READY signals the device that data are ready for it. When the device has captured the data, it signals on OUTPUT CAPTURED, which may generate an interrupt to the microprocessor. The microprocessor program can then supply more data or respond in some other way. Similarly, when the device has data for the microprocessor, it signals on the INPUT READY line. The parallel interface may then generate an interrupt to the microprocessor, which would then read the data now present in the IN DATA REGISTER. The act of reading that register causes the parallel interface to generate the signal INPUT CAPTURED to the device.

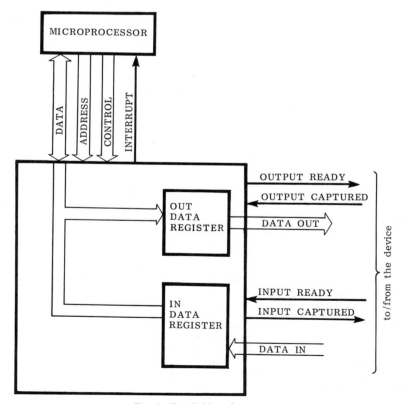

Fig. 4 Parallel interface.

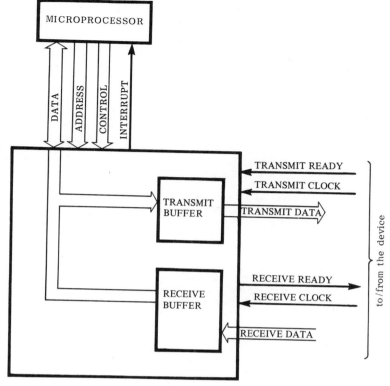

Fig. 5   Serial interface.

Serial Interface

This family of integrated circuits is designed to simplify the attachment of devices requiring serial data transfer. An example of such a serial interface device, called a *universal synchronous asynchronous receiver transmitter* (*USART*), is shown in Fig. 5 (see also Fig. 1.18.7). The signals between the microprocessor and the serial interface (on the memory bus) are those required by any I/O attachment. The signals between the serial interface and the device consist of status signals (TRANS-MIT READY, RECEIVE READY), clock signals (TRANSMIT CLOCK, RECEIVE CLOCK), and data (TRANSMIT DATA, RECEIVE DATA). When the device has data for the microprocessor, it signals those data, serial by bit, on the RECEIVE DATA line in synchronism with a clock signal on RECEIVE CLOCK. Usually, the data are prefixed by a 1 bit (the "start" bit), indicating the start of data, and the data are from 5 to 8 bits long. A 1 bit (the "stop" bit) may be suffixed to the data. After all bits of the data have been received by the serial interface, the stop and start bits are stripped and an interrupt may be generated to the microprocessor to indicate that data may be read from the RECEIVE BUFFER. The mode of data transmission in which one 5- to 8-bit character is transmitted at a time is called *start/stop*.

When data are to be sent to the device, the microprocessor sets the data in the TRANSMIT BUFFER. The data are then serialized, prefixed with the start bit and suffixed with the stop bit, and sent to the device on TRANSMIT DATA in synchronism with a clock on TRANSMIT CLOCK.

Other Attachments

Another form of general-purpose attachment is the IEEE 488 General-Purpose Interface Bus,* a standard for the connection of laboratory instrumentation. Integrated-circuit manufacturers supply

*IEEE Standard Digital Interface for Programmable Instrumentation, IEEE Std 488-1975, IEEE, New York.

interface devices that connect to a microprocessor bus on one side and to the IEEE 488 bus on the other (see also Sec. 1.13.8).

1.12.5 Device Attachment Examples

This section contains a number of examples of specific I/O attachments for microprocessors.

Keyboard attachment

Figure 6 shows how a keyboard can be constructed as an array of contacts connected to a parallel interface. The DATA OUT signals are used to select a row of contacts for sensing; the DATA IN signals give the state of each contact in the row. The microprocessor sets only one bit to 0 at a time in the OUT DATA REGISTER; otherwise, several rows might be selected simultaneously. All inputs to the IN DATA REGISTER are tied to a logical 1 and will remain 1 if no contact is closed. Only those contacts tied to an OUT DATA REGISTER line that is 0 can affect the corresponding IN DATA REGISTER bit.

Since the contacts may open and close rapidly for up to 10 ms after a key is depressed, the state of a contact should be sampled several times before the microprocessor program decides that the key has been depressed. This process is called *debouncing*. As peak keying rates may exceed 20 keystrokes per second, the keyboard scanning rate should be at least 40 scans per second to allow for at least two scans per key per keystroke.

Communications Attachment

When microprocessors are used in communications systems, more complex and efficient modes of transmission than start/stop (Sec. 1.12.4) must often be supported. Higher-data-rate devices require a *synchronous* or continuous mode of transmission that transmits a continuous sequence of transitions,

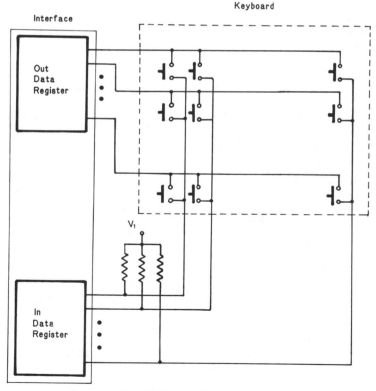

Fig. 6 Nonencoded keyboard.

allowing the receiver to maintain clock synchronization. Messages are transmitted according to a link protocol, where a message consists of a destination address, control information, a block of characters, and an error control unit.

Typical of the devices that can be used to implement these communications protocols is the Motorola MC6854 Advanced Data Link Controller (ADLC). The general form of this device is similar to that of the serial interface (Sec. 1.12.4). Among the differences are the three-stage transmitter and receiver buffers, capable of buffering up to three characters, allowing the processor more time to respond to an interrupt. The ADLC computes a 16-bit polynomial check code (Vol. 2, Secs. 2.16 to 2.18), which is automatically appended to transmitted messages and stripped from received ones. Provision is made for the ADLC to work with DMA (see Sec. 1.12.1) so that data link rates too fast to be processed by the microprocessor with interrupts can be supported. This device must be serviced continually once a message is begun; if not, a data overrun or underrun condition will cause a portion of a message to be lost. This is a "real-time" device whose internal buffering is minimal and whose data rate is determined by the link speed, not by the microprocessor program.

Display Attachment

Alphanumeric CRT displays are often designed with an internal microprocessor. This processor can be used to scan, debounce, and encode the keyboard; to provide the interface, either to a computer or to a communications line; and to perform editing functions in response to keyboard entries. Earlier we described the I/O attachment of a keyboard and communications. This section describes the attachment of the display.

The display considered here is a raster CRT whose beam moves horizontally left to right across its screen. The beam is then shut off, moved downward by one beam width, and retraced to the left. The beam is then moved horizontally from left to right. This process is repeated many times per second. When the beam reaches the bottom of the screen, it is retraced to the top. To display characters with this beam, a signal must be supplied to an unblanking circuit as the beam moves horizontally left to right.

Figure 7 shows the circuitry necessary to convert a buffer of character codes from the microprocessor memory into the serial bit stream of data necessary to unblank the beam. This circuitry is called a *character generator*. When the beam begins its scan at the top of the screen, the character buffer CB1 contains the codes of all the characters to be displayed on that scan line. The code for the leftmost character is in the rightmost end of the character buffer and is used to address a memory (the

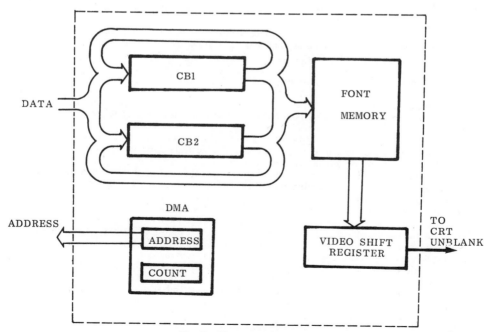

Fig. 7   Character generator.

FONT ROM) containing the bit image of the character. A horizontal slice of the character image is then accessed from the FONT ROM and placed in the VIDEO SHIFT REGISTER, which serializes the slice to the unblanking amplifier of the CRT. As the horizontal slice of the first character is displayed, the character buffer is shifted circularly one position to the right, bringing the code for the next character to be displayed to the right end of the character buffer. That code is now in position to address the FONT ROM. In this way the character codes are converted to their serial video representation.

While one of the character buffers is being shifted to access the FONT ROM and create the character images, the other is being filled from microprocessor memory using the DMA controller. Successive character codes are retrieved from microprocessor memory and stored in the character buffer. At the bottom of the screen, the DMA address register and counter must be reset so that codes for characters at the top of the screen are the next to be accessed. This process of alternately filling the two character buffers continues for as long as an image is required on the display screen.

1.13 BUSES

Kenneth J. Thurber

A bus is a communication device used to interconnect components in a digital system by providing a data highway between system elements. There are many forms of buses; however, the general context of a computer bus is that of a digital structure designed to support high-speed traffic (rates of many megabits per second) over short distances (millimeters to kilometers), in contrast to more general circuits designed to handle low-bandwidth/long-distance traffic (e.g., phone lines). Typically, the bus consists of a set of lines that carry information, such as addresses (memory location, device ID, etc.), control signals, and data. The primary function of a bus is to provide the system with a means of device interconnection which supports the allowable communication modes.

The operation of a bus may be viewed as a sequence of functions: the devices that use the bus make requests for allocation of the bus, the bus requests are arbitrated and a device selected, the bus is allocated to the device, the data are transferred, the transmission errors are resolved, and the bus is released for allocation. Arbitration may be performed implicitly (i.e., it may be designed into other system functions). For example, in an intra-ALU (arithmetic-logic unit) bus, one central unit may make all decisions. In other cases, the arbitration may be an explicit function provided by a unit or series of units. Clearly, many of these functions may be overlapped; for example, it is quite common to develop a bus that is arbitrating for bus usage at time t_1, is transferring data for devices selected during the arbitration at $t_1 - t$, and is providing error control for data transferred at time $t_1 - 2t$ by a third set of devices.

All bus operations and concepts will be functionally described as explicit implementations. In an actual design, some functions would be combined or even deleted via some implicit design decision intended to simplify the hardware.

1.13.1 Terminology and Definitions

There are a number of terms that are commonly used to describe design parameters of digital bus structures. The major terms necessary for understanding the remainder of this article are defined below.

There are two general forms of buses: *dedicated* and *nondedicated*. A dedicated bus may be dedicated to a pair of devices or to the performance of a particular function. Nondedicated buses are shared between multiple devices or functions or both.

The *arbitration*/control mechanism consists of the algorithm and hardware structure necessary to resolve which device (among requesting devices) is to be allocated the bus for the next communication period. Arbitrators may be *centralized* (the arbitration mechanism is at a single location) or *decentralized* (the arbitration mechanism is physically or logically dispersed among the devices).

After a device has gained control of a bus for communication, the device must be connected to the bus to permit the actual transfer of information. The actual transmission occurs between a source device and a destination device. If prearranged timing agreements between the devices exist, the transmission is called *synchronous*; if not, it is called *asynchronous*. Asynchronous transmissions may require interlocking transmissions between source and destination devices; this procedure is known as *handshaking* or *request/acknowledge* asynchronous communication.

The *length* of a bus is its physical distance from beginning to end. In a loop, length can be measured as either the maximum distance between any pair of devices or the total of all distances between pairs. Generally, loop length is the total of distances. The number of circuits (wires) in the bus is called the number of lines or *bus width*. The transmission capacity of the bus in bits (or bytes, words, etc.) per second is known as bus *bandwidth*. Bus *latency* is the time necessary to effect a transaction on the bus.

A *transaction* consists of all steps from the initial source device request through all communication steps until the source device ascertains that the destination has correctly received the data.

1.13.2 Types of Buses

At least two distinct views of a bus exist: *hierarchical* and *functional*. The hierarchical approach notes that buses occur repeatedly in a computer system. They are used to interconnect registers on a chip, to connect chips together inside a computer, and to interconnect computers. This view notes that buses at different levels in a system differ in implementation rather than kind (i.e., all buses perform the same basic functions); however, for hardware efficiency reasons, functions that may be explicit in one bus may be implicit in another bus.

The hierarchical approach [1] categorizes the bus as dedicated or nondedicated. Further, these terms may apply to either function or physical characteristics. That is, a bus may be physically dedicated to a pair of devices while being used for a variety of functions performed between the devices.

The function approach [3] generally classifies buses into groups. The most common grouping breaks out bus categories as follows:

1. CPU–memory
2. Input/output controller–memory
3. CPU–input/output controller
4. Input/output controller–peripheral device
5. Input/output controller–external communication lines

Table 1 illustrates the characteristics generally associated with such buses.

Inside a central processor there are also buses. Some of these are used to interconnect register structures (interregister buses), and some are used to connect various functional units in the ALU (intra-ALU buses). Generally, these buses are very simple. There may be implicit arbitration done by the microprogrammer, who specifies the use of the bus via the microprogram sequences; no error control other than bus parity causing a hardware fault; and so on.

1.13.3 Arbitration/Control Units

One of the key functions performed by the bus structure is to allocate the bus. In general, a bus may be viewed as a shared data highway in which users (devices) compete on the basis of some performance measure (e.g., priority) to use the data highway. One integral portion of this concept is that of the bus control unit/bus master or arbitrator. The function of the arbitrator is to accept and process requests to use the bus. The control unit then selects the next device to receive the bus and allocates the bus to the appropriate device. This function may be either centralized (i.e., there exists a specific unit, sometimes called the bus master) or decentralized (there are multiple units capable of being the bus master). One way of building a decentralized controller is to replicate the bus controller at every device location. This may improve fault tolerance, but also increase cost, size, power, and weight. This same type of function, arbitration, is performed at other parts in the computer system;

Table 1. Functional Bus Types

Requirement	CPU–Memory	Controller–Memory	Type CPU–Controller	Controller–Peripheral	Controller–External
Memory addressing	Large (2^{32})	Large (2^{32})	None	None	None
Number of connections	Small (2^4)	Small (2^4)	Medium (2^6)	Small to large $(2^4$ to $2^8)$	Small to large $(2^4$ to $2^8)$
Bandwidth	High (5 Mbyte/s)	Medium (1.2 Mbyte/s)	Low (0.1 Mbyte/s)	Low to high (0.1 to 5 Mbyte/s)	Low to high (0.1 to 5 Mbyte/s)
Length	Short (3 m)	Medium (30 m)	Long (300 m)	Medium to long (30 to 300 m)	Medium to very long (30 to 3000 m)
Information carried	Instructions and data	Addresses and data	I/O commands, status, interrupts, and data	Control signals and data	Control signals and data
Transferred unit	Word	Block	Word	Word and block	Arbitrary

Table 2. Arbitration Taxonomies

Thurber–Masson Taxonomy	Chen Taxonomy

Centralized
  Daisy chain
  Poll
  Independent request
  Implicit request
Decentralized
  Daisy chain
  Poll
  Independent request
  Implicit request
	Arbitrator location
	  Distributed
	  Centralized
	  Static
	  Dynamic
	Sorting priority
	  Comparison
	  Counting
	Addressing
	  Priority
	  Unit
	Information passing
	  Encoded
	  Decoded

Levy Taxonomy

Arbitration Category	(a) Fixed with Respect to Data Transfer	(b) Variable with Respect to Data Transfer
1. Centralized, priority	Centralized, priority, fixed	Centralized, priority, variable
2. Centralized, democratic	Centralized, democratic, fixed	Centralized, democratic, variable
3. Centralized, sequential	Centralized, sequential, fixed	Centralized, sequential, variable
4. Distributed, priority	Distributed, priority, fixed	Distributed, priority, variable
5. Distributed, democratic	Distributed, democratic, fixed	Distributed, democratic, variable
6. Distributed, sequential	Distributed, sequential, fixed	Distributed, sequential, variable

Luczak Taxonomy

Configuration
  Bidirectional shared channel
  Dual unidirectional shared channel

Channel access (arbitration)
  Selection
  Random-access contention
    Access control
    Collision resolution
    Message protocol
  Reservation

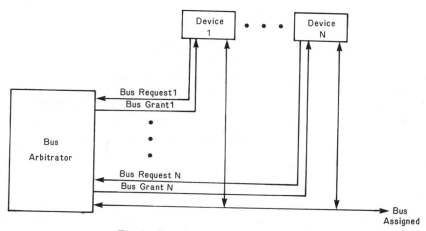

Fig. 1   Centralized independent requests.

for example, at the memory multiport (a multiport is a priority sorting device that determines which of several requestors is allowed access to a specific memory bank). In fact, a memory multiport may be viewed as one form of a bus structure in which all arbitration for a given memory bank is centralized in the memory multiport front end.

There are four important categorizations of bus arbitration mechanisms as illustrated in Table 2. The details of these categorizations are beyond the scope of this discussion. The schemes are simply summarized in the table so that the reader will not have to develop the taxonomies while reading the appropriate references.

An example of a centralized bus control unit operation for independent requests [1] is shown in Fig. 1. In this case, each device has a separate pair of bus request and bus grant lines, which it uses for bus controller communication. When a device requires use of the bus, it generates a bus request signal, which is sent to the controller. The controller selects the next device to receive service via an algorithm and generates a bus granted signal to the selected device. The selected device lowers its request and generates a bus assigned signal, indicating bus busy to all other devices. After the transmission completes, the device lowers the bus assigned line; the bus controller lowers bus granted, and then selects the next device to use the bus.

From the perspective of the bus controller, at the start of the arbitration algorithm, all pending bus requests appear to be presented simultaneously to the bus controller; thus the overhead time required for allocating the bus can be short—namely, the time to compute the algorithm. The controller can use any desired algorithm, such as a fixed device priority scheme, a programmable (modifiable) device priority scheme, or a circular allocation (round-robin) scheme. It is also easy to disable requests from a device that is suspected to have failed.

The major disadvantage of independent requests is the potentially large number of lines and connectors. Furthermore, the complexity of the allocation algorithm will be reflected in the bus controller hardware.

1.13.4   Communication

There are two main communication strategies: synchronous communication (explicit timing agreements exist between devices) and asynchronous communication (no explicit agreements) [1, 2]. Generally, communication design depends on timing trade-offs which specify the allowable sequencing of specific control lines (e.g., the relationship between data ready and data accept lines).

In the digital data communications environment, in general, and the computer network environment, in particular, paths are usually the point-to-point links characteristic of common-carrier systems. Sharing these paths, line sharing, involves the use of units known as "multiplexers" and "concentrators" for connection of (other) nodes to the path (multiplexing is discussed in Sec. 1.13.6).

"Synchronous" devices are normally defined to be those that exchange data based on advance agreements as to timing (i.e., without synchronization signals). Frequently, the devices have either a common clock or separate clocks which are "implicitly" synchronized (i.e., within a specified tolerance of one another). One of the primary techniques of implicit systems is to have the sender and receiver of information both contain local clocks of a specified accuracy. A series of special signals is sent between devices to allow them to synchronize these clocks. Then transmissions can occur at a predefined rate, as long as the accuracy of the clocks remains within a specified tolerance. Periodically, the clocks will have to be resynchronized.

As an example of a form of synchronous communication, consider Fig. 2. This figure illustrates a logical clocking mechanism in which local clocks are synchronized and used to derive the data from an encoded waveform. In the example shown, the receiver is assumed to be synchronized onto the time standard of the sender. The sender sends a signal that is encoded as follows. In a time slot (t between two successive clock pulses) a 0 is represented by no change in the signal and a 1 is represented by a change (either high to low or low to high) during the time slot. This coded information is transmitted on the bus. The receiver derives the data by detecting when the signal changes level near the center of the time slot (data = 1) and when it does not (data = 0). Since there is always a transition at the beginning of every time slot, the receiver can maintain synchronization with the sender's clock.

As a detailed asynchronous communication example, asynchronous request/acknowledge communication will be illustrated (see Sec. 1.9.7). The request/acknowledge method of asynchronous communication is separated into three cases: non-interlocked, half interlocked, and fully interlocked.

Figure 3a illustrates the noninterlocked case. The source puts data (D) on the bus and raises data ready (DR), and the destination stores D and responds with data accept (DA), which causes the source to drop DR and to place new D on the lines. If an error is found in the data, the receiving device raises a data error line instead of DA. This signal interchange provides error control and permits operation between devices of any speeds. The price paid is speed and added logic complexity compared to a noninterlocked, one-way command interface, which would simply send the data and hope it would arrive. The exact timing is a function of the implementation. There are two lines, DA and DR, susceptible to noise, and twice as many bus length delays as in a one-way noninterlocked interface.

Improper ratios of bus propagation time and communication signal pulse widths could allow a second DR to come and go while DA is still high in response to the first DR. This could hang up the entire bus, because the destination would never send a second DA, having missed the second DR. Therefore, the second transmission would never be completed.

This can be avoided by making DR remain up until DA (or data error) is received by the source, as seen in Fig. 3b. In this half-interlocked interface, if DR comes up while DA is still high, the second transfer will only be delayed. When the source of the first transmission sees DA, it "drops" DR. The second transmission holds up until this event, ensuring a proper sequence of interlocks. The variable width of DR tends to protect it from noise. In Fig. 3a a noise pulse could be interpreted as DR, but not in the half interlocked case. There is no speed penalty and little hardware cost associated with these improvements over the noninterlocked case.

Assume that the source generates outputs from a buffer register, which has a cycle time called the buffer reload period. One more potential timing error is possible if DA extends over the source buffer reload period and masks the leading edge of the next DR (i.e., DR's leading edge is sent before DA is

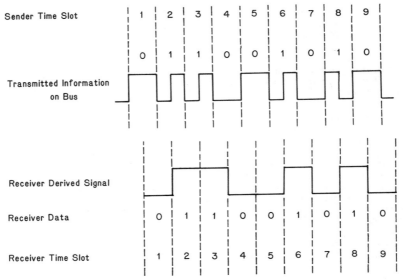

Fig. 2 Biphase synchronous communication.

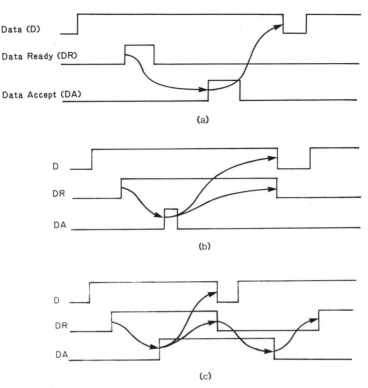

Fig. 3 Asynchronous request/acknowledge communication: (*a*) non-interlocked; (*b*) half-interlocked; (*c*) fully interlocked.

dropped). Figure 3*c* shows how this can be avoided with a fully interlocked interface, where a new DR does not occur until the trailing edge of the old DA (or data error) signal has been received. Both communication signals are now comparatively noise immune. The device logic is more complex. The major disadvantage is that the bus delays for the fully interlocked case have doubled over the half-interlocked case, thus halving the maximum possible transfer rate.

Other examples of bus handshaking appear in Secs. 1.9.7 and 1.10.4.

1.13.5 Error Control

The function of error control is to provide means for checking, detecting, and correcting transmission errors (see Vol. 2, Secs. 2.16 to 2.20). The most basic error control concepts are:

1. VRC (vertical-redundancy checks): parity or M-out-of-N codes
2. LRC (longitudinal-redundancy checks): e.g., check-sum procedures (cyclic error checking or polynomial codes)

In the VRC technique, a parity bit or other encoding is added to each character transmitted. LRC adds parity bits to each message. The M-out-of-N code technique uses a special code set in which characters are mapped onto the code assignments in such a manner that all N-bit characters contain M bits set to the value 1. Check-sum procedures compute a correctness value based on either a cyclic error code or a polynomial error code. Of course, combinations of these techniques could be used.

Some techniques (polynomial codes) provide for both error-detection and error-correction capabilities. If an error-correcting technique is selected, enough redundant information is added to each transmission so that not only can transmission errors be detected, but they can also be corrected automatically by the destination device. This approach is expensive. Encoding and decoding redundant data require complex computational capabilities and use significant transmission bandwidth.

The error-detecting approach is efficient in terms of bandwidth utilization for systems with a small percentage of bad transmissions. The concept requires retransmission of any erroneous incoming information. The destination typically must return an acknowledgment (ACK) signal to the source before some specified event occurs at the source (e.g., a clocked time-out period is completed), or the information will be retransmitted. After a specified number of transmissions have failed to complete (generate a received ACK within the allowable clock time-out period), the line and/or destination device will be declared inoperable.

1.13.6   Signal Lines

The width of a bus affects many aspects of the system, including cost, reliability, and throughput. Signals have been discussed as if separate lines exist dedicated to specific functions. In an actual implementation, this may not be true. Techniques exist designed to minimize/combine the number of lines associated with functions, such as device addressing lines, data lines, and control. The objective is to achieve the smallest number of lines consistent with the necessary types and rates of communication.

Bus lines require drivers, receivers, cable, connectors, and power, all of which tend to be costly compared to logic. Physically and electrically, the bus can be viewed as drivers, connectors, cabling, connectors, and receivers—in that order. The connectors physically connect the cable ends into the electrical system. The drivers and receivers convert the signals into a form for transmission through the cable. Clearly, media other than cable are available and would use different connectors, drivers, and receivers. Because of media, distance, and speed, conventional logic generally cannot be used to drive the bus; thus special circuits and interfaces must be designed. Connectors occupy a significant amount of physical space and are also among the least reliable components in the system. Reliability is often diminished even further as the number of lines increases, because of the additional signal switching noise.

Line combination, serial/parallel conversions, and multilevel encoding are some of the fundamental techniques for reducing bus width. These are discussed in detail in the next three paragraphs.

Combination is a method of reducing the number of lines based on function and direction of transmission. Complementary pairs of simplex lines might be replaced with single half-duplex lines. Instead of dedicating individual lines to separate functions, a smaller number of time-shared lines might be more cost-effective, even if extra logic is involved. This includes the performance of bus control functions with coded words on the data lines.

Serial/parallel trade-offs are frequently employed to balance bus width against system cost and performance. Transmitting fewer bits at a time saves lines, connectors, drivers, and receivers, but adds conversion logic at each end. It may also be necessary to use higher-speed circuits (thus more expensive) to maintain effective throughput. Serial/parallel converters at each end of the bus can be augmented with buffers that absorb traffic fluctuations and permit the use of a slower bus, relieving the device of having to accept each input by allowing inputs to be buffered automatically into larger quantities of information before requiring device attention. Independent of bus width considerations, this concept can minimize communication delays due to busy destination devices. Bit-serial transmission generally is the slowest, requires the most buffering and the least line hardware, produces the smallest amount of noise because only one line is changing state at a time, and is the most applicable approach in cases with long lines. Parallel transmission, although faster, uses more line hardware, generates greater noise, and is more cost-effective over shorter distances.

Multilevel encoding converts digital data into analog signals on the bus. It is occasionally used to increase bandwidth by sending parallel data over a single line, but there are numerous disadvantages, such as complexity, line voltage drops, and lack of noise immunity.

Time-division multiplexing (TDM) provides the capability to share the set of lines in time rather than by space or electrical implementation. At time T_1, the line set may appear (be interpreted) as control lines; at time T_2, as data lines; and so on. Whether the interpretation is performed periodically or at an arbitrary time, under control of a set of specification lines, differentiates the concept of pure time-division multiplexing from the concept of statistical multiplexing (STDM). Statistical multiplexing requires more lines (interpretation codes) but promises more efficient use of bandwidth.

TDM can be viewed as dividing the system bus bandwidth among a set of devices. A device wishing to transmit simply waits until it is assigned time, and transmits information of the form: data, destination. If a device does not transmit, its slot goes unused, wasting bandwidth. However, there is no need for an arbitration function. (Another perspective is that polling is used; thus the source device is known.) STDM allows any device to use any slot. Devices compete for slots; thus all slots could be used. However, arbitration must be provided for each slot allocation, and devices must know the source. Typically, the transmitted information is: source, data, destination.

1.13.7   Implementation

There are a number of technologies available to implement a bus structure. This section discusses briefly the available transmission media and the coupling circuitry between the system and the medium.

Typical implementation media are:

1. Copper wire
   (a) Twisted pair
   (b) Microstrip or stripline
   (c) Coaxial cable or shielded twisted pair
   (d) Triaxial cable
2. Waveguides
3. Optical fibers
4. Free space

The main advantages of twisted pairs are that they are inexpensive, lightweight, easy to modify (splice), and emit low levels of radiation. Their primary disadvantages are bandwidth and distance limitations.

Striplines, like twisted pairs, are inexpensive. They are especially suitable for parallel bus structures. Like twisted pairs, striplines are primarily bandwidth and distance limited.

Coaxial cables and shielded twisted pairs provide lightweight, low-cost, low-emission, medium-distance, and medium-bandwidth media. However, their connectors must be more complex than twisted pairs or striplines. Triaxial cables are essentially double-shielded coax, and thus have the advantages of coaxial cable while worsening the connector problem.

Waveguides provide a high-bandwidth medium in which very little radiation is emitted. However, they are very bulky, delicate, and mechanically inflexible.

Fiber-optic filaments come in two primary forms: multimodal and single mode. The multimode form is near 60 to 200 μm and is made up of a tight bundle of single-mode fibers; single-mode fibers are on the order of 2 μm. Single-mode fibers have properties similar to waveguides. Multimodal fibers provide essentially little emitted radiation, complete electrical isolation, low weight, and high bandwidth. The primary disadvantage of fiber optics is the need for optical interfaces and special connectors.

Free space used in a broadcast system provides a low-cost bus medium with unlimited bandwidth; however, the medium is uncontrolled and vulnerable to eavesdropping and uncontrollable interference or noise. Further, radios, satellites, and microwave systems are used in the interface to the medium, making this potentially a very expensive system.

A number of techniques exist to allow the system to interface to the transmission medium, including:

1. Tristate logic
2. Transformers
3. Repeaters
4. Directional couplers
5. Radio, microwave, and others

These are briefly discussed below.

Tristate logic is a low-cost logic-based technique good for distance-limited buses which desire to utilize standard logic levels. This technique is effective over reasonable distances with any type of balanced lines or coaxial cables.

Transformer coupling using inductive power transformers through a diode current source (utilizing balanced receivers) is used for coaxial systems that need high speed and electrical isolation.

Active repeaters are special logic elements which essentially employ any desired coupler technique with the signal being accepted at every device and then repeated if necessary. The advantage of this technique is that it allows an unlimited number of taps on the bus.

Directional couplers are available in many forms for such media as coax, striplines, and optical fibers. Their properties and implementations are beyond the scope of this discussion, as are radio and microwave techniques, which are useful for free-space media.

1.13.8 Case Study Example

Many bus standards are appearing [12–14]. They are too numerous to enumerate in this section. Thus a brief summary of one standard, the IEEE standard digital interface for programmable instrumentation, is provided [11].

The objective of the standard is to provide a communication bus over which messages can be effectively carried between interconnected devices. Messages belong in one of two categories: (1) those that manage the interface system (interface messages) and (2) those carried by the interface (device-dependent messages). For a bus communication network to organize and manage information, it must contain three elements: (1) a listener device, (2) a talker device, and (3) a controller device.

The IEEE interface contains 16 lines to carry all communication. Messages are coded onto one line or a set of lines. The bus is divided into three line sets: data (eight lines), data byte transfer control (three lines), and general interface management (five lines). The eight data bus lines carry interface messages and device-dependent messages. The three transfer control lines synchronize the data transfers. The five interface management lines control the device-to-bus interface functions. Messages are carried on the data input/output lines in an asynchronous, bidirectional, bit-parallel, byte-serial manner.

From a standards strategy viewpoint, a device may be viewed as a physical object designed to perform a specific application and separated from the interface and bus. The interface is the element through which a device receives, processes, and sends messages. The IEEE standard defines a set of available interface functions. A designer can select a particular set of interface functions from the available defined set for each application. These functions, together with the message coding and routing decisions, specify the function aspects of the IEEE standard that the designer can work with. The standard stipulates basic functions that interfaces must contain while allowing for a communications hierarchy.

1.13.9   Conclusion

Buses are the cornerstone of digital communications. They are a hierarchial concept that provides the designer the ability to interconnect functional elements (e.g., ALU to registers) or complete systems (e.g., HYPERchannel) [9]. Buses differ in implementation, with a set of common functions being implemented via either implicit or explicit functional capabilities rather than in kind. This article summarized the most important trade-offs in the area of bus design. The functional and physical parameters discussed will provide a designer the capability to exploit fully contemporary hardware technology via a state-of-the-art interconnection system specialized to a specific requirement.

To date, even though buses are very important, there exists little published work on the subject. Most work on the subject tends to be contained in general system descriptions: Thurber et al. [1] performed the first comprehensive design study of buses; Chen [2] first described exhaustive bus communication modes and bus deadlock problems; Levy [3] provided a detailed description of minicomputer buses; and Luczak [4] included a description of random-access bus arbitration. Finally, Jensen et al. [5] and Thurber [6–8] provided overviews that detail the relationship of buses, packet switches, and circuit switches.

REFERENCES

1. K. J. THURBER ET AL., "A Systematic Approach to the Design of Digital Busing Structures," *Proc. FJCC*, 1972.

2. R. C. CHEN, "Bus Communication Systems," University Microfilms Dissertation 74-20493, Ann Arbor, Mich., 1974.

3. J. V. LEVY, "Buses, the Skeleton of Computer Structures," in *Computer Engineering: A DEC View of Hardware System Design*, C. G. Bell et al. (eds.) Digital Press, Bedford, Mass., 1978.

4. E. C. LUCZAK, "Global Bus Computer Communication Techniques," *Comput. Networking Symp.*, Dec. 1978.

5. E. D. JENSEN ET AL., "A Review of Systematic Methods in Distributed Processor Interconnection," *ICC '76*.

6. K. J. THURBER and G. M. MASSON, *Distributed-Processor Communication Architecture*, Lexington Books (D. C. Heath), Lexington, Mass., 1979.

7. K. J. THURBER, *Distributed Processor Architecture: A Tutorial*, IEEE Computer Society, Long Beach, Calif., 1979.

8. K. J. THURBER, "Computer Communication Techniques," *COMPSAC '78*.

9. J. E. THORNTON ET AL., "A New Approach to Network Storage Management," *Comput. Des.*, 14(11), 81–85 (Nov. 1975).

10. D. E. KNOBLOCK, ET AL., "Insight into Interfacing," *IEEE Spectrum*, May 1975.

11. *IEEE Standard Digital Interface for Programmable Instrumentation*, IEEE Std. 488-1975, IEEE, New York.

12. D B. GUSTAVSON, "Standards Committee Activities: An Update, "*Computer*, 12(7), 61–64 (July 1979).

13. Proposed IEEE Standard 696: K. A. ELMQUIST, "Standard Specification for S-100 Bus Interface Devices, "*Computer*, 12(7), 28–52 (July 1979).

14. IEEE Computer Society draft standard P796, "Microcomputer System Bus."

1.14   LOGIC SYSTEM IMPLEMENTATION

Walter J. Kleinfelder and Walter V. Vilkelis

The implementation of a logic system is accomplished in a number of steps. All steps are required to reduce a logic design to actuality, but in any specific example some steps may become trivial or may be determined prior to the implementation. The larger the computer system, the more emphasis will be given to the division of the implementation into discrete stages, while smaller systems may find practically all steps being done simultaneously and trade-offs being made across the entire span of the project. Specific steps in the design and implementation of a logic system include the following (see also Sec. 1.18.1):

1. *Definition of architecture.* The specification of what the system is to perform at the highest level is defined as the architecture. Instruction sets, data types, addressing schemes, and so on, are defined. The machine programmer or user operates at this level of definition.

2. *Hardware organization.* At the first stages of design, a division of the computer into hardware and software components is made. From the architecture, a hardware organization is made of the system elements (i.e., memory, control, I/O, processors, etc.). Decisions will be made in larger logic systems as to what elements of the architecture will be implemented in microcode, arrays, or other physical implementations. In addition, technological considerations produce other broad specifications for the system which designate the system performance to be achieved, the power available, the physical constraints of size and shape, and the reliability, testing, and repair strategies for these elements.

3. *Logical design.* The logical design is a detailed design of a logic organization which is capable of achieving the objectives of the architecture and hardware organization. Many of the decisions at this phase are made by anticipating how the system will be implemented in hardware and what technologies are available.

4. *Implementation.* The logical design must finally be implemented in a physical form that achieves all aspects of the system design. The implementation that is chosen must be partitioned into physical pieces and organized in physical space. Information must be assigned physical attributes such as voltages or currents. Devices to perform logical decisions must be selected from alternatives offered by the technologies available. Consideration is given to the interconnection of the physical elements, the distribution of electrical power, and the extraction of heat from the elements of the system. Finally, the implementation must allow for testing, diagnosing failures, and repair of defective parts, first as the system is designed, and continuously during subsequent manufacture and as failures occur when the system is in use.

1.14.1   Partitioning

The system design proceeds from the architecture definition through the various stages of hardware organization and logic design to a point where the computer system is described in diagrammatical form, called the logical definition, and also in a more descriptive form in which the flow of information and the control of the system are described. Concurrently with the system design process, the implementations of the physical components of the system in terms of memory cells and logic gates are being defined. This is usually done with very little direct knowledge of the final system design other than empirical knowledge of the general configuration the physical components will take in the final system. Each of these procedures may be done completely independently of each other, as an example, by independent corporations.

At some point, the logical definition must be partitioned to a physical description of the components that will provide the system functions. The first step in this process is partitioning the logical description into physically definable parts. Only on rare occasions will the logical partitions defined during system design coincide exactly with the physical partitions provided by the technology chosen. The process of partitioning is enhanced if the design of the system is reviewed in its entirety in the early stages, so that logical design can be carried out with an adequate knowledge of the physical implementation and the technology can be synthesized toward the system requirements. Such is the case in small system projects or if the "logical" design has specific design procedures which result in a one-to-one mapping of the logical system into physical parts. With the advent of silicon technology at very high levels of integration and batch fabrication procedures being used to provide highly functional, lower-cost computer elements, the one-to-one correspondence of logical to physical partitions has been harder to achieve. As the logical function realizable in a physical part becomes larger, partitioning with respect to physical components must be done earlier in the implementation stages of design.

Figure 1 describes the logical function of an 8-bit ALU with a register array, at a high level of abstraction. The physical implementation may be done in various ways (see Sec. 1.5.3).

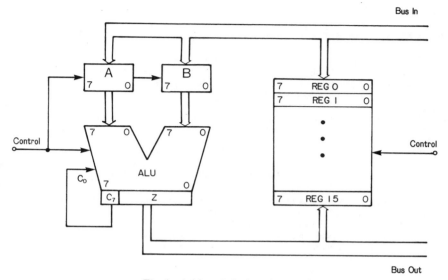

Fig. 1   Arithmetic-logic unit control.

As a first example, the logical design is carried out to a lower level. The physical parts available may not be the equivalent function to the level of design of Fig. 1, or this function would be optimized further at a lower design level. Figure 2 shows a section of the adder of the ALU described as composed of primitive logic blocks. Generally, it is not economically feasible to construct the system with a one-to-one correspondence of logic block to physical part. Many logic blocks of the same type may be integrated in a single physical element. In Fig. 3 the function of a simple binary adder is shown partitioned into parts of the type just described, each containing two similar gates.

At today's level of circuit integration, the implementation of physical parts is at a higher level of circuit integration than that of the first example. If parts of similar functions to those pictured in Fig. 1 are not available, it may be possible to modify the logical design so that the physical parts may be an exact fit for the logical design. Figure 4 describes how custom parts that fit the design of the ALU of Fig. 1 can be selected if we modify the design slightly and add external logic to provide the function specified. Note that some of the functions provided by the components shown in Fig. 4 are not needed.

The function shown in Fig. 1 may also be provided as a single part or even as part of a larger functional part. In the latter case, it may be economical to proceed up one level of the design hierarchy to a higher-level functional design that contains the required logical function as a subset. This strategy

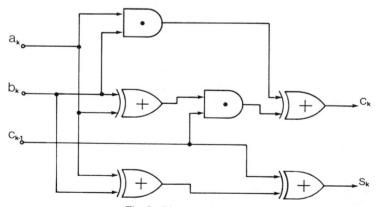

Fig. 2   Binary adder logic.

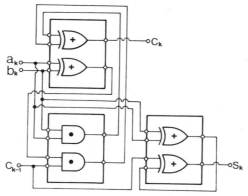

Fig. 3 Binary adder.

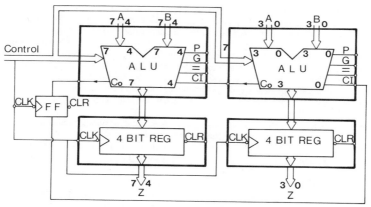

Fig. 4 Arithmetic-logic unit.

may require modification of the design to accommodate the differences between the desired function and the larger functional part already available. The physical to logical equivalence of partitions and parts is then achieved at a very high level.

At the extreme, it may be required to change the architecture definition completely because of the availability of extremely complex physical components. An example of this would be if the function given in Fig. 1 were part of the design of a complex control system. If the architectural definition of the control system could be accomplished by utilization of an available microprocessor component, the entire function shown in Fig. 1 could be incorporated within the physical implementation of the microprocessor itself. Part of the function provided by the hardware definition of the control system may also appear in coding within the software structure of the microprocessor architecture. With levels of integration on the rise and more and more highly functional parts becoming available, partitioning of hardware and software functions is affecting the implementation phase of design earlier in the design process and is dictating changes in architectural definition, especially in small to medium-scale computer system applications.

1.14.2 Packaging Logic Systems

The design of logic systems is usually accomplished by the multiple use of a small number of different logical elements. The physical embodiment of logic systems has also resulted in the interconnection of a large number of similiar physical parts. The layout and construction of the computer system from these physical structures is called packaging. The system package is required to support the electrical circuits, distribute power to the circuit elements, implement the electrical connections that carry the information required by the logical design, and remove the power dissipated in the form of heat generated in the course of operating the system. The physical constraints on the implementation of logic systems utilizing these structures are determined by the technology that is employed.

Definition of Structures

In integrated structures such as those associated with semiconductor circuits (also magnetic bubble circuits and Josephson circuitry), the first level of packaging consists of a number of switching circuits fabricated on a single part called a chip. The number of permissible circuits available on the chip is limited by many factors, such as power dissipation, ability to provide electrical interconnection, design complexity, and most important, by the manufacturing yield or ability to produce nondefective parts. Since there is no effective repair strategy for the chip level, all parts must be defect free at the level of integration of the chip component (or employ redundancy to allow operation in the presence of defective parts). Figure 5 shows the historical trend for the level of integration limits due to yield for the most complex logic parts available.

The chip is mounted in a structure called a module, which provides environmental protection for the chip and permits electrical interconnection to be made to the next level of package. In most cases only one chip component is mounted in a module, although in larger logic systems specialized packages may be provided in which several chips may be housed in a single module package. Modules are normally provided in standard configurations to allow for the design of general-purpose manufacturing equipment and higher-level packages.

Modules are mounted on printed-circuit cards which provide for the distribution of power to the modules and for the interconnection of signal lines between modules and to higher packaging levels. Printed-circuit cards are most commonly laminated of glass-filled epoxy insulating layers and layers of etched copper conductors. The simplest interconnection structure consists of a single layer of insulation made of a glass-filled epoxy and a single layer of copper conductors. More complex structures consist of numerous layers of conductors and insulators which are divided into power distribution layers, signal layers, and ground plane layers. Signal layers are grouped in pairs which carry electrical information in orthogonal directions (x, y pairs) and are located adjacent to ground layers. This provides a uniform impedance for the electrical signals and prevents electrical coupling of signals among adjacent conductors.

Signal wires carry logical information between modules and between modules and input/output connections to the card. The terminals that carry the logic signals to the modules and to the input/output terminals are called logic service terminals (LSTs), and connections between wiring layers in the package are called vias (VSTs). Figure 6 shows the cross section of a typical multilayer structure and a typical connection between modules.

In some structures the card does not contain wires that carry logic information. These connections are placed on the card structure as discrete wires, uniquely for each application, by automated attachment and routing equipment. The card is used only to distribute power and support the modules.

Interconnections between cards are normally made by discrete or bundled wires, twisted pairs, or cables which are attached to connectors mounted on a frame. Connectors mounted on the card plug

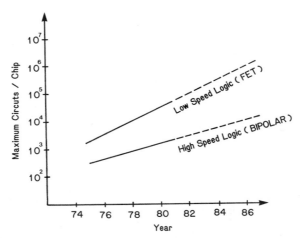

Fig. 5 Integrated-circuit complexity.

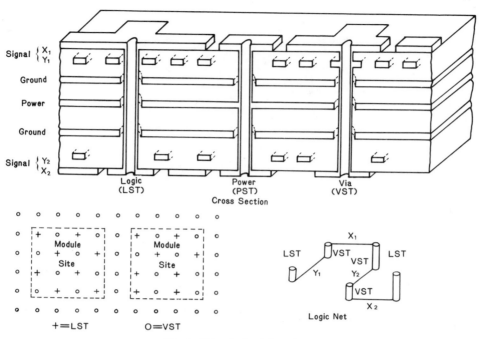

Fig. 6   Printed-circuit board.

into the frame connectors and permit removal of the logic cards for service and replacement. In smaller logic systems the logic cards may be interconnected by cables that plug directly into the card, the card being more permanently mounted to the frame. In large logic systems, cards may be plugged orthogonally into other printed-circuit structures called boards, forming a card-on-board (COB) arrangement. Interconnections between boards are then made by pluggable discrete or bundled wires or cables routed within the mounting frame.

Wiring Limitations

Many forms of logic systems must be permitted to be implemented in general-purpose packaging structures. The packaging structures are designed prior to the final logic design, and the exact interconnection for any specific logic system is described only in the final embodiment of that logic system. For that reason it is necessary to estimate the requirements placed on the wiring of physical packages in a general way so that the wiring structures may be configured prior to the implementation of any specific logic system design. The following describes the attributes of partitioned logic as it affects the wiring load placed on the interconnection structure elements of the logic system.

Definitions

n_c: Number of unit logic circuits/partition

n_{c_M}: Maximum circuits allowed/partition

n_{c_m}: Minimum circuits expected/partition

$\bar{n}_c$: Average number of circuits used/partition

N_{IO}: Number of input/output ports/partition

N_{IO_M}: Maximum number of input/output ports/partition

N_{IO_m}: Minimum number of input/output ports expected by a partition

$\overline{N_{IO}}$: Average number of input/output ports required by a partition

$\epsilon = \dfrac{\bar{n}_c}{n_{c_M}}$: Efficiency of use of circuits/partition

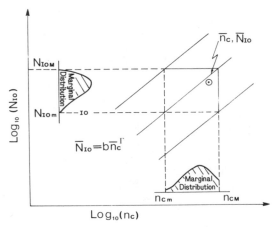

Fig. 7   Distribution of I/Os and circuits/partition.

Figure 7 indicates the observed statistical relationship that exists between the number of circuits per partition (n_c) and the number of input/output ports (N_{IO}) which are provided for logic interconnections to other partitions in the system. It has been observed that the partition states form a "cloud" of possible parts that is about one decade wide and rises to the right: $\overline{N_{IO}} = b\overline{n}_c^{\Gamma}$ (commonly known as Rent's rule). The particular decision for N_{IO_M} and n_{c_M} depends on electrical, thermal, technological, and cost constraints. Generally, most choices lead to

$$0.6 < \epsilon < 0.7$$

and to values of

$$2.2 < b < 2.5$$

$$0.63 < \Gamma < 0.67$$

In printed wiring structures such as that depicted in Fig. 6, where the space occupied on the board by a single module is a uniformly distributed array of LST, VST, and power terminals, the area required by a module is given by

$$A = \left(N_{IO_M}(1 + Vg) + P + DC \right) d^2 \geq N_{IO_M}(1 + Vg) d^2$$

where

    V_g = VST/LST ratio
    P = Number of LST-like sites required to carry electrical power to the module
    DC = number of LST-like sites required to carry power supply decoupling and regulating
        elements
    d = lattice spacing between LST and VST sites (assuming the wiring lattice is isotropic)

An interconnection net consists of a series of conductor segments between LSTs and VSTs that form a single electrically connected structure which carries logical signals among similar structures such as modules on a printed-circuit board (Fig. 6). One must estimate the demand of a logic system on wiring structures so that sufficient space can be provided for the interconnections required by the logic.

Figure 8, derived from observation, shows that as a partition increases in average circuit capacity, the bulk of the nets between partitions are simply cut into two pieces by the partition boundaries. At the unit logic level (one circuit per partition), an average of 4 LSTs per net are required; and at >100 circuits per partition, an average of <2.5 LSTs per net are required. The circuit packing density has the average value:

$$\bar{\rho} = \frac{\bar{n}_c}{A} < \frac{\bar{n}_c}{N_{IO_M}(1 + V_g)d^2} = \frac{\epsilon}{b_M} \frac{n_{c_M}^{1-\Gamma}}{(1 + V_g)d^2}$$

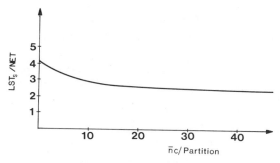

Fig. 8 Average LSTs as a function of partition size.

where

$$b_M = \frac{N_{IO_M}}{n_{c_M}^{\Gamma}}$$

At constant ϵ, the ratio ϵ/b_M is also constant; therefore,

$$\bar{\rho} \propto n_{c_M}^{1-\Gamma}\big|_{\Gamma \approx 2/3} \approx n_{c_M}^{1/3}$$

if the d of the printed circuit is kept constant. Thus, as the partition gets larger, the electrical power density and thermal power density to the cooling medium get greater.

The lengths of wires in the packaging structures are dependent on the configurations of the connections between levels of the packaging hierarchy. If a configuration is chosen as a square area, such as that shown in Fig. 6, the minimum amount of wire is used for module-to-module wiring, and the wiring loads in the x and y directions of the printed circuit are identical. Under these conditions the average length of a wire interconnecting two LSTs, one LST in one partition and the other LST in a second partition, is

$$\overline{L_{++}} \propto \sqrt{A} \geqslant (1 + V_g)^{1/2} d\, b_M^{1/2} n_{c_M}^{\Gamma/2}$$

The number of LSTs per unit area is a constant because of the assumption of fixed d. If the area of the printed circuit is very large compared to the area required to support a partition, and if DC and P are assumed zero to facilitate discussion, the number of LSTs to be connected in the printed circuit is

$$N_{LST} = \frac{A_{PC}}{d^2(1+V_g)} \frac{\overline{N_{IO}}}{N_{IO_M}} = \frac{A_{PC}}{d^2(1+V_g)} \left(\frac{b}{b_M}\right) \epsilon^{\Gamma}$$

where A_{PC} is the area of the printed-circuit card. Thus the total length of wire required per card for a given partition size is proportional to

$$\frac{A_{PC}}{d^2(1+V_g)} \left(\frac{b}{b_M}\right) \epsilon^{\Gamma} \overline{L_{++}}$$

$$\propto \frac{A_{PC}}{d(1+V_g)^{1/2}} \frac{b}{b_M^{1/2}} \epsilon^{\Gamma} n_{c_M}^{\Gamma/2}$$

$$\propto n_{c_M}^{\Gamma/2}$$

$$\simeq n_{c_M}^{1/3}$$

Under these assumptions, each time the value of n_{c_M} increases by 8, the number of xy-plane pairs required goes up by a factor of 2. Note the assumptions that ϵ is kept constant and that there are more than 10 partitions in the logic system.

1.14.3   Semiconductor Logic Components

For the last decade, the preferred embodiment of logic circuits for computer systems has been silicon integrated circuits, and it will undoubtedly be the dominant technology for at least another decade. The realization of logic systems in highly integrated silicon semiconductor circuits has lead to distinct forms of physical design. Figure 9 shows in graphic form the range of design options available within this technology. "Degrees of freedom" spans the range from the situation in which the class of structure under consideration may be fixed in all its attributes, through the situation in which a selection may be made among fixed alternatives, to one in which complete freedom of design may be exercised. The hierarchy of physical design level ranges from materials to circuit interconnection or wiring. Logical representations of system designs usually do not progress any lower in definition than the interconnection of unit logic circuits. The three areas of the two-dimensional space subtended by the available options and level of design may be classified as custom designs, array designs, and programmable logic arrays. Each design will be discussed in turn.

Custom Designs

In the custom design of silicon integrated logic systems, all design levels down to the selection of materials and processing steps are assumed to be available as design variables to be optimized for each specific design. In memory array components, the custom design approach is usually used in adjusting all elements of the design to optimize cost, performance, reliability, size, and power. Rarely is the custom approach used in its pure form in realizing logic components, because of the amount of design effort involved. Early microprocessor designs and to some extent register stacks and local high-speed storage within large logic systems may be considered as examples of custom logic designs. As the level of integration increases, it is becoming more and more difficult to contemplate complete custom design of logic systems. Portions of semiconductor components may still be done by custom design techniques, while the entire design of the overall part may be done in one of the following fashions.

Gate Arrays

In logic system implementation in the gate array environment, shown in Fig. 10, the degrees of freedom in design are restricted in comparison to custom designs. The design of the interconnection of a fixed array of elements represents the only freedom of design. Circuits or other functional parts form a finite set from which a selection may be made for any specific design, while devices within the circuits and the selection of the process and materials are fixed by the technology. One particular implementation of this design methodology especially suited to implementation of unit logic system designs is the logic gate array. One example of this structure will be used to illustrate this design option. Figure 10 illustrates a fixed pattern into which the cells may be placed. The pattern, number, and physical location of the cells are fixed by the technology. During design, the designer selects from a fixed set of logical elements which should correspond to the elements of the lowest level of logic design, places them in the available sites in the array, and then interconnects them according to the desired function dictated by his logical design. The result of this implementation for the design given

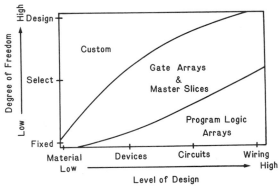

Fig. 9   Logic chip design.

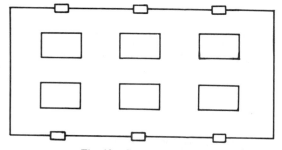

Fig. 10 Gate array chip.

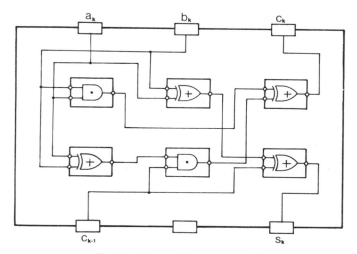

Fig. 11 Binary adder gate array chip.

in Figure 2 may take the form shown in Figure 11. Variations in gate arrays include: a more restrictive array in which the physical sites and the function of each cell are given by the technology, wiring of the cells being the only variable; a more permissive design in which the size and function of each cell may be varied and only minor restrictions are given as to their placement; and an array design, which is becoming more useful in higher levels of integration, in which each cell itself may be a custom, array, or PLA design with substantial function. This design methodology then becomes hierarchial in much the same way that logic design is; higher-order cells, called macros, are made from lower-order cells on the same physical part. This extension of this concept can be carried to more than two levels. A binary adder gate array chip is shown in Fig. 11.

PLAs*

A PLA may be considered a custom designed physical part in which the logic function performed by the part is implemented only by varying the interconnection structure of the part in a trivial way, by making or breaking a fixed number of interconnections in an ordered structure similar to an array of memory storage elements. The PLA allows physical design to proceed without the necessity of knowing the detailed logical design of the system in which it is to be employed. In this sense, it is an optimum physical realization of logic systems as the level of integration increases in component manufacture. The higher the level of physical design and integration and the more universal the part is in logical system design, the more optimum is the match that may be obtained in the logical to physical translation.

*See also Vol. 1, Sec. 7.4, as well as Sec. 1.9.4 in this volume.

Trade-offs

Trade-offs are made in selecting the methodologies described in any particular realization. Custom designs are the most complete in optimizing for performance, size, reliability, and power requirements; however, they require proportionally longer design times and generate physical embodiments that have very restrictive applications. PLAs, on the other extreme, are the most universal and have much broader applicability but are not optimized for size, performance, or power in any single application. Gate array designs represent a compromise.

BIBLIOGRAPHY

A. J. KHAMBATA, *Introduction to LSI*, Wiley, New York, 1969.
C. G. BELL and A. NEWELL, *Computer Structures: Readings and Examples*, McGraw-Hill, New York, 1971.

1.15 RELIABILITY, AVAILABILITY, AND SERVICEABILITY

William C. Carter

1.15.1 Dependable Computing

This article, with its bibliography of books and symposia proceedings, attempts to aid engineers in creating their own dependable systems. References for specific statements will not be given, since the material can be found in many of the books and proceedings.

A *failure* of a system occurs when that system does not perform its service as specified. An internal state is *erroneous* if there are circumstances in which further processing by the normal algorithms will lead to a failure. A *fault* is a mechanical or algorithmic construction such that this construction will cause the system to assume an erroneous state. The preceding definitions include faults due to inadequate specifications, program bugs, algorithmic flaws, and erroneous hardware designs as well as the standard hardware component faults due to aging or environment. The goal of dependable computing is to detect errors, find and overcome the fault that caused the error, and resume system operation without a failure.

1.15.2 Relationship between Faults and Errors

The lack of a direct connection between the occurrence of faults and the occurrence of the associated errors is a fundamental difficulty in reliability, availability, and serviceability (RAS) theory. Physical faults are classified by (1) their duration—permanent or transient; (2) their value—determinate or indeterminate; and (3) their extent—local (independent) or distributed (correlated, multiple). The usual theory assumes that physical faults are single, permanent, determinate [stuck-at-1 (s-a-1) or stuck-at-0 (s-a-0)], randomly occurring, independent malfunctions which affect module inputs or outputs or logic gate inputs or outputs only. The effect of such faults on an AND gate $f = xyz$ is shown in the following table.

Input: x y z	Output: f	Fault Description	Output After Fault
0 0 0	0	Any input s-a-1	0
0 0 1	0	x or y s-a-1	0
		z s-a-0	0
0 1 1	0	x s-a-1	1
		y or z s-a-0	0
1 1 1	1	Any input s-a-0	0

If f is s-a-1, then seven out of eight input combinations will cause an error, any input s-a-0 and the output s-a-0 are indistinguishable, and cause an error in one out of eight cases. Each input s-a-1 causes an error in one out of eight cases. Dually, for an OR gate $g = x + y + z$, any input s-a-1 and the output s-a-1 are indistinguishable and cause an error in one out of eight cases. Each input s-a-1 causes an error for a single input pattern, and the output s-a-0 causes an error in seven out of eight cases.

The multilevel circuit $f = \bar{x}(y + z)$ can be implemented as in Fig. 1. To test for y s-a-v (either 0 or 1), the erroneous signal at the output of the OR gate must be propagated to the output circuit output f. From the previous example, p will have the same value as y only if $z = 0$, and f will have the same value as p only if $q = 1$. Tracing q back to the input shows that $x = 0$. Thus the input pattern

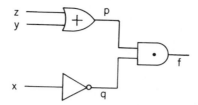

Fig. 1   Multilevel logic circuit.

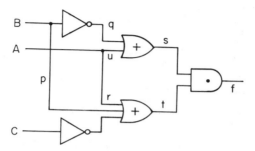

Fig. 2   More complex logic circuit.

$x = y = z = 0$ with output $f = 0$ tests y for s-a-1. It also tests z, p, and f for s-a-1. The input pattern $x = z = 0$, $y = 1$ with output $f = 1$ tests y for s-a-0. It also tests p and f for s-a-0, and x for s-a-1. The same technique proves that there is one pattern which shows that y (or z or p) is s-a-1, and one pattern each which shows that y or z is s-a-0; three patterns each show x or q s-a-0 or 1; p s-a-0 or f s-a-0 or f s-a-1 is shown by five patterns.

This simple example shows that although faults may be static, errors are produced only if the input conditions propagate the effects of the fault to an output. Thus all errors are intermittent, and all faults have intermittent manifestations.

The circuit $f = (A + \bar{B})(A + B + C)$, shown in Fig. 2, has the test set $A = B = 1$, C any value; $A = B = C = 0$; $A = 0$, $B = C = 1$; $A = B = 0$, $C = 1$; and $A = C = 1$, $B = 0$. It tests all inputs, the output, and internal lines s and t. The input A fans out to gate inputs u and r, which are tested. The input B fans out to gate inputs q and p; q is tested, as is p s-a-1. The line p s-a-0 cannot be tested, as the test inputs must be $B = 1$, $A = 0$, and $C = 1$. Now $(A + \bar{B}) = 0$, so $f = 0$ regardless of p's value.

Designing circuits with fan-out all of whose lines cannot be tested is easy. Without circuit fan-out, tests for all gate inputs and outputs can be found.

1.15.3   Architectural Techniques to Achieve High RAS

The two basic approaches are fault avoidance and fault tolerance. Fault avoidance attempts to assure reliability by elimination of the causes of faults. In fault tolerance, faults are expected to occur, but their effects are counteracted.

The principal hardware fault avoidance technique is to develop reliable components by careful analysis of possible physical faults, conservative design, and component burn-in. The components are packaged to screen out expected forms of interference and environmental stresses, and tested to ensure that they are fault free. Software fault avoidance techniques use extensive testing or verification.

Fault-tolerant design approaches may be divided into two types, static or dynamic. In static redundancy, the effect of a fault is masked by permanent concurrent operations. In dynamic redundancy, the algorithms and the set of modules in use varies depending on the number of detected faults. Recovery, the continuation of system operation with data integrity, is performed after error detection.

Fundamental techniques for static redundancy are duplication and comparison, two-out-of three voting [often called triple modular redundancy (TMR)], or coding. Storage and data transmission are usually checked using parity, or single-error-correcting, double-error-detecting codes (see Vol. 2, Sec. 2.16). Using codes adds to the cost of the computer by increasing word length, and by adding checking circuits and also the circuits to report and control the results of checking.

The basic design specification for dynamic recovery requires the following: (1) all errors should be detected, their existence signaled, and their contamination of data restricted; (2) the system status information before error must be determined; and (3) functions must be rescheduled and operation restarted. Recovery control uses a combination of hardware and software, and is an important part of the system design.

1.15.4 Static Redundancy

The necessary procedures to apply static redundancy can be best shown by an example. Consider TMR, or two-out-of-three voting. A TMR voter circuit has three inputs, and its output has the logic value of the majority of the inputs. A voter between modules contains one voter circuit for each module input. As shown in Fig. 3, TMR configurations have one or three voters between modules. The module, voter, and configurations a and b reliabilities are $R, R_v, R_a = R_v R^2(3-2R)$ and $R_b = R_v^2 R^2(3-2RR_v)$ respectively. Figure 4 shows that the simplex system is best when the points defined by values of R and R_v lie below the lower curves. Otherwise, $R_a \geqslant R$ and $R_b \geqslant R$. The minimum value of R_v is $\frac{8}{9}$, on both $R_a = R$ and $R_b = R$. If a TMR configuration is to be used for greater reliability, then $R_v > \frac{8}{9}$ and $R_v > R$ for configuration a.

If a module is bad initially, the TMR system will fail whenever one of the two remaining good modules fails. In this case the TMR reliability is less than the module reliability. To avoid this in the Saturn V Launch Vehicle, the configuration used was TMR/simplex; in addition to the voters, each pair of lines used as inputs to the voters was compared. This allowed testing each module to be tested, so it could be shown before launch that all modules were working. During operation, if one module was consistently in error, it and another module were disconnected, further improving the system reliability.

When TMR is used to increase the reliability of modules containing sequential circuits, a transient fault may cause an erroneous state. Even though the transient fault disappears, the sequence of module states may continue to be erroneous. Then a fault in another processor will cause TMR system failure. Since a major reason for using TMR is to overcome short transients, during normal operation each replicated processor must frequently receive a synchronizing sequence to reset any possible erroneous states.

The steps to follow when designing for static redundancy are as follows. First, variations of the proposed scheme must be mathematically analyzed to determine the optimum. Second, the hypotheses assumed in the mathematical analysis must be shown to hold in practice. Finally, operational conditions must be considered.

In summary, the use of static hardware redundancy is based on the assumption that failures of the redundant modules are independent. Other difficulties are the cost, the difficulty of ascertaining that the components are initially operating correctly, the difficulty of testing and repair, and the absence of warning when the redundant system finally fails. The advantages of static redundancy are its conceptual simplicity and its instant action, entirely transparent to the user.

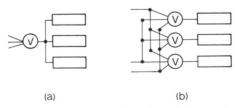

(a)　　　　　　　　　　(b)

Fig. 3 Triple modular redundancy configurations: (*a*) one voter; (*b*) three voters.

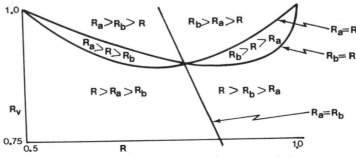

Fig. 4 Relationships among TMR reliabilities.

1.15.5 Dynamic Redundancy

As stated earlier, dynamic redundancy depends on error detection, fault isolation, determination that data are valid, then the restarting of operation at the correct place. Reliability evaluation is as important for dynamic redundancy as for static redundancy, but it is more difficult. In the classical standby spare configuration, connections go from each sending module to each receiving module, and status register connections determine which sending module inputs are used by the receiving modules. Each module should contain the switching circuitry needed for its part in computer system operation and the checking circuitry needed to determine if a faulty component has caused an error. The status register must work correctly. The reliability depends on the active circuit failure rate λ, the number of spares s, the standby circuit failure rate σ, and the coverage c. The coverage is the conditional probability that if an error occurs, the system will recover. If the module reliabilities satisfy the exponential distribution, the configuration reliability R is

$$R = e^{-\lambda T} \sum_{k=0}^{s} \binom{(\lambda/\sigma)+k-1}{k} c^k (1-e^{-\sigma T})^k$$

$$< \left[\frac{e^{-\sigma T}}{1-c(1-e^{-\sigma T})} \right]^{\lambda/\sigma} < 1$$

No matter how many spares, perfect coverage is never attained. Since it is advantageous to repair the module that has failed as soon as possible, the system should be designed so that one module can be repaired while the others are in use.

As an example, consider the popular case of one spare. Now, $R = e^{-\lambda T}[1+(c\lambda/\sigma)(1-e^{-\sigma T})]$. Again, λ is the sum of the failure rates for the original simplex module, the switching circuitry, the checking circuitry, and any built-in test circuitry, which together compose the circuitry for the modules in the standby spare system. To get the true reliability, one must multiply R by the reliability of the status register. But in this case the register is small and can easily be made redundant (TMR), and so this contribution to the reliability will be disregarded. The mean time between failure is

$$\text{MTBF} = \int_0^\infty R \, dt = \frac{1}{\lambda} + \frac{c}{\lambda+\sigma}$$

If one module can be repaired while the other is running, and both modules have the same failure rate,

$$\text{MTBF} = \frac{(2+c)(1+r_1)\lambda + \mu}{(1+r_1)\lambda[2\lambda(1+r_1)+\mu(1-c)]}$$

which is higher than the case of no repair, as long as the amount of extra circuitry for repair ($r_1\lambda$) is small.

Some problems of detection and checking may be bypassed by using the TMR operation of three units with standby spares, called hybrid redundancy. The TMR voting unit has disagreement detectors on each pair of lines, and when a unit is is disagreement with the others, it is switched out. The reliability formula with n modules ($n-3$ spares) is

$$R_{\text{hybrid}} = R_v \{ 1-(1-R)^{n-1}[1+(n-1)R] \}$$

1.15.6 Comparison of Configuration Reliabilities

Comparing the reliability attributes of different systems is difficult, since reliabilities are probabilities and have little intuitive meaning. A plan for system operation may assume periodic repair of faults before failure at intervals of length T, and repair of system failure when it occurs. In this case, a meaningful measure to use for comparison of configuration reliabilities is mean time before first failure (MTFF), defined as $\text{MTFF} = (\int_0^T R \, dt)/1 - R(T)$. The following table indicates the relationship between these measures for the TMR and simplex systems, under the assumptions that the voter has $\frac{1}{8}$ the circuitry in the module with reliability R.

R	R_v	R_b	$(\text{MTFF}/T)_{\text{simplex}}$	$(\text{MTFF}/T)_{\text{TMR}}$
0.774	0.968	0.844	3.90	5.55
0.842	0.979	0.918	6.06	12.7
0.911	0.988	0.972	10.8	35.7
0.956	0.994	0.993	22.2	131.

Compare these results with those for a system with one spare, with 20% added circuitry for switching, checking and testing.

$R_{simplex}$	R		$(MTFF/T)_{simplex}$	$(MTFF/T)_{one\ spare}$	
	$c = 0.95$	$c = 0.99$		$c = 0.95$	$c = 0.99$
0.774	0.9402	0.9472	3.90	13.0	13.8
0.842	0.9576	0.9637	6.06	28.4	29.4
0.911	0.9840	0.9855	10.8	81.9	85.0
0.956	0.9947	0.9967	22.2	344.	376.

The standby system has better potential if c is high enough and the added circuitry is small.

1.15.7 Detection, Diagnosis, and Recovery

To be successful, recovery strategy must be an initial system specification, and be guided by mathematical analysis at all stages of design. Improving coverage is the main goal. The most sophisticated recovery methods are only as good as the fault detection procedures which initiate their action. All major components must be self-contained and separated from each other by well-defined simple interfaces. For example, a code may be defined for each subunit interface and a check added which will detect the errors caused by the expected faults. Examples are parity checks, k-out-of-n checks, and comparison checks. Self-checking checking circuits have been designed for these and other codes.

Other types of checks test that information has expected properties. For example, storage areas are properly addressed, or data have the proper type. The choice of checking type is made by considering whether analyzing the effect of a class of physical faults in a computer is easier than determining the set of all important errors for that computer. Combining both types of checks is frequently done. Remember, an overlooked fault remains latent and may cause a succession of undetected errors (two errors defeat a parity check).

An independent interval timer that causes an error trap when it becomes zero and can be reset by the operating machine will signal unanticipated errors and is the best defense against catastrophic faults.

General guidelines for checker placement are: (1) the error should be detectable before it corrupts other information; (2) errors should be locatable to a replaceable unit; and (3) the cost should be minimized. Containment of erroneous information is achieved by using the error signal to interrupt the running procedure before the destruction of the essential parts of the previous state. Saving this state will aid later diagnosis.

Software testing routines can be used to replace or supplement hardware detection. The design trade-offs are between the cost and speed of checking circuits and the cost and flexibility of software checks. Supplemental software testing is frequently used to test maintenance logic, noncritical functions, or redundant hardware present for fault tolerance.

Diagnostic tests are called after an error is signaled, to locate the fault to a replaceable unit. To do this effectively, two facilities are necessary. The first is to have available information about the system state when the error occurred, as stated above. Second, the number of circuit elements that are accessible to direct program control and interrogation must be as large as possible. The interval between points at which the system state status can be determined must contain as few intermediate system states as possible. Microdiagnostics satisfy these conditions well. In microprogrammed units, the control store should be organized so that part of it can be used for microdiagnostic routines called from the operating level.

The necessary hardware efforts for recovery can be quickly stated. For transient errors, the first standard technique is retry. During the operation of an instruction (microinstruction) the module state at the beginning of the previous instruction is saved until the propagation of error signals from the checking circuits indicates no error. The amount of extra storage required is not great, but determining the propagation of the error signals requires careful design. If an error is detected, the computer saves the appropriate state information in a protected area for later analysis, then attempts to reexecute the previous instruction. If successful, the computer operation proceeds; if unsuccessful, the process described above is usually repeated a specified number of times before a complete diagnostic procedure begins. For permanent errors, after diagnosis, if standby redundancy is being used, the faulty unit is replaced by a spare, and repair begins if possible. If the redundancy is unit removal with degraded performance, the unit is disconnected, and repair begins.

Backward error recovery (checkpoint/restart) procedures are now begun. These techniques place the system in a state from which consistent processing can proceed without incurring the error that has just been diagnosed. It involves backing up one or more of the processes of the system to a previous state (usually called a checkpoint) before attempting to continue operation.

1.15.8 Recent Developments

Microprocessors, LSI modules and PLAs are widely available. These modules are more reliable than the modules they replace as long as the system functions remain approximately the same. However, no fault model exists which is generally accepted. For LSI, stuck-at-v faults are only one of the important classes of faults. The fault of two wires shorted together is becoming more common. Depending on the circuit technology, shorts act as logical AND or logical OR, and the circuit function is thus changed from $f(a, b, ...)$ to $g(a, b, c, ...)$. Shorts occur frequently between module input lines, and capacitance causes interference between lines. These faults not only cause errors, but also affect the detection of faults in other fault classes.

The increased logic facilities available have usually resulted in increased system function and complexity, making design faults more important. Similarly, greater program complexity has made program design faults more important. Unfortunately, no good methods for reducing the effect of design faults have been found.

Most current proposals for high-RAS systems use distributed processing. The advantages are that units are applied to a small part of the problem, changes are relatively easy, growth is simple, the system is flexible, and adverse environments are more easily handled. The difficulties are in communication and in determining system integrity.

As an example of such new techniques, the SIFT (software-implemented fault-tolerance) computer consists of a set of independent general-purpose computing units, each with its own processor and memory. Error detection is achieved by software voting on the outputs of replicated tasks (replicated one to six times, depending on circuitry). After error detection, software damage assessment and reconfiguration is carried out.

1.15.9 Conclusions

The key to successful application of protective redundancy is the systematic and balanced selection of fault tolerance techniques that complement and reinforce the most appropriate selection of fault avoidance techniques. The basic principles seem simple, but their successful application to real problems requires tremendous attention to detail and constant system evaluation if the desired specifications are to be met. Faults must be carefully traced through all circuits, including the redundant circuits added to give system fault tolerance. Although a system might make extensive use of redundancy, unless the software or hardware mechanisms that manage the redundancy are correct, the system will still be unreliable. Similarly, the formulation and use of elaborate reliability models is to little avail if it cannot be assured that these models actually reflect the behavior of the system.

BIBLIOGRAPHY

T. ANDERSON and B. RANDELL (eds.), *Computing Systems Reliability, an Advanced Course*, Cambridge University Press, New York, 1979.

M. A. BREUER and A. D. FRIEDMAN, *Diagnosis and Reliable Design of Digital Systems*, Computer Science Press, Potomac, Md., 1976.

Proceedings of 197– *Ann. Int. Symp. Fault Tolerant Comput.* IEEE Computer Society, annual since 1971.

Proceedings of 197– *Ann. IEEE (Semiconductor) Testing Symp.* (Cherry Hill Conf.), annual since 1972.

F. F. SELLERS, M. Y. HSIAO, and L. W. BEARNSON, *Error Detecting Logic for Digital Computers*, McGraw-Hill, New York, 1968.

1.16 SPECIAL ARCHITECTURES

Philip H. Enslow, Jr.

For the purposes of this handbook, "special system designs" refers to any system differing from the basic computer organization discussed in the introduction to Sec. 1. The differences may be either in the number or type of functional units or in the interconnections and flows between these units. One such system design has been covered in Sec. 1.10.5—the introduction of a *channel* to control input and output operations.

For many years, "special architectures" was a topic closely associated with "supercomputers," owing primarily to the fact that the expense of special designs and the special hardware components with which to implement designs were appropriate only for those systems having extremely heavy computational requirements. Today, that situation has changed quite dramatically. The availability of low-cost hardware components implementing both general and special functions, which can be easily interconnected with a wide degree of flexibility, has resulted in a situation whereby special computer architectures can also be considered for even moderate-size computing installations.

1.16.1 Motivations for Special Architectures

Throughput

Throughput is evaluated by measuring the amount of data that the system can process in a given amount of time. To be of real value, the measure of throughput must consider the total processing job, including input, processing, and output of results. The most immediately obvious technique to improve throughput is to build a faster processor; however, special architecture systems often achieve this goal by introducing into the system parallelism or simultaneous operation as well as by utilizing functional units that are designed to optimize the execution of specialized tasks, such as input/output and matrix arithmetic.

System Control

It is often possible to obtain the desired values of system throughput by constructing a single, superfast processor that executes a large number of tasks concurrently in a multiprogramming environment (see Secs. 2.20 and 2.25). However, very large multiprogramming operating systems introduce problems of their own, the most important of which is the increase in complexity of system control with resultant increases in overhead and decreases in reliability. This is especially true when there are time constraints imposed on the execution of some of the processing activities. If the overall processing job can be partitioned into separate tasks that have very little interaction with one another, the problems of system control and the system resources that have to be devoted to that function can be greatly reduced by designing a system in which the different tasks are executed on separate processors that communicate and/or interact with one another only to maintain some basic synchronization of activities.

Simplified Programming

For reasons somewhat similar to those cited above for system control, it is also possible to simplify the programming tasks, especially the development and implementation of the operating systems, if the job is partitioned into small, disjoint tasks. Special systems architectures can also simplify programming of applications by providing hardware designed to perform specific functions, such as matrix or floating-point arithmetic and Fourier transforms. These special hardware units effectively take the place of complex subroutines.

Ease of Incremental Growth

If the total job to be done can be partitioned appropriately, and if increases in work load require only the execution of more of the disjoint pieces of the program, it is often possible to design a system that can be expanded very easily by adding additional processing units. Unfortunately, it is usually not possible to partition the entire job into such separate, noninteracting pieces.

Reliability and Availability

An obvious motivation for the use of a special architecture containing multiple processing units is to increase the overall system reliability and availability through redundancy. These techniques are discussed in Sec. 1.15.

Summary

It should be obvious that the primary application of special architectures is in areas in which the overall processing job can be partitioned into separate tasks that have only low levels of interaction with other tasks or into tasks that can be executed more effectively by special-purpose hardware. If the work to be done is a single, monolithic job in which all tasks are tightly bound one to another, and the job contains no appreciable amount of code that can benefit from special hardware, then special architecture systems are usually not very appropriate, and increases in "performance" can usually be obtained just as effectively from the utilization of a faster, general-purpose processor.

1.16.2 Operational Characteristics of Special Architectures

Before proceeding with a discussion of specific examples of special architectures, it is useful to describe the general classification schemes that may be applied to such systems. Note that a single system might fall into more than one of the classifications given below.

Parallel Operations: Simultaneous and / or Concurrent

Simultaneous operation refers to two streams of execution that are proceeding independently of each other, at least to the extent that they share no resources during execution. In this situation, it can truly be said that events in the separate streams take place *at the same instant*. On the other hand, it is also possible to have two streams of activities that are executed *concurrently* with one another. That is, events from the different streams of actions take place *during the same interval* of time. Concurrent operation often involves the sharing of some resource, either hardware, software, or data.

Obviously, in order to have simultaneous operation in a system, there must be more than one set of processing hardware. This replication of hardware may occur at the highest level—multiple-computer systems with each component capable of independent operation. If only a portion of the complete computer is replicated, (e.g., all functional units except the central memory), a tightly coupled multiprocessor might result if suitable control software is provided. If only a smaller portion of the system, such as the ALU, is replicated, an array or vector processor results, depending on how the various arithmetic units are interconnected and interact with one another. Another example of parallel operation that is discussed below is the pipeline system, in which portions of the arithmetic and control units are divided into separate parts, such as the positions along an automotive assembly line.

Specialized Operations

Special architectures may include functional components or units designed to perform single specialized tasks in a highly efficient manner (e.g., input/output processors, fast Fourier transform processors, and signal processors).

A large number of combinations of the foregoing categories is possible. One that is discussed below is an associative processor.

Modes of Operation

As pointed out below in the section on array and vector processors, "special architectures" are often characterized more by their mode of operation than by any specific hardware organization. The terms that are commonly encountered when describing the mode of operation of a processor are discussed below.

Serial Processing. Serial processing of data is directly analogous to serial transmission of data. A single stream of data is processed, and it is not necessary that the same operations be performed on successive units of data.

Parallel Processing. There are two or more streams of data, not necessarily independent, which are processed *simultaneously*. In the general case, the operations being performed on the streams of data need not be identical nor even necessarily directly related to each another.

Array Processing. Array processing refers to operations performed on arrays of data. In such a system, identical or very closely related operations are performed on adjacent data elements in the array. In addition, there may be direct interaction between the processing activities on individual elements. In order to achieve high performance, array processors usually contain some degree of parallelism or replication in their hardware; however, that is not an essential characteristic of a system performing array processing.

Vector or String Processing. A stream of data is processed, and the operations to be performed on successive data elements in the vector or string are identical. There may be parallel operations supported by the hardware, as discussed in the next paragraph.

Pipeline Processing. Pipeline processing refers to a mode of operation in which the basic steps in the arithmetic operations are performed by separate hardware components. A stream of data elements is processed by moving it through these hardware components.

Associative Processing.   Associative processing might be considered a subclass of array processing; however, in associative processing, the data elements to be processed are selected by values or attributes of the data elements themselves and not by their physical location within the array.

Instruction and Data Stream Categories

Another characterization technique based on the operation of the system describes the number of instruction streams being executed and the number of data streams being processed.

SISD: Single Instruction Stream/Single Data Stream.   The basic computer structure discussed in the Introduction to Sec. 1 is the classic example of an SISD architecture. As can be seen in Fig. 1*a*, SISD implies a single stream of instructions flowing from the memory unit to the control unit and a single stream of data flowing from the memory through the ALU back to the memory.

Even though there are additional instruction and data paths present in the basic computer with an input/output channel, the only paths that are considered for the instruction and data stream classification scheme are those in the central processor pertaining to the memory, ALU, and control units.

SIMD: Single Instruction Stream/Multiple Data Streams.   In this type of system, shown in Fig. 1*b*, all of the ALUs perform identical operations on multiple, separate data streams. Vector and array processors might be examples of SIMD machines.

MIMD: Multiple Instruction Streams/Multiple Data Streams.   If both the ALU and the control unit are replicated, a system may be organized such that there are multiple instruction streams and multiple data streams present, as in Fig. 1*c*. A multiprocessor is an example of an MIMD system.

MISD: Multiple Instruction Streams/Single Data Stream.   As mentioned earlier, parallelism may also be introduced into a system by partitioning the ALU and the control unit into separate portions that function like a pipeline. If this is done, the system has s single data path with effectively

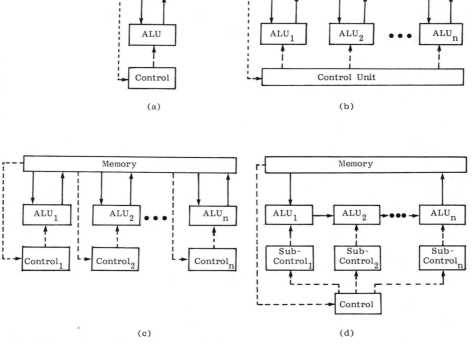

Fig. 1   Instruction and data stream classification: (*a*) SISD; (*b*) SIMD; (*c*) MIMD; (*d*) MISD.

multiple instruction paths (Fig. 1*d*). A pipeline processor might be considered an example of an MISD system.

1.16.3 Interconnection Techniques and Topologies

The techniques utilized to interconnect the functional units of the computer form the basis on which "computer organization" is usually described. What is being referred to here is the type of bus structures utilized and the topology or organization of those buses. Within the computer itself, where there are short distances and very high transfer-rate requirements, bus structure can be categorized into three basic topologies: the time-shared bus, crossbar switch, and multiport memory. Topologies that apply more to the communication paths established *between* complete systems rather than internal buses are trees, rings or loops, and meshes.

Shared Bus Organization

The simplest method by which the different functional units of a computer system can be interconnected is the single time-shared bus (Fig. 2*a*) (see Sec. 1.13). All of the functional units share a common interconnection path. Any unit can transfer data to any other unit; however, *only one* transfer can be taking place at any one time, and the system must include the means for bus allocation and control. One variation is illustrated in Fig. 2*b*, in which an additional bus has been introduced. Obviously, in such a system, two transfers can be taking place simultaneously; however, there is also a large increase in the amount of control that is necessary to control bus usage. Blocking of transfers may still occur, since all functional units cannot transfer data simultaneously.

Although smaller systems provide for the transfer of data directly from a processor to the I/O, such paths are not normally implemented into the larger systems, which utilize powerful input/output processors to control the interfaces to the I/O devices (see Sec. 1.10.2). In those systems, the primary data paths are between the central processors and the memories and between the I/O processors and the memories. If the number of buses in the system is increased to the point where there is one available at all times for each memory, the resulting interconnection topology is known as a crossbar switch.

Crossbar Switch

The crossbar switch (see Fig. 2*c*) provides for the simultaneous transfer of data to or from all of the memory units present in the system. Blocking may still occur when two processors wish to utilize the same memory unit simultaneously; however, the crossbar switch does provide for the maximum number of transfers possible with a given number of memory units.

The drawback to the crossbar switch is the complexity of the hardware required to control the allocation of each of the buses connected to the memory units. This control hardware must be replicated at each intersection in the crossbar switch.

Multiport Memories

If the control logic that is distributed throughout the cross-points in the crossbar switch is concentrated within the memory units, a multiport memory system topology results (Fig. 2*d*). It might well be argued, correctly, that the same amount of control logic is required for either the crossbar switch or the multiport memory; however, there are other factors to be considered, such as the capability to expand the system more easily. These are discussed in more detail in Refs. 4 and 5.

Tree or Star

Although some of the interconnection topologies described above might also be utilized to interconnect separate computers through communications links, a number of additional topologies are also utilized for such external connections.

The first of these is the tree (Fig. 2*e*), in which additional forking or splitting of the communication paths is allowed at each level of the tree. If only one level of splitting is allowed in the tree, a star topology results (see Fig. 2*f*).

Loop or Ring

If a *single* closed path is established connecting all the nodes or computers, a loop or ring results (Fig. 2*g*).

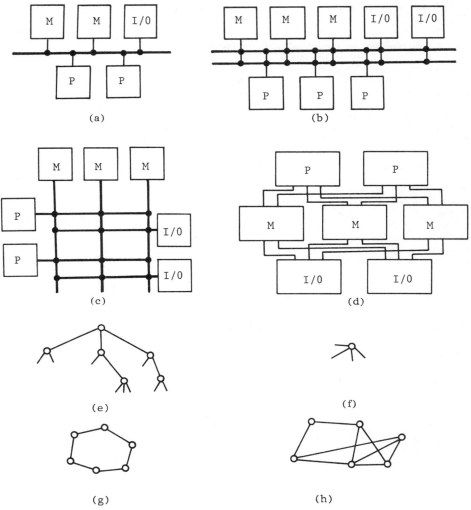

Fig. 2 Interconnection topologies. (*a*) shared bus; (*b*) multiple shared buses; (*c*) crossbar switch; (*d*) multiport memories; (*e*) tree; (*f*) star; (*g*) loop or ring; (*h*) mesh. P, processor unit; M, memory unit; I/O, I/O unit.

Mesh

If multiple paths between the nodes are permitted, and if the topology includes multiple loops, the resulting structure is known as a mesh (Fig. 2*h*).

1.16.4 "Single-Computer" Special Architectures

Input/Output Operations

One area of computer operations offering high potential for the introduction of parallelism is input/output. These operations, which proceed at much slower transfer rates than those applicable to the other functional units of the computer, are usually asynchronous with the operation of the rest of the system. They present a heavy load to the central processor if the central processor control unit is responsible for the detailed, low-level control of the input/output operation and if the path for data entering or leaving the system is through the ALU. In that case, all processing must cease during input/output operations. Two approaches that have been taken to improve this situation have been direct memory access (DMA) and the input/output channel. These are discussed in Sec. 1.10.5.

It is possible to extend the concept of parallelism in input/output operations even further by including multiple channels or input/output processors in the system. Such a technique can be of great benefit when there is a large amount of I/O activity within the system compared to the amount of processing that must be done on the data.

Multiple Sets of Registers

When a computer system is operating in an environment producing a large number of asynchronous interrupts, the system must frequently execute a context change (see Sec. 1.2). That is, the processor control unit must interrupt the program that it is currently executing, save the partial results and other information required to restart the program at the point of interruption (e.g., instruction counter, index registers, arithmetic registers, etc.), and then load the machine registers with appropriate values to initiate the interrupt-handler routine. This process of frequent context switching also occurs in generalized multiprogramming systems. One architectural technique that has been utilized to speed up this process is providing multiple sets of registers, so that one set can be devoted to the applications program being executed, while a completely different set can pertain to the interrupt handler, with additional sets assigned to other appropriate software components. In this situation it is not necessary to unload and load registers to switch from one process to another.

Multiple Functional Units

The inclusion of a specialized functional unit or multiple copies of "general-purpose" functional units has become a very common example of special architectures. Such systems are especially easy to assemble when the basic organization of the processor is bus oriented. Some of the functional units that have been added to systems to create special architectures are quite powerful in their own right and perhaps should not be called basic functional units: for example, components that perform a complete vector addition or some other form of array or vector processing.

Multiple Arithmetic Units

If the accepted definition of a computer requires that it consist of both an ALU *and* a control unit, a system containing only one control unit but multiple copies of the ALU (see Fig. 1b) might still be called a "single computer." It is obvious that such a hardware organization can provide a large amount of parallelism if there is work to be done for which each data element must receive identical processing.

Specialized Functional Units

Specialized functional units are becoming extremely popular as a means to improve the performance of basic computer systems. Floating-point operations can be implemented in hardware; however, including such hardware capabilities in the ALU adds greatly to its cost, and such features might not be required by everyone who wishes to purchase that processor. Therefore, floating-point operations are frequently not implemented as part of the basic instruction set of a processor. Optional floating-point processors were provided as early as 1960 as a means to improve the performance of a system. Such processors are utilized in a manner similar to input/output devices. Three data elements, the two operands and the designation of the operation to be performed, are transferred to the special processor, and one data element, the resulting floating-point number, is transferred back to the central processor.

Many specialized functional units or processors have been introduced. Examples of these are fast Fourier transform processors, signal correlation processors, array processors (discussed below), and display processors.

1.16.5 Parallel Operation at Higher Levels

Although most of the special architecture systems that are being designed currently under the influence of very low cost LSI components are variations on the single-computer architectures, there are also a large number of special architectures which provide parallelism at higher levels of operation.

Multiple-Computer Systems

Two or more computers processing separate data streams certainly provide parallel operation. However, if these systems are totally disjoint and have no communication one with the other, that is certainly not a "special architecture." A very good discussion of systems consisting of multiple, interconnected processors which includes details on quantitative design issues is given in Ref. 7.

Interprocessor Communications. The communication between processors, and the processing of the messages that are transferred, can constitute a major overhead activity of the operating system in multiple computer systems. Interprocessor communication must be reliable and robust (recover quickly and easily from failures that do occur) while presenting minimal overhead to the operating system. One method that can be used to characterize the form of interprocessor communication utilized is by defining the degree of coupling present. Another is by describing the interconnection subsystem.

System Coupling. The generally accepted terms used to describe the forms of system coupling are "loose" and "tight."

1. *Loose coupling.* Two systems are said to be loosely coupled physically and/or logically if the transfers of data between the two systems are performed in the same manner as transfers between a system and its I/O.

2. *Tight coupling.* Systems that are tightly coupled physically have access to a common main memory. It is also essential that this memory be "executable memory" and that each processor can directly access memory locations in the shared memory. The physical transfer of data between the two systems is then accomplished by placing the information to be transferred in "shared" memory locations.

Tight logical coupling is not as easy to characterize as loose logical coupling. Obviously, when two processors share access to the same memory space, one may insert data directly into working storage locations of the other without the recipient being aware that a transfer has taken place. In early systems, this mode of operation was quite common; however, it was soon obvious that transferring data in this way was very dangerous. Currently accepted practice is that transfers between systems that are physically tightly coupled should be handled in the same manner as those in loosely coupled systems. That is, one system will send a "message" to the other, utilizing an agreed-upon communication "mailbox" as the transfer point. The receiving system will then move the information from the mailbox to the proper location within its own data space and process it there.

Interconnection Subsystems. The form of the interconnection subsystem must be selected after a decision is made as to the type of physical coupling to be implemented. Although any of the interconnection topologies might be utilized for loosely coupled systems, the time shared bus, crossbar, and multiport memory are obviously much more suitable for tight physical coupling.

Multiple-Computer Organizations

Attached Support Processors. An attached support processor system is one in which two computers are loosely coupled, with one of them devoted to input/output processing and the other assigned to the primary processing tasks (Fig. 3).

Multiprocessors. Multiprocessors are tightly coupled systems that share access and utilization of a common main memory as well as a common set of input/output channels and devices, while the entire system is controlled by a single, multiprocessor operating system (see Fig. 2c).

1. *Control software problems.* Certainly, the greatest deterrent to growth in the utilization of multiprocessors is the problem of designing and implementing suitable control software. Multiprocessor operating systems have characteristically incurred a large amount of operational overhead.

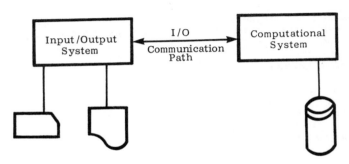

Fig. 3   Attached support processor.

In addition, these operating systems have been designed to control only a small number (two to four) of separate processors. Extending the number of processors involved adds to the complexity of the operating system, increasing both the execution overhead required and the likelihood of system failure due to failures within the control program. Although there have been some interesting proposals recently for basic improvements in the design of multiprocessor operating systems, such ideas have not yet been fully reduced to practice, so their overall applicability can only be estimated. The designer of a tightly coupled multiprocessor system should give careful consideration to the important problem of system control.

2. *System throughput.* Improvement in system throughput as a result of additional processors is a function of numerous factors. Some of these are:

What constraints are placed on data transfers by the interconnection subsystem or the utilization of a common resource such as primary memory?

What overhead is added by the control software?

How well do the characteristics of the work to be performed match the special capabilities of the hardware?

Does the organization of the tasks within the work to be done lend itself to partitioning?

Two sets of performance figures are shown below. System 1 is a common bus system, and the throughput is constrained by conflicts in access to that bus [8]. An additional processor adds almost nothing, owing to a further increase in access conflicts. System 2 is a multiport memory system in which the throughput is lowered by the effects of the control software as well as memory access [4].

| Number of | Relative Payoff | |
Processors	System 1	System 2
1	1.0	1.0
2	1.8	1.8
3	2.3	2.1
4	2.5	

Array, Vector, and Pipeline Processors

There is a large amount of confusion as to the meaning of these three terms when used to describe specific types of processors. The basic misunderstanding results from not clearly differentiating between a mode of operation or type of processing and a hardware system designed to support that specific form of processing. The "processing" point of view has been discussed above. Introduced below are some special hardware features.

Pipeline Systems. The classical example of a pipeline processor is one in which the basic arithmetic steps have been implemented by separate hardware components so that operands are passed from one state to the next (see Sec. 1.9.5). Each stage is designed to provide the optimum performance in executing a very basic operation. Figure 4 shows an example of pipelined arithmetic hardware. The paths through the hardware components to be followed by the operands when executing two different instructions are shown. The details of the FLOATING ADD (see Sec. 1.5.5) are discussed below.

Major improvements in performance for a pipeline system result when there is a series of operands on which identical operations are to be performed. Consider, for example, the floating-point addition of vectors A and B with n elements each, resulting in a new vector C. The floating addition requires the five steps described. Typical execution times for each step are also given.

1. Receive operands: 100 ns
2. Subtract exponents: 60 ns
3. Alignment of mantissas (fraction):   100 ns
4. Addition of mantissas (fraction):   120 ns
5. Normalization of results (removal of leading zeros in mantissa):   100 ns

A *single* floating addition would require at least 480 ns; however, once all the steps in the pipeline are filled with operands, a new result will be produced at each clock pulse, which could be as short an interval as 120 ns.

A very complete discussion of pipeline architectures is presented in Ref. 9.

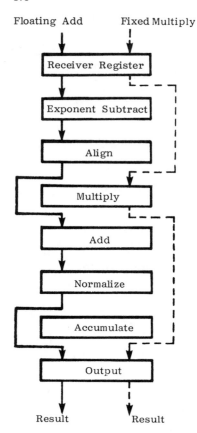

Fig. 4 Examples of the pipeline flow for two different instructions (based on the Texas Instruments Advanced Scientific Computer).

Vector Processors. Vector processors are systems that utilize hardware and software designed specifically to provide for the high-speed execution of loops, processing indexed data arrays while not lowering the performance for "nonlooping' portions of the program. Obviously, pipelining of the arithmetic functions is very effective in such systems, as well as the inclusion of multiple pipelines. Large-scale systems containing vector capabilities, such as the Cray-2, also utilize a large number of registers to hold temporary results and allow chaining of operations without intervening memory accesses.

Array Processors. It is possible to design an array processor utilizing an array of arithmetic units, as was done in the ILLIAC IV (Fig. 5; see Ref. 11). However, there are several disadvantages to this approach, in addition to the high cost and low mean time between failures that may result from the large amount of equipment involved. The primary weakness of such a system is the fact that its "power" in any application depends directly upon how well the structure of the data matches the physical structure of the array of processing elements.

Another approach is a system in which the "array processor" is a specialized functional unit operating in conjunction with a general-purpose host (Fig. 6). The programmable array processor may have its own set of peripheral devices, or it may transfer data only to and from the host. Internally, the array processor unit may contain multiple, parallel arithmetic units as well as pipelining within those execution units.

Associative / Content - Addressable Processors

"An *associative processor* can generally be described as a processor that has the following two properties: (1) stored data items can be retrieved using their content or part of their content (instead

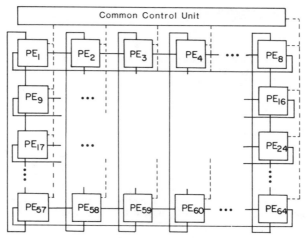

Fig. 5 Illiac IV. Solid lines, data transfer paths; dashed lines, control signal paths. Each PE (processing element) consists of an ALU and its own memory.

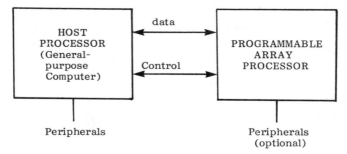

Fig. 6 Array processor as an attached unit.

of their addresses) [see Sect. 1.7.2]; and (2) data transformation operations, both arithmetic and logical, can be performed over many sets of arguments with a single instruction" [13]. Thus associative processors exhibit high degrees of parallelism in both data accessing as well as in data operations.

The conventional method of accessing data is to utilize its physical address. However, a situation often encountered in data processing is to be presented with a collection of data elements, such as a table or a general data base, with the requirement to locate the specific data element(s) within that collection that meet specific characteristics. The normal method utilized to perform this operation is to access each data element individually and to transfer it into the ALU, where the appropriate arithmetic and logical tests may be performed to determine if it meets the "search criteria." Obviously, for large collections of data, this can become a very time consuming operation. The first goal of an associative processor is to facilitate this data access, test, and retrieve operation.

To facilitate the execution of these operations, a special form of memory is often utilized (see Sec. 1.7.2). The distinctive feature of this memory is that there is processing hardware associated with *each* word of the entire memory. This special hardware might implement the comparison operations described above as well as the capability to modify the current values in the memory. Obviously, such memory is more expensive than standard, address-accessed memory. Therefore, associative processing memories are usually quite small, and if the number of data elements to be searched and/or processed exceeds the size of that memory, the complete data collection must be processed in separate batches. Content addressable memory units are currently available to install as specialized functional units on bus-organized microcomputers. A representative example with 4096 8-bit words or 16 256-byte words cost approximately $350 in 1980.

Comprehensive discussions of associative processors are presented in Refs. 6, 10, and 13.

1.16.6 Other Special Architectures

Data Base Computers

The increased utilization of data base management systems has greatly increased the interest in developing special hardware to improve their performance. In very general terms, the four activities that must be performed in such a system are:

1. Application program execution
2. Data base management
3. Input/output control
4. Device control

In the conventional, general-purpose system, the first three of these activities are performed by the host computer, with the fourth activity being supported by a device controller (Fig. 7*a*). The various approaches that have been taken to developing special data base computers consist primarily of providing additional hardware so that activities 2 and/or 3 may be removed from the central host.

The first step that might be taken is to place the data base management system and the I/O control system in a back-end processor (Fig. 7*b*). The work load on the host processor is greatly reduced;

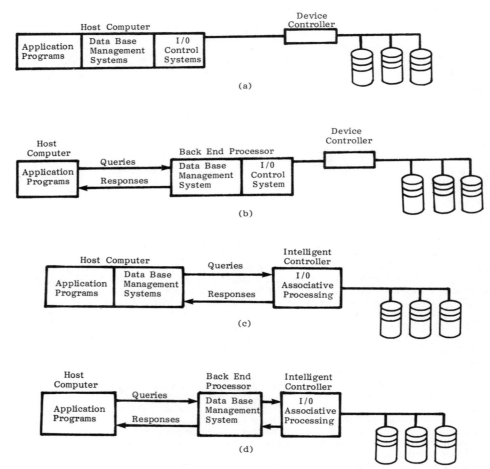

Fig. 7 Data base computer systems: (*a*) conventional general-purpose computer; (*b*) host computer with back-end data base processor; (*c*) host computer with intelligent device controller; (*d*) host computer with back-end processor and intelligent controller.

however, the overall performance is usually governed by the time required to access records on the devices. Attempts to improve the performance of the system in accessing specific records or portions of records from the storage devices have centered on the introduction of an intelligent controller which might contain built-in capabilities for performing associative processing on the records as they are read (Fig. 7c). The data base management system is still executed on the host processor. Another approach is to include a separate back end processor as well as an intelligent controller (Fig. 7d).

Multilevel Microprogramming

As discussed in Sec. 1.9.3 microprogramming may be utilized to provide more flexibility in supporting "basic" hardware operations. The conventional method for implementing microprogramming is shown in Fig. 8a, in which the microprogram that controls the basic hardware is stored in the control store, with the object program being kept in main memory. Although such a system does provide a great deal of flexibility in establishing the "machine language instruction set" of the processor, there are still a number of limitations that strongly affect the performance of such a system when it is used in an application such as general-purpose emulation. The basic hardware has a given word size and a

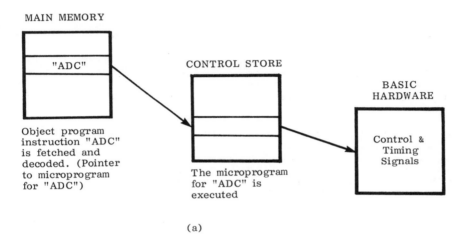

(a)

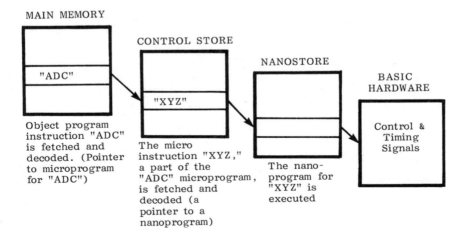

(b)

Fig. 8 Multilevel microprogramming: (a) "conventional" microprogramming; (b) nanoprogramming.

given set of operations, and the resulting overall performance can be quite poor if these are poorly matched to those of the target machine. One approach to improving this performance is the introduction of another level of microprogramming (see Sec. 1.9.3). The introduction of an additional level of programmable control, as shown in Fig. 8*b*, provides the system designer with the ability to develop a much better match between the basic hardware and the microprograms stored in the control store.

Stack Machines

The basic concepts of stack architecture are discussed in Sec. 1.1.3. The utilization of stacks for program execution has become so commonplace that it probably should not be referred to as a "special architecture"; however, there are some special aspects of stack machines that should be mentioned. Primarily, these are the utilization of stacks as the basic control mechanisms for the machine. Excellent discussions of many of the aspects of stack machines are given in Refs. 1, 2, and 3.

Language - Based Processors

It is obvious that the performance of a processor would be greatly improved if there were a better match between operations specified by the programming language and the primitive operations that are implemented in the hardware. For example, the ADD operation implemented in most processors is not a very good match to the ADD statement in COBOL when the operands are decimal values. Two approaches have been taken in improving the match between the programming language and the hardware. The first of these has been to include operations in the hardware which implement specific instructions in the source code. The second has been to build a machine that supports the complete processing operation—the execution of the operating system as well as the execution of the translated source code.

Special Instruction Set Machines.   The first examples of this type of machine were systems that included special "data processing" or "commercial" instruction sets to support the faster execution of object programs generated from COBOL statements. The primary capabilities added by these special instruction sets were the decimal arithmetic and decimal manipulation operations.

Another example of special instruction set machines were the INTERLISP machines produced by changing the microcode in some models of IBM System 360 processors.

Complete Architecture Systems.   Recently, there has been much more activity in this area as a result of the availability of low-cost microprogrammable processors that can be easily interconnected. Early examples of machines that were oriented toward specific programming systems were the APL machine and the Symbol processor; however, in the early 1980s, the major interest is in Pascal-based architectures that are specifically designed to support the execution of Pascal as well as the execution of the UCSD (University of California, San Diego) Pascal operating system. Other activity has continued in designing special processors for languages that have traditionally been very slow in execution, such as LISP.

Certainly not in the small-computer category, but of considerable importance in this area, has been the development of families of processors by Burroughs Corporation. These processors were greatly influenced by the decision to utilize ALGOL as the primary systems programming language. The hardware greatly facilitates the execution of ALGOL-type languages as well as the operating system, which is highly stack oriented.

1.16.7 Summary

Recent technological advances in the development of LSI microprocessors and other components that are extremely flexible and highly adaptable, as well as the economic trends that have accompanied these technological developments, have produced a condition in which many different forms of special architectures are both technically and economically feasible, even when the anticipated production quantities are quite small. This is in marked contrast to the previous eras of computer design, during which the high cost of design and implementation dictated high production quantities to justify economically a special architecture design, or when the performance requirements were so critical that the high cost of a single special architecture machine could be justified. When these special systems have been embedded in larger assemblies and had no direct interface to users, they have been quite successful; however, the complexities of these systems have inhibited user acceptance of special architectures.

REFERENCES

1. R. P. BLAKE, "Exploring a Stack-Architecture," *Computer*, May 1977, pp. 30–39.
2. D. M. BULMAN, "Stack Computers," *Computer*, May 1977, pp. 14–16.
3. D. M. BULMAN, "Stack Computers: An Introduction," *Computer*, May 1977, pp. 18–28.
4. P. H. ENSLOW, JR. (ed.), *Multiprocessors and Parallel Processing*, Wiley, New York, 1974.
5. P. H. ENSLOW, JR., "Multiprocessor Organization—A Survey," *Comput. Surv.*, **9**(1), 103–129 (1977).
6. C. C. FOSTER, *Content Addressable Parallel Processor*, Van Nostrand, New York, 1976.
7. B. H. LIEBOWITZ, "Multiple Processor Minicomputer Systems, Parts 1 and Part 2: Implementation," *Comput. Des.*, Part 1: Oct. 1978; Part 2: Nov. 1978, pp. 121–131.
8. D. MOSS, "Multiprocessing Adds Muscle to MicroPs," *Electron. Des.*, **24**, 238–244 (May 1978).
9. C. V. RAMAMOORTHY and H. F. LI, "Pipeline Architecture," *Comput. Surv.*, **9**(1), 61–102 (Mar. 1977).
10. K. J. THURBER and L. D. WALD, "Associative and Parallel Processors," *Comput. Surv.*, **7**(4), 215–255 (Dec. 1975).
11. K. J. THURBER, *Large Scale Computer Architecture — Parallel and Associative Processors*, Hayden, Rochelle Park, N.J., 1976.
12. K. J. THURBER, "Parallel Processor Architectures: Part 1: General Purpose Systems and Part 2: Special Purpose Systems," *Comput. Des.*, Jan. 1979, pp. 89–97, and Feb. 1979, pp. 103–114.
13. S. S. YAU and H. S. FUNG, "Associative Processor Architecture—A Survey," *Comput. Surv.*, **9**(1), 3–27 (Mar. 1977).

1.17 POWERING COMPUTER SYSTEMS

George C. Feth

Computer systems and peripheral equipment require high-quality power systems to maintain proper and reliable computer operation, to protect both the equipment and the operators from harm, and to avoid degrading the power system from which they are energized. The load requirements presented by the energy-using components of the computer include both ac loads (e.g., drive motors for fans and disk files) and dc loads (e.g., logic and memory circuitry, dc motors for capstans and servos, stepping motors, high-voltage CRT accelerating and deflecting voltages, analog circuits, print hammers, and actuators). Many of these are active loads, and the current drains of some fluctuate widely and rapidly. A well-regulated voltage supply is crucial for proper operation of most dc loads.

Functions of the power system may include: connecting to and disconnecting from the energy source, isolating the computer system from the source, protecting against overload or overvoltage or undervoltage, voltage transformation, frequency conversion (i.e., rectification and/or inversion), voltage regulation, filtering, and distribution of power.

1.17.1 Energy Source

The most common energy source is the electrical utility. For large computing systems, a separate transformer is usually used for powering only the computing system; this is to reduce the sensitivity of the computer to transients in other loads on the power system. To guard against loss of power, an uninterruptible power system (UPS) may be included in the computer power system. The energy source for the UPS may be electrical storage batteries, fuel cells, or an engine-generator, each of which converts chemical energy to electrical energy. The UPS includes an energy source, an inverter or converter to supply ac power or dc at some other voltages, and switchgear and controls. In some systems a motor-generator with a flywheel is used to protect against power transients. For portable systems, storage batteries are the usual energy source; a battery charger may be included for charging secondary cells or for operation from the utility line when it is available.

1.17.2 Converter/Regulator

Transformers are commonly used to provide both voltage transformation and electrical isolation of the computer circuits from the utility, so that the secondary can be grounded at a single point. Since the computer usually requires numerous voltages, the transformer may use multiple secondary windings to provide the various voltage levels. A common unregulated dc supply employs simply a transformer and rectifiers; the volage regulation of such a supply is the sum of line regulation, which may be of the order of 10%, and load regulation. The required degree of regulation (including ripple from incomplete filtering) varies with the application: 8 to 10% represents a fairly relaxed requirement; 3% may be required for high-performance circuitry; and sensitive analog circuits may require 1% or tighter regulation.

Ferroresonant transformers are used to supply open-loop regulation in the range 8 to 12%. A ferroresonant transformer combines a capacitor and the nonlinear (saturating) properties of the ferromagnetic core in such a way that the output voltage remains nearly constant over a range of input voltage because of the "ferroresonance" of the core and capacitor.

Linear regulators are commonly used for the tightest regulation. Series linear regulators employ a series or "pass" transistor between an unregulated voltage source and the load, to absorb the excess of the applied voltage above the desired regulated-voltage output. A feedback circuit is used to compare the output voltage with a reference voltage to form an error signal, which may be amplified and then fed to the base of the pass transistor. This regulates against both line and load variations at the point where the voltage is sensed. Integrated regulator circuits are available for a variety of voltage, current, and regulation specifications. The power efficiency of such a regulator is often quite small, especially where line-voltage and load-current variations are large. Hence series regulators are often used together with a ferroresonant transformer and rectifiers, which provide a partially regulated dc source. The efficiency of such a combined system may be of the order of 50 to 60% under favorable conditions, but can be as low as 20% for an output voltage of only a few volts. Linear regulation may also be achieved using the regulator in parallel with the load if there is sufficient series impedance in the source; this is called a shunt regulator.

Nominally dissipationless regulation can be achieved by using a switch to controllably connect and disconnect the power source to the load with a duty cycle which supplies the right average voltage; this is a time-ratio control. However, it requires reactive elements to store energy in order to maintain a smooth flow of power to the load. By using high-frequency switching, the size of reactive components can be greatly reduced. This is also a feedback-controlled regulator. Switching semiconductor devices —bipolar transistors, silicon-controlled rectifiers (SCRs), or power MOSFETs—are used as the switches. Dc-to-ac conversion without isolation is obtained using buck, boost, or buck/boost converter circuits to provide, respectively, reduction of voltage, increase of voltage, or both. [The Cuk converter (see Ref. 1) provides all of these capabilities.] For operation directly from the ac line, a line-operated converter/regulator system is used. The ac line voltage is rectified and filtered, providing unregulated dc voltage of about 200 to 400 V. A high-frequency (20 to 50 kHz) inverter converts to ac, transforms the voltage to the output level and provides isolation by means of a high-frequency transformer (ferrite), provides regulation by feedback control of the switching element, and rectifies and filters the output. Schottky-barrier rectifiers are used for the low-voltage output rectifiers to reduce the forward drop and to eliminate reverse recovery currents. Both single-ended inverters (e.g., flyback), and push-pull inverters are used. Careful attention is required to filtering and grounding to avoid radio-frequency interference (RFI) and to meet electromagnetic compatability (EMC) requirements. The cost of switching regulators is comparable to or slightly larger than that of linear regulators, and regulation is somewhat looser, albeit 3 to 8% regulation is achievable. However, switching regulators can provide power efficiencies commonly from 60 to 80%, and cooling problems are reduced.

For powering large computing systems, motor-generator sets are often used, the generator commonly being a 400-Hz three-phase alternator. Regulation at low-frequency is obtained by control of the field excitation of the alternator. In one system, for example, the regulation is extended to higher frequencies by using phase control (by means of SCRs which rectify and control the conduction interval to the load by means of their feedback-controlled firing angle—ideally, a dissipationless regulator) and shunt regulators.

All regulators have limited frequency response, their cutoff frequency being far below the frequencies that correspond to load changes in switching of the active loads; these frequency components are of the order of the reciprocal of the machine cycle or subcycle. Decoupling capacitors are used close to the loads to bypass these high-frequency components of load-current change (ΔI), and larger decoupling capacitors can be used at intermediate points in the packaging hierarchy or power distribution network for medium-frequency components, down to the cutoff frequency of the regulator itself (of the order of a few kilohertz for linear or switching regulators). In this way the regulating system is designed to provide a low output impedance over the whole frequency range of interest.

REFERENCE

1. S. CUK, "General Topological Properties of Switching Structures," *IEEE Power Electron. Specialists Conf., 1979 Record.*

BIBLIOGRAPHY

E. R. HNATEK, *Design of Solid-State Power Supplies*, Van Nostrand, New York, 1971.

1.18   DESIGNING WITH MICROPROCESSORS

Earl E. Swartzlander, Jr.

The development of microprocessors is one of the most significant events in electrical and computer engineering. By integrating memory, logic, and a programmable control unit on a single chip (or a few chips), a high level of design flexibility and computational efficiency is achieved.

This article begins with an overview of the design process, to establish a perspective of the microprocessor system design environment. Subsections on hardware design and software design follow, with an emphasis on the available components and design tools. Finally, the use of microprocessor development systems is examined; these are invaluable aids to debugging and greatly simplify system integration.

1.18.1   Overview of the Design Process*

Microprocessor system design requires a balanced mixture of closely cross-coupled hardware and software design. This departs from previous approaches, which could be (and often were) segregated into separate hardware and software activities with little or no interaction until the final system integration.

The sequencing of the major activities is shown in Fig. 1. The first step is requirements definition, which is performed jointly by the hardware and software staffs. Then design and development of the hardware and software are performed by the respective groups, with a high level of cooperation. Finally, the joint staffs perform system integration and checkout.

This process was developed in response to two basic observations: (1) closer interaction between the hardware and software groups produces better systems; and (2) changes are significantly easier to implement during the definition and design phases than in later phases.

This design process emphasizes requirements definition, which terminates with a specification design review. In this review the customer and the hardware and software groups meet to review the requirements, their interpretation by the design groups, and preliminary high-level design approaches. At the completion of the design activities, hardware and software preliminary design reviews are held among the customer and both design groups. Participation by both design groups in both of the reviews helps to ensure their close cooperation. Reviews of the specifications and the initial designs help to solidify the designs (both hardware and software) before the implementation phase. It is during implementation that seemingly small changes tend to cause significant "ripples," which often impact the entire design. A final design review after development of the hardware and software helps to minimize changes during system integration.

Even in the tasks that are performed primarily by the hardware or software groups, much intergroup cooperation is required. Development of hardware and software to facilitate fault detection and location is an integral part of the design process. Often the software group will identify weaknesses in the hardware design, and vice versa. Corrections are best done as needed, in a spirit of close cooperation, instead of waiting until design review; again, the sooner design ideas are implemented, the easier their implementation. During development, close interaction between the hardware and software teams is necessary for hardware checkout and debugging of the software.

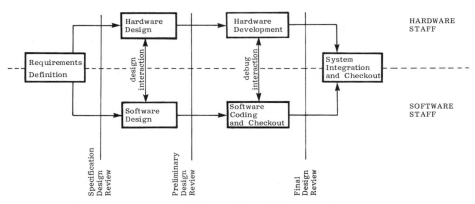

Fig. 1   Microprocessor design process.

*See also the introduction to Sec. 1.14.

In the system integration and checkout phase, the total deliverable system is assembled and tested. Teamwork in the previous phase has resulted in relatively clean hardware and software packages, with minor problems during integration. This task is often performed primarily by the software group with assistance (in hardware debugging) by the hardware group.

The approach shown here is one that has been used on a number of microprocessor systems ranging from a single processor (of roughly 100 chips and 1K instructions) to distributed processors (comprising thousands of chips and millions of instructions).

1.18.2   Requirements Definition

In developing a microprocessor system, one must ensure that the hardware and software performance capability is adequate to solve the problem. Requirements definition involves assessing the characteristics of the system problem in machine design terms. Typically, problem requirements will demand certain levels of machine throughput, word size, and memory capacity, and may also impose requirements for special functions.

Throughput

The primary measure of processor performance is throughput, which is commonly expressed as millions of operations per second (MOPS) or millions of instructions per second (MIPS). The "Gibson mix" is a well-known frequency distribution of instructions measured for general-purpose data processing [1]. It is shown in Table 1. Arithmetic comprises only 10% of the load, which is typical of many commercial data processing applications. Special-purpose processors, on the other hand, generally have operation distributions that are dominated by the arithmetic requirements, because most of the nonarithmetic operations are executed in specialized control logic. Typically, the arithmetic mix is 50 to 80% addition/subtraction and the remainder multiplication. The dominance of add, subtract, and multiply is due to the prevalence of the sum of products in signal processing and other applications of special-purpose processors.

Word Size

To analyze word size requirements in a microprocessor, one must understand the specific application. Figure 1 in the introduction to Sec. 1 shows a high-level block diagram of a typical stored program computer. There are three major paths: (1) op codes and control and timing signals from the control unit to the ALU and registers, (2) data and instructions from memory to the ALU and registers and the control unit, and (3) addresses from the control unit to memory. The path between the control unit and the ALU indicates which ALU operation is to be performed and provides timing signals. Typically, an 8-bit op code is adequate for ALU operation selection, although high-performance systems may have a higher level of parallelism and may require more lines to control instruction selection and register transfers within the ALU. Status signals are often sent to the control unit from the ALU; typically, 4 bits are used.

Data and instructions from the memory to the ALU and the control unit are often 16 bits wide. This provides adequate dynamic range for data in signal-processing systems and is a standard general-purpose minicomputer word size. High-precision data may be as wide as 32 bits (either floating point with 8-bit exponent and 24-bit mantissa, or fixed point), but the majority of microprocessor applications use 16-bit or smaller data words. The instructions to the control unit can be conveyed in 8 bits in most cases, but if the data word is wider, the extra bits allow passing literal data to the control unit.

Table 1.   Gibson Mix

Instruction	Frequency (%)
Fixed add/subtract	6
Fixed multiply	3
Fixed divide	1
Move	25
Conditional branch	20
Compare	24
Branch on character	10
Edit	4
Initiate input/output	7

The address path to memory from the control unit must be wide enough to allow direct addressing of the memory. Most 16-bit single-chip microprocessors have 20 to 24 address lines, providing direct addressing to more than 1 million words of memory. Earlier 8-bit processors often provided 16-bit addressing, which is adequate for 64K words of memory. With the decreasing cost of semiconductor memory, it is often desirable to provide more than 64K, and the 20- to 24-bit address space can provide protected memory areas and more than ample addressing for most microprocessor applications.

In microprocessor design, it is necessary to determine the width requirements for each of the major data paths of the machine. In systems that use multiple microprocessors, the data widths may increase or decrease due to a change in data precision. For example, in image processing, the input data may be 8 bits wide, which is adequate for most image data. In image enhancement, it is often desirable to compute the two-dimensional spectrum of the image and apply various filtering operations in the spectral domain. As the spectrum is computed, it may be necessary to allow the word size to increase to 12 bits to prevent excessive round-off error. The word size is further increased in the course of the filtering, but is rounded down to 8 bits for display, since the human visual system can rarely perceive differences in quality as the displayed data increases above 8 bits.

Memory

The memory requirements comprise program memory and data memory. In some situations, the memories are implemented as a single physical entity, but in others, different memories (and even different types of memory) are used. The latter situation arises in cases where the program will be fixed and thus may be implemented in a read-only memory (ROM), whereas only the data are stored in random-access, read–write memory (RAM).

Often, a large RAM will be used for program storage in the prototype system. Once the programs have been written and checked out, the requirement is known, and a ROM of the correct size or slightly greater size (to allow the addition of new programs) is provided.

1.18.3   Microprocessor Hardware

An important aspect of microprocessor design is awareness of current and future hardware technology. This section summarizes the state of the art (as of 1980) and identifies areas where future development is most likely.

Current Microprocessors

Two broad classes of microprocessors have been developed: single-chip processors and bit-slice arithmetic units. The former are one-chip central processing units which perform 4-, 8-, 12-, or 16-bit fixed-point arithmetic (likely to increase to 32 bits in the early 1980s), while the latter are universal 4-bit-wide building blocks which may be cascaded to perform arithmetic of arbitrary precision (see Sec. 1.3). In general, the single-chip processors are implemented with MOS technology and, as a result, are relatively slow (i.e., up to 1 MIPS). The bipolar bit-slice processors achieve 2 to 20 MIPS at a cost of greater system complexity.

The first microprocessor was the Intel 4004, which is a 4-bit single-chip processor. It is still used for some low-speed applications in industrial systems where low cost is the primary concern. Later single-chip microprocessors include the Fairchild F8, the Motorola 6800, the Intel 8080, and the Zilog Z-80.* These are 8-bit processors with instruction execution times on the order of 1 to 5 μs.

The basic architecture of the Intel 8080 is shown in Fig. 2. The 8-bit arithmetic logic unit (seen on the left side of the figure) has two registers, the accumulator and the temp register, associated with it. Data from off-chip (via the bidirectional data bus buffer/latch) or from the internal register array (shown on the right side of the figure) can be loaded into the accumulator or the temp register by way of the internal bus; the ALU output can be routed off-chip or into the register array for further processing. An instruction decoder and an interruptable timing and control unit are on-chip.

The 16-bit single-chip microprocessors include the Intel 8086, Motorola MC 68,000, Texas Instruments TMS 9900, and Zilog Z8000. These achieve throughputs on the order of $\frac{1}{2}$ MIPS and offer features that are similar to minicomputers.

A bit-slice microprocessor is essentially an arithmetic-logic unit combined with a register file on a single chip. A commonly used bit-slice processor is the Advanced Micro Devices AMD 2901. The architecture of the AMD 2901 is shown in Fig. 3, where the shaded lines are 4-bit-wide data buses. Basically, this chip consists of a 16-word by 4-bit register file with three ports (one for input and two for output), which is coupled to an ALU. The two register file outputs pass through a selector into the

*Although specific vendors' devices are cited, each is available from multiple sources.

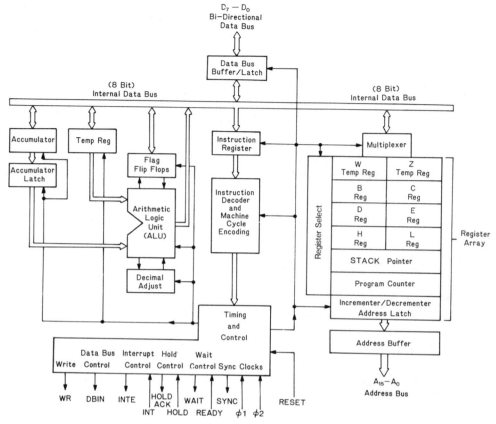

Fig. 2   Intel 8080 microprocessor architecture.

ALU inputs; the ALU output passes through a shifter to the register file. It also includes a Q register which is used in iterative multiply and divide routines and other operations.

Several new bit-slice processors are under development; for the most part they are evolutionary enhancements of existing designs. Most of the new devices are being implemented with Schottky TTL and may be expected to be comparable in speed to the machines currently available, with word size (i.e., slice width) increasing to 16 bits. The new processors will presumably be optimized for specific applications and will have features appropriate to the target application (e.g., multiple-precision arithmetic for navigation and guidance, bit manipulation for data encoding/decoding, etc.).

Microprocessor Support Functions

As a microprocessor-based system is developed, it quickly becomes evident that the microprocessor chip does not solve all the problems. Much support circuitry is required for such functions as microprogram sequencing, priority interrupt, and I/O interface. Each of these functions and applicable devices which are currently available are described.

A microprogram sequencer (see Secs. 1.9.3 and 1.9.4) generates the addresses for a microprogram memory as explained in Sec. 1.9.3. Sequencers are used to implement microprogrammed control units for bit-slice microprocessors. Sequencers are not required for single-chip microprocessors, which contain built-in sequencing logic. Current commercial devices are available in either 4-bit-wide expandable slices or 12-bit-wide (nonexpandable) chips, both of which provide considerable operating flexibility. Specifically, as the block diagram of the AMD 2909 (Fig. 4) shows, the microprogram memory address $y_0 - y_3$ is selected from a fixed address of zero, the direct inputs (D), a previous input held in a register (R), the top word in a four-word last-in-first-out (LIFO) stack, or a counter. The counter is used for most operations, while the external inputs and the LIFO stack are used for subroutine operation (i.e., the subroutine address is input via the external inputs, and the stack stores the return address). The OR inputs from the left side of the figure and "zero" gates are used for program jumps and resetting, respectively.

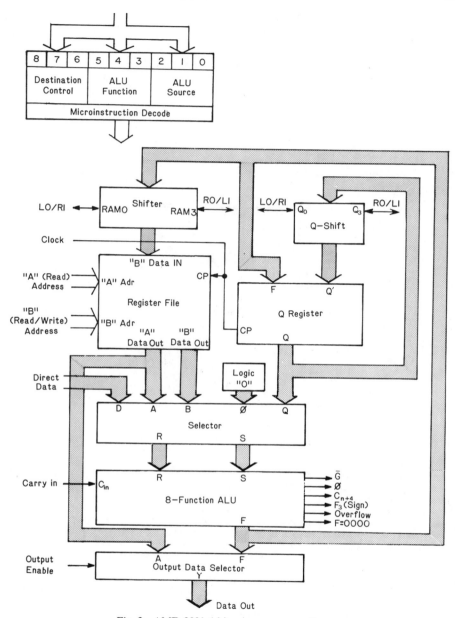

Fig. 3 AMD 2901 4-bit microprocessor slice.

The Fairchild Macrologic 9406 program stack performs a similar function, although it is organized differently, as Fig. 5 shows. The program stack is a 16-word by 4-bit LIFO stack and counter. It is used to implement instruction counter and return address storage for nested subroutines. The device executes four instructions: call, return, branch, and fetch, as specified by a 2-bit control field. When initialized, the instruction counter is in the top location of the stack. As a new program counter value is "pushed" onto the LIFO during subroutine calling, all previous instruction counter values effectively move down one level. The top location of the LIFO is the current program counter. Up to 16 instruction counter values can be stored, affording 15 levels of nesting. The return instruction, used during subroutine return, brings the most recent counter to the top of the LIFO. The remaining two instructions affect only the top location of the LIFO. In the branch operation, a new counter value is

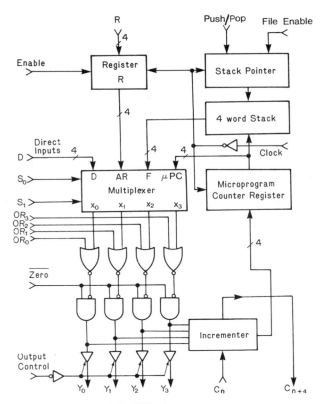

Fig. 4   AMD 2909 microprogram sequencer.

loaded into the top LIFO location from the data inputs, replacing the previous value. In the fetch operation, the contents of the top stack location (current counter value) are provided at the output, and the current counter value is incremented.

An example of a current commercial priority interrupt chip (the AMD 2914) is shown in Fig. 6. It assists processors having very few input interrupt lines (only one necessary) to process interrupt signals from up to eight devices (see also Sec. 1.12.3). It provides interrupt latching, encoding, prioritization, and gating. Asynchronous interrupt pulses are captured by the latch register. Since the processor can service only one interrupt request at a time, the chip has the ability to prioritize the requests and determine which has the highest priority. In this unit the relative priority of interrupt requests is established by the relative physical position of the inputs to the latch register. The priority encoder identifies the highest interrupt request, as a binary encoded number. The ability to selectively inhibit, or "mask," individual interrupt requests under program control is provided by the mask register. The bit-by-bit AND of the contents of the mask and request registers is formed at the input of the priority encoder. Thus the mask register can be used to select which interrupt requests will pass through to the rest of the hardware. The mask register is loaded by the processor. The ability to establish a priority threshold is provided by the status priority register and comparator. The register's contents are compared with the current request level output from the priority encoder. Only if the current request level is higher will the "combined interrupt request" signal to the processor be generated. A common mode of operation is for the status register to be automatically updated with 1 plus the current level each time an interrupt request is generated by the unit. This permits an interrupt service routine for one request to be interrupted in turn only by a higher-priority interrupt request. The status register can be loaded by the processor. Means are also provided to clear the interrupt currently being serviced.

Interface between processors and users is facilitated with universal synchronous receiver/transmitters (USRT) and universal asynchronous receiver/transmitters (UART). Since both perform similar functions, only the former is described here (see also Sec. 1.12.4). The universal synchronous receiver/transmitter (USRT) is a single-chip device (usually implemented in MOS technology) that provides the serial-to-parallel and parallel-to-serial conversion logic required to interface character

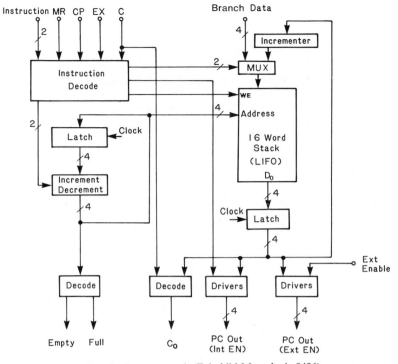

Fig. 5 Program stack (Fairchild Macrologic 9406).

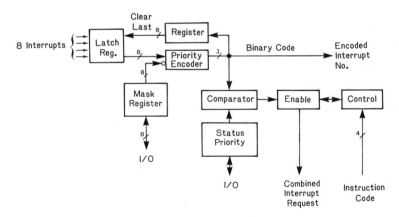

Fig. 6 Priority interrupt unit (AMD 2914).

data from a CPU, microprocessor, or other parallel processor to a bit-serial, synchronous communication link. The AMI S2350 USRT shown in Fig. 7 consists of separate receiver and transmitter sections with independent clocks, data lines, and status lines. Data are received and transmitted in continuous bit synchronous streams at rates up to 500 kHz. The USRT receiver is initialized to a "character" mode when power is applied and when initiating. In this mode, the receiver repeatedly collects 8 bits of data and then provides an 8-bit parallel output. An output buffer register allows a full character time to transfer the data out. Receiver status outputs indicate received data available and receiver overrun. The data lines have three-state outputs. Like the receiver, the transmitter is buffered to allow

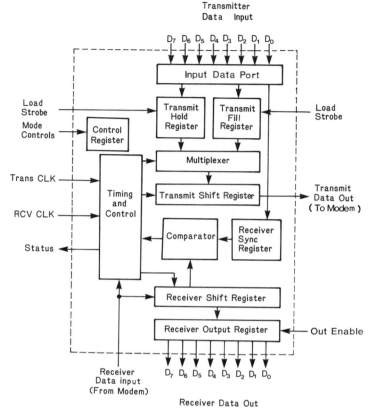

Fig. 7   USR T block diagram (AMI S2350).

a full character time to respond to a "transmitter buffer empty" request for data. Data are transmitted in a NRZ format (see Sec. 1.11.2), changing on the positive edge of the transmitter clock.

Memory

Two main classes of memories are required for microprocessor systems: ROM and RAM, (see Sec. 1.6). The general area of ROM technology is rich with variations. A few of the many types are:

    Mask programmed ROM
    Programmable ROM (PROM)
    Programmable logic arrays (PLA)

    Mask programmed ROMs are used to store fixed programs or fixed data constants (e.g., cosine tables or window functions). ROMs are available in large sizes (e.g., up to 64K bits), organized in words of 4 to 8 bits in width, with access time (depending on technology) from under 100 ns (for TTL devices) to 1 μs (for MOS memories).

    Programmable ROMs (or PROMs) are like ROMs; they are used to hold data that will not be changed. However, because they can be encoded or programmed by the user, the mask charge of a ROM is avoided. In its place, the recurring cost of a PROM is higher than the cost of a ROM of the same size. Often PROMs are used in the early phase of a program; when the patterns have been fixed, mask programmed ROMs are used for production.

    Recently, programmable logic arrays (PLA) have become available (see Vol. 1, Sec. 7.4, and Sec. 1.9.4 of this volume). They allow specific logic functions to be implemented in much the same manner

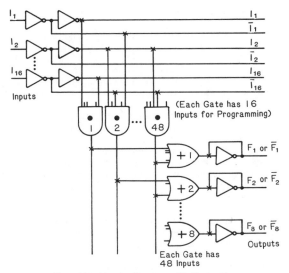

Note: X is Mask– Programmable Connection

Fig. 8 Logic diagram of programmable logic array.

as a PROM or ROM, with, for example, the capacity of forming up to eight unique functions of any combination of 16 input variables for a maximum combined total of 48 intermediate terms. A logic diagram of the Signetics 82S100 is shown in Fig. 8. Both mask programmed and field programmable devices are available, and work has been done in streamlining the design process with PLA-oriented computer-aided design (CAD) programs.

In terms of RAM, the primary applications in microprocessor systems are program storage and data memory where dynamic "constants" and intermediate results are stored.

Static memories are generally used for fairly small high-speed storage, such as scratchpad memory for a CPU. In such applications it is desirable to have the memory speed comparable to the ALU cycle time. Wide-memory-word formats (e.g., 1K×8) are desirable, since only a few wide-word memories are necessary.

In contrast, dynamic memory designs (see Sec. 1.6.3) emphasize large capacity with 1-bit width. The user of dynamic memory must ensure that each row of each memory chip is accessed at some specified rate (typically on the order of 1 kHz). This is generally accomplished with a refresh circuit that periodically locks out all users of the memory and accesses all rows. This means that the memory is only 97% available, which may not be a limitation unless refresh occurs at a critical time. Often, however, if a fixed pattern of data accessing occurs, it can be modified to automatically refresh the memory simply by arranging the data on the correct rows of the memory.

Technology Trends

The trend in single-chip microprocessor support devices is to develop chips that ease interfacing to external circuits. This will continue and will become more general with the development of support chips which will simplify interface to dynamic RAMs, and other devices. Support circuitry for the bit slices is less developed and more important to the processor performance, so considerable activity is expected. Continued development of program stacks, priority interrupt units, and I/O systems is likely.

With memory technology, continued speed and capacity growth are anticipated. By analogy to Grosch's law of computer costs [2] (the user cost decreases as the square root of the increase in machine speed), an intuitive memory cost relation has been developed: memory cost will drop at a rate proportional to the square root of the rate at which chip density increases. This relation appears to apply equally to ROM, PROM, and RAM technology. Specifically, density should continue to quadruple biannually, while the cost per bit is halved biannually. The largest memories will continue to be dynamic, but as special refresh chips are developed, this will pose less of a problem to users.

1.18.4   Microprocessor Software*

Microprocessor hardware resources have provided desirable design flexibility, although the lack of ready-to-use integrated systems and the complexity in creating them frustrate some potential users. The utility of a component or building-block design approach depends on how easily the individual elements can be assembled, separated, and reassembled to test ideas. This versatility, which is reflected in both the hardware and the software architecture of microprocessors, has improved at a phenomenal rate, although the fast-moving microprocessor industry has not yet paused to establish firm interface standards.

As with early computers, most microprocessor programming has been done at the assembly language level (see Sec. 2.11). Although assemblers are available for most microprocessors, memory constraints or I/O limitations on the configurations used for development have meant that users sometimes have no alternative to working in machine language (programming at the bit level). Even with access to an assembler, one finds that editing source programs is often clumsy, and entering changes into memory or patching a paper tape is sometimes easier than reassembling.

Influence of Large Computers

The biggest difference between the evolution of software for microprocessors and that of large computers has been the presence of the large systems. To date, microprocessor software development has, in fact, generally used assemblers, compilers, and simulators running on larger computing systems (so called cross-assemblers and cross-compilers). Indeed, most commercial time-sharing services now offer libraries of utility programs designed to support microprocessor software development.

This "cross-development" of software usually starts with the creation of a source program with assistance from an interactive text editor. Next, the source program is translated by a cross-assembler or cross-compiler into the machine language of the target microprocessor. The cross-compilers and cross-assemblers have themselves been written in languages suitable for the time-sharing computer. FORTRAN is used primarily because of its portability. A FORTRAN cross-assembler can be run without major modifications on almost any general-purpose computer. To test the correctness of the program, the object file of machine instructions is sometimes processed on the time-sharing system by a program that simulates the operation of the microprocessor.

This testing is facilitated by an assortment of debugging aids, particularly breakpoints, traces, and the direct interrogation and alteration of CPU register and memory contents (these topics are discussed in detail later in this section). When errors are detected and corrective action is determined, the cycle is repeated by reediting the source program, reassembling or recompiling, and again simulating the execution of the machine code. When the simulation performs as desired, the object file is ready for additional testing by executing it on the microprocessor. This execution is usually accomplished in one of two ways. One way is to "burn" the machine code into a PROM module and then insert the PROM into the microprocessor system. An alternative to the expense and slow turnaround time of this approach is to punch the object file into paper tape and load it into a RAM module connected to the microprocessor, but this option requires paper tape facilities.

This "resident" phase of program development (resident on the microprocessor hardware itself) often reveals problems that were not apparent during simulation. In particular, timing-dependent events and their consequences, which are difficult to simulate, show up in this phase. (In addition, the overhead costs of simulation are high and often prevent exhaustive testing.)

Software Development

Recently, resident microprocessor hardware/software development systems (MDSs) have emerged, which are aimed at reducing the dependence on time sharing and its concomitant expense. These systems, as shown in Fig. 9, consist of the microprocessor, memory, I/O interfaces, and a variety of peripheral devices, such as a user console with keyboard input, CRT display, hard-copy output, and auxiliary storage (e.g., a floppy disk unit). Minimum configuration front panels are kept simple, as their cost is large compared to other components, and traditional front-panel operations are largely assumed by the keyboard input and hard (or soft) output at the user console. Peripheral I/O equipment dominates the cost of these systems, but these peripheral devices are sophisticated, fast, and inexpensive. The software support supplied with such configurations usually includes a text editor, debugging aids, a resident assembler, and file maintenance capability. Although the hardware and software features of these systems are modest compared to those of a time-sharing system, the cost is about an order of magnitude lower, and the software development tools exist in a dedicated and "live" environment, which significantly improves the fidelity of testing.

*This section is based upon the paper "A Perspective on Microcomputer Software," by C. Bass and D. Brown, in *Proc. IEEE*, **64**, 905–909 (1976).

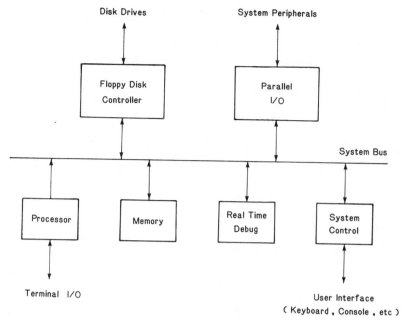

Fig. 9   Development system configuration.

The dedicated nature of a microprocessor system and the ability to monitor and record the state of CPU interface lines (by use of a logic analyzer) provides the ability to suspend the execution of a program, interrogate and modify the operating environment, and resume execution at any point without adding overhead or affecting normal execution conditions. In addition, specialized hardware can be attached directly to the development hardware to include the actual I/O interfaces and peripheral devices which are to be used in the end product, thus assuring the design engineer that the development environment corresponds accurately to the intended operating environment. The combined attributes of this resident testing enable an execution quality which cannot be matched by simulation, no matter how sophisticated it is, particularly with regard to time-dependent events and environmental influences.

Microprocessor Compilers and Debugging

Resident compilers and interpreters for high-level languages (HLLs) such as FORTRAN, Pascal, and ADA are generally available as standard software on microcomputer development systems. Although the arguments for and against programming in an HLL are well known, it is undoubtedly a fact that more and more people will program in HLLs as translators for these languages become widely available, code optimization techniques improve, and the costs of primary memory and auxiliary storage decline. An intermediate step already being used in this move toward HLLs is to "hand optimize" the object code produced by a compiler. The HLL allows potentially better formulation of algorithms and provides a nucleus of correct code which can then be tightened by hand to meet size and speed constraints. Only the code along the critical path needs to be examined and, in some instances, this can be a relatively small part of the total compiler output.

By combining translation with existing debugging capabilities, microcomputer program development can be significantly enhanced. Debugging aids, which now operate at the level of registers, memory locations, and machine cycles, can be raised to the level of variables, statement labels, and control structures. Consider the following development system command:

BREAK ON identifier REFERENCE

This requests that execution be suspended whenever there is a reference to the indicated identifier or variable. For example,

BREAK ON SALARY REFERENCE

will cause execution to be suspended whenever the variable SALARY is either read or written.

The request is implemented by setting special breakpoint registers, built into the development system hardware, which monitor CPU control lines. These registers are accessed by the system development software in the same way as I/O devices. In this case, the value placed in the appropriate register is the memory address of the variable SALARY. During the execution of a memory READ or WRITE cycle, whenever the designated memory location appears on the address bus, the development system forces the CPU to suspend its execution, and a breakpoint occurs. When the breakpoint occurs, control is transferred to the development system software, which saves the status of the CPU in order to maintain the integrity of the user's program and allow it to continue execution later. This transition between user and system software execution is accomplished by either employing a separate CPU and associated memory exclusively for system purposes or by employing the same CPU that serves the user and simply passing control to a ROM segment containing the system software. In either case, the user's program remains intact and accessible for interrogation.

During the breakpoint, variables can be displayed and changed at the request of the user at the keyboard/console, and additional breakpoint commands can be issued. If an interpretive translation technique is used, individual program statements can also be changed at this time. Execution can then be resumed at the point of suspension or at any specified memory location.

Another form of the breakpoint directive,

$$\text{BREAK ON identifier WRITE}$$

requests that execution be suspended whenever the value of a variable is changed. When the specified memory address appears on the address bus during a memory WRITE cycle, execution is suspended.

Another command form,

$$\text{BREAK ON identifier RANGE} = r_1 : r_2$$

requests that execution be suspended when a variable is set to any value between r_1 and r_2. If only r_1 is specified, execution stops when the variable equals r_1. For example,

$$\text{BREAK ON SALARY RANGE} = 1200$$

will suspend execution whenever SALARY is set to 1200. This is implemented by setting one breakpoint register as before to the memory address of SALARY and another register to the data value 1200. When the appropriate memory address appears on the address bus together with 1200 on the data bus during a memory WRITE cycle, a breakpoint occurs. This comparison is performed directly in the development system hardware.

System commands can also specify that breakpoints be associated with the number of times that a statement is executed: for example,

$$\text{BREAK ON label EXECUTE} = n$$

The same criteria used for setting breakpoints can also be used to record a history of execution by using the TRACE command. For example,

$$\text{TRACE ON identifier REFERENCE}$$

requests that a history of execution be established which records each reference to the specified variable. This is implemented by setting special trace registers within the development system, which, like the breakpoint registers, monitor CPU control lines. Unlike the breakpoint operation, however, when a condition specified by these registers is detected, the current status of the CPU is recorded in a storage module, but execution is not suspended. This storage module acts like a pushdown stack, providing last-in-first-out access to its records. In this way, real-time execution can be traced without affecting timing-dependent operations. When the user program terminates or is suspended, the contents of this storage module can be retrieved by the development system software and related to variable, statement, and logical program block activity. The realism of such a mechanism is especially valuable in control and I/O applications.

These commands represent debugging techniques that programmers have traditionally used by strategically placing extra conditional branching and I/O statements in their programs to monitor execution. The design of future development systems, as well as microprocessors themselves, should be influenced by the study of existing debugging strategies.

Software Development Trends

Currently, the predominant users of microprocessors are electronic design engineers. This is in contrast to the mathematicians and physicists who programmed and used early computers. The economy and utility of microprocessors will introduce computing to a new spectrum of users whose needs will challenge traditional microprocessor methodology.

The dramatic reduction in hardware costs achieved by micros should precipitate dramatic software cost reductions. By dedicating microprocessors to specific tasks with software only as complex as the situation demands, the software will become easier and less expensive to produce. Throughout the computer spectrum, software costs have come to exceed hardware costs. The difference is most pronounced with microprocessors, but it is likely that the biggest savings will also be achieved in this environment.

1.18.5 Microprocessor System Development*

An important problem is the testing and debugging of the microprocessor based systems at the factory and in the field. Thus a measure of a company's competitiveness will be its ability to develop new products rapidly and to manufacture and service them effectively.

Design Approaches

Microprocessor chips, as they are being utilized today, service two philosophically diverse areas: "microcomputers" and "embedded microprocessor systems." The term "microcomputer" as used here means a card or system with a microprocessor, memory, and I/O. These cards or systems resemble a minicomputer in almost every respect. As used here, the term "embedded microprocessor system" denotes the microprocessor chips together with memory and I/O chips that are designed and packaged by a user into a specific product. In this case, the microprocessor is embedded, because it is not a separately packaged entity. Historically, the embedded microprocessor system grew out of sequential hardware logic, whereas the microcomputer grew directly from the minicomputer. Microcomputers do not represent a dramatic departure in concept from minicomputers. On the other hand, embedded microprocessor systems do represent a dramatic new concept, as well as a complete new set of problems.

Microcomputers generally have the following characteristics:

1. They tend to be used in low volumes, and they are purchased by the user in an already packaged and working state.
2. They are usually RAM based. Most programs are not packaged in ROM, so that peripherals are required for loading software.
3. The development system is part of the product itself; a terminal is usually attached for controlling and loading software, which both resides on the system for development and diagnostic purposes and forms a portion of the product.
4. Testing of the microcomputer can usually be performed in a manner independent of the product application. In other words, testing is not application specific.

The software development approaches for microcomputers are similar to those used with general-purpose computers (i.e., minicomputers, mainframes, etc.).

Embedded microprocessor systems usually have the following characteristics:

1. They tend to be used in high volume.
2. The final products are usually ROM based, meaning that very little RAM is available to test software and few if any peripherals are available for loading software.
3. The development system must be totally separate from the product, because the product generally does not contain the functions needed for a development system.
4. The peripherals for a microcontroller are usually special IC logic. The special logic usually constitutes the greatest percentage of hardware in the system. Thus more problems in development and production will occur in the peripheral logic than in the microprocessor or memory. Microprocessor chip families are attempting to minimize TTL random logic designs, but today much TTL I/O logic surrounds the microprocessor.
5. Testing of software and hardware must be directed toward demonstrating that the product performs the specific tasks for which it was designed. Therefore, the testing is application dependent and concentrates on peripheral I/O logic.

Software development approaches for embedded microprocessor systems follow somewhat from the approaches used with sequential logic design. Software is written with the idea that it will be executed from ROM, not RAM. It is carefully segmented into ROM chip-size boundaries (e.g., 1K- or 8K-byte

*This section is based on the paper "Advances in Microcomputer Development Systems," by L. Krummel and G. Schultz, in *Computer*, **10**, 13–19 (Feb. 1977).

boundaries), and addresses are assigned accordingly. Memory space is usually critical because of product volume, and software must be coded as tightly as possible.

Developing Microprocessor Systems

The *initial* hardware debug effort for any microprocessor system is simply one of stimulating each memory and peripheral device on the system and verifying its operation. It is important to be able to stimulate the system even if it is not working properly. This can only be accomplished if the user can perform the following four primary functions:

Write memory.
Read memory.
Write I/O devices.
Read I/O devices.

Other functions that use combinations of these four may speed the debug process. For instance, a memory test that writes and reads memory over a range of addresses is very useful in initial hardware debug. If implemented correctly, the memory test will verify address decoding as well as memory handshake circuits. Also, the user may apply the four primary functions repeatedly as a "scope loop" to track down specific hardware malfunctions, once they are isolated within the system. All of these functions are possible via in-circuit emulation (described in the following paragraphs), since the emulator can generate the bus signals even if there is no operational user software. After the initial hardware debug phase, the software must be integrated, in order to exercise the system.

In-circuit emulation (ICE), as the name implies, involves simulating all the operations of a CPU in its normal physical position. The purpose is to emulate the CPU while monitoring it with surrounding circuitry that is not desirable to build into the user's product. To be most effective in performing in-circuit emulation with a particular microprocessor, it is necessary to be able to implement the following functions:

1. Detect the beginning of each instruction execution.
2. Suspend instruction execution at a defined point where execution can begin later.
3. Perform single simulated memory read, memory write, I/O read, and I/O write sequences.
4. Recover the contents of the CPU registers without destroying their contents.

The concept of in-circuit emulation may be more easily understood by considering an actual implementation for the 8080 microprocessor. Figure 10 shows the architecture of the Ramtek MM80, a typical single-processor approach to in-circuit emulation. This emulator uses a single 8080 CPU which resides on a bus with memory and I/O devices used by the emulator. The ICE has a cable that is plugged into the socket on the user's microprocessor system board into which his microprocessor chip is normally plugged. This connects the memory buses of the user system and the emulator. When the 8080 CPU is operating as part of the user's system (user mode), all the memory and I/O devices inside the emulator are disabled by the mode control logic, but the address stack is enabled to store instruction addresses for tracing software.

The user may set or examine memory or I/O devices from the console of the emulator. It performs memory transfers with the user's memory system by utilizing the 8080 move instructions. These transfers correspond to the display and set commands that are issued at the emulator console. In executing these commands, the in-circuit emulator software first issues an I/O command to its mode control logic followed by the move instruction. The mode control logic disables the emulator memory during the portion of the move instruction when the transfer occurs (last cycle), and it turns on the logic interconnection to the user system which is represented by the in-circuit emulator cable. User I/O devices are loaded or examined in a similar manner, except that the input and output instructions are substituted for the memory move instructions.

When the emulator's 8080 CPU is required to change from a mode of operation within its own memory and I/O devices (called emulator environment) to the user's memory and I/O devices (called user environment), it first saves its program state and then loads the user's last program state into its registers. The emulator then issues an I/O command to its mode control logic followed by a jump instruction. The jump instruction serves to load the program counter with the address of the first user instruction to be executed. At the end of execution of the jump instruction, the emulator mode control logic switches the 8080 to the user environment and disables the emulator environment.

The in-circuit emulator provides the fundamental capability needed to allow the user to easily work with memory or I/O devices in a system by entering simple commands at the emulator console. Some of the commands perform complex sequences which save the user considerable time. A few examples

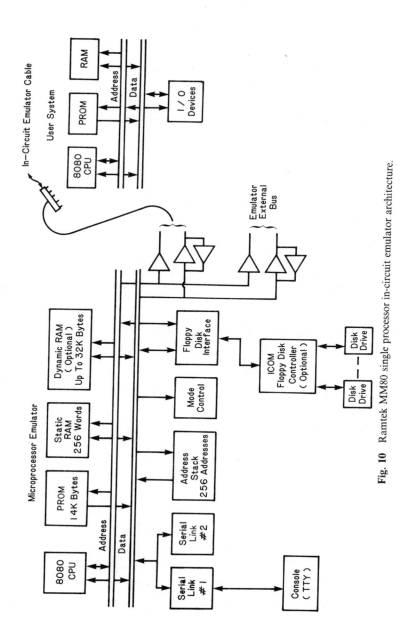

Fig. 10 Ramtek MM80 single processor in-circuit emulator architecture.

197

are:

1. Fill memory with a pattern.
2. Search memory for a pattern.
3. Verify that all of memory contains a particular pattern.
4. Continuously read or write memory or I/O devices with a pattern.
5. Run memory tests.

The important result is that these commands allow a test technician to perform comprehensive product tests without having to understand how to write software.

An alternative approach to implementing in-circuit emulation is the multiple-processor architecture. The Intel MDS system is an example of such a system. In these systems a "master" processor provides a basic facility that controls a general-purpose set of development resources, and a slave processor tailors the programming, in-circuit emulation, and diagnostic functions to a particular class of microprocessors. This configuration is very much like a minicomputer, with in-circuit emulation as a peripheral which is capable of gaining full use of the master processor's environment. Figure 11 depicts the block diagram for a typical multiprocessor architecture. Note the many similarities between the two approaches of Figs. 10 and 11. The multiprocessor-organized bus shown in Fig. 11 is somewhat more complex, because the in-circuit emulator must become the system master when using user main memory and peripherals. The "slave" in-circuit emulator of Fig. 11 performs its emulation functions in much the same manner as described for the single-processor approach.

The advantage of the dual-processor approach is that more than one microprocessor type may be emulated without redesign of basic general-purpose development resources such as file management, text editing, and system I/O. Peripheral device controllers need be designed only once to be applicable to a wide range of microprocessor families with varying bus structures and instruction sets.

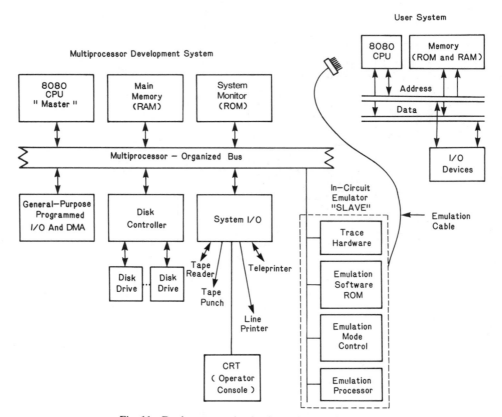

Fig. 11 Dual processor in-circuit emulator architecture.

Other Microprocessor Development Aids

It is not surprising that today's development aids for microprocessor systems have evolved from time-sharing and minicomputer systems on one extreme, and from hardware sequential logic on the other. Figure 12 indicates the spectrum of microprocessor development aids presently offered. The left-hand columns list aids that are primarily hardware oriented; the right-hand columns list aids that are primarily software oriented.

On the hardware development end, oscilloscopes and logic analyzers give the user pulse characteristic measurement and pulse trace capability. Pulse tracing, like its software tracing counterpart, allows the user to "look back" to see what occurred prior to the time of a selected event. These aids are obviously useful for debugging specific logic functions once a problem has been isolated. They are of little value in isolating a problem from the beginning, because they do not provide a way to stimulate the system, and if the system is not operating, it cannot be expected to stimulate itself. On the other hand, tracing microprocessor software flow with these devices is an inefficient use of time.

Microprocessor analyzers display instructions, addresses, and logic levels for handshake lines or any external logic. The Hewlett-Packard 1611 is an example of such an instrument. Although microprocessor analyzers have no way of stimulating the system, they allow the user to view the program flow in mnemonic format. A desirable characteristic of microprocessor analyzers is that they are portable and provide easy-to-use pushbutton operation. The user does not need to have knowledge of a lot of software and peripherals such as floppy disks just to perform simple functions.

On the other end of the spectrum are software development systems such as the Intel MDS. These systems are intended to solve software development problems, and they perform well in this area. They make use of floppy disks and large amounts of RAM. They are characteristically large and stationary. Historically, these systems have been complex to use because they are primarily intended for programmers, not technicians. As a result, they are not ideally suited for hardware debugging, especially in both product final test areas and in the field. In other words, they lack the instrument-like operation.

Developing software in large RAM-based microprocessor development systems is not totally consistent with most "user-packaged" final products, which are ROM based. One reason is that most ROM-based products are documented and released to manufacturing on a hardware basis. The ROMs contain software, but they are treated like pieces of the hardware. They are documented as assemblies and controlled by ordinary engineering documentation control procedures. The user must be able to correct an error in one ROM without affecting all the other ROMs in the system. Thus software must be planned and generated on ROM chip address boundaries. Users cannot simply reassemble the whole memory; they must set aside spare locations in each section and always work within a section. It would help if the development system were consistent with this philosophy. Large RAM-based systems simply do not encourage users to plan their systems for ROMs. As a result, they are often forced into a significant software redesign effort when integrating into ROMs.

The use of time sharing for software development is especially useful for static software (i.e., when the input/output relationship is unaffected by time). A floating-point package is static in the sense that the output of a floating-point add should depend only on the input, not on other variables. The careful use of time sharing can avoid large initial capital outlays, and it will also easily support a

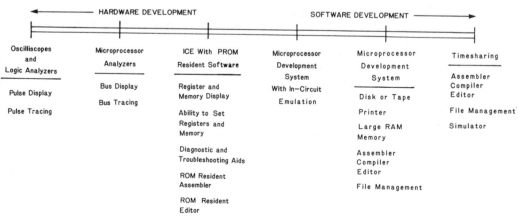

Fig. 12   Range of microprocessor development aids.

number of programmers on the same project. A time-sharing system provides file space and software facilities (editing, etc.) which will usually surpass any microcomputer development system.

The arguments against using time sharing for software development are twofold: cost and real time. If the time-sharing user is not aware of costs, he or she can spend more on time sharing in a month than would be spent on a stand-alone development system. If the user is aware of time-sharing cost factors, time sharing can be a very effective tool for functions that are not real time.

REFERENCES

1. C. G. BELL, J. C. MUDGE, and J. E. McNAMARA, *Computer Engineering*, Digital Press, Bedford, Mass., 1978, p. 551.
2. H. R. J. GROSH, "High Speed Arithmetic: The Digital Computer as a Research Tool," *J. Opt. Soc. Am.*, **43**, 306–310 (1953).

1.19 GLOSSARY

Jack L. Rosenfeld

Access Time.   *See* Cycle Time.

Accumulator.   Register in CPU used to hold data and results of arithmetic and logic operations (e.g., accumulation); occasionally, this is the only such register.

Adder.   *See* ALU; Carry.

Address.   Number specifying location of item in memory, on device, etc.

Address Space.   Set of all addresses that can be generated by CPU.

ALU (Arithmetic-Logic Unit).   Combinatorial logical circuitry in CPU that performs arithmetic and logic functions; main component is generally an "adder"—a combinatorial circuit that performs binary (perhaps decimal) addition of input words; ALU sometimes contains buffer registers; *see* Carry.

Arbitration.   Process of deciding which one of contending requesters (usually units attempting to use a bus or to interrupt a CPU) may use the requested facility.

Architecture.   Characteristics of a computer system visible to the programmer (e.g., instruction set, registers, interrupt structure).

Arithmetic-Logic Unit.   ALU.

Array Processor.   Processor executing identical operations on multiple elements within an array, allowing interactions between results and operations on adjacent array elements.

ASCII.   *See* Code.

Assembler.   *See* Machine Language.

Assembly Language.   *See* Machine Language.

Associative Memory = Content-Addressable Memory.   Memory in which selection of a word is based on the information stored in a portion of the word, rather than its location; "key field" is that part of a memory word searched for match; used for address translation and other special purposes.

Associative Processing.   Selecting data elements for processing by value—not by location within memory.

Asynchronous.   *See* Synchronous.

Attached Storage = Secondary Storage.   *See* Memory.

Attached Support Processor.   Computer dedicated to a specialized function in a multicomputer organization (e.g., input/output and array processing).

Availability.   Fraction of time a system is able to perform its required function.

Backing Store.   Memory subsystem with larger capacity, slower access, and lower cost per bit than main memory; usually used for storing information needed less frequently than information kept in main memory; generally not accessed like main memory.

Base Register.   CPU register holding base address; *see* Effective Address.

Bidirectional.   *See* Tristate.

Bit = Binary Digit.   0 or 1.

Bit Slice.   Slice.

Board.   *See* Packaging Hierarchy.

Borrow.   *See* Carry.

Branch Instruction. CPU instruction causing control to jump to another instruction, generally out of the normal sequence; "conditional branch" instruction causes control to jump only if specified conditions are satisfied (e.g., if a result is 0).

Break Point. (for debugging). Point in program under test at which control is caused to pass to the debugging system.

Buffer. Storage element, between data transmitter and receiver that are not synchronized, used to hold data temporarily; "memory buffer" is area in memory device to hold block of several words written by transmitter before being read by receiver; similarly, "buffer register" is device to hold a word of information; *see* Stack.

Bus. Communication hardware interconnecting components in a digital system; "memory bus" connects main memory, CPU, and I/O control; "I/O bus," controlled by I/O channel, transmits data and control information between I/O channel and attached device controllers.

Byte. Data word, generally 8 bits wide.

Cache. Very high speed buffer memory interposed between CPU and main memory, holding recently referenced information; used to improve system performance.

CAM (Content-Addressable Memory). Associative memory.

Card. *See* Packaging Hierarchy.

Carry. (in an adder). Signal from one stage to the next-higher-order stage denoting a sum greater than or equal to the radix; "carry propagation" is passing carry from each stage to the next-higher stage; a "ripple-carry" adder propagates carries between neighboring stages; "carry lookahead" is determination of carry from a stage according to inputs to that stage and several lower-order stages, but without carry propagation, thus increasing the speed; "borrow" is like carry for subtraction process; *see* Full Adder.

Central Processing Unit. CPU.

Channel. I/O channel.

Character. Symbol used to represent data (e.g., alphabet, numerals).

Characteristic. *See* Floating Point.

Chip. *See* Packaging Hierarchy.

Clock. Electronic circuitry for generating periodic timing signals.

Code. Bit pattern used to represent computer instruction, data character, etc.; "EBCDIC" (Extended Binary Coded Decimal Interchange Code) uses 8 bits to represent alphanumeric and control characters; "ASCII" (American National Standard Code for Information Interchange) is a different code, using 7 bits plus parity bit.

Compiler. *See* High-Level Language.

Complement. The opposite; for example, binary bits 0 and 1 are complements.

Computer. System for performing sequences of arithmetic and logical operations specified by a program; includes CPU, memory, and I/O.

Conditional Branch. *See* Branch Instruction.

Console. Device by which operator or user interacts with a computer; generally has input means (e.g., keyboard and switches) and output means (e.g., cathode-ray-tube display and lights).

Content-Addressable Memory. Associative memory.

Control Program = Supervisor. *See* Operating System.

Control Store. *See* Microprogrammed Control.

Control Store Sequencer. Logic unit that provides the machine instruction decode logic and specifies the "next-control-store address" generation scheme for fetching microinstructions from a control store; *see* Microprogrammed Control.

Control Unit. Part of a computer's CPU that issues timing and control signals to direct the activity of the entire system; device controllers are sometimes called control units.

Coupling (in a multiple-processor system). The nature of physical interconnection or level of logical interaction; "loosely coupled" systems interact in the same manner as they perform input/output operations; "tightly coupled" systems share directly addressable, executable main memory, interacting by sharing each other's address space.

CPU (Central Processing Unit). Section of a computer system that includes ALU, control unit, and registers.

Cross-Assembler. Assembler that runs on one computer and produces code to run on another computer; *see* Machine Language.

Cross-Compiler. Compiler that runs on one computer and produces machine language to run on another computer; *see* High-Level Language.

Cycle Stealing.   Mode of operation in which I/O channel or DMA controller has priority over CPU with regard to requests for memory access cycles.

Cycle Time   (in a memory system).   Total time for a memory operation, from initiation until memory is ready for the next such operation; "access time" is the part of memory read cycle time from initiation until data are available at memory output; (for CPU) interval during which basic operations occur.

Cylinder.   *See* Track.

DASD (Direct-Access Storage Device).   Storage device such as disk or drum in which access time is relatively independent of location of data, in comparison with, for example, magnetic tape unit; *compare* Sequential-Access Memory.

Data Channel.   I/O channel.

Data-Flow Processing.   Machine organization in which successive operations on data are executed as soon as the data are available.

Destructive Read.   Memory read operation in which original information is not preserved (e.g., for charge storage cells and magnetic cores); means are generally provided for regeneration of the information.

Device Controller = I/O Device Controller (sometimes called *Control Unit).*   Hardware that attaches peripheral devices to I/O interface, generating control signals to the device, serializing and deserializing data, monitoring status, and performing other functions.

Direct-Access Storage Device.   DASD.

Direct Addressing.   Simplest CPU addressing method, in which unmodified address specifies memory location of operand; *see also* Indirect Addressing; Relative Addressing.

Direct Memory Access.   DMA.

Disk.   Magnetic disk.

Diskette = Floppy Disk.   Flexible Disk for magnetic recording; drives for diskettes are generally less expensive and slower than drives for stiff disks.

Displacement.   *See* Effective Address.

Division.   *See* Restoring Division.

DMA (Direct Memory Access).   Transmission of data on memory bus directly between memory and a device controller; a "DMA controller" manages a sequence of DMA transmissions for a peripheral device.

Dynamic Allocation = Folding.   Process in which different subsets of programs and data in the address space occupy different areas of main memory at different times; "paging" is one technique for dynamic allocation.

Dynamic Memory.   Memory device in which information must be regenerated periodically, generally due to loss of charge; *see* Static Memory.

Dynamic Redundancy.   *See* Static Redundancy.

Dynamic Relocation.   Process in which programs and data may occupy different areas of main memory at different times.

EAROM.   Electrically alterable read-only memory.

EBCDIC (Extended Binary Coded Decimal Interchange Code).   See Code.

ECC.   Error Checking and correction.

Effective Address.   Address used to access main memory, the sum of several quantities: a "base address" is generally the address of the start of a block of storage; an "index" is usually the distance between an element of an array and the origin of the array; a "displacement" is the difference in addresses between the start of a block and an element of interest (e.g., a single word or the origin of an array).

Embedded Microprocessor System.   Microprocessor, memory, and I/O, all packaged into a specific product.

Emulation.   Use of microcode to simulate an architecture; hardware on which microcode is executed is called "host"; architecture simulated is called "target" architecture; host may or may not be designed specifically to emulate target; host may be capable of switching emulation among two or more targets; *see* Microprogrammed Control.

Enable Signal.   Signal sent to a device to cause it to become active.

EPROM.   Erasable programmable read-only memory.

Erroneous State.   Internal system state for which circumstances exist such that further processing by the normal system algorithms will lead to a failure; *see* Failure.

Error Checking and Correction (ECC). Process by which additional checking bits are added to data by a transmitter so that if any of the bits (data or checking) are received incorrectly by a receiver, the error can be detected and the erroneous bits corrected.

Exponent. See Floating Point.

Failure. Event said to occur when system does not perform its service as specified.

FAMOS. Floating gate avalanche injection metal-oxide semiconductor.

Fault. "System fault" is a mechanical or algorithmic construction that will cause a system to assume an erroneous state; *see also* Paging.

Fault Avoidance. Design approach to assure reliability by elimination of causes of faults; *see* Fault.

Fault Tolerant. Able to function satisfactorily despite occurrence of faults.

FHF. Fixed-head file.

FIFO (First in First Out). Rule for specifying order of processing data, requests, etc.; *see* LIFO; Stack.

File. A large unit of information on a secondary storage device; also, a secondary storage device itself; *see* Memory.

Firmware. Microcode; *see* Hardware.

Fixed-Head File (FHF). Magnetic disk or drum storage device in which reading and recording transducers do not move; *compare* Moving-Head File.

Fixed Point. Representation of numbers and the associated arithmetic in which radix point (e.g., decimal or binary point) is considered to be in the same position for all such numbers; *see* Floating Point.

Floating Point. Representation of numbers and the associated arithmetic using a movable radix point (e.g., decimal or binary point); representation (e, f) of a number N comprises a fraction or "mantissa" part f and an "exponent" or "characteristic" part e ($N = f \times r^e$, where r is the radix); occasionally, a bias quantity is subtracted from the characteristic to give the true exponent; *see* Fixed Point; Radix.

Floppy Disk. Diskette.

Folding. Dynamic allocation.

Fragmentation. Creation of partitions in memory with alternating used and unused sections, due to a succession of storage allocations.

Full Adder. One stage of a binary adder with two operand inputs and a carry input, which produces a sum and a carry output; *see* Carry.

Gate Array = Masterslice. Logic integrated circuit in which the primitive logic circuits (AND, OR, etc.) are in a fixed pattern, and different functions are implemented by creating interconnections among the logic circuits.

Handshaking. Means of coordinating two units, in which signals are exchanged in a prescribed sequence.

Hardware. The physical components of a computer system; "software" is the collection of programs executed on the system; "firmware" is the microcode for a CPU that has microprogrammed control; *see* Microprogrammed Control.

Hardwired Control. Implementation of the control unit of a CPU by means of discrete logic elements and sequential circuits; *see* Microprogrammed Control.

Head (in a magnetic-recording system). Transducer that converts electrical signals to magnetic, or vice versa; also, physical module holding read, write, and/or erase transducers.

Hexadecimal. Base 16 representation of numbers.

Hierarchy. See Memory Hierarchy; Packaging Hierarchy.

High-Level Language (HLL). Programming language using statements close to user's normal expressions, such as $A = B \times (C + D)$ to express an arithmetic operation and IF $A = B$ THEN $I = I + 1$ to represent a control function; a "compiler" is a program that translates from an HLL to machine language; *see* Machine Language.

Hit. See Miss.

HLL. High-level language.

Horizontal Microinstruction. Microinstruction that encodes several microoperations to be executed concurrently; *see* Microprogrammed Control; Vertical Microinstruction.

Host. See Emulation.

ICE. In-circuit emulator.

In-Circuit Emulator (ICE). Device, including microprocessor, attached to microprocessor system to aid in debugging.

Index. *See* Effective Address.

Index Register. CPU register to hold index; automatically added to address of origin of array to calculate address of array element in main memory; "indexed addressing" is this mode of calculating address; index register also used for counting iterations; *see* Effective Address.

Indexed Addressing. *See* Index Register.

Indirect Addressing. Mode for CPU to access operand, in which access is first made to location holding address of operand rather than operand itself; *see also* Direct Addressing.

Instruction. A command to be executed by a computer's CPU; a "program" is a sequence of such commands (perhaps in a high-level language) for performing a useful function.

Instruction Counter = Program Counter. CPU register holding address in main memory of instruction currently being executed (or next instruction).

Instruction Register. CPU register holding instruction being executed.

Interrupt. Signal to CPU causing it to suspend execution of current program and execute another program ("interrupt handler") designed to respond to the source of the signal; a "trap" is an interrupt generated internally to the CPU; *see* Priority Interrupt Device.

I/O (Input/Output). Subsystem of computer for reading in and writing out data and programs.

I/O Channel = Data Channel = Channel. Unit to control transmission of blocks of data between I/O interface of a CPU and memory; *see* Bus.

I/O Device Controller. Device controller.

I/O Interface. Connection between device controllers and channel or CPU; usually completely specified in terms of a description of physical connection and a description of all permissible signal sequences with their timing constraints.

K. Abbreviation for 1024 (2^{10}); often used in referring to memory size; "M" is abbreviation for 1,048,576 ($2^{20} = 1\text{K} \times 1\text{K}$).

Key Field. That part of a block of data that contains identification of the block; *see also* Associative Memory.

Latency. Interval between request for data and availability of data, often applied to rotation time of magnetic disk or drum device.

LIFO (Last in First Out). Rule specifying order of processing data requests, etc.; *see* FIFO; Stack.

Local Memory. Small memory integrated in CPU to hold intermediate results.

Logic Analyzer. Laboratory instrument for storing and observing sequences of digital signals; *see* Microprocessor Analyzer.

Logic Service Terminal (LST). Physical connection point for transmission of logic signals between two levels of the packaging hierarchy; *see* Packaging Hierarchy; Power Service Terminal; Via Service Terminal.

Lookahead. "Instruction lookahead" is a technique to overlap instruction fetching, decoding, and execution times by fetching instructions and operands in advance of execution; *see also* Carry.

Loose Coupling. *See* Coupling.

M. *See* K.

Machine Language. Programming language consisting of instructions ("machine-level" instructions) for a computer's CPU, encoded in binary form and interpreted by the control unit; "assembly language" is the same instruction set encoded in alphanumeric form with added instructions understood by the assembler; an "assembler" is a program that translates a program written by a programmer in assembly language to its machine language equivalent, for execution by the CPU; *see* High-Level Language.

Magnetic Disk = Disk. Storage device using one or more disks of magnetic material as the storage medium.

Magnetic Drum. Storage device using cylinder coated with magnetic material as the storage medium.

Magnetic Tape Drive. Storage device using magnetic tape as the storage medium.

Mainframe. CPU and memory of large computer system (slang).

Main Memory. *See* Memory.

Mantissa. *See* Floating Point.

Mask. Bit pattern designating which bits of a word are to be examined or processed (e.g., in selecting which of several external interrupt signals to accept).

Masterslice. Gate array.

MDS. Microprocessor development system.

Memory. Computer component for storing data and instructions; "main memory" in this handbook section refers to memory directly addressed by CPU; "attached storage" or "secondary storage" refers to slower memory that can be accessed only by first moving contents to main memory; "file" is sometimes used to refer to attached storage devices (e.g., tape file, disk file, fixed-head file).

Memory Address Register (MAR). Register in CPU or main memory holding address for memory word being accessed.

Memory Hierarchy. Assemblage of storage devices with different speeds, costs, and sizes linked together so as to appear to have the speed of the fastest device and the size of the largest device; a "staging" hierarchy permits movement of data between adjacent members of the hierarchy only, although several such movements may be performed in sequence.

Memory-Mapped I/O. Principle of CPU accessing device controllers attached directly to memory bus as if they were memory locations.

MHF. Moving-head file.

Microcode = Microprogram = Firmware. *See* Microprogrammed Control. (*Note*: microcode is *not* code for a microcomputer.)

Microcomputer. *See* Microprocessor.

Microinstruction. *See* Microprogrammed Control.

Microinstruction Register (MIR). Register receiving microinstructions from control store in microprogrammed control system; *see* Microprogrammed Control.

Microoperation. Primitive operation of a computer system (e.g., open gates between two registers, start memory cycle).

Microprocessor. CPU implemented on a single semiconductor chip or a small number of chips; a "microprocessor system" is controlled by one or more microprocessors; a "microcomputer" comprises a microprocessor, main memory, and I/O.

Microprocessor Analyzer. Laboratory instrument for storing sequences of microprocessor signals and displaying them as sequences of instructions and addresses; *see* Logic Analyzer.

Microprocessor Development System (MDS). Microcomputer with software and hardware for developing programs for microprocessor systems; has facilities for writing, testing, and storing programs.

Microprogram = Microcode. *See* Microprogrammed Control. (*Note*: a microprogram is *not* a program for a microcomputer.)

Microprogrammed Control. Implementation of the control unit of a CPU using information found in a storage unit (generally read-only) called the "control store"; "microinstructions" are the binary words in the control store, containing encodings of the microoperations to be performed (microinstructions may specify that several microoperations occur simultaneously); "microcode" or "microprogram" is the collection of all microinstructions in the control store, analogous to a machine language program in main memory; *see* Control Store Sequencer; Hardwired Control; Microoperation.

Microprogram Sequencer. Control store sequencer.

MIPS (Millions of Instructions per Second). Unit of CPU performance.

MIR. Microinstruction register.

Miss. (in a paging or cache system). *Reference to a block not currently found in main memory or the cache; a "hit" is a reference to a block currently in main memory or the cache; see Paging.*

Module. *See* Packaging Hierarchy.

Moving-Head File (MHF). Magnetic disk storage device in which reading/recording transducers are on access arms that move to access tracks at different radii; *see* Fixed-Head File.

MTBF. Mean time between failures.

MTFF. Mean time before first failure.

Multiplex. Share a facility; in "time multiplexing" (e.g., of a bus) each user is assigned a time interval for using the facility; in "frequency multiplexing," each user uses a different frequency range so all can transmit simultaneously; "space multiplexing" permits use of different physical parts simultaneously; a "multiplexer" is a device that controls multiplexing; a multiplexer is also a device with more than one input and one output in which any one of the inputs at a time can be connected to the output.

Multiport Memory. *See* Port.

Multiprocessor. Computer system with two or more CPUs that are controlled by a single operating system and that communicate with each other.

Nondestructive Read. Opposite of "destructive read."

Nonrestoring. *See* Restoring Division.

Non-Return-to-Zero (NRZ). *See* Return-to-Zero.

Nonvolatile. Opposite of "volatile."

NRZ (Non-Return-to-Zero).   *See* Return-to-Zero.

Off-Line.   *See* On-line.

One's-Complement.   Binary representation of numbers in which negative number $-n$ is represented by the bit-by-bit complement of the binary representation of n; *see also* Sign-Magnitude; Two's-Complement.

On-Line.   Physically connected and capable of performing normal functions; "off-line" means not capable of performing normal functions: not logically connected, but may be physically connected.

Op Code.   Operation code.

Operand.   Data manipulated by a computer instruction.

Operating System (OS).   Software to manage all the resources of a computer: storage, processing time, system programs, I/O, etc.; the "control program" or "supervisor" is the part of the operating system that manages the execution of other programs.

Operation Code (Op Code).   Part of computer instruction that specifies what operation is to be performed.

OS.   Operating system.

Packaging Hierarchy.   Set of Physical structures used to construct computer system; in contemporary systems, the most common hierarchy is: "chip," a semiconductor entity on which integrated circuits are fabricated; "module," which houses one or more chips, provides protection for them, and provides interconnection between them and the card; "card," composed of laminated insulation and conductor layers, which provides support and interconnection structures for many modules; cards may be plugged orthogonally into "boards," which provide pluggable connections and wiring structures for the cards.

Page.   *See* Paging.

Page Fault.   *See* Paging.

Page Frame.   *See* Paging.

Page Table.   *See* Paging.

Paging.   Technique for implementing virtual memory; address space and main memory are divided into equal, fixed-size blocks called "pages" and "page frames," respectively; "paging algorithm" is used to determine what pages to move between secondary storage and main memory, and when to move them; a "page table" records status of pages and page frames; when a page referred to by the program is not in main memory, a "page fault" interruption occurs, and the paging algorithm is used to determine what action to take; *see* Miss; Virtual Memory.

Parameter.   *See* Subroutine.

Partition.   A grouping of logical or physical objects for the purpose of defining a higher-order function or packaging part; an example of a logical partition may be a group of lower-order logical elements such as a binary adder, storage cells, and gates to form a "bit slice;" a physical partition may be defined by all the chips to be included in a single module or all logic circuits on a single chip, etc.

Peripheral Device.   Input and/or output device attached to a computer.

Pipeline.   A type of ALU design for improved performance in which an arithmetic operation is performed on operands by automatically moving them through a set of individual units, each unit performing a separate part of the arithmetic operation; more than one set of operands are generally in the pipeline simultaneously.

PLA (Programmable Logic Array).   Combinatorial logic device, usually consisting of AND gates feeding OR gates, in a physical array; used as a ROM; the logic function is generally established ("programmed") at time of manufacture.

Poll.   To interrogate status repeatedly (e.g., to test status of devices one after the other).

Pop.   *See* Stack.

Port.   Location where data can enter or exit; "multiport memories" permit simultaneous entrance and/or exit of data.

Power Service Terminal (PST).   Physical connection point for supplying primary power between two levels of the packaging hierarchy; *see* Logic Service Terminal; Packaging Hierarchy; Via Service Terminal.

Printer.   Computer output device that prints information on paper; a "line printer" prints one line at a time; a "serial printer" prints a character at a time.

Priority Interrupt Device.   Semiconductor device used in small computer systems to select one of several input interrupt signals on the basis of some priority algorithm, and generate interrupt signal to CPU if specified conditions are satisfied.

Program.   *See* Instruction; also, to write a specified bit pattern in a permanent or semipermanent storage device (e.g., ROM, PROM, PLA).

Program Counter. Instruction counter.

Programmable Logic Array. PLA.

Programmable Read-Only Memory. PROM.

Programmer. Person who writes programs; also, device for writing specified bit patterns in a permanent or semipermanent storage device (e.g., PROM programmer).

PROM (Programmable Read-Only Memory). Memory that can be written selectively ("programmed") only once—after that, it behaves like ROM.

Protection. "Storage protection" is prevention of access to designated areas of memory by unauthorized programs.

Protocol. Rules for communication; specifically, the sequence of signals that must be interchanged and the actions that must be taken to complete a communication.

Push. See Stack.

Pushdown Stack. See Stack.

Radix. Base of a number system (e.g., 2 for binary numbers, 10 for decimal, 16 for hexadecimal).

RAM (Random-Access Memory). Memory system in which words can be accessed in any sequence and access time is independent of location; memory capable of both read and write operations; *see* ROM.

Random-Access Memory. RAM.

Read-Only Memory. ROM.

Read-Only Store (ROS). ROM.

Record. Basic block of data on input or output device.

Refresh. (in dynamic memory). To restore the original physical quantity (e.g., charge) that represents stored information.

Register. Set of flip-flops to hold information; usually, all flip-flops of the register (or a subset of them) are set simultaneously, and information is read out from all (or a subset) simultaneously.

Register File. Group of registers in CPU.

Relative Addressing. Mode for CPU to generate address by adding displacement to address of current instruction; *see also* Direct Addressing.

Reliability. Probability of being able to perform specified function.

Relocation. Process of moving program or data to a new main memory location for execution there.

Replacement Algorithm (in a paging system). A rule for selecting which memory page frame is to be replaced by new page from secondary storage; *see* Paging.

Requirements Definition. Initial phase of design process involving specification of product.

Restoring Division. Division algorithm involving making trial divisions and restoring original dividend when trial fails; "nonrestoring division" does not restore when trial fails.

Return-to-Zero. Method of magnetic recording or digital communication in which signal returns to 0 between excursions to positive or negative limits; "non-return-to-zero" is method in which signal is always at either positive or negative limit.

Ripple-Carry Adder. See Carry.

ROM (Read-Only Memory) = ROS. Memory whose information contents cannot be changed after manufacture.

ROS (Read-Only Storage). ROM.

Search (for input device). To scan data until the desired information is located.

Secondary Storage = Attached Storage. See Memory.

Seek (for moving-head file). To move access arm(s) from one track position to another.

Segment. See Segmentation.

Segmentation. Technique for implementing virtual memory in which address space is divided into variable-size blocks called segments.

Self-Modifying Code. Program that modifies parts of its own instructions.

Sequencer. Control store sequencer.

Sequential-Access Memory. Memory system in which words can be read only in the order in which they were written (or reverse order); (e.g., magnetic tape); *compare* DASD.

Serviceability. Ability to be repaired or maintained.

Sign-Magnitude. Binary representation of numbers with one bit for plus or minus sign and other bits for the magnitude; *see also* One's-Complement; Two's-Complement.

Slice. Building-block section of ALU, registers, memory, or other components, performing a function for m bits of a word; generally, several of these (n) are used in parallel to provide the function for $n \times m$ bits; provides flexible means of designing CPUs or other subsystems to satisfy special requirements.

Software. *See* Hardware.

Source – Sink I/O. Input or output between system and original source of data or final recipient of data, as opposed to I/O with attached storage device intended for temporary storage.

Stack. Mechanism, implemented by hardware, software, or both, for storing a variable number of units of information; a "pushdown" or "LIFO" stack has a single port, and the order of retrieval is the inverse of the order of storing [i.e., the item most recently written ("pushed") onto the stack is the first item read ("popped") from it]; a "FIFO" mechanism has a port for writing and another for reading, and the order of retrieval is the same as the order of storing (i.e., the first item written is the first item read); *see* Buffer.

Staging. *See* Memory Hierarchy.

Static Memory. Memory device that retains information as long as power is applied to it; *see* Dynamic Memory.

Static Redundancy. Approach to system reliability using redundant components, with a permanent system configuration (e.g., triple-modular redundancy); "dynamic redundancy" is an approach to reliability using redundant components with a configuration that is changed according to the errors detected.

Storage. *See* Memory.

Store-Through = Write-Through (in cache system). Process of writing both in the cache and the corresponding location in main memory when a memory write operation is called for, to avoid subsequently writing entire cache block to memory.

String Processor = Vector Processor. Computer system designed specifically to optimize execution of the same arithmetic or logical operation on a continuous series of data elements; often uses ALU with pipeline.

Subroutine. Program sequence invoked ("called") from one or more points in another program (the "calling" program); generally returns control to instruction immediately after point of invocation; the "parameters" of the subroutine are operands passed to it by the calling program and manipulated by the subroutine.

Supervisor = Control Program. *See* Operating System.

Synchronous. Associated with clock having fixed cycle time; "asynchronous" is not associated with clock, so asynchronous events can occur at any time.

Target. *See* Emulation.

Three-State. Tristate.

Throughput. Rate of work completed by a computer system; *see* MIPS.

Tight Coupling. *See* Coupling.

Time Sharing (in computer system). Permitting more than one user to use system concurrently by causing the CPU to execute a part (or all) of each user's program, one at a time.

TMR. Triple-modular redundancy.

Track. Circular path on disk or drum storage medium, or linear path on magnetic tape; contains data recorded by single head, without motion of access mechanism; (in moving-head file) "cylinder" is the set of tracks that can be accessed for a single position of the access mechanism.

Transaction (for communication along a bus). All steps required to complete transmission of a unit of data.

Trap. *See* Interrupt.

Triple-Modular Redundancy (TMR). Approach to high reliability in which three copies of system modules are provided, all fed with same inputs, and in which the three module outputs are compared by "voters" that select final outputs according to majority vote.

Tristate = Three-State. Logic circuit capability to force a line to one of two different voltages to represent two different logic values or to assume a high-impedance state so that another circuit can place a voltage on the line; a "bidirectional" line is one with tristate drivers at both ends.

Two's-Complement. Binary representation of numbers in which a negative number $-n$ is represented by the binary representation of $2-n$; *see also* One's-Complement; Sign-Magnitude.

UART (Universal Asynchronous Receiver/Transmitter). Device for communicating along a serial bus, one character at a time, with facilities for serializing and deserializing data.

UPS. Uninterruptible power system.

USART (Universal Synchronous/Asynchronous Receiver/Transmitter). Device able to operate like either UART or USRT.

USRT (Universal Synchronous Receiver/Transmitter).   Device similar to UART, except for transmitting or receiving streams of characters rather than one at a time.

Variable Field Length (for instructions and data).   Having more than one possible length.

Vector Processor.   String processor.

Vertical Microinstruction.   Microinstruction with format similar to machine instruction format; *see* Horizontal Microinstruction; Microprogrammed Control.

Via Service Terminal (VST).   Physical path used to transmit signals between two levels of conductors in a multilayer planar package (e.g., a plated hole connecting two conductor layers in a glass-filled epoxy card structure); *see* Logic Service Terminal; Packaging Hierarchy; Power Service Terminal.

Virtual Memory.   System whereby main memory is made to appear larger than it actually is by automatically moving blocks of memory from secondary storage as needed; generally, implemented by a combination of hardware and software; *see* Paging.

Volatile (in memory system).   Losing information when power is removed or interrupted.

Word.   Group of characters or bits treated as a unit for purposes of reading or writing to memory and performing arithmetic or logic operations; multiple-word units and fractional-word units, however, are often encountered.

WOROM.   Write-once read-only memory.

Write-Through.   Store-through.

BIBLIOGRAPHY

American National Dictionary for Information Processing, Computer and Business Equipment Manufacturers Association, Washington, D.C., 1977.

ISO Vocabulary of Data Processing, International Standards Organization, Geneva, Switzerland.

IBM Data Processing Glossary, Publication GC20-1699, IBM Corporation, White Plains, N.Y., 1977.

1.20   SOURCES OF INFORMATION

David F. Bantz

Information on computer systems, microprocessors, and computer peripheral devices can be obtained from manufacturers and from the trade press. This section lists some standard sources of such information.

EEM — The Electronic Engineers Master Catalog, published annually by United Technical Publications, 645 Stewart Avenue, Garden City, N.Y. 11530. A large listing of electronic equipment and component manufacturers, together with many pages excerpted from their catalogs.

The Electronic Industry Telephone Directory, published annually by the Harris Publishing Company, 2057-2 Aurora Road, Twinsburg, Ohio 44087. Telephone numbers and addresses of many firms.

Electronic Design's Gold Book, published annually by the Hayden Publishing Company, 50 Essex Street, Rochelle Park, N.J. 07662. Similar to the *EEM*.

Association for Computing Machinery, Special Interest Group (SIG) publications (1133 Avenue of the Americas, New York, N.Y. 10036):

> *Computer Architecture News*, informal bimonthly publication of ACM SIG on Computer Architecture (SIGARCH)—computer design, organization, and structure.

> *SIGSMALL Newsletter*, informal bimonthly publication of the ACM SIG on Small Computing Systems and Applications (SIGSMALL)—all aspects of small computing systems.

> *SIGMICRO Newsletter*, informal quarterly publication of the ACM SIG on Microprogramming (SIGMICRO)—minicomputer and microcomputer systems: hardware, software, and firmware.

BYTE, published monthly by BYTE Publications Inc., 70 Main Street, Peterborough, N.H. 03458. Devoted to microprocessor and home computer systems.

COMPUTER, published monthly by the IEEE Computer Society, 5855 Naples Plaza, Suite 301, Long Beach, Calif. 90803. Current survey papers of interest in computer design.

Computer Design, published monthly by Computer Design Publishing Corporation, 11 Goldsmith Street, Littleton, Md. 01460. Articles and advertisements of practical interest to implementers.

Datamation, published monthly by Technical Publishing, 1301 South Grove Avenue, Barrington, Ill. 60010. Computer systems and management.

Digital Design, published monthly by Benwill Publishing Company, 1050 Commonwealth Avenue, Boston, Mass. 02215. Articles on computer and peripheral design.

EDN, published semimonthly by Cahners Publishing Company, 221 Columbus Avenue, Boston, Mass. 02116. Articles on electronic components and systems.

Electronic Design, published biweekly by Hayden Publishing Company, Inc., 50 Essex Street, Rochelle Park, N.J. 07662. Articles on electronic components and systems.

Electronic Products, published monthly by United Technical Publications, 645 Stewart Avenue, Garden City, N.Y. 11530. Articles on electronic components and systems.

Electronics, published twice a month by McGraw-Hill, Inc., 1221 Avenue of the Americas, New York, N.Y., 10020. Articles on electronic components and systems.

IBM Journal of Research and Development, published bimonthly by the IBM Corporation, Armonk, N.Y. 10504. Highly technical papers on computer and peripheral design concepts and implementations.

IEEE Transactions on Computers, published monthly by The Institute of Electrical and Electronics Engineers, Inc., 345 East 47th Street, New York, N.Y. 10017. Highly technical papers on computer design concepts and implementations.

Mini-Micro Systems, published monthly by Cahners Publishing Company, 221 Columbus Avenue, Boston, Mass. 02116. Articles on small computer systems and applications.

SECTION 2
COMPUTER SOFTWARE

ARTHUR J. BERNSTEIN, EDITOR
Department of Computer Science
State University of New York at Stony Brook

S. SALVETER
Mathematics Department
Boston University
Boston, Massachusetts

P. HENDERSON
Department of Computer Science
State University of New York at Stony Brook

D. MAIER
Department of Computer Science
and Engineering
Oregon Graduate Center
Beaverton, Oregon

J. HELLER
Department of Computer Science
State University of New York at Stony Brook

F. SCHNEIDER
Department of Computer Science
Cornell University
Ithaca, New York

D. TYCKO
Technicon Instruments Corp
Tarrytown, New York

D. ROSENKRANTZ
Department of Computer Science
State University of New York at Albany

J. CHERNIAVSKY
Computer Science Section
National Science Foundation
Washington, D.C.

DOMINIC SERAPHIN
Computing Center
State University of New York at Stony Brook

PAUL SEIGEL
Paul Seigel Computer Enterprises, Inc.
Hauppauge, New York

K. EKANADHAM
IBM Thomas J. Watson Research Center
Yorktown Heights, New York

MANFRED RUSCHITZKA
Department of Electrical and
Computer Engineering
University of California
Davis, California

M. HOFRI
Technion
Haifa, Israel

ARIE SHOSHANI
Lawrence Berkley Laboratory
Berkeley, California

GREGORY R. ANDREWS
Department of Computer Science
University of Arizona at Tucson

S. WECKER
Technology Concepts
Sudbury, Massachusetts

S. RAPPAPORT
Department of Electrical Engineering
State University of New York at Stony Brook

G. CAMPBELL
Applied Mathematics Department
Brookhaven National Laboratory
Upton, New York

YIH-CHYUN JENQ
Bell Laboratories
Holmdel, New Jersey

RICHARD E. SCHANTZ
Bolt, Beranek & Newman
Cambridge, Massachusetts

HAROLD A. ANDERSON, JR.

IBM Thomas J. Watson Research Center
Yorktown Heights, New York

H. C. FORSDICK

Bolt, Beranek & Newman
Cambridge, Massachusetts

The area of computer software has seen such explosive growth over the last several decades that it is not possible to compress in a single handbook section a useful summary of what is currently understood about the subject. Instead, the goal is to touch on much of the information that is most likely to be of interest and use to electrical and computer engineers. This information has been subdivided into four categories: data structures, basic support software and techniques, operating systems, and network software and algorithms.

Sections 2.1 to 2.10 contain a summary of the underlying data structures with which virtually all applications software must deal. An algorithm is expressed as a sequence of operations on such structures. The basic operations for each structure are described in this section. This is well-established and stable material that has been incorporated in many texts and is a prerequisite for effective programming of any kind.

Sections 2.11 to 2.18 contain brief descriptions of software packages, languages, and techniques with which the electrical and computer engineer is likely to come in contact. Assemblers, loaders, and compilers fall into this category. No attempt has been made to provide the details of any particular language; the reader is referred to appropriate manuals for that purpose. Rather, the goal here is to focus on mechanisms basic to all languages and certain common programming techniques.

Sections 2.19 to 2.26 are concerned with operating systems, the software that controls the computer. These are among the most complex of programs since they must deal with the asynchronism inherent in the hardware. The material included describes commonly accepted algorithms and techniques used in most operating systems, as well as some of the newer developments in the area. In particular, kernel systems, hierarchical architectures, and high-level languages will be key concepts in the operating systems built in the 1980s. The introduction of microcomputers will accelerate this trend as these devices find their way into more and more applications.

Sections 2.27 to 2.32 are concerned with computer networks, an area that has come into its own in the last decade. This material bridges the gap between the more traditional areas of computers and communications. It is a subject that is still very much in flux, one in which standards are just beginning to be established. Central to it is the issue of protocols, the agreements between entities on how communication between them is to take place.

It is hoped that the articles will serve as introductions to these subjects and that the references will provide the reader with pointers (see Sec. 2.2) to more detailed discussions.

2.1 ARRAY

S. Salveter

An *array* is an ordered collection of objects of the same type. Unlike scalers, where a name refers to one object, the *name* of an array refers to the entire collection of objects. An object in the collection is called an *element* or *cell* of the array. *Subscripts* (or *indices*) are used to reference individual elements. The *dimension* of an array is the number of subscripts required to reference an element. In the general case, an array may be an n-dimensional rectangular structure. If A is an n-dimensional array, then an element of A is referenced by $A[I_1, I_2, \ldots I_n]$, where $L_j \leq I_j \leq U_j$. L_j and U_j are, respectively, the *upper bound* and the *lower bound* of the Jth subscript, I_j.

Figure 1 shows a one-dimensional array named LIST that consists of 10 elements, LIST[I], $1 \leq I \leq 10$. LIST is a collection of characters. The value of LIST[7] is the character M. Figure 2 shows a two-dimensional array (or *matrix*) named TABLE that contains 30 elements organized into five rows and six columns. TABLE is a collection of integers. TABLE[I, J], $-2 \leq I \leq 2$ and $4 \leq J \leq 9$, references the element in the Ith row and Jth column. TABLE[0, 8] has the value 20. For further information, see Ref. 1.

REFERENCE

1. E. HOROWITZ, and S. SAHNI, *Fundamentals of Data Structures*, Computer Science Press, Potomac, Md., 1976.

LIST

1	A
2	N
3	
4	E
5	X
6	A
7	M
8	P
9	L
10	E

Fig. 1   One-dimensional array.

TABLE

	4	5	6	7	8	9
−2	100	95	90	85	80	75
−1	70	65	60	55	50	45
0	40	35	30	25	20	15
1	10	5	0	−5	−10	−15
2	−20	−25	−30	−35	−40	−45

Fig. 2   Two-dimensional array.

2.2 POINTER

S. Salveter

A *pointer* (or *link*) is a variable whose content is interpreted as a memory address. Rather than containing the value to be used as a data item, a pointer indicates where to go in memory to get the data item. Pictorially, pointers are represented by the symbol → , since one is generally not concerned with the actual address contained in the pointer, only with the fact that it refers to another memory location. The *null value* of a pointer, often represented by λ, nil, or ∅, is used to indicate that the pointer is not currently referring to any memory location.

Pointers are commonly used to build linked structures such as lists and trees. A singly linked linear list has a pointer, sometimes referred to as a *list header*, which locates the first node on the list. Each node in the list contains a pointer field that indicates where to find the next item on the list (see Secs. 2.4 and 2.7).

Pointers are useful when several lists share common data items. Rather than have multiple copies of the item, one for each list, each node will have multiple pointer fields, one for each list on which it may reside. All lists that reference the item point to it. A set of three lists that share nodes is shown in Fig. 1. A traversal of LIST1 will access nodes with data fields A, C, B, D, and G; of LIST2 will access C, B, D, and E; and of LIST3, F, C. G, E, and B.

Pointer variables may be used for *dynamic memory allocation*, in which a program requests a block of storage from the operating system during its execution. Since the space was not allocated at compile time and therefore cannot be named, the operating system can only provide the program with a pointer to the allocated block of storage. For further information, see Ref. 1.

REFERENCE

1. D. KNUTH, *The Art of Computer Programming*, Vol. 1: *Fundamental Algorithms*, Addison-Wesley, Reading, Mass., 1969.

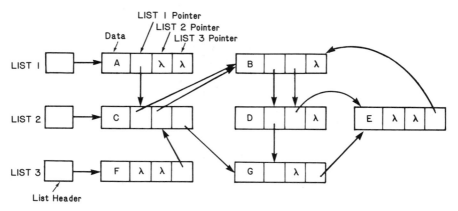

Fig. 1 Use of pointers in a list structure.

2.3 STACK

S. Salveter

A *stack* (or *pushdown list*) is an ordered list in which all insertions and deletions are made at one end, called the *top*. The word *push* is used to describe the operation of adding an item to a stack; the item will be added to the top of the stack. *Pop* describes the operation of removing an item from a stack; the item at the top of the stack will be removed. Since the last item added to a stack will be the first one removed, a stack is called a *last-in-first-out* (LIFO) list. *Stack overflow* occurs when trying to push an item onto an already full stack. *Stack underflow* occurs when trying to pop from an empty stack. In addition, operations for reading (but not popping) the top element of the stack and testing for an empty stack may be provided.

Stacks may be implemented using arrays or linked lists. Figure 1 shows an array used to implement a stack. An integer variable, TOP, indicates the subscript of the item at the top of the stack. If TOP = 0, the stack is empty; if TOP = 100, the stack is full. Figure 1a shows the result of the sequence of operations PUSH(89), PUSH(67), PUSH(106), PUSH(2) performed on array STACKA. Figure 1b and c illustrate, respectively, the result of PUSH(72) and POP performed on STACKA. In a PUSH operation, we first test for available space (TOP < 100 in this case). If no space is available, stack overflow occurs. If space is available, we increment TOP and insert the data item at the TOPth

	STACKA	
1	89	
2	67	TOP = 4
3	106	
4	2	
5		
6		
⋮		
100		

	STACKA	
1	89	
2	67	TOP = 5
3	106	
4	2	
5	72	
6		
⋮		
100		

	STACKA	
1	89	
2	67	TOP = 4
3	106	
4	2	
5	72	
6		
⋮		
100		

(a)   (b)   (c)

Fig. 1 Sequential stack: (a) four-item stack; (b) pushing 72 onto the stack; (c) popping the stack.

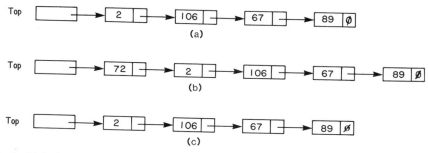

Fig. 2 Linked stack: (*a*) four-item stack; (*b*) pushing 72 onto the stack; (*c*) popping the stack.

position in the array. The POP operation requires that we first check for a nonempty stack (TOP > 0 here). If the stack is empty, we have an underflow condition. Otherwise, the item at position TOP is removed and TOP is decremented.

A linked list used to implement a stack is shown in Figure 2. A pointer variable, TOP, is used to point to the top node on the stack. TOP = ∅ indicates an empty stack. The stack is full only when no more nodes are available to construct new stack entries. Figure 2 shows the results of the same sequence of operations described for Fig. 1. For further information, see Refs. 1 and 2.

REFERENCES

1. D. KNUTH, *The Art of Computer Programming*, Vol. 1: *Fundamental Algorithms*, Addison-Wesley, Reading, Mass., 1969.
2. E. HOROWITZ and S. SAHNI, *Fundamentals of Data Structures*, Computer Science Press, Potomac, Md., 1976.

2.4 LINKED LIST

S. Salveter

2.4.1 Terminology

A *linked list* is an ordered list in which the logical order of the nodes is not the same as their physical order in memory. Each node in the list consists of several items of information, or *fields*, some that contain data and some that contain pointers or links to other nodes in the list. The *list header* is a pointer to the first node in the list. An empty list is indicated by the null pointer in the list header.

Operations performed on linked lists include:

Traversal. Access each node in the list in the logical order in which it occurs.

Search. Traverse the list until a particular data item is located.

Insertion. Insert a new node in the list at some arbitrary position or in accordance with a specified ordering.

Deletion. Remove a node from the list.

Insertion and deletion are easy to accomplish in linked lists since only the updating of a few pointers is involved. By contrast, if a sequence of items is stored so that successive entries must occupy successive physical locations, insertion or deletion involves moving an arbitrary amount of information to make room for a new item or to close the space created by deleting an existing item. Such movement is not required in a linked list since the physical location of an item does not reflect its order in the list. For further information on list structures, see Refs. 1 and 2.

2.4.2 Singly Linked Lists

A *singly linked list* has one pointer field in each node. This pointer indicates the location of the next node in the list. Figure 1a shows an example of a singly linked list pointed to by list header L. The data field of each node contains a string of characters. To traverse the list, the first node of the list is accessed through the list header; subsequent nodes are accessed by following the link in each node. Figure 1b illustrates insertion into the list. Given a pointer, P, to a node in the list, a new node pointed

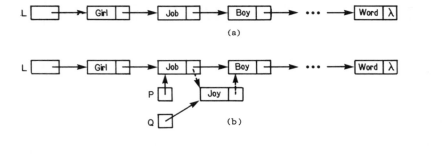

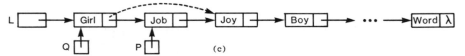

Fig. 1   (a) Two singly linked lists. (b) Insertion. (c) Deletion.

to by Q is inserted after the node referred to by P by changing the two links shown by dashed arrows. Note that given only P and Q, it is not possible to insert the node referred to by Q before the node referred to by P, since we need access to the pointer in the node which precedes the point of insertion (i.e., the pointer in the node containing "girl"). An example of deletion is shown in Fig. 1c. If we wish to delete the node pointed to by P, we must have available a pointer to the previous node, here pointed to by Q, since the latter's link field must be altered to bypass the deleted node.

2.4.3   Doubly Linked Lists

A *doubly linked list* has two pointer fields in each node: a *forward pointer* to the next node in the list and a *back pointer* to the previous node in the list. The back pointer of the first node and forward pointer of the last node are null. Figure 2a shows a doubly linked list of ordered integers. Traversal of a doubly linked list is the same as for a singly linked list, using the forward pointers to access the nodes in order. The insertion of a new node is illustrated in Fig. 2b. The node referred to by Q is to be inserted after the one referred to by P. Four pointers must be changed, as indicated by dashed arrows. Note that, unlike the case with singly linked lists, inserting the node referred to by Q *before* the node

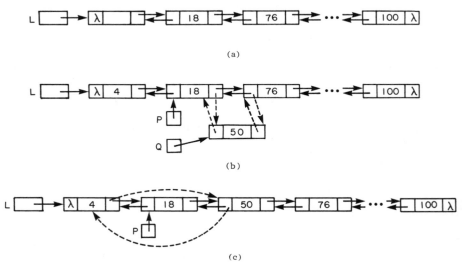

Fig. 2   (a) Doubly linked list. (b) Insertion. (c) Deletion.

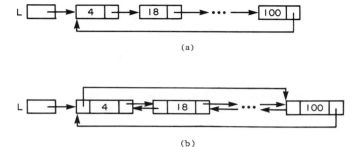

Fig. 3   (a) Singly linked circular list. (b) Doubly linked circular list.

referred to by P may be done without difficulty, since the back pointer of the latter gives access to the previous node. The back pointers are especially useful when deleting a node pointed to by P from the list, as shown in Fig. 2c. Unlike deletion from singly linked lists, it is no longer necessary to maintain a pointer to the node before the node referenced by P, since this information is contained within the node. Thus although deletion is easy in a singly linked list if the node to be deleted is located by traversing the list from the starting point (thus making it possible to keep track of the pointer in the previous node), a doubly linked list will be necessary if the deletion is not preceded by a traversal.

2.4.4   Circularly Linked Lists

In a *circularly linked list* the last node in the list points to the first node. Figure 3a shows an example of a singly linked circular list. A doubly linked list may also be circular, as shown in Fig. 3b. In this case, the forward pointer of the last node points to the first node and the back pointer of the first node points to the last node. Circular lists have the advantage that the entire list may be easily traversed when starting at any node in the list. Insertion and deletion operations are similar to those for noncircularly linked lists.

REFERENCES

1.   D. KNUTH, *The Art of Computer Programming*, Vol. 1: *Fundamental Algorithms*, Addison-Wesley, Reading, Mass., 1969.
2.   E. HOROWITZ and S. SAHNI, *Fundamentals of Data Structures*, Computer Science Press, Potomac, Md., 1976.

2.5   HASH TABLES

P. Henderson

A hash table is a structure that can be used to efficiently implement symbol tables (Sec. 2.6) and table-lookup problems. Here we use the symbol itself as a "key" or index into the table. Hence searching for a specified symbol in the table is usually extremely fast. To gain this improvement in speed, however, some memory space is usually wasted.

Conceptually, we may view a hash table as an array of N locations indexed by $1, 2, 3, \ldots, N$, where one or more symbols may be stored at each location. We also define a function h, called a *hashing function*, which maps symbols to integers in the range 1 to N. To determine the location in the table of a specified symbol s, we simply evaluate $h(s)$ and use the resulting integer as an index into the hash table.

In many practical applications the number of possible symbols is much greater than N. For example, there are more than 100 billion possible PASCAL identifiers, whereas N (the size of the identifier symbol table) is typically in the range 500 to 5000. Clearly, h hashes many elements of the set of possible identifiers to the same location. The set of symbols that are actually used in a particular application may or may not map to distinct locations under h. If two distinct symbols are used that hash to the same location, a *collision* is said to result.

If each location holds a maximum of M symbols, the hash table holds at most $N \times M$ symbols. When an attempt is made to insert a new symbol into a location that currently holds M symbols, an *overflow* is said to occur. In this case we may either abort, or attempt to find an alternative free location where the symbol can be stored. The latter is preferred, and techniques for systematically searching for a symbol or finding a free location for symbol insertion—if one exists—will now be discussed.

2.5.1 Techniques for Handling Overflow

Linear Probing. Linear probing is one method for resolving an overflow. If a symbol is not stored in its hashed location and that location is full, we "probe" the next adjacent location. If the symbol is found there, the search succeeds. Otherwise, there are two possibilities. If the adjacent location is not full and the symbol is not found there, the symbol is not in the table and the search fails. If it is full, we repeat the preceding steps. This process continues until either (1) the symbol is found, or (2) the symbol is not found in a partially filled location, or (3) we return to the initial hashed location, implying that the table is full. If an insertion is being attempted and the search fails (i.e., case 2), the symbol is stored in that partially filled location.

One disadvantage of linear probing is that symbols are not usually uniformly distributed in the table. They tend to cluster into several groups of adjacent locations. This clustering leads to a dramatic increase in the variance of the search and insertion times. Ideally, we would like nearly uniform search and insertion times for all symbols.

Quadratic Probing. To reduce clustering, quadratic probing uses a quadratic function of the number of attempted probes to determine the next location to probe. Techniques for selecting an appropriate table size and quadratic function are presented in Refs. 1 and 3–5.

Rehashing. Here a series, $h_1, h_2, h_3, \ldots, h_N$, of distinct hash functions are applied to symbol s until the search fails or succeeds or a full table is encountered. Hence on the ith probe, $1 \leq i \leq N$, location $h_i(s)$ is examined.

Rehashing can also be accomplished by using a series, $h_1, h_2, h_3, \ldots$, of (possibly identical) hash functions applied successively. On the ith probe, $1 \leq i \leq N$, location $h_i(h_{i-1}(\ldots(h_2(h_1(s)))\ldots))$ is examined. An interesting application of this technique is *random rehashing*, where h_1 maps s to an initial location i, $1 \leq i \leq N$, and the functions $h_2, h_3, \ldots$ are identical and are implemented using a pseudo-random number generator [1]. This method ensures a uniform distribution of symbols in the table, resulting in more uniform symbol search and insertion times.

The preceding techniques are used primarily for implementing structures that do not require the deletion of symbols. Because of the nature of the algorithms employed, symbol deletion may require complete reorganization of the table. For example, consider the consequences of deleting a symbol from a full location when using linear probing. One method for resolving this deficiency is chaining.

Chaining. All preceding methods assume that each location holds at most M symbols. With chaining, each location is the head of a linked list (see Sec. 2.4) of symbols, called a chain. Thus each location may hold a variable number of symbols. Given a specified symbol s, hash function $h(s)$ is initially used to determine a location for s. Linked list techniques are then used to implement searching, insertion, and deletion.

2.5.2 Hashing Functions

The hashing function required to transform a symbol to an integer i, $1 \leq i \leq N$, is critical to the development of a good hashing scheme. Such a function should have the following desirable properties: (1) easy to compute; (2) minimizes collisions; and (3) unbiased. An example of a biased function is one that maps all symbols with the initial character A to the same location.

Some common hashing functions include midsquare, division, folding, and digit analysis [3]. The "middle of the square" scheme squares the integer representation of the symbol and then extracts the middle r bits for use as the index. Here it is assumed that the table has 2^r locations, with indices 0 to $2^r - 1$.

The division technique divides the integer representation of the symbol by the table size and uses the remainder as the location. This simple scheme may be highly biased for certain table sizes. Selection criteria for table sizes that yield unbiased results with this technique are presented in Ref. 5 (p. 261).

Folding partitions the symbol into components of size r bits. These components are then arithmetically summed to yield an r-bit location in the range 0 to $2^r - 1$.

Digit analysis can be effectively used for implementing static symbol tables (see Sec. 2.6). Here, a prior knowledge of the symbols in the table can be used to construct an almost optimal hashing function.

REFERENCES

1. A. V. AHO and J. D. ULLMAN, *The Theory of Parsing, Translation and Compiling*, Vols. 1 and 2, Prentice-Hall, Englewood Cliffs, N.J., 1973.
2. D. GRIES, *Compiler Construction for Digital Computers*, Wiley, New York, 1971.
3. E. HOROWITZ and S. SAHNI, *Fundamentals of Data Structures*, Computer Science Press, Potomac, Md., 1976.
4. E. HOROWITZ and S. SAHNI, *Fundamentals of Computer Algorithms*, Computer Science Press, Potomac, Md., 1978.
5. D. E. KNUTH, *The Art of Computer Programming*, Vol. 3: *Sorting and Searching*, Addison-Wesley, Reading, Mass. 1973.
6. V. Y. LUM, P. S. T. YVEN, and M. DODD, "Key to Address Transformation Techniques—A Fundamental Performance Study on Large Existing Formatted Files," *Commun. ACM*, **14**, 228–239 (Apr. 1971).
7. R. MORRIS, "Scatter Storage Techniques," *Commun. ACM*, **11**, 38–44 (Jan. 1968).

2.6   SYMBOL TABLES

P. Henderson

A symbol table is a data structure for associating symbols with information which those symbols represent. It simulates an associative memory in the same way that the human mind associates written words or symbols with their meaning (information). Symbol tables are used in computer language translators (e.g., assemblers, compilers, interpreters, etc.) and other information-processing systems where symbols are used extensively (e.g., data base management systems, interactive systems, etc.).

Conceptually, we may view the structure of a symbol table as a table of symbols with their associated information. This is illustrated in Fig. 1 (here, for example, symbols may be names, FORTRAN keywords, or Pascal identifiers). In addition, we require a set of operations on this structure which may permit us to make inquires about the symbols and information in the table, or to modify the table. Five desirable operations are:

1. Search for a specified symbol.
2. Obtain the information associated with a specified symbol.
3. Insert a new symbol.
4. Modify the information associated with a specified symbol.
5. Delete a specified symbol and its associated information.

Hence a symbol table represents one example of an abstract data type (Sec. 2.10) since it is conceptually an "abstract" data structure with a set of operations on that structure. Subsequently, we will illustrate "concrete" ways of implementing symbol tables.

In many applications of symbol tables the symbols may not be unique and/or all five operations given above may not be required. Some common restrictions, with examples, are presented next.

A symbol table is said to be *static* if the symbols in the table never change. A common application of a static symbol table is in a compiler for a programming language with a fixed set of keywords.

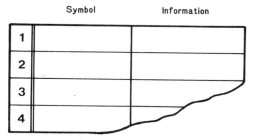

Fig. 1   Conceptual structure of a symbol table.

Here, operations 3 through 5 are not utilized, and frequently operations 1 and 2 are combined into a single SEARCH operation which returns the information associated with the specified symbol when the search for that symbol is successful.

A *dynamic* symbol table is one whose size (number of symbols) may change. For example, in a system that determines word-frequency counts for English language text, the table would initially be empty. As new words are discovered they would be inserted into the table. Words encountered that are already in the table would have their associated frequency count information updated (i.e., incremented). Such a "word dictionary" symbol table would use operations 1 through 4. Clearly, in such a dictionary all symbols are unique. An example of a dynamic symbol table that utilizes all operations and may have nonunique symbols is a table for maintaining identifier symbols in a block-structured language such as ALGOL [1].

2.6.1   Implementation of Symbol Tables

Several different data structures and numerous algorithms operating on these structures are used for implementing symbol tables. The three most common approaches are based on lists, trees, and hash tables.

Lists.   Lists (see Sec. 2.4) represent the simplest approach to implementing symbol tables. However, for large tables they are inefficient, since searching is done sequentially.

Lists are implemented using either array or linked list data structures [1, pp. 336–339]. Array structures may be used for small to medium-size static tables (approximately 5 to 1000 symbols) using either a sequential or sorted binary search algorithm, or they may be used for small dynamic tables (without random symbol deletions) using a sequential search algorithm.

Linked list structures may be used for small dynamic tables where random deletions are required and efficiency is not a primary concern. There are two different approaches to using linked lists for implementing symbol tables: the direct approach, where insertions are at the head or tail of the list [4], and self-organizing lists, where both insertions and inquiries reorganize the list in such a way that symbols which are accessed frequently move toward the head of the list [1, p. 338]. This generally reduces the average search time; however, some extra overhead cost is incurred in list reorganization.

Trees.   Binary trees (see Sec. 2.7) may be used for the implementation of static or dynamic symbol tables [4, pp. 422–456]. For medium-size to large tables there is a substantial reduction in search time over sequential search techniques. However, algorithms for inserting and deleting symbols become more complex because of the problems associated with maintaining a "balanced" tree structure [5]. In addition, as with linked lists, more memory space is required to store the pointers used to implement the trees.

Hash Tables.   Hash tables (see Sec. 2.5) generally provide a good compromise between execution time, memory space efficiency, and implementation difficulty [4, pp. 456–471]. Algorithms for searching and inserting are very efficient when the number of symbols is not close to the maximum size of the table.

A summary of the important characteristics of these implementation methods for symbol tables is presented in Table 1.

Table 1.   Comparison of Symbol Table Implementation Techniques

Technique	Efficiency of Operations			Memory Utilization	Implementation Difficulty
	Search	Insert	Delete		
Static sorted array	Fast	×	×	1	1
Dynamic array	Slow	Slow	Slow	1	1
Linked list	Slow	Slow	Slow	2	2
Self organizing list	Slow	Slow	Slow	2	3
Static tree	Fast	×	×	3	2
Dynamic tree	Fast	Fast	Fast	3	4
Array hash table	Very fast	Slow	Slow	4	3
Chained hash table	Very fast	Very fast	Very fast	4	3
				Efficient → Wasteful 1 4	Easy → Difficult 1 4

REFERENCES

1. A. V. AHO and J. D. ULLMAN, *Principles of Compiler Design*, Addison-Wesley, Reading, Mass., 1978.
2. A. V. AHO and J. D. ULLMAN, *The Theory of Parsing, Translation and Compiling*, Vols. 1 and 2, Prentice-Hall, Englewood Cliffs, N.J., 1973.
3. D. GRIES, *Compiler Construction for Digital Computers*, Wiley, New York, 1971.
4. E. HOROWITZ and S. SAHNI, *Fundamentals of Data Structures*, Computer Science Press, Potomac, Md., 1976.
5. D. E. KNUTH, *The Art of Computer Programming*, Vol. 3: *Sorting and Searching*, Addison-Wesley, Reading, Mass., 1973.
6. C. E. PRICE, "Table Lookup Techniques," *Comput. Surv.*, **3**, 49–65 (June 1971).

2.7 TREE

D. Maier

2.7.1 Terminology

Definitions of terms related to trees are given in this section. Further information on this subject can be found in Refs. 1 and 2.

Trees and Nodes

A *tree* is a generalization of a list. In a list, each item has at most one predecessor and one successor. In a tree, each item has at most one predecessor, but any number of successors. The items in a tree are called *nodes*. Figure 1 depicts a tree. The circles labeled by letters A through K represent the nodes. Each node generally stores some item of information called the *value* at the node. In Fig. 1, the values are the integers in the circles. For example, 4 is the value at node G.

Relationships between Nodes

An immediate successor of a node is a *child* of the node. In Fig. 1, node D is a child of node B, as are nodes E and F. Each node is the *parent* of its children, so node B is the parent of nodes D, E, and F.

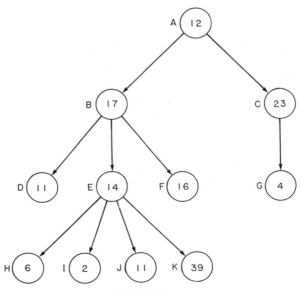

Fig. 1 Tree.

The restriction on predecessors and successors in a tree dictates that a node have at most one parent, but it may have any number of children. Two nodes with the same parent are *siblings*, such as nodes *B* and *C* in Fig. 1. The genealogical terminology extends to nodes that are not immediate predecessors. An *ancestor* of a node is either:

1. The parent of the node, or
2. The parent of an ancestor of the node.

In Fig. 1, the ancestors of node *J* are nodes *E*, *B*, and *A*. If node *x* is ancestor of node *y*, then node *y* is a *descendent* of node *x*. The descendents of node *B* in Fig. 1 are nodes *D*, *E*, *F*, *H*, *I*, *J*, and *K*.

Properties of Nodes

The *degree* of a node is the number of children it has. In Fig. 1, nodes *A*, *B*, and *H* have degrees 2, 3, and 0, respectively. The unique node in a tree with no parent is the *root node* of the tree, such as node *A* in Fig. 1. Any node with degree 0 is a *leaf node* or *terminal node*. The leaf nodes in Fig. 1 are nodes *D*, *F*, *G*, *H*, *I*, *J*, and *K*. Any node that is not the root node or a leaf node is an *interior node* or *branch node*. Nodes *B*, *C*, and *E* are the interior nodes in Fig. 1.

Subtrees

It is useful to consider parts of a tree as trees themselves. Given a tree *T* and a node *x* in *T*, the *subtree of T headed by node x* is a tree *T'* consisting of node *x* and all its descendents in tree *T*. The parent–child relationships are preserved from *T*, except that node *x* has no parent in *T'* and is hence the root node. In Fig. 1, the subtree headed by node *B* is composed of nodes *B*, *D*, *E*, *F*, *H*, *I*, *J*, and *K*.

Paths

A *path* through a tree is a sequence of nodes $X_1, X_2, \ldots, X_k$ such that node X_i is the parent of node X_{i+1} for $1 \leq i < k$. The path $X_1, X_2, \ldots, X_k$ *connects* nodes X_1 and X_k. There is at most one path connecting two nodes in a tree; there may be no such path. The length of a path is one less than the number of nodes in the path, which is the number of arrows in the graphical representation of the path. In Fig. 1, *A*, *B*, *E*, *J* and *C*, *G* are both paths, with lengths 3 and 1, respectively. For every node in a tree there is a path connecting the root to the node. The *depth* or *level* of a node in a tree is the length of the path from the root to the node. In Fig. 1, node *J* has depth 3 and node *C* has depth 1. The *height of a node* is the length of a longest path connecting the node to a leaf node. The *height of a tree* is the height of the root. The tree in Fig. 1 has height 3 because node *A* has height 3.

Types of Trees

Ordered Trees. An ordered tree is a tree in which the children of every node have an ordering. That is, there is a first child, a second child, a third child, and so on, counting from the left. If the tree in Fig. 1 is considered to be ordered, node *J* is the third child of node *E*. In an ordered tree, a node has (possibly) a *left sibling* and a *right sibling*: the nodes immediately before and after the node in the ordering. In Fig. 1, node *C* is the right sibling of node *B* and node *I* is the left sibling of node *J*. Node *K* has no right sibling.

Binary Trees. A binary tree is an ordered tree in which every node has degree at most 2, such as the tree in Fig. 2. The two children of each node are designated as the *left child* and the *right child*. In Fig. 2, node *G* is the left child of node *D*, node *H* is the right child of node *D*, and node *E* has a right but no left child. Note that it is necessary to indicate whether the only child of a node is a left child or right child. For a node *x* in a binary tree, the *left subtree* of node *x* is the subtree headed by the left child of node *x* and the *right subtree* of node *x* is the subtree headed by the right child of node *x*.

Trees of Higher Degree. Analogous to a binary tree is a *ternary tree*: an ordered tree in which every node has degree at most 3. In general, an *n-ary tree* is an ordered tree with node degree at most *n*. Any ordered tree of degree higher than binary is a *multiway tree*.

2.7.2   Representation of Trees

For trees to be useful data structures, there must be a means to store them that is both concise and easy to manipulate. In order to express the tree representations, a simplified computer memory is

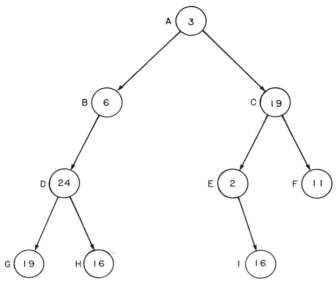

Fig. 2   Binary tree.

assumed, with memory locations addressed by positive integers and each memory location holding a signed integer.

Binary Tree Representation

When storing a tree, the name of a node is unimportant. The important pieces of information are the value at the node and the children of the node. In the following examples, each node is represented in three contiguous memory locations: the first to store the value at the node, the second and third to store the address of the memory locations of the left child and right child, respectively. (If the value of a node were not a single integer, but rather, for example, a character string, more memory locations would be set aside for the value.) Figure 3 is a portion of the representation of the tree in Fig. 2. The representation of node *B* occupies memory locations 103, 104, and 105. Location 103 contains the value at *B*. Location 104 contains the memory address of node *D*, the left son of node *B*. Location 105 contains 0 to show that node *B* has no right son. Whereas the three memory locations for a node must be contiguous, the memory locations for the entire tree need not occur together, nor do the locations need to appear in any particular order. This representation of a binary tree is like a linked representation of a linear list in that additions and deletions do not require changing the contents of a large number of memory locations.

Multiway Tree Representation

A node in an *n*-ary tree can be represented in a manner similar to a node in a binary tree: one memory location for the value at the node and *n* locations to store memory addresses for the first child, second child,..., *n*th child. In some applications this representation is unsuitable. Only a few nodes may have all *n* children, so much memory space is wasted storing zeros. Sometimes the value of *n* is not known in advance, so there is no means to determine how many memory locations to set aside for each node.

There is an alternative representation for a multiway tree that avoids both problems. Three memory locations are needed to represent each node. The first location holds the value at the node. The second location holds the memory address of the first child of the node. The third location holds the memory address of the right sibling of the node. Figure 4 is a portion of the representation of the tree in Fig. 1. The representation of node *E* occupies memory locations 212, 213, and 214. Location 212 holds the value at node *E*, location 213 holds the address of node *H*, the first child of *E*, and location 214 holds the address of node *F*, the right sibling of node *E*. The value 0 is used when a first child or right sibling does not exist.

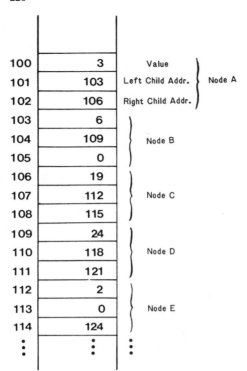

100	3	Value
101	103	Left Child Addr.	Node A
102	106	Right Child Addr.
103	6	
104	109	Node B
105	0	
106	19	
107	112	Node C
108	115	
109	24	
110	118	Node D
111	121	
112	2	
113	0	Node E
114	124	

Fig. 3 Portion of the representation of the tree shown in Fig. 2.

2.7.3   Binary Tree Traversal

In some applications it is necessary to perform some operations on every node of a binary tree exactly once, such as printing the value at the node. A (*binary*) *tree traversal* algorithm is a method of moving through a tree and visiting each node once. *Visit* is a generic term standing for whatever operation is to be performed at the node. In a binary tree, each node has a left and right subtree (although either may be the tree with no nodes). A subtree is a tree in its own right. This property implies that the tree traversal algorithm can be formulated recursively (see Sec. 2.15), incorporating three subproblems:

1. Visit the root of the tree.
2. Traverse the left subtree of the root.
3. Traverse the right subtree of the root.

The left and right subtrees are themselves trees, and traversing each of them can in turn be decomposed into three subproblems. Since a subtree that has no nodes requires no action to traverse, the problem of traversing such a subtree is no longer decomposed.

Applying this traversal algorithm to the tree in Fig. 2 and letting visit mean "print the label of the node" (assuming that the label is stored as part of the value), the result is

$$A \ B \ D \ G \ H \ C \ E \ I \ F$$

The order in which the subproblems are solved affects the order the nodes are visited. The traversal algorithm using the order above is called *preorder traversal*, because the root is visited before either subtree is traversed.

Another possible order for the subproblems is to visit the root between traversing the subtrees. This order gives an *inorder traversal*. An inorder traversal of the tree in Fig. 2, printing the label of the node at each visit, gives

$$G \ D \ H \ B \ A \ E \ I \ C \ F$$

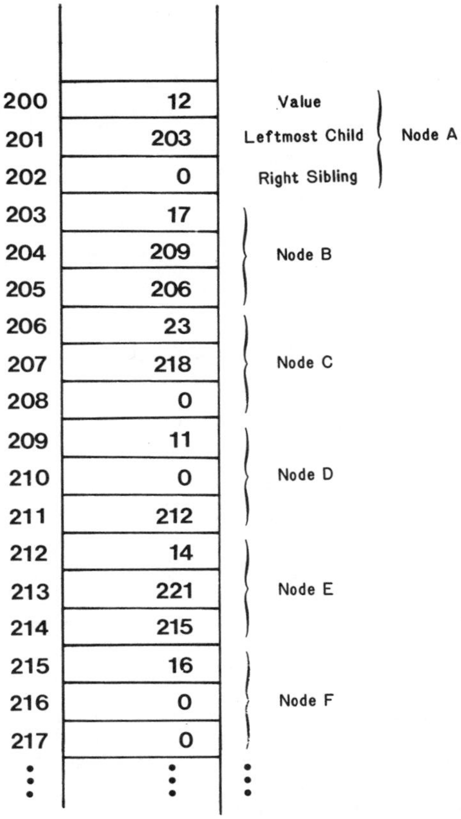

200	12	Value ⎫
201	203	Leftmost Child ⎬ Node A
202	0	Right Sibling ⎭
203	17	⎫
204	209	⎬ Node B
205	206	⎭
206	23	⎫
207	218	⎬ Node C
208	0	⎭
209	11	⎫
210	0	⎬ Node D
211	212	⎭
212	14	⎫
213	221	⎬ Node E
214	215	⎭
215	16	⎫
216	0	⎬ Node F
217	0	⎭

Fig. 4 Portion of the representation of the tree shown in Fig. 1.

The other common order for the subproblems is to visit the root after traversing both subtrees. This order gives a *postorder traversal*. A postorder traversal of the tree in Fig. 2 yields

$$G\ H\ D\ B\ I\ E\ F\ C\ A$$

When implementing a traversal algorithm, a stack is used to keep track of the node being visited and the path taken to reach the node.

2.7.4 Tree Searching

Search Trees

The most common use of trees in computer programming is to organize a set of linearly ordered values so that membership in the set of values can quickly be determined. A *search tree* is a binary tree with the values at the nodes organized according to the following rule:

The value at a node is greater than the values at all the nodes in its left subtree and less than the values at all the nodes in its right subtree.

Figure 5 shows a search tree for the set of values $\{1,3,7,9,10,17,20,22,25,28\}$. For example, node *B* has value 9. The values in its left subtree are 1, 3, and 7; the value in its right subtree is 10. The tree is not unique; there are other search trees for this set of values. If an inorder traversal of the tree is made, the nodes are visited in order of increasing value.

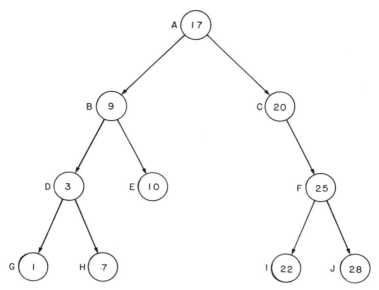

Fig. 5   Search tree.

Searching a Tree

To determine if a value, k, is in the search tree, the following procedure is used. Compare k to the value at the root. If the values are the same, the search is successful; stop. If k is less than the value at the root, proceed to the left child of the root; otherwise, proceed to the right child.

Compare k to the value at the node proceeded to. If the values are equal, stop. If k is smaller, proceed to the left child of the node; otherwise, proceed to the right child.

Continue the process of comparison and proceeding to the left or right child until either a match for k is found or the bottom of the tree is reached. In the second case, the value k is not in the tree.

A search of the tree in Fig. 5 with $k = 7$ proceeds as follows. Compare 7 to 17, the value at A. Since 7 is smaller, proceed to node B, the left child of node A. Compare 7 to 9, the value at B. Proceed to node D, since 7 is smaller. Compare 7 to 3, the value at D. Since 7 is larger, proceed to H, the right child of D. The value at H is 7, so the search is successful. If k were 8 instead of 7, the search proceeds along the same path to node H. However, at node H, since 8 is greater than 7, an attempt is made to proceed to the right child of node H. Since there is no right child, the search fails.

Balanced Trees

The maximum number of steps for tree searching depends on the depth of the deepest node in the tree. For tree searching to be faster than list searching, there must be some limitation on the form of the search tree. For example, if the tree is one where every node except a single leaf node has a left child but no right child, the tree is actually a linked list and tree searching becomes list searching.

To ensure a fast search, a *balance constraint* is imposed on the search tree. A balance constraint is a restriction on the form of a tree meant to guarantee low maximum depth of the nodes. One constraint is to require that every nonleaf node, except possibly one, have two children and every leaf node have depth i or $i + 1$ for some i. A tree meeting this constraint is a *depth-balanced tree*. The maximum depth for such a tree is approximately i or $\log_2 n$, where n is the number of nodes in the tree. (A binary tree with every leaf node having depth at most i has at most $2^{i+1} - 1$ nodes.) Therefore, tree searching a depth-balanced tree with n nodes involves looking at about $\log_2 n$ nodes at most (as compared to a worst case of n nodes in a list search).

Another variety of constrained tree is a *height-balanced tree*, in which, for any node, the height of the left and right subtrees may differ by at most one. Note, however, that the depth of leaf nodes in other subtrees may be quite different. Height-balanced trees are also called *AVL trees*, for G. M. Adel'son-Vel'skii and E. M. Landis [3], who introduced them. The maximum depth for a height-balanced tree with n nodes is about $1.4 \log_2(n + 2)$, which is slightly worse than for a depth-balanced tree. However, height-balanced trees are easier to maintain when nodes are being added to or deleted from the tree.

A third type of constrained tree is the *weight-balanced tree*. The weight of a tree is one plus the number of nodes in the tree. In a weight-balanced tree, for every node

$$\sqrt{2} - 1 < \frac{\text{weight of left subtree}}{\text{weight of right subtree}} < \sqrt{2} + 1$$

The maximum depth in a weight-balanced tree with n nodes is about $2\log_2(n+1)$. This bound is worse than the bound for height-balanced trees, but the representation of a weight-balanced tree takes slightly less storage space. Weight-balanced trees were introduced by J. Nievergelt and C. K. Wong [4].

REFERENCES

1. D. E. KNUTH *The Art of Computer Programming*: Vol 1, *Fundamental Algorithms*, 2nd ed.; Vol. 3, *Sorting and Searching*, Addison-Wesley, Reading, Mass., 1973.
2. C. C. GOTLIEB and L. R. GOTLIEB, *Data Types and Structures*, Prentice-Hall, Englewood Cliffs, N.J., 1978.
3. G. M. ADEL'SON-VEL'SKII and E. M. LANDIS, "An Algorithm for the Organization of Information," English trans. in *Sov. Math. Dokl.*, **3**, 1259–1262 (1962).
4. J. NIEVERGELT and C. K. WONG, "On Binary Search Trees," in *Information Processing Letters 71*, Vol. 1, North-Holland, Amsterdam, 1972, pp. 91–98.

2.8 FILES

J. Heller

Whenever the amount of data processed by a computer system is very large or is needed for future processing, the data are stored on files that can be archived and physically detached from the system. There are two types of files: sequential and direct access. The data in *sequential* files are stored so that they must be read sequentially from the beginning of the file. Similarly, a write adds the data to the end of the file. The data in direct access files can be read and written in any order desired.

Sequential files can be viewed as a sequence of data stored in a linear fashion. A sequential file is constructed by writing blocks of data starting at the beginning of the file and adding each block after the last written block. When stored, successive blocks are separated by an interrecord gap. Each block is frequently referred to as a *physical record*.

From the point of view of the application, the file can be viewed as a sequence of *logical records*. Each logical record contains a unit of related information (e.g., all the information describing a particular employee or stored on a single punched card). Several logical records can be stored within a block. This is referred to as *blocking* (see Fig. 1). The blocking size can be determined by the user. A transfer of a block from the *high-speed storage* (a write) streams the data onto the storage device after the last written block. After a sequential file is written, its end is marked by a special set of characters recognizable as the *end-of-file mark* (EOF).

Only after a sequential file is constructed by a sequence of writes and terminated with an EOF mark can transfer of a block of data (a read) into the high-speed storage commence. The reading of a sequential file starts at its beginning. Each read scans a complete block of data, although not all the data need to be actually transferred into the high-speed storage. The next read starts after the gap and reads up to the next gap on EOF mark.

If an already constructed sequential file is positioned at the EOF mark, the next write will overwrite the EOF with the new block of data and append a new EOF at the end. All the previously written blocks still exist. However, if the sequential file is positioned at its beginning, a write transfers a block of data onto the file at that location and all previously written data are lost, since a new EOF marker is automatically appended after the newly written block.

A *direct access* file can be viewed as a set of blocks of data which can be written or read in any order. After any block is written, it can later be read or overwritten without destroying the other previously written blocks. In the direct access file, not only must programmers manage the data within each block, they must also manage the location of each block within the file. Each block is known by a unique item of information called a *key*.

In the simplest direct access file, the keys are the sequence numbers of the blocks and the operating system provides a mapping between sequence numbers and corresponding blocks. When such a direct access file is first created, the blocks are written sequentially and the physical keys to locate a block are viewed as the integers $1, 2, 3, \ldots$ (see Fig. 2). It is necessary for the programmer to manage which blocks are free and which blocks contain written logical data. In Fig. 2 three logical blocks of information have been written. The first of these, block 1, contains the index of the first free block, 4. The second and third contain application-related information.

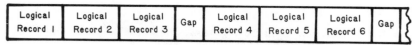

Fig. 1 Sequential file with a blocking of three records.

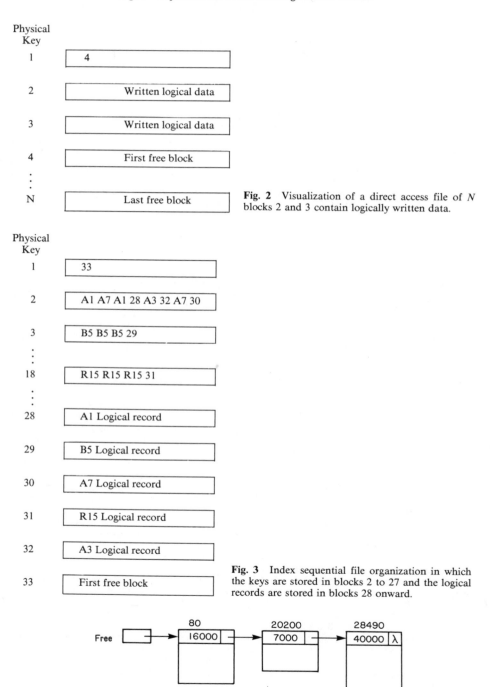

Physical
Key

1	4
2	Written logical data
3	Written logical data
4	First free block
⋮	
N	Last free block

Fig. 2 Visualization of a direct access file of N blocks 2 and 3 contain logically written data.

Physical
Key

1	33
2	A1 A7 A1 28 A3 32 A7 30
3	B5 B5 B5 29
⋮	
18	R15 R15 R15 31
⋮	
28	A1 Logical record
29	B5 Logical record
30	A7 Logical record
31	R15 Logical record
32	A3 Logical record
33	First free block

Fig. 3 Index sequential file organization in which the keys are stored in blocks 2 to 27 and the logical records are stored in blocks 28 onward.

Fig. 1 Linked list of free blocks.

230

Another type of direct access file is the *index sequential file*. In this case each physical block is associated with a unique item of data within the file called a *logical key*. These logical keys are also stored in an index portion of the file, which associates each one with the physical key of the corresponding block.

Starting with a logical key, a sequential search is made through the index portion of the file to locate the corresponding physical key. This sequential search can be shortened by storing the logical keys in lexical order. Each block in the index portion will then start with a header indicating the smallest and largest logical key contained in the block. Only the header needs to be examined to determine if a particular key is in the block. If this logical key is found, the physical key associated with it is used to access the corresponding block of data.

Figure 3 gives a view of an index sequential file in which the index portion of the file is contained in blocks 2 to 27. Each index block starts with a header containing the lowest logical key, the highest logical key, and a list of logical keys with their corresponding physical block number. Block 1 contains the number of the first free block and blocks 28 to 32 contain the data.

2.9 STORAGE ALLOCATION

S. Salveter

2.9.1 Storage Allocation and Deallocation

Computer operating systems and language processors need to be able to allocate and reclaim contiguous blocks of memory. The operating system must provide storage when programs are initiated and subprograms are linked together. A language processor must allocate storage for dynamically created variables.

Storage allocation is the process of providing contiguous blocks of memory of a requested size. A *deallocation* or *reclamation* mechanism for returning blocks of memory that are no longer being used is also necessary to prevent programs from halting due to lack of storage when, in fact, free storage is available. *Fragmentation*, the proliferation of many small unused and unusable blocks, often occurs because request sizes do not usually match available block sizes. A process of *consolidation* is used to examine the neighbors of released blocks and combine them if they are free. Further information on this subject can be found in Refs. 1 and 2.

The blocks of available storage are generally maintained as a linked list sequenced by address; each block minimally contains its size and a pointer to the next available free block. Such a list is shown in Fig. 1. Three blocks are available, starting at locations 80, 20200, and 28490 with sizes 16,000, 7000, and 40,000 locations. To aid the consolidation process, two *boundary tags* may be kept in the first and last locations of each block to indicate whether or not the block is available or in use. The use of these tags in the consolidation process is explained below. Three common allocation algorithms are first fit, best fit, and buddy system.

First Fit

The *first fit* storage allocation strategy searches down the list of available space to find the first block large enough to satisfy the request. If the request is for N locations, the first block with size greater than or equal to N is chosen. N locations out of the block are allocated and the rest remain on the free list. If only a portion of the block is allocated, the allocation is made from the bottom of the block so that the links need not be changed. Figure 2 shows the result of applying the first fit strategy with a request for 5000 locations to the free list shown in Fig. 1. Pointer P points to the allocated block, which starts at location 11080.

One problem with the first fit approach is that small blocks tend to congregate at the front of the list, making it necessary to traverse farther down the list to find larger blocks. One solution is to maintain the free list as a circular list and always begin the new search at the point where the last search ended. This technique distributes the smaller blocks throughout the free list.

To prevent the proliferation of small adjacent blocks of memory on the free list, we wish to coalesce any adjacent free blocks. To determine if the blocks adjacent to a returned block are free, boundary tags and block size are kept in the first and last locations of each block. The boundary tags indicate whether the block is used or free. Since the address and size of the released block are known, the first word of the next block may be interrogated. If its boundary tag indicates that it is free, it may be merged with the newly released block. Similarly, the last word of the previous block may be inspected and merged if its boundary tag indicates that it is not currently in use. In this scheme, the first and last locations of allocated blocks cannot actually be used. Since this may not be satisfactory in some

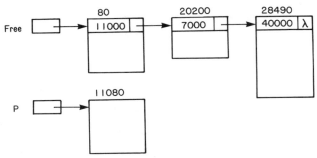

Fig. 2   Result of first fit strategy given a request for 5000 locations.

applications, an alternative is to store the starting addresses and sizes of blocks in the operating system rather than in the blocks themselves. Thus a list containing one entry for each free block, and sorted on starting address, can be maintained to keep track of free storage. Coalescing of adjacent free blocks can easily be carried out with such a data structure.

Best Fit

The *best fit* allocation strategy searches the free list to find the smallest block that will satisfy the request. As with first fit allocation, if the size of the selected block is larger than the request size, locations are allocated from the bottom of the block and the extra locations are left on the free list. Figure 3 shows the result of applying the best fit strategy with a request for 5000 locations to the list in Fig. 1. P points to the allocated block, which starts at location 22200.

A problem with the best fit strategy is the tendency for very small blocks to proliferate. One solution to this problem is to require that if a portion of a block is to be allocated, at least some minimum size block must be left behind; otherwise, the entire block is allocated. For example, if the threshold is to be 100 and a request for 550 locations is to be taken from a 600 location block, the entire 600 locations will be allocated. Consolidation of a freed block with its free adjacent blocks can be accomplished using the boundary tag method described above.

Buddy System

The *buddy system* allocation strategy only allows allocation of blocks of length 2^k, where memory consists of 2^m locations (addressed 0 through $2^m - 1$), $k \leq m$. If the request size is not a power of 2, the next higher power of 2 is chosen and the entire block of that size is allocated.

A binary tree can be used to describe the operation of the buddy system. The leaf nodes of the tree refer to the blocks of storage. Initially, only one block of size 2^m is available. When a request for N words is received, we determine the value of k such that $2^{k-1} < N \leq 2^k$. If a block of size 2^k is available, it is allocated. If no block of that size is available, a larger available block is split into two

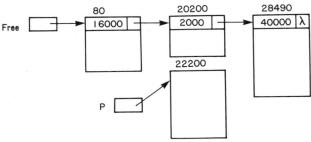

Fig. 3   Result of best fit strategy given a request for 5000 locations.

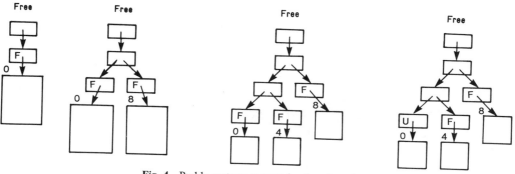

Fig. 4 Buddy system: request for three locations.

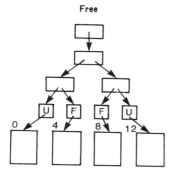

Fig. 5 Determining buddies.

equal parts called *buddies*. The process continues until a block of size 2^k is created. Figure 4 shows the sequence of trees generated when a request for three locations is made from a memory of size 16. The block of size 16 is split into two buddies, each of size 8. One of those buddies is split into two buddies of size 4. Leaf nodes marked with F point to free blocks; those marked with U point to blocks that are in use.

The buddy system is generally implemented using lists. A particular list contains entries representing all available free blocks of a particular size. We will refer to the list containing free blocks of size 2^k as list k. Note that there may be some lower limit on the size of blocks that can be allocated. If 2^s is the size of the smallest block to be allocated, $m - s + 1$ lists are required.

When a block of size 2^i is to be split into buddies, its entry is removed from list i and entries for the buddies are added to list $i - 1$. The process continues until a block of the desired size is created.

Consolidation in the buddy system is accomplished by coalescing buddies into a single block whenever possible. Note that two adjacent blocks of the same size may not always be buddies; they are buddies only if they were both originally created out of the same block. For example, blocks starting at locations 4 and 8 in Fig. 5 will not be merged, since they are not buddies. Given the address and size of a block, we can determine the address of that block's buddy since the address of a block of size 2^k is a multiple of 2^k. If we have a block of size 2^k starting at location L, the address of its buddy will be

$$L + 2^k \qquad \text{if } L \bmod 2^{k+1} = 0$$
$$L - 2^k \qquad \text{if } L \bmod 2^{k+1} = 2^k$$

To determine whether the buddy of a block of size 2^k is free, a tag field may be used in each allocated block, or, if that is not possible, a search through the appropriate list can be performed. If the buddy is free, the blocks are merged. The entry for the buddy of the freed block is removed from list k and an entry for the merged block is added to list $k + 1$. Whenever a larger block is created from

(a)

(b)

Free

(c)

Free

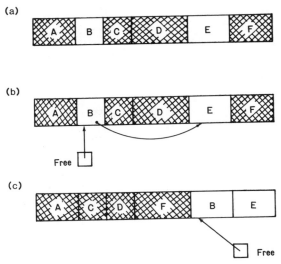

Fig. 6 Garbage collection: (*a*) after marking; (*b*) after returning unused blocks to the free list; (*c*) after compaction.

two buddies, the merging process continues to check if the buddy of the newly created block is free. The process terminates when all free buddies have been merged.

Note that the buddy system may allow two adjacent blocks to be free without merging them. Simulation has shown [3], however, that after an initial startup period it is not often necessary to split or merge blocks at all; blocks tend to remain on the commonly used lists.

2.9.2   Garbage Collection

This term is used to describe the storage reclamation process that is used in a multilist environment, where each node may be pointed to by a number of other nodes. A node deleted from one list may not be returned to the free list, since it may still be part of another list. If there is no simple way of determining when a node is no longer a part of any list, a new technique for recovering unused storage may be needed. The garbage collection process consists of two subprocesses: marking and collection. The *marking* process identifies the storage blocks available for release. *Collection* gathers the free blocks identified in the marking phase. There are two possible collection schemes: compaction and return to a free list.

The marking process requires that all nodes have a header containing a special bit, the marking bit (generally all nodes are the same size). The process starts by setting the mark bit in each node to zero. Then each list is traversed and the mark bit in each node encountered is set to one (or marked), indicating that the node is in use. At the end of this process, all allocated storage will be marked and all free storage will be unmarked. If the unmarked blocks are to be returned to a free list, memory is traversed once more; the unmarked blocks are linked together and a pointer is set to the first free block.

If compaction is used as the collection process, all allocated blocks will be copied into new, more tightly packed storage. As memory is traversed, the information in the marked locations is copied into one "end" of the storage area; the other "end" of the storage area will be one contiguous block of free space. Unlike consolidation, which only coalesces adjacent free blocks, compaction results in all free space forming one contiguous block. Thus, instead of maintaining lists of different-size blocks as in the buddy system, after compaction it is necessary only to keep a pointer to the boundary between allocated and free storage.

For example, suppose that after marking memory is as shown in Fig. 6*a*, where shaded areas indicate marked locations. If returning unmarked blocks to a free list is the collection scheme, memory will look like Fig. 6*b* afterward. Blocks and B and E have been linked together and the freelist pointer, FREE, points to B. If compaction is used instead, memory will look like Fig. 6*c*. Marked areas, C, D, and F, have been copied to the left end of memory and FREE indicates the start of available space.

REFERENCES

1. D. KNUTH, *The Art of Computer Programming*, Vol. 1; *Fundamental Algorithms*, Addison-Wesley, Reading, Mass., 1969.
2. E. HOROWITZ and S. SAHNI, *Fundamentals of Data Structures*, Computer Science Press, Potomac, Md., 1976.
3. P. W. PURDOM and S. M. STIGLER, "Statistical Properties of the Buddy System," *J. ACM*, **17**, 682–697 (1970).

2.10 ABSTRACT DATA TYPES

F. B. Schneider

Most modern digital computers implement a variety of data types in the hardware. For example, floating-point numbers, fixed-point numbers (a subset of the integers), and characters and character strings are data types often available to the machine language programmer. For each data type implemented in hardware, a collection of machine instructions is defined to manipulate values of that type. Thus, on a machine that supports both floating- and fixed-point numbers, two addition instructions might be provided: one for addition of floating-point values and the other for addition of fixed-point values. When using a hardware-implemented data type, a programmer need not be aware of exactly how values are represented (e.g., is 1's complement or 2's complement used for negative values?) or how operations are realized (e.g., is multiplication implemented by repeated addition?).

Often, high-level programming languages (see Sec. 2.13) also provide the programmer with a collection of data types and convenient operations on these types. It is not unusual for a language to support data types that are not directly implemented in hardware. Values of instances of such types are represented in terms of values of instances of types that are supported by the hardware. For example, an array is represented in terms of the values of its components. Similarly, operations on the new types are implemented in terms of operations (machine instructions) on the hardware-supported types [1].

This approach can be extended to allow a programmer to define new data types by specifying a representation for values of that type, the set of operations on instances of that type, and the implementation of those operations on the chosen representation. Such data types are called *abstract data types*, and programming languages that allow such user definition of data types are called *extensible* [3].

2.10.1 Defining Abstract Data Types

The syntax of an abstract data type definition facility in a hypothetical high-level language appears in Fig. 1; ⟨typename⟩ is the name of the abstract data type. A variable v of type ⟨typename⟩ may be instantiated by declaring it as follows:

$$\textbf{var } v : \langle \text{typename} \rangle$$

This results in the allocation of an instance of each of the variables defined in the representation portion of the abstract data type definition for ⟨typename⟩, and execution of the initialization code.

```
type  ⟨typename⟩ = abstract data type;
    representation... define variables needed to represent an instance of ⟨typename⟩...
    ⟨operationl⟩ procedure(...parameters...);
        var... local variables required for implementation of ⟨operationl⟩...
        begin
            ...code to implement ⟨operationl⟩
        end;
    ...definitions of other operations...
    begin
        ...code to initialize an instance of ⟨typename⟩...
    end;
```

Fig. 1 Abstract data type definition.

Variables defined in the representation portion of an abstract data type definition may be referenced only from within the operations or the initialization section of that type definition. Furthermore, the values of these variables persist as long as the instance of the abstract type is allocated (such as ALGOL **own** or PL/1 **static** allocation). Alternatively, variables declared local to an operation of the abstract data type are instantiated when the operation is invoked and its execution commences, and deallocated when the operation completes.

The only way to manipulate an instance of an abstract data type is by invoking operations. To invoke operation ⟨OP⟩ on ⟨V⟩, an instance of an abstract data type whose definition includes ⟨OP⟩, one codes

$$⟨V⟩.⟨OP⟩(\ldots \text{actual values for parameters}\ldots);$$

2.10.2   Example

A *stack* is a last-in-first-out data structure (described in Sec. 2.3). Figure 2 is an abstract data type definition for a bounded stack of integers. Given this definition, it is possible to allocate an instance of such a stack, called *LIFOSTORE*, by coding the following:

var LIFOSTORE : stack of int;

Subsequently, a value L can be placed on the top of the stack by executing

LIFOSTORE. push (L);

By executing

LIFOSTORE.value (L);

(where L is a variable of type *integer*), the top value in *LIFOSTORE* is copied to L. The topmost element in *LIFOSTORE* is deleted by executing

LIFOSTORE. pop;

```
type   stack of int = abstract data type;
       representation   s : array[1..10] of integer;
                        top : 0..10;
       push procedure (val : integer);
           begin
                        if top = 10 then error; (*stack overflow*)
                        top: = top + 1;
                        s[top]: = val;
           end;
       pop procedure;
           begin
                        if top = 0 then error;  (*stack underflow*)
                        top: = top − 1;
           end;
       value procedure (var topval : integer);
           begin
                        if top = 0 then error;  (*empty stack*)
                        topval: = S[top];
           end;
           begin                                    (*initialization*)
                        top: = 0;
           end;
```

Fig. 2   Example of an abstract data type.

2.10.3   Implications of Abstract Data Types

Programming is a difficult task, in part, because of the extraordinary number of details to which a programmer must attend [1]. Use of abstract data types frees the programmer from keeping track of all these details all of the time. This is because when using an instance of an abstract data type, a programmer need not be aware of the details of the representation of the abstraction or the implementation of the operations on it. Similarly, when defining an abstract data type, the implementor need not be concerned with how and when instances of this type will be manipulated. Rather, the implementor's only concern should be to provide operations that implement the required manipulations on the representation.

Programs that use abstract data types tend to be well structured, hence easy to read and understand. This is because the details concerning the manipulation of each abstraction are localized in the abstract data type definition. Furthermore, algorithms that use instances of an abstract data type are not cluttered with details concerning the manipulation of a representation of the abstraction—they need only reference the operations that are implemented in the abstract data type definition. The idea of partitioning a program into components, where each implements some abstraction and therefore hides implementation details from its users, is not new. This idea of *information hiding* is the basis for most system decompositions into *modules* [2]. In fact, modules and abstract data types are very similar notions.

Most programs are subject to continual change. The use of abstract data types can help to avoid some of the problems associated with making changes to programs. This is because abstract data type definitions can be changed without having any effect on a program (other than on performance), provided that the functionality of the abstraction is unaltered by the changes. Abstract data types also allow a good deal of control over the representation of data structures. Often, the "optimal" representation of an abstraction depends on the frequency with which the various operations will be performed. (The data type "set" is a good example of this.) When such an abstraction is built into a high-level language, a general representation scheme is usually employed. Such a scheme may not be optimal for all applications. Abstract data types, however, provide the programmer with the ability to design a representation well suited for each application. This is called *representational optimization*.

Finally, note that abstract data types provide a facility for constructing hierarchical systems (Sec. 2.24). The representation of a particular abstraction need not be only in terms of primitive data types, but could involve instances of other abstractions. A hierarchy of abstract data types results.

REFERENCES

1. O. J. DAHL, E. W. DIJKSTRA, and C. A. R. HOARE, *Structured Programming*, Academic Press, New York, 1972.

2. D. L. PARNAS, "On the Criteria to Be Used in Decomposing Systems into Modules," *Commun. ACM* **15**(12), 1053–1058 (Dec. 1972).

3. *Proc. Conf. Data: Abstraction, Definition and Structure, SIGPLAN Not.* **8**(2) (Vol. II).

2.11   ASSEMBLY LANGUAGE

D. H. Tycko

2.11.1   Basic Concept

Conventional computers are capable of executing programs expressed in a language that is directly interpretable by the hardware. This language is referred to as machine language. The machine language instructions that comprise a program to be executed are stored in the computer's memory as strings of bits. For example, the PDP-11 instruction for copying the contents of register 4 into register 5 is 0001   000100   000101. The leftmost group of 4 bits in this instruction is the binary code for the copy (or move) operation, the middle group of 6 bits specifies the source of the information (register 4), and the rightmost group of 6 bits indicates the destination register (register 5). Although it is possible to write a program of arbitrary complexity in the machine language of the computer on which the program is to be run, in practice symbolic programming languages are used almost exclusively. In most cases, the programming language employed is unrelated to a machine language (e.g., FORTRAN or COBOL), but in certain situations it is advantageous to use a language that is essentially a symbolic form of the machine language of interest. Such a language is called an *assembly language* and a program that translates an assembly language program to its corresponding machine language program is an *assembler* for that machine. When programming in an assembly language, alphabetic mnemonic symbols are used in place of binary operation codes, and alphabetic symbols or nonbinary numerals are used in place of binary representations of register and memory addresses. The example above from the PDP-11 instruction set could be written as MOV R4, R5 in the PDP-11 assembly language, MACRO-11.

In order to write a program in the machine language of many machines the programmer must specify the absolute memory locations of both the instructions and the data. That is, memory allocation must be done at the time the program is being written. Assembly languages relieve the programmer of this responsibility. The use of symbols to designate memory locations causes the assembler to produce a relocatable form of the machine language program in which instruction and data addresses are specified relative to more or less arbitrary points in the program. In this case the absolute address, at the time the program is executed, of an item of information does not effect the outcome of the computation. Only its relative position with respect to other items of information in the program is important. The final binding of these relative addresses to physical memory locations is subsequently done by utility programs of the operating system (linkers and loaders) just prior to execution of the program.

2.11.2 Assembly Language Statements

An assembly language program is comprised of a sequence of statements. An assembly language statement is made up of four ordered fields:

1. Label field
2. Op code field
3. Operands field
4. Comment field

The op code field, used to specify an operation, is always present. The label and operands fields, whose uses depend on the operation specified in the op code field and the context of the statement, may be empty. The comment field is provided for documentation purposes and its use is completely at the discretion of the programmer. Examples of assembly language statements are given in Figs. 1, 2, and 3, which contain programs written in the assembly languages of the IBM 360/370, UNIVAC 1100 series, and PDP-11 computers, respectively.

Assembly language statements are divided into three classes: machine-instructions, assembler-instructions, and macro-instructions. The three sets of operation codes corresponding to the three statement classes are disjoint, making classification of a given statement a simple matter.

Labels	Op Codes	Operands	Comments
1.	TITLE	'EXAMPLE PROGRAM—IBM 360/370'	
2. R14	EQU	14	MAKE R14 STAND FOR 14.
3. FIRST	BALR	2,0	SET REG 2 FOR USE AS BASE
4.	USING	*,2	REG & INFORM ASSEMBLER.
5.	L	5,X	LOAD REG 5 WITH X.
6.	A	5,Y	ADD Y TO REG 5.
7.	S	5,Z	SUBTRACT Z FROM REG 5.
8.	M	4, = F'99'	MULTIPLY BY 99 (LITERAL).
9.	ST	5,R	STORE THE RESULT.
10.	BR	R14	EXIT VIA REG 14.
11. X	DC	F'1234'	DEFINE THE CONSTANT X.
12. Y	DC	F'3189'	DEFINE THE CONSTANT Y.
13. Z	DC	F'2399'	DEFINE THE CONSTANT Z.
14. R	DS	1F	RESERVE A FULL WORD FOR RESULT.
15.	END	FIRST	SPECIFY STARTING ADDRESS.

Fig. 1 Program written in the assembly language of the IBM 360/370 computer systems. This program evaluates the expression $99*(X+Y-Z)$ for the values $X=1234$, $Y=3189$, and $Z=2399$ and leaves the result in the memory word labeled R.

Labels	Op Codes	Operands	Comments
1.	EXAMPLE PROGRAM—UNIVAC 1100 SERIES		
2.	AXR$		. USE STANDARD MNEMONICS
3. R	RES	1	. RESERVE A WORD FOR RESULT
4. FIRST	LA	A4, X	. LOAD REG A4 WITH X
5.	AA	A4, X + 1	. ADD Y TO REG A4
6.	ANA	A4, $ + 13	. SUBTRACT Z FROM REG A4
7.	MSI	A4, (99)	. MULTIPLY BY 99 (LITERAL)
8.	SA	A4, R	. STORE THE RESULT
9.	L$LSNAP	'RESULT', 0, 1, R	. USE MACRO TO PRINT RESULT
10.	ER	EXIT$	. TERMINATE EXECUTION
11. X	+ 1234		. DEFINE THE CONSTANT X
12. Y	+ 3189		. DEFINE THE CONSTANT Y
13. Z	+ 2399		. DEFINE THE CONSTANT Z
14.	END	FIRST	. SPECIFY STARTING ADDRESS

Fig. 2 Program written in the assembly language of the Univac 1100 series computer systems. The program evaluates the same expression as the one evaluated by the program of Fig. 1. In addition, it prints an octal representation of the result through the use of the system macro L$SNAP. In this assembly language, a period followed by a space indicates the beginning of a comment.

Labels	Op Codes	Operands	Comments
1.	.TITLE	EXAMPLE PROGRAM—PDP-11	
2. ;			
3. ;	DEFINE A MACRO FOR MULTIPLICATION USING THE KE11		
4. ;	EXTENDED ARITHMETIC UNIT		
5.	.MACRO	MULT A, B, PROD	
6.	MOV	A, @ # 177304	
7.	MOV	B, @ # 177306	
8.	MOV	@ # 177304, PROD	
9.	.ENDM		
10. ;			
11.	.RADIX	10	; USE DECIMAL NUMBER SYSTEM
12. R:	.BLKW	1	; RESERVE A WORD FOR RESULT
13. FIRST:	MOV	X, R4	; LOAD REG 4 WITH X
14.	ADD	Y, R4	; ADD Y TO REG 4
15.	SUB	Z, R4	; SUBTRACT Z FROM REG 4
16.	MULT	R4, # 99, R	; USE MACRO TO MULTIPLY BY 99
17.	HALT		; STOP
18. X:	.WORD	1234	; DEFINE THE CONSTANT X
19. Y:	.WORD	3189	; DEFINE THE CONSTANT Y
20. Z:	.WORD	2399	; DEFINE THE CONSTANT Z
21.	.END	FIRST	; SPECIFY STARTING ADDRESS

Fig. 3 Program written in the asembly language of Digital Equipment Corporation PDP-11 computer systems. The same expression is evaluated by the program that is used in the programs of Figs. 1 and 2. In this case, a user-defined macro, MULT, is employed for multiplication of $(X + Y - Z)$ by the immediate constant 99. In this assembly language, comments are preceded by semicolons.

Machine-Instruction Statements

A machine-instruction statement directs the computer to perform a particular operation on the specified operands during the execution of the program. Each statement of this class is translated by the assembler into one machine language instruction. Lines 3 and 5 to 10 of Fig. 1, lines 4 to 8 and 10 of Fig. 2, and lines 13 to 15 and 17 of Fig. 3 are the machine-instruction statements in the example programs. Lines 6 to 8 of Fig. 3 are also machine-instruction statements, appearing in the context of a macro definition (see the discussion of macro-instruction statements below).

The label field of a machine-instruction statement is used to define a symbol (label) which stands for the address of the memory location that the corresponding machine instruction occupies during execution of the program. The label may then be used in other parts of the program to refer to this instruction. Labels are strings of nonblank characters, usually starting with an alphabetic character. The maximum length of these strings is generally limited to a value that depends on the particular assembly language (typically 6 to 12 characters). In the example programs, the symbol FIRST is defined through its use as a label in a machine-instruction statement.

The op codes for machine-instruction statements are short alphabetic mnemonics related in a one-to-one fashion to the binary operation codes of the target computer (e.g., MOV corresponds to 0001 for the PDP-11). The mnemonics and their correspondence with the computer's binary codes constitute an important part of the definition of an assembly language.

Operands fields of machine-instruction statements are used to indicate the operand address to be used in the execution of the instruction and to specify addressing modes [e.g., indirect, indexed, (see Sec. 1.1)]. The operands may be specified as absolute (physical) register or memory addresses (expressed in decimal, octal, or hexadecimal notation) or as relative memory addresses using symbols (labels) and expressions. For example, in Fig. 1, line 5, the operands field designates register 5 (absolute) as the destination operand of the load instruction using the register number explicitly while specifying the source address using the symbolic address X (relative), defined in line 11 through the use of the DC assembler-instruction (see the following section for an explanation of assembler-instructions). The octal numbers 177304 and 177306 appearing in lines 6, 7, and 8 of Fig. 3 are examples of the use of absolute memory addresses in operands fields. The prefixes @# in these operands specify a particular addressing mode of the PDP-11 and serve as examples of the use of special characters in operand fields to designate addressing modes. Arithmetic expressions involving symbols and constants

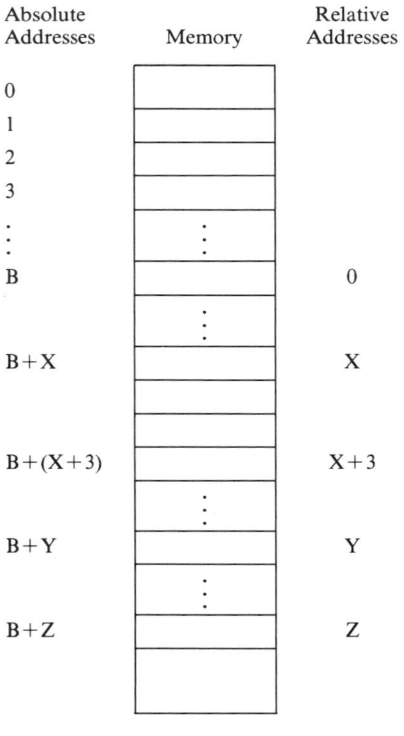

Fig. 4 Relationship between symbolic relative addresses and absolute addresses. A relative address, X, is mapped into an absolute address by adding it to a base address, B, which is determined at the time the program is loaded (stored in the computer's memory) just prior to its execution.

are generally allowed as operands provided that they evaluate to either an absolute or relative address. For example, $X+Y$ is not an allowed expression but $Y-X$ and $X+3$ are. To understand this, recall that symbolic addresses $X, Y, Z, \ldots$ represent displacements of their associated memory addresses from some common origin or base address, B, which is the actual first address of the program and is determined at the time the program is loaded into memory. Consequently, when the program is executed, the corresponding absolute addresses are $B+X$, $B+Y$, $B+Z, \ldots$ (see Fig. 4). Thus a relative address S is mapped into an absolute address through the relation $S \rightarrow B+S$. Since the expression $X+Y$ maps into $2B+X+Y$, $X+Y$ is not a relative address. It is also not an absolute address because $2B+X+Y$ depends on the base address, B. On the other hand, $Y-X$ maps into a constant (the number of locations separating Y and X) independent of B, which is interpretable as an absolute address, while $X+3$ maps into $B+(X+3)$, a relative address. Hence the latter two expressions are allowed as operands. Lines 5 and 6 of Fig. 2 illustrate the use of expressions as operands. Line 6 also is an example of the use of a special character, "$", to represent the relative address of the instruction in which the symbol is used (3, in this case), the so-called current value of the location counter (see Sec. 2.11.3).

Most assembly languages include a feature, called *literal operands*, which allows the programmer to define program constants by writing their values in the operands fields rather than their addresses. In both line 8 of Fig. 1 and line 7 of Fig. 2 the program constant 99 is defined as a literal operand. The assemblers automatically generate the literal constants, assign them memory addresses at the end of the program modules, and use these addresses in the associated machine language instructions.

Assembler-Instruction Statements

An assembler-instruction statement directs the assembler to take a particular action during the translation of the source program. Some assembler-instruction statements effect the memory requirements of the machine language program, whereas others do not. Assembler instructions are also called assembler directives or pseudoinstructions in the literature.

Assembler instructions for defining program constants and reserving blocks of memory are universally included in assembly languages. The symbolic addresses of data are defined through the use of the symbols in the label fields of statements of this kind. Examples appear in Fig. 1, lines 11 to 14; Fig. 2, lines 3 and 11–13; and Fig. 3, lines 12 and 18 to 20. Thus in Fig. 1, line 11, the DC statement assigns the constant 1234 to the memory location following the BR instruction and gives it the symbolic address X.

The END statement that appears as the physically last statement in all assembly language programs (see Figs. 1, 2, and 3) is an assembler instruction that does not generate machine instructions; it tells the assembler where the end of the program is to be found and, through its operand field, usually identifies the starting address of the program.

In addition, assembler instructions include those for controlling the listing of the program during assembly (e.g., the TITLE instructions in the first lines of Figs. 1 and 3), instructions for defining or equating mnemonic symbols (e.g., the EQU of Fig. 1, line 2 indicates that the symbol R14 stands for the number 14), instructions for specifying the number system the programmer is using in his coding (e.g., Fig. 3, line 11), instructions for controlling base register addressing (e.g., Fig. 1, line 4; see Secs. 1.5 and 2.12.1), instructions for identifying externally defined symbols and entry points, and a number of others.

Macro-Instruction Statements

A macro-instruction statement is a statement that is expanded by the assembler into a sequence of machine-instruction statements called a *macro*. For example, a macro-instruction statement for adding two numbers and storing the result could be written as

$$\text{SUM} \quad A, B, C$$

For a single-accumulator, single-address machine, the expansion of this statement might be

$$
\begin{array}{ll}
\text{LOAD} & A \\
\text{ADD} & B \\
\text{STORE} & C
\end{array}
$$

Certain macro instructions, called *system macros*, are predefined in the system software and are available to the programmer as extensions of the machine instruction set. These system macros usually deal with input/output operations and other functions handled by the operating system. Line 9 of Fig. 2 contains an example of the use of the UNIVAC system macro L$SNAP.

Macros can also be defined within the text of the assembly language program itself. A macro definition starts with a special assembler instruction which informs the assembler that a macro definition is beginning and specifies the macro name and parameters. The sequence of statements that define the macro follow. Finally, the macro definition terminates with another assembler instruction used for that purpose. The hypothetical macro SUM presented above might have been defined as follows:

```
MACRO    SUM      P1,P2,P3
LOAD     P1
ADD      P2
STORE    P3
MEND     SUM
```

where P1, P2, and P3 are dummy arguments and MACRO and MEND are the assembler instructions marking the beginning and end of the macro definition. Note that the macro definitions in the text of a program do not result directly in machine instructions. They only serve as templates for the expansions that occur when macro-instruction statements are processed. The actual arguments listed in the macro-instruction statements replace the dummy arguments of the macro definitions. Another example of the definition and use of macros is given in Fig. 3, where lines 5 to 9 contain the definition of the macro MULT with dummy arguments A, B, PROD, and line 16 contains the corresponding macro-instruction statement with actual parameters R4, #99, R. During the assembly of the program, line 16 would be expanded into the three statements

```
MOV    R4,   @#177304
MOV    #99,  @#177306
MOV    @#177304,   R
```

Modern assembly languages provide quite sophisticated macro capabilities, including such features as nesting of macros and conditional macro expansion.

2.11.3 Assemblers

Assemblers are programs that read files containing assembly language source programs and produce files of relocatable machine language programs. They also create listings of the source programs together with octal or hexadecimal representations of the associated machine language programs.

The first phase of the translation process involves an initial statement-by-statement examination of the source program. Depending on the contents of its fields, a given statement may or may not require memory space for its translation. Each time a statement requiring space is encountered, an integer variable, called the *location counter* (LC), is incremented by the appropriate number of units. The LC is initialized to zero and is, therefore, essentially a pointer to the next available location in the relative address space.

During this first pass over the statements of the source program several tables are generated. First, the macro definitions, which must precede the main body of the source program, are collected into a *macro-definition table* (MDT). Second, a *symbol table* (ST) is constructed relating labels to the LC values associated with their occurrences. Finally, a list of literal constants, called the *literal pool* (LP), is developed in such a way that multiple uses of a given literal results in a single entry in the LP. When the first pass is completed, the final LC value becomes the relative address of the first entry in the LP (often called the literal origin).

During the first pass, macro-instruction statements are expanded when they are encountered by referring to the MDT for programmer-defined macros or to similar tables provided by the system software for the system macros. The macro expansion process involves the substitution of the actual parameters specified in a macro-instruction statement for the corresponding dummy arguments in the macro definition statements. The resulting sequence of assembler language statements are inserted into the source program text at the point where the macro-instruction statement appeared. First-pass processing then proceeds from the first statement of the macro expansion.

It is not possible to make the complete translation to machine language in a single pass through the source program because a statement may contain a symbolic operand that is not defined until a later statement is processed (e.g., see Fig. 1, lines 5 and 11). Also, the addresses of the literals cannot be known until the literal origin is determined at the end of the first pass. Therefore, assemblers require a second pass through the input file, during which the information in the ST and LP is utilized to make the final translation and produce the output file and listings.

To illustrate second-pass processing, consider the example program in Fig. 2. Each Univac 1100 machine instruction occupies one 36-bit memory word, the addressable unit of memory for these machines. Therefore, after completion of the first pass the ST would contain the symbols R, FIRST, X, Y, and Z, having values (relative addresses) 0, 1, 14, 15, and 16, respectively. The LP would contain the binary representation of the decimal constant 99 with a relative address of 17. Consequently,

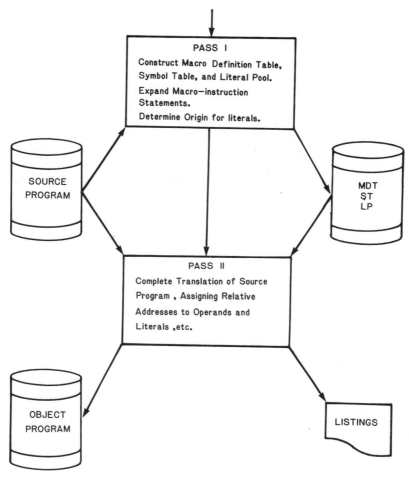

Fig. 5 Schematic representation of a two-pass assembler.

during the second pass the operands X, X+1, (99), and R would be translated into the binary representations of 14, 15, 17, and 0, respectively, and inserted in the operand fields of the corresponding relocatable machine instructions.

The general organization and information flow of assemblers is shown in Fig. 5. Additional information on this subject can be found in Ref. 1.

REFERENCES

1. C. W. GEAR, *Computer Organization and Programming*, McGraw-Hill, New York, 1969.

2.12 LINKING AND LOADING

P. Henderson

Presently, almost all programming is done using symbolic assembly or higher-level languages. These languages are translated to machine language using assemblers or compilers, respectively. Certain compilers, such as compile-and-go processors, used for short student jobs (e.g., WATFIVE) store their resultant machine language code directly into memory for subsequent execution. However, most assemblers and compilers produce machine code modules, called *object modules*, which can be saved on magnetic tape, disk, cards, and so on, for subsequent use. These modules are created so that they can be adapted to execute anywhere in memory. They are frequently referred to as relocatable object modules and the adaptation is called *loading*. Also, they can be "linked" to other user-generated object modules, or to system library modules that support operations such as input, output, mathematical functions, and sorting.

2.12.1 Loaders

A *loader* is a program that loads machine code programs into the memory of a computer. The simplest loader is the *absolute* or *binary loader*, which copies an "absolute" binary module directly into memory. One representation of a binary module is as a sequence of pairs of memory addresses and binary words. The loader reads each pair, storing the binary word into its corresponding address.

A *bootstrap loader* is a binary loader that can be initiated using a hardware switch, usually labeled LOAD, on the console panel of the computer. The loader is wired into the hardware. Typically, it reads the contents of a single record, generally containing several instructions and data items, into successive positions in memory starting from some preset initial location. After the record has been loaded, control is transferred to that initial location. Generally, when a bootstrap loader is used, the contents of the record is a simple binary loader capable of loading larger programs (e.g., operating system, compilers, etc.). Bootstrap loading is used for initial loading when the system is first turned on, or is restarted.

A *relocating loader* loads a relocatable object module (i.e., relocatable data and machine instructions) into memory. The language processor that produces such modules assumes, for reference purposes, that the address of the first word of the module is zero and that subsequent words follow in consecutive addresses. Such addresses are called *relative addresses*. Upon loading, the first word is usually stored at some address other than zero, and hence the module requires relocation if it is to execute correctly. Accordingly, the values of all "location-sensitive" words must be adjusted by adding an appropriate *relocation constant*. An example of a location-sensitive word is an instruction containing the address of another instruction or data item in the module (e.g., a transfer instruction). An instruction that shifts the contents of a register in the CPU would not be location sensitive. Location-sensitive words are designated in an object module by either "flagging" each such word or by providing an index table, called a *relocation directory*, of such words. These words can be modified later by the loader [2].

The ease with which relocation of an object module can be performed depends on the architecture of the computer hardware. On some machines (e.g., PDP-8, HP-2115), location-sensitive words must be adjusted on loading by adding the appropriate relocation constant. For machines with base register addressing (e.g., IBM 360; see Sec. 1.1.5) instructions and data can be relocated without code modification at load time. Here the base register is set by the module itself at execution time to contain the module's starting location in memory [6, p. 86]. Location-sensitive instructions use the base register during effective address computation. Thus relocation is performed by the program at execution time. In architectures implementing one-dimensional virtual memories (see Sec. 2.19) relocation is also done by the hardware at execution time. This differs from the base register addressing scheme in that the contents of the hardware memory mapping registers are under the control of the operating system, and their use is transparent to the user.

The relocation constant for an object module depends on the location in memory where that module will reside. Usually, the relocation constant is the loading address of the first word of the object module. That is, since the relative address of the first word (assumed to be zero) is mapped to an absolute memory address, all references to data and instruction words must be adjusted by this absolute address, which is the desired relocation constant. When several object modules are to be linked to form a single program and loaded into contiguous memory locations, the loader determines the relocation constant for a particular module from (1) the loading address of the first module, (2) the specified order of module loading, and (3) the size or number of words in each module preceding the module in question in the order of (2). Thus in hardware architectures implementing one-dimensional virtual memories, the first module need not be relocated, but subsequent modules must be relocated by the loader within the virtual memory of the process.

2.12.2 Linking

A routine for *linking* (linkage editor, linking loader, consolidator, map routine) constructs one object module from several independently generated object modules. The resultant object module may either be a complete executable machine code module, or another object module. Thus a linkage editor "consolidates" several independent object modules into a single, possibly executable object module. To understand this linking process, the concepts of an *undefined symbol* and an *externally referenceable symbol* must be understood.

Whenever an object module is created, whether it be by assembly, compilation, or consolidation of several object modules, the resulting object module will most likely have a set of symbols which are not defined, that is, symbols whose value cannot be resolved at module creation time. These *undefined symbols* may represent references to constants, data variables, or procedures and functions used in that module but which are defined in other object modules (e.g., system library modules). For example, an object module for a FORTRAN program which invokes the standard function SIN will have "SIN" as an undefined symbol, or in other terms, an unresolved external (to that module) reference. Here "SIN" represents the "entry" address of the sin function. This address will be resolved when this object module is linked with the library object module that implements this function.

Now consider the object module for the SIN function. In this module there are symbols that must be referenced from other modules (e.g., SIN), and local symbols that cannot be so referenced (e.g., local variables, constants, labels, etc.). The former are called *externally referencable symbols*. Such symbols can be identified in a source language by using designated language constructs (e.g., ENTRY PROCEDURE, or ENTRY for assemblers).

Hence we may conceptually view a relocatable object module as consisting of six distinct components:

1. A module name for identification
2. The length of the module
3. A definition table consisting of externally referenceable symbols, with associated values
4. A use table consisting of undefined symbols and, associated with each, a list of "places" (addresses, expressions, etc.) where that symbol is used
5. Data and machine instructions
6. A relocation directory or flagged location sensitive words

Note that some systems allow undefined symbols to be used in expressions (e.g., in the operand field of an assembly language instruction). In this case the expression must be saved with the object module for subsequent evaluation when the values of the undefined symbols are resolved during linking [2, Chaps. 4 and 5].

Most linkers use two passes. The first reads all information associated with each module, creating tables of module names, lengths, and undefined and externally referenceable symbols. On the second pass the modules are consolidated, by resolving undefined symbols where possible, and relocated.

A *linking loader* stores the resulting machine code directly into memory. This code can be executed provided that all undefined symbol values are resolved (i.e., by searching the desired object modules or the system library modules). A *linkage editor* or map routine stores its output in secondary memory. If all symbol values are resolved, the resulting relocatable load module can be loaded into memory. Otherwise, the result is another relocatable object module.

Thus far it has been assumed that symbol values are resolved prior to loading. This may not always be the case. The time at which a symbol's value is known is called its *binding time*. This may range from program creation (declaration of a constant) to the instant of execution of a machine instruction using that symbol [6, p. 335]. On machines with virtual or paged memory, *dynamic linking* of program segments is done during program execution as segments are swapped in and out of memory. See Ref. 3 and Sec. 2.19 for further information on dynamic linking.

REFERENCES

1. A. S. TANENBAUM, *Structured Computer Organization*, Prentice-Hall, Englewood Cliffs, N.J., 1976.
2. J. J. DONOVAN, *Systems Programming*, McGraw-Hill, New York, 1972.
3. L. PRESSER, and J. R. WHITE, "Linkers and Loaders," *Comput. Surv.*, **4**, 150–167 (Sept. 1972).
4. D. GRIES, *Compiler Construction for Digital Computers*, Wiley, New York, 1971.
5. A. V. AHO and J. D. ULLMAN, *Principles of Compiler Design*, Addison-Wesley, Reading, Mass., 1978.
6. A. V. AHO and J. D. ULLMAN, *The Theory of Parsing, Translation and Compiling*, Vols. 1 and 2, Prentice-Hall, Englewood Cliffs, N.J., 1973.
7. E. HOROWITZ and S. SAHNI, *Fundamentals of Computer Algorithms*, Computer Science Press, Potomac, Md., 1978.
8. E. HOROWITZ and S. SAHNI, *Fundamentals of Data Structures*, Computer Science Press, Potomac, Md., 1976.
9. A. V. AHO, J. E. HOPCROFT, and J. D. ULLMAN, *The Design and Analysis of Computer Algorithms*, Addison-Wesley, Reading, Mass., 1974.
10. D. E. KNUTH, *The Art of Computer Programming*, Vol. 1: *Fundamental Algorithms*, 2nd ed., Addison-Wesley, Reading, Mass, 1974.

11. D. E. KNUTH, *The Art of Computer Programming*, Vol. 3: *Sorting and Searching*, Addison-Wesley, Reading, Mass, 1973.

12. D. W. BARRON, *Assemblers and Loaders*, American Elsevier, New York, 1969.

13. V. Y. LUM, P. S. T. YVEN, and M. DODD, "Key to Address Transformation Techniques—A Fundamental Performance Study on Large Existing Formatted Files," *Commun. ACM*, **14**, 228–239 (Apr. 1971).

14. R. MORRIS, "Scatter Storage Techniques," *Commun. ACM*, **11**, 38–44 (Jan. 1968).

15. C. E. PRICE, "Table Lookup Techniques," *Comput. Surv.*, **3**, 49–65 (*June* 1971).

2.13   HIGH-LEVEL LANGUAGES

D. Rosenkrantz

2.13.1   Language Levels

A programming language is used to specify algorithms in a form that is precise enough for a specified algorithm to be performed by a computer. In a low-level language, such as assembly language, algorithms are specified in terms of the instructions and registers of a given computer. In a high-level language, such as FORTRAN, they are specified in a form that is closer to the way people think. For instance, the description and manipulation of data is expressed more in terms of properties of the data than in terms of the internal representation of the data. High-level languages are used by most programmers, and are increasingly being used for tasks formerly programmed in assembly language. There is trend toward the availability of very high level languages, in which algorithms are expressed in a way that is even further removed from the details of their machine implementation, so that an algorithm might even be automatically constructed from a sufficiently precise statement of a problem to be solved.

2.13.2   Advantages of High-Level Languages

The main advantages of high-level languages are increased programmer productivity because of ease of use, and increased program portability. Programs written in a high-level language are usually easier to write, easier to debug, easier to prove correct, easier to read, and easier to modify than programs written in a low-level language. The life-cycle cost of the program is less, and less total programmer effort is involved. These benefits accrue because a program written in a high-level language is usually easier to understand and more "natural" than if it were written in a low-level language. Furthermore, the programmer need not bother with those details that are handled automatically by the implementation of the language. The programmer need only bridge the gap between a conceptual understanding of an algorithm and its high-level-language specification. The gap between the high-level-language specification and the machine implementation is bridged automatically.

Use of a high-level language vastly increases the portability of a program, that is, the ease with which it can be made to run on a different computer. Ideally, if the new computer can process the language in which a program is written, the program can be used unchanged. In practice, conversion may require more effort because the program contains machine or system dependencies, or exploits peculiarities of the programming language implementation on the original computer.

2.13.3   Kinds of High-Level Languages

Since a major advantage of using a high-level language is its naturalness, it is desirable for the concepts relevant to the problem solved by a given program to be naturally expressible in the language in which the program is written. Thus high-level languages have been developed that are oriented toward various kinds of problems, in the sense that a given language contains features to facilitate the natural expression of an algorithm for solving certain kinds of problems. Major types of programming problems include scientific, which typically involves the solution of numerical problems; commercial, which typically involves processing large quantities of business data; artificial intelligence, which typically involves the manipulation of a representation of some human activity; systems programming, which typically involves constructing a program that processes other programs; and simulation, which typically involves determining the effect of random sequences of events.

There are hundreds of high-level languages in use, and many languages are used for a great variety of problems [5]. FORTRAN [3] and ALGOL are major scientific languages. COBOL is the major commercial language. PL/1 is a multipurpose language used for scientific and commercial programming. Pascal [6] is widely used for systems programming. LISP and SNOBOL are often used for artificial intelligence applications. SIMULA is a simulation language. The features in a number of languages are described in Refs. 1, 2, and 4.

2.13.4   Language Features

Some typical features contained in high-level languages will now be described. Note that a given language feature may not be present in all high-level languages, and may be expressed differently in different languages. Usually (but not always), a Pascal-like form will be used in this article.

Since a program is generally stored as a long string of characters, perhaps on a computer file or on a deck of cards, everything expressible in a language must be represented as a string of characters. A language is specified by giving its syntax and semantics. The syntax is a description of which character strings are considered to be valid programs. The semantics is a description of what a program does when it is executed (i.e., what happens when the algorithm specified by a program is performed).

Data-Oriented Language Features

Constants.   A constant is a data value. For instance, 371, 0, and 4 are integer constants. Also 37.2, −.0021, and 67.3E26 are real constants. Note that this last constant would be expressed as 67.3×10^{26} in the usual scientific notation.

A typical string constant is expressed as "xyzx," representing the string consisting of the characters x, followed by y, followed by z, followed by x.

There are only two Boolean (also called logical) constants. They are *true* and *false*.

Identifiers.   An identifier is a name, such as *andrea*, that is associated with data values during the execution of a program.

Data Types.   A data type is a collection of possible values. Examples of types are *integer*, *real*, *string*, and *Boolean*. Generally, a type has associated operations that can be performed on member values, and an associated internal machine representation. The generality of the word "type" may vary considerably from one language to another.

Declarations.   A declaration is a specification that associates a type with certain identifiers. For instance

var *arthur*, *jack*, *gary*: *integer*

declares that identifiers *arthur*, *jack*, and *gary* are of type *integer*, and so can take on integer values. They are said to be integer variables. The word "variable" connotes that the value of *arthur* might change during the execution of the program.

Arrays.   An array is a collection of data values, all of the same type, organized in a regular pattern with a fixed number of dimensions. For instance,

var *velio*: **array**[1..100] **of** *integer*

specifies that *velio* is a one-dimensional array, or vector, consisting of 100 integers. The twenty-third member of the array is referred to as *velio* [23].

As another example,

var *raymond*: **array** [1..20, 1..30] **of** *real*

declares *raymond* to be a two-dimensional array whose members are of type *real*. The array can be considered to have 20 rows and 30 columns. The element in row 6 and column 5 is referred to as *raymond* [6, 25]. The same element can be referred to as *raymond* [*i*, *j*] if the variable *i* and *j* are of type integer having value 6 and 25, respectively.

Record Structures.   A record structure is a collection of data values, possibly of different types, arranged in a hierarchical manner. For instance,

> **var** *partdesc*:**record** *name*: *string*;
>
> > > *partnumber*: *integer*;
> > >
> > > *weight*: *real*
>
> **end**

declares *partdesc* as a record consisting of string-valued *name*, integer-valued *partnumber*, and real-valued *weight*. The entire record is referred to as *partdesc*, and its three elements are referred to as *partdesc.name*, *partdesc. partnumber*, and *partdesc.weight*, respectively.

As another example, the following declares variable *person*:

> **var** *person*: **record**
>> *name*:   **record** *firstname*: *string*;
>>>   *middlename*: *string*;
>>>   *lastname*: *string*
>>
>>   **end**;
>>   *identification*: *integer*;
>>   *address*: **record** *housenumber*: *integer*;
>>>   *street*: *string*;
>>>   *city*: *string*;
>>>   *state*: *string*
>>
>>   **end**
>
> **end**

Variable *person* is a record having several components, some of which are records. For instance, *person.name* is a subrecord of *person*, and consists of three strings.

User-Defined Types.   High-level languages sometimes have facilities for a user to introduce new types. For instance, for a language with type *real* built in, the user might be able to declare *complex* as a new type, specified as a record structure whose components are of an already defined type.

> **type** *complex* =**record** *realpart*:   *real*;
>>   *imagpart*:   *real*
>
>   **end**

The user can then subsequently use *complex* like any other type. For instance, variables, arrays, and record components can be of type *complex*, as illustrated by the following declaration:

> **var** *poles*: **array** [1..10] **of** *complex*

In some languages, the user can define operations on newly introduced types. For instance, the user might define arithmetic operations such as addition and multiplication on the newly defined type *complex* (see Sec. 2.10).

Block Structure.   Some languages permit a program *block*, or module, to be nested inside another program block. Furthermore, they permit the inner block to contain its own declarations. The declarations occurring in the inner block are in effect for that block only. For instance, consider a program with the following skeleton, where each block is bracketed by the reserved words **begin** and **end**.

> **begin**   **var** *sheldon*, *ann*: *real*;
>>   ⋮
>>   **begin var**   *sheila*, *ann*: *integer*;
>>>   ⋮
>>
>>   **end**;
>>   ⋮
>
> **end**

The *real* variable *sheldon* can be referred to in the entire program. The *integer* variable *sheila* can only be referred to in the inner block. A use of *ann* in the inner block refers to the *integer* variable *ann* declared in the inner block, and the use of *ann* elsewhere in the program refers to the *real* variable *ann* declared in the outer block.

Action-Oriented Language Features

Operators. Operators combine data values to produce new data values. For instance, assume that x, y, and z are *real* variables. Then

$$x + y$$

represents the $+$ operator applied to operands x and y to give a *real* result. The result of an operator may itself be the operand of another operator, as in the following expression:

$$x * (y + z) + 45.621$$

Besides arithmetic operators that are applied to numeric operands and produce a numeric result, there are relational operators that are applied to numeric operands and produce a *Boolean* result, and there are *Boolean* operators that are applied to *Boolean* operands and produce a *Boolean* result. For instance, the relational operator $>$ is used in the relational expression

$$x > y$$

producing result *true* if x is greater than y, and result *false* otherwise. Typical *Boolean* operators are **and, or,** and **not.** The following expression uses these operators, where b is a Boolean variable.

$$(x > y) \text{ and not } (b \text{ or } y = z)$$

Assignment Statements. An assignment statement "assigns" the value of some expression to a variable. The variable then retains that value until a subsequent assignment to the variable (or perhaps exit from the block in which the variable is declared, if that occurs first, in which case the variable simply disappears). For instance, if $: =$ represents the assignment operation, the following assignment statement assigns the value 23 to *integer* variable i:

$$i: = 23$$

The following assignment statement assigns a value to a component of **array** a:

$$a[j]: = a[j] * 6 + x$$

Input/Output. An input statement reads a value or values from a computer terminal, card reader, computer file on a disk, or some other device, and assigns the values read to some program variables. For instance, the statement

$$read(x, y, z)$$

would input three values and assign them to variables x, y, and z.

An output statement writes a value or values onto a computer terminal, printer, computer file on a disk, or some other device. For instance, the statement

$$write(x, y, z)$$

would output the values of variables x, y, and z.

Programming languages usually include features for specifying the format that input data or output data should have.

Conditional Statement. A conditional statement selects a statement to execute based on the value of a *Boolean* expression or expressions. For instance, the **if** statement

$$\text{if } x > 3 \text{ then } write(y)$$

will only output y if x is greater than 3.

The **if** statement

$$\text{if } y < z \text{ and } q > 9.2 \text{ then } w: = z + 1 \text{ else } write(x)$$

will select the assignment statement when the condition is true, and will select the output statement when it is false.

A convenient language feature to use in combination with the **if** statement is the ability to group a sequence of statements into a single, compound statement by bracketing the sequence with the reserved words **begin** and **end**. This feature makes it convenient to refer to the group as a single entity, as in the following **if** statement:

```
if y < 3 then begin read(t, w);
              z: = t * 6;
              if z < w then print(z)
      end
```

When y is less than 3, the compound statement is selected, where the compound statement consists of an input statement, an assignment, and an **if** statement.

For an example of **if** statements embedded in a program, consider the following program:

```
program richard;
  var temperature: real;
  begin
       read(temperature);
       if temperature > 100 then write ("temperature too high");
       if temperature < 10 then write("raise temperature by", 10 − temperature)
  end.
```

This program is named *richard*, and contains a declaration followed by a compound statement.

Loops. A loop, or iteration statement, repeats some statement or statements until some conditions are met. For instance, suppose that a program contains the following declarations:

```
var i: integer;
var max, min: real;
var a, b, c: array [1..100] of real;
```

Now consider the following **for** statement:

$$\textbf{for } i: = 1 \textbf{ to } 100 \textbf{ do } a[i]: = b[i] * c[i]$$

The effect of the **for** statement is to execute the assignment statement

$$a[i]: = b[i] * c[i]$$

100 times, first with i equal to 1, then with i equal to 2, then with i equal to 3, and so on. Thus if a, b, and c are regarded as vectors, the **for** statement computes the inner product of b and c.

In the following example, the loop involves a compound statement.

```
max: = a[1];
min: = a[1];
for i: = 2 to 100 do begin
                if max < a[i] then max = a[i];
                if min > a[i] then min = a[i]
        end
```

The sequence of statements above assigns the largest value in a to *max* and the smallest value in a to *min*.

Procedures

A procedure is a named module, or part of a program, that can be called (i.e., have its execution initiated) at various places in a program. As an example, the following program contains a procedure named *sortxy* which ensures that the value of x does not exceed the value of y, interchanging the two values if necessary.

```
program robert;
    var x, y: integer;
    procedure sortxy;
        begin var temp: integer;
            if x > y then begin temp: = x;
                             x: = y;
                             y: = temp
                        end
    end;
begin
    read(x, y);
    sortxy;
    write(x, y)
end.
```

In the example, identifier *sortxy* is declared to be a procedure. This particular declaration consists of the word **procedure**, the procedure name, and a procedure body consisting of a statement (which in this example is a block enclosed by **begin** and **end**). Note that the procedure body refers to both the local variable *temp* that is declared within the procedure body, and the global variables *x* and *y* that are declared outside the procedure. The procedure body is not executed until it is called when the *procedure call statement*

$$sortxy$$

is executed. Thus the first statement executed in the program is *read*(x, y).

As another example, consider the following program.

```
program alice;
    var x, y, z: integer;
    procedure sort2 (var a, b: integer);
        begin var temp: integer;
            if a > b then begin temp: = a;
                             a: = b;
                             b: = temp
                        end
    end;
begin
    read(x, y, z);
    sort2(x, y);
    sort2(y, z);
    sort2(x, y);
    write(x, y, z)
end.
```

In this example, procedure *sort2* has two formal parameters, *a* and *b*, that are referred to in the procedure body. These two formal parameters are specified to be of type *integer*. When the procedure is actually called, an actual parameter is supplied for each formal parameter. For instance, in the first call of *sort2*, actual parameter *x* corresponds to formal parameter *a*, and actual parameter *y* corresponds to formal parameter *b*. When the procedure is executed, a reference to formal parameter *a*, as in

$$temp: = a$$

has the effect of using the corresponding actual parameter instead. Thus *temp* would be assigned the value of *x*. The second time *sort2* is called, with actual parameters *y* and *z*, execution of the same statement in *sort2* would assign the value of *y* to *temp*. Thus the effect of the preceding program is to input three numbers and then output them in sorted order.

Formal parameters designated by the reserved word **var** in the heading of the procedure declaration (e.g., *a* and *b* in *sort2*) are referred to as reference parameters since they are, in reality, references back to the corresponding actual parameters. If the **var** designation is removed in the procedure heading, the formal parameter is referred to as a value parameter. In this case the value of the corresponding actual parameter is used only to initialize the formal. Thereafter, references in the procedure to the formal parameter have no connection to the corresponding actual. In particular, since a modification of the formal within the procedure does not affect the corresponding actual, no information can be passed from the procedure back to the point in the program where the procedure was called through a value parameter.

A *function* is a special kind of procedure that returns a value when it is called. A function can be used in an expression. For instance, in the expression

$$y := chi * sin(x)$$

sin is a function that returns a *real* value, and has a single real-valued parameter.

The following program includes a declaration of function *ramp*.

> **program** *kenneth*;
>
> **var** *x, y, z*: *real*;
>
> **function** *ramp* (*john*: *real*): *real*;
>
> > **begin if** *john* < 0 **then** *ramp* := 0 **else** *ramp* := *john* **end**;
>
> **begin**
>
> > *read(x)*;
> >
> > *y* := *ramp(x)*;
> >
> > *write(y)*;
> >
> > *z* := *ramp(x + 1) * ramp(x − 1)*;
> >
> > *write(z)*
>
> **end**.

Function *ramp* is declared to return to a *real* result, and to have a single *real* parameter.

2.13.5   Structured Programming

Programs are complex objects, and it is usually difficult to construct a program to perform a desired task. Programs tend to be easier to design, write, debug, prove correct, and modify when constructed in a disciplined way that produces a program with an easily understood structure. A carefully designed programming language can facilitate structured programming.

It is widely believed that programs should be designed by a process of *stepwise refinement*. A task to be performed by a program is divided into several subtasks. Each subtask is, in turn, divided into subtasks, until the subtasks are small enough to be intellectually manageable. Furthermore, at each step, in order to make the division of a given task into its subtasks intellectually manageable, many details of these subtasks are not considered. These details are filled in as a task is converted, via a series of steps, from an abstract expression of what is to be accomplished, to a concrete program that accomplishes it.

A programming language facilitates this process by supporting program modularity. For instance, subtasks may become procedures and functions. Parameters and the naming conventions in a block-structured language help permit a module to be designed by itself.

Control structures, such as conditional statements, loops, and compound statements, encourage structured programming by permitting the construction of programs where each portion of a program has a single entrance and a single exit. This facilitates consideration of such a program portion as a subtask.

Often, a given programming language is deliberately designed so as to not contain or to make unnecessary certain features that are considered inimical to good programming practice. Use of the programming language naturally guards the programmer from the temptation offered by these features. For example, a control structure that permits a programmer to cause transfers of control to occur between arbitrary points in the program (the **goto** statement) encourages the construction of programs in which portions have more than one entry or exit. It has been shown that such a control structure adds no additional power to a language that already contains well-designed looping and conditional structures, although it may be convenient in a few cases.

The data types of a programming language can also facilitate structured programming. By having data types that permit data objects to be specified and manipulated in a natural way, details of the representation of these objects may not have to be considered. Structuring can be further facilitated through the use of abstract data types (see Sec. 2.10).

REFERENCES

1. J. E. NICHOLLS, *The Structure and Design of Programming Languages*, Addison-Wesley, Reading, Mass., 1975.

2. E. I. ORGANICK, A. I. FORSYTHE, and R. P. PLUMMER, *Programming Language Structures*, Academic Press, New York, 1978.

3. E. I. ORGANICK and L. P. MEISSNER, *FORTRAN IV*, 2nd ed., Addison-Wesley, Reading, Mass., 1974.

4. T. W. PRATT, *Programming Languages: Design and Implementation*, Prentice-Hall, Englewood Cliffs, N.J., 1975.

5. J. E. SAMMET, *Programming Languages: History and Fundamentals*, Prentice-Hall, Englewood Cliffs, N.J., 1969.

6. N. WIRTH and K. JENSEN, *PASCAL User Manual and Report*, Springer-Verlag, New York, 1975.

2.14 INTERPRETERS AND COMPILERS

D. Rosenkrantz

2.14.1 Distinction between Interpreters and Compilers

A *translator* is a piece of software that converts programs from one programming language, called the *source language*, to another, called the *object language* or *target language*. A compiler is a translator for which the source language is a high-level language, such as FORTRAN or COBOL, and the object language is a low-level language, such as machine language or assembly language. The input to a compiler is a *source program*, written in the source language, and the output of the compiler is an equivalent *object program*, written in the object language. Whenever the program is to be used, the object program is loaded into memory (if it is a machine language program) and executed. Compilers are needed because computers operate by executing machine language instructions, whereas people find it easier and more efficient to specify algorithms in a high-level language. Compilers perform the translation between the two languages.

An *interpreter* is a piece of software that inputs a source program and performs the algorithm specified by the program. It does not produce a machine language version of the source program. When processing a source language statement, it performs the action specified by the statement, rather than translating the statement into machine instructions that can perform the action.

The main advantage of a compiler over an interpreter is that the execution of the machine language version of a program is usually much more rapid that the interpretation of the program. Various reasons for using an interpreter are that interpreters can usually be written more easily than compilers, they can more easily produce meaningful error messages for errors detected during program execution, they may occupy less storage than a compiler, the version of a program that is interpreted may occupy less storage than the machine language version would occupy, and some high-level languages are extremely difficult to translate into machine language because the meaning of certain statements is not known until the program is executed.

2.14.2 Intermediate Languages

Usually, interpreters do not directly interpret the original source language version of the input program. Rather, the source program is first translated into an *intermediate language*, and then the intermediate language version of the program is interpreted. Thus the translation of a statement from source language to intermediate language is done only once, rather than each time the statement is encountered during execution of the program.

Compilers also usually do not translate directly from source language to object language. Rather, the source program is first translated into an intermediate language, and then into the object language. Typically, each statement in an intermediate language represents a single operation. An intermediate language statement might be

$$\text{MULTIPLY} \quad \text{A} \quad \text{B} \quad \text{C}$$

where A and B represent the operands of the multiplication, and C represents the result. The source language statement

$$x := y + z * q$$

might be translated into the following sequence of intermediate language statements, where T1 and T2 are new names constructed by the translator:

$$
\begin{array}{llll}
\text{MULTIPLY} & \text{Z} & \text{Q} & \text{T1} \\
\text{ADD} & \text{Y} & \text{T1} & \text{T2} \\
\text{ASSIGN} & \text{X} & \text{T2} &
\end{array}
$$

In practice, the intermediate language statements would be represented in a more efficient manner than the character strings displayed above (e.g., "MULTIPLY" would be represented not as a string of eight characters, but as a small integer). This more efficient representation is an advantage of the intermediate language version of the program over the source language version. Another advantage is that operations usually occur in the intermediate language in the order in which they should be performed; for example, in the example above, multiplication is to be done first, then addition, and then assignment.

2.14.3 Parts of a Compiler

A compiler usually breaks its total job of translation into several *phases*. A typical compiler might consist of three phases. The first phase is a *lexical analyzer*, which translates the source program, which is a string of characters, into a representation of the program called the *token string*. The second phase is a *syntax analyzer*, which translates the token string into intermediate language. The third phase is a *code generator*, which translates from intermediate language to machine instructions. The compiler would also have several tables, which might be accessed by more than one phase. For instance, there is typically a *symbol table* (see Sec. 2.6) with an entry for each identifier that occurs in the program. The compiler would also have an *error processor* for handling and displaying errors in the input program. The error processor might be distributed between several phases, each of which detects different errors.

There might be additional phases besides the three described above. For instance, there might be an *optimizer*, which is invoked before the code generator. The optimizer modifies the intermediate language version of the program so that the object program will be more efficient. For instance, if the program has a loop that contains an *invariant expression* (i.e., an expression whose value is the same each time around the loop), an optimizer would typically move the expression to the entry point of the loop, so that the expression would be evaluated only once, just before entering the loop, rather than each time around the loop. An "optimizer" generally does not attempt to produce a mathematically optimum version of the program, but rather attempts only to improve the efficiency of the program.

There might also be a *semantic analyzer* which processes the uses of an identifier, based on the declarations for that identifier. For instance, for programming languages that permit several declarations for a single identifier, the semantic analyzer would determine which declaration is relevant for each use of an identifier. The task of semantic analysis is often incorporated into the syntactic analyzer or code generator rather than being a separate phase.

In some compilers, the syntax analyzer translates into some data structure other than intermediate language, and an additional phase called the *intermediate language generator* performs the translation into intermediate language.

Although a compiler consists of several phases, a given phase need not produce its entire output representation of the program before calling the next phase. Rather, the phases are grouped into *passes*. If two successive phases are in the same pass, then whenever the first phase produces an output, the second phase is invoked and supplied with that output. Whenever the second phase requires an input, the first phase is invoked and requested to supply the input. The final phase of a pass accumulates its output into a representation of the entire program before the next pass is invoked. When there is not much memory available, the compiler is often broken up into many passes, each of which can fit in the available memory.

2.14.4 Lexical Analysis

The lexical analyzer translates the source program, represented as a character string, into a *token string*. The token string has a single symbol, called a *token*, for each string of source language characters that represents a natural unit. Thus lexical analysis involves breaking the input character string into natural units and replacing each unit with a new symbol. For instance, the character string

$$\text{IF } xyz > \, = 3.97 \text{ then } zip : \, = xyz$$

might be translated into the following eight tokens:

IF
IDENTIFIER XYZ
COMPARISON $> \, =$
CONSTANT 3.97
THEN
IDENTIFIER ZIP
ASSIGN
IDENTIFIER XYZ.

In practice, the tokens would be represented more compactly than displayed above. For instance, token IDENTIFIER XYZ would typically consist of a small integer indicating that the token type is IDENTIFIER, accompanied by a pointer to a table entry for XYZ. Similarly, token CONSTANT 3.97 might consist of the small integer indicating token type CONSTANT, accompanied by the internal machine representation of the value of the constant.

2.14.5 Syntax Analysis

Syntax analyzers are usually based on *context-free grammars*. A context-free grammar is a mathematically precise way to specify a set of strings. *Backus – Naur form* (BNF) is a widely used notation for expressing a context-free grammar. As an example, the following is a context-free grammar, expressed in BNF notation, for generating integer constants in a typical programming language.

$\langle\text{digit}\rangle :: = 0\,|\,1\,|\,2\,|\,3\,|\,4\,|\,5\,|\,6\,|\,7\,|\,8\,|\,9$

$\langle\text{unsigned integer}\rangle :: = \langle\text{digit}\rangle\,|\,\langle\text{digit}\rangle\langle\text{unsigned integer}\rangle$

$\langle\text{sign}\rangle :: = +\,|\,-$

$\langle\text{integer}\rangle :: = \langle\text{sign}\rangle\langle\text{unsigned integer}\rangle\,|\,\langle\text{unsigned integer}\rangle$

In this grammar, the symbols

$$0\ \ 1\ \ 2\ \ 3\ \ 4\ \ 5\ \ 6\ \ 7\ \ 8\ \ 9\ \ +\ \ -$$

are the *terminal symbols*, and compose the strings specified by the grammar. The symbols

$$\langle\text{digit}\rangle\ \ \langle\text{unsigned integer}\rangle\ \ \langle\text{sign}\rangle\ \ \langle\text{integer}\rangle$$

are *nonterminal symbols* that are names for sets of strings. In BNF notation, each nonterminal is enclosed by the triangular brackets "$\langle$" and "$\rangle$." Each nonterminal has a defining *rule* that specifies how to construct an example of that nonterminal (i.e., how to construct the strings represented by the nonterminal). The rule consists of the name of the nonterminal being defined, the symbol ":: = ," and a list of alternative construction methods, where the vertical bar "$|$" separates the alternatives. The defining rule for $\langle\text{digit}\rangle$ specifies that an example of a $\langle\text{digit}\rangle$ can be constructed by writing down 0, or by writing down 1, or by writing down 2, and so on. The first alternative in the rule for $\langle\text{unsigned integer}\rangle$ says that an example of an $\langle\text{unsigned integer}\rangle$ can be constructed by writing down an example of a $\langle\text{digit}\rangle$. The second alternative says that an example of an $\langle\text{unsigned integer}\rangle$ can be constructed by concatenating any example of a $\langle\text{digit}\rangle$ with any example of an $\langle\text{unsigned integer}\rangle$. Thus because the string 2 is a $\langle\text{digit}\rangle$ and 7 is an $\langle\text{unsigned integer}\rangle$ (because it is an example of a $\langle\text{digit}\rangle$), 27 is an $\langle\text{unsigned integer}\rangle$. Furthermore, because 6 is a $\langle\text{digit}\rangle$ and 27 is an $\langle\text{unsigned integer}\rangle$, 627 is an $\langle\text{unsigned integer}\rangle$.

The compiler designer writes a context-free grammar that specifies the set of token strings corresponding to valid programs; other token strings will produce an error message. The grammar associates a *parse tree* with each valid string. The parse tree for the string $+4627$, shown in Fig. 1, indicates how the string is constructed in accordance with the grammar given above. As another example the statement

$$xyz : \, = zap - 79 * t$$

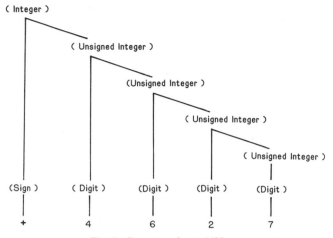

Fig. 1   Parse tree for $+4627$.

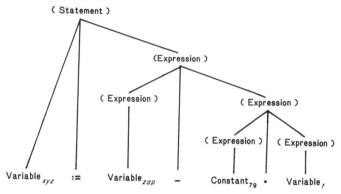

Fig. 2   Parse tree for a typical statement.

might have the parse tree of Fig. 2. Notice that the parse tree implies that $79*t$ is a subexpression to be evaluated, while $zap-79$ is not. Thus the grammar reflects the *precedence* of the language operations: for instance, that the multiplication should be done before the subtraction when the statement above is executed.

Sometimes, a specification is given of how the parse tree for the input string can be converted into a parse tree for an output string, thereby specifying a *syntax-directed translation* from the input string to the output string. Sometimes an *action routine* is associated with each node of the parse tree, where the action routines produce outputs, update table entries, and so on. When the input string is processed, the action routines associated with the nodes of its parse tree are to be called.

The task of a given syntax analyzer might be to output the parse tree, or perform a syntax directed translation, or call the appropriate sequence of action routines. Syntax analyzers usually perform their task by simulating a device called a *pushdown automaton*, whose main data structure is a *stack*. Once the input/output function of the syntax box is specified in a grammar-based manner, there exist algorithms to assist in producing a pushdown automaton that performs that specified input/output function.

2.14.6   Symbol Table Entries

There are a number of tables that a compiler uses to keep track of objects referred to in the program being compiled. An example is a *symbol table* (see Sec. 2.6), with an entry for each identifier occurring in the program. Usually, the lexical analyzer, using some search method, such as *hashing* (see Sec. 2.5), finds the symbol table entry corresponding to each occurrence of an identifier in the program. For a programming language that permits only one declaration for an identifier, the symbol table entry is used to record information extracted from the declaration for the identifier. For a block structured language, where a program may contain several different declarations for the same identifier, a separate table entry is created for each declaration. Each of these entries, which can be called a *declaration entry*, records information extracted from the relevant declaration. Typically, when the syntax box processes a declaration, it calls routines to create and fill in these entries.

A table entry typically indicates whether an identifier is being declared as a simple variable, array, function, procedure, formal parameter, and so on. It might indicate the type (real, integer, Boolean, etc.) of the identifier. For an array, it might indicate the number of dimensions, and the array bounds if supplied as constant. In addition, information about the run-time location of the declared object is kept in the table entry. This information is vital since the generated instructions must refer to the run-time location of the object. The method actually used for mapping run-time storage allocation of data objects to memory locations depends on the language being compiled.

2.14.7 Code Generation

The code generator converts each intermediate language statement into machine instructs. For instance, the intermediate language statement

$$\text{MULTIPLY Z Q TI}$$

might be converted into the two instructions

$$\text{LOAD, REGISTER5} \qquad \text{Z}$$
$$\text{MULTIPLY, REGISTER5} \qquad \text{Q}$$

and the code generator would remember that the value of T1 is in register 5. The specifics of the instructions generated would depend on information stored in the relevant table entries for Z and Q. For instance, the types of these variables determines whether fixed-point or floating-point instructions should be generated.

Designing a code generator involves planning a run-time implementation of the features, such as data types and control structures, of the programming language being compiled. For instance, typical issues are what sequence of instructions should be used to access an array element, or to call a recursive procedure.

An important task of the code generator is keeping track of changes in the run-time location of data items. In particular, the code generator usually decides what to keep in which machine register at any given time during execution of the object program. Effective use of the machine registers can have a significant effect on the efficiency of the generated object program.

2.14.8 Error Processing

A compiler must be able to handle errors in the source program. The compiler must first *detect* the existence of an error. Then the compiler produces an *error message*, which usually describes the error and indicates its location in the source program. Unfortunately, it is sometimes hard to give an accurate description of the error, and the position in the program where the compiler detected the error may not be the position where the programmer would want to modify the program in order to correct the error. Finally, the compiler should *recover* from the error, that is, resume processing the program. An error can be either a *fatal error*, in which case the compiler does not produce an executable object program, or a *nonfatal error*, in which case the error message is only a *warning*, and object code is produced. Even for fatal errors, error recovery is desirable since it permits the detection of additional errors in the program.

2.14.9 Cross-Compilers

A *cross-compiler* is a compiler that operates on one machine, called the *host machine*, and produces an object program for a different machine, called the *target machine*. A cross-compiler is most likely to be constructed when the host machine has a large memory and the target machine has a small memory. The larger host machine memory permits the compiler to be constructed more easily, to be more powerful (e.g., do better optimization and produce better error messages), and to compile larger programs.

2.14.10 Run-Time Package

To implement a given programming language, it may be necessary not only to write a compiler for the language, but also to write a number of run-time routines. When an object program is to be executed, the run-time routines that it needs are loaded along with it. There may be run-time routines for input/output, standard mathematical functions, storage management, displaying error messages, and interfacing with the operating system.

REFERENCES

1. A. V. AHO and J. D. ULLMAN, *Principles of Compiler Design*, Addison-Wesley, Reading, Mass., 1977.
2. D. GRIES, *Compiler Construction for Digital Computers*, Wiley, New York, 1971.
3. P. M. LEWIS, II, D. J. ROSENKRANTZ, and R. E. STEARNS, *Compiler Design Theory*, Addison-Wesley, Reading, Mass., 1976.

2.15 RECURSION

J. Cherniavsky

Recursion is a term used in several contexts, all of which involve a notion of self-reference. In its most general form, recursion is a method of function definition where the definition of a function involves the function itself (hence self-reference). A typical example is the definition of the Fibonocci function, Fib(n), which produces the nth Fibonocci number.

$$\text{Fib}(0) = 0, \quad \text{Fib}(1) = 1, \quad \text{Fib}(n) = \text{Fib}(n-1) + \text{Fib}(n-2)$$

The value of a recursive function is determined by substituting the function definition for every occurrence of the function within the definition. As an example, consider the definition of Fib(4) (the substitutions are indicated by underlines):

$$\text{Fib}(4) = \underline{\text{Fib}(3)} + \text{Fib}(2) = \left(\underline{\text{Fib}(2)} + \text{Fib}(1)\right) + \text{Fib}(2)$$

$$= \left(\left(\underline{\text{Fib}(1)} + \text{Fib}(0)\right) + \text{Fib}(1)\right) + \text{Fib}(2)$$

$$= ((1+0)+1) + \text{Fib}(2) = 2 + \text{Fib}(2)$$

$$= 2 + \left(\underline{\text{Fib}(1)} + \text{Fib}(0)\right) = 2 + (1+0) = 3$$

The recursive definition of functions may be elaborated by allowing systems of equations of the form

$$f_1(x_1,\ldots,x_n) = E_1(f_1,\ldots,f_m, x_1,\ldots,x_n)$$

$$\vdots \qquad \vdots$$

$$f_m(x_1,\ldots,x_n) = E_m(f_1,\ldots,f_m, x_1,\ldots,x_n)$$

Each E_i is an expression that involves at most the functions $f_1,\ldots,f_m$ and the variables $x_1,\ldots,x_n$. The function being defined is the first named function (f_1 in the case above) and its value is determined by substituting the function definitions of $f_1,\ldots,f_m$ (i.e., $E_1(f_1,\ldots,f_m, x_1,\ldots,x_n),\ldots, E_m(f_1,\ldots,f_m,x_1,\ldots,x_n)$) for $f_1,\ldots,f_m$ in the expression $E_1(f_1,\ldots,f_m,x_1,\ldots,x_n)$.

As an example, consider the following definition of multiplication, which uses a subsidiary definition of addition:

$$M(n,m) = P(M(n,m-1),n)$$

$$P(n,m) = P(n,m-1) + 1$$

$$M(n,0) = 0$$

$$P(n,0) = n$$

We evaluate $M(2,2)$ to illustrate the evaluation mechanism.

$$M(2,2) = P(M(2,1),2) = P(M(2,1),1) + 1$$

$$= P(M(2,1),0) + 1 + 1 = M(2,1) + 2$$

$$= P(M(2,0),2) + 2 = P(M(2,0),1) + 1 + 2$$

$$= P(M(2,0),0) + 1 + 3 = M(2,0) + 4$$

$$= 0 + 4 = 4$$

In the context of programming language control structures, a programming language that allows recursion is one in which a procedure or function may include, within its body, one or more calls to itself. Not all programming languages allow recursion. Programming languages such as Pascal, PL/1, and ALGOL allow recursion, whereas programming languages such as FORTRAN and COBOL do not. A programming language that does not allow recursion is not necessarily less powerful than one that does. As will be shown below, it is frequently possible to simulate recursion within such a programming language. Hence the utility of recursion lies not in adding computational power, but in the implementation of algorithms whose most natural description is recursive. We illustrate this point in Fig. 1 and 2 by programming Fib in FORTRAN and Pascal. To avoid possible infinite executions, we extend the definition of Fib so that $Fib(n) = 0$ if $n < 0$. It is clear that the Pascal implementation of Fib is direct; its correctness is immediately seen. The FORTRAN implementation, however, requires some thought to ascertain its correctness; it is less direct and hence more prone to implementation error.

Recursion may also occur less directly (i.e., a recursive computation may occur even though a procedure does not contain a call to itself within its body). For example, suppose that we had three procedures, A, B, and C. A contains a call to B, B contains a call to C, and C contains a call to A. Then ultimately, A's definition involves a call to itself using B and C as agents. This type of recursion is similar to recursion involving systems of equations and goes by the name *daisy-chain recursion*.

The disadvantage of using recursion to implement functions is that it is generally less efficient than an implementation that does not use recursion. In the example above, the running time of FIB(N) in

```
        INTEGER FUNCTION FIB(N)
        IF (N .LEQ. 0) FIB = 0
        IF (N .EQ. 1) FIB = 1
        IF (N .LEQ. 1) RETURN
        IFIB1 = 0
        IFIB2 = 1
        DO 20 I = 2, N
        ITEMP = IFIB2
        IFIB2 = IFIB1 + IFIB2
        IFIB1 = ITEMP
20      CONTINUE
        FIB = IFIB2
        RETURN
        END
```

Fig. 1   FORTRAN program for computing a Fibonocci number.

```
function FIB(N: integer): integer;
begin
    if N < = 0 then FIB: = 0 else
        if N = 1 then FIB: = 1 else
        FIB: = FIB(N − 1) + FIB(N − 2);
end;
```

Fig. 2   Pascal program for computing a Fibonocci number.

the FORTRAN version will be proportional to N. On the other hand, for the Pascal version it is proportional to 2^N.

Compilers implement recursion using a stack of activation records. Each activation record contains storage for the variables used in the recursive procedure (e.g., N in Fig. 2). At the point of a recursive call (i.e., when the recursive procedure calls itself), the return address in the calling procedure as well as a new activation record for the called procedure are stored on top of the stack. The called procedure uses this new activation record for its computations. Thus, returning to the example, the value of N that it uses may be different from the value of N at the calling site.

The direct simulation of recursion in, say, FORTRAN follows the compiler implementation of recursion. A stack is simulated using a one-dimensional array and a separate variable to record the current top of the stack. Return addresses are stored as labels and returns to the calling procedure are implemented using the computed address capability of FORTRAN [1]. Although direct simulation of recursion is possible, it frequently pays to look for iterative definitions of the recursive function (the FORTRAN implementation of Fib is one such example). Such definitions, when implemented, are frequently much faster than the original definition's implementation.

REFERENCES

Reference

1. D. E. KNUTH, "Structured Programming with GO TO Statements," *Comput. Surv.*, **6**(4), 261–301 (1974).

2.16   BUFFERING TECHNIQUES

Arthur J. Bernstein

Early computer systems operated in a purely synchronous mode, with only one unit active at a time. Thus if a program executing on the processor requested an I/O transfer, the processor would initiate that function and then enter a wait state until the transfer had completed before resuming execution of the program. As processor speeds increased, the inefficiency of such a mode of operation became acute and asynchronous systems, involving channels, were introduced. In such systems processor execution could continue after an I/O transfer had been initiated and the two activities would then progress concurrently and asynchronously.

Special programming techniques are required if a program is to take advantage of the increased speed that asynchronous hardware is capable of delivering. For example, in a typical data processing application, a program accesses one or more files in a sequential fashion (see Sec. 2.8). Since a file generally contains a large amount of information, it cannot all be made accessible to the program at the same time. To program around this shortcoming, a directly accessible buffer is allocated with the program to serve as a window over the file. The program, using I/O transfers, fills the buffer with successive portions of information from the file and, after each transfer has completed, processes the

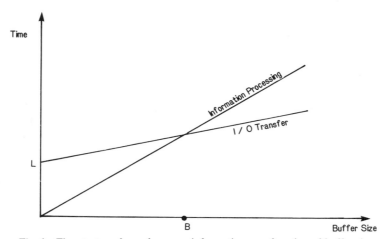

Fig. 1   Time to transfer and process information as a function of buffer size.

information. Thus the main loop of a program that processes information from a sequential file might take the form

loop

    Perform an I/O operation using the buffer;

    Process the information in the buffer

end

Unfortunately, such a program does not take advantage of the concurrency that the hardware is capable of providing since the program calls for sequential execution of the two statements. Thus useful computation does not occur while an I/O transfer is in progress.

Double buffering is a programming technique frequently employed to overcome this deficiency. In such a scheme two buffers are used and the program attempts to cause the processing of information in one of the buffers to occur concurrently with an I/O transfer into the other. When both the processing and the transfer have completed, the activity in the buffers is switched. Thus an I/O transfer is initiated using the buffer that had formerly been involved in the computation while the program resumes its computation using the buffer that had been involved in the previous I/O transfer. The main loop of a program utilizing such a technique might take the form

loop

    cobegin

        Perform I/O transfer using buffer i;

        Process information in buffer $(i+1)$ MOD 2

    coend;

    $i := i+1$ MOD 2

end

In this program the buffers are numbered 0 and 1 and the reserved words **cobegin** and **coend** bracket statements which are executed concurrently.

The effectiveness of this technique in exploiting concurrency depends on the relative execution times of the concurrent statements. Clearly, if the time to perform the I/O transfer, for example, is very much greater on average than the time to process a buffer filled with data, the processor will be idle much of the time. In many cases the average execution time of these functions is linearly proportional to the size of the buffer, as shown in Fig. 1. Here we have assumed that the file is stored on a device with an average latency of L (see Sec. 2.21) and that the average time to process a unit of information (slope of the processing curve) is greater than the average time to transfer a unit (slope of the transfer curve). The buffer size at the intersection of the two curves, B, is the optimal buffer size for maximizing concurrency.

Since this analysis is based on average values, we must still expect significant processor and channel idle time due to the fact that the actual transfer or processing time for a particular block of information will fluctuate around the mean. An additional technique to compensate for this is to use a buffering scheme involving more than two buffers. In this case the buffers can be used in a circular fashion. On completion of the processing (transfer) of a particular block of information, the processor (channel) moves on to the next buffer in the ring. The additional buffers reduce the probability of having no information (buffers) available when the processing (transfer) of a block of information has completed.

2.17 JOB CONTROL LANGUAGE

Dominic Seraphin

A computing system may be used interactively or in batch mode. In *interactive mode* the user enters commands at a terminal. The computing system carries out the commands one at a time and communicates the results to the user through the terminal. In *batch mode* a set of commands is presented to the computing system all at once. In this case the commands are submitted in some machine-readable medium, such as punched cards, magnetic tapes, or disk files. These commands will constitute a JOB in the scheduling queue of the computing system and will be performed at a later time when permitted by its scheduling priorities.

In either mode of operation a set of commands are necessary to communicate the needs of the user to the computing system. The language of these commands is referred to in this article as control language (CL). Each system has its own version of CL. Our discussion is limited to the common characteristics seen in major control languages.

2.17.1 Elements of a Control Language

The alphabet of CL consists of the alphanumeric character set and a few special characters. The exact set of special characters will vary from language to language. One character from the special character set is singled out as the recognition character. The basic unit of CL is a statement. One statement of CL will be one line of input for the operating system. In the classical case this will be one punched card or one line entered from a computer terminal. One or more recognition characters are used as leading characters of a CL statement. This is necessary to distinguish CL statements from other input data in the job stream. We will express a CL statement in the form

$$\langle R\rangle\langle \text{statement body}\rangle$$

where $\langle R\rangle$ denotes one or more recognition characters.

Some examples of CL statements are:

//SYSLIB DD UNIT = 3330, VOL = SER = MYPACK,	
DSN = SYS2.USERLIB,DISP = OLD	(1)
@ASG,C SYS∗FILE.,F/10/TRK/200,MYPACK	(2)
$ FILE AC,X2R,20R,NEW,OUTFILE	(3)

The recognition characters in these examples are /, @, and $. As a rule the recognition character will not appear in the statement body.

A CL statement can be divided into three distinct fields. All fields are not mandatory. We shall refer to the three commonly used fields as

1. Name or label
2. Operation
3. Operand

With this notation a CL statement can be expressed as

$$\langle R\rangle\langle\text{name}\rangle\ \langle\text{operation}\rangle\ \langle\text{operand}\rangle$$

The different fields in the examples above are:

Field			
$\langle R\rangle$	//	@	$
$\langle\text{name}\rangle$	SYSLIB	None	None
$\langle\text{operation}\rangle$	DD	ASG	FILE
$\langle\text{operand}\rangle$	UNIT = 3330,..	SYS∗FILE..	AC,..

The field terminator is a blank or a special character.

Name or Label

The name or label field begins immediately after the recognition character(s) and serves to identify the statement itself. In some control languages the label field is used to identify a statement to which control is to be transferred as a result of a conditional branch. This field is optional in many control languages.

Operation Field

The operation field indicates the function to be performed for the user and in that sense is the most significant part of a control statement. All control languages have a keyword in the operation field.

Operand Field

To augment the operation field, all control languages use the operand field. When more than one piece of information is required to be specified in the operand field, the field is subdivided into several subfields. A special character is used to delimit the subfields.

In example (1) there are four subfields. A comma is used to indicate the end of a subfield. In (2) there are three subfields. Two different techniques are used in coding a subfield. To continue the examples above, the first uses keywords and second and third use position. When keywords are used, a subfield takes the form

$$\langle keyword \rangle = \langle value \rangle$$

With this method subfields can be specified in any order and the keyword chosen usually will have some obvious meaning or association. This is very convenient for the user and minimizes coding errors.

In the second method each subfield will have a specific meaning by virtue of its position. Although users do not have to remember keywords, they must be careful about the position. The same text appearing at a different position can have a different meaning.

The subfield itself can be further divided into smaller items. The items in a subfield also can use keywords or make use of their position to signify meaning.

2.17.2   Types of Statements

There are four distinct functions to be performed by control statements. One statement has to identify a job stream to the operating system, a second has to invoke a processor or a program, a third has to define various files and other resources required for the processor, and a fourth is needed to act as the terminator of data entered as a part of the input stream. Based on the function performed by a CL statement, we may classify them as:

1. Job statement
2. Processor statement
3. Facility statement
4. Delimiter statement

This classification is based on the keyword used in the operation field of the statement. Some types may have more then one keyword in that category. But it is possible to include all statements found in any control language of an operating system in one of the four categories defined above.

2.17.3   Job Statement

This is the statement that identifies a job to the operating system and as such is mandatory in the batch mode in any operating system. The job statement must be the first control statement in an input stream and there should not be more than one job statement in a given job stream.

The job statement contains the following information:

1. The name by which the job is to be identified in the system.
2. The name or other identification of the person who initiated the job.
3. The account number to which the cost of the job is to be charged.
4. The estimated duration of the job in the operating system. This is usually given in standard units of the specific operating system.
5. The estimated amount of printed and punched output to be generated by the job.
6. Special processing options to be used for the job.

The operand field is optional in the job statement of all control languages, but most control languages make the name field mandatory. Also, some installations make some of the accounting and identification subfields mandatory. Here are three examples of job statements:

```
//XYZ12 JOB 98765,SMITH,TIME = 25,PRTY = 13
@RUN,A/R XYZ12,98765/SMITH,PROJECT,25,200
$        SNUMB XYZ12,13
```
(4)

(5)

(6)

XYZ12 is the identifier of the job in all; in the first it appears in the name field and in the other two it appears as a subfield in the operand field. 98765 is the account number and SMITH the identification of the user. 25 units is the estimated time. PRTY = 13 in (4) and 13 in (6) are the desired priority of the job. In (5) the A in the option field signifies priority.

2.17.4   Processor Statement

The processor call statement indicates to the operating system that the user desires to invoke a program which is in one of the files known to the operating system. In most operating systems a job stream will contain at least one processor statement. The processor statement has the following information:

1.   The name of the processor to be invoked.
2.   Options, if any, to be used while executing the processor.

In some control languages, there is a provision to specify the name of the file containing the desired program. Other control languages use a separate facility statement to accomplish this. The next three examples invoke programs or processors called PROG, ACOB, and FORTRAN.

//STEP1 EXEC PGM = PROG,PARM = (ONE,'TWO = B',EIGHT)   (7)
@FN.ACOB,S ONE,TWO/B,EIGHT   (8)
$ FORTRAN LSTIN,DECK   (9)

In (8) FN is the name of the file that contains the program ACOB. The remaining information in these statements consists of parameters. These will be passed to the program by the system to enable the program to make logical decisions.
The first example uses a name STEP1 and has the unique keyword EXEC in the operation field. In the last two examples the operation field is not unique, but is the name of the processor being invoked.

2.17.5   Facility Statement

This type of statement forms the majority in any control language. Its main purpose is to define and identify files that are necessary for the processor under invocation or which will be invoked later. The facility statement provides the operating system with a complete description of the file implicitly or explicitly. For a file cataloged in the system file directory, the description is implicit. Any information not specified explicitly on the control statement will be obtained from the system directory. For files that are new or not yet cataloged, all pertinent details are stated explicitly on the facility statement.
Consider the following examples of facility statements:

//FILE1 DD UNIT = 3330,
            VOL = SER = USB001,SPACE = (CYL,20,5),
            DCB = (RECFM = FB,LRECL = 80,BLKSIZE = 1600),
            DSNAME = MYFILE,DISP = (NEW,CATLG)   (10)
@ASG,U MYFILE.,16N//////Q,REEL01   (11)
$ TAPE   AB,X1D,,REEL01,,MYFILE   (12)

The six consecutive slashes in (11) indicate that five positional items of information are omitted from a subfield. DD, ASG, and TAPE are operation fields in these examples.

The facility statement defines the following:

1.   File identification
2.   Physical location of the file
3.   Size of the file
4.   File attributes
5.   Special processing options

File Identification

An external name is needed for referring to the file and is given as part of the file identification in a facility statement. It is to be stated whether it is an existing file in the system or is being newly created.

The final disposition of the file—whether it is to be retained or deleted at the end of the processing—is to be specified.

The values expressed for keywords DSNAME and DISP in example (10) provide the name, initial status, and final disposition of the file. The same function is accomplished in example (11) by the option U in the operation field and the first subfield in the operand. In (12) the last subfield is the file identifier.

Physical Location

The facility statement identifies the peripheral device on which the file resides. This will include the type of device—whether it is a drum, disk, magnetic tape, or paper peripherals—and identification of the physical units themselves. The UNIT, VOL, and SER keywords indicate the physical location in example (10). In example (11) the second subfield, 16N, and third subfield, REEL01, indicate the location of the file. In (12) X1D indicates a logical device and REEL01 is the reel identifier for the tape reel.

File Size

The space needed for the file can be specified through the subfields of a facility statement. This is a safeguard against erroneous or malicious use of mass storage facilities of a computing system. When the file exceeds the specified limit, the operating system will generate an error condition and the job in question will not be allowed to proceed further. This information is needed only for mass storage devices such as drums and disks. Files residing on tapes or defined through paper peripherals do not require information about file size.

In our example the keyword SPACE provides the information about size. The second example describes a tape file, so does not need the file size.

File Attributes

The operating system will require the logical attributes of data contained in a file. With the help of a facility statement, attributes that are not specified internally in a program can be specified externally on a control statement. This provides data independence to the program and great flexibility in program coding to the user. The attributes given on the control statement will be those that are not defined in the processing program. Some systems require that all data attributes be given in the processing program. In such cases the control statements will not accept data attributes.

In systems where this information is specified on the control statement the following attributes are given (see Sec. 2.8):

1. The organization of data—whether it is sequential, indexed sequential, partitioned, or direct access.
2. The length of buffer to be used in reading or writing data from or to the file.
3. The format of the physical blocks—whether they are fixed- or variable-length blocks.
4. The length of logical records in the file. A logical record is the amount of data accessed by a single READ or WRITE statement or equivalent thereof in a high-level programming language.
5. The length of a physical record. This may be equal or greater than the logical record. The length of physical record is decided by the hardware characteristics of the recording medium. Usually, a physical record length will be a multiple of logical record length.

In example (10) the subfield containing the keyword DCB describes the data attributes. The system from which example (11) is taken does not accept any attributes from the control statement. However, the letter Q appearing in one of the items of the second subfield indicates quarter-word format, meaning that one computer word will contain four characters.

Special Processing Options

The facility statement may also contain some special options to be considered by the operating system while processing the file. These options may be specified by means of keywords in the operand field or as options in the operation field.

The special options may include:

1. *Separation or affinity of a file with another file.* This is usually done to optimize the input/output operations through the assignment of files on separate channels or units to avoid contention.

2. *The type of translation required.* In some files the data format on the medium may be different from the data format in the computer memory, and some form of translation may be necessary to convert one to the other.

3. *The access control of a file.* For security or other reasons the access on a file may have to be restricted. By appropriate options at the time of creation of a file, it can be made read only for one user while providing read and write privilege to another user; or a file can be made accessible globally to all users or be restricted to a specific group of users.

2.17.6 Delimiter Statement

The purpose of the delimiter statement is unique. The input stream always contains control statements as well as data. When there are no ambiguities, any control statement will act as a data delimiter. But when control statements themselves are part of the data to be processed, an ambiguity arises. The delimiter statement solves this problem. All control languages reserve one or more keywords to indicate delimiter statements.

2.17.7 Procedures in Control Languages

In any operating system, an inexperienced user is apprehensive of the control language in spite of the flexibility it provides. Some control languages provide a technique that takes away much of the pain in coding control statements.

A group of control statements that are frequently used are kept in a library under a specific name. By referring to the name given to this group of statements, a user can effectively introduce the entire group of statements in the input stream, thus avoiding a lot of coding of control statements. Such a group of control statements is called a *procedure* in a control language.

Procedures may also contain what is known as *symbolic parameters.* A symbolic parameter is a variable defined in a procedure to which a user can assign specific values according to his or her need when the procedure is called. This enhances the power of procedures to a great extent. An analogy can be drawn between the symbolic parameters of a procedure and the arguments of a subroutine. By changing the values of the argument, the subroutine can be made to perform predetermined actions or computations on different sets of data. In a sense the symbolic parameter is an "argument" of a procedure.

2.17.8 Programming-Language-Like Control Languages

So far, what have been described are the structure and characteristics of control languages generally in use in the industry. The present direction in control language design is toward procedure-oriented languages, which are more programming-language-like in their structure and with ALGOL or PL/1-like rules on their syntax specification. But they are still in the design stage and have not reached the point of being used widely in the industry. However, the Work Flow Management system used by Burroughs is an ALGOL-like language and is an exception among generally used control languages.

2.18 STRUCTURED SYSTEMS DEVELOPMENT

Paul Siegel

Software engineering refers to the process of creating software systems, but today the term has come increasingly to apply to those identifiable techniques that reduce high software cost and complexity while increasing realiability and modifiability. Software projects often fail to be completed on schedule and within budget, and the delivered systems are frequently unreliable and expensive to maintain. In recent years, efforts have been made to see how projects proceed, to collect data about project performance, and to devise methods that will produce better systems faster.

Together with the development of separate design techniques, or tools, has come the attempt to integrate a collection of them into coherent design methodologies that will lead to higher-quality software. A design methodology will generally be made up of a number of design methods, tools, representations, and management rules for their application. For example, a design methodology might prescribe the order in which certain classes of decisions are to be made, ways of making decisions, ways to represent the developing design, and so on. The objective of these methodologies is to improve the productivity and accuracy of a software development organization.

This article concentrates on those aspects of a structured methodology that can increase productivity, whatever the application. Although references to specific computers and programming languages are generally avoided, some languages that lend themselves to the principles discussed here are mentioned by name.

Most systems evolve through a set of successive stages from initial recognition of a problem or requirement to final acceptance and utilization of the system. This set of stages is often referred to as the *system life cycle* and its phases can be listed as follows (see Fig. 1):

1. Functional analysis and definition
2. System design
3. Implementation and test
4. System installation (with conversion, if necessary)
5. Operation, review, and evaluation

Phase I determines whether or not a need exists for the new system. It includes an analysis of the current system, if one exists, of ideas and goals for the proposed system, of organization factors, and of financial considerations. It culminates in the generation of a functional specification and project plan. It is at this stage that effective documentation originates; the documentation will provide a means of coordinating the various stages and must always be kept up to date throughout all phases of the development cycle.

In the past, the output of the analysis stage of functional specification has generally been tedious to read, excessively wordy, and unbearably redundant. It will be seen that structured analysis produces a much more useful and maintainable document which bears a greater relationship to the design stage

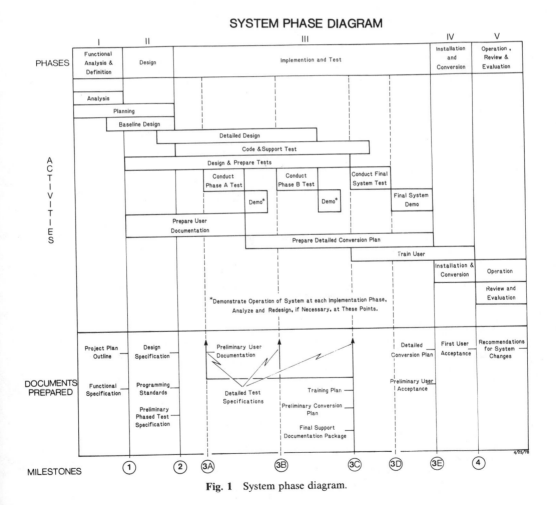

Fig. 1   System phase diagram.

than does the traditional type of specification. Indeed, the preliminary structured design is derived directly from its associated specification.

Phase II, the design phase, is concerned with the hierarchical structure of the new system and the functions that are performed at each level and by each component of the system. A set of design specifications is generated that will be used during the development stage.

During *phase III*, the design specifications can be implemented as software modules, with each module unit tested to ensure that it operates according to specifications. The components of the system would then be assembled and the complete system tested to ensure that the interfaces between the components are properly designed and that the entire system meets its operational objectives.

An alternative approach is to use top-down development, where the modules are developed in natural order from the control structures downward. "Stubs," or skeleton replacement modules, are employed to test module interfaces, so a massive integration effort is not required at the last stage of implementation. The only module that is unit tested in isolation is the top module in the program structure. When a module calls a lower module that currently does not exist, stub modules are coded to simulate the functions of the missing modules. Such modules may merely print an entry statement and return, or return a fixed output instead of the particular output that will eventually result from the module's operations.

Phase IV, system installation, refers to the process of putting a new system into operation, conducting acceptance tests, training operations personnel, disseminating information regarding the capabilities of the new system to prospective users, completing any necessary data conversion, and phasing out the old system in an orderly manner.

The last phase, *phase V*, involves monitoring the new system during the early periods of operation, evaluating its performance, and analyzing its contribution to the goals outlined in the feasibility study. Some of the same cost/benefit analyses that were performed in anticipation can now be performed in actuality. Most important, phase V also includes "maintenance" or changes to correct errors and to modify function.

A large number of programming errors can ultimately be traced back to faults in the analysis and design phases of a project. Since maintenance is a significant item in any analysis and can account for 50 to 80% of the total system cost [13], the discussion will focus on how structured designs and top-down implementation can decrease the maintenance costs.

2.18.1 Methodologies

Most methodologies attempt to match the activities of different phases of the development cycle to form a coherent whole, on the assumption that producing a reliable system is an activity that must be spread over the complete development process. A useful methodology should be flexible so that it can be applied to different design tasks and problem environments. It should also be sufficiently general so that it can be employed by different organizations.

A number of methodologies are currently being used and refined. Many have elements in common, such as: structured programming; use of structured languages; emphasis on hierarchical structure and modularity; employment of design languages which incorporate decision tables and other graphic diagramming techniques; and various organizational innovations such as chief-programmer teams, structured walkthroughs, and development support libraries. Each methodology offers a notation for representing the allowed constructs and hierarchical structure. There are, however, areas of philosophical difference.

A fuller discussion of procedures in common use can be found in Refs. 5, 6, and 12. In this article we discuss the methodology called structured design [14]. A detailed discussion of its notation and concepts will serve to illustrate the modern development process.

Systems Analysis and the Analyst

The title *systems analyst* can mean something different in every organization. In the context of structured development, however, the analyst is the person who communicates with the user, studies the present system and new requirements, and describes these in sufficiently understandable terms to the person responsible for designing an appropriate computer system. The main product of the analyst's efforts is a set of functional requirements otherwise known as functional specifications or, in this case, a structured specification.

This aspect of phase I, problem definition or requirements analysis, is frequently given short shrift on many projects. Since most failures of systems to do what the user had in mind, or to make sufficient allowances for projected change, can be traced to misunderstandings at this stage, a good job of determining the requirements and constraints is crucial to the success of the project. Questions regarding resources needed for implementation, security levels that will be necessary, schedules, and existing software should be answered before a solution is specified.

The analyst obtains information by interviewing key personnel, learning the mechanics of the operations involved, studying any written documentation that exists, and observing the crucial data flows (both those which are automated and those which are not). He or she defines the problem clearly and proposes a solution. In addition to the facts and figures leading to his recommendation, the primary output of this phase of development is a set of data flow diagrams, a data dictionary, and the mini-specs or descriptions of primitives that together form the final product of phase I.

It is wise to make as few design decisions as possible during phase I, and to allow for change in these areas so that the design will not be unnecessarily constrained. It is quite common for the analyst to follow up a proposed system throughout the system's life cycle, and for the designer to take an active interest in the specifications and implementation stages as well.

2.18.2 Structured Analysis

In the context of the project life cycle, analysis takes place near the beginning, preceded only by the feasibility study, if one is performed. Structured analysis applies the principles of top-down partitioning to the analysis phase. Its output is the structured specification, which has the following characteristics:

1. It is graphic; made up mostly of diagrams.
2. It is partitioned; not a single specification, but a network of connected subspecifications whose purpose is to divide the system into reasonably independent pieces, and to declare the interfaces among the pieces.
3. It is top-down; presented in a hierarchical fashion, progressing from the most abstract upper level to the most detailed bottom level [4].

Structured analysis creates a system model consisting of *data flow diagrams* and a *data dictionary*. A data flow diagram (DFD) is a portrayal of a situation from the data's point of view rather than that of any one user or set of users (a flowchart is documentation from the system's point of view). A DFD shows the set of possible paths a datum may follow. The diagrams present the system in terms of its component processes, and declare all the interfaces among the components. The dictionary defines the interfaces shown on the diagrams.

Data flow diagrams are constructed in leveled sets, beginning with the top of the hierarchy, and proceeding to create a more detailed DFD for each component process down to the bottom level. The resultant functional specification makes an excellent starting point for the design phase.

For example, suppose that a company decides to market computerized language instruction. Such instruction is called *computer-assisted instruction* (CAI) or computer-based instruction. In a CAI system, the computer displays drills, exercises, and information at a terminal, asks for a response, processes the student's response, and proceeds differentially through a program according to features of the individual student's responses.

The top-level, or context, diagram of a language school subsidiary called COMPU-SPEAK might appear as shown in Fig. 2. Diagram 0, or the next level if we were to "zoom in" on the bubble to obtain more information about the processing going on in COMPU-SPEAK, would resemble Fig. 3.

Note that the notational symbols are relatively simple and can be readily understood when examining a diagram. These clear pictures alleviate the communications problems that arise between analyst and user. A named vector (data flow) portrays a data path; a bubble (process) portrays some transformation of the data; a straight line portrays a file or data base; and a box (source or sink) portrays a net originator or receiver of data.

The rules governing the use of these symbols are also simple. For the data flow:

1. Items that travel together are represented by a single data flow.
2. Data flow names represent what we know about the data; no two data flows have the same name.

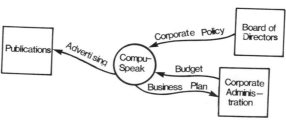

Fig. 2   Context diagram.

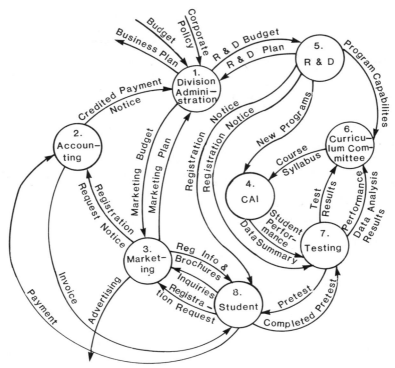

Fig. 3   0. COMPU-SPEAK.

3. The data flow name is defined in the data dictionary in terms of its constituent data flows and self-defining data items unless it is a self-defining data item.
4. Data flows moving into and out of simple files do not require names—the file name suffices.
5. The ⊕ symbol means that either of the two adjacent data flows, but not both, will be present (Fig. 4).
6. The * symbol means that both of the adjacent data flows will always be present if either is present (Fig. 4).

Processes show some amount of work performed on data. Each process should have a descriptive name and each bubble is numbered with reference to its position within the set of diagrams.

For instance, suppose that we want to specify a system for the delivery of instruction to the student (i.e., those functions performed inside the bubble called "CAI" in Fig. 3). We want a system that can present and modify instructional materials and sequences in response to student performance. It must also give tests, compute grades, diagnose needs, and evaluate student progress.

The next-level partitioning of bubble 4 will look like Fig. 5. The incoming and outgoing data flows (those that cross the dashed line) are the same as those found in the higher-level diagram. Data flows into and out of a bubble on a parent diagram are equivalent to *net* inputs and outputs to and from a child diagram. This equivalence is called "balancing." The data dictionary entry for the pretest results might be:

$$\text{pretest results} = \text{Name} + \text{Sex} + \text{Date-of-Birth} + \text{Test-Date}$$
$$+ \text{Score-Part I} + \text{Score-Part II}$$

This tells us that the test will have at least one score and can generate two.

The dashed line in Fig. 5 shows the CAI bubble, which has now been divided up into three parts. The relationship between the parts and the data flows and the role of two major files is indicated. Unlike conventional flowcharts, no attempt is made to show flow of control in this diagram; there is no attempt to show what initiates or terminates the data flows from bubble to bubble. These questions will not be addressed until the bottom levels. (Note that the bubble numbers do not indicate any form

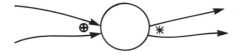

Fig. 4   Various data flows.

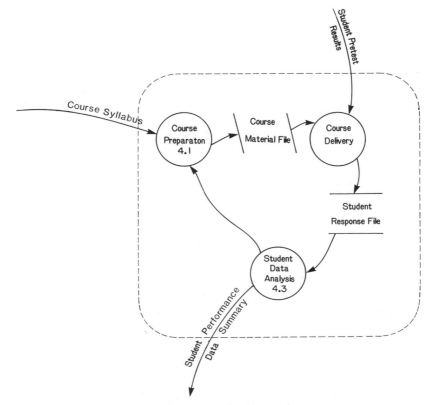

Fig. 5   Computer-assisted instruction.

of precedence, or the order in which they should be considered.) The purpose is to partition the system into reasonably independent pieces and to declare the interfaces among the pieces; the data flow diagram (DFD) is a tool for the functional decomposition of the system.

Figure 6 presents the lower-level diagram for bubble 4.2 of Fig. 5 (i.e., a detailed presentation of the bubble bearing that number on the parent diagram). The child diagram, in this case, portrays the transformation of course material into student performance data as shown on the parent; this transformation is divided into five component pieces, and we can see the interfaces among these pieces. Diagram 4.2 also shows the human–machine boundary (i.e., the interface between human being and automated procedure), which, in this case, is the set of data flows moving into and out of bubble 4.2.3.

While "walking through" diagram 4.2, we will answer any questions that come up. For example, exactly what sort of performance data should be saved, and how can we provide for change in this data base in ways that are not too costly? We also update the data dictionary to show the content of other new data flows, such as:

$$\text{display} = \begin{bmatrix} \text{text} + \text{request-for-signal-to-proceed} \\ \text{text} + \text{request-for-response} \end{bmatrix}$$

$$\text{text} = \begin{bmatrix} \text{instructions} \\ \text{problem} \\ \text{data} \end{bmatrix}$$

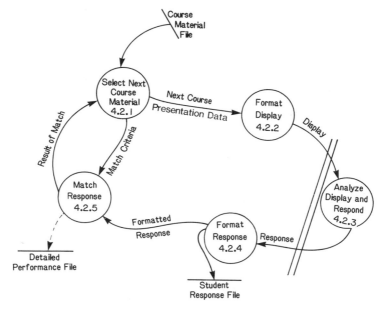

Fig. 6 Course delivery.

where brackets indicate alternative data flows. Furthermore, we will decide which bubbles require additional lower-level data flow diagrams and which qualify as functional primitives.

Within our course delivery system, bubbles 4.2.1 and 4.2.5 appear complex enough to require lower-level exposition, especially if responses other than those which match the target exactly are to be identified for special processing. Bubble 4.2.2, however, fulfills all the criteria for a primitive:

1. Its name is made up of an action verb and a single concrete object.
2. It has single input and single output.
3. Each input will eventually cause one output.
4. Most important, its allocated work can easily be described in one page or less.

Figure 7 shows one technique for specifying a primitive. There are a number of other ways, including decision tables and Nassi–Schneiderman diagrams [10]. The latter have the advantage of modeling the

Process Number: 4.2.2
Process Name: Format Display

Clear screen.
 	
For each line of text:
    Determine line number.
    If no line number specified, use next available line.
    Determine column number.
    If no column number specified, use leftmost column.
 	
Determine position of cursor.
If no cursor position specified, use next
        available line, starting at leftmost column.

Fig. 7 Primitive specification.

process in simply ordered structures which prevent unrestricted transfers of control. Decision tables may be preferable when subpolicy selection depends on many combinations of conditions.

Several aspects of a structured specification are easily seen from this example:

1. It presents an overall view first and works its way smoothly from the abstract to the detailed.
2. It is graphic; the decomposition of the system is highly visible and quickly understandable.
3. It is maintainable (i.e., easily modifiable).
4. It does not depend on or specify any physical elements of the system.
5. It provides a smoother transition to the design phase; there is a natural relationship between the structured specification and the early activities of structured design.

2.18.3 Structured Design

Whereas the functional specification document describes *what* tasks or functions are to be performed by the proposed system, the design specification is a detailed description of *how* these functions will be carried out. The program design is specified in a notation that can support the organization and management of the implementation process as well as provide the essential communication of the design to those outside the design phase processes.

The designer gets a set of functional and performance requirements (the performance requirements are the limiting conditions under which the specified functions are to be realized by the software design). If the structured development methodology is adhered to, the designer receives a readable document that already takes a hierarchical view of the system, has already isolated the detail at the lowest levels, and has already divided the system into manageable parts.

From the products on the analysis phase, it is the goal of the designer to produce the structure of a system in which complexity is controlled, which will be easy to test and to prove out, and which will be easy to maintain. Ill-designed systems often display a high degree of connectivity among subsystems; many of these interconnections are hidden in that they represent unstated assumptions made by one subsystem about other subsystems and can lead to unforeseen side effects when seemingly trivial changes are made.

One way of combating complexity is modularity. A program is modular if it is written in many relatively independent parts which have well-defined interfaces such that each module makes no assumptions about the operation of other modules except what is contained in the interface specifications; these modules can be compiled and tested separately.

A measure of the interdependence of modules is the degree of coupling, or association, between them. The higher the coupling, the more likely that changes in one module will affect the functioning of another; the fewer and simpler the connections between modules, the easier it is to understand each module without reference to other modules. A high degree of coupling affects readability; minimal coupling makes it possible to read through a given module without having to refer to another for complete understanding.

The complexity of a system is affected by the total number of connections and by the degree to which each connection couples the modules, making them interdependent. For example, when two or more modules share a common environment (area of storage, data elements, etc.), they are coupled without regard to their functional relationship. The type and amount of data passed between two modules affects their interdependence. References from one module to another module's data have a strong influence on coupling, as do some types of transfers of control.

Coupling is minimized, all other things being equal, when only input/output data flow across the interface between two modules (i.e., output from one module serves as input data to the other). The passing of control information, that information which governs the operations or execution of another module (flags, branch labels, etc.), introduces a strong and largely unnecessary form of coupling; most systems can be constructed so that almost all coupling is I/O coupling.

In addition to the kinds of dependencies already discussed, higher coupling results from pushing back the binding time (see Sec. 2.12) of the connection (i.e., connections bound to fixed referents at execution time result in lower coupling than binding that takes place at earlier stages, such as loadtime, link-edit time, assembly time, or coding time, in that order). An example of binding is that of variables to values. The values of parameters are dependent on data from outside the module; when they are fixed late rather than early, they are more readily changed and the system becomes more adaptable to changing requirements.

Another sign of poor partitioning is the presence of many modules which lack a high degree of "cohesion" [8, 14]. Functionally, cohesive modules perform only one task, or several related tasks that use the same data items. Modules lack cohesion when they perform unrelated tasks and are bound together only by time dependencies (things that happen at the same time) or order dependencies (things that happen one after the other). There is a strong relationship between coupling and cohesion; the greater the cohesion within each individual module in the system, the lower the coupling will be between the modules.

Structured design utilizes a diagram called a *structure chart*. There is a strong correlation between a structure chart (showing *how* the requirement will be met) and the associated data flow diagram (stating *what* is to be accomplished). Two relatively simple procedures, transform analysis and transaction analysis, help derive a structure chart from a DFD.

Transform Analysis

Many systems can be represented by a DFD consisting of one or more inward flowing data branches and one or more outward flowing data branches with what is called a "central transform" in the middle. Such a system is shown in Fig. 8. In *transform analysis*, the input and output portions of the structure chart correspond on a one-to-one basis to bubbles of the input and output legs of the DFD. For each input bubble there is one "get" module and one "transform" module on the structure chart. For each output bubble on the DFD, there is one "transform" module and one "put" module. The transform itself results in one or more modules which effect the transformation from the inputs to the outputs (see Fig. 9).

Considering the specifications for the course delivery portion of the CAI system (Fig. 6) and ignoring the human interaction to the right of the double lines, it is easy to see the derivation of the structure chart shown in Fig. 10. The data elements are now represented by small labeled arrows moving along the connecting arrows. Bubbles 4.2.4 and 4.2.2 are the input and output portions of Fig. 6; the central transform is contained in 4.2.5 and 4.2.1. At this stage we have an initial design which, with respect to modularity, is reasonably good.

Transaction Analysis

Transaction analysis is very similar to transform analysis. However, instead of locating the transform center of the DFD, it locates the transaction center, which is the place where the various processing *actions* are performed, depending on the input type. The transaction center is readily identified. It consists of a number of bubbles which are each connected to a single bubble accepting input, as well as a single bubble producing output. The corresponding box in the structure chart looks much as it would in the transform-centered analysis except that there are many processing modules between the input and output transform modules at the highest level (see Fig. 11).

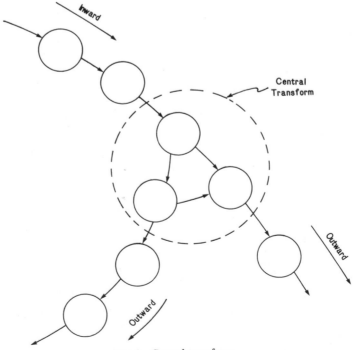

Fig. 8 Central transform.

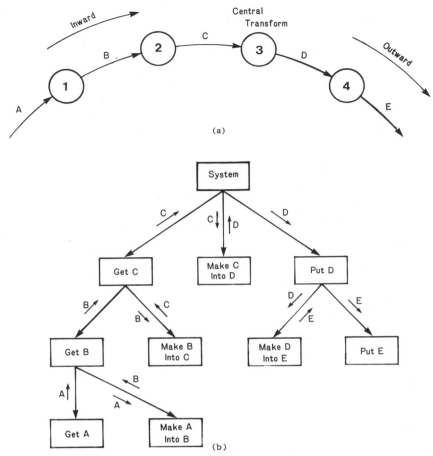

Fig. 9 Transform analysis: (*a*) DFD illustrating a transform; (*b*) Structure chart corresponding to the DFD of part (*a*).

The primary strategy for most systems will be transform analysis, but there are special situations in which additional strategies can be used to supplement this basic approach. Transaction analysis is suggested by a DFD where a transform splits an input data stream into several discrete output substreams. A transaction center of a system gets each transaction in raw form, analyzes it to determine its type, and dispatches it to the proper processing module for its type.

A system may include any number of transaction centers which the designer can learn to recognize and specify. The steps of a transaction analysis are described at greater length in Ref. 14.

Packaging and Optimization

Changes related to efficiency should be introduced as late as possible, and only those parts where efficiency really matters should be tuned up. The more efficiency is considered, the less flexible and easy to modify the system will be.

A rule of thumb is that more than 90% of efficiency can be realized by concentrating on 10% of the system (in some systems, 98% of the code contributes to less than 2 s of computer time per *year*). The trick is to find and remove the real bottlenecks in the system.

Well-structured, highly modular systems, with highly cohesive modules and low coupling, make these bottlenecks easier to identify and much easier to change. Walkthroughs (see Sec. 2.18.4) of the system help find potential bottlenecks and instrumentation can confirm their existence. However, each proposed optimization must be evaluated in terms of the added cost to other design goals, such as clarity and maintainability.

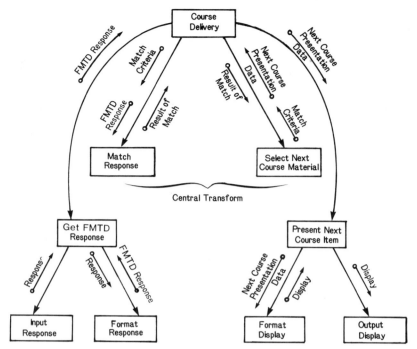

Fig. 10   Course delivery partial structure chart (see Fig. 6).

Packaging is the process of combining previously designed and programmed modules into larger units which can be loaded into the machine and executed directly. After having developed a good design and taken into account factors such as coupling and cohesion, the necessary packaging decisions for execution of the programs on specific equipment can be addressed.

For example, consider the structure chart shown in Fig. 12. It would be desirable to package C with A since they appear to be used together more frequently than will other modules. Another consideration may be the volume of data transferred between modules. The general rule is simple: include, where possible, modules connected by a reference that is used or accessed many times during execution within the same load unit. Wherever possible, optional functions (ones that, for some executions, may not be used at all) and functions that are used only once per execution should be packaged separately.

Packaging considerations should come to the fore only at the end of the design phase. Mechanical restrictions on memory size or execution time should *not* affect the modular structure of the system.

2.18.4   Walkthroughs

A walkthrough is simply a peer-group review of any product. At various stages of the structured development life cycle, it is appropriate to conduct formal walkthroughs of, for instance, the structured specification and the design specification in order to improve the quality of the final product. Walkthroughs have been found by many organizations to increase productivity and reliability, encourage better dissemination of technical information, and provide greater familiarity with partially completed work among members of the group should takeover become necessary because of illness or the departure of its author.

The formal walkthrough is conducted according to set procedures so that the benefits will be maximized while the potential negative aspects will be minimized. Roles of participants are carefully delineated in advance, and adequate preparation is encouraged. The concept of a walkthrough is made much more practical within the context of structured development, since it is only possible to review thoroughly a product that is readable and comprehensible. See Ref. 15 for further details on walkthroughs.

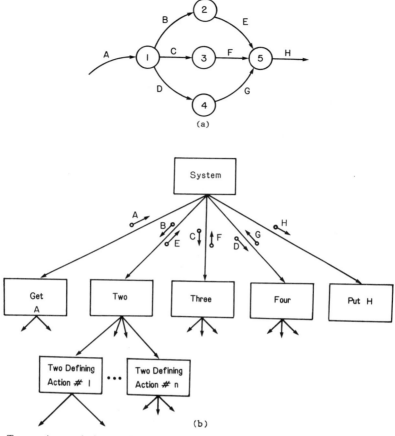

Fig. 11 Transaction analysis: (*a*) DFD illustrating a transaction center; (*b*) structure chart corresponding to the DFD of part (*a*).

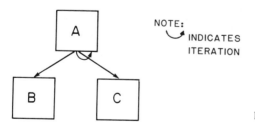

NOTE:
⤷ INDICATES
ITERATION

Fig. 12 Packaging considerations.

2.18.5 Structured Programming

The philosophy of structured programming (see Sec. 2.13.5) is based on modularization and was formulated by innovators such as Edsger W. Dijkstra and C. A. R. Hoare some time before the concepts of structured analysis and design were developed. The rules of structured programming actually represent an expansion of the rules of modularization. In addition to the decomposition of the program into independent, discrete units each having one entry point and one exit point, structured programming attempts to control complexity by limiting program paths even further (i.e., by restricting the set of and use of control structures).

Within a well-structured program, only the following control structures are permitted:

1. Concatenation (normal sequencing from one statement to its successor)
2. Selection of the next statement based on the testing of a condition (e.g., IF, CASE)
3. Iteration (e.g., WHILE, FOR)

Connection of two statements by a GOTO is avoided [3]. These restrictions make the program more readable, make walkthroughs more practical, and thereby increase reliability and maintainability. Efficiency considerations that violate these constructs should be entertained if absolutely necessary and only if the program remains sufficiently manageable.

Some programming languages, such as Pascal [2], MODULA, and Ada have good control and data structures. For the ancient but still widely used FORTRAN, preprocessors exist which supply these structures.

2.18.6 Top-Down Implementation

Structured programs are typically developed from the top down, in levels. The highest level describes the flow of control among major functional components of the system; component names are introduced to represent the components. The names (or stubs consisting of dummy code) are subsequently associated with code which describes the flow of control among still-lower-level components, which are again represented by their component names, or stubs. The process stops when no undefined names remain.

Among the advantages of this method are the identification of problems in the most important areas first and the elimination of massive end-of-project integration problems. At each level, previously existing code has been tested and debugged so that, if the partitioning is correct, new bugs can be easily traced to the new module(s).

Frequently, especially when large systems are involved, it is suitable to employ a hybrid top-down technique. For example, if a critical module, or set of modules, that is used frequently is located somewhere at the lower levels, as shown in Fig. 13, it may make sense to implement an entire section of the design, from the top down, and then complete other sections. Alternatively, it may be the case that an input or output device is located at the bottom of a particular branch of the design, and it would be useful to be able to test with actual data. For such legitimate purposes, hybrid variations are acceptable while the underlying principles are adhered to.

2.18.7 Chief-Programmer Teams

A natural outgrowth of top-down development, this organizational innovation assigns a small, highly specialized nucleus of experienced people to complete the system architecture. After this, additional programmers can begin to work in parallel, with the chief programmer supervising the development process. He is also the technical interface with the user or customer. Large projects may have multiple chief-programmer teams, responsible for the development of subsystems.

Each team consists of the chief programmer (an excellent programmer, and a creative and well-disciplined individual), the backup programmer (also an excellent programmer who can take over

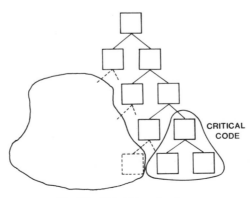

Fig. 13   Hybrid top-down.

the project should the chief programmer leave), two or three junior or less experienced programmers, and a librarian to manage the development support library.

The team concept recognizes that programmers have different levels of competence, and seeks to set up a productive entity within which personnel are maximally utilized and technical help is available on the required levels.

For further information, see Ref. 1.

2.18.8   Testing

Since the bug-free program is an abstract theoretical concept, the modern techniques described above promote the construction of programs in a way that tends to isolate bugs, and to apply a strongly disciplined testing procedure to large systems during their development. The test plan should, in fact, be designed early and most of the test data specified during the design stage of the project.

Systems testing comprises (1) creating or obtaining test data to simulate all possible conditions, and (2) observing and approving the final results. If the system is coded from the bottom up, each module is unit tested with test drivers simulating the actual software environment of the module. Then groups of modules are tested together, and eventually all the components are tested together in an integrated test which frequently reveals errors missed in module tests. Correcting such errors, at this stage, can account for one-fourth of the total effort. The top-down procedure, recommended for structured development, avoids this.

Structured development also facilitates the derivation of tests from the structured specification, where all data paths are clearly visible. A set of tests that demonstrates the acceptability of the system should include:

1. **Normal Path Tests.**   Derived from the data dictionary. A number of valid test inputs is made up for each input data flow. These inputs should include boundary values as well as midrange values.
2. **Exception Path Tests.**   Invalid values for each data element, designed to test the system's capacity to deal with errors. Each test involves *one* error. Exception path tests also deal with format-type errors (null fields, too many fields, etc.)
3. **Transient State Tests.**   Tests the normal path inputs for each of the states that can be generated in memory for the particular input data flow (no match on field N, limit surpassed, status HOLD, all tests pass, etc.). For example, if the previous test input produced a state of "no match," or "upper limit surpassed," will this have any effect on the correct processing of the next input? If so, is it an unanticipated effect?
4. **Performance Tests.**   Test the quantitative standards previously set (throughput, response time, etc.).
5. **Special Tests.**   Test any peculiarities of the system.

2.18.9   Operation and Maintenance

Users may also insist on their own acceptance tests, on-site, to demonstrate that the system performs all functions described for it in the specifications. If they already have a system performing these functions, conversion is the next step in the cycle. This can be accomplished all at once if the system is small, by phasing in the new system if both use the same machine, or by running a parallel operation for some period of time. The third approach is safest for large, complex projects, although it is costly and difficult to manage. Structured development, because it cuts down significantly on errors that turn up in the final stages of a project, will ensure significantly less angst and expense during this phase.

Finally, even if errors are kept to a minimum, the user will probably request changes in the delivered system. The combination of error correction and necessary modifications can dwarf the original development costs. It is here that the ultimate rewards of structured development are reaped. A program that is properly partitioned and readable will significantly reduce this major chunk of development costs.

REFERENCES

1. F. T. BAKER, "Chief Programmer Team Management of Production Programming," *IBM Syst. J.*, **11**(1), 56–73 (1972).
2. R. CONWAY, D. GRIES, and E. C. ZIMMERMAN, *A Primer on Pascal*, Winthrop Publishers, Cambridge, Mass., 1976. (A structured programming language gaining wide acceptance in the industry.)
3. O. J. DAHL, E. W. DIJKSTRA, and C. A. R. HOARE, *Structured Programming*, Academic Press, New York, 1972.

4. T. DeMARCO, *Structured Analysis and System Specification*, Yourdon Press, New York, 1978.
5. *IEEE Transactions on Software Engineering*, **SE-3**(1) (Jan. 1977). (Issue devoted to Structured Analysis.)
6. M. A. JACKSON, *Principles of Program Design*, Academic Press, New York, 1975.
7. B. W. KERNIGHAN and P. J. PLAUGER, *Software Tools*, Addison-Wesley, Reading, Mass., 1976.
8. G. J. MYERS, *Reliable Software through Composite Design*, Petrocelli/Charter, New York, 1975.
9. W. MYERS, "A Statistical Approach to Scheduling Software Development," *Computer*, Dec. 1978.
10. I. NASSI and B. SCHNEIDERMAN, "Flowchart Techniques for Structured Programming," SUNYSB Dept. of Computer Science, Aug. 1972.
11. K. T. ORR, *Structured Systems Development*, Yourdon Press, New York, 1977.
12. D. L. PARNAS, "On the Criteria to Be Used in Decomposing Systems into Modules," *Commun. ACM*, Dec. 1972.
13. L. H. PUTNAM, "A General Empirical Solution to the Macro Software Sizing and Estimating Problem," *IEEE Trans. Software Eng.*, **SE-4**(4), July 1978.
14. E. YOURDON, and L. CONSTANTINE, *Structured Design*, 2nd ed., Yourdon Press, New York, 1978.
15. E. YOURDON, *Structured Walkthroughs*, Yourdon Press, New York, 1977.

2.19 VIRTUAL MEMORY

K. Ekanadham

2.19.1 Concept of Virtual Memory

A system is said to have *virtual memory* if the address space of a process (i.e., the addresses it generates to reference instructions and data) is not identical to the physical address space (i.e., the machine addresses actually occupied by the process while running) [1]. A run-time translation must therefore take place from the address space of the process to the physical address space. This is done with the help of specially designed *virtual memory hardware*. The address space of the process is then known as the *virtual address space* or *virtual memory*.

The virtual address space may be larger or smaller than the physical address space. When a larger virtual memory is provided, part of it resides on an auxiliary storage device and only that portion of it that is currently being accessed is kept in primary memory. As the execution progresses, some portions may be transferred to the auxiliary device and new portions may be brought into primary memory. These transfers are done by the software supporting the virtual memory and are invisible to the process. Thus, from the viewpoint of the process, it has a (potentially large) virtual memory, all of which is directly accessible. The process has the illusion that the whole of its address space is residing in primary memory at all times.

Since a program generates addresses in its own address space without making any assumptions about the machine addresses at which it resides, its physical location can be changed during execution. Information in the virtual memory hardware must be modified to reflect the new mapping. Furthermore, if the virtual memory is large enough, the programmer is relieved of the burden of overlaying code or data (file buffers) in order to accommodate processing in a limited physical memory. This is done automatically by the virtual memory support.

In a *one-dimensional virtual memory* the process views its entire address space as a linear array of words. Reference to a word is made by simply providing the corresponding index of the word in the array. *Segmented virtual memory* is *two-dimensional*. The virtual memory is divided into segments [2]. Each segment is a one-dimensional virtual memory of arbitrary size. A segment is a convenient unit in which the programmer groups related information (e.g., a program, an array). To refer to the ith word in a segment s, the virtual address (s, i) is used.

A segmented virtual memory has a number of advantages from the programmer's point of view. Since the size of a segment can vary dynamically, it can conveniently be used to represent variable-size data structures (e.g., pushdown stacks). This is more difficult in a one-dimensional virtual memory since the programmer must reserve enough space to handle the worst case, or, alternatively, check for overflow each time the data structure grows. In the case of code, a segment can be allocated to each program module. As a result, changes in one module do not affect the name (i.e., virtual address) and internal references of another module. (This is not the case in a one-dimensional virtual memory, as expanding a program will change the virtual addresses of all programs following it in the virtual memory.) Sharing of information between processes is more easily accomplished in a segmented virtual memory since the unit of information to be shared can be stored in a separate segment. This segment can then more easily be incorporated into the address spaces of the processes accessing it. If the unit of information to be shared is a code segment (see pure procedure Sec. 2.19.2), care must be taken to ensure that the addresses it generates during execution on behalf of each process correspond to the layout of information in the virtual memory of that process. Techniques for handling this have been developed for segmented virtual systems [2].

A further advantage of segmented virtual memory is that access to information can be controlled on a segment basis. When information is shared, the owner of the information generally regulates the way in which others access it. For instance, whereas one user may be allowed to read and write the information, another may only be allowed to read it. In a one-dimensional virtual memory it is extremely difficult to enforce different access rights since there are no natural boundaries between the various portions of information. In a segmented virtual memory, separate checks can be done for each segment at the time of address translation. Thus, while in a one-dimensional virtual memory all portions of information are equally accessible, a segmented virtual memory provides much finer control, enabling a user to have different access privileges to different segments (see Sec. 2.23).

2.19.2 Virtual Memory Implementation (Hardware and Software)

A simple way of mapping a virtual memory into contiguous locations in physical memory is by using a *base and bound register*. The register is manipulated by the operating system to implement a one-dimensional virtual memory and is not accessible to user programs, which can neither read nor modify its contents. The base field of the register contains the physical address at which the first word of the process is stored and the bound field contains the total number of words in the process. A virtual address generated by the process is first checked to determine if it is less than the bound. If not, instruction execution is aborted and a *memory fault* is generated, causing entry to the operating system. The physical address is then obtained by adding the base address to the virtual address produced by the CPU. Since the physical address thus produced must be within the space allocated to the process, a base and bound register performs the functions of both relocation and protection of addresses. In this scheme contiguous virtual addresses map into contiguous physical addresses. It should be noted that a base register (see [1] and Sec. 2.12.1), such as is used in the IBM 360, operates in a different fashion. Although it performs relocation, the user can freely change the contents of the register and hence it offers no protection. Furthermore, if a process has to be moved during execution, the base register presents a problem since the process may have stored an absolute address in it. The base and bound register presents no such problem since the new base address can be loaded into the register by the system when the process next runs.

The base and bound register scheme discussed above does not permit the sharing of the same copy of a program by two users. This may be achieved by having *multiple base and bound registers*. For instance, the virtual memory of each process can be divided into two parts, program and data, which are stored in two contiguous sections of the memory. One base and bound register is used for each section. The sharing of a program by two processes, each of which has its own data (segment), is depicted in Fig. 1.

In order for the procedure to be shared, it must be pure. A *pure procedure* is one that does not modify itself during execution. Otherwise, modifications made when the procedure is executed by one process will effect the execution of another process sharing the same code. Thus a pure procedure contains unmodifiable code and read-only constants. Any modifiable variables or process-related data and intermediate results must be stored outside the procedure (and usually constitute part of the state of the process). Consequently, the same procedure can compute different results when executed with different process states (registers, stacks, etc.).

The procedure portion of the process must be read-only, whereas the data portion can be read or written. This can be enforced by extending the base and bound registers with an access field indicating the mode of access permitted to the corresponding segment, as shown in Fig. 1. On each reference, the hardware can check these bits and ensure that the program is not modified, while the data can be overwritten. If the check fails, a *protection fault* occurs, causing entry to the operating system.

The notion of multiple base and bound registers can be extended to a table in the implementation of a segmented virtual memory. Each process now has a *segment descriptor table*, in which there is an entry called the *segment descriptor word* (SDW), for each segment. An SDW contains (1) a flag indicating whether the segment is currently in main memory or not, (2) the base address in main memory at which the segment starts, (3) the length of the segment, and (4) protection bits indicating the mode of access allowed to the segment. The entire table is kept in main memory when the process is running and is referred to by a special register called the *descriptor base register* (DBR). This contains the base address and length of the table.

The scheme to translate a virtual address (s,i) using the DBR and segment descriptor table is shown in Fig. 2. When a virtual address (s,i) is presented, s is checked by the hardware to determine whether it is less than the bound in the DBR. Then, using the base address in the DBR, the sth entry in the segment descriptor table is located. This contains the SDW for segment s. By checking the flag in the

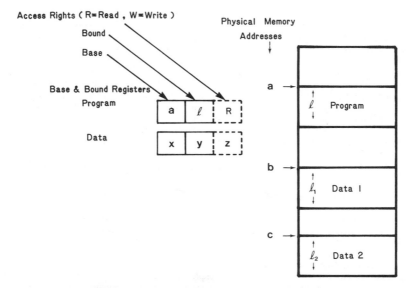

Fig. 1 Two base and bound registers (one for program and one for data) enable processes to execute the same copy of a procedure with different data. When the first process executes $x = d$, $y = l_1$ and $z = (R, W)$. When the second process executes $x = c$, $y = l_2$ and $z = (R, W)$.

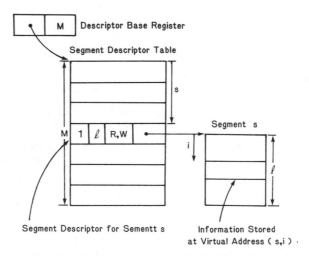

Fig. 2 Accessing a word at virtual address (s, i) using the descriptor base register and the segment description table.

descriptor, it is determined if the segment is in main memory (a value of 1 is assumed to mean that the segment is in main memory). If so, the attempted access is validated with the protection bits and the index i is checked to determine whether it is less than the length of the segment. Using the base address of the segment, the physical address of the ith word can be determined. This entire algorithm is implemented by the address translation hardware. If the segment is not present, a *segment fault* is said to occur, which traps the process and causes the operating system to initiate a transfer from auxiliary memory. Invalid values of s or i produce a memory fault, while an attempted access which is inconsistent with the protection bits produces a protection fault.

The use of multiple base and bound registers (appropriately extended) to store the segment descriptor table would be very efficient, but is highly expensive in view of the large number of segments a process may have. On the other hand, keeping the table in the memory adds an additional memory reference for each access and hence is inefficient. Some form of associative memory is generally used to speed the translation (see Sec. 1.7.2).

Use of a base and bound register to implement a one-dimensional virtual memory is too restrictive for two reasons. First, it requires a contiguous block of physical memory for a segment, and second, it assumes that the physical memory is larger than the virtual memory. Paging is adopted to alleviate these problems. The virtual memory of each process is divided into blocks of fixed size called *pages*. Correspondingly, main memory is treated as if it were divided into a set of page frames, each of which is capable of accommodating a page from the virtual memory of some process (see Fig. 3). Thus the contents of each page are stored in contiguous locations, but the pages of a process can be scattered arbitrarily in main memory. A *page table* for each process is maintained in the operating system. The jth entry in the table refers to the jth page of the virtual memory. Each entry contains a flag indicating whether the page is currently present in memory or not (a value of 1 indicates presence) and the base address of the page. If p is the page size, i DIV p (the integral part of the quotient) is the page number of virtual address i, and i MOD p (the remainder) is the index of the word in that page. These are easily obtained if p is a power of 2, since then the virtual address is simply the concatenation of the word number and the index. By indexing into the page table using the page number, the starting address of the page is determined, and from this the address of the desired word is obtained by adding the index of the word in the page. If the page is not in main memory, a *page fault* occurs. This is analogous to a segment fault and indicates to the operating system that a page transfer from auxiliary storage is necessary. Keeping the page table in main memory as opposed to special registers doubles the number of memory references. An associative memory can be used to alleviate this problem in the same manner as described for segments (see Sec. 1.7.2).

Paging has several advantages over a base and bound register scheme. First, the entire virtual memory need not be mapped into physical memory at any time. Only the pages currently being referenced need be accessible. This makes it possible for a process to have a virtual memory larger than main memory and is referred to as demand paging. Second, it is not necessary to obtain contiguous blocks to store the pages of the virtual memory. This tends to increase the efficiency of the memory allocation algorithm.

It should be noted that while segmentation and paging may seem similar, they are fundamentally different. Segmentation is visible to the user; it is created for the user's convenience. The user can name segments, refer to them, create and destroy them, and assign access modes to them. Segments are varying in size. Paging is invisible to the user and is created for efficient management of memory. Pages are usually of fixed size.

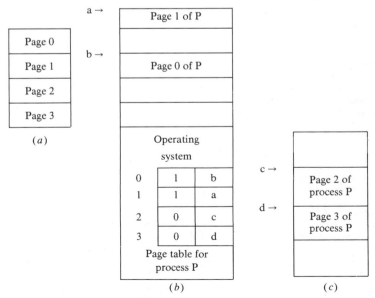

Fig. 3 Pages in the virtual memory of a process are distributed in main and auxiliary memories and can be located using the page table for process P: (*a*) virtual memory of process P; (*b*) main memory; (*c*) auxiliary memory.

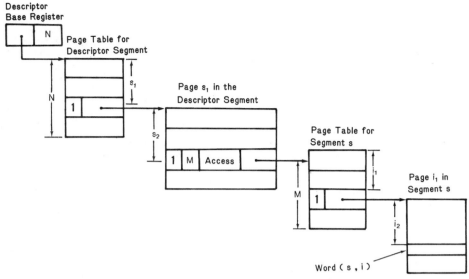

Fig. 4 Segmentation and paging are combined. The schematic shows the chain of actions leading to the access of the word whose virtual address is (s, i).

In the implementation of segmentation described earlier, each segment was assumed to be a one-dimensional virtual memory which, when stored in main memory, occupied contiguous locations. It is possible to combine segmentation and paging by causing each segment to be paged. The situation is depicted in Fig. 4. The SDWs are stored in a segment called the descriptor segment (DS). The following notation is used in the translation of virtual address (s,i), where p is the page size.

$s_1 = s \ DIV \ p =$ page number of page in DS in which SDW for segment s is stored

$s_2 = s \ MOD \ p =$ index into page s_1 at which the SDW for segment s is stored

$i_1 = i \ DIV \ p =$ page number of page in segment s in which the desired word is stored

$i_2 = i \ MOD \ p =$ index into page i_1 at which the desired word is located

The descriptor segment is itself a segment and hence is paged. The DBR points to the page table of the descriptor segment and the bound in DBR is the total number of pages in the descriptor segment. $s_1 = s \ DIV \ p$ gives the index into the page table of the entry for the desired page in the descriptor segment. $s_2 = s \ MOD \ p$ gives the index into that page, thus locating the SDW for segment s. The descriptor contains the address of the page table of segment s and its length in pages. A word in segment s can be obtained by repeating the process above using the page table of segment s and the index i. Further details on this subject may be found in Ref. 3.

2.19.3   General Considerations

In addition to the preceding implementation strategy, a virtual memory system has to consider a number of other problems regarding policies of placement and replacement of segments and pages. At any given time in a nonpaged system, memory is divided into a sequence of arbitrary-size regions each of which either contains a segment of some process or is unoccupied (a hole). When a new block of information is to be read in, some hole must be selected. There are two popular methods of selection: first bit and best fit (see Sec. 2.9). With both methods it is possible to encounter a situation of *overflow* in which no hole is large enough to accomodate a new block, but the sum of the sizes of all the holes is larger than the new block size. Such a situation is the result of *external fragmentation*, where the holes become too small to be useful. The problem can be solved by *compacting memory* (see Sec. 2.9) and thus coalescing all the holes into one large block of free storage. Compaction is time consuming, however, and may yield only marginal overall benefits. If the memory size is at least 10 times larger than the average segment size, it is felt that this problem is not serious [1].

A paged system avoids external fragmentation, since memory is divided into uniform-size page frames which can exactly accomodate a single page (organization of a paging drum is described in Sec.

2.21.2). However, an integral number of page frames must be assigned to a segment. The last page may only be partially filled with information, so some storage is wasted, as it cannot be assigned to another segment. This is known as *internal fragmentation* and its effect is more pronounced in systems having a large page size. On the other hand, a smaller page size increases the size of the page table and hence is expensive. Thus the page size has to be optimally chosen and some analysis in this regard is reported in Refs. 1 and 4.

In general, paged systems tend to result in better memory management than nonpaged systems. An attempt to make optimal use of main storage has resulted in a strategy called *demand paging*. Here pages are brought into main memory only on demand, that is, when a reference is made to information on the page. When a new page has to be brought in and there are no free page frames, a page must be swapped out. The selection of the page for swapping is governed by a policy known as the *page replacement policy*. Ideally, it would be appropriate to remove the page in the memory that will not be referenced by any process for the longest time; that is, every other page in the memory will be referenced before the page selected for replacement. But this entails the prediction of the pattern of future references by a program and is not feasible.

Denning [1,5,6] has formulated the principle of locality for this purpose. It states that in a small interval of time, the references made by a program are not random, but tend to be confined to a subset of the pages of the process, and these pages will be the most recently referenced. Denning defines a *working set* at any time to be the set of all pages referenced in the preceding t units of time. It is assumed that references in the near future will most likely be to information contained in pages in the working set. The choice of the small interval t depends on various considerations, such as the memory available, page size, nature of the programs, and system characteristics; hence it has to be tuned for each system. For many programs, the working set varies gradually with time. The general strategy is to run a program only when all its working set is in main memory. When a page fault occurs, the *least recently used* page is replaced. The principle of locality suggests that this approach tends to optimize the page fault rate.

One serious pitfall in demand paged systems is the phenomenon of *thrashing*. This occurs when the system is attempting to multiprogram too many processes and as a result the number of page frames allocated to any one process is insufficient. The processes commit page faults at a rapid rate and as a result, the system spends most of its time swapping pages in and out with little computational progress. The only way to prevent this is to regulate the number of processes to be run at any given time in relation to their memory requirements and available memory.

2.19.4   Linking

Programs are written using symbolic name references to segments. Before the program runs, the names must be translated into indices into the virtual memory [(s,i) pairs]. Usually, this translation is performed at the time of compilation and/or loading (i.e., linking the various compiled modules into an executable module). For this purpose, all symbolic references made in the programs must be collected and translated into segment indices before the programs run. This is known as *static linking*. If the segments being referenced are retained in the system (e.g., files on auxiliary devices), they must be made known (i.e., table entries will be set up so that the virtual addresses can be mapped to the appropriate device addresses). Such linking is called static, as the linkage is done prior to execution and regardless of whether the segments are actually accessed during run time or not. Furthermore, linking segment references embedded in shared segments is difficult.

Alternatively, linking may be done *dynamically* at runtime when a segment is first referenced. The first reference causes what is known as a *linkage fault* and the system searches the directory of symbolic names, allocates a virtual address, and establishes the necessary translation tables. All further references must use the translation tables. This is done by having all symbolic references done indirectly through a separate segment called the *linkage segment*. Each process has its own linkage segment where the virtual address is stored after the first reference. The method can be very complex and involves careful design of the indirections and table-entry manipulations involved. Details of this scheme may be found in Ref. 3.

REFERENCES

1. P.J. DENNING, "Virtual Memory," *Comput. Surv.*, **2**(3) (Sept. 1970).
2. J. B. DENNIS, "Segmentation and the Design of Multiprogrammed Computer Systems," *J. ACM*, **12**(4) (Oct. 1965).
3. E. I. ORGANICK, *The MULTICS System: An Examination of Its Structure*, MIT Press, Cambridge, Mass., 1972.
4. E. WOLMAN, "A Fixed Optimum Cell Size for Records of Various Lengths," *J. ACM*, **12**(1) (Jan. 1965).

5. P. J. DENNING, "The Working Set Model for Program Behaviour," *Commun. ACM*, **11**(5) (May 1968).
6. E. G. COFFMAN and P. J. DENNING, *Operating System Theory*, Prentice-Hall, Englewood Cliffs, N.J., 1973.

2.20 PROCESSES

K. Ekanadham

A process is probably the most frequently used, but least precisely defined, term in operating systems. A number of intuitive definitions appear in the literature [1–4]. A more formal treatment of the subject may be found in Ref. 5. Intuitive concepts of a processor, a process, and their interaction are presented below.

A *processor* is a machine that has a set of memory registers and a control to execute (step by step) a program stored in the memory. The contents of the registers (which include the program counter indicating the next step to be executed in the program) at any time is called the *state of the processor*. Each step of the execution transforms one processor state into another. There will be *start and stop* mechanisms by means of which a processor may be initialized with a state, and started and stopped after encountering a desired state or executing a certain number of steps.

A *process* is an abstract entity consisting of a set of values, called an *address space* and a program counter. The address space includes the program to be executed as well as data. The program counter refers to the next step to be executed in the program. The contents of the address space at any time is called the *state of the process*. A process is said to be *running* when a processor is associated with the process by initializing the state of the processor with that of the process and executing the program. As a process runs, it goes through a sequence of *state transformations*. A process is said to be *dormant* when no processor is currently associated with the process.

Although not explicitly stated in the definition of a process, the following are generally assumed to be the implicit properties of all processes. A process is designed to accomplish a specific *well-defined task* for the external world. The outcome of the execution of a process is the *final state* it produces for a given *initial state*. This *functional behavior* of a process is unaffected by arbitrary *variations in the grain of time* a processor takes to execute each step. Thus a process behaves the same way for any speed of its associated processor. A process is *deterministic* and *sequential* in the sense that after the execution of a step, the resulting state will uniquely determine the next step to be executed and any state produced by the process is obtained only by applying its fixed state transformation function in a step-by-step fashion starting from the initial state (some exceptions to this are mentioned later).

For a process to accomplish a meaningful task, it must be able to communicate with the external world. In the model above, the inputting and outputting of information between the external world and a process are assumed to be embedded in the initial/final state. However, in practice, a large task is subdivided into many tasks (for the sake of efficiency in terms of parallelism and modularity) which can be executed in parallel almost independently except for some interactions at well-defined points. Each such task can be structured as a process. The interaction between the processes can occur through a *shared address space* or through *process communication*. In either case, special mechanisms must be made available for proper interaction and these are provided by an operating system (see Sec. 2.26). When two processes share some address space, the execution of one process may cause a change of state in the other. Such a process is not strictly deterministic as defined above and it becomes difficult to characterize its behavior functionally (independent of other processes). For example, the relative time at which the state change occurs will affect the outcome of the process.

An operating system is the software that provides (among other things) the *abstraction of a process*. A multiprogrammed operating system records the states of a number of processes and runs them by associating the processor(s) with different processes at different times using some scheduling policy (see Sec. 2.21). Whenever the processor is taken away from a process, the current state of that process is saved by the operating system in a *save area* and is restored later when the processor is reassigned to that process. The save area could be in main memory or on auxiliary memory or both. For this purpose, the operating system maintains a *process table* in which there is one entry for each process. A *process entry* contains all information about the process, such as its priority, whether it is running or dormant, whether it is in main memory or on auxiliary memory, and a pointer to its save area.

The term *state of a process* is also used at a macro level to refer to the running/dormant condition of a process. Whether "process state" refers to the contents of its address space or to its running/dormant conditions (macro state) is usually clear from the context. The dormant state is further subdivided to indicate the reason the process is dormant. The *ready* state indicates that the process is dormant because a processor is not associated with it at that time. The *blocked* state indicates that the process cannot run until some event occurs. The reasons for being blocked have to do with communication and synchronization with other processes (see Sec. 2.26) or synchronization with a device (see Sec. 2.22.1). A process undergoes changes in its macro state according to the pattern indicated in Fig. 1. Usually, a process is created in the ready state with its address space stored on

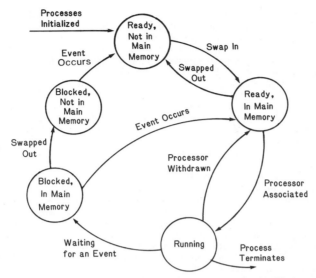

Fig. 1 Macro states of a process and possible transitions during the lifetime of a process.

auxiliary memory. When main memory is available, it is swapped from auxiliary into main and is then ready to run as soon as a processor is available. The processor may be periodically taken away from the process (to service another process) and reassigned later. When a process is running it may request a change to the blocked state if it has to wait for some event to occur. As a result, the processor can be assigned to another process. When the desired event occurs the process becomes ready again. The process entry is modified to record the current macro state as time progresses. The process may from time to time be swapped out to auxiliary memory to create room for other processes.

The sequence of events in a demand paged system (see Sec. 2.19) is somewhat more complicated since the entire address space of the process need not be in main memory when the process is running. Thus the distinction in Fig. 1, between a process in main memory and a process not in main memory, is not as clear.

REFERENCES

1. "IBM System/360 Operating System: Concepts and Facilities," Form (28-6535-0). Data Processing Div., IBM Corporation, White Plains, N.Y., 1965.

2. J. H. SALTZER, "Traffic Control in a Multiplexed Computer System," MAC-TR-30, Ph.D. thesis, Dept. of Electrical Engineering, MIT, Cambridge, Mass., 1966.

3. E. W. DIJKSTRA, "The Structure of the T.H.E. Multiprogramming System," *Commun. ACM*, **11**(5) (May 1968).

4. P. BRINCH HANSEN, "The Nucleus of a Multiprogramming System," *Commun. ACM*, **13**, (Apr. 1970).

5. J. J. HORNING, and B. RANDELL, "Process Structuring," *Comput. Surv.*, **5**(1) (Mar. 1973).

2.21 RESOURCE SCHEDULING ALGORITHMS

Manfred Ruschitzka, M. Hofri, and Arie Shoshani

2.21.1 CPU Scheduling

M. Ruschitzka

The Scheduler

The progress of a process toward completion within a computer system depends on the availability of the system resources required. For each resource type, an allocation algorithm determines the order in which competing processes are serviced. The operating system module responsible for the allocation of central processing units (CPUs or processors) is called the *scheduler*. The performance objectives of the scheduler and the allocators of other major system resources, notably main memory and I/O channels, are to provide satisfactory response times (i.e., limited delays) to all processes and simultaneously maintain acceptable ranges of resource utilization. These two objectives are potentially conflicting. In order to utilize resources optimally, processes with resource requirements that best match the available resources should be scheduled first. These processes, however, may differ from those requiring the fastest response. For example, the concurrent servicing of a suitable set of CPU-bound and I/O-bound processes will keep processors and channels highly utilized, but in view of response-time constraints it may be more important to service a different set of interactive processes first even if utilization factors decrease. In general, different allocation algorithms achieve different performance compromises for specific process and system types. Since processes typically require the concurrent allocation of several resource types, some coordination of the various allocators is necessary (see the discussion of working-set management in Sec. 2.19.3). In this section we deal only with processor allocation.

The scheduling status of a process may be *running*, *ready* (to run), or *blocked* (see Sec. 2.20). A blocked process requires an event to occur (e.g., an I/O completion interrupt) before it can continue to run. When that event occurs, its status changes to ready. A ready process is waiting for a processor to become available. A running process is executing on a processor. The major data structures of the scheduler are the process tables of the ready and running processes. For efficiency, they are commonly linked on the *ready queue* and the *run queues* (one per processor, with at most one entry per run queue), respectively. Figure 1 illustrates the components of a scheduling system. An arriving (newly created or unblocked) process—or, more precisely, its process record—is inserted in the ready queue by the appropriate operating system module (e.g., the initiator or file system). At certain instants in time, the scheduler is invoked and reallocates the processors to the set of processes with the currently highest priorities. If a running process is not a member of this set, it is recycled to the ready queue. A process departs for one of two reasons: termination or blocking (e.g., for I/O). The time between arrival and departure of a process is called the *response time*. It is the sum of the service requirement and the total waiting time in the ready queue. Note that in this more restricted use of the term, only CPU service is being considered.

A scheduling algorithm can be specified in terms of a decision mode, a priority function, and an arbitration rule. The *decision mode* defines the instants in time at which the scheduler is invoked. The most common decision modes are: nonpreemptive, preemptive, and quantum-oriented. In *nonpreemptive* mode, the scheduler is invoked only when a process departs or when an arriving process finds the

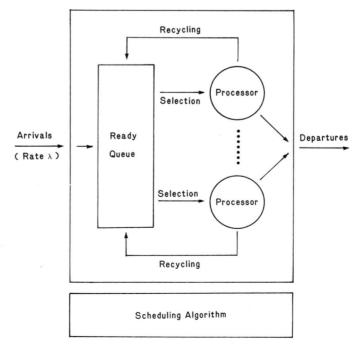

Fig. 1   Components of a scheduling system.

Table 1. Response Functions of Different Scheduling Algorithms in M/G/1 Systems[a]

Algorithm	Response Function
First-come first-serve	$$\dfrac{\lambda ES^2}{2(1-\lambda ES)}+x$$
Shortest job first	$$\dfrac{\lambda ES^2}{2\left[1-\lambda\int_0^x y\,dB(y)\right]^2}+x$$
Preemptive shortest job first	$$\dfrac{\lambda\int_0^x y^2\,dB(y)}{2\left[1-\lambda\int_0^x y\,dB(y)\right]^2}+\dfrac{x}{1-\lambda\int_0^x y\,dB(y)}$$
Preemptive shortest remaining processing time	$$\dfrac{\lambda\int_0^x y^2\,dB(y)+\lambda x^2(1-B(x))}{2\left[1-\lambda\int_0^x y\,dB(y)\right]^2}+\int_0^x\dfrac{dy}{1-\lambda\int_0^y s\,dB(s)}$$
Highest response ratio next	$$x\int_x^\infty\dfrac{\lambda ES^2}{2\left[y-\lambda y\int_0^y s\,dB(s)+\lambda\int_0^y s^2\,dB(s)\right]^2}dy+x$$
External static priority groups	$$\dfrac{\lambda ES^2}{2\left(1-\lambda ES\displaystyle\sum_{i=p+1}^N f_i\right)\left(1-\lambda ES\displaystyle\sum_{i=p}^N f_i\right)}+x$$
Preemptive external static priority groups	$$\dfrac{\lambda ES^2\displaystyle\sum_{i=p}^N f_i}{2\left(1-\lambda ES\displaystyle\sum_{i=p+1}^N f_i\right)\left(1-\lambda ES\displaystyle\sum_{i=p}^N f_i\right)}+\dfrac{x}{1-\lambda ES\displaystyle\sum_{i=p+1}^N f_i}$$
Processor-sharing round robin	$$\dfrac{x}{1-\lambda ES}$$
Processor-sharing feedback	$$\dfrac{\lambda\int_0^x y^2\,dB(y)+\lambda x^2(1-B(x))}{2\left[1-\lambda\int_0^x y\,dB(y)-\lambda x(1-B(x))\right]^2}+\dfrac{x}{1-\lambda\int_0^x y\,dB(y)-\lambda x(1-B(x))}$$
Preemptive two-level feedback	$$\dfrac{\lambda\int_0^q y^2\,dB(y)-\lambda q^2(1-B(q))}{2\left[1-\lambda\int_0^q y\,dB(y)-\lambda q(1-B(q))\right]}+x,\qquad x\le q$$ $$\dfrac{[\lambda ES^2/2(1-\lambda ES)]+x}{1-\lambda\int_0^q y\,dB(y)-\lambda q(1-B(q))},\qquad x>q$$

[a] x, specific service requirement; λ, process arrival rate; $B(y)$, ES, and ES^2, distribution function, first moment, and second moment of the service requirement; p, specific priority group; f_i, fraction of processes of priority group $i(i=1,2,\ldots,N)$; q, quantum of level 0.

system empty. Additional decisions are made upon process arrivals in *preemptive* mode, and at quantum completion times in *quantum-oriented* mode. The latter is called *processor-sharing* mode when the quantum size approaches zero; performance measures for this mode serve as good approximations for small quantum sizes.

The *priority function* is an arbitrary function of process and system parameters. The current priority of a process is obtained by evaluating the priority function for the current values of its parameters. Process parameters such as memory requirement, attained service, time of arrival, I/O measures, and job group are kept in the process table. System parameters include load, time of day or week, and the number of ready processes. The *arbitration rule* resolves ambiguities when two or more processes have the same priority.

When process priorities change dynamically, priorities must be reevaluated and compared whenever the scheduler is invoked. To avoid overhead, simple priority functions are advisable. For *time-invariant* algorithms, the difference between the priorities of any two processes does not change as long as neither of them receives service. They are particularly efficient, since the ready queue can be kept sorted in decreasing order of process priorities. The scheduler simply selects the process at the head of the queue for execution, and overhead is limited to inserting an arriving or recycled process at the appropriate queue position. The most common algorithms are time invariant, and it is often more convenient to describe them in terms of the structure of the ready queue rather than the underlying priority function.

A common performance measure for scheduling algorithms is the *response function*, the average response time of a process conditioned on its service requirement. Analytic expressions for this measure can be derived for appropriate queueing models. The shorthand notation A/B/C is used to describe such models, where A specifies the distribution of the interarrival times, B that of the service requirements, and C the number of processors. For example, M/G/1 denotes a single-processor

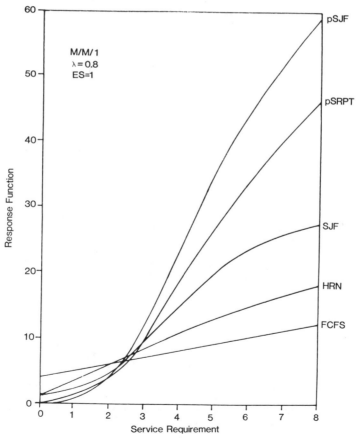

Fig. 2 Response functions of batch-processing algorithms in $M/M/1$ systems with a load of 80%.

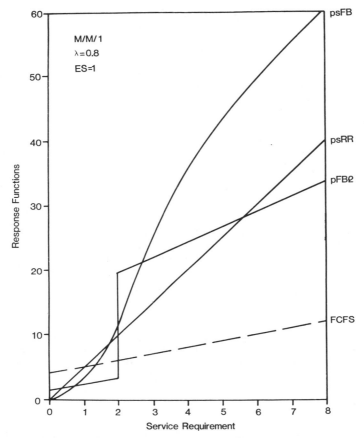

Fig. 3 Response functions of time-sharing algorithms in $M/M/1$ systems with a load of 80%.

system with exponential (Markov) interarrival times and an arbitrary (General) service requirement distribution. For a variety of algorithms, Table 1 summarizes the response functions in steady-state $M/G/1$ systems. In Figs. 2 and 3, some of these response functions are plotted for exponential service times ($M/M/1$ systems) and a load (arrival rate λ times expected service requirement ES) of 80%.

Batch - Processing Algorithms

In batch-processing systems, users do not interact with their processes while they reside in the system and thus equate service quality with turnaround time. Turnaround times in the order of minutes to hours are often adequate. The primary performance criterion is system throughput. To reduce overhead, nonpreemptive algorithms are favored. Memory allocation usually precedes processor allocation and thus reduces the performance impact of the latter.

The simplest batch-processing algorithm is the *first-come, first-serve* (FCFS) algorithm. It is least discriminatory in the sense that it does not base priorities on either the service requirement or the attained service time of a process. Arrivals join the ready queue at the tail and the scheduler always selects the process at the head of the queue for execution. The expression for the response function is given in Table 1 and plotted in Fig. 2 for exponential service requirements. The average waiting time in the ready queue is the same for all processes.

The *shortest job first* (SJF) algorithm requires that the service requirement of a process, or an estimate for it, is known at the time of arrival, typically from the job card. The ready queue is maintained in increasing order of these service requirements. The response function is given in Table 1 and plotted in Fig. 2. SJF minimizes the overall average response time among *all* nonpreemptive algorithms. The favorable treatment of short processes is obtained at the cost of increased waiting times for long processes. The *preemptive* version of SJF (pSJF) further accentuates the discrimination of short and long processes. Its major drawback is the overhead resulting from the preemption of processes which reduces system throughput. The response function is given in Table 1 and plotted in Fig. 2. A related algorithm, the *preemptive shortest remaining processing time* (pSRPT) algorithm, minimizes the overall average response time among all scheduling algorithms. When a process is preempted, the entry for the remaining processing time (service requirement minus attained service time) in the process table is updated and the ready queue is kept in increasing order of this quantity. The response function is listed in Table 1 and plotted in Fig. 2. As in pSJF, preemption affects throughput and may outweigh the advantage of minimal response.

The priority function of the *highest response-ratio next* (HRN) algorithm is defined as the quotient of the time a process has spent in the ready queue and its service requirement. The response function is presented in Table 1 and plotted in Fig. 2. HRN strikes a balance between FCFS and SJF by reducing the waiting time of long processes while still favoring short ones. This property and nonpreemption make the algorithm attractive, but the priorities of all processes must be reevaluated on every invocation of the scheduler.

A class of algorithms is based on *static, externally assigned priority groups*. The assignment of priority p ($p = 1, 2, \ldots, N$), where N is the highest priority, to a process may be based on its importance, memory requirement, or other factors. SJF belongs to this class with priorities based on service requirements. The ready queue is kept sorted in decreasing order of process priorities and processes of the same group are linked in the order of arrival. Nonpreemptive and preemptive versions of these algorithms exist. Their response functions are listed in Table 1. The discrimination between high-priority and low-priority processes is analogous to that of SJF and pSJF for short and long processes, respectively. With increasing priority, a process encounters a decreasing number of competitors and thus experiences a lighter system load.

Irregular process arrivals cause peak loads and, consequently, a deterioration of response. When the process characteristics are at least partially known, *production schedules* which are set up periodically by the system manager reduce this effect. Essentially, a process is given a reservation for a particular time interval on a certain processor. Processes submitted ahead of time are delayed in a separate queue before they are released to the ready queue. Production schedules can be used to guarantee completion times. System throughput can also be improved by scheduling those processes concurrently that are compatible in the sense that their cumulative resource requirements match the system resources. In time-sharing systems, such compatibility is difficult to achieve since interactive processes arrive at random and their resource requirements are typically not known in advance.

Time - Sharing Algorithms

The interactions of users with their processes in a time-sharing system necessitate response times of the order of seconds. Although users tolerate increasing response times for increasingly complex tasks, their productivity decreases rapidly when the response becomes sluggish for simple tasks. Thus time-sharing algorithms discriminate against long processes in favor of short ones. The attained service time is used to achieve the desired discrimination since the service requirement of a process is typically not known in advance. In view of the importance of the response characteristics, preemptive and quantum-oriented algorithms predominate. Throughput plays a secondary role as long as the overhead resulting from frequent preemptions remains tolerable.

The *quantum-oriented round-robin* algorithm allocates quanta to the ready processes in a cyclic manner. The scheduler selects the process at the head of the ready queue for the next quantum and recycles it to the tail when the quantum expires. New arrivals may be inserted at the head or at the tail. The response function of the *processor-sharing round-robin* (psRR) algorithm is presented in Table 1 and Fig. 3. On the average, the response time of a process is proportional to its service requirement. The algorithm is eminently fair in the sense that all processes are serviced at the same rate. This property also implies that short processes are delayed less than long ones.

In *quantum-oriented feedback* algorithms, the priority of a process is a monotonic decreasing function of its attained service. The ready queue is kept sorted in increasing order of this parameter and the FCFS rule is used as the arbitration rule. Alternatively, the ready queue may be viewed as consisting of multiple levels (numbered $0, 1, 2, \ldots$) with new arrivals joining level 0. Processes having received j quanta and requiring more service join level j. When the scheduler is invoked, it selects the process at the head of the lowest-numbered nonempty level. The response function of the *processor-sharing feedback* (psFB) algorithm is given in Table 1 and plotted in Fig. 3. Among all algorithms that do not consider the service requirement of a process, feedback algorithms are most discriminatory in favor of short processes and against long ones. The *quantum-oriented n-level feedback* algorithm implements only a finite number of queue levels. When a processes is selected from level $n - 1$ (the highest-numbered level) and, after receiving a quantum, requires further service, it is recycled to level $n - 1$. Thus processes with an attained service of $n - 1$ quanta or more are serviced in round-robin fashion, provided that there are no ready processes with less than $n - 1$ quanta. This scheme still favors short processes, but without the excessive delays of long processes under the pure feedback scheme. In general, the quanta allocated at different levels need not be the same. Since frequent preemptions (i.e., short quanta) imply overhead and since processes are only selected for service when all lower-numbered levels are empty, it is advantageous to increase the quantum size with increasing level numbers. Optionally, new arrivals may preempt running processes which have been selected from the highest-numbered level. The response function of the *preemptive 2-level feedback* (pFB2) algorithm with quantum sizes q for level 0 and ∞ for level 1 is listed in Table 1. It is plotted for $q = 2$ in Fig. 3.

With an increase in the number of ready processes, the average number of quanta that a process receives in a given interval decreases. Feedback algorithms assure continued service to short processes by effectively ignoring processes in higher levels. Under the round-robin algorithm, the cycle time required to execute one round-robin through all ready processes equals the quantum size times the number of ready processes. To maintain rapid response for short processes, the quantum size may be dynamically redefined by dividing a predetermined acceptable cycle time by the number of ready processes. Excessive preemption overhead is avoided by specifying a minimum quantum size.

Process priorities may also be based on the arrival source. To assure rapid response for interactive processes, processes that completed a terminal-I/O operation, a secondary storage transfer, and a quantum are favored in this order. For this purpose, levels within the ready queue are affiliated with arrival sources and treated like a feedback system. By definition, a process arriving at the ready queue has no attained service. To distinguish between interactive processes and those cycling between the ready queue and secondary storage queues, however, the attained service times of the latter may be maintained cumulatively. Exponential dampening of this quantity in time reduces excessive delays of noninteractive processes with only minor effects on interactive ones.

Real-Time Scheduling

Real-time systems are characterized by interactions of processors and peripheral devices with strict timing constraints. Depending on the nature of the devices, processes must be run within seconds, milliseconds, or even microseconds of the time of occurrence of some device-related event (e.g., interrupt). The most time-sensitive processes involve the acquisition of data that are available for short periods only. (Availability may be limited due to the periodic nature of a device, or the sampling of dynamic signals.) The generation of output signals in process control applications may be equally time-sensitive. Data-reduction processes are less time-sensitive and may be run in the background (i.e., when no other processes are ready). The real-time constraints require a *worst-case analysis* of the possible scheduling sequences based on the given process characteristics (maximum service requirement, maximum tolerable response time, memory need, frequency of invocation, etc.). In designing a system, these quantities are first estimated and later refined. Because of the severe response constraints, throughput considerations are limited to the selection of appropriate hardware equipment; a system load of as low as 50% is often considered adequate. The dynamic allocation of system resources, like memory, is limited to background processes, since the time taken to allocate resources to time-sensitive processes dynamically may make it impossible for them to respond to events quickly enough.

Context switching represents the basic limitation to fast response. When an interrupt occurs, the state of the executing process must be saved and the state of the interrupt handling process must be set up. With R registers per state and a memory access time of A nanoseconds, context switching takes $2RA$ nanoseconds. If a scheduler is invoked to give control to the corresponding process, the minimal response is at least an order of magnitude larger. The most time-sensitive processes are therefore implemented as interrupt processes (i.e., invoked directly by the interrupt without scheduler intervention), and suitable real-time processors offer large interrupt vectors for this purpose. Preemption of interrupt processes involves context switching and should be kept minimal; a few levels of interrupt processes, where processes of the same level do not interrupt each other, suffice. When the capacity of a single processor is insufficient, multiple processors must be employed and a message facility is needed for coordination. In this case, fast and intelligent communications channels are desirable in order to keep the potentially extensive delays in forwarding a message tolerable.

Processes with less severe response time may be dispatched by the scheduler. *Static, external priorities* are assigned according to real-time sensitivity (see the section on batch-processing algorithms). Both nonpreemptive and preemptive algorithms are suitable; the latter are more responsive to high-priority processes but cause additional system overhead. Alternatively, a *scheduling cycle* may be defined as a sequence of phases, each of which is dedicated to the nonpreemptive execution of processes of a specified group. When invoked, the scheduler selects the next process as a function of the current phase. Background processes are run when there are no ready processes of the specified group. High-priority processes have several phases dedicated per cycle. This scheme is advantageous when the ratio of service time to required response time is small for most processes.

A more flexible, preemptive algorithm determines process priorities dynamically based on maximum service requirement, maximum tolerable response time, time in system, and attained service time. Highest priority is given to the process that must *complete soonest*. A refinement of this algorithm avoids preemptions when a currently running process can run to completion without violating the maximum tolerable response time of the new arrival.

BIBLIOGRAPHY

E. G. COFFMAN JR. and L. KLEINROCK, "Computer Scheduling Methods and Their Counter-measures," *Proc. AFIPS 1968 SJCC*, Vol. 32, AFIPS Press, Montvale, N.J., pp. 11–21.

G. S. GRAHAM, (ed.), "Queueing Network Models of Computer System Performance" (special issue), *Comput. Surv.*, **10**(3) (Sept. 1978).

L. KLEINROCK, *Queueing Systems*, Vol. 2: *Computer Applications*, Wiley, New York, 1976.

R. B. MILLER, "Response Time in Man–Computer Conversational Transactions," *Proc. AFIPS 1968 FJCC*, Vol. 33, Thompson Book Co., Washington, D.C., pp. 267–277.

M. RUSCHITZKA, "Policy Function Scheduling," *Perf. Eval.* **1**(1), 31–47 (Jan. 1981).

2.21.2 Latency Reduction

M. Hofri

In a random-access storage device, the time to access a unit of information is independent of the location on the device at which the information is stored. The term "latency" has come to signify certain forms of delay which occur when *nonrandom* devices are accessed. Latency is related to the physical technique the device employs to access the information, as well as to the state of the device when the access is attempted.

Other forms of delay exist. Some are incurred when random storage is accessed, for example, when several simultaneous accesses are attempted by different processors or channels but only one can be performed at a time. This is commonly referred to as cycle contention and is resolved autonomously by the device (i.e., by hardware). Delays that arise when nonrandom devices fail to react fast enough to satisfy incoming requests are termed waiting (or queueing) times. The implied queues are managed by software. These delays are highly dependent on the latency experienced by serviced requests. Thus reducing latency decreases queueing delays, which will not be further discussed. Another form of delay that is not considered in this article is due to the organization of storage in hierarchies (e.g., cache–main store–secondary storage– · · · –mass storage) and the required "staging" operations.

Latency reduction is the term used for any policy of sequencing accesses—and sometimes rearranging data—at a nonrandom storage unit so as to reduce the *average* latency experienced by an access. The following types of latency can be distinguished:

1. Rotational latency (drums and drum-like devices; shift registers).
2. Linear latency (in moving-arm disks, which exhibit, in addition, rotational latency).

Drum

Here, and in similar devices with one mechanical degree of freedom, latency arises when the data path from the unit to the computer can be activated, but the read–write mechanism (RWM) is not positioned at the desired location, as seen in Fig. 4. If requests are honored in order of arrival, the data path will idle for approximately one-half a revolution time. A well-known technique to reduce this is the shortest-latency-time-first (SLTF) algorithm, which selects for transmission the request with the starting address closest to the RWM in the direction of rotation (some arbitrary rule may be used to resolve ties). The expected reduction in latency increases with increasing load on the device, since this increases the likelihood of finding among the waiting requests one that has the minimal possible latency, approximately equal to the interrecord gap. Assuming that a track holds N records, and that under heavy load the device transmits continuously, this technique increases the throughput of the drum by a factor of $N/2$. An analytical treatment of this approach can be found in Refs. 1 and 2. The latter also contains a discussion of the waiting delay experienced by the queued requests.

This technique requires the implementor to distinguish between two forms of drum organization. Figure 4*a* shows the so called "file drum"—data are recorded in segments of arbitrary length which may begin at arbitrary addresses. Figure 4*b* represents the "paging drum," where all requests are for fixed-size segments, often called sectors, which have the same address at all the tracks. The latter organization simplifies space allocation and prevents fragmentation if the sector size is a natural unit of transmission between storage levels; otherwise, it creates internal fragmentation and leads to multiple-sector records (see Secs. 2.9 and 2.19.3). The first organization requires maintaining the list of pending requests sorted by beginning word address. For the paging drum a better method is to maintain N distinct request queues, one for each sector, across all tracks. Within these queues the

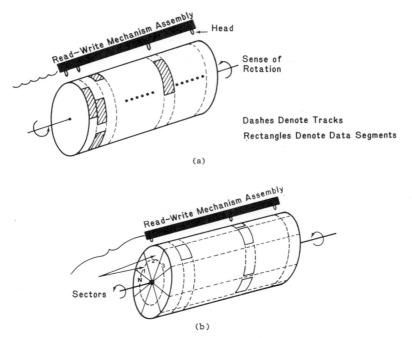

Fig. 4 Drum memory: (*a*) file drum; (*b*) paging drum. Dashes denote tracks; rectangles denote data segments.

order is immaterial to the throughput of the device. For this organization SLTF is optimal. For a drum with the organization of Fig. 4*a*, if the objective is to sequence a given *finite* list of requests so as to minimize the time until completion, SLTF can be shown to yield a good schedule usually, but not necessarily the optimal one (finding it requires a substantially more complicated procedure [2]). For an arbitrary arrival process again SLTF is normally quite good; the optimum is not known.

An effective latency reduction measure which is rarely used for drums—because of the large number of tracks—but is used for fixed-head disks, provides *several* RWMs per track. This arrangement will approach its maximum increase in throughput under SLTF even under much lower loads than with a single RWM per track. When SLTF is not used, the use of *n* equally spaced RWMs per track will cut the average latency by a factor of approximately *n*.

Shift Registers

The 1970s witnessed the emergence of a few novel technologies for the fabrication of large electronic storage. Notable among those are magnetic bubbles and charge-coupled devices. These lend themselves to the organization of shift registers, with a considerable saving in addressing and refresh circuitry. The transmission unit is the contents of a register. For the saving to be meaningful the registers must be fairly long ($\geqslant 512$ bits, and often much more). Reading data that are a small portion of such a register encounters "rotational" latency, since only after the complete register content is transmitted can the necessary data be located.

As of this writing there are no general-purpose methods to reduce these delays, which are smaller by one to three orders of magnitude than those discussed above; but in applications where the latency poses a problem proper care (which is algorithm sensitive*) must be taken to time the access requests to best avail. It may be of interest to note that shift registers were among the first forms of *main* storage organization used for computers, and programmers were expected then to be cognizant of the implied timing constraints.

Magnetic bubble storage modules have special organizations (e.g., major–minor loops) which can be used to link such registers under program control. This capability makes it possible to implement various permutation schemes so as to speed up certain operations (e.g., sorting). See Ref. 3 for an example and further references.

---

*A simple example would occur when an array of such registers stored a matrix row-wise, but occasionally column-wise processing was necessary.

Moving-Arm Disks

These devices present a further source of latency: the time required to move the arm, or seek, to the addressed cylinder. This time usually depends only on the number of cylinders to be traversed, not on the initial position of the arm. It typically varies from 1 to 10 times the disk revolution time, so it should not be ignored.

All approaches to seek latency reduction are based on arranging the queued requests according to their target cylinder, and not moving the arm as long as some request can be served at the current position. A shortcoming of this approach is that an occasional burst of references to some cylinder (a burst that temporarily exceeds the rate at which these requests can be serviced) could subject requests for other portions of the disk to intolerably long delays. It has been suggested that this can be overcome by simply using an upper bound on the number of requests that will be serviced between successive seeks.

The various recognized linear latency reduction policies differ in the criterion they use to select the "seek" address. There are two main policies, each of which has a few obvious variants [4]. Cylinder queues as described above are maintained in all of them. Shortest-seek-time-first (SSTF) selects the cylinder with nonempty queue nearest to the cylinder currently under the head. This policy is probably the one that minimizes average waiting time when the arrival of requests is independent of the current queues, and the seek decision is based only on testing whether queues are empty or not, but not on comparative queue lengths. SSTF exacerbates, however, the danger of a spate of references to some set of adjacent cylinders monopolizing the disk—as described above—to the detriment of other users, especially those requesting access to extreme cylinders.

The second main policy, SCAN, eliminates the last problem at the cost of a slight increase in the mean waiting time. It causes the arm to appear as if it scans the entire disk surface—hence the name. The policy is always in one of two modes: "move up" (to higher numbered cylinders) or "move down." When a seek is to be selected, the nearest cylinder with nonempty queue in the direction indicated by the mode is addressed. The mode is switched when an extreme cylinder is reached or (in some variants) when there are no requests for cylinders in the direction called for by the mode. The resistance of SCAN to having the arm monopolized by input to part of the disk is especially noticeable when the input is of a highly nonuniform rate (i.e., when periods of quiescence alternate with periods when queues are built up fast). When the rate of requests is nearly uniform, as can be expected in a system with a high degree of multiprogramming or in a multiprocessing system, the difference is negligible compared with SSTF.

Disks lend themselves even better than drums to operations with multiple arms. This is so because if the number of "active" cylinders is not larger than the number of arms each, such a cylinder will have an arm assigned to it and seeks will be quite infrequent. This can also be done relatively inexpensively by making only a subset of the cylinders accessible to each arm, and placing files that are expected to interact (i.e., to be active simultaneously) in disk regions accessible by distinct arms.

Disks also obviously generate rotational latency. It does not appear, however, that SLTF has much to offer here, since cylinder queues are generally too short to warrant maintaining a sector-queue structure as was described for drums. It can obviously be done, though.

Although normally outside the scope of latency reduction techniques, it is easy to see that the distribution of data on the surface has a considerable impact on the resultant latency. It can also seriously affect the effectiveness of the techniques mentioned above. Only rather vague directives on distributing such data can be given:

1. In drums, record addresses should be evenly distributed over all sectors.

2. In disks, popular files should be stored on midway cylinders (e.g., in the middle third). Files that are frequently used simultaneously should be on distinct packs, unless multiple arm drives are used.

Two impediments to the implementation of these techniques should be pointed out:

1. Particularly in the case of drums, the selection of next requests to be serviced must be prompt, or a sector is missed. If this is done by the CPU, it puts a stringent timing constraint on the servicing of drum interrupts. If done by the channel, it requires more local storage and processing capability than is usually relegated to a channel.

2. I/O requests may have external priorities associated with them (typically representing those of the tasks that issued the requests). These priorities will not normally agree with the latency reduction policy.

REFERENCES

1. C. ADAMS, E. GELENBE, and J. VICARD, "An Experimentally Validated Model of the Paging Drum," *Acta. Inf.*, **11**, 103–117 (1979).

2. S. FULLER, *Analysis of Drum and Disk Storage Units*, Lecture Notes in Computer Science 31, Springer-Verlag, New York, 1975.

3. G. C. BONGIOVANI and F. LUCCIO, "Permutation of Data Blocks in Bubble Memory," *Commun. ACM*, **22**, 21–25 (1979).

4. T. J. TEOREY and T. B. PINKERTON, "A Comparative Analysis of Disk Scheduling Policies," *Commun. ACM*, **15**, 177–184 (1972).

2.21.3   Deadlocks: Detection and Prevention

A. Shoshani

Background

Whenever there is a need to share resources, a condition called *deadlock* (or more graphically, "deadly embrace" [4]) may arise. Certain conditions, however, have to be met in order for deadlocks to occur. Even when these conditions exist, deadlocks may not occur. Therefore, techniques for the detection of deadlocks are needed in order to determine whether a deadlock condition exists. Alternatively, one can choose techniques to prevent deadlocks altogether by eliminating one (or more) of the conditions that lead to deadlocks. Before we spell out these conditions, we examine some examples.

Deadlock is a situation in which resources have been allocated to two or more processes in such a way that they can never proceed. Each deadlocked process is waiting for another deadlocked process to release some resources, while at the same time it holds on to the resources it has already acquired. Imagine a machine shop where tools are shared among workers. Suppose that the making of a certain part requires two tools simultaneously, for example a hammer and a screwdriver, and there is only one of each. Suppose that two workers making this part have one tool each: one has the hammer and the other the screwdriver. Realizing that they need another tool, they leave the tool they have on their bench, and go to the shared area, waiting for the other tool to be returned. Clearly, they cannot proceed unless the situation is discovered. This deadlock situation can involve more workers and more tools. For example, worker 1 has tool A and needs tool B; worker 2 has tool B and needs tool C; and worker 3 has tool C and needs tool A. Note that a deadlock involves a circular waiting condition.

In the example above, the processes are the making of parts, and the resources are the tools. In an operating system environment, processes are the execution of programs. Resources can be physical devices, such as disks, channels, CPU, or main memory. In addition, data and programs, such as tables, files, and subroutines, can be treated as resources. In general, any entity that may be needed by a number of processes, but can only be used by one process at a time, qualifies as a resource.

There are many other areas where deadlock potential exists. In the network communication area, the shipping of a message (or packet) corresponds to a process and resources are the buffers in each network node. In the data management area, a process may require exclusive access to files or subfiles to ensure the validity of information in the face of concurrent reads and writes. Similarly, deadlock conditions can arise in production management, information flow control, and so on. Even problems as mundane as traffic jams can be modeled by cars representing processes, and the space they occupy representing resources.

Notice that in the machine shop example there was a restriction that only one tool of each type exists. Clearly, deadlocks can arise in the more general case where there are multiple resources of the same type which can be used interchangeably. The problem of deadlocks is usually treated in this general context, while special cases lead to more efficient solutions.

In the next sections we discuss different approaches for handling the deadlock problem. As can be seen from the examples, process and resource characteristics may vary. Thus some resources may be easy to release, or "preempt" (e.g., a process running on the CPU can be preempted by saving the "current program status"; see Sec. 2.20). Others may be difficult to preempt (e.g., interrupting a disk write). Therefore, analysis is required to determine which approach is best suited to each situation.

Deadlock Conditions

The following conditions are necessary (but not sufficient) for the occurrence of deadlocks: that is, deadlocks cannot occur unless all these conditions are met, but their existence does not guarantee a deadlock. The actual occurrence of a deadlock depends on having a conflict of resource requirements by a subset of processes running concurrently. These conflicts are more likely to happen when resource utilization is high and there is a very small reserve of unused resources.

1. *Mutual exclusion condition.* Processes require exclusive use of resources. If there are many resources of the same type, this condition implies exclusive use of a particular resource of that type.

2. *Wait-for condition.* This condition means that processes are allowed to hold resources while waiting for additional resources to become available. Wait-for conditions exist mainly because processes can proceed to do useful work with some resources, and then need additional resources to

continue. Furthermore, sometimes processes know what additional resources they need only after they use previous resources.

3. *Circularity condition.* This condition exists if processes are allowed to behave in such a way that they can become dependent on each other in a circular fashion. In the section on deadlock prevention we discuss a subtle technique that prevents this condition.

The concept of *preemption* is related to the wait-for condition. If it is possible to preempt resources, wait-for conditions can be removed. However, one still has to detect the need to preempt a resource.

A deadlock condition can be described as a directed graph, where nodes represent resources and an arc from node A to node B represents a process that holds resource A but needs, in addition, resource B. A directed loop (cycle) in that graph indicates the existence of a deadlock. An alternative graph could be constructed where nodes represent processes, and an arc from node A to node B represents the fact that process A is waiting for a resource held by process B. Again, cycles represent deadlocks. Graph representation is suitable when there is only one resource of each type. A representation for the general case of multiple resources of the same type is given in the next section to explain detection algorithms.

Deadlock Detection

Suppose that the state of a system at a particular point in time is represented by two matrices. The *allocation matrix* represents the current state of resources as they are allocated to processes, and the *request matrix* represents the additional resources currently requested by processes. Note that entries in the request matrix may be 0 if the process is executing. Thus position (i, j) of the allocation and request matrices represents the number of resources of type i allocated to and requested by process j, respectively. In addition, an *available resource vector* can be computed by subtracting the allocated resources from the total number available for each type.

To detect whether a deadlock exists, one can check whether there is a way to sequence processes such that all their pending requests can be satisfied. A detection algorithm described more fully in Ref. 1 achieves this as follows. It checks if there is a task whose request matrix entry (called the *request vector*) can be satisfied (i.e., that the number of resources it needs of each type is less than the number currently available in the available resource vector). If so, it makes the optimistic assumption that the process will complete in some finite time and return all its resources to the pool. Thus its allocation vector is added to the available resource vector, and another process is searched. If all processes can be satisfied, the system is not currently deadlocked. Otherwise, a deadlock exists. This algorithm runs in time proportional to the square of the number of processes but can be run in time linear with the number of processes provided that resource requests are ordered by size as described in Ref. 2.

Notice that there is no guarantee that processes will complete and return their allocated resources to the pool, and indeed a deadlock can develop at a future time. Therefore, a detection algorithm has to be applied periodically.

If a deadlock is found, it has to be removed by preempting some of the resources. Depending on the application, one can associate a cost with preempting particular resources, and use these costs to select the least expensive solution. A crude but simple preemption strategy would be to back up one or more processes involved in the deadlock. In an operating system environment a backup mechanism usually exists for crash recovery purposes.

Deadlock Prevention

The prevention of deadlocks can be achieved by violating one of the necessary conditions mentioned previously, thus removing the possibility of deadlocks altogether. Let us consider techniques that apply to each condition.

1. *Mutual exclusion condition.* Removing this condition is often impossible because of the nature of the resources involved. However, specific types of resources can be simultaneously shared, at least part of the time. Examples are program modules with reentrant code, and files that can be shared when read by more than one process. Another approach is to logically partition resources, such as files, into smaller units, thus permitting the use of different sections of files simultaneously, creating the effect of sharing.

2. *Wait-for condition.* This condition can be avoided by requiring that processes acquire all the resources at one time rather than in stages. Often, this condition cannot be met since all needs are not known ahead of time. However, if processes can be broken into steps, such that they return all resources at the end of each step, the same effect is achieved. In the machine shop example above, this approach implies that workers return all their tools to the shared area and then get all the tools they need for the next job step. If this approach is used, care must be taken that a process with large resource demands is not perpetually postponed, while processes with smaller demands continue to run as small amounts of resources are returned.

3. *Circularity condition.* An interesting technique to prevent circularity was first given in Ref. 3. One can order all resource types linearly, and require that processes acquire resources in this order only.

Suppose that process A is waiting for process B to release a resource. Process B cannot be waiting for process A (or any other process waiting for A) because it will be requesting a resource higher in the linear order, in violation of the condition above.

Another approach to avoiding the circularity condition is to check, whenever a request for resources is made, that granting this request will still allow all processes to complete. This approach requires advance information about process needs, and involves finding a sequence of the processes such that all processes can eventually complete. The algorithm was introduced by an example in Ref. 4, called the *banker's algorithm*. The banker has a fixed amount of money to be loaned to customers. Money represents multiple resources (dollars) of the same type. Each customer specifies in advance the maximum amount of dollars he or she may borrow, but can borrow or return smaller amounts. The problem is to determine whether it is *safe* to grant the next request, in the sense that all customers are guaranteed to get their loan requirements eventually. The more general problem of many resource types can be modeled by having many currencies that customers may loan.

A technique for solving this problem was given in Ref. 5 and is similar to the detection algorithm explained previously. However, the request matrix now represents the maximum amount of money specified by each customer less the amount already allocated to that customer. The next request is assumed to be granted, and the detection algorithm above is applied to see if a deadlock was introduced. If so, we conclude that it is unsafe to grant the request, and it must be postponed. As in the detection algorithm, determining whether it is safe to grant a request can be performed in time linear with the number of processes [2].

Since the maximum amounts specified may not actually be required, it is possible to deny a request unnecessarily. A more detailed model of process needs can be assumed, such as breaking processes into process steps, to permit a more efficient utilization of resources. Techniques to handle this situation are discussed in Ref. 1.

REFERENCES

1. E. G. COFFMAN, JR., M. J. ELPHICK, and A. SHOSHANI, "System Deadlocks," *Comput. Surv.* 3(2), 67–78 (June 1971).

2. R. C. HOLT, "Some Deadlock Properties of Computer Systems," *Comput. Surv.*, 4(3), 179–196 (Sept. 1972).

3. H. W. HAVENDER, "Avoiding Deadlocks in Multi-tasking Systems," *IBM Syst. J.*, **2**, 74–84 (1968).

4. E. W. DIJKSTRA, "Cooperating Sequential Processes," in *Programming Languages*, F. Genuys (ed.), Academic Press, New York, 1968.

5. A. N. HABERMANN, "Prevention of System Deadlocks," *Commun. ACM*, **12**, 373–377, 385 (July 1969).

2.22 FILE SYSTEMS

K. Ekanadham

A *file* is a collection of related information that has a name. Its size can change dynamically and it is usually stored on an auxiliary storage device. A file can be accessed by invoking access methods provided by a *file system*, parts of which are generally embedded in an operating system. Typically, portions of a file may be read, modified, and deleted, or new information may be appended (see Sec. 2.8) by invoking file system routines. A number of file system designs appear in the literature which are tailored to particular operating systems. A systematic treatment of a level structured (see Sec. 2.24) file system design may be found in Ref. 1. There are two aspects of file system design. The *physical aspect* deals with the organization of storage in the auxiliary memory. It is concerned with efficient manipulation of files and depends on the physical characteristics of the auxiliary storage device. The *logical aspect* is concerned with providing a user interface with a convenient naming facility and flexible methods to access and share data.

2.22.1 Physical Considerations

A file system must have routines that deal with the idiosynchrosies of a device and perform physical I/O operations. The function of these routines is to provide I/O service for users in a timely fashion and to make efficient use of the devices. Such routines must respond to two types of events: requests for I/O service from users (perhaps filtered through higher, logical levels of the file system) and signals from the physical I/O interface (e.g., interrupts) indicating completion of I/O transactions initiated previously. It is convenient to organize the I/O handling code for a particular asynchronous device into two routines, or processes, one for handling the user request event and the other for handling the completion event. The former will be referred to as a *feeder* and the latter as a *driver*.

Since during a particular interval of time more requests may arrive than can be serviced, the feeder must employ a data structure to record each request that has arrived but has not yet been serviced. Generally, some form of linked list (see Sec. 2.4), referred to as an I/O queue, is used. Each entry on the list contains information describing one such request (e.g., identity of the issuing process, amount of information to be transferred, buffer address). In simple situations the list is treated in a first-come, first-served fashion. More complicated disciplines may be employed to increase the efficiency of use of certain types of devices (see Sec. 2.21.2).

The function of the driver is to respond to interrupts that signal the completion of an I/O service. It must delete the I/O queue entry describing the I/O transaction whose completion has just occurred and, depending on the conventions of the overall system, arrange for the return of status information describing the outcome of the transaction (e.g., the actual number of words transferred, parity error) to the requesting process. This may involve awakening a blocked process (see Sec. 2.20). The driver reinitiates the device if the I/O queue is not empty. If the device is idle when a new request arrives (the I/O queue is empty), provision must also be made for the feeder to initiate an I/O operation.

When multiple asynchronous I/O units are present, each would typically have a feeder/driver pair and a unique I/O queue. They may all share a common free list which serves as a pool of storage from which I/O queue entries can be constructed. In this case extreme care must be taken to ensure that access to the free list is mutually exclusive (see Sec. 2.26.2). This is a particularly sensitive concern since the drivers are interrupt driven. It must be guaranteed that one routine which is in the midst of accessing a data structure (such as the free list) not be interrupted by another which then proceeds to access the same data structure. The same considerations apply to a particular feeder/driver pair with respect to the I/O queue that they both use.

If such mutual exclusion is guaranteed, generally by completely inhibiting interrupts in critical regions of code, it is possible to allow certain interrupts to occur when execution is in progress in other parts of the I/O handlers. This is generally done in accordance with some rules of priority so that device interrupts that must be serviced quickly can delay the servicing of interrupts from lower-priority devices, but not vice versa. Such a priority structure is implemented by selectively masking interrupts at priority levels less than or equal to i when servicing an interrupt at level i using some form of interrupt mask register. By taking into account interrupt priority and the execution time of each driver, it is possible in many situations to calculate the worst-case delay a system can experience in responding to an interrupt.

Each time an interrupt occurs, the state of the executing process must be preserved so that it can be resumed after the interrupt has been serviced. In a priority interrupt structure it may be necessary to save many states since one driver may interrupt another of lower priority. A stack is generally used for this purpose (see Sec. 2.3). Thus a priority interrupt structure involves some complications that can be avoided in systems in which interrupts are completely inhibited in all I/O handling code. Such systems will not, however, be as responsive to interrupts.

User references to files on file-oriented devices are generally formulated in terms of logical addresses, or offsets, within the file as opposed to physical addresses on the device. This insulates the user from the details of physical addressing on the device and allows the operating system to reorganize information on the device without having to inform users. It implies, however, that the operating system must maintain information about the physical location of all files so that it can translate logical addresses supplied by users to physical addresses when requests for I/O service are made.

The allocation of physical space on mass storage devices (e.g., disk, drum) to files can be done in several ways. When contiguous allocation is used, a block of physically contiguous space is set aside for the file at the time it is created. The file can then expand and contract in this space and arbitrary portions of it can be easily accessed (random access) since conversion between logical and physical addresses is simple. Implementation of such a scheme is straightforward since the operating system need only record the starting address and size of the allocated block. Disadvantages include the inability to expand the block (if the file grows beyond the originally anticipated size), since the physically contiguous space may be allocated to another file, and the waste involved in reserving unused space for the file.

In linked allocation the file may be stored in physically noncontiguous blocks on the mass storage device which are linked together in a list (see Sec. 2.4). Each block contains a header, in which the size of the block and a pointer to the next block in the file, is stored. Although the space allocated to the file is now expandable (since blocks need not be contiguous) and unused space need not be reserved, the file is now accessible only in a sequential fashion (see Sec. 2.8), since a particular block in the file can only be reached by traversing the previous blocks in the list. Thus access to an arbitrary portion of the file in reality involves accessing all preceding information.

In paged allocation (see Sec. 2.19) space for the file is allocated in uniform size blocks and a page table is maintained in the operating system. This complicates the operating system, which must now manipulate (potentially bulky) tables, but since all information about physical allocation is directly accessible to the system (as opposed to stored in the blocks themselves, as in linked allocation) sequential access is no longer required. Furthermore, space can be allocated dynamically, thus eliminating waste.

In addition to keeping track of the physical location of each file on the mass storage device, the operating system must also keep track of free storage. This can be done using a linked list approach, with the operating system maintaining a pointer to the first free block on the list. Unfortunately, this does not give the operating system directly accessible information about all free storage, thus preventing the system from employing various storage allocation strategies (e.g., coalescing free blocks, attempting contiguous allocation where possible). Another technique is the use of a bit vector in the operating system in which storage is divided into uniform-size blocks and the ith bit represents the storage state of the ith block. Bit vectors used for this purpose can, of course, be quite large.

Internal to the file system, a file is identified by means of a unique *file index* assigned to it at the time of its creation. Given the file index, the file system can retrieve from its tables information describing the file, including the address translation information.

2.22.2 Logical Considerations

Users choose symbolic names relevant to their application to refer to files. The file system uses the name to locate information about the file, such as its location on auxiliary storage. To avoid the conflicts that can arise when the same name is chosen by different users, the name of the file can be prefixed by the user name. This concept of forming a file name by the concatenation of different parts can be generalized so that a user may create file names composed of many *elementary names* reflecting the application. For example, a user, JOHN, may have files named: JOHN·ENERGY·SOLAR, JOHN·ENERGY·NUCLEAR, JOHN·PERSONAL, and so on. The dot notation indicates the concatenation of elementary names.

All the file names in the system are stored in a hierarchy of directories. A *directory* is a list of cells (sometimes called branches), each of which refers to and contains information describing a file or another directory, and each of which contains an elementary name associated with that item. A *directory hierarchy* is a tree structure (see Sec. 2.7) in which intermediate nodes refer to directories and leaf nodes refer to files. The *path name* (sometimes called tree name) of an item is the concatenation of elementary names encountered on the path from the root of the hierarchy to the cell that refers to the item. Figure 1 shows a directory hierarchy containing a first-level directory with cells JOHN·ENERGY and JOHN·PERSONAL. The latter refers to a file while the former refers to a second-level directory with cells JOHN·ENERGY·NUCLEAR and JOHN·ENERGY·SOLAR, both of which refer to files. Cells referring to files not only contain the associated elementary name, but also the file length, the file index, an indication of whether the file is currently in use, and so on. A cell may also contain a password and other information whose purpose is to restrict access to the file to appropriate users (see Sec. 2.23).

The hierarchical structure has the advantage of giving users a flexible naming scheme. All names in a particular directory must be unique; however, the same name may appear in different directories (see Fig. 1). The search for a particular cell is minimized by using its path name. If a directory is maintained as a linked list, it is easy to add and delete entries at any level. The number of levels is arbitrary and is under user control through the naming convention.

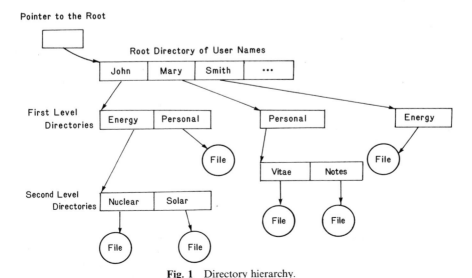

Fig. 1 Directory hierarchy.

2.22.3 Servicing Requests

Each time a user accesses a file, information contained in the corresponding cell must be used. For example, users generally refer to information in a file logically. Thus a file address may be a pair (path name, offset within file). Such a logical address must be translated to a physical address. To do this, the file index stored in the associated cell must be used to locate the storage map. Unfortunately, a search through the hierarchy to locate the cell is time consuming since the directory structure is generally too large to be contained in main memory and must itself be stored on an auxiliary storage device. The efficiency of the system would be severely degraded if such a search had to accompany each file access. To overcome this problem a subset of the information contained in the hierarchy, describing only those files that are actively in use, is generally stored in main memory in the file system for fast reference when a user requests access to a file. The organization of these tables differs from one system to the next [1–4]. In some systems users must first open the file using an appropriate request directed to the file system. The purpose of this is to cause the file system to locate relevant file information in the directory hierarchy and copy it into the tables in main memory. A corresponding close command, issued when the user has finished using the file, indicates when this information can be purged from the tables. Between the time of open and the time of close the user may continue to refer to the file by its path name or, more commonly, may use some simpler name that the file system creates at open time.

The information describing the file falls into two categories. In the first category is the information that must be available to all users of the file. An important example is the storage map used for address translation. In the second category is access information. Different users must have different access rights to a particular file [e.g., user 1 may have read/write permission while user 2 may only have read permission (see Sec. 2.23)]. This information must be used to validate each file operation requested by a user. The access rights possessed by one user, however, are of no relevance to another. In a system in which several users may simultaneously have opened the same file, it is generally the case that information in the first category is held in a single global table, whereas information in the second category is held in tables local to individual users. One such table is uniquely associated with each user. Both global and local tables are manipulated solely by the operating system.

2.22.4 Access Methods

The lowest levels of a hierarchically organized file system (see Sec. 2.24) generally treat a file as a linear array of units of information (bytes, words) with no concern for the internal structure a file may possess. Requests at this level are typically for transfers of particular blocks of information to/from the file. However, in many applications a file may be internally structured (e.g., as a series of variable-length logical records) and a convenient interface would allow a user to deal with the file in terms of that structure (e.g., read the next record). This facility can be provided by higher levels of the file system, which would interpret such requests in terms of the simpler requests implemented at lower levels. These higher levels may or may not be a part of the operating system and, depending on their sophistication, may be referred to as a *data base management system*. For further information on this subject, see Sec. 2.8 and Ref. 5.

REFERENCES

1. S. E. MADNICK and J. W. ALSOP, "A Modular Approach to File System Design," *Proc. AFIPS 34, SJCC*, 1969.
2. J. B. DENNIS and E. C. VAN HORN, "Programming Semantics for Multiprogrammed Computations," *Commun. ACM*, **9**(3) (Mar. 1966).
3. E. I. ORGANICK, *The MULTICS Systems: An Examination of Its Structure*, MIT Press, Cambridge, Mass., 1972.
4. R. C. DALEY and P. G. NEUMANN, "A General Purpose File System for Secondary Storage," *Proc. FJCC*, AFIPS Press, Montvale, N.J., 1965.
5. Special Issue on Database Management Systems, *Comput. Surv.*, **8**(1) (Mar. 1976).

2.23 PROTECTION

K. Ekanadham

Protection is a general term used to refer to the control and regulation of the use of various items in a system. Examples of protected items are instructions, devices, storage, files, and so on. Furthermore, each process must be protected within itself so that one portion does not inadvertently destroy another. The latter form of protection is done to a large extent by compilers in checking parameters, calling sequences, and the scope of variables. Some operating systems also provide run-time protection, so that certain program parts have, for example, access to a file while others do not. A process must also be protected from either malicious or inadvertent damage by other processes. For example, a process should not ordinarily be able to read or modify the address space of another process or access the file of another process without permission. Finally, the operating system must be protected from damage caused by user processes. This is crucial since the operating system implements the protection schemes in addition to managing the system's resources. Protection within a computer system can be broadly classified into three parts: the basic protection system, access control, and information flow control. These are briefly discussed in the following sections.

2.23.1 Basic Protection System

Since not all programs are written in high-level languages and since the actions that programs take frequently depend on the data they operate on, not all protection violations can be detected at compile time. Thus, in most environments, secure systems require run-time checking and, if this is to be performed efficiently, hardware support is required. A basic protection system provides three features: (1) memory protection, (2) device protection, and (3) instruction protection. All of these are implemented using special features in the hardware.

1. *Memory protection.* Various processes and the operating system reside in memory simultaneously. Each process must be allowed to use only that part of the memory assigned to it. Any attempts to access outside its limits must be detected and prevented. This is achieved by interpreting addresses produced by the processor as virtual addresses (see Sec. 2.19) and translating them to physical addresses using some form of memory mapping hardware. Since the mapping information used by this hardware is under the control of the operating system, the physical addresses produced are guaranteed to be within the space allocated to the process. Consider, for example, a system that uses base and bounds registers for address mapping. When a process runs, the base and bound of its space are loaded in the registers. If the process attempts to access outside the limits, the hardware traps to the operating system, which can take corrective action.

2. *Device protection.* The central processing unit is a principal device that is shared by many processes. It must be guaranteed that no single process monopolizes its use. This is accomplished using an *interval timer*, which is a register that automatically decrements its value at each time unit and causes a trap to the operating system when it reaches zero. The operating system can use this device to limit the execution time of a process to some specified interval by loading it with a number proportional to that interval prior to transferring control to the process. The interval timer will cause an interrupt at the end of the interval and control will be transferred back to the operating system. Thus the use of the CPU can be regulated as desired.

    Access to I/O devices must be protected, as most of them are shared by many processes. This can be enforced by allowing only the operating system to execute I/O instructions and receive interrupts from all devices. A process wishing to access a device must make an explicit request to the operating system, which can then validate it. The manner in which processes are prevented from executing I/O instructions directly is discussed next.

3. *Instruction protection.* As discussed above, a number of instructions, such as loading address mapping registers, loading the interval timer, device I/O instructions, and so on, must be executed only by the operating system and not by user processes. These are called *privileged instructions*. The CPU is equipped with two modes of operation, called *privileged mode* and *user mode* (indicated by a mode bit in the CPU's state). The privileged instructions can be only executed in privileged mode. An attempt to execute a privileged instruction in user mode causes a trap. All interrupts or traps occurring during the execution of a process not only cause a transfer to the operating system but also cause the CPU to switch to privileged mode. Consequently, the operating system always runs in privileged mode. When the operating system transfers control to a process, provision is made to change back to user mode. Thus processes always run with the CPU in user mode.

    The integrity of the operating system cannot be guaranteed if it is not entered at an appropriate instruction. It follows from the discussion above that any event that causes entry to the system (i.e., an attempt by a process to execute a privileged instruction or access a location outside its address space, decrementing the interval timer to 0, an explicit request for service from a user process, an interrupt) causes a trap, an enforced transfer to a hardware-specified location. These locations reside in the operating system and are its only entry points.

2.23.2 Access Control Systems

In order to generalize the concept of protection beyond the standard features discussed above, the notions of subject and object have been introduced [1, 2]. A *subject* is an active agent, such as a process, that is capable to accessing an object. An *object* is any item in the system (e.g., file, segment, device, data base, etc.) which can be uniquely referenced and upon which a set of operations or *accesses* (e.g., read, write, start I/O, update, etc.) can be performed. Such accesses may be implemented in hardware or software. An *access right* is a permission, granted to a subject, to perform an operation of a particular type on a particular object. An *access control system* is a mechanism that performs the following functions: (1) It provides a means of specifying the subset of accesses any subject may perform on any object. The specifications may be changed dynamically, but within a fixed framework of rules as to who can change an existing specification and the extent to which it can be changed, (2) it provides a means of enforcing the specification at the time that a particular subject attempts to access an object. The access will be allowed if it conforms to the specification in effect at that time; otherwise, a protection fault is generated, preventing the access.

Access control systems can generally be classified into two groups: *list oriented* and *ticket oriented* [3]. A typical list-oriented implementation is one in which a list of user names and their corresponding access rights is associated with each object. Thus an entry of the form (SMITH-R,W) associated with file F would be interpreted to mean that user Smith had permission to read or write F. The union of these lists constitute a specification of the current state of all access rights for all files. Typically, the owner of the file creates the list and can dynamically add or revoke access rights. Since such lists can become long and consume considerable space, a common technique is to specify a set of access rights available to all (most) users of the system and reserve the list for users who are exceptions to the general policy. Such a list is commonly called an *access control list*. Information of this type is generally stored in the cell associated with the file in the directory hierarchy (see Sec. 2.22.2).

Enforcement can be accomplished by copying the access rights possessed by a user for a file from the directory entry into the tables maintained in main memory at the time the user opens the file (see Sec. 2.22.3). Since the user must invoke the operating system in order to access the file, each such access can then readily be validated by the system at the time it is requested. Further discussion of list-oriented systems can be found in Refs. 1, 2, 4, and 5.

A ticket-oriented system, on the other hand, does not maintain a list of allowed accesses, but issues tickets, called *capabilities*, to processes. A capability specifies an object and access rights to that object which can be exercised using that capability. A process attempting to perform an access presents the capability and the access is permitted if the corresponding access right is contained in the capability.

It is assumed that a process is not able to change a capability. This may be implemented in the following two ways. In the first approach the operating system maintains a list of capabilities for each process called the *C-list* [6]. A process refers to a capability by its index in the C-list. Primitives are provided by the operating system so that processes can manipulate capabilities appropriately (e.g., pass a capability to another process). Alternatively, a *tagged architecture* may be used [7]. In such an organization a few bits have been appended to each location in memory to serve as a tag. The tag is used to indicate the kind of information currently contained in the location and is checked by the hardware to guarantee that all operations performed on the location are appropriate. Such an organization can be used to detect an attempt to execute data. In the context of capability systems it can be used to guarantee that capabilities can only be modified in privileged mode (i.e., the operating system). Thus capabilities can be tagged so that user processes can store them in their programs or in data segments but cannot modify them. They can be copied and passed, and can be used by presenting them to the operating system.

In a capability-based system, the possession of a capability permits the access specified in it. Granting an access right is easily accomplished by simply copying the capability and passing it to another process. However, revocation of privileges is complicated, as the system has to keep track of how capabilities are copied and passed. Some stratagies to deal with this problem are discussed in Refs. 8–10.

A further refinement in the organization of an access control system is to regulate access to objects not only on the basis of a subject but also on the basis of the context (or procedure) from which the access can occur. For instance, a sensitive data file may be accessible to any process only through the execution of a specially designed procedure, but not otherwise. Thus any subject may have access to the file, but only by calling that procedure. The concept of *domain* is introduced for this purpose [2,11]. A domain is an abstract entity that represents the collection of access rights available to a process at a particular time. The system maintains a current domain as part of the state of a process and during execution a process jumps from one domain to another. Domain switches occur at well-defined points by specific calls to the system. Usually, domain switches occur at procedure calls. A number of designs of domain architectures appear in the literature [2,4,5,11,12].

2.23.3 Information Flow Control

When a subject has READ access to an object, it may copy information from the object into other objects accessible to other subjects. Thus, although a subject may be barred from accessing an object directly, information originating in that object may become accessible to it. Sometimes it is desirable to regulate how the information contained in an object is propagated and such regulation is called *information flow control*.

A classic example is the *confinement problem* [13] in which a program accessing sensitive data must be prevented from leaking any information about the data to any place other than the specified output parameters. Such a regulation involves either preventing the program from accessing any other output objects/communication (*total confinement*) or carefully destroying all information generated by the program (*partial confinement*). In general, this problem is difficult and some covert ways in which information can be leaked are discussed in Ref. 13.

Another facet of the problem is to divide the variables of a computation into different classes and enforce certain rules regarding the flow of information from one class to another. An approach to this problem using tags associated with variables may be found in Ref. 14.

REFERENCES

1. B. W. LAMPSON, "Dynamic Protection Structures," *Proc. AFIPS 35, FJCC*, 1969.

2. B. W. LAMPSON, "Protection," *Proc. 5th Annu. Princeton Conf. Inf. Sci. Syst.*, 1971.

3. J. H. SALTZER and M. D. SCHROEDER, "The Protection of Information in Computer Systems," *Proc. IEEE*, **63**(9) (Sept. 1975).

4. M. SCHROEDER, "Cooperation of Mutually Suspicious Subsystems in a Computer Utility," Ph.D. dissertation, MAC-TR-104, MIT, Cambridge, Mass., 1972.

5. E. ORGANICK, *The MULTICS System: An Examination of Its Structure*, MIT Press, Cambridge, Mass., 1972.

6. J. B. DENNIS and E. C. VAN HORN, "Programming Semantics for Multiprogrammed Computations," *Commun. ACM*, **9** (3) (Mar. 1966).

7. E. A. FEUSTEL, "On the Advantages of Tagged Architecture," *IEEE Trans. Comput.*, **C-22** (July 1973).

8. D. REDELL, "Naming and Protection in Extendible *Operating Systems*," Ph.D. thesis, (MAC-TR-140) University of Calif., Berkeley, 1974.

9. E. COHEN and D. JEFFERSON, "Protection in the HYDRA Operating System," *Proc. 5th ACM Symp. Oper. Syst. Principles*, Austin, Tex., 1975.

10. K. EKANADHAM and A. J. BERNSTEIN, "Conditional Capabilities," *IEEE Trans. Software Eng.*, **SE-5** (Sept. 1979).

11. M. SPIER, T. HASTINGS, and D. CUTLER, "An Experimental Implementation of the Kernel/Domain Architecture," *ACM Oper. Syst. Rev.*, **7** (Oct. 1973).

12. M. D. SCHROEDER and J. H. SALTZER, "A Hardware Architecture for Implementing Protection Rings," *Commun. ACM*, **15**(3) (Mar. 1972).

13. B. W. LAMPSON, "A Note on the Confinement Problem," *Commun. ACM*, **16**(10) (Oct. 1973).

14. D. E. DENNING, "A Lattice Model of Secure Information Flow," *Commun. ACM*, **19**(5) (May 1976).

2.24 HIERARCHICAL ORGANIZATION

Gregory R. Andrews

2.24.1 Basic Concepts

A software system consists of a number of modules, each of which defines some abstraction (see Sec. 2.10) and provides operations to manipulate that abstraction. For example, a file system (Sec. 2.22) typically contains several modules. A file management module defines file directories and provides operations such as create or open a file. A file access module defines the structure of files and provides read and write operations for accessing them. A buffer management module implements buffer storage and provides operations for requesting and releasing buffers. Finally, device drivers define I/O devices and provide routines for reading and writing those devices.

In implementing one module, it is often convenient to make use of the operations provided by another module. Thus a file access module might use a device driver module. If one module, M1, uses the operations of another, M2, we say that M1 *depends on* M2. The *dependency graph* of a system is the graph that is obtained from all depends on relations between modules. (It has one node for each module and a directed arc from node M_i to node M_j if module M_i depends on module M_j.) A system is *hierarchically organized* if its dependency graph is acyclic. By contrast, a system has circular dependencies if some module depends directly or indirectly on itself.

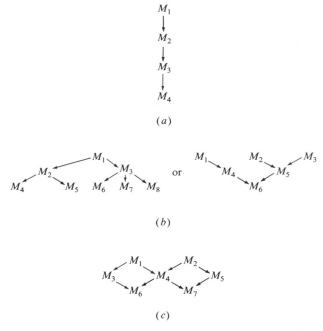

Fig. 1 Examples of hierarchical organizations: (*a*) chain or linear structure, (*b*) tree structure, (*c*) level structure.

The simplest hierarchical organization is a *linear* one, in which the modules are connected in a chain. More common are a *tree-structured organization*, in which the dependency graph forms a tree, or a *level-structured organization*, in which the dependency graph consists of two or more levels of nodes (such a graph is called a series–parallel graph). These three types of hierarchical organizations are illustrated in Fig. 1. In a level-structured organization, each level can be thought of as a virtual (abstract) machine whose modules provide operations used by higher levels and use operations provided by lower levels. (The lowest level interfaces to the physical machine.) Note that trees and chains are special cases of level structures.

2.24.2 Implementation of Hierarchies

Software systems are typically organized in a hierarchical fashion because a hierarchically organized system can be implemented one level at a time, starting with the lowest level (the one closest to the machine). Once a level is correctly implemented, the next higher level can be implemented. This is repeated until the entire system has been constructed.

There are three important benefits that result from this approach. First, it enables a system to be constructed a module at a time since each level can use the operations of the lower levels without concern for how they were actually implemented. Second, it makes it possible to change the implementation of one module without affecting any other module as long as the operation interfaces remain unchanged. Third, it aids debugging since once a level has been correctly implemented no errors in the implementation of higher levels can affect its correctness.

The modules of the highest level of a hierarchically organized asynchronous system are generally processes. Such processes are users of the system. The other levels can be implemented using procedures, processes, monitors, and so on (see Sec. 2.26). The choice depends on the amount of concurrency desired and the need for protecting shared data from simultaneous access. A module is implemented as a process if one wants to ensure that its local data can be accessed by only one process and also wants to allow the module to execute concurrently with other computation. A module is implemented as a monitor if one wants to ensure that its data are accessed by at most one process at a time and if one wants to synchronize users of the module. A module is implemented as a procedure if one wants to allow it to be used concurrently by more than one other module.

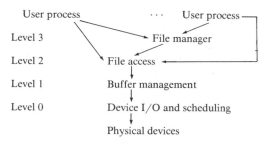

Fig. 2 Unix file system structure.

2.24.3 Examples

Two examples of hierarchically organized systems will illustrate the concepts discussed above. The T.H.E. system is an operating system developed at the Technological University of Eindhoven in the mid-1960s by a group led by E. W. Dijkstra [1]. The system consists of the following levels:

Level 4	User programs
Level 3	Input/output controllers
Level 2	Message interpreter
Level 1	Segment controller
Level 0	Processor allocation

Level 0 is a monitor that defines processes and provides semaphore operations (see Sec. 2.26.2) which are used for process synchronization. (Level 0 is a kernel, described in Sec. 2.25.) Level 1 manages a drum and implements virtual segments. Level 2 manages the console keyboard and provides facilities for user processes to communicate with the operator. Level 3 contains controllers for each peripheral device that implement I/O access and buffering operations. Level 4 consists of the processes that manage and execute user programs. Each level, except level 4, defines and implements an abstraction that is used by the higher levels. For example, above level 0 each module is implemented as a process and synchronizes with other modules by using semaphores. In Ref. 1, Dijkstra describes the levels in detail and discusses the advantages of organizing the system hierarchically.

As mentioned earlier, a file system typically contains several modules and is usually organized hierarchically. An excellent description of the hierarchical approach to file system design is contained in Ref. 2. A specific example is the file system in the Unix time-shared operating system [3]. In Unix, there is at least one process for each active user at a terminal. Each user process executes commands or programs, which may use the file system. At the top level of Unix, therefore, there are several processes that use the file system. At the top level of the file system itself is the file manager module, which defines directories and implements operations such as create and open. Once a file is opened, a user process can use the file access module's operations, such as read and write. The file access module is logically below the file manager in the file system since it is also used by the file manager, for example to search directories. To the caller of a file-access operation such as read, input appears to be unbuffered and synchronous (immediately after the completion of read, the data are available). Actually, the file access module depends on another level that implements a fairly complex buffering mechanism. The buffering mechanism in turn employs the lowest-level file modules, which schedule and actually perform I/O transfers. The resulting structure is summarized in Fig. 2. Most of the Unix file modules are implemented as procedures to allow the greatest possible amount of concurrent execution. Only the modules that perform I/O, buffer management, and other critical operations, such as directory manipulation, are implemented as monitors.

REFERENCES

1. E. W. DIJKSTRA, "The Structure of the T.H.E. Multiprogramming System," *Commun. ACM*, **11**(5), 341–346 (May 1968).

2. S. E. MADNICK and J. W. ALSOP II, "A Modular Approach to File System Design," *Proc. 1969 Spring Joint Comput. Conf.*, pp. 1–13.

3. D. W. RITCHIE and K. THOMPSON, "The Unix Time-Sharing System," *Commun. ACM*, **17**(7), 365–375 (July 1974).

2.25   KERNEL SYSTEMS

G. R. Andrews

2.25.1   Nature of a Kernel

An operating system contains the software that manages and provides access to the hardware resources of the machine on which it is implemented. In particular, it contains modules that manage memory, schedule the processor(s), control I/O devices, and implement a file system. The organization of an operating system can be based upon either of two concepts: a monolithic monitor or a kernel.

In a system based on a *monolithic monitor*, all the operating system modules are grouped into one large program that provides the means for all interactions between user programs and the hardware. Each module consists of a collection of procedures together with large tables that record the status of each system resource and user program. To preclude timing errors that could result from asynchronous interrupts, the monitor modules are executed with interrupts inhibited or employ a complex interrupt stacking and state-saving protocol.

By contrast, in a system based on a kernel, there is a small monitor, called the *kernel* or *nucleus*, that implements processes and provides an interface to the host machine. All other operating system modules are moved from the monitor to distinct, interruptable processes. The role of the kernel is to support multiprogramming, namely the concurrent execution of more than one system or user program. It provides a virtual (abstract) machine that is more attractive than the bare machine since it implements processes, handles interrupts, and provides mechanisms for process communication. The advantages of a kernel-based system relative to a monolithic monitor are that system programs can execute concurrently with each other as well as with user programs, system modules are more cleanly separated, interrupt processing is more efficient, and fewer large tables are required.

2.25.2   Components of a Kernel

To support multiprogramming on any contemporary machine, all kernels contain the following components:

1. Interrupt handlers, which receive hardware interrupts from I/O devices and relay status information to device-handling processes.
2. Primitive operations for synchronizing process execution [e.g., to allow processes to send and receive messages (see Sec. 2.22) and perhaps to create and destroy processes.
3. A process scheduler or dispatcher, which allocates the processor to executable processes.

To support the other hardware management functions of an operating system, a kernel may also contain:

4. Input/output routines, which initiate I/O on peripheral devices on command from device handling processes.
5. Memory management routines, which allocate and manage the main memory used by processes.
6. Protection mechanisms, which control access to memory and files.

Input/output routines are sometimes included since I/O requires the use of special machine instructions which may only be executable by the kernel. Memory management routines are included if memory-mapping information, such as page tables, are maintained by the kernel. Protection mechanisms are included for systems where the security of stored data is of concern. (Such a kernel is often called a security kernel.) It should be noted that the kernel merely provides mechanisms that support I/O, memory management, or security; the modules that implement these functions usually reside within processes outside the kernel. For example, in a kernel-based system there is typically one I/O driver process for each device; each driver process employs the kernel-implemented mechanisms to communicate with other processes, initiate I/O, and wait for hardware interrupts.

2.25.3   Implementation of a Kernel

The relationships in a typical system among a kernel, the host hardware, and the system and user processes are shown in Fig. 1. Also shown are the flow of control into and out of the kernel and the kernel's internal organization.

The kernel is always entered through the interrupt handlers. There is one handler for each kind of interrupt that can occur. Each handler saves the state of the interrupted process in the process's

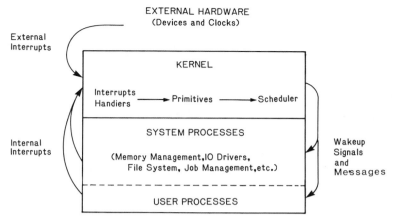

Fig. 1   Kernel organization.

descriptor (see Sec. 2.10), then handles the interrupt. To illustrate the functions of the interrupt handlers, the IBM 370 machine will be considered. (Other machines are similar at this level of detail.)

The 370 has five kinds of interrupts: supervisor call, I/O, clock, memory, and program check. A supervisor call is used to invoke a kernel primitive such as "create a process"; the appropriate kernel primitive is therefore executed. An I/O interrupt signals the completion of an I/O operation; the appropriate I/O process is notified, usually by sending it a message. A clock interrupt signals that a clock has reached a specified value (usually zero); the clock handler notifies the kernel scheduler or an appropriate system or user process. A memory fault interrupt signals an addressing exception; the appropriate memory management function is notified either by sending it a message (if it is implemented as a process) or by branching to it (if it is implemented as a procedure in the kernel). Program check interrupts signal program exceptions such as overflow or division by zero; the appropriate trap handler, which is generally a special routine in the offending process, then receives control.

The primitives consist of the routines that implement process management and synchronization, and, if included in the kernel, the routines that implement I/O, memory management, or protection mechanisms. The primitives are invoked by the interrupt handlers, execute the appropriate program, and then call the scheduler.

The scheduler (sometimes called a dispatcher) selects a process to run and then loads the machine registers and program counter with the appropriate information, which was stored in the process's descriptor when the process was created or last interrupted. The selected process may be the one that was interrupted, or it may be another process. The scheduler may employ any of the CPU scheduling algorithms described in Sec. 2.21. (An alternative kernel organization that is sometimes employed is to have the interrupt handlers call the primitives as procedures, then call the scheduler if necessary, and then load the state of the interrupted or newly scheduled process.)

Most machines distinguish between (at least) two modes of execution: supervisor mode, in which any machine instruction may be executed, and user or problem mode, in which only the nonprivileged instructions may be executed. The kernel executes in privileged mode; all processes, except possibly for I/O drivers, execute in user mode. In this way the kernel is the only software module that may affect hardware status registers. Another distinction between the kernel and the processes is that the kernel executes with interrupts inhibited, whereas processes may be interrupted. The kernel must be noninterruptable (unless greater care is taken) since it maintains critical status tables, such as process descriptors. The processes may be interrupted, however, because the kernel ensures that asynchronous interrupts are correctly synchronized with the recipient process.

2.25.4   Examples and References

One of the first operating systems to be based on a kernel was the T.H.E. system developed at the Technological University of Eindhoven under the leadership of Dijkstra [1]. The T.H.E. system kernel implements processes and semaphores. All other system modules are implemented as processes that synchronize by means of semaphores.

A brief, classic description of a nucleus (kernel) is given in Ref. 2, which describes the RC4000 multiprogramming system developed for a Danish machine by Brinch Hansen. The RC4000 nucleus provides primitives for process management and message passing. Using the message passing primitives, user processes can communicate with I/O and file processes.

The components of a kernel, their implementation, and their relation to the other parts of the system are described in the book by Holt et al. [3]. A complete description of a comprehensive nucleus (kernel), which includes protection and memory management mechanisms, is included in the book by Shaw [4].

REFERENCES

1. E. W. DIJKSTRA, "The Structure of the T.H.E. Multiprogramming System," *Commun. ACM*, **11**(5), 341–346 (May 1968).
2. P. BRINCH HANSEN, "The Nucleus of a Multiprogramming System," *Commun. ACM*, **13**(4), 238–241, 250 (Apr. 1970).
3. R. C. HOLT, ET AL., *Structured Concurrent Programming with Operating System Applications*, Addison-Wesley, Reading, Mass., 1978.
4. A. C. SHAW, *The Logical Design of Operating Systems*, Prentice-Hall, Englewood Cliffs, N.J., 1974, Chap. 7.

2.26 SYNCHRONIZATION AND CONCURRENT PROGRAMMING

Fred B. Schneider

A sequential program consists of some variables and a sequentially executed list of statements. At any point during its execution the next statement to be processed is completely determined by the program. This is called a *sequential process* [3]. If during execution the identity of the next statement to be processed is not completely determined by the program, the process is referred to as *nonsequential*. An example of a nonsequential process is one in which parallelism is explicitly expressed (e.g., using **fork** as described below) or whose sequential flow can be interrupted so that it can respond to the occurrence of an asynchronous event (e.g., the completion of an I/O request). Of particular interest are those programs that involve execution of more than one sequential process at a time. They are called *concurrent programs*. A concurrent program is often a useful way to formulate a computation. For example, an airline reservation system that involves processing transactions from many terminals would have a natural specification as a concurrent program—each terminal would be monitored by a sequential process.

Even when simultaneous execution of processes is not intended (or involved), it is often easier to structure a system as a collection of cooperating processes than as a single sequential program. This approach frequently finds application in operating systems and data base management systems. For example, a simple operating system could be viewed in terms of three concurrent processes: a card reader process, a job manager process, and an output process. The card reader process reads cards from the card reader and places card images in an input buffer. The job manager process reads card images from the input buffer and processes them, generating line images that are stored in an output buffer. The output process obtains line images from the output buffer and writes them to the line printer. One advantage of this structure is that the effects of speed variations of each process can be damped, as long as the average rate that images are stored in a buffer is the same as the average rate they are removed. The amount of speed variation that can be smoothed depends on the size of the buffer used. This sort of producer–consumer relationship appears frequently in concurrent programs.

One way to execute a concurrent program is to use a multiprocessor. Each process is executed on a separate processor, and any shared variables are kept in a store that is accessible to all processors. A more common way to execute a concurrent program is to time-multiplex the concurrent processes on one (or more) processors (see Sec. 2.20). This creates the illusion that processes are executing on a "variable-speed" processor, as opposed to being periodically suspended and resumed.

Coroutines provide a mechanism that allows the programmer explicit control over this process switching [4]. Recall that the subroutine **call** instruction always causes control to be transferred to the first instruction of the named routine. The coroutine **resume** instruction, like the **call** instruction, causes control to be transferred to the named routine. However, the **resume** instruction causes execution to commence at the instruction following the last **resume** instruction executed in that routine. This is illustrated in Fig. 1.

Usually, process switching is not under the control of the programmer, but is implemented by the kernel or lowest level of an operating system (see Sec. 2.25). Process switching may occur periodically— in response to timer interrupts—or randomly— in response to other events that cause the kernel to receive control. It may be assumed that each process will progress at some finite speed; however, no assumption can be made about that speed and its relation to the speeds of other

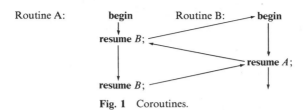

Fig. 1   Coroutines.

processes. Consequently, processes executing in this manner are referred to as *asynchronous*. Further-more, since process switching may in general occur between any two instructions, the programmer may not assume that high-level language statements are necessarily executed as indivisible actions.

2.26.1   Expressing Concurrency

Numerous language constructs have been proposed to allow specification of concurrent computations. The constructs differ primarily in the level of implementation detail to which the programmer is exposed. Three common constructs are described below.

fork/join [4].   A **fork** statement is like a **call** statement—it specifies that execution of a designated routine should commence. However, in a **fork** statement, execution of the statements following the **fork** (i.e., the invoking routine) and the invoked routine proceed concurrently. (In a **call** statement the caller is suspended until the invoked routine terminates.) For example, in Fig. 2 the **fork** statement causes concurrent execution of *Program2* with the statements following *L0* in *Program1*.

The **join** statement causes the invoker to be suspended until the previously "forked" routine terminates. In Fig. 2 *Program1* cannot progress beyond *L1* until *Program2* terminates.

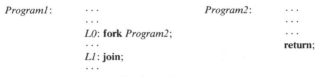

Fig. 2   fork/join.

cobegin [1].   The **cobegin** statement is a structured way to denote the concurrent execution of a set of statements. Thus

$$\textbf{cobegin } S_1 // S_2 // \cdots // S_n \textbf{ coend}$$

results in an arbitrary interleaving of the execution of $S_1, S_2, \ldots, S_n$. Each of the S_i's may be any statement (including **cobegin**). Execution of **cobegin** terminates only when each of the S_i's has terminated. Execution of each S_i can be viewed as a process.

process [2].   Large programs are often structured as a collection of sequential routines (modules or subroutines, see Sec. 2.20). One routine initially receives control and invokes other routines, as required. A **process** declaration identifies a routine that executes concurrently with its caller. Activation of a **process** is accomplished by executing a **start** instruction. Using this, a concurrent program can be structured as a collection of these modules and a main routine that initially receives control and starts them. For example, Fig. 3 shows the program outline for the simple operating system discussed earlier in terms of **process** modules.

2.26.2   Synchronization

To cooperate in performing a task, processes need some means to communicate. Shared variables (variables accessible to more than one process) are often used for this purpose. However, certain problems may occur when execution of processes that access shared variables is interleaved in an

```
main:        start cardreader_process;
             start output_process;
             start job_manager_process;

cardreader_process: process;
             var card : cardimage;
             do forever
                begin
                   read card from cardreader;
                   store card in input_buffer;
                end;
             end;

output_process: process;
             var line : lineimage;
             do forever
                begin
                   obtain line from output_buffer;
                   print line on lineprinter;
                end;
             end;

job_manager_process: process;
             var card : cardimage;
                 line : lineimage;
             do forever
                begin
                   obtain card from input_buffer;
                   process card generating line;
                   store line in output_buffer;
                end;
             end;
end;
```

Fig. 3   System composed of three processes.

arbitrary manner. To illustrate this, consider the following program:

$$(I) \qquad A := a;$$

```
             cobegin
                 R:   A := A+1;
             //
                 Q:   A := A+1;
             coend;
             Print (A)
```

Note that the statement "$A := A + 1$" might be implemented in machine language as follows:

$$
\begin{array}{ll}
\text{Load} & \text{Reg}, A \\
\text{Add} & \text{Reg}, \text{``1''} \\
\text{Store} & \text{Reg}, A
\end{array}
$$

One possible interleaving that might result from execution of the **cobegin** statement in (I) is shown in Fig. 4. In that description, "a" represents the initial value of variable A. Note that in this case, the final value of A is $a+1$, not $a+2$, as might be expected. Furthermore, this seemingly pathological behavior is purely a consequence of the interleaving of the Load instruction in process Q and the Store instruction in process R.

Often, execution of a sequence of statements must be made indivisible. For example, the manipulation of a complex data structure may be in terms of operations that are implemented by sequences of

Process R	Process Q	Description
Load Reg1, A		Reg1 = a
Add Reg1, "1"		Reg1 = a + 1
	Load Reg2, A	Reg2 = a
	Add Reg2, "1"	Reg2 = a + 1
	Store Reg2, A	A = a + 1
Store Reg1, A		A = a + 1

Fig. 4 Interleaved execution.

statements. If processes concurrently perform operations on the same shared data object, pathological results like those described earlier might be observed because of interleaving of the execution of those operations. A sequence of one or more statements that should be executed as an indivisible action is called a *critical section*. The *mutual exclusion problem* is concerned with preventing the interleaving of processes executing in critical sections. Clearly, if all accesses to a given shared data structure are made from statements within critical sections, and execution of critical sections is mutually exclusive, the integrity of shared data objects will be preserved.

Another situation where it is necessary to coordinate execution of concurrent processes occurs when a shared data object is not in a state conducive to execution of a particular operation. A process attempting such an operation should be delayed, since the state (i.e., value of the variables that comprise the object) of the data object may subsequently change, as a result of operations performed by other processes. This is called *condition synchronization*. An example of this appears in the simple operating system discussed earlier. In that system, the card reader process must be delayed when it attempts to store a card image in the input buffer if all the buffer frames are full. (This might happen if the card reader process was reading cards faster than the job manager process was using them.) Thus a process executing a store operation on a buffer must be delayed if there was no space in that buffer. Similarly, a process attempting to remove a card image from the buffer should be delayed if there is nothing in the buffer to remove.

Synchronization mechanisms are used to restrict the possible interleavings of concurrently executing processes. In the sequel, a number of common mechanisms will be discussed. They provide a convenient way for a programmer to regulate access to shared data. In particular, they facilitate the definition of critical sections and mutual exclusion, as well as provide ways to prescribe other constraints on interleavings in the execution of concurrent programs.

Note that it is possible to coordinate execution of concurrent processes solely by use of shared variables because of the atomic nature of a memory reference. Unfortunately, programs that use only shared variables to implement synchronization tend to be complex, hence difficult to understand and formally verify. Typically, these programs set and repeatedly test the value of a shared variable, waiting until that variable has a certain value. Waiting is accomplished by performing the test operation in a tight (short) loop. Thus, in order to delay itself, a process may cause the processor to *busy wait* (also known as *spinning*)—execute instructions for no purpose other than to pass time. Clearly, this is wasteful of CPU cycles.

Semaphores

A *semaphore* is a data type that assumes nonnegative integer values on which two operations are defined: P and V [3]. If s is a semaphore, then $V(s)$ causes s to be incremented by one in an atomic action. $P(s)$ causes s to be decremented by one in an atomic action, provided that s will remain nonnegative. If the decrement operation would cause s to become negative, execution of the P operation is delayed. Semaphore implementations are expected to exhibit *fairness*. This means that no process delayed while executing a P operation on a semaphore s will remain suspended forever if V operations are performed on s by other processes. The notion of fairness is required since a number of processes may be simultaneously delayed, all attempting to execute a P operation on the same semaphore. Clearly, a choice exists as to which one will be allowed to proceed when a V is ultimately performed by another process. A simple way to ensure fairness is to awaken processes in the order they were suspended, as V operations are performed.

Implementation of critical sections that mutually exclude each other in execution is possible using semaphores. Each sequence of statements that is to be a critical section is preceded by a P operation on a semaphore, and followed by a V operation on the same semaphore. All mutually exclusive critical sections use the same semaphore, which is initialized to one. Below, program (I) has been modified to ensure that statements R and Q are each executed as atomic actions. A semaphore, S, initialized to 1 has been introduced.

$$(\text{II}) \qquad A := a;$$
$$\textbf{cobegin}$$
$$\qquad P(S); R: A := A+1; V(S)$$
$$//$$
$$\qquad P(S); Q: A := A+1; V(S)$$
$$\textbf{coend};$$
$$Print\,(A)$$

The pathological interleaving described earlier cannot occur here because of the semantics of P and V. Thus program (II) always establishes the truth of the assertion: $A = a + 2$.

It is sometimes necessary to coordinate execution of a number of processes so that at most k processes can be executing in critical sections at any time. When $k = 1$ this is the mutual exclusion problem, for which a solution has already been given. A solution for the case when $k > 1$ can be obtained by changing the initialization of the mutual exclusion semaphore from 1 to k.

Semaphores can also be used to solve mutual exclusion problems when the critical sections are partitioned into sets, and execution must be constrained so that no two members of the same set are executed concurrently, although execution of critical sections in different sets can be interleaved. (Presumably, the critical sections in a given set all involve references to the same shared variables.) This is illustrated in Fig. 5, where initially $S1 = S2 = 1$. Execution of $\langle CS1\rangle$ and $\langle CS3\rangle$ is mutually exclusive, and execution of $\langle CS2\rangle$ and $\langle CS4\rangle$ is mutually exclusive. However, concurrent execution of $\langle CS3\rangle$ and $\langle CS4\rangle$ is permitted.

Semaphores can be used to implement condition synchronization, as well as various types of mutual exclusion. V operations are used to signal occurrences of events, and P operations to cause process execution to be delayed if an event has not yet occurred. This use of semaphores can be seen in Fig. 6, a somewhat expanded version of the simple operating system illustrated in Fig. 3.

The *input_mutex* and *output_mutex* semaphores are used to implement mutual exclusion of operations on *input_buffer* and *output_buffer*, respectively, and are initialized to 1. However, an operation on *input_buffer* may proceed concurrently with an operation on *output_buffer*. The *no_cards* and *no_lines* semaphores are used to ensure that processes do not attempt to obtain values from empty buffer frames. Since the buffers are initially empty, they have initial value 0. V operations are performed on these semaphores after each store in a buffer, and P operations prior to removal of information from the buffer. Finally, the *free_input* and *free_output* semaphores are employed to delay a process attempting to store an item in a buffer if that buffer is already full. Their initial values reflect the size of *input_buffer* and *output_buffer*, respectively. Thus their values at any time record the number of free slots in each buffer.

Program1: **process**;   *Program2*: **process**;   *Program3*: **process**;

	.		.		.
	.		.		.
	.	$P(S1)$;			.
$P(S1)$;		$\langle CS3\rangle$		$P(S2)$;	
$\langle CS1\rangle$		$V(S1)$;		$\langle CS4\rangle$	
$V(S1)$;			.	$V(S2)$;	
	.		.		
	.		.		.
	.				.
$P(S2)$;					
$\langle CS2\rangle$					
$V(S2)$;					
	.				
	.				
	.				

Fig. 5   System of processes with multiple critical sections.

```
           var input_mutex, output_mutex, no_cards, no_lines,
               free_input, free_output : semaphore;
main:      start job_manager_process;
           start cardreader_process;
           start output_process;
cardreader_process: process;
               var card : cardimage;
               do forever
                  begin
                     read card from cardreader;
                     P (free_input);
                     P (input_mutex);
                        store card in input_buffer;
                     V (input_mutex);
                     V (no_cards);
                  end;
               end;
output_process: process;
               var line : lineimage;
               do forever
                  begin
                     P (no_lines);
                     P (output_mutex);
                     obtain line from output_buffer;
                     V (output_mutex);
                     V (free_output);
                     write line on lineprinter;
                  end;
               end;
job_manager_process: process;
               var card : cardimage;
                   line : lineimage;
               do forever
                  begin
                     P (no_cards);
                     P (input_mutex);
                     obtain card from input_buffer;
                     V (input_mutex);
                     V (free_input);
                     process card, generating line;
                     P (free_output);
                     P (output_mutex);
                        store line in output_buffer;
                     V (output_mutex);
                     V (no_lines);
                  end;
               end;
end;
```

Fig. 6 Synchronization using semaphores.

Semaphores can be implemented by using a test-and-set instruction, which is found on most modern-day computers (for exactly this reason). The operation of the test-and-set instruction is as follows:

```
TS(x, y):  As an atomic action do;
              x := y;
              y := true;
           end;
```

Usually, y is a shared variable, and x is local to the invoking process.

A *binary semaphore* is a semaphore that is always either 0 or 1. Using test-and-set, the operations on a binary semaphore P_b and V_b can be implemented as follows:

$$P_b(s): \quad \textbf{var } slocal : \textbf{boolean};$$
$$L: \ TS(slocal, s);$$
$$\textbf{if } slocal \textbf{ then go to } L;$$
$$V_b(s): \quad s := false;$$

It is possible to implement a general semaphore, *sem* (i.e., a semaphore with no upper bound on its value), by using an integer variable, *value*, a binary semaphore, *mutex*, for mutual exclusion, and a binary semaphore, *delay*, to delay process execution. *Mutex* is initialized to 1; *delay* to 0; and *value* to the initial value of semaphore *sem*.

$$P(sem): \quad P_b(mutex);$$
$$value := value - 1;$$
$$\textbf{if } value < 0 \textbf{ then do begin } V_b(mutex);$$
$$\qquad\qquad\qquad\qquad\qquad P_b(delay);$$
$$\qquad\qquad\qquad \textbf{end}$$
$$\qquad\qquad\quad \textbf{else } V_b(mutex);$$

$$V(sem): \quad P_b(mutex);$$
$$value := value + 1;$$
$$\textbf{if } value \leq 0 \textbf{ then } V_b(delay);$$
$$V_b(mutex);$$

Notice that busy waiting is used to delay process execution.

In a single-processor machine with a kernel system (see Sec. 2.25) P and V operations can be implemented as kernel calls that do not involve busy waiting. Recall that the kernel implements the process abstraction. To do this, the kernel maintains a queue of all processes that are eligible to run on the processor. This queue is called the *ready list*. The kernel switches the processor among these processes. In addition, the kernel maintains a queue of the processes that are suspended on each semaphore. Processes are not executed while they are on these queues. Execution of a V operation moves a waiting process from the corresponding semaphore queue to the ready list, thereby making that process eligible for execution. Execution of a P operation may or may not remove the executing process from the ready list, depending on the value of the semaphore. Crucial to the correctness of this implementation is that the kernel not be interrupted while performing these operations. This is because the ready list, the values of the semaphores, and the semaphore queues are shared data objects, and therefore arbitrary interleaving of concurrent accesses (by invoking processes and interrupt handlers) might yield pathological results. Thus execution in the kernel occurs with interrupts masked off (disabled). Consequently, each kernel operation is atomic. Such a technique is not suitable in multiple-processor systems, and busy waiting may be required to ensure the integrity of these variables. This is because it may become necessary to delay a processor that is attempting to access one of these variables if it is concurrently being manipulated by a second processor. Furthermore, no other process could be executed by the first processor because access to the ready list would be required to run such a process.

Monitors [2]

Although semaphores can be used to program any synchronization problem, P and V are rather unstructured primitives. It is therefore easy for a programmer to make coding errors when using semaphores. For example, the programmer might forget to include all statements that access shared variables in critical sections, or might perform operations on the wrong semaphore. *Monitors* provide a somewhat more structured synchronization mechanism. When using monitors, many of these problems can be avoided, or detected by a compiler.

The monitor enforces a very disciplined use of shared variables. Consequently, it is easy to write concurrent programs, although the amount of concurrency in such programs may be somewhat restricted. A monitor is essentially an abstract data type (see Sec. 2.10) extended for use in an asynchronous environment. It consists of a collection of permanent variables and a set of procedures, which are used to manipulate these variables. The values of the permanent variables are retained between activations of monitor procedures, and may be accessed only from within those procedures.

```
⟨monitor_name⟩: monitor;
      var ... define permanent variables ...
      procedure entry ⟨operation_1⟩ (... parameters ...);
            var ... define local variables ...
            begin
                  ... code to implement ⟨operation_1⟩ ...
            end;


      procedure entry ⟨operation_n⟩ (... parameters ...);
            var ... define local variables ...
            begin
                  ... code to implement ⟨operation_n⟩ ...
            end;
      begin
            ... initialization ...
      end;
```

Fig. 7   Monitor syntax.

The permanent variables are generally related, and they are referred to as a *resource*. For example, a buffer can be implemented in terms of an array and two pointer variables. These three variables comprise the buffer—a resource. The syntax of a monitor is shown in Fig. 7. Generally, each monitor procedure implements an operation on the resource defined by the permanent variables of the monitor. A procedure is invoked by coding

call ⟨monitor_name⟩.⟨procedure_name⟩ (... argument list ...);

Execution of monitor procedures is guaranteed to be mutually exclusive. Thus, at most one process can be executing in a given monitor at any time. This ensures the integrity of the permanent variables in the monitor. Notice that a monitor is really just a grouping of all the critical sections that reference a set of shared variables.

The use of monitors allows programmers to ignore the implementation details of a resource when using it, as they need only be concerned with the monitor procedure interfaces. Similarly, the circumstances surrounding the use of the resource may be ignored when the monitor is being coded, as long as the implementation satisfies its interface specification.

Within a monitor, *condition variables* are used to delay a process when the values of the permanent variables of the monitor are not conducive to continued execution by that process. Two operations are defined on condition variables: send and wait. If *cond* is a condition variable, *cond*.wait causes the invoker to be suspended and to relinquish control of the monitor. If a process is currently delayed on *cond*, execution of *cond*.send causes that process to be resumed. The process executing the *send* is suspended. A process suspended due to a **send** operation is reactivated when control of the monitor has been relinquished. A new process is granted entry into a monitor procedure only if there are no processes delayed as a result of having performed a **send** operation and there is no process actively executing in the monitor.

Figure 8 is the operating system example programmed using monitors.

Message Passing [1]

The synchronization mechanisms described thus far involve the explicit use of shared variables to implement interprocess communication and synchronization. A second approach to the coordination of concurrent processes uses message passing for this. The programmer defines logical communications channels between processes that must communicate. Two operations are defined on a channel: **send** and **receive**. The **send** primitive causes a message to be transmitted on the designated channel. The **receive** primitive removes a message from the designated channel. It may delay the invoker until a message has been sent on that channel.

Although shared memory can be used in the implementation of message passing, it is not required. This makes such a synchronization mechanism suitable for distributed processing and network applications, where there is no shared memory. Furthermore, since there need not be any shared variables, there is no need for the programmer to be concerned with mutual exclusion and critical sections. A consequence of this is that it is easy to understand in isolation each of the processes that comprise the concurrent program. The message passing primitives designate the only places in that code that can be affected by execution of other processes.

```
inbuff: monitor;
        var no_cards: integer;
                in_full, in_free: condition;
                ... other variables to represent input_buffer ...
        procedure entry deposit (c: cardimage);
                begin
                    if no_cards = input_buffer_size then in_free.wait;
                    ... code to store c in input_buffer ...
                    no_cards := no_cards + 1;
                    in_full.send;
                    end;
        procedure entry retrieve (var c: cardimage);
                begin
                    if no_cards = 0 then in_full.wait;
                    ... code to remove a cardimage from input_buffer and place it in c ...
                    no_cards := no_cards - 1;
                    in_free.send;
                    end;
        begin (*initialization of inbuff*)
                no_cards := 0;
                ... initialization of other variables ...
                end; (*of inbuff*)
outbuff: monitor;
                ... similar to inbuff ...
                end; (*of outbuff*)
main: start cardreader_process;
        start output_process;
        start job_manager_process;
cardreader_process: process;
        var card: cardimage;
        do forever
            begin
                read card from cardreader;
                call inbuff.deposit (card);
                end;
        end; (*of cardreader_process*)
output_process: process;
        ...similar to cardreader_process ...
        end; (*of output_process*)
job_manager_process: process;
        var card: cardimage;
                line: lineimage;
        do forever
            begin
                call inbuff.retrieve (card);
                process card, generating line;
                call outbuff.deposit (line);
                end;
        end; (*of job_manager_process*)
```

Fig. 8 Operating system constructed with monitors.

Message passing can be organized in a number of different ways. It may be required that a channel connect exactly one sender and receiver. Alternatively, more than one receiver and/or sender may be associated with each channel. Second, a channel may or may not have the capacity to buffer messages. If it does, a **send** operation will delay the invoker only if the capacity of the buffer has been exhausted by messages that have been sent, but not yet accepted, by a receiver. There are good reasons to require that a channel have no buffering capacity, a finite buffering capacity, or an infinite buffering capacity. Note that if the channel has no buffering capabilities, a **send–receive** pair defines a synchronization point in the execution of the invoking processes (one process must wait for the other to do the corresponding operation before either can proceed).

```
main:      start cardreader_process;
           start output_process;
           start job_manager_process;
cardreader_process: process;
  var card: cardimage;
  do forever
    begin
           read card from cardreader;
           send (job_manager_process, card);
           end;
    end;
output_process: process;
  var line: lineimage;
  do forever
    begin
           receive (job_manager_process, line);
           write line on lineprinter;
           end;
    end;
job_manager_process: process;
  var card: cardimage;
      line: lineimage;
  do forever
    begin
           receive (cardreader_process, card);
           process card, generating line;
           send (output_process, line);
           end;
    end;
  end;
```

Fig. 9   Synchronization using message passing.

The use of message passing for synchronization is illustrated in Fig. 9. There, the operating system example has been coded using the following typical message passing primitives:

send(x, m)	send to process x message m
receive(x, m)	receive from process x message m

Note that the buffer capacity of the channels has no effect on the correctness of this particular program.

2.26.3   Synchronization Mechanisms and System Structure

A system can be viewed as a collection of objects and tasks. The tasks use the objects to perform a computation. Shared objects may be implemented in one of two ways. In the following these two approaches are discussed, and their implications are explored.

In the *passive* model of objects, each shared object is represented in a portion of shared memory, perhaps with some procedures to facilitate access and manipulation of the abstraction implemented by the object. To perform an operation on an object, a task invokes one of these procedures. Thus objects are manipulated directly by the process that requires the service. Since objects are subject to concurrent accesses by processes, the programmer must be concerned with defining critical sections and arranging for their mutual exclusion.

The *active* model of objects associates a process with each shared object. This "caretaker" process performs all operations on its object. When a process requires that an operation be performed on an object, a message is sent to the caretaker for that object. The caretaker performs the actual operation, and may respond with a completion message when the operation has been performed. Thus objects are never directly manipulated by tasks, as was the case in the passive model. Furthermore, although concurrent processes interact and in fact may be synchronized through the use of these shared objects, the objects are never actually subject to concurrent access. Rather, operations are performed on objects by the caretaker process on behalf of other processes.

2.26.4 Deadlock [4]

Deadlock or *deadly embrace* (see Sec. 2.21) is a phenomenon that can be exhibited by concurrent programs. It occurs (in its simplest form) when one process waits for an action to be performed by another process, while this second process is waiting for an action to be performed by the first process. Clearly, in that case neither process can progress. In more complicated situations, deadlock may result from some interleavings of a concurrent program's execution, but not from others. Clearly, when writing a concurrent program it is necessary to ensure the absence of the possibility of deadlock for all possible interleavings.

REFERENCES

1. P. BRINCH HANSEN, *Operating System Principles*, Prentice-Hall, Englewood Cliffs, N.J., 1973.
2. P. BRINCH HANSEN, *The Architecture of Concurrent Programs*, Prentice-Hall, Englewood Cliffs, N.J., 1977.
3. E. W. DIJKSTRA, "Hierarchical Ordering of Sequential Processes," *Acta Inf.*, **1**, 2 (1971).
4. A. C. SHAW, *The Logical Design of Operating Systems*, Prentice-Hall, Englewood Cliffs, N.J., 1974.

2.27 GENERAL NETWORK DESIGN CONSIDERATIONS

S. Wecker

2.27.1 Definition

A network is any system that *interconnects*. Specifically, a *computer network* is a collection of computers and I/O devices connected by a system of communication channels. A computer network is a tool providing a communication path for the flow of information between the objects or components interfaced to the network. The network in Fig. 1, for example, interfaces host computers, terminals, printers, and disk devices.

2.27.2 Design Requirements

A computer network must effectively meet the communication requirements of the connected components. They must be able to address each other easily and transport their information in a form compatible with the network mechanisms. These network communication mechanisms must support the *communication characteristics* of the applications, including stream or block orientation, data integrity, data sequencing, addressing, priority, security, data formats, code sets, throughput, and delay. These characteristics will vary across network applications [1].

A computer network may be designed to meet the requirements of a single specific application or be a more general purpose tool, such as an operating system, to be used by many varying applications. In this case options are usually provided, via the *user interface*, the user view of the network, to tailor the characteristics of the communication mechanism to the user application requirements. The interfaces to a computer network and the network internal design, structure, and communication mechanisms define the *network architecture* [2].

Communications in a network may be for the purposes of sharing resources, distributing computing, or communicating remotely. In *resource sharing networks*, resources on one system, such as I/O devices and disk files, are shared or made available to other systems. Examples of resource-sharing

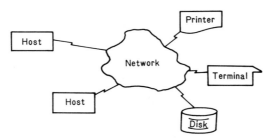

Fig. 1 Computer network.

activities include remote file access, intercomputer file transfer, and distributed data base queries. In *distributed computing networks*, cooperating programs executing in different computers exchange information much the same as program modules communicate via subroutine calls. Examples of distributed computing networks include process control systems and parallel processing structures. In *remote communication networks*, remote interactive and batch terminals are connected to computing systems via the network. By sharing communication facilities, communication channels and computer I/O interfaces can be more effectively utilized.

2.27.3 Communication Model

Modeling can be an effective tool in the design of computer systems. A model of network usage and communication techniques provides the basis for the design of the network user interface and ultimately the architecture of the network. An analysis of the network uses listed above leads to such a model. In all these networks there is a similarity of communication function, a communication between objects or resources in the network systems. Application programs communicate directly in the network, while other resources (e.g., disk files, terminals, I/O devices) communicate via inter-mediate *network access programs* (NAPs). These network access programs communicate with both the network and the local managed resource, providing a translation between the two communication paths, network and local (see Fig. 2). Clusters of resources, network access programs, and network communication channels may be grouped into work stations. A *work station* is a clustered set of activities that perform a well-defined set of functions. These functions are executed by procedures (programs) within the work station. Work stations communicate with each other via their message communication channels. Thus communication between resources becomes a communication between work stations, programs that control or interface resources to the network.

In addition, an examination of the communication characteristics of network applications divides them into those with a sequential stream orientation (e.g., file transfer), and those with a message or transaction-like orientation (e.g., data base access). Thus a communication mechanism providing for *program-to-program* communication, for both application and network access programs, and offering both a *stream* and *message* mode will satisfy the requirements of a very wide range of applications and network uses.

2.27.4 Communication Characteristics and Switching Techniques

The basic function of the network is to create a *communication mechanism* via an *interface* to work stations (programs) so that they can *communicate*, transport information to each other. These work stations communicate via their message channels. The characteristics of these channels depend on the requirements of the application and can be grouped by data flow into virtual circuits, datagrams, and transactions (see Secs. 2.28.1 and 2.28.2). *Virtual circuits* are telephone-like communication channels for transmitting a stream of data as a sequence of blocks. *Datagrams* are post-office-like, each message block of information transmitted independently of every other message. *Transactions* are like datagrams but relate a message with a corresponding reply.

Data sent over a communication channel, whether virtual circuit, datagrams, or transaction in orientation, are *addressed* to a destination. This destination may be one resource interfaced into the network, *single-destination addressing*; a group of resources, *multicast addressing*; or all resources, *broadcast addressing* (see Sec. 2.28.3). The *topology*, physical arrangement of channels and nodes, of the network will determine the ease with which multicast and broadcast can be accomplished. In addition, other characteristics of the user communication channel will be affected by the topology and the properties of the individual circuits of the network. These include: *data integrity*, the probability of the transport of data without errors; *flow control*, controlling the rate at which data are transmitted; *information representation*, the permissible code sets and data formats; and *performance*, the through-put and delay of the communications.

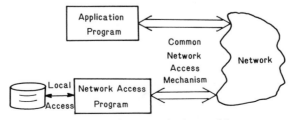

Fig. 2 Network communication model.

The communication mechanism is realized from a combination of hardware circuits (data communication channels), switching nodes, and associated software. The switching nodes and software connect the channels into an end-to-end pathway via the *switching* or *routing* function (see Sec. 2.29). There are several alternative switching technologies (see Sec. 2.28) [4]. In *circuit switching* a connection or pathway is established between the end communicating users by either creating a direct electrical connection between them or concatenating dedicated, fixed-bandwidth physical channels and dedicated intermediate node switching resources (CPU, buffers, etc.). In *message switching* no dedicated end-to-end path is created; instead, an entire message is first assembled at the source node and then forwarded from node to node toward its destination, being stored at each intermediate node along the way. *Packet switching* is a compromise between the two extremes of circuit and message switching. As in message switching, no resources are dedicated at intermediate nodes; they simply forward data blocks based on a destination node address and routing algorithm. Messages are segmented, however, into medium-size blocks, called *packets* (usually 128 to 256 bytes in length), as the data are generated. Packet switching tries to provide the advantages of both of the previous techniques: the smooth data flow and low delay achieved with static allocation and the shared resource utilization of message switching [5]. Note that these switching techniques can be used to support a virtual circuit, datagram, or transaction interface between work stations, although some techniques are more suitable than others for a particular interface and will result in different levels of performance.

2.27.5   Layered Structure and Protocols

Network structures are typically implemented via a *hierarchy of communication layers* (see Secs. 2.24, 2.31, and 2.32). That is, the network functions are divided or *decomposed* into a hierarchical set of functions, higher layers building on the capabilities of lower layers. Each layer consists of interfaces to the layers above and below it and a set of functions performed by the layer. Each layer presents a communication function, via its interface, to the layer above it and uses the functions of the layer below it (see Fig. 3) [2].

The lowest layer in the structure is the physical communication channel layer. The highest layer in the basic communication network is the layer creating the connection interface to the users. Intermediate layers in the structure perform such functions as error control, switching, and flow control and bridge the gap between the physical channels and the user interface (see Sec. 2.30). Additional layers, above the user interface, perform *application-oriented functions*, such as file access and terminal control (see Sec. 2.32) [6,7], Organizing the network in this way forces a well-specified and documented structure, provides points of convenient interface for standardization, and allows for debugging, maintenance, and evolution on a layer-by-layer basis.

The decomposition of functions into layers is usually done to minimize the communication between layers, and to group common functions together. The decomposition coincides with the physical and logical boundaries of the system. A common set of layers has been used in many of the current architecture, designs (see Sec. 2.31) [3]. Each layer in the structure creates a wider communication path. First over physical channels, then between switches, then between end nodes, and finally between the end communicating users.

Each layer in the hierarchy performs a communication function, that is, a transformation or change in the communication characteristics of the data entering and exiting the interfaces of a layer. The characteristics of the physical communication channels and the topology affect both the choice of layering and the functions performed within each layer. The layer functions may be centralized or distributed. When distributed, the distributed parts must communicate to synchronize and coordinate their operation. This is done via a *protocol*, a well-defined and agreed-upon set of messages and rules for their exchange. Peer layers communicate using protocols by sending protocol information via their

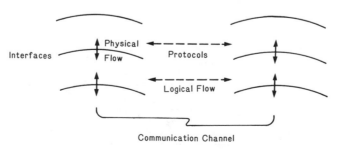

Fig. 3   Layered protocol communications.

interface through the layer hierarchy (see Fig. 3). Protocols form part of the state and operation of the distributed layers. When protocols are combined with the layering concept, the result is a set of *layered protocols*, each one performing higher-level functions in the hierarchy [8]. At the application layer, the network access programs communicate via *application-oriented protocols* for the access and control of I/O devices and resources such as terminals and disk files (see Sec. 2.32) [6, 7].

2.27.6 Communication Channels

The communication channels form the lowest layer in the structure. Their function is to transmit bits over a physical channel connecting a pair of nodes. Communication media include wire pairs, coaxial cable, microwave, radio, satellite channels, and optical fibers. Bits are transferred over the channel either synchronously or asynchronously. In *synchronous transmission* the transmitter and receiver use a common clock. The receiver knows when each bit will arrive by reference to the clock. Transmission is usually uniform in time. The clock signal may be sent: over a separate signal channel, or combined with the data by using either digital or analog techniques, or via a combination of a local clock and periodic clock information used for clock adjustment (e.g., phase-locked-loop receiver). In *asynchronous transmission* the transmitter and receiver each use separate local clocks. Bits are grouped together preceded by a start signal. The clocks must be accurate enough so they do not drift within a bit group more than a fraction of a bit time. The time between the transmission of groups is not necessarily uniform [9].

Communication channels may be *bit serial* or *bit parallel*. Bit parallel channels have skew problems (i.e., not all bits in the parallel transmission arrive at the same instant at the destination) and require high driving current and many interface pins on LSI chips. Thus serial channels, even though slower, are very desirable in data communication environments. In addition, serial signals may be sent over *leased* or *switched* (dialed) telephone channels. The functions of parallel to serial conversion, clocking, and buffering between a channel and a computer interface has been standardized into a 40-pin LSI chip called a universal synchronous/asynchronous receiver/transmitter (USART). There is a version for asynchronous use only, the UART [9].

Data may be transmitted in analog or digital form. Digital transmission may be used on relatively short (1 to 2 km) wire channels without significant deterioration. Beyond this, capacitive and resistive effects of the wire distort the signal. For longer distances using digital transmission, *digital repeaters* are used to recreate the signal. Optical fibers do not suffer as much from these problems and will see increased usage in the future. Digital transmission in this form without a carrier is called *baseband* transmission.

For longer distances it is common to use analog transmission on private or leased telephone-type channels. Transmission on these channels must fit within the channel bandwidth of 300 to 3000 Hz. The data are *modulated*, converted from digital to analog form, and combined with a carrier signal for transmission over these channels. At the receiver the reverse process occurs, *demodulation*. The device that performs these transformations is a *modem* (modulator–demodulator). The data may be modulated by varying the amplitude (loudness) of the carrier, *amplitude modulation* (AM), by varying the frequency (tone), *frequency modulation* (FM), or by varying the phase of the carrier, *phase modulation* or phase shift keying (PSK) [10].

The number of analog levels or possible states determines the number of digital bits that may be conveyed with each analog signal state. The digital information rate is measured in *bits per second* (bps). The analog signal change rate is measured in *baud*. An analog signal with only two states conveys one digital bit (0 or 1) with each state and bps equals the baud rate. However, if there are 2^n analog states, n digital bits are conveyed with each state and the bps rate is n times the baud rate. For example, an AM signal with four amplitudes or levels can convey 2 bits of information per level (e.g., $00, 01, 10, 11$). There is a limit to the number of states, however, as the signal-to-noise ratio makes it difficult to detect smaller state changes, increasing the error rate on the channel.

The interface between a *computer serial data port* and a *modem* has been standardized by a number of standards organizations. The most common *standard* today is the RS-232C (EIA) or V.24 (CCITT) standard [11]. The standard defines the physical and logical characteristics used for communication between the modem and the computer. The physical components include the wire, connector plug, and signal levels. The logical components are the meaning of the signals and the rules and states of their operation.

Errors on communication channels are usually *bursty*. That is, unlike the single and double bit errors common to computer memories, errors on communication channels extend over many bits (a burst). On telephone channels the average error rate is 1 error every 10^5 bits. On private channels, such as coaxial cable, the error rate could be as low as 1 error every 10^9 bits. Because of these relatively low error rates and the ability to retain copies of messages in memory at the data source, the usual error correction technique for recovering from bit errors on communication channels is to use an *error-detection-only code* and correction via *retransmission*. Because of the burstiness of the errors, block codes, such as cyclic codes (cyclic redundancy checks), are usually used for the detection of bit errors [9, 12].

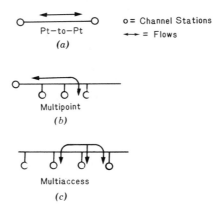

Fig. 4 Channel configurations; (*a*) point to point; (*b*) multipoint; (*c*) multiaccess. Circles denote channel stations; arrows denote flows.

The performance of a channel is measured by its throughput and delay. *Throughput* is the rate of flow, usually measured in bits per second. *Delay* is the time for the first bit to traverse the channel. Delay on a channel can vary from a few microseconds on a 1-km private channel to 0.5 s on an 80,000-km satellite channel. Throughput can also vary from a few hundred bits per second (typical of an asynchronous dialed channel) to 1 to 50 million bits per second (private coaxial cable or fiber-optic channel). On telephone (voice) channels using analog transmission via modems, data rates can vary from 110 to 9600 bps.

Channels connect nodes in the network. A channel may connect only two nodes (*channel stations*) or many nodes. Channels connecting only two stations are *point-to-point channels* (see Secs. 2.28.1 and 2.28.2). A channel connecting one station with many others is a *multipoint channel*. A channel connecting many stations to each other is a *multiaccess channel* (see Fig. 4 and Sec. 2.28.3). Leased telephone channels may be point to point or multipoint. Multiaccess channels are used primarily in local (1 to 2 km) environments to connect many nodes together via a single physical channel. Another use of multiaccess channels is for satellite communication, the satellite and radio communication being the single channel connecting the ground stations together. In addition, channels may also be *simplex*, unidirectional data flow, as for a doorbell, *half-duplex*, unidirectional and reversible, as for shortwave radio, or *full-duplex* (two simplex channels), bidirectional, as for the telephone.

On full-duplex point-to-point channels both stations may transmit simultaneously. On half-duplex channels there must be a way to pass control to transmit back and forth between the stations. This is done via a protocol (message format) defined for use on the channel. On multipoint channels messages must be *addressed* to specific receivers and there must be a mechanism to pass transmit control in an orderly way among the stations. Multiaccess channels have much the same problems and must include both a source and destination address. The passing of control can be via a centralized algorithm, *polling*, or a distributed one, *contention*. Addressing is done by including an address field in the header of messages being transmitted. On point-to-point channels only a single destination can be addressed. On multiaccess channels all stations compare the received destination address with their own. Using this technique, a message can be addressed to a group of stations, *multicast*, or to all stations, *broadcast*, on such channels [4].

Channels can be local (1 to 2 km) or geographically distributed. *Local channels* usually have low error rates (1 error in 10^9 bits), low delay (a few microseconds), and high throughput (1 to 50 Mbps). They may be point to point, multipoint, or multiaccess in configuration. *Geographically distributed channels* are usually leased from the telephone company. If voice-grade channels, they are limited to 9.6 Kbps and either point to point or multipoint. Higher speed channels (up to 56 Kbps) are also available and will become more common in the future. *Satellite channels* offer speeds equaling those of local channels but with much higher delay (0.25 to 0.5 s).

2.27.7 Network Topology

Channels are connected together via switching nodes to form the *switching network*. The *topology* is the physical arrangement of channels and switches to form this network. The network may consist of only a single channel, (e.g., a multiaccess channel or bus), and thus not require a switching function. The

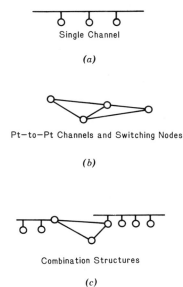

Single Channel

(a)

Pt—to—Pt Channels and Switching Nodes

(b)

Combination Structures

(c)

Fig. 5 Network topology examples: (*a*) single channel; (*b*) point-to-point channels and switching nodes; (*c*) combination structures.

network may also consist of point-to-point channels connected by switching nodes, or a combination of both channel types (see Fig. 5). In these cases the topology may be regular (e.g., trees, rings, or lattices), or general. Some of the properties of different topologies are:

Multiaccess Bus or Channel

On such channels all stations may communicate with each other directly. Since the stations all share the channel, there must be a way to schedule or arbitrate its use. This is done via an arbitration algorithm, which decides which station can transmit next on the channel. This algorithm can be centralized within one of the stations on the channel or distributed among them via a common distributed algorithm. No path selection is required on multiaccess channels since all stations are connected on only the single channel. Broadcast and multicast are easily done via the message addressing. The routing function is inherent in the operation of the channel.

Ring

A ring is a circular connection of point-to-point channels and interface nodes connecting them. As for the multiaccess channel, messages include both a source and a destination address. Messages enter the ring via the sending interface, are received by one or more destinations whose addresses match, and are later removed by the sending interface when they have traveled around the ring. Each interface connects the ring segments with a minimum amount of delay (at least one bit time). On a ring there is no route or path selection. Broadcast and multicast are easily done via the addressing information in the messages. An additional feature is the ability to alter the message as it traverses the ring and thereby add acknowledgment information, telling the sender which stations have accepted the message (see Fig. 6).

Tree

A tree is a regular structure of point-to-point channels and nodes. By a proper assignment of addresses to nodes in the tree, the location of a node can be determined by its address. In addition, the path from one node to another can be determined from their addresses, eliminating the need for routing

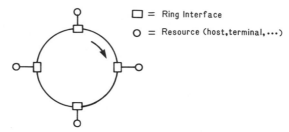

□ = Ring Interface

○ = Resource (host,terminal,...)

Fig. 6   Ring structure. Squares denote ring interfaces; circles denote resources (host, terminal, (etc.).

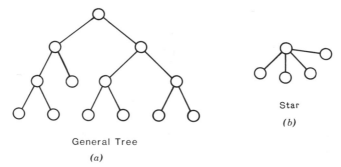

Star

(b)

General Tree

(a)

Fig. 7   Tree structures: (a) general tree; (b) star.

path tables (see Fig. 7). A star is a special configuration of a tree with a depth of one and a single central node.

General

A general or random topology requires routing via a table of node addresses and paths. The algorithm for creating this table can be centralized or distributed (see Sec. 2.29). That is, it can be computed in one location and sent to each node or it can be computed by each node using information distributed through the network. This table can be static or dynamic, adapting to failures in the network [13].

2.27.8   Communication Subnetwork

The communication functions and layer structure can be divided into those functions that provide the basic communication between the end communicating nodes, computers, and those functions that are at higher layers in the structure. This lower-layer transport facility forms the *communication subnetwork* or *backbone network*. Its function is to provide the basic communication facilities of the network. It creates the communication path between the computers within which the resources reside. In some networks the subnetwork provides error-free, block-oriented, sequential paths directly. In others, the communication subnetwork provides a more primitive service (unreliable block transmission) and the hosts provide the necessary enhancements.

The choice of service level within the subnetwork depends on the capabilities of the switching nodes and the reliability and performance requirements of the network. The division of function will also be influenced by the ownership of the service (i.e., user or communication carrier) and on the physical boundaries of ownership between the circuits, switches, and hosts. The communication network is a *logical network*. That is, it may share physical hardware (processor, memory) with higher-level functions such as host support or it may exist independently, interfacing to host systems.

When host systems are either heavily utilized or a separation of functions is desirable, the communication functions may be moved to an outboard *front-end processor*. This processor performs the functions outlined earlier in the discussion of layered architectures. In addition to relieving the host of basic communication functions, these systems also perform a routing or switching function, selecting outgoing channels for messages either generated by their attached host or arriving on incoming channels and not destined for the host. The difference between a front-end processor and a *communication processor* or network switch is the intimacy of the coupling and support for a particular host system. Communication processors are usually more distant from their attached hosts and may provide general communication functions to a number of host systems. Front-ends are generally more closely coupled to their host operating systems. The architecture of front-end or communication processors must support rapid manipulation of data. This support includes such architectural features as memory management support for flexible buffer management and I/O interfaces supporting varied data structures. Many current small minicomputers are well suited for this function.

Communication networks may be used to connect only homogeneous host systems or heterogeneous ones. If the systems are similar, specialized interfaces to the network, connecting the host and communication processor (e.g., channel adapters, parallel channels), may be used. If the hosts are heterogeneous, a standard interface to all hosts is very desirable. Such an interface has been standardized by the world organization of communication carriers, the CCITT. This interface specification, named X.25, defines the physical, electrical, and logical standards used to connect the common-carrier processor [the data communication equipment (DCE)] and the user or customer system [the data terminal equipment (DTE)]. The interface provides the host with a virtual circuit service and is implemented via a layering of three interfaces or protocols. The lowest layer provides the electrical signaling on the link and conforms to the X.21 specification. The second layer creates an error-free path via the HDLC standard. The third layer creates and manages the virtual circuits that are multiplexed on the physical channel [14].

REFERENCES

The volumes listed in Refs. 1–4, 9, and 10 are general references and include material covering the entire area of computer communication networks.

1. J. LICKLIDER and A. VEZZA, "Applications of Information Networks," *Proc. IEEE,* **66**(11), 1330–1346 (Nov. 1978).

2. S. WECKER, "Computer Network Architectures," *Computer,* **12**(9), 58–72 (Sept. 1979).

3. H. ZIMMERMAN, "ISO Reference Model—The ISO Model of Architecture for Open Systems Interconnection," *IEEE Trans. Commun.,* **COM-28**(4), 425–432 (Apr. 1980).

4. D. DAVIES, ET AL., *Computer Networks and Their Protocols,* Wiley, New York, 1979.

5. L. KLEINROCK, "Principles and Lessons in Packet Communications," *Proc. IEEE,* **66**(11), 1320–1329 (Nov. 1978).

6. R. SPROULL and D. COHEN, "High-Level Protocols," *Proc. IEEE,* **66**(11), 1371–1386 (Nov. 1978).

7. J. DAY, "Resource Sharing Protocols," *Computer,* **12**(9), 47–56 (Sept. 1979).

8. L. POUZIN and H. ZIMMERMAN, "A Tutorial on Protocols," *Proc. IEEE,* **66**(11), 1346–1370 (Nov. 1978).

9. J. MCNAMARA, *Technical Aspects of Data Communication,* Digital Press, Bedford, Mass., 1977.

10. D. DAVIES and D. BARBER, *Communication Networks for Computers,* Wiley, New York, 1973.

11. H. FOLTS, "Status Report on New Standards for DTE/DCE Interface Protocols," *Computer,* **12**(9), 12–19 (Sept. 1979).

12. W. PETERSON, *Error-Correcting Codes,* MIT Press, Cambridge, Mass., 1961.

13. M. SCHWARTZ and T. STERN, "Routing Techniques Used in Computer Communication Networks," *IEEE TRans. Commun.,* **COM-28**(4), 539–552 (Apr. 1980).

14. A. RYBCZYNSKI, "X.25 Interface and End-to-End Virtual Circuit Service Characteristics," *IEEE Trans. Commun.,* **COM-28**(4), 500–510 (Apr. 1980).

2.28 NETWORK COMMUNICATION

Stephen Rappaport and Graham Campbell

In this article various issues connected with computer communication in networks are discussed. Related material, concerned with terminal communications, can be found in Sec. 2.10.

The media used to effect computer communications may include wire (coaxial cable), terrestial radio, satellite radio, optical links, or some combination of these. When dedicated point-to-point links are used to connect a number of sites in a communication network, various circuit-, message-, or packet-switching strategies can be used. These are described in Secs. 2.28.1 and 2.28.2.

In many cases of practical interest, however, the transmission medium is pervasive and can be easily and directly accessed by many system users. Typical of these are certain radio and satellite channels, although some wire facilities with simple user taps have similar properties. The use of such channels in combination with packet switching has given rise to an important special class of techniques collectively known as packet broadcasting. The context and essential features of these are explained in Sec. 2.28.3.

2.28.1 Classification of Switching Techniques

Graham Campbell

Network switching techniques for computer-to-computer communication may be characterized by two basic attributes, the use of intermediate storage for data along the transmission path and the use of static/dynamic allocation of resources for communication between two specified hosts. When intermediate storage is used, a block of data is transmitted from the storage of one node to the storage of the next, then the second node initiates transmission to the third, and so on until the final destination is reached. The term *store-and-forward* is used to describe this mode of operation.

When dynamic resource allocation is used, the resources necessary for communication, such as buffer space, communication line bandwidth, and route through the network, are assigned for each data block and released when that block is transmitted. Usually, these allocation decisions are made independently at each node. In this case some care must be taken in the design of the routing algorithm [16]. A route through the network requires the cooperation of the network nodes, since a local routing algorithm can only determine the next node to which the data are forwarded. In a complicated network it might be possible to keep sending the data around a loop without delivering them to their destination unless the routing algorithm is properly designed.

When static allocation is used, there must be a technique for initially reserving the necessary resources (e.g., buffer allocation, bandwidth allocations, specific path through the network), then transmitting a number of blocks of data using those resources, and finally releasing the resources. In this case a central resource manager is sometimes used to make the allocation decisions, since this allows use of algorithms for global optimization in the use of resources.

The three useful combinations of these characteristics are:

1. *Static allocation, no storage.* This is called *circuit* or *line switching.* The switched telephone network is the best known example of circuit switching. In the design of these networks, the major concerns are techniques for selecting a path through the network and allocation of bandwidth on shared communication lines.

2. *Static allocation with storage.* In this mode of operation a store-and-forward technique is used. A major concern in the design of these networks is the degree to which the allocation decisions are centralized. Since allocation decisions are made only once at the beginning of a communication period, the extra overhead of sending a request to a central site and waiting for a resource allocation determination may well be paid back by the more efficient use of the resources.

3. *Dynamic allocation with storage.* There are two subtypes of this mode of operation, *message switching* and *packet switching.* With message switching, an entire message is treated as the unit of data to be moved from node to node using a store-and-forward technique. Since a message may be quite long, auxiliary storage (e.g., disk) is normally required at each node. With packet switching the message to be sent is broken into small units (at either the sending host or within the network) called *packets.* Each packet is sent independently and they are reassembled at the ultimate destination.

The major concerns here are the algorithms for resource allocation. Since the allocation decisions are made very frequently, fast algorithms are necessary, yet they must be moderately sophisticated to achieve good overall use of resources when the decisions are made independently at each node.

Although the previous classifications are convenient for explaining the principles involved, they are not rigidly adhered to in practice. For example, the static allocation technique is frequently used without bandwidth preallocation, thus introducing some additional contention. Some dynamic allocation schemes keep buffers assigned in anticipation of use, thus approximating a static allocation scheme for a period of time.

2.28.2 Characteristics of Switching Techniques

Graham Campbell

Circuit Switching

Circuit switching offers to the connected hosts a direct electrical connection. It is the most transparent connection technique, requiring only hardware interfacing, with no software interface needed. The software designer may specialize communication techniques to optimize usage and, since there is no network overhead, very effective use of available bandwidth is possible. The initial establishment of the circuit may be quite time consuming (several seconds for the switched telephone network); thus this is best adapted for lengthy communication. Because of the physical connection, both source and destination must use the same transmission speeds, character codes, communication protocols, and so on.

Static Allocation with Storage

This shares with circuit switching the predictability of network characteristics since resources, such as bandwidth, are preallocated. Thus once a connection has been established, contention is minimized. Because incoming data are completely received and stored before being transmitted, the transmission speeds, character codes, and communication protocols need not be the same for output from a node as present in the input to the node (provided, of course, that there is sufficient intelligence in the switching node to perform the translation). Accounting for resource usage (and hence billing for them) is simplified, which makes the technique attractive for some commercial networks. Because of the delays in allocating resources prior to transmission, this is best adapted for lengthy communication.

Dynamic Allocation with Storage

Because of the contention possibilities inherent in any dynamic allocation scheme, network characteristics such as response time and throughput are subject to random variations and will change with general network load. Since this is a store-and-forward technique, speed, character code, and protocol transformations are possible between source and destination. There is no delay for initial establishment of a connection; however, there is network overhead as extra information must be transmitted with each unit of data (addressing information, etc.).

Message Switching. This subtype is a low-performance, high-reliability technique. Performance is limited since the entire message must be received (and stored) at each network node before transmission to the next node is started. Thus if a message must transit n intermediate nodes from source to destination, the total transmission time is $(n + 1)t$, where t is the time it takes to transmit a message between two consecutive nodes. Reliability is high because disk storage (the usual auxiliary storage medium) is more reliable than random-access storage and because host or node failures while a message is in transit can be handled in a direct manner, retaining the message in the network until it can be correctly delivered. This scheme also allows a higher apparent system availability, since a message may be accepted for a destination that is not operating at that time. The message is simply stored within the network until the destination is again available. Because of the inherent performance limitation, this scheme is normally used only when relatively long delivery times (say the order of minutes) are acceptable. This means that low-speed transmission lines may be used and their usage highly optimized. If the network is multiply connected (more than one path from source to destination is available), performance may be improved by sending different messages on alternate paths.

Packet Switching. This subtype is generally used for high-performance, general-purpose networks. The major improvement in performance compared to message switching comes from allowing each node to be transmitting one packet of a message while receiving another, thus stacking the packets into a "pipeline" effect [17]. If there are p packets in a message that must be sent across n intermediate nodes, and if the time to send a single packet between two consecutive nodes is t, the total transmission time is $(n + p)t$. Note that, in the same notation, the transmission time using message switching would be $(n + 1)(pt)$. Additional performance improvements may be made by sending packets along alternate routes (if they exist), thus using two or more paths in parallel to transmit a single message. The dynamic selection of a path through the network on a packet-by-packet basis offers both performance and reliability advantages. Performance is improved by selecting the least congested path from source to destination. Reliability is improved since packets may be automatically sent around failing communication lines (if an alternate path exists). However, the price paid for this adaptation is a variation of network delays depending on the network loading that is, in general, not predictable.

2.28.3 Packet Broadcasting

Stephen S. Rappaport

Channel-Sharing Concepts

Digital data communication is the process of transferring digital information from one geographical location to another. If a single transmitter is connected by wire to a single (dedicated) receiver, there is no problem concerning *access* to the medium; it is available to the transmitter for its exclusive use 100 percent of the time. This is called *fixed access*, or fixed assignment. If the medium were a satellite link, the transmitter/receiver pair might be linked by a fixed frequency channel centered at a carrier frequency reserved for the exclusive use of this pair using any suitable modulation–demodulation scheme. Many such frequency channels may be provided by a single satellite transponder, with each channel reserved for a particular transmitter/receiver pair. In this way *many* separate users have *access* to the *common facilities* (satellite transponder bandwidth). This is called *multiple access*. Since the transponder channels are separated in the frequency domain (as in frequency-division multiplexing), the above is an example of *frequency-division multiple access*, commonly denoted FDMA. Furthermore, since the FDMA channels are dedicated to specific transmitter/receiver pairs, this is fixed assigned FDMA.

Another way to provide multiple access to a common bandwidth is to separate signals in the time domain, as in time-division multiplexing. In this case a system clock would be used to enable all users to establish common system timing. The time axis would be divided into fixed time periods called *frames*, and each frame in turn subdivided into smaller time periods called *slots*. The first slot of each frame can be fixed assigned to the first transmitter/receiver pair, the second to the next, and so on. This scheme then provides for bandwidth sharing using fixed assigned *time-division multiple access* (TDMA).

In many cases of practical interest, fixed assignment of communication system resources to users (or user pairs) is grossly inefficient. For example, data communications generated by computer–computer transactions and terminal equipment are typically very bursty. The ratio of peak to average data rate can be as high as 2000 : 1, depending on line speed. A fixed assigned high-speed link from a bursty source would be idle most of the time; a low-speed link (with appropriate buffering) would introduce inordinate delay in the transmission of each data burst. The low channel utilization due to fixed assignment of resources to bursty users can be alleviated by allowing the high-speed channel or channels provided by the medium to be used by more than just one single user. Without fixed assignment there will in general be contention among system users for communication resources. Part of the communication protocol must be devoted to resolving such contention. Packet switching can provide a satisfactory solution for computer communication networks with dedicated point-to-point links between switching nodes. Various forms of polling may also be appropriate in certain applications.

Certain types of communications channels by their nature are essentially of *broadcast* type. That is, the transmissions of a user are "heard" by many other users. Typical of these are satellite channels where downlink transmissions are heard by all users within the satellite's field of coverage, and nondirectional terrestrial radio channels. Such channels can also easily be used in multiple-access modes since many users can transmit on the channel. A significant feature of such *broadcast channels* is that they provide complete connectivity among users within the system's field of coverage.

Packet broadcasting refers to the use of broadcast channels for transmitting data *packets*. Such techniques are characterized by special features that offer significant advantages in particular situations. Notable among these are the elimination of the need for routing and network switches (and the complex algorithms they entail), and the ability to communicate relatively easily with mobile users in the field of coverage.

Much of the pioneering work on such schemes was performed in connection with the University of Hawaii's ALOHA System. In the simplest of these schemes (*pure Aloha*), users in the coverage area organize the information to be sent into *packets*, containing a header with ID and control information, data, and parity check bits. Users transmit their packets on the broadcast channel without any user–user synchronization. A short segment of unmodulated carrier preceding the header information is used to facilitate acquisition of the packet by the intended receiver. Typically, individual users have low duty cycles. Transmissions on the broadcast channel are therefore characterized by short high-rate bursts occurring at random time instants. Since each user makes use of the channel at random time instants, this is called *random access*.

In the Aloha system, the basic problem was to provide communications between any individual system user and a single central station. The individual system users were geographically dispersed. Two 100-kHz broadcast channels were used. The *forward* channel for communications to the central station was operated in the unsynchronized random access mode described above. Transmissions are relatively short bursts because individual users attempt to use the full 100-kHz bandwidth. The *reverse* channel, which is broadcast from the central to the users, is used without contention since only the central may transmit on it. A user who has a data packet to send to the central transmits it on the forward channel immediately and maintains the contents of the packet until an acknowledgment from the central is received via the reverse broadcast channel. No new packets are originated by this user until the contents of the previously transmitted packet are released. The elapsed time before release must be greater than the round-trip propagation time (from the user to central and return) plus the processing time required at the central and at the user.

The central monitors the forward channel and checks parity of the packets that it receives using a suitable error-detecting code. A positive acknowledgment (addressed to the sending user) is broadcast by the central via the reverse channel for any packet that it receives without error. A *cyclic redundancy check code* can provide essentially perfect error detection (probability of undetected packet error less than 10^{-9}) with 32 check bits. The central will not respond to packets with detected errors or to packets that it did not successfully demodulate because of failure to acquire the accompanying pilot.

When two or more packets overlap one another in time, a "collision" is said to occur. If the *signal-to-noise ratio* on the forward channel is sufficiently high, most damaged packets will be caused by such overlapping packet transmissions (collisions) on the random-access channel. No acknowledgments will be sent for these packets.

If a user who has transmitted a packet to the central does not receive an acknowledgment for that packet by the end of the waiting period, the user enters a retransmission mode and retransmits the packet after a random retransmission delay. This randomization of retransmission time is required to prevent recurrent interference among the same users.

Figure 1 schematically shows the activity on a random-access Aloha channel. Each letter denotes the user that generated the corresponding packet. New packets are shown unshaded, retransmissions are shaded. Since the users have a low duty cycle, the collision probability will be small if there are not too many users sharing the channel. However, if either the number of users or the duty cycle of each is increased, the number of collisions will tend to increase. The channel can then become saturated with retransmissions. Few, if any, users will be in their origination mode; most users will be *retransmitting* packets that will be continuously colliding with one another.

Throughput and Delay

An elegantly simple approximate analysis has been put forth to describe the Aloha channel and its characteristics [1,2]. In this model it is assumed that the start times of packets on the channel (as shown by the points in Fig. 1) comprise a *Poisson point process* with a parameter Λ packets per second. Strictly, the Poisson model is inconsistent with the collision–retransmission procedure described above; a Poisson point process is memoryless and the procedure clearly is not. Nevertheless, if the random rescheduling delays are generally large compared with a packet duration, the effect of this assumption on the *expected value measures* of system performance to be described is small. The probability of there being exactly k points (start times) in any interval of length T is given by

$$P(k) = \frac{(\Lambda T)^k}{k!} e^{-\Lambda T} \tag{1}$$

The *normalized channel traffic* is defined as

$$G = \Lambda \tau \tag{2}$$

where τ denotes the duration of each packet on the channel. G is a dimensionless quantity that is indicative of activity on the random-access channel. It is, in fact, the average number of packet transmissions (including both new and retransmitted packets) during a packet duration.

For sufficiently high SNR, those packets that do not collide will be received correctly by the central. A given packet on the channel will not collide with any other if there is no other starting time τ seconds before or after its own. Under the Poisson assumption (1) the probability of this event is $e^{-2\Lambda\tau}$. Letting Λ_0 denote the rate at which packets are received correctly, one finds

$$\Lambda_0 = \Lambda e^{-2\Lambda\tau} \tag{3}$$

Multiplying both sides of (3) by τ yields

$$S = G e^{-2G} \tag{4}$$

where

$$S \triangleq \Lambda_0 \tau \tag{5}$$

is the *normalized channel throughput*. If a channel were perfectly scheduled and if there were sufficient demand, all new packets could be placed end to end without overlap. The throughput S would be equal to unity. The normalized throughput represents the utilization of the forward channel (ignoring the overhead cost of pilot, control information, and parity-check digits.) Values of S less than unity indicate wasted channel time attributable to idle time (because of random arrivals) and destructive

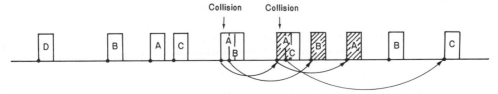

Fig. 1   Activity on random-access (unslotted) Aloha channel.

interference (*collisions*). A sketch of (4) is shown in Fig. 2, from which it can be seen that the pure Aloha channel can achieve a maximum utilization of only $1/2e \simeq 0.184$ when the channel traffic G is 0.5. This maximum utilization is called the *Aloha capacity* of the channel.

This concept should be distinguished from both the information theoretic (*Shannon*) *capacity*, and from the concept of *line speed*, which is also sometimes (loosely) called capacity. It is important to note that in general it may be neither possible nor desirable to operate an Aloha channel at capacity when consideration is given to resulting packet delay and to marginal stability of the system. Thus only values of utilization lower than $1/2e$ can be obtained by this scheme in practice; and this still does not account for the forward channel overhead mentioned above. These low values of utilization are in a sense the price paid for the extreme simplicity of both the scheme and the equipment required.

The delay in getting a packet through the channel will depend on the number of times it has to be retransmitted before succeeding. The average number of retransmissions per new packet is $(G/S)-1$ $= e^{2G}-1$, and the average normalized delay (measured in packet durations) is given approximately by

$$\overline{D} = R + 1 + \left(e^{2G} - 1 \right)\left(R + 1 + \overline{T}_r \right) \tag{6}$$

where $R=$ round-trip delay (in packet durations) from user to receiver and return
$\quad\quad \overline{T}_r=$ average rescheduling delay in packet durations

(*Note:* Here the value $\overline{T}_r = 0$ would imply that packets are retransmitted immediately after the waiting period.) On terrestrial channels the value of R can be quite low, that is, of the order of a normalized packet duration (unity), or less. However, for channels using satellites in geostationary orbit, R typically would be much greater than unity. A conceptually simple variation of the scheme suitable for multiple point-to-point communications between system users themselves employs acknowledgments on the Aloha channel [3].

Because of the low channel utilization of pure Aloha, some effort has been devoted to variations of the basic scheme that provide greater throughput. All of these in some sense require increased coordination among the system users. A simple modification of the basic scheme is to use a central clock to establish a common time base for all active system users [4]. Since all active users monitor the reverse channel, the needed timing can be derived from this channel. The time base is used to segment the forward channel into slots of the same duration as a packet. Users who have packets to transmit must begin transmission at the beginning of a slot. Partial overlapping of packet transmissions on the channel is thereby eliminated. In this *slotted Aloha* scheme a given packet on the channel will not collide with any other if no other user gets ready during the previous slot interval. Using (1), the probability of this event is $e^{-\Lambda\tau}$. Thus the average rate at which packets are received correctly in this scheme is

$$\Lambda_0 = \Lambda e^{-\Lambda\tau} \quad\quad \text{packets/second} \tag{7}$$

Multiplication of both sides of (7) by τ gives

$$S = Ge^{-G} \tag{8}$$

as the relation between normalized throughput and channel traffic in this scheme. This relationship is also sketched in Fig. 2 from which it can be seen that the slotted Aloha channel can achieve a maximum utilization of $1/e$ when the channel traffic G is 1.0. Thus by the introduction of slotting the capacity of the forward channel is doubled but is still less than 37 percent of what could be attained if the channel were perfectly scheduled.

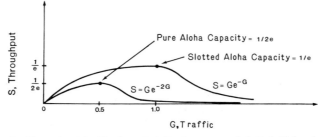

Fig. 2   Throughput-traffic characteristics for pure and slotted Aloha channels.

It is interesting to note that system capacity is affected by the relative demands of user access. For example, if a slotted Aloha system has a large number of low-duty-cycle users (typical of data terminals) and a single user who accesses the channel more often (perhaps a file transfer device), the capacity of the channel will exceed $1/e$ even though all users access at random. Physically, this is because the packets of the single heavy user will not interfere with one another; the significant component of traffic contributed by the heavy user faces less contention than an equivalent amount of traffic from independent users. This phenomenon has been termed *excess capacity*.

In calculating the average normalized delay experienced by a packet in the slotted Aloha scheme, it must be noted that randomized rescheduling delays for packets that have previously collided are still needed to prevent recurrent interference among users. A detailed analysis of delay characteristics is given in Ref. 5. If (when required) a packet is *retransmitted* (with equal probability of $1/K$) in any of the K slots following the propagation delay R, the average normalized delay is given by

$$\bar{D} = R + 1.5 + (e^G - 1)\frac{R + 1 + (K - 1)}{2} \tag{9}$$

which includes a half-packet delay to account for a user's being ready to transmit at any time before the beginning of a slot interval [6].

By letting G take on various values in (4) and (6), a plot of average delay ($\bar{D}$) versus throughput (S) can easily be obtained for the unslotted scheme. A similar plot can be obtained for slotted Aloha using (8) and (9). Typically, for very small values of G (and therefore of S), pure Aloha gives smaller delays for the same throughput. This is because in pure Aloha a user does not have to wait for the beginning of the next slot before packet transmission. However, for larger values of S the effect of collisions and retransmissions becomes more pronounced and slotted Aloha not only gives smaller delays but can also achieve higher throughputs (up to twice the capacity of pure Aloha).

Additional related schemes have been proposed which can achieve throughputs somewhat greater than the $1/e$ of slotted Aloha. Generally, these fit into one or the other of two categories: those employing carrier sensing and those employing reservations (demand assignment).

In the carrier-sensing schemes, just prior to transmission each user senses the broadcast channel and defers packet transmission if the presence of another transmission is detected. A family of such packet broadcasting protocols has been proposed and analyzed in detail [7]. Members of the family differ in the action taken by deferring users. In networks where the maximum signal propagation time is small compared to the duration of a packet, carrier-sensing techniques can provide significant increases in channel throughput compared with pure and slotted Aloha. They are useful mostly for terrestrial packet broadcasting configurations. These may include radio propagation over several hundred miles, or wire communications over only several miles, as in Ethernet [8]. A notable feature of the architecture of Ethernet is its use of packet broadcast techniques similar in nature to those of the Aloha concept but on a "broadcast channel" provided by a simple coaxial cable into which individual system users are tapped. Thus packet broadcasting is not limited to radio or satellite channels as one might at first suppose; rather, it can be a reasonable alternative to polling and to ring-switched configurations on local wire networks.

In the reservation schemes, users generally first contend for space on the channel, but then use the channel in a well-ordered manner for message transmission. In one such scheme, users employ two types of packets and the forward channel employs frames as well as slots [9]. The frames consist of $M + 1$ slots, each having the same duration as a message packet. One of the slots is subdivided into smaller request slots. A user who has a message packet to transmit first sends a smaller request packet in a randomly selected request slot. The request packet may collide with requests transmitted by other users. A user whose request succeeds obtains a reservation to transmit its message packet in the earliest unreserved message slot. Reservations for requests that succeed in the same frame are ordered by prior agreement according to position of the corresponding request slot. Thus, as in slotted Aloha, there is random-access contention for reservations; however, an orderly queue for message slots develops during system operation. This queue is a single-server queue, even though the waiting packets are distributed throughout the system at the user stations. When there are no reservations outstanding, all slots in the frame become reservation slots; this reduces reservation delay for low values of traffic.

In a properly sized system with sufficient traffic demand, few message slots will be idle; and since there are no collisions in the message slots, most of each frame will be used for successful data transfer. Channel utilizations (throughput) which are significantly greater than the basic Aloha schemes are attainable.

An important issue is supervision of the reservation queue; there can be a central controller or control can be distributed among system users. In the former case all users listen to reservations by monitoring communications from a central station. This affords some simplicity. but a minimum two-hop propagation time (user to central and return) is required to secure a reservation. In a system employing a satellite in geostationary orbit, this two-hop delay is considerable; it is about 0.54 s if the users and the central are on the ground, but is halved if the central controller is on the satellite itself.

If distributed control is used, each system user can monitor the satellite's downlink transmissions and hear successful requests of its own as well as that of other users. Each user can maintain a counter indicating the number of outstanding reservations; the counters are incremented for each successful request and decremented for each message slot as time progresses. In this way distributed control is achieved by having each user execute the same algorithm based on downlink transmissions and the state of its own counter. To avoid destructive interference of message transmissions, it is critical that all users' counters be in synchronism. It is therefore necessary to incorporate additional algorithms whereby individual users can identify their own lack of *queue synchronization* and also acquire such synchronization [10] with minimal impact on normal system operation. This may entail some additional complexity in hardware and software and some additional overhead in packet transmissions.

A number of other reservation schemes have also been proposed and are described briefly in Ref. 10, which contains an extensive bibliography. One uses a frame structure; each user is assigned a slot in the frame which it uses both to send data and to make reservations for unused slots. Another employs reservation-by-use, wherein a user is assured a reservation in the corresponding slot of the next frame. Although many *packet broadcasting* schemes (inspired by Aloha) employ *collision-type channels*, the two concepts are quite distinct; a reservation scheme using fixed assigned request slots is described in Ref. 10. A demand assigned scheme which employs *multiple-collision-type request channels* and *multiple message* channels is described and compared with alternatives in Ref. 11.

Stability

In schemes that employ collision channels, the possibility of system instability is an important issue; care must be taken to assure stable operation. Unstable operation may arise when a large number of interfering transmissions occur in a short time. The number of users in the retransmission mode and the rate of retransmission will then increase. This will further increase the collision rate, even more users will enter the retransmission mode, and so on.

The approximate analytical description of the stability problem given below is based on the more complete and rigorous accounts of Refs. 12 and 13. Consider a pure Aloha system with a large number of active users M, of which n are at some time in the retransmission mode. We assume that a user in the origination mode generates new packets with an average interarrival interval of Λ_0^{-1} seconds and that a user in the retransmission mode retransmits packets with an average interarrival interval of Λ_r^{-1} seconds. Thus the total average rate of packet transmissions on the collision channels is $\Lambda_0(M-n)+\Lambda_r n$. Assuming that these arrivals follow a Poisson point process, the average number of packets that succeed during a packet duration τ is given by (4), where the channel traffic, G, is given by

$$G = \Lambda_0\tau(M-n)+\Lambda_r\tau n \tag{10}$$

The average number of *new* packets that are offered to the system per packet duration is

$$S_{\text{in}} = \Lambda_0\tau(M-n) \tag{11}$$

The difference $S_{\text{in}} - S$ is proportional to the average net rate at which users enter the retransmission mode (i.e., the rate at which n tends to increase). With Λ_0, λ_r, τ, and M fixed, a plot of S_{in} versus G can be obtained as n assumes values from 0 to M. With $\Lambda_r > \Lambda_0$, G increases and S_{in} decreases with increasing n. A plot of G versus S_{in} is a straight line having a G intercept of $M\Lambda_r\tau$ and a slope of $-(\Lambda_r - \Lambda_0)/\Lambda_r$. Several such "load lines," labeled a–f, representing different choices of parameters, are shown in Fig. 3. As the number n of users in the retransmission mode changes, the system operating point moves along the load line. Also shown in the figure is the relation (4) required by the Aloha channel.

When S_{in} exceeds S, the average *net* number of users entering the retransmission mode per packet duration is positive and n tends to increase. Conversely, n tends to decrease for $S_{\text{in}} < S$. The arrows in Fig. 3 indicate the direction of expected net drift of the system operating point. Circles indicate locally stable operating points.

It can be seen that, depending on parameter choices, a "load line" can intersect the channel contour in one, two, or three points. If there is one intersection, the system has a unique stable operating point. This can be at a point where few users are in the retransmission mode and S_{in} is below or near capacity, as shown by load lines a and b. On the other hand, the intersection can be at a point that is much less than capacity and almost all users are in the retransmission mode, as depicted by load lines c and d. If there are three intersections, as shown by load line e, there are two stable operating points. One corresponds to a relatively large S and small G and is a desirable point since it corresponds to relatively small delays; the other, with a small S and large G, is undesirable. For the choice of parameters represented by load line e, the system packet transmission instants will cause the system to shift from one point to another (system thrashing) and even to linger about the undesirable equilibrium point for considerable periods of time. If there are two intersection points, as shown by

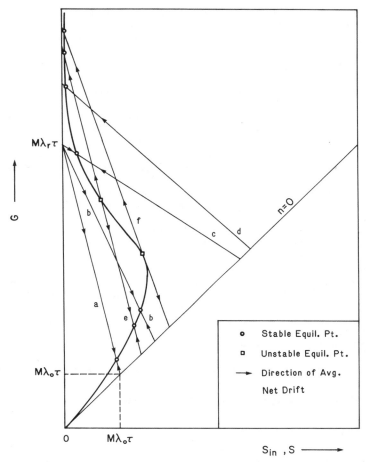

Fig. 3 Stability of Aloha channels. Circles denote stable equilibrium points; squares denote unstable equilibrium points; arrows denote the direction of the average net drift.

load line f, there is again only one stable equilibrium point, and this yields a throughput somewhat less than capacity; operation at this point is undesirable.

In practice, the assurance of stable behavior by selecting appropriate values of M, Λ_0, Λ_r, and τ may lead to unreasonable parameter choices in some situations; hence some effort has gone into developing dynamic control procedures for potentially bistable systems [14]. Roughly, these procedures vary Λ_0 and Λ_r as a function of n. Each user must therefore obtain estimates of n from the system and adjust transmission rates appropriately. Note that with Λ_0 and Λ_r dependent on n, the curve of S_{in} versus G may no longer be linear. Stability problems and dynamic control procedures for carrier-sense schemes have also been described in the literature [15].

The reader's attention is called to the special issues of the journals in which Refs. 2 and 10 appear. These issues contain many pertinent articles and references.

REFERENCES

1. N. ABRAMSON, "The Aloha System," in *Computer Communication Networks*, Prentice-Hall, Englewood Cliffs, N.J., 1973.

2. N. ABRAMSON, "The Throughput of Packet Broadcasting Channels," *IEEE Trans. Commun.*, **COM-25**(1), 117–128 (Jan. 1977).

3. T. J. KLEIN, "A Tactical Packet Radio System," *Proc. Natl. Telecommun. Conf.*, New Orleans, La., Dec. 1975.

4. L. G. ROBERTS, "Aloha Packet System with and without Slots and Capture," *Comput. Commun. Rev.*, **5**, 28–42 (Apr. 1975).

5. L. KLEINROCK and S. S. LAM, "Packet-Switching in a Slotted Satellite Channel," *AFIPS Conf. Proc.*, **42**, 703–710 (June 1973).

6. M. SCHWARTZ, *Computer Communication Network Design and Analysis*, Prentice Hall, Englewood Cliffs, N.J., 1977, Chap. 13.

7. L. KLEINROCK and F. A. TOBAGI, "Packet Switching in Radio Channels: Parts I and II," *IEEE Trans. Commun.*, **COM-23**, 1400–1433 (Dec. 1975).

8. R. M. METCALFE and D. R. BOGGS, "Ethernet: Distributed Packet Switching for Local Computer Networks," *Commun. ACM*, **19**(7), 395–404 (July 1976).

9. L. G. ROBERTS, "Dynamic Allocation of Satellite Capacity through Packet Reservation," *Natl. Comput. Conf. AFIPS Conf. Proc.* **42**, 711–716 (1973).

10. I. M. JACOBS, R. BINDER, and E. V. HOVERSTEN, "General Purpose Packet Satellite Networks," *Proc. IEEE*, **66**(11), 1448–1467 (Nov. 1978).

11. S. S. RAPPAPORT, "Demand Assigned Multiple Access Systems Using Collision Type Request Channels: Traffic Capacity Comparisons," *IEEE Trans. Commun.*, **COM-27**(9), 1325–1331 (Sept. 1979).

12. A. B. CARLEIAL and M. E. HELLMAN, "Bistable Behavior of Aloha-Type Systems," *IEEE Trans. Commun.*, **COM-23**(4) 401–409 (Apr. 1975).

13. L. KLEINROCK and S. S. LAM, "Packet Switching in a Multiaccess Broadcast Channel: Performance Evaluation," *IEEE Trans. Commun*, **COM-23**(4), 410–422 (Apr. 1975).

14. S. S. LAM and L. KLEINROCK, "Packet Switching in a Multiaccess Broadcast Channel: Dynamic Control Procedures," *IEEE Trans. Commun. Technol.*, **COM-13**, 891–905 (Sept. 1975).

15. F. A. TOBAGI and L. KLEINROCK, "Packet Switching in Radio Channels, Part IV: Stability Considerations and Dynamic Control in Carrier Sense Multiple Access," *IEEE Trans. Commun.*, **COM-25**(10), 1103–1119 (Oct. 1977).

16. R. J. CYPSER, *Communications Architecture for Distributed Systems*, Addison-Wesley, Reading, Mass., 1978, Chap. 16.

17. L. KLEINROCK, *Queueing Systems*, Vol. 2: *Computer Applications*, Wiley, New York, p. 292.

2.29   ROUTING IN PACKET-SWITCHED NETWORKS

Yih-chyun Jenq

One of the basic problems in the design of modern data communication networks is to establish efficient routing procedures for fast delivery of messages to their destinations. Many routing algorithms have been proposed and implemented and some classifications and discussions of various algorithms have been reported [1–3,11]. One can classify these routing algorithms into three categories: static routing, quasistatic routing, and dynamic routing. Another classification distinguishes between centralized computation and distributed computation depending on whether the routing algorithm is executed at a control node or is done at each individual node in a coordinated manner.

In static routing, given fractions of the traffic at a node of the network destined for each of the other nodes are routed on each of its outgoing links. These fractions are predetermined based on some network information such as topology and average traffic requirement, and are fixed in time. Shortest-path and minimal-cost-flow algorithms [4,6] and the flow deviation algorithm [5] are typical methods for static routing. They are described in detail in Secs. 2.29.1 and 2.29.2, respectively.

In quasistatic routing, changes of routes are allowed only at given intervals of time and/or whenever extreme situations such as dramatic changes in traffic pattern or network topology occur. Dynamic routing allows continuous changes of routes to adapt to quick-changing traffic requirements. Both centralized computation and distributed computation techniques can be used for quasistatic routing. However, the problem of communicating control and traffic information through the network rules out the possibility of using centralized computation for dynamic routing. In Sec. 2.29.3 we describe a quasistatic algorithm using distributed computation [8,9,12] and in Sec. 2.29.4 the dynamic routing used for ARPANET is presented.

2.29.1   Shortest-Path and Minimal-Cost-Flow Algorithms

In this section we first describe an algorithm for finding a shortest path from a given starting node to another node in the network. A minimum-cost multicommodity flow algorithm is given in the second part of this section.

Consider a network $[N, L]$, where N is a set of n nodes and L is a set of b links. Every link L_{ij} of the network has associated with it a positive distance d_{ij}. The problem is to find a path from node N_s to node N_t with the sum of the distances d_{ij} of links in the path a minimum. The algorithm to be described is due to Hu [4] and Dijkstra [13]. It involves assigning labels to the nodes, either temporary or permanent, in a sequential manner. The label for node p is of the form $[q, \pi(p)]$, where $\pi(p)$ is the length of the shortest path found, as yet, between node N_s and p and the node immediately preceding p on this path is q. The labels are developed as follows:

Step 1. Assign a permanent label $[-, 0]$ to node N_s and a temporary label of $[-, \infty]$ to all other nodes. Go to step 3.

Step 2. Let T be the set of nodes with temporary labels. Find a node, p, in T such that

$$\pi(p) = \min_{k \in T} \pi(k)$$

Declare the label of p permanent. If $p = N_t$, the shortest path between N_s and N_t has been found. Otherwise, proceed to step 3.

Step 3. For each permanently labeled node p, consider every directly connected node, j, with a temporary label. If

$$\pi(p) + d_{pj} < \pi(j)$$

assign to each such j the new temporary label $[p, \pi(p) + d_{pj}]$. Go to step 2.

If this algorithm is expanded so that it terminates when all nodes have permanent labels, the shortest path between N_s and p has been determined for every node p in the network. Consider the network shown in Fig. 1, where the numbers beside the links are the distances and links are undirected. The labels derived sequentially are

N_s	1	2	3	4	N_t
$[-, 0]^0$	$[-, \infty]$	$[-, \infty]$	$[-, \infty]$	$[-, \infty]$	$[-, \infty]$
	$[N_s, 3]^3$	$[N_s, 3]$	$[N_s, 1]^1$		
		$[3, 2]^2$			$[3, 8]$
				$[2, 4]^4$	
					$[4, 7]^5$

where superscripts indicate the order in which labels are declared permanent. In this example the shortest path from N_s to N_t is N_s–3–2–4–N_t and the length is 7.

TYMNET, a computer-communication network developed in 1970 by Tymshare, Inc., uses a generalized version of the shortest-path algorithm for assigning message routes [3]. The path is newly selected each time a user comes on the network, but while the user maintains his or her current connection, the path chosen is unchanged. In this respect the route selection process is the same as that used in telephone circuit-switched networks. However, the messages are switched in a store-and-forward fashion, hence the technique is called virtual circuit switching (see Sec. 2.28). The routing algorithm, contained in the supervisory program, finds the path of current least cost from source terminal to destination computer. The distance d_{ij} assigned to each link expresses the cost associated with the transmission of data through the link. For example, the number 16 is assigned to a 2400-bps link, 12 to a 4800-bps link, and 10 to a 9600-bps link. A penalty of 16 is added if one node of the link complains of overloading and the penalty is 32 if both nodes complain. An infinite cost is added for nonfunctional links.

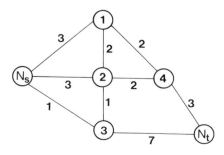

Fig. 1 Shortest-path algorithm.

We now consider the minimum-cost multicommodity flow problem. The algorithm presented here is due to Tomlin [6]. Consider the network $[N, L]$ with n nodes and b directed links. Assign each link L_{ij} a capacity $c_{ij} \geq 0$ and associate with it a cost $d_{ij} \geq 0$ per unit flow. For each commodity $k = 1, 2, \ldots, K$ denote the source node N_s^k and the sink node N_t^k and let the required flow of commodity k between these two nodes be r_k. Let f_{ij}^k be the flow of commodity k along the link L_{ij}. The problem is to find a set of flows $\{f_{ij}^k\}$ to meet the flow requirements and capacity constraints over an existing network at minimum cost. It is not difficult to see the analogy between the minimum-delay routing assignment and this minimum-cost multicommodity flow problem if we consider the message for a source-destination pair a commodity. There is a critical difference between these two problems, however. In the minimum-cost multicommodity flow problem considered here, the cost d_{ij} associated with link L_{ij} is a preassigned and *fixed* quantity, whereas for the minimum-delay routing assignment problem the delay (considered to be the cost) d_{ij} associated with each link L_{ij} is a function (in general a nonlinear function) of the flow assignment $\{f_{ij}^k\}$. This fact significantly complicates the problem. This problem can be handled by the flow deviation algorithm, which is the subject of Sec. 2.29.2.

The capacity constraints are

$$\sum_{k=1}^{K} f_{ij}^k \leq c_{ij}, \qquad i, j = 1, 2, \ldots, n \tag{1}$$

Each commodity must also satisfy the flow conservation requirements

$$\sum_{j=1}^{n} f_{ij}^k - f_{ji}^k = \begin{cases} r_k & \text{for } i = N_s^k \\ -r_k & \text{for } i = N_t^k \\ 0 & \text{otherwise} \end{cases} \tag{2}$$

In matrix notation, (2) can be expressed by

$$A\mathbf{f}^k = \mathbf{e}^k \tag{3}$$

where $\mathbf{f}^k$ is the flow vector $[f_{11}^k, f_{12}^k, \ldots, f_{1n}^k, \ldots, f_{nn}^k]^t$, where t represents the transpose operation, $\mathbf{e}^k$ is the n-dimensional vector obtained from the right-hand side of (2), and A is an $n \times n^2$ matrix obtained from the incidence matrix of the network. If we eliminate those flow variables associated with nonexistent links, the dimension of A will become $n \times b$.

Letting $\mathbf{c}$ be the vector of link capacities and $\mathbf{s}$ be the vector of slack variables, the capacity inequality constraints (1) become equality constraints and can be combined with (3) to form

$$\begin{bmatrix} I & I & \cdots & I \\ A & 0 & \cdots & 0 \\ 0 & A & & \cdot \\ \cdot & \cdot & & \cdot \\ \cdot & \cdot & & \cdot \\ 0 & 0 & \cdots A & 0 \end{bmatrix} \begin{bmatrix} \mathbf{f}^1 \\ \mathbf{f}^2 \\ \vdots \\ \vdots \\ \mathbf{f}^k \\ \mathbf{s} \end{bmatrix} = \begin{bmatrix} \mathbf{c} \\ \mathbf{e}^1 \\ \mathbf{e}^2 \\ \vdots \\ \vdots \\ \mathbf{e}^k \end{bmatrix} \tag{4}$$

where I is the n^2-dimensional identity matrix. The matrix on the left in (4) has the dimension $(nK + n^2) \times (n^2K + n^2)$. If we eliminate all flow variables associated with nonexistent links, I becomes b-dimensional and the dimension of that matrix becomes $(nK + b) \times (bK + b)$. We wish to minimize the total cost D,

$$D = \mathbf{d}^t \cdot (\mathbf{f}^1 + \mathbf{f}^2 + \cdots + \mathbf{f}^K) \tag{5}$$

where d is the cost vector $[d_{11}, d_{12}, \ldots, d_{1n}, \ldots, d_{nn}]^t$, subject to constraint (4) and $\mathbf{f}^k \geq 0$ for all $k = 1, 2, \ldots, K$.

The special structure of the matrix in (4) means that the linear program can be attacked by the decomposition principle. Let $W^k = \{\mathbf{w}_1^k, \mathbf{w}_2^k, \ldots, \mathbf{w}_{N_k}^k\}$ be the set of extreme point solutions to $A\mathbf{f}^k = \mathbf{e}^k$, where N_k is the number of extreme point solutions in each set $k = 1, 2, \ldots, K$. Then we may write $\mathbf{f}^k$ as a convex combination of the elements of W^k:

$$\mathbf{f}^k = \sum_{j=1}^{N_k} \lambda_j^k \mathbf{w}_j^k \tag{6}$$

where

$$\sum_{j=1}^{N_k} \lambda_j^k = 1 \quad \text{and} \quad \lambda_j^k \geq 0 \qquad \text{for all } j, k$$

Our original problem is then equivalent to

$$\min \left(\sum_{j=1}^{N_1} \lambda_j^1 \mathbf{d}^t \cdot \mathbf{w}_j^1 + \sum_{j=1}^{N_2} \lambda_j^2 \mathbf{d}^t \cdot \mathbf{w}_j^2 + \cdots + \sum_{j=1}^{N_K} \lambda_j^K \mathbf{d}^t \cdot \mathbf{w}_j^K \right) \tag{7}$$

subject to

$$\sum_{j=1}^{N_1} \lambda_j^1 \mathbf{w}_j^1 + \sum_{j=1}^{N_2} \lambda_j^2 \mathbf{w}_j^2 + \cdots + \sum_{j=1}^{N_K} \lambda_j^K \mathbf{w}_j^K + \mathbf{s} = \mathbf{c}$$

$$\sum_{j=1}^{N_1} \lambda_j^1 \qquad\qquad\qquad = 1 \tag{8}$$

$$\sum_{j=1}^{N_2} \lambda_j^2 \qquad\qquad = 1$$

$$\ddots \qquad\qquad\qquad \vdots$$

$$\sum_{j=1}^{N_K} \lambda_j^K \quad = 1$$

where $\lambda_j^k \geq 0$ for all $j = 1, 2, \ldots, N_k$ and $k = 1, 2, \ldots, K$.

This is a problem with $b + K$ equations and a large number of variables, where b is the number of (directed) links in the network.

Suppose that we have a basic feasible solution to this linear program and assign simplex multipliers $\pi_1, \pi_2, \ldots, \pi_b$ to the first b rows of (8) and $\alpha_1, \alpha_2, \ldots, \alpha_K$ to the remaining rows. Then, according to the column selection criterion for the revised simplex method [4], the column corresponding to $\mathbf{w}_j^k$ is introduced if

$$\mathbf{d}^t \cdot \mathbf{w}_j^k - \left(\boldsymbol{\pi}^t \cdot \mathbf{w}_j^k + \alpha_k \right) < 0 \tag{9}$$

But since $\mathbf{w}_j^k$ is an extreme point solution of $A\mathbf{f}^k = \mathbf{e}^k$, the most improving column, j, for commodity k can be found by solving the subproblem

$$\min (\mathbf{d} - \boldsymbol{\pi})^t \cdot \mathbf{w}^k$$

subject to $A\mathbf{w}^k = \mathbf{e}^k$, where $\mathbf{w}_k \geq 0$.

This subproblem involves finding a minimum cost flow without capacity constraints in a network with link costs obtained from $(\alpha - \pi)$. This subproblem can be solved by using the shortest-path algorithm described earlier in this section.

To obtain the initial basic feasible solution, we can use the "phase I" procedure [4] by adding artificial variables $x_1, x_2, \ldots, x_K$ to the last K rows of (8) and minimizing the new objective function $\sum_{i=1}^{K} x_i$ to zero.

2.29.2 Flow Deviation Method [5]

Consider a network of n nodes and b links. For each node N_i, it is required to route r_{ij} amount of data to another node, N_j. The matrix R with r_{ij} as its (i, j) element is called the traffic requirement matrix. Let $f_{kl}^{(ij)} \geq 0$ be the portion of data traffic from N_i to N_j flowing on the directed link L_{kl}. Then, similar to (2), we have the flow conservation equations

$$\sum_{k=1}^{n} f_{kl}^{(ij)} - \sum_{m=1}^{n} f_{lm}^{(ij)} = \begin{cases} -r_{ij} & \text{if } l=i \\ r_{ij} & \text{if } l=j \\ 0 & \text{otherwise} \end{cases} \quad \text{for all } i, j \qquad (10)$$

If we number links by $1, 2, \ldots, b$, the capacity constraint equations can be written as

$$\sum_{i=1}^{n} \sum_{j=1}^{n} f_k^{(ij)} \leq c_k, \qquad k = 1, 2, \ldots, b \qquad (11)$$

where c_k is the capacity of the kth link.

The routing problem can now be expressed in the following way:

Given: A network with n nodes and b links with capacities c_k, $k = 1, 2, \ldots, b$ and the traffic requirement matrix R.

Objective: To find a flow $\{f_{kl}^{(ij)}\}$ that minimizes a delay function D subject to the constraints (10) and (11).

The delay function D is assumed to be a function of total flow $f_k = \Sigma_i \Sigma_j f_k^{(ij)}$ on each link k. To emphasize this dependence we write $D = D(\mathbf{f})$, where $\mathbf{f}$ is the flow vector $\mathbf{f} = [f_1, f_2, \ldots, f_b]$. A frequently used formula for $D(\mathbf{f})$ is $D(\mathbf{f}) = [\Sigma_{k=1}^b f_k/(c_k - f_k)]/(\Sigma_i \Sigma_j r_{ij})$ [3]. We also assume that $D(\mathbf{f})$ is continuous with its first partial derivatives.

The key concept that leads to the flow deviation method is stationarity. The point $\mathbf{f}$ is said to be stationary if for any infinitesimal perturbation $\delta \mathbf{f}$, we have $D(\mathbf{f} + \delta \mathbf{f}) \geq D(\mathbf{f})$. The most general perturbation around a feasible point $\mathbf{f}$ can be obtained as a convex combination of $\mathbf{f}$ with any other feasible flow $\mathbf{v}$,

$$\mathbf{f}' = (1 - \lambda)\mathbf{f} + \lambda \mathbf{v} = \mathbf{f} + \lambda(\mathbf{v} - \mathbf{f}), \qquad 0 \leq \lambda \leq 1$$

If λ approaches zero, the flow deviation $\lambda(\mathbf{v} - \mathbf{f})$ is infinitesimal. For $\lambda = \delta\lambda \ll 1$, we have

$$\delta D(\mathbf{f}) = D(\mathbf{f}') - D(\mathbf{f})$$

$$= \delta\lambda \sum_{k=1}^{b} \frac{\partial D}{\partial f_k}(v_k - f_k)$$

where $\partial D/\partial f_k$ is evaluated at $\mathbf{f}$. Hence the flow $\mathbf{f}$ is stationary if $\Sigma_{k=1}^b (\partial D/\partial f_k)(v_k - f_k) \geq 0$ for any feasible flow $\mathbf{v}$. Possible perturbations of $\mathbf{f}$ include those in which only $\mathbf{f}^{(ij)}$ is changed. Thus the preceding argument also applies to each individual commodity. Therefore, we have

$$\sum_{k=1}^{b} \frac{\partial D}{\partial f_k}(v_k^{(ij)} - f_k^{(ij)}) \geq 0$$

for an feasible flow $\mathbf{v}$, where the feasibility here refers to the constraints for commodity (ij) only.

The condition $\Sigma_k (\partial D/\partial f_k)(v_k - f_k) \geq 0$ for all feasible flow $\mathbf{v}$ can be rewritten as

$$\min_{v \in V} \sum_{k=1}^{b} \frac{\partial D}{\partial f_k} v_k \geq \sum_{k=1}^{b} \frac{\partial D}{\partial f_k} f_k$$

where V is the set of all feasible flows. But since $\mathbf{f}$ itself is a feasible flow, we have

$$\min_{v \in V} \sum_{k=1}^{b} \frac{\partial D}{\partial f_k} v_k = \sum_{k=1}^{b} \frac{\partial D}{\partial f_k} f_k$$

Similarly, for each (ij) commodity, we have

$$\min_{v \in V^{(ij)}} \sum_{k=1}^{b} \frac{\partial D}{\partial f_k} v_k^{(ij)} = \sum_{k=1}^{b} \frac{\partial D}{\partial f_k} f_k^{(ij)}$$

The discussions above indicate that if $\mathbf{f}$ is not a stationary flow, the minimum-cost multicommodity flow with link metric $d_k = [\partial D / \partial f_k]$ evaluated at the current flow $\mathbf{f}$, $k = 1, 2, \ldots, b$, represents the flow deviation of steepest decrease for $D(\mathbf{f})$. This fact suggests the flow deviation method to be described below, for finding the stationary point. If $D(\mathbf{f})$ is a convex function, the stationary flow, if it exists, is unique and is a global minimum.

We now describe the flow deviation algorithm.

Step 1. Find a feasible starting flow $\mathbf{f}^{(0)}$.

Step 2. Compute $\mathbf{v}^{(m)}$, the minimum-cost multicommodity flow with link metric $d_k = [\partial D / \partial f_k]_{\mathbf{f} = \mathbf{f}^{(m)}}$, $k = 1, 2, \ldots, b$.

Step 3. Let $\bar{\lambda}$ be the minimizer of $D((1-\lambda)\mathbf{f}^{(m)} + \lambda \mathbf{v}^{(m)})$, $0 \leqslant \lambda \leqslant 1$. Let $\mathbf{f}^{(m+1)} = (1-\bar{\lambda})\mathbf{f}^{(m)} + \bar{\lambda}\mathbf{v}^{(m)}$.

Step 4. If $|D(\mathbf{f}^{(m+1)}) - D(\mathbf{f}^{(m)})| < \epsilon$, then stop and $\mathbf{f}^{(m)}$ is optimized to within the given tolerance. Otherwise, let $m = m + 1$ and go to step 2.

To find the feasible starting flow, $\mathbf{f}^{(0)}$, we first pick a flow $\mathbf{f}$ satisfying (10) without the capacity constraints (11), and then reduce the flows in all links by a scaling factor S until a feasible flow $\mathbf{f}^{(0)} = S \cdot \mathbf{f}$, satisfying the capacity constraints (11), is obtained. This flow, $\mathbf{f}^{(0)}$, satisfies a reduced traffic requirement matrix $R_0 = S \cdot R$. The flow deviation method is applied using $\mathbf{f}^{(0)}$ as the starting flow and R_0 as the starting traffic requirement matrix. After each iteration the value of scaling factor S is increased up to a level very close to saturation on links. The search for a feasible flow terminates when one of the following two cases occurs: either $S \geqslant 1$, and a feasible flow is found; or the network is saturated, $D(\mathbf{f})$ is minimized, and S converges to a number less than 1. In the latter case the problem is infeasible.

The computation of the minimum-cost multicommodity flow $\mathbf{v}^{(m)}$ can be carried out by the algorithm described in the previous section. The flow deviation method, as described above, provides only the optimum global flow $\mathbf{f}$. If complete information about the routes taken by each commodity is required, an updating of routing tables at each iteration should also be carried out.

2.29.3   Quasistatic Routing Using Distributed Computation

In this section we present a routing algorithm using distributed computation. This algorithm is due to Gallager [8] and is suitable for quasistatic environments. For stationary input traffic, the average delay per packet through the network converges, with successive updates of the routing tables, to the minimum average delay over all routing assignments. This algorithm also guarantees a loop-free routing—an important characteristic for distributed computation algorithms.

Consider a network $[N, L]$ with n nodes and b links and let us assume that if the link (i, k) exists, the link (k, i) does also. Let $r_i(j)$ be the expected traffic entering the network at node i and destined for node j, and $t_i(j)$ be the total expected traffic at node i [including $r_i(j)$ and traffic routed through node i] destined for node j. A routing policy is defined in terms of the fraction $\phi_{ik}(j)$ of the node flow $t_i(j)$ that is routed through the link (i, k). A routing variable set ϕ must satisfy the following conditions:

1. $\phi_{ik}(j) = 0$ if (i, k) is not a link.
2. $\sum_k \phi_{ij}(j) = 1$.

If we further assume that for each i, j $(i \neq j)$ there is a routing path from i to j, i.e., there is a sequence of nodes $i, k, l, \ldots, m, j$ such that $\phi_{ik}(j) > 0, \phi_{kl}(j) > 0, \ldots$, and $\phi_{mj}(j) > 0$. Then the following conservation equations have a unique solution [8]:

$$t_i(j) = r_i(j) + \sum_k t_k(j)\phi_{ki}(j), \qquad \text{all } i, j \quad \text{and} \quad i \neq j$$

Let D_{ik} be the expected number of packets per unit time transmitted on link (i, k) times the expected delay per packet on the link. It is assumed to be a function only of the total link flow $f_{ik} = \sum_j t_i(j)\phi_{ik}(j)$. Since the total packet arrival rate $\sum_i \sum_j r_i(j)$ is independent of the routing assignment, we can minimize the expected delay per packet on the network by minimizing the total delay per unit time, D, where

$$D = \sum_{i,k} D_{ik}(f_{ik})$$

It was shown in Ref. 8 that if $D_{ik}(f_{ik})$ is convex cup (U) and continuously differentiable for $0 \leqslant f_{ik} \leqslant c_{ik}$ where c_{ik} is the link capacity, then a sufficient condition for a routing variable set ϕ to minimize D is

$$D'_{ik}(f_{ik}) + \frac{\partial D}{\partial r_k(j)} = \min_{m:\,(i,m)\in L} \left[D'_{im}(f_{im}) + \frac{\partial D}{\partial r_m(j)} \right] \qquad \text{for all } i \neq j$$

where $(i,k)\in L$ for $\phi_{ik}(j) > 0$ and $D'_{ik}(f_{ik})$ is the derivative $dD_{ik}(f_{ik})/df_{ik}$.

The algorithm is based on this result and can be described as follows. A routing variable $\phi_{ik}(j)$ is said to be improper if $\phi_{ik}(j) > 0$ and $\partial D/\partial r_i(j) < \partial D/\partial r_k(j)$. A node k is said to be blocked relative to j if node k has a routing path to node j containing some link (l,m) for which $\phi_{lm}(j)$ is improper and

$$\phi_{lm}(j) \geq \frac{\eta \left[D'_{lm}(f_{lm}) + \partial D/\partial r_m(j) - \partial D/\partial r_l(j) \right]}{t_l(j)} \tag{12}$$

where η is a scaling factor to be discussed later.

The set $B_i(j)$ is defined to be the set of nodes, k, for which either node k is blocked relative to j and $\phi_{ik}(j) = 0$ or there is no link from node i to node k.

The algorithm is not permitted to increase $\phi_{ik}(j)$ from 0 for those nodes in the set $B_i(j)$. This is required if the algorithm is to guarantee loop-free routing. The procedure for determining the set $B_i(j)$ will be given later.

The algorithm A, on each iteration, maps the current routing variable ϕ into a new set $\bar{\phi} = A(\phi)$. For $k \in B_i(j)$,

$$\bar{\phi}_{ik}(j) = 0$$

For $k \notin B_i(j)$, define

$$a_{ik}(j) = D'_{ik}(f_{ik}) + \frac{\partial D}{\partial r_k(j)} - \min_{m \notin B_i(j)} \left[D'_{im}(f_{im}) + \frac{\partial D}{\partial r_m(j)} \right] \tag{13}$$

$$\Delta_{ik}(j) = \min \left[\phi_{ik}(j), \frac{\eta a_{ik}(j)}{t_i(j)} \right]$$

Let $\bar{k}_i(j)$ be the node (a value of m) that minimizes the rightmost term in (13). Then

$$\bar{\phi}_{ik}(j) = \begin{cases} \phi_{ik}(j) - \Delta_{ik}(j), & k \neq \bar{k}_i(j) \\ \phi_{ik}(j) + \sum_{k \neq \bar{k}_i(j)} \Delta_{ik}(j), & k = \bar{k}_i(j) \end{cases}$$

Notice that the nonnegativity of ϕ and $\Sigma_i \phi_{ik}(j) = 1$ are preserved in the updating equation presented above.

In this algorithm a key quantity to be determined for each node at each iteration is the marginal delay $D'_{ik}(f_{ik}) + \partial D/\partial r_k(j)$. The algorithm is designed to decrease those routing variables for which the marginal delay is large, and increase those for which it is small. To determine $D'_{ik}(f_{ik})$, we can either calculate it from the formula if it is available, or estimate it through the traffic statistics; one such estimation procedure can be found in Ref. 12. To see how a calculation of $\partial D/\partial r_i(j)$ can be made at node i for a neighboring node k, define node m to be downstream from node i with respect to j if there is a routing path from i to j passing through m. Similarly, we define node i to be upstream from node m if m is downstream from i. A routing variable set ϕ is loop free if for each destination j, there is no i, m ($i \neq m$) such that i is both upstream and downstream from m. The procedure for updating is now as follows. For each destination node j, each node i waits until it has received the value $\partial D/\partial r_k(j)$ from each of its downstream neighbors $k \neq j$. Node i then calculates $\partial D/\partial r_i(j)$ according to

$$\frac{\partial D}{\partial r_i(j)} = \sum_k \phi_{ik}(j) \left[D'_{ik}(f_{ik}) + \frac{\partial D}{\partial r_k(j)} \right]$$

and then broadcasts this quantity to all its neighbors (actually only upstream neighbors). It is easy to see that this procedure is free of deadlocks if and only if ϕ is loop free.

A heuristic derivation of the updating equation above for $\partial D/\partial r_i(j)$ is as follows. Let us assume a small increment δ in the input $r_i(j)$. For each neighboring node k, there will be an increment $\delta\phi_{ik}(j)$

of traffic flowing over link (i, k). This increment, to first order, will cause an incremental delay on link (i, k) of $\delta\phi_{ik}(j)D'_{ik}(f_{ik})$. If node k is not the destination node, the extra traffic $\delta\phi_{ik}(j)$ at node k will cause the same increment in delay from node k onward as an extra input traffic at node k. This incremental delay will be, to first order, $\delta\phi_{ik}(j)\partial D/\partial r_k(j)$. Summing over all neighboring nodes k, we thus have the equation above for $i \neq j$.

It is noted that the algorithm is executed independently at each node based on information communicated between adjacent nodes. There is no control node in the network; therefore, it is a routing algorithm using distributed computation.

To complete the algorithm, we now turn to the problem of determining $B_i(j)$. The procedure for determining this set is as follows. Each node l, when it calculates $\partial D/\partial r_l(j)$, determines, for each downstream m, if $\phi_{lm}(j)$ is improper and satisfies the inequality (12). If any downstream neighbor satisfies these conditions, node l adds a special tag to its broadcast of $\partial D/\partial r_l(j)$. The node l also adds this special tag if the received $\partial D/\partial r_m(j)$ from any downstream m contained a tag. In this way all nodes upstream of l also send the tag. The set $B_i(j)$ is then the set of nodes k for which either (i, k) is not a link or the received $\partial D/\partial r_k(j)$ was tagged. The proof of the loop-free nature of the algorithm can be found in Ref. 8.

The choice of η is influenced by the following consideration. For small η, the convergence of the algorithm is guaranteed but rather slow. As η increases, the speed of convergence increases but the danger of no convergence also increases. In general, it is rather difficult to choose an appropriate scaling factor η. A detailed discussion can be found in Ref. 9.

2.29.4 Dynamic Routing Algorithm of ARPANET [10]

The original ARPANET algorithm was designed in 1969. Since then, various problems have been encountered and methods to deal with those problems have also been suggested and introduced into the system. Interested readers should consult Ref. 10, which contains detailed discussion of the problems discovered during the evolution of the ARPANET routing algorithm.

Here we describe the basic part of the ARPANET algorithm. It can be briefly stated as follows. Each packet is directed toward its destination along the path for which the total estimated delay is minimum. Unlike the algorithms presented in Secs. 2.29.1 and 2.29.2, this path is not determined in advance. Instead, each IMP (interface message processor), the switching computer at each node, individually decides which outgoing link to use in transmitting a packet to its final destination IMP, based on estimated delay information from its neigborhing IMPs.

Each IMP maintains several tables to perform two basic functions: to determine which other IMPs are reachable, and to calculate the path of least delay to those IMPs that are reachable. To estimate the delay, each IMP maintains a *network delay table*, which gives an estimate of the delay it expects a packet to encounter in reaching every possible destination IMP over each of its outgoing links. The table is illustrated in Fig. 2. The estimated delay of a packet destined for IMP 3 is 7 if it is sent out on link 2. Periodically, the IMP selects the minimum estimate delay to each destination to form a *minimum delay table*. It also marks the outgoing link which gives the minimum estimated delay for each destination IMP to form a *routing table*. The IMP also passes its minimum delay table to each neighboring IMP (i.e., it sends the minimum delay table out through each of its outgoing links).

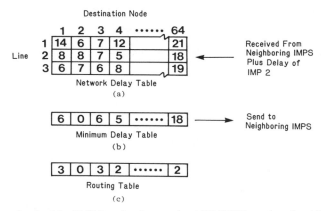

Fig. 2 Tables maintained by IMP 2 to implement the ARPANET routing algorithm: (*a*) network delay table; (*b*) minimum delay table; (*c*) routing table.

Periodically, an IMP receives a minimum delay table from each neighboring IMP. As each table arrives it is read in over the row of the network delay table corresponding to the link it arrived on. After all the neighboring IMPs estimated minimum delay tables have arrived, the IMP adds its own contribution to the total delay (e.g., by adding the number of packets queued at each outgoing link) to each row of the network delay table. Thus the IMP has the updated network delay table and hence can update its minimum delay table and its routing table. An example of a typical network delay table, a minimum delay table, and a routing table are shown in Fig. 2 [10]. In this example, there are 64 IMPs in the network. The tables shown are kept by IMP 2, which has three outgoing links connecting to three neighboring IMPs. Notice that both the second elements of the minimum delay table and routing table are zeros.

To determine the reachability of other IMPs, each IMP, in a similar fashion, also computes and propagates shortest-path information (minimum number of intermediate IMPs), termed the *hop count*. An upper limit of the number of hops in the longest path in the network is used as the threshold for disconnected or nonexistent nodes. This is known as a *reachability test*.

One of the main problems of this routing algorithm is that the estimated delay for traffic at one instant is a function of the traffic that existed several seconds earlier due to the propagation delays from one IMP to another. This situation could potentially lead to oscillations and poor performance. The ARPANET algorithm attempts to prevent this undesirable phenomenon by biasing delay heavily toward the shortest path. That is, the estimated delay contributed by an IMP is measured by the number of packets on an output queue plus a fixed increment, so that even an empty queue represents additional delay. Although this shortest time plus bias routing policy leads to stable flow, the bias makes the algorithm somewhat insensitive to changes in traffic patterns.

Another problem with this algorithm is that it reacts quickly to good news and slowly to bad news. This property comes from the fact that an IMP sends only the minimum delay table to its neighboring IMPs. IMP *i* tends to think that there is a good alternative path, in case of link or node failure or sudden heavy traffic development, based on information from its neighboring IMPs, which in turn construct their minimum delay table based on information from IMP *i* before the problem developed. Therefore, it tends to react slowly to bad news. Similar consideration shows that it acts quickly to good news. A partial solution to this problem is the so-called *holddown*. The routing algorithm should continue to use the "best route" to a given destination, both for updating and forwarding, for some time period after it gets worse. The idea is to purge the surrounding nodes of any out-of-date information before the nodes will accept any new information.

REFERENCES

1. G. L. FULTZ, "Adaptive Routing Techniques for Message Switching Computer-Communication Networks," Ph.D. dissertation, UCLA, July 1972.

2. J. M. McQUILLAN, "Routing Algorithms for Computer Networks—A Survey," *Natl. Telecommun. Conf. '77.*

3. M. SCHWARTZ, *Computer-Communication Network Design and Analysis*, Prentice-Hall, Englewood Cliffs, N.J., 1977.

4. T. C. HU, *Integer Programming and Network Flows*, Addison-Wesley, Reading, Mass., 1969, Chap. 10.

5. L. FRATTA, M. GERLA, and L. KLEINROCK, "The Flow Deviation Method: An Approach to Store-and-Forward Communication Network Design," *Networks*, **3**, 97–134, (1973).

6. J. A. TOMLIN, "Minimum-Cost Multi-Commodity Network Flow," *J. ORSA*, **14**(1), 45–51 (Feb. 1966).

7. D. G. CANTOR and M. GERLA, "Optimal Routing in a Packet-Switched Computer Network," *IEEE Trans. Comput.*, **C-23**, 1062–1068 (Oct. 1974).

8. R. G. GALLAGER, "A Minimum Delay Routing Algorithm Using Distributed Computation," *IEEE Trans. Commun.* **COM-25**, 73–85 (Jan. 1977).

9. R. G. GALLAGER, "Scale Factors for Distributed Routing Algorithm," *Natl. Telecommun. Conf. '77.*

10. J. M. McQUILLAN, G. FALK, and I. RICHER, "A Review of the Development and Performance of the ARPANET Routing Algorithm," *IEEE Trans. Commun.*, **COM-26**, 1802–1810 (Dec. 1978).

11. H. RUDIN, "On Routing and Delta Routing: A Taxonomy and Performance Comparison of Techniques for Packet-Switched Networks," *IEEE Trans. Commun.*, **COM-24**, 43–59 (Jan. 1976).

12. A. SEGALL, "The Modeling of Adaptive Routing in Data-Communication Networks," *IEEE Trans. Commun.*, **COM-25**, 85–95 (Jan. 1977).

13. E. W. DIJKSTRA, "A Note on Two Problems in Connection with Graphs," *Numer. Math.*, **1**, 269–271 (1959).

2.30 FEATURES OF NETWORK COMMUNICATION PROTOCOLS

Richard E. Schantz

For communication to take place, certain conventions must be established between the sender and receiver. Agreed-upon conventions, or *protocols*, for the orderly exchange of data in a network environment typically address aspects of establishing and controlling the data path between the communicating entities. Protocols are used to augment an existing transmission medium, providing a more idealized, virtual communication facility. In this section we describe a number of general features that are part of many communication protocols, and various approaches or techniques that have been used to support these features.

In its most general forms, network communication is a complex matter whose implementation is typically organized as a hierarchy of levels, each new level adding to the sophistication of the communication facility. At the lower levels there are concerns for items such as electrical interconnection and link control. At the higher levels issues such as addressing and support for virtual connections become paramount. Both data and control signals share the communication medium to support each additional layer.

Figure 1 illustrates a typical message-switching computer network environment. In such a configuration data passed between communicating processes P_1 on Host$_1$ and P_2 on Host$_2$ are handled by the network interface programs on each of the hosts, as well as some number of communication processors (CP), as the data are routed from H_1 to H_2. Taken together, the CPs are often referred to as the communication subsystem. During the lifetime of a message in the system it is subject to a number of protocols as it traverses the network from P_1 to P_2. In our example, as the message is passed from CP to CP, it is subject to link control protocols; transmission between the network interface program OS$_1$, and its counterpart on Host$_2$ adhere to what is commonly called a host-to-host protocol; exchanges between the communicating processes obey higher-level-function-oriented protocols. In this model it is easily seen that there are a number of perspectives on the concept of source-to-destination or end-to-end protocols. There remains considerable controversy among network designers as to which level of protocol should be responsible for supporting certain desirable source-to-destination or end-to-end features, such as ensuring correct message delivery or maintaining message order. In some network designs (e.g., ARPANET [1]), the communication subsystem plays a large role in these areas. In other network designs (e.g., CYCLADES [2]), the network interface program protocols accept this responsibility. In simpler networks, the transmission medium itself may ensure in-order message delivery. In other cases the user processes themselves must organize their own protocols to achieve similar goals. Regardless of which level supports these end-to-end transmission procedures, the issues surrounding them remain the same, as do the approaches to the problems they

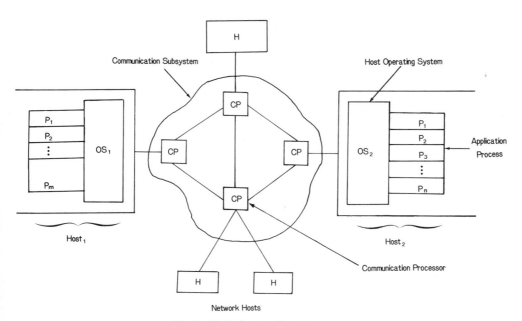

Fig. 1 Typical network environment.

must address. The specific end-to-end features we discuss here are performance considerations, error control, flow control, and message sequencing.

2.30.1   Desirable Properties of Source-to-Destination Protocols

The effectiveness of a communication system is largely measured by a combination of its performance, its reliability, and its cost. Typical measures of performance are throughput and delay. *Throughput* measures the total flow of data per unit time, while *delay* measures the waiting and transmission time associated with an individual message delivery. High throughput and low delay are often in conflict with one another in the following senses. A network optimized for high throughput will support large messages in order to avoid the additional overhead associated with each new message, whereas optimizing for low delay usually means that short messages are desirable, so that an ongoing transmission will not block other pending transmissions for long periods. To achieve low delay, it may be necessary to dedicate certain resources to the communication path so that as data are ready they can be transmitted. This may imply lower utilization of the resource and hence lower throughput.

Communication systems can be designed to support both low delay and high-throughput traffic (see Sec. 2.28). Allowing multiple simultaneous messages in transit between a source and a destination (*pipelining*) attempts to increase end-to-end throughput. Breaking large messages up into a number of smaller independent transmissions (commonly known as packet switching) attempts to reduce the end-to-end delay characteristics of the network. Supporting these (as well as other) features of a communication facility requires additional protocol-related control messages. Because the control data shares the communication medium with the actual message data, it should be clear that they diminish the overall effective bandwidth of the physical transmission medium for carrying the data. The protocol to support additional features of a communication facility may also impose requirements on the sender or receiver which limit throughput and adds to delay by blocking message transmission at certain times or by requiring additional control messages to precede data transmission. An important element of adding a feature to a communication protocol is to limit any adverse effect it may have on the performance of communication using the protocol.

For reliable message transmission, most protocols provide an *error control mechanism*. Errors in data transmission may arise from noise or hardware malfunction either in the transmission medium or in the transmission-handling equipment, or in some cases, may result from too much contention for transmission resources. There are three classes of errors usually considered. One type of error is the corruption of one or more bits of data of a successfully delivered message. Another type of error is the failure of a message to be delivered at all (a so-called "lost message"). This may result from a temporary failure in the network during message transmission. A third type of error occurs when the same message is delivered more than once ("duplicate message"). This usually happens as a result of prematurely invoked error recovery mechanisms built into the network or into the end-to-end protocol. In all three cases, it is the job of the error control protocol feature to detect such errors, and provide for their correction. In most cases, there are multiple mechanisms to support the various aspects of error control. Section 2.30.2 discusses a number of techniques for error control.

Since a network usually connects equipment having different speeds, there is a need in the steady state to match the rate at which the network accepts data from the source to the rate at which it is being accepted by the destination. Protocol features for regulating the data flow from source to destination to account for varying processing rates are known as *flow control mechanisms*. Flow control mechanisms are used to ensure available buffer capacity at the destination for transmitted messages to avoid congestion in the network or at the destination site. If flow control is not adequately handled, this congestion leads to increased errors or inefficient use of bandwidth capacity in recovering from those errors or both. Flow between source and destination is usually controlled in terms of a specified amount of storage available or a specified number of messages allowed to be processed before blocking further transmission. Techniques for handling flow control in a network are discussed in Sec. 2.30.3.

As a result of the combination of the desire to have multiple simultaneous messages outstanding to improve throughput, the multiple physical connectivity of many current network configurations, and embedded techniques for error recovery from transient network failures, it is possible that messages arrive at the destination site in a different order from that originally sent. Another feature that is sometimes part of a communication facility and supported by its protocols is the *sequencing of messages*. That is, the destination site delivers the messages to the receiver in the order in which they were sent, independent of their order of arrival. When messages are guaranteed to be delivered in the order sent, users can view the channel between the source and the destination as a single virtual pipe. In the absence of such a facility, users can include sequencing data in the message itself to be processed by the receiver. Alternatively, users can limit process-to-process conversations to a single outstanding message at a time to ensure in-order processing.

As noted previously, a packet-switching network may break up a single message into a number of independent smaller transmissions. When this happens, *packet reassembly* of the original message at the destination site makes this decomposition transparent to the message sender. Packet reassembly is conceptually similar to in-order delivery of individual messages. In both cases control information included with each data transmission identifies the logical position of the data with respect to the sequence of transmissions.

2.30.2   Techniques for Error Control

There are two aspects to error control: error detection and error correction. The nature of error detection in a network environment is influenced by the physical distribution of the communicating entities and the independent failure patterns they follow. In such an environment, error detection is most commonly supported by a *positive acknowledgment* discipline. Under such a protocol, a message (or a packet) from a source which is correctly received by the destination requires a message in the reverse direction confirming (or acknowledging) successful receipt of the message. Since either the message or the acknowledgment can be lost, the sender must guard against waiting indefinitely for an acknowledgment. To handle this, the source site sets a *time-out* interval, after which it will assume a failure of the transmission. This is the error-detection phase at the sending site. Error correction is most often handled by *retransmission* of the message by the source to the destination after the expiration of the time-out interval. Notice that the retransmission error-correction strategy involves buffering the original message at the source site until it is positively acknowledged by the destination.

Check sums or more general error-detecting codes included with the message data are most often used for detecting bit errors in arriving messages. More sophisticated error-correcting codes can be used, but the transmission error rates do not generally warrant the additional overhead. A simple way to correct a bit transmission error is for the destination to discard the message, relying on the expiration of the time-out to force message retransmission. However, when time-out intervals are large, it is sometimes appropriate to add a *negative acknowledgment* message to the protocol. These control messages serve to indicate the error detected in a particular message and force its retransmission immediately, without waiting for the time-out interval to expire. Negative acknowledgments alone cannot be used as the basis for an error detection protocol because they are subject to being lost in the same manner as the original message. This situation would lead the sender to believe that a message had been correctly delivered when in fact it had not.

In situations where it is the positive acknowledgment and not the message that has been lost, the expiration of the time-out interval and subsequent message retransmission can lead to a duplicate message received at the destination. To detect these errors, messages are generally identified with embedded *sequence numbers*. The sequence number of an arriving message can be used to determine whether the message represents new data or a duplicate of previously received data, provided that the receiver maintains a record of correctly received sequence numbers. When a message has been detected as a duplicate, it can be discarded by the receiver. However, for both new and duplicate messages a positive acknowledgment is sent, which includes the sequence number of the message that has been correctly received. The strategy of retransmitting acknowledgments when duplicate messages are received provides error control on the acknowledgment stream.

Sequence numbers which are incremented by some predictable value (e.g., by one) by the sender for each new message or data transmission unit allow the recipient to detect that there are *missing messages*. Various strategies for handling missing messages are possible, and are dependent on factors such as an in-order delivery requirement, and availability of extra message buffering capacity. Another major issue associated with sequence numbers is selecting the size of the sequence field so that it does not recycle during an interval in which a late-arriving duplicate message may appear. In addition, a properly designed protocol must provide mechanisms to resynchronize reliably sequence numbers at startup and failure recovery time. For a more complete discussion of sequence numbers, see Refs. 3 and 7.

A number of optimizations associated with error control protocols are possible. Two of these are multiple acknowledgments with a single message, and piggyback acknowledgments. The positive acknowledgment protocol can be augmented to provide that a single sequence number acknowledgment can also serve as the acknowledgment for all preceding previously unacknowledged sequence numbers. This multiple-message acknowledgment can reduce the acknowledgment traffic when multiple messages from a source to a destination are outstanding simultaneously. However, batching acknowledgments in this way may increase the cost of retransmission should the acknowledgment be lost. Care must also be taken to ensure that the acknowledgment traffic proceeds in a timely fashion to avoid unnecessary time-out-related retransmission. Another performance optimization is to provide for acknowledgments to be included (to piggyback) with message traffic from the destination to the source. This avoids much of the additional overhead associated with each new message. It is obviously applicable only when there is frequent traffic in both directions between a given source and destination pair.

We conclude our discussion of error control by noting the importance for performance of selecting an appropriate time-out interval. If the time-out interval is too long, the system does not respond promptly to error conditions, resulting in potentially poor utilization of the communication channel since a sender may delay a transmission until the previous one is acknowledged. If the time-out interval is too short, messages are often needlessly retransmitted, wasting some of the effective bandwidth of the channel. For more complete discussions of error control, see Refs. 4 and 5.

2.30.3 Techniques for Flow Control

Controlled flow of data from source to destination is always required to avoid congestion and inefficient use of communication resources. In some simple cases, flow control may be implicit in the nature of the communicating entities. For example, in a simple communication system, the data receiver can be designed to operate at a rate which guarantees that it processes the data faster than it can be produced. However, in the more general case, rates of consumption cannot be accurately predicted or guaranteed to be greater than rates of production. For this reason, explicit flow control mechanisms are usually part of the communication protocol between sender and receiver.

A common form of flow control is to have the receiver indicate to the sender via a control message the amount of data (or the number of messages with a fixed maximum size) it is willing to accept. As data (or a message) are sent, the sender decrements its count of available buffering capacity allocated at the receiver by the amount of data sent. When the allocation has been depleted, the sender is not permitted further transmission on that data stream until receiving a control message indicating a renewal of buffering commitment by the receiver. To avoid interrupting a steady flow of data and increasing delay by having the sender wait for a renewal control message, the receiver may issue its next buffering commitment before the old allocation has been completely exhausted. This allocation and renewal protocol for handling flow control ensures that no transmission bandwidth is consumed by message data which cannot be accepted by the destination. However, communication resources are consumed in handling the additional control messages. Further, a lost renewal message can stop data transmission entirely, unless error control is applied to the renewal control messages.

Another approach to flow control can be developed out of the techniques for error control discussed previously. In a transmission protocol that requires the sender to retransmit any messages that go unacknowledged for too long, the receiver may discard messages simply because it cannot process them at the rate they are being sent. The unacknowledged messages will be retransmitted until there is capacity at the destination to handle them. Under this protocol, the sender sends data whenever they are available. Although such a scheme is conceptually very simple and is part of the error control protocol, this approach to flow control can under some circumstances become unstable and result in reduced throughput and limited effective bandwidth because of excessive retransmission.

A refinement to the flow control by retransmission model defines a moving *window* over the numbered sequence of messages (or other agreed-upon units of data) on a data stream. A source site may send a message to a destination site immediately provided that the consecutively assigned sequence number to be given to the new message lies within the current window. Thus the window defines the maximum extent of the pipelining of unacknowledged data at any point in time. As messages are correctly received and processed at the destination, the window can be advanced at the source either implicitly based on acknowledgment traffic, or explicitly based on additional window control messages. Usually, an acknowledgment for a particular message sequence number serves both to acknowledge all lower-numbered unacknowledged messages within the window, and to advance the window so that it now begins immediately after the acknowledged sequence number. Within the allowable transmission window, the time-out-driven retransmission procedure provides both error control and destination site flexibility to discard a message should its buffer capacity become temporarily overcommitted. A time-out could mean retransmission of the entire unacknowledged portion of the current window (i.e., all messages sent after the unacknowledged one). When this overhead is likely to be extensive, additional protocol in the form of negative acknowledgments can be added to support selective retransmission of particular segments of the message stream. Additionally, time-outs can be used as a signal to the sender to limit the extent of message pipelining.

A variety of strategies for controlling the width of the allowable transmission window can be adopted. Window size can exactly match reserved buffer space to eliminate all non-error-related retransmission overhead. Alternatively, windows that nominally overcommit memory may be effective in increasing throughput under some patterns of network traffic.

The insertion of flow control mechanisms into a transmission protocol means that at times, further transmission may be blocked if the destination is not processing the data as fast as it has been produced. In some cases, it may still be important to signal the destination of an important event. An example might be a signal to abort processing of a job that may be looping and not processing its backlogged input. To handle such situations, communication protocols usually support a limited transmission capability which bypasses the flow control mechanism. Destination sites may be required to reserve the storage necessary to accept these limited transmissions, independent of the resource commitments to flow-controlled data paths.

Further discussion of the issues associated with flow control can be found in Refs. 4 and 6.

REFERENCES

1. J. M. McQUILLAN and D. C. WALDEN, "ARPANET Design Decisions," *Comput. Networks*, **1**(5) (Sept. 1977).
2. H. ZIMMERMAN, "The Cyclades End-to-End Protocol," *Fourth ACM/IEEE Data Commun. Symp.*, Quebec, Oct. 1975.
3. V. CERF and R. E. KAHN, "A Protocol for Packet Network Interconnection," *IEEE Trans. Commun.*, **COM-22**(5) (May 1974).
4. W. R. CROWTHER, ET AL. "Issues in Packet Switching Network Design," *AFIPS Conf. Proc.*, **44** (June 1975).
5. S. W. EDGE and A. J. HINCHLEY, "A Survey of End-to-End Retransmission Techniques," *Comput. Commun. Rev.*, **8**(4) (Oct. 1978).
6. CORNAFION GROUP, "A Critical Study of Different Flow Control Methods in Computer Networks," *Comput. Commun. Rev.*, **9**(3) (July 1979).
7. R. S. TOMLINSON, "Selecting Sequence Numbers," *Oper. Syst. Rev.*, **9**(3) (July 1975).
8. G. FALK, "A Comparison of Network Architectures—The ARPANET and SNA," *AFIPS Conf. Proc.*, **47** (June 1978).

2.31 HOST-TO-HOST PROTOCOLS

Harold A. Anderson, Jr.

During the 1970s the implementation of the ARPA network triggered many parallel developments in data communications. One of the most significant was the development of different data communications system (DCS) architectures by every major data processing product manufacturer. All these DCS architectures have a similar layered structure. However, the details of the protocols and message formats used to implement the services provided by each layer differ from architecture to architecture. These differences make it difficult to implement a heterogeneous network consisting of data processing products from various manufacturers. For this reason the CCITT International Standards Organization formed the Open System Interconnection Subcommittee and chartered it to develop a generic model of existing DCS architectures that can serve as a framework for developing protocol standards [5]. The subcommittee has defined and published a description of a generic seven-layered DCS architecture model that can be tailored to represent any type of node connected to a data network. Their model is referred to as the *ISO Model* for Open System Interconnection Architecture.

The ISO model of a network node provides the framework used in this article to describe *host-to-host protocols* (Fig. 2.27.3). The seven layers of the ISO model are as follows:

The *application process (AP) layer* consists of *application processes (APs)* that make use of the communication services of the lower layers to intercommunicate according to some application protocol.

The *presentation services (PS) layer* provides a set of services that are selected during session initiation by the two APs desiring to communicate to transform the data they exchange into a form each understands. The PS layer makes it possible for an application program to transmit and receive data units from an end user without regard to the type of terminal being used by the end user.

The *session control (SC) layer* provides services needed to establish interconnections (sessions) between APs desiring to communicate, and to control the data exchange over these sessions. Each session has a tailored set of presentation services associated with it.

The *transport network control (TNC) layer* provides services to establish point-to-point transport connections between network nodes, and controls the data exchange over these connections. Any number of sessions between APs in the same two network nodes can be multiplexed on a transport connection. The TNC layer insulates sessions from the physical characteristics of a network by representing it as a collection of logical point-to-point connections between network nodes.

The *network control (NC) layer* provides services to establish the routes between network nodes required to support the activated transport connections, and controls the flow of data over these routes. The NC layer deals with the physical topology of the network and performs routing by selecting the next node to route a data unit to and the corresponding data link to be utilized.

The *data link control (DLC) layer* provides services to activate the data links between adjacent nodes used in next-node routing, and controls the flow of data over these links. The DLC layer insulates the NC layer from the details of the data link protocols (BSC, HDLC, SDLC, start/stop, 370 channel, etc.) utilized.

The *physical control (PC) layer* is the lowest layer. It deals with the electrical characteristics and signaling required to set up, operate, and take down the data circuits used as the data links of a network.

For the purposes of this article, host-to-host protocols will be represented as the hierarchy of protocols provided by the three adjacent layers of the ISO model under the AP layer (i.e., the PS layer, SC layer, and TNC layer). The primary differences in supporting different types of AP-to-AP communication can be isolated to the presentation services they require. All the communication services required of the other lower layers are generally the same.

2.31.1 Review of Data Communications System Architecture

The terminology used to describe the ISO model will be defined first [5]. The *end users* of a data communications system consist of *APs* (*applications processes*) representing application programs, terminal operators, and various operator-attended or unattended work stations. To support the interconnection and communication among such a diversity of AP types requires an architectured structure of distributed subsystems providing a broad range of communication services. The *principles of layering* first developed in the late 1960s by Dijkstra to structure the services of an operating system (see Sec. 2.24) has been applied to the development of DCS architectures.

In all DCS architectures, the APs are the *entities* making up the highest layer. Except for the AP layer, each layer provides the entities in the next highest layer with a set of *services* that are accessed by means of an *interface*. The cooperating entities of a layer which are providing a service can be distributed over one or more network nodes. Before two entities can cooperate to provide a service, a *connection* has to be established between them. Requiring the formal establishment of a connection ensures that a communication path exists between the two entities, that both entities are active and available, and that both possess the complementary capabilities needed for them to cooperate in providing a service. Each layer supports its own entity connection protocol, and once a connection is established, the cooperation between entities is governed by a set of protocols specific to that layer. Therefore, both the establishment of a connection and the transmission of *data units* between APs are made possible and supported by a hierarchy of protocols.

The transmission of a data unit through the layers of a DCS architecture proceeds as follows. An AP requests the PS layer to provide a specific type of presentation service in transmitting a data unit over a session to the AP at the other end. As the data unit is routed down through the layers at the origin network node, the appropriate entity in a layer provides the service requested by the next highest layer and appends a layer-specific header of control information on the data unit received. When the data unit arrives at the destination network node and is routed up through the layers, each layer's header is removed and the appropriate entity in that layer takes action based on the control information specified in the header. Only the original data unit arrives at the AP layer in the destination node and is routed to the specified AP (Fig. 1).

As mentioned above, in order for two entities in layer N to communicate, a connection must already exist between the appropriate two entities in the source and destination nodes in layer $N - 1$. Except

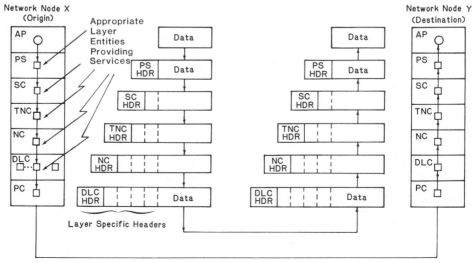

Fig. 1 Routing and servicing of a data unit passing through the ISO layers of the origin node and destination node.

for the lowest layer, communicating entities in a given layer have to be assigned to a connection in the next-lower layer. The connections in layer $N-1$ are identified as *service ports* to entities in layer N. Each service port in a layer is assigned a unique *network address*. For each layer below the AP layer a directory is maintained to record the network addresses of the interconnected entities (connections) in the adjacent higher layer. These layer directories are used to record the connections between entities at level N as well as the information that must be provided to accompany a request for data transmission between those entities.

2.31.2   Presentation Services Layer

The PS layer insulates APs from each other's data presentation idiosyncrasies. This layer is partitioned to provide different classes of presentation services (i.e., display terminal support, printer/keyboard terminal support, file transfer support, etc.) [3, 5]. These classes are defined based on the presentation services required to support the communication between different types of APs. The appropriate presentation entities are created and a connection is established between them when two APs are establishing a communication connection. At that time, a one-to-one correspondence is also set up between the presentation entity and the session entity at each end of the connection. For more detailed information on presentation services, see Sec. 2.32.

2.31.3   Session Control Layer

AP-to-AP connections are commonly referred to as *sessions*. The terms *dialogues* and *liasons* have also been frequently used in the past to refer to sessions [3].

An AP gains access to the SC layer by being assigned a network service port (network address). The PS-to-SC interface is used by an AP to request session initiation and termination services, while the AP-to-PS interface is used to request a presentation service as part of a request to transfer a data unit over a session. If no presentation service is required, an AP can request a data transfer service directly at the PS-to-SC interface. This interface is rather complicated, because of the different types of information that pass across it, such as session initiation/termination service requests, session status indicators, data transfer service requests, data transfer status indicators, and flow control commands [1].

The SC-to-TNC interface is not as complex as the previous interface. The dialogue between a session entity and its transport entity is rather limited. The information passing across this interface includes data units and SC commands that are transmitted over transport connections to the SC layers on other nodes, and requests to establish transport connections, transport connection status indicators, session failure notifications, and flow control commands that flow between the entities in the SC and TNC layers in the same node.

The SC layer consists of a *session services component* and a *data transfer control component* in each network node. The latter consists of the entities that support the initiated sessions. Figure 2 depicts the entities supporting sessions between two APs in node x with three APs in node y. Not shown is the interface to the session services component required by an AP to initiate and terminate sessions.

Session Services Component

The session services (SS) component is concerned with session initiation and termination. In any DCS architecture a wide variety of session initiation service options are available. Only a simple ARPA-like session intiation scenario need be described to portray what is involved in initializing a session [2, 3]. For example, AP1 requests its SS component to initiate a session for it with AP2. If the SS component can resolve the network address of AP2, it will format a session initiation request and use the services of the TNC layer to deliver the request to the SS component servicing AP2. If AP2 is active and willing to go into session with AP1, it informs its SS component of its decision. The SS component formats a session intiation response and uses the services of the TNC layer to deliver the response to the SS component servicing AP1. AP1 is then notified whether its session initiation request was accepted. There are many possible variations to this scenario. The most common one, which is SNA-like, occurs when the SS component does not have the capability to resolve the network address of an AP [1]. In this case, a centralized network directory management facility is introduced into the network, and the session initiation protocol is modified to include the services of a network directory manager to assist in session initiation.

The session services protocols have to be designed to handle and recover from all sorts of unusual circumstances that can arise when a session is being initiated or terminated [3]. For example, it is possible for two APs to attempt to initiate a session between themselves at the same time, or for the SS components involved in initiating a session to lose synchronization. Circumstances like these have to be dealt with to prevent protocol deadlocks or unpredictable results from occurring when initiating or terminating sessions.

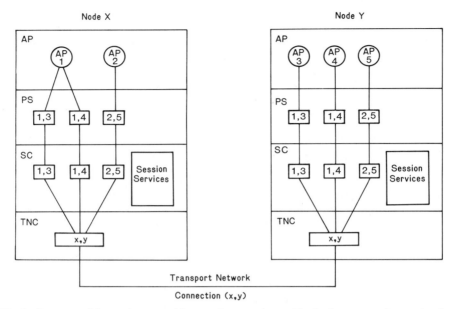

Fig. 2 Structure of the session control layer and supporting entities in the presentation services layer and transport network control layer.

The presentation services and data transfer control services that are available to tailor the support of a session are extensive. As it happens, only a few subsets of services are ever used. This makes it possible to define a small number of session types, each identified by a profile of supported services [1]. Just as presentation services are partitioned into presentation service classes, the data transfer control services can be partitioned based on whether sequence numbers are to be used, full-duplex transmission is supported, and so on. A *session type profile* specifies the presentation service class and the data transfer control services supported. During session initiation, the two APs involved identify to their respective SS component the services they require. If the services required are complementary, they are set up in the PS layer and SC layer. This entails creating presentation entities and session entities with the required capabilities and assigning network addresses to them for routing data units. There are other approaches to setting up the required services, including the situation where the SS components involved attempt to negotiate a set of complementary services through exchanging a series of SC commands.

Data Transfer Control Component

The data transfer control component controls the exchange of data units over the active sessions. It consists of session entity pairs that represent each session. These entity pairs enforce the rules governing data exchanges over a session that were agreed to at session initiation. They employ data transfer control protocols which also involve the exchange of SC commands between session entities to recover from errors or resynchronize when something unexpected occurs during a data exchange [3].

A session may support full-duplex transmission, half-duplex transmission, simplex transmission, or a complex transaction-oriented transmission. In *full-duplex transmission* both APs in session can be transmitting data units simultaneously, while in *half-duplex transmission* only one AP can be transmitting at a time. In this case, there are generally two types of dialogues, either an AP systematically alternates (flip-flops) between transmitting and receiving a data unit, or an AP continuously contends for permission to transmit with its session partner. In the latter situation, a tie-breaking rule is used to grant permission to one of the APs whenever both are attempting to transmit simultaneously. *Simplex transmission* is transmission in only one direction over a session.

An airline reservation system is typical of a data processing system where the basic unit of work flowing over a session is a transaction. A *transaction* consists of a series of related information exchanges between a computer and a terminal operator. The uncertainty in the number of exchanges and the number of data units within an exchange complicates the data transfer control protocol used to provide a transaction transmission service. The protocol has to enforce a rule for granting permission to an AP for initiating the transmission of a transaction, keeping track of the flow of data units making up a transaction, and detecting and attempting to recover from any error. If an unrecoverable error occurs, the whole transaction has to be retransmitted.

The SNA *bracket protocol* is an example of data transfer control protocol for transaction transmission [1]. It is used primarily to support the communications employed in data base management systems. In the bracket protocol, one AP in a session always has the right to initiate the transmission of a transaction, and upon receiving a request to transmit a transaction from the other AP, can either grant or refuse it permission to do so. Once a transaction is initiated it may consist of an alternating sequence of data units transmitted in one direction, followed by a sequence of data units transmitted in the opposite direction.

The decision to assign sequence numbers (see Sec. 2.30.2) to all data units transmitted over a session is made at session initiation. The sequence number placed in the header appended to a data unit by the transmitting session entity is checked by the receiving session entity to detect whether a data unit was received in the proper order, a duplicate data unit was received, or a data unit is missing. If a data unit is missing, the receiving session entity may wait for some predetermined time to receive the missing data unit before discarding all data units received out of order and transmitting an SC command back indicating that a transmission error has occurred. Since the transmission of data units and SC commands can be interspersed over a session, a different set of sequence numbers should be used for each to ensure the highest integrity. To eliminate any ambiguity in identifying a received data unit, the size of the sequence number field in the SC header should be based on the number of data units expected to be in transit over a session. The use of sequence numbers complicates data transfer control protocols, but enables both ends of a session to recover from network failures and resynchronize data transmission.

When a session entity detects that an error has occurred, it initiates an exchange of SC commands to attempt to recover from the error, and resynchronize its state with that of its peer. The error recovery procedure may be as follows: A signal to initiate recovery is transmitted, all data traffic is cleared and transmission is halted, sequence numbers are reset, and then data transmission is resumed. In order to be responsive in recovering from errors, a session supports two types of flows: *expedited flow* for SC commands involved in error recovery, and *normal flow* for all other session traffic [1]. Expedited session traffic is treated with higher priority than normal session traffic by the supporting transport connection. There are times when session entities cannot recover from an error. They must then notify the APs they support that session outage has occurred.

Assigning a sequence number to a data unit is one way of associating an identifier with a data unit. An identifier can be used to implement various types of delivery confirmation services [3]. One type of service provides delivery confirmation or acknowledgment to a transmitting AP for every data unit delivered correctly over a session. Another type of delivery confirmation service allows an AP to select the data units for which it wants to receive delivery confirmations. Alternatively, there are times when an AP only wants to be notified when a specific data unit has been delivered in error or that something unexpected happened in delivering the data unit. In addition to requesting positive or negative acknowledgments, there are times when transmitting a data unit or an SC command that a response is wanted to determine what course of action was taken at the other end of the session.

Whenever some form of response (delivery confirmation, etc) is requested, the transmitting session entity makes an entry in a correlation table indicating this fact. Upon receipt of the response, the session entity searches the correlation table, removes the entry, and if the response was for a data unit, notifies its AP; otherwise, it processes the response.

When an AP attempts to transmit data units over a session faster than the AP at the other end can process them, the danger exists of buffer overflow at the receiver. A flow control mechanism is required to prevent this. A common form of session flow control employs a pacing mechanism (see Sec. 2.30.3). In *session pacing*, the transmitting session entity sets a pacing request indicator in the header it appends to a data unit to indicate that it is requesting to receive a stand-alone pacing response when the receiving session entity can accept N more data units. When the transmitting session entity has sent N data units without receiving a pacing response, it becomes blocked and stops transmitting until it receives the pacing response; otherwise, it continues to transmit. The pacing request indicator can be set in the header of any of the N data units to be transmitted in a *session pacing window*. Session pacing is selected and the session pacing control parameters for both directions are set when a session is initiated. The control parameters specify when to set the pacing request indicator and the *pacing window size*, N. If a session entity becomes blocked, it may still continue to accept data units from its AP and enqueue them. After awhile, however, a blocked session entity may experience a buffer shortage, and have to stop accepting data units until it becomes unblocked. In a similar fashion, a session entity may receive feedback from its transport entity not to transmit additional data units until notified, because the transport entity is experiencing too much congestion in the network.

2.31.4   Transport Network Control Layer

The TNC layer represents the network to sessions as consisting of point-to-point transport connections between source and destination nodes [4, 5]. The initiation of a session between an AP in node 1 and an AP in node 2 requires the existence of a transport connection between the two nodes. Many sessions may be multiplexed on a transport connection. One of the primary purposes of the TNC layer is to insulate sessions from the details of a network's configuration and the telecommunication facilities employed. This is very important because the configuration of a large network is continuously being changed. In the future it will be common for a large network to be configured as interconnected subnetworks implemented out of different telecommunication facilities (i.e., packet-switching networks and/or subnetworks configured from switched and nonswitched data circuits of various speeds). Routing data units through such a network may require data transformations at the subnetwork boundaries (Fig. 3). There is even a distinct possibility that data units may become lost or delivered out of order due to congestion or failures in the network. The TNC layer solves these problems by providing services to prevent network congestion and to ensure the proper delivery of all session traffic on a transport connection. Alternatively, delivery confirmation services can be provided to particular sessions by the SC layer. (Note that certain functions, such as error control, may be provided at either or both the TNC and SC levels, depending on the requirements of a particular architecture.)

Transport connections provide full-duplex transmission. They may be permanent connections or dynamic connections. *Permanent transport connections* are established at network startup, while *dynamic transport connections* are established at network startup, while *dynamic transport connections* are established as needed to support sessions. The TNC layer consists of the transport connection services component and the transport transfer control component. The latter consists of the entities that support the activated transport connections. Figure 4 depicts the entities supporting the transport connections between three network nodes. Two transport connections between nodes x and y, having different classes of service, are shown multiplexed on the route (network connection) between nodes x and y. Not shown is the interface to the transport connection services component used by the session services component to determine the status of a transport connection.

Transport Connection Services Component

The SS component in the SC layer requests the transport connection services (TCS) component to assign a session to a transport connection with a given class of service when the session is being initiated. If the connection has not been activated, the TCS component communicates using the services of the NC layer with the TCS component in the other network node to activate a transport connection with the desired class of service. This requires, of course, that a route already be available between the two network nodes. The transport connection activation/deactivation protocols are similiar to the session initiation/termination protocols. They have to be error tolerant, permitting recovery from all types of errors, and involve communication between TCS components. A connection validation protocol is required to ensure that a transport connection is working properly and to permit recovery from intermittent failures that may occur along the assigned route.

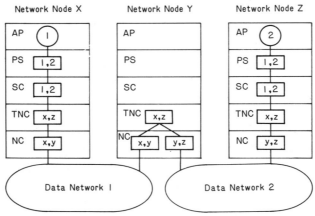

Fig. 3   Role of the transport network control layer in providing an interconnection for a session that spans two separate data networks.

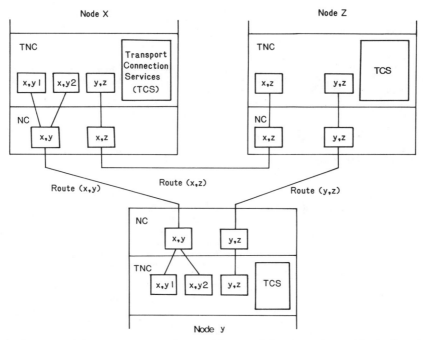

Fig. 4 Structure of the transport network control layer and the supporting entities in the network control layer.

The TCS component supports the activation of multiple transport connections between two network nodes. Each connection could provide a different class of service [5]. There are several attributes of a connection that can be used to define *transport service class profiles*. The most common ones are availability, delivery services, performance, and security. The availability of a transport connection depends on many factors. For connections requiring high availability, a nondisruptive alternative route-switching procedure may be used to recover from network failures. In contrast, those connections that either do not need or cannot afford the overhead to ensure high availability may shut down whenever a network failure occurs somewhere along the assigned route. The possible delivery services offered by a transport connection can be as varied and equivalent in intent to those offered by a postal system (i.e., registered mail, special delivery, first-class mail, etc.). The performance of a transport connection is measured in terms of throughput and transit delay, which in turn are effected by the connection's transmission capacity and the data traffic offered. Providing connections that offer performance guarantees requires network-wide performance monitoring to ensure that these guarantees are met. Equipping selected routes with facilities to encrypt the data being transmitted and assigning some transport connections to these routes is a way to provide security services in the transport network. The transport service class supported by a transport connection is set up at connection activation.

Transport Transfer Control Component

The transport transfer control (TTC) component controls the flow of session traffic over the active transport connections. It consists of transport entity pairs that represent the active transport connections. These entity pairs support full-duplex transmission and provide the transport services requested at connection activation. Transport transfer control protocols are used to support error recovery, resynchronization, and flow control over transport connections. These protocols involve the exchange of TNC commands between transport entities to initiate the following actions: clear all data traffic on a connection, signal the occurrence of an unusual event, exchange connection status information, reset connection status, and halt/resume/restart data transmission. To ensure responsive management and control of a transport connection, special provision has to be made to ensure that these TNC commands receive high priority in being transmitted through the transport network.

The TNC layer provides a transparent transport network interface to sessions. If the transport network is limited in the size of a data unit it can transmit, and sessions are not limited, transport entities may have to segment and reassemble data units. Alternatively, if data unit sizes are too small to make efficient use of the transport network, transport entities may have to block and unblock data units to make efficient use of the network.

The support of interconnected subnetworks in the TNC layer is very important, because there will be no one dominant communication facility in the 1980s [4, 5]. A data network configured from interconnected packet-switching networks will probably be a common type of network. Transport connections that are routed through more than one subnetwork will have to be supported. These connections will require a transport entity to be located in each subnetwork boundary node along their assigned routes. Such a transport entity forwards session traffic on the same transport connection from one subnetwork to another. In the process it may have to transform data units from one packet size to another before routing them on, provide special error recovery and network failure procedures, and perform inter-subnetwork flow control.

One of the primary purposes of the TNC layer is to provide delivery confirmation [5]. This is accomplished by the placement of a sequence number in the transport header appended by a transport entity. The sequence number allows a transport entity receiving data units to deliver them in the proper order, detect when a data unit is missing, and provide acknowledgments for correctly delivered data units. The acknowledgment procedure may be selective or nonselective. When a transport entity has been set up to have retransmission capability, it will keep a copy of every data unit transmitted. The copy is destroyed only when an acknowledgment has been received indicating that the data unit has been delivered. If an acknowledgment is not received within some predetermined time, a retransmission procedure will be invoked. This procedure may initiate retransmission starting with the oldest data unit awaiting acknowledgment, or it may transmit a request to the other transport entity to determine which data units have not been received.

Typically, the traffic from more than one session are multiplexed onto a transport connection. A transport connection has to provide flow control to prevent the session traffic from flooding the network [5]. The importance of flow control in the TNC layer cannot be overstated. If the session traffic is not regulated to match the transmission capacity of a transport connection, serious network-wide performance degradation will result. Various flow control mechanisms have been proposed. The most commonly employed mechanism employs end-to-end pacing to open and close a "window" to allow N data units to flow into the network (see Sec. 2.30.3). The mechanism is similar to session pacing. The primary difference is that the window size, N, may be adaptive, changing in value to respond to changes in network congestion. When a transport connection becomes congested (blocked), it notifies the sessions assigned to stop transmitting until further notice.

REFERENCES

1. R. J. CYPSER, *Communications Architecture for Distributed Systems*, Addison-Wesley, Reading, Mass., 1978.

2. G. FALK, "A Comparison of Network Architectures—The ARPANET and SNA," *AFIPS Conf. Proc.*, **47**, 755–763, (June 1978).

3. J. M. McQUILLAN and V. G. CERF, *Tutorial: A Practical View of Communication Protocols*, IEEE Catalog No. EHO 137-0, IEEE Computer Society, Long Beach, Calif., 1978.

4. K. NAEMARA ET AL. "Data Communication Network Architecture—Objective and Concepts," *Rev. Electr. Commun. Lab.*, (NTT Public Corp.), **27**(5–6), 298–311 (May-June 1979).

5. H. ZIMMERMANN, "OSI Reference Model—The ISO Model of Architecture for Open Systems Interconnection," *IEEE Trans. Commun.*, **COM-28**(4), 425–432 (Apr. 1980).

2.32   HIGH-LEVEL PROTOCOLS

H. C. Forsdick

2.32.1   What is a High-Level Protocol?

A high-level protocol (HLP) is the highest layer of communication conventions followed by interacting processes. This basic definition can be augmented by several alternative, but consistent views. From the standpoint of an application program, HLPs are the agreements on application program-specific information exchanged between the multiple components of an application. To the communications network, HLPs are the last layer of communications conventions followed by autonomous, interacting processes. An example of an intermediate-level protocol is a data transfer protocol, which uses a low-level protocol for byte stream communication and is used in turn by an HLP, such as a file transfer protocol for transferring complex data items. For the programmer of a distributed application program, HLPs are the high-level languages of a distributed computing environment [1,2]. Components of a distributed computation interact in the language specified by the HLP. For a protocol designer, HLPs, like all other protocols, represent standards for communication. In terms of the ISO model (see the introduction to Sec. 2.31), aspects of HLPs may be implemented in both the presentation services layer and the session control layer.

2.32.2 Examples

There are many examples of HLPs which emphasize different aspects, views, or levels of sophistication. The earliest well-publicized HLPs were developed for the ARPANET [3]. As a result, many HLPs dealing with the same subject are similar to the ARPANET protocols in spirit, if not also in detail. In the following discussion we draw on many of the ARPANET protocols as examples and include references to other similar HLPs.

Telnet: A Terminal-to-Process Protocol

In the ARPANET Telecommunications Network (Telnet) Protocol [4], an example of a terminal-to-host protocol (THP), the participants in the protocol are one process connected to a terminal (called the *user* process) and a second process (the *server* process) which passes characters to and from a third process (the *remote* process). The server and remote processes are located on the same host, whereas usually, the server and user processes are on different hosts. The Telnet Protocol is the means of creating and controlling a process running on a remote host.

Issues stressed in Telnet include standardization on a network virtual terminal (NVT) which serves as a common basis for terminal–process interactions, and option negotiation about the exact features of the NVT to handle the different types of terminals and processes that exist. The communication path between the user and server processes is called a Telnet connection, a full duplex connection used to transmit both data and command information. Each end of a Telnet connection (user and server) is assumed to be an NVT. The NVT eliminates the need for user and server hosts to keep information about characteristics of each other's terminals and host-specific ways of handling terminals. Users and servers map their local terminal device characteristics so as to appear to be dealing with an NVT over the network. The NVT is an input and output character device with a printer (e.g., a video display) and a keyboard. The printer responds to incoming data from the Telnet connection and the keyboard produces outgoing data to the Telnet connection. The standardized character set of an NVT is an extended 7-bit ASCII code in an 8-bit field. Other issues that center around the NVT include: the handling of both half-duplex and full-duplex terminals within the same NVT model, standard representations for control functions not standardized by the 7-bit ASCII codes (e.g., erase a character, erase a line, etc.), and standardized ways of interrupting the normal sequencing of data transmission and synchronizing the input and output sides of a Telnet connection. This set of mechanisms allows terminal users to regain control of runaway processes.

Option negotiation is included in the Telnet protocol because many sites wish to provide additional services over and above those available within an NVT. The various options to an NVT allow a user and server to agree on different conventions for their Telnet connection. The approach to the negotiation is for either party to request that a specific option be in effect. The other party may either accept or reject the request. Examples of optional NVT features supported by Telnet include remote echoing of characters and control over the output line width so that lines that overflow an agreed-upon width can be handled properly.

File Transfer Protocol

There are several different existing file transfer protocols (FTPs); two good examples are the ARPANET FTP [5] and the AUTODIN II FTP [6]. In all, the purpose is to move a data file stored on one host to a data file stored on a different host, with the possibility that the two hosts are very dissimilar in their representation of data or their view of files. Issues stressed include standard representations of data items and files, translation from this standard to the specific host representation of data items and files, and transfer of control and status information facilitating good feedback to the user (or process) who initiated the file transfer. In some sense the issues associated with FTPs are very similar to the issues associated with THPs (e.g., Telnet). Unlike the latter protocols, a concise standardization of a network virtual file (NVF) has yet to reach acceptance, perhaps because of the relatively wide variation between files on the many different host operating systems. Developing such an NVF is clearly a desirable goal.

In a file transfer protocol, there are usually three components: a controller, a donor, and a recipient. The controller interacts with the human user, accepting commands and reporting progress of the file transfer. In addition, the controller interacts with the other two components, causing the donor to transfer the file to the recipient. As stated, each of the three components could reside on a separate host. In some FTPs, the controller and the donor or recipient are merged into one component and a file transfer involves only two hosts: the one on which the human user resides and the one to or from which the file is being transferred.

Issues associated with standard representations of data and translation to and from this representation for FTPs are similar to the same issues for THPs. With FTPs, because such translations must be performed on large amounts of data (relative to THP), there is usually a way to avoid such translations when both donor and recipient share the same internal representation. Since file transfer is a much less interactive task than interacting with a terminal, many FTPs contain provisions for reporting the current status of an ongoing file transfer.

Network Graphics Protocal and Network Voice Protocols

The purpose of a network graphics protocol [7] is to provide a standard way for an application program to control a graphics display. In this sense it is a natural extension of a THP, such as Telnet. For a different representation of information, such as spoken words, yet another protocol is required, a network voice protocol [8]. Although there are many structural differences between such protocols, one common goal exists: to develop an efficient yet flexible and powerful representation of the information being transferred.

Data Language: Data Base Access Protocol

An example of a protocol tailored to a particular application is the ARPANET Data Language Protocol [9]. Data Language can be viewed as a further refinement of a file transfer protocol used for accessing subsets of records in a file. In addition to data transfer, emphasis is placed on ways of expressing record selection based on values of fields in the record.

2.32.3   Features of HLPs

From a sufficiently high level view, most HLPs provide a generic set of architectural features.

Master/Slave versus Symmetric

High-level protocols fall into one of two categories: *master/slave* applications, where a service is offered by the slave and is used by the master, and *symmetric* applications, where both parties following the protocol are equally likely to make use of a protocol feature. Examples of master/slave protocols (also known as user/server protocols) in the ARPANET include Telnet, FTP, and the Data Language. In the case of Telnet, the process connected to the Terminal is the master because the human user interacting with the terminal is the source of most decisions about optional protocol features. The process connected to the remote host is the slave, offering a service. An example of a symmetric HLP is the ARPANET Network Voice Protocol. The NVP is intended to support two-way voice transmission by two symmetric parties.

Language: Commands and Parameters

A protocol is a language for transmitting information. A feature of every HLP is the specification of the form, syntax, and semantics of that language. Much of the effort in designing a protocol is finding the minimum expressive power needed to satisfy the requirements of the application under consideration. The language needs to be simple, so that it is easy for a program to understand (parse) the language as it comes from the other party. On the other hand, the language must be able to express possibly complex orders from one party to the other, which may refer to previous statements in the language.

A promising approach to HLP design is based on the view that an HLP is really an underlying support mechanism for a high-level language. In this sense, the HLP should model the interactions between components programmed in the high-level language.

The language of most existing HLPs is expressed in commands and parameters—the verbs and nouns of HLP languages. A *command* is an order or request to perform a specific operation. The *parameters* included with a command are used as data values when executing the command. There is a strong similarity between HLP languages and programming languages: A command is analogous to a procedure name and a parameter is analogous to an argument to a procedure. An example of a command in the ARPANET FTP for transmitting a file is the STOR command, which directs the recipient to accept the data that follow the command as the contents of a named file. The parameter included with the STOR command is a string which is the name of the destination file. Although not all HLPs are expressed as a set of commands and parameters, almost all could be restated from this viewpoint.

Responses

Where there is the possibility of erroneous specification, optional features or contention for resources, there is also a need for responses to commands. A *response* indicates whether or not a command was obeyed, the nature of the problem when a command was not obeyed, and possibly a value for a parameter when a previous command asked for a selection from a range of choices. An example of the last type of response would be a value selected for a check point interval. Responses are actually quite similar to commands in that they convey an action that the receiver must take (e.g., perform a cleanup action for a negative response) and may reference a value for a parameter (a citation of a value for a parameter that caused a problem for a negative response). In some HLPs responses are just another type of command.

Exceptions / Interruptions

During the normal action of an application program, situations arise where either an abnormal event occurs or where a momentary diversion from the main task is required. Examples include an abnormal disk allocation overflow and a momentary departure while status information about the progress of a main task is reported. When application programs are distributed among multiple components, the HLPs coordinating the communication between the components must have techniques for providing communication outside the normal flow of exchanges. This gives rise to the *exception* or *interruption* mechanism of many HLPs. Such mechanisms provide a means of breaking into a relatively long exchange of information either to stop the exchange or to send additional information during the long exchange. In the AUTODIN II File Transfer Protocol, all commands are sufficiently short so that exceptions and interruptions are treated as ordinary commands.

2.32.4 Issues in the Design of New HLPs

In designing new HLPs, a set of common design strategies can be followed. On analysis most HLPs also display a common set of internal features or topics that must be addressed in the protocol. These strategies and features are derived from early generations of computer communications protocols.

Well-Structured Protocols

An important first step in HLP design is to develop a good model of the intercomponent communication requirements for the application. Does this application require symmetric or asymmetric interactions? (This is inherent in the application. For example, in a network voice protocol, each speaker is equally likely to talk, and thus a symmetric protocol is required.) How frequently will messages interactions between components occur? How much data will be exchanged between components? (With large amounts of data, the overhead associated with each bit of data should be low, so that most of the bandwidth of the communication channel is used for transmitting application data. With small amounts of data, protocols with more elaborate features can still be effective.) Once answers to these questions are known, the basic architecture for the HLP can be specified. The goal is to develop a framework for information exchange which covers all the requirements in as regular a manner as possible with the least number of different mechanisms. Such well-structured protocols enhance one's ability to understand, implement, and evaluate an HLP.

Options, Option Negotiation, and Extensions

Very few HLPs are ironclad, unchangable agreements. Hosts and implementations vary in their capabilities, yet there is still the desire to support the greatest common application functionality. In addition, requirements change, equipment changes, and experimental features are invented. Protocol options, option negotiation, and protocol extensions by option negotiation are used to achieve this flexibility. A common practice is to specify a core protocol which incorporates the minimum number of application features necessary to be part of a multicomponent application. Part of the information exchange that occurs when a multipart application program is initiated is to negotiate the set of optional protocol features supported by each component. Option negotiation occurs by the exchange of standard commands, parameters, and responses. Extensions to a protocol fit naturally into the option negotiation strategy and can be viewed as previously undefined options to the protocol. For example, a new protocol feature can be tested by two parties by their negotiation to use the new experimental option without any of the other parties having to know about the experimental option.

Use of Data Paths

The nature of the data paths provided by underlying data transport protocols (host-to-host protocols; see Sec. 2.31) has an impact on the HLP making use of those paths. Most HLPs in the ARPANET rely on connections (i.e., virtual circuits; see Sec. 2.27) through which error-corrected, sequenced streams of data flow. HLPs built on top of other types of data paths, for example, datagrams (see Sec. 2.27), which may arrive in a different order from the one in which they were sent, will choose different approaches to solving problems. Although there is a desire to have the features of an HLP motivated solely by the application, there must be some exploitation of (and compensation for) the strengths (and weaknesses) of the underlying data transport mechanism.

Coding and Data Representations

A significant part of protocol design is the development of schemes for coding information to be transferred along the data paths. In terms of the commands and parameters of an HLP, there are two types of coding: a mapping between the commands of the HLP and a set of command codes (usually, small integers) and a convention for the transfer of parameter values. A parameter value has an associated data type. For example, the file name parameter in a file transfer protocol would be a variable-length character string. For each different data type in an HLP, the protocol must specify the convention used for transmitting values of that type along data paths. For example, if the HLP utilizes floating-point numbers, it must also specify a standard representation for such data items.

Errors and State Resynchronization

Provision must be made for errors and state resynchronization in the interaction of components following an HLP. A component following a command received on a data path must know what to do in the event that an error occurs in the performance of actions implied by the command or if an error occurs in the use of the protocol by another component. Simply aborting the interaction may not be the best action to take, especially when resources have been allocated in response to previous commands. The components need to resynchronize their action so that further actions can occur. At the lowest level of a protocol, a standard method for resynchronizing the interpretation of data items needs to be specified. At the highest level, resynchronization needs to be performed in the terms and objects pertinent to the application in question. For example, in an FTP, if a file is specified to which a user has no access, what is the next command to be exchanged between the controller and the donor? Should the user be allowed to continue issuing commands, or should connections be closed and further file transfers prevented? In some highly secure environments, the latter action may be warranted.

2.32.5   Issues in the Implementation of HLPs

High-level protocols that display regularity and order are easier to implement and maintain than HLPs where each mechanism has been added in an ad hoc manner. As usual, in any implementation, protocols that make use of symmetry, repeated structures, and recursive structures are easier to implement than are less-well-structured protocols.

Finally, we should not lose track of the purpose of a high-level protocol: to transmit information between components of a multicomponent application program. The extent to which the HLP is tuned to the specific application will determine the ease of implementing the distributed application.

REFERENCES

1. L. POUZIN and H. ZIMMERMAN, "A Tutorial on Protocols," *Proc. IEEE*, **66**(11), 1346–1369 (Nov. 1978).

2. R. F. SPROULL and D. COHEN, "High Level Protocols," *Proc. IEEE*, **66**(11), 1371–1386 (Nov. 1978.)

3. L. G. ROBERTS and B. D. WESSLER, "Computer Network Development to Achieve Resource Sharing," *AFIPS Conf. Proc.*, **36**, 543–549 (June 1970).

4. J. DAVIDSON ET AL. "The ARPANET Telnet Protocol: Its Purpose, Principles, Implementation and Impact on Host Operating System Design," *Proc. 5th ACM-IEEE Data Commun. Symp.*, 4.10–4.18 Sept. 1977.

5. E. FEINLER and J. POSTEL, (eds.), "File Transfer Protocol for the ARPANET," *ARPANET Protocol Handbook*, 1976 ed., pp. 117–235; available for NTIS, DDC AD A027964.

6. H. C. FORSDICK, "AUTODIN II File Transfer Protocol," Bolt Beranek and Newman, Inc., Technical Report No. 4246, Cambridge, Mass.

7. R. F. SPROULL and E. L. THOMAS, "A Network Graphics Protocol," *Comput. Graphics*, **8**(3) (Fall 1974).

8. D. COHEN, "Specification for the Network Voice Protocol," ISI/RR-75-39, DDC AD A023506. USC/Information Sciences Inst., Marina del Rey, Calif., Mar. 1976.

9. T. MARILL and D. H. STERN, "The Datacomputer: A Network Utility," *Proc. AFIPS Natl. Comput. Conf.*, Vol. 44, AFIPS Press, Montvale, N.J., 1975.

SECTION 3

COMPUTER-AIDED CIRCUIT ANALYSIS AND DESIGN

SHELDON S. L. CHANG, EDITOR

Department of Electrical Engineering
State University of New York at Stony Brook

I. HAJJ

Department of Electrical Engineering
University of Illinois at Urbana

S. SUSSMAN-FORT

Department of Electrical Engineering
State University of New York at Stony Brook

Computer circuit analysis and design programs are very effective engineering aids. They can be instructed to do the routine analysis, parameter optimization, and circuit layout work with a minimum of programming. By taking over such drudgery, they relieve their user to concentrate on creative thinking and design which only a human being can do.

The present section gives an introduction to computer circuit analysis and parameter optimization, their algorithms, and input/output representations. The subject is still being developed, and much of the state-of-the-art material is not published; our discussion is necessarily limited by this constraint. However, by acquainting readers with the basic principles and techniques, it is expected that they will be able to use an existing program intelligently, provide user input effectively, and in case of necessity, write special programs to fit their own needs.

3.1 ELEMENTS OF COMPUTER CIRCUIT ANALYSIS AND DESIGN PROGRAMS

S. S. L. Chang

A computer-aided circuit analysis program has three essential components:

1. *An input program with its structured library.* The input program is designed for users to communicate their circuit analysis problem unambiguously to the computer. A structured library makes this possible with a minimum amount of required input programming.

2. *The modeling and analysis program.* The modeling program expresses each physical device (e.g., transistor, diode, etc.) as an equivalent circuit of mathematically defined circuit elements, linear or nonlinear, which is then integrated into the global circuit to be analyzed. At the end of the modeling stage, each and every circuit element is defined mathematically. The required performance, dc, and frequency or transient response are then calculated from the global circuit.

3. *The output program.* The output program communicates the computed results to the user in a numerical and/or graphical format.

Computer-aided circuit design is based on a circuit analysis program, as shown in the flowchart of Fig. 1. The blocks with rounded corners indicate stages in which user input is usually necessary. With a given design specification, a preliminary design is made, and an overall or integrated performance cost function F is formulated. The performance of the preliminary design is then calculated with the circuit analysis program, and the results are used to determine the circuit's cost F. A number of preselected parameters in the circuit are adjusted to minimize F according to a parameter optimization algorithm, and F is recalculated. The optimization loop is represented by the heavy flow lines in Fig. 1. The loop is traversed repeatedly until the parameters are optimized. If the optimized performance is satisfactory, the program ends with the finalized circuit, circuit parameters, and performance as its output. If the optimized performance is not satisfactory, changes are made in the preliminary design and/or the circuit topolgy, and the process is repeated.

3.1.1 Input Format and Structured Model Library

The circuit to be analyzed is defined by (1) $N + 1$ nodes and (2) devices and circuit elements connected to the nodes. The node 0 is generally taken as the ground or reference node. Each device, subcircuit, or circuit element is specified by its name, nodes to which its terminals are connected, and parameter values. Sometimes it is not necessary to supply all the parameter values. A set of "default" parameter values is stored in the library. The default values are assumed for the parameters that are not explicitly specified.

There are two types of models in a structured model library: (1) *permanent models*, and (2) *temporary models*. The permanent models are part of the analysis program, and the temporary models are user defined. A model may be no more than a set of numerical values defining the parameters of another model, or it may be the equivalent circuit of a device, or a subcircuit comprised of circuit elements, devices, and/or other subcircuits.

Figure 2 illustrates the hierarchy in a structured model library. At the base are idealized circuit elements that are admissible to the analysis program. Note that the set of admissible circuit elements can be different at different stages of the analysis. For instance, a nonlinear resistance is admissible in the dc and transient analysis, but is not admissible for linearized small-signal frequency-response calculations. The Ebers–Moll model of bipolar transistors or one of its modified versions is used in the

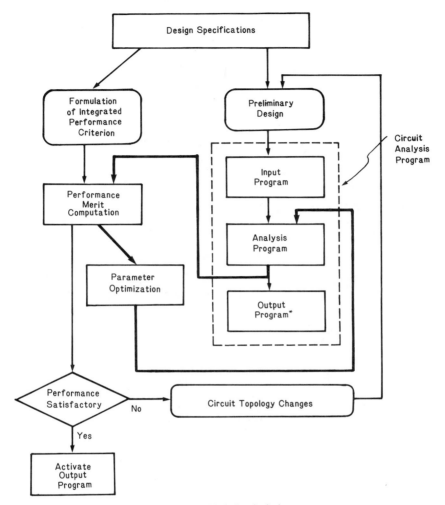

Fig. 1 Computer-aided circuit design program.

dc analysis. Once the operating condition (I_C, V_{CE}) is determined, the linearized transistor parameters are calculated and used in the small-signal analysis programs. As a rule, both the nonlinear and linear versions of a device model are stored.

One level above the circuit elements are the device models, each of which is an equivalent circuit made up from the set of admissible circuit elements. Similarly, each stored subcircuit is made up from stored subcircuits of lower levels, devices, and circuit elements. The software for defining circuit models at various levels is similar to that used in nesting of subroutines.

A stored subcircuit in computer-aided circuit analysis can be compared to a block in system analysis. However, it has entirely different implications. A block is represented by its transfer characteristics, and interacts as a single unit with other components in the system. A stored subcircuit is no more than a convenient means of user input to the computer. At the beginning of the analysis program, each subcircuit or device model is replaced by its equivalent circuit and integrated into the global circuit. The circuit elements are treated alike in the analysis program, as their origins are completely disregarded.

However, within the framework described above, it does offer the user freedom to substitute a simpler equivalent version for the complete circuit. For instance, an operational amplifier is usually represented as a controlled source with appropriate input and output circuits in lieu of the complete transistor circuit.

In the following, we illustrate these concepts with some commonly used circuit analysis programs.

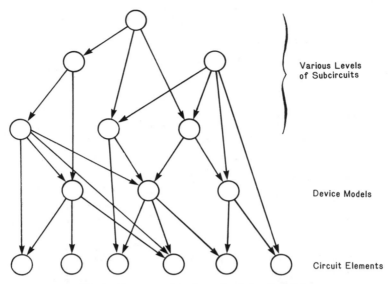

Fig. 2   Structure of device and subcircuit models.

EXAMPLE 1. SCEPTRE [27].   The devices and circuit elements in SCEPTRE are entered into the program with the following format:

ELEMENT NAME, NODE-NODE ... = DESCRIPTION

The first letter in an element name specifies the nature of the element:

E	Voltage source
J	Current source
R, L, M, C	Resistance, inductance, mutual inductance, and capacitance, respectively
D	Diode
T	Transistor (bipolar, FET, or MOSFET)

For instance, a step-response computation of the emitter-follower circuit of Fig. 3 can be entered as follows:

CC-CC EMITTER FOLLOWER
ELEMENTS
EIN, 0-1 = TABLE 1 (TIME)
EV, 0-3 = 12
RL, 0-5 = 0.65
RS, 1-2 = 15
T1, 2-3-4 = MODEL 2NXXXX (TEMP)
T2, 4-3-5 = MODEL 2NYYYY (TEMP)
OUTPUTS
VRL, PLOT
FUNCTIONS
TABLE 1
0,4
0,4.1
1,4.1
1,4
2,4

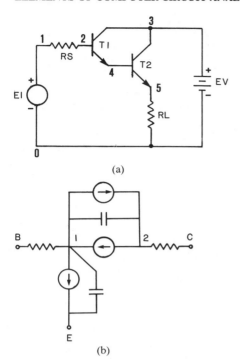

(a)

(b)

Fig. 3   CC-CC emitter follower: (a) actual circuit;
(b) transistor model.

Under the heading ELEMENTS, the first line enters the input voltage EIN as connected between nodes 0 and 1 with positive polarity at 1. The description part means that EIN is a function of time as given by TABLE 1, which specifies a pulse input of 100 mV. The second line enters the 12-V battery EV as connected between 0 and 3 with positive polarity at 3. The next two lines enter RL and RS with resistances of 0.65 Ω and 15 Ω, respectively. The next two lines enter transistors T1 and T2 with B-C-E connected to 2-3-4 and 4-3-5, respectively. We note that the input statements above completely specify the circuit of Fig. 3a without any need of referring to Fig. 3a itself. The stored transistor equivalent circuits are illustrated in Fig. 3b. The transistors T1 and T2 are replaced by the equivalent circuits at the beginning of the analysis program. By entering the models in lieu of the equivalent circuits, considerable user time and effort are saved. In the analysis program the nodes $0,1,2,\ldots$ of the equivalent circuit for T1 become $1T1, 2T1,\ldots$, and no ambiguity will arise.

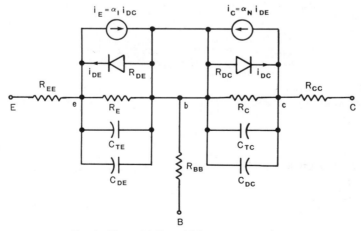

Fig. 4   Ebers–Moll model for an *npn* transistor.

The circuit of Fig. 3*b* is a reduced model for operation in the transistor's forward active region. A complete model is illustrated in Fig. 4. It is basically an Ebers–Moll model, but the coefficients θ_E, θ_C,... (see page 372) are to be determined experimentally. It turns out that the experimentally determined θ_E is approximately equal to $1/kT$, but θ_C is much lower. Procedures for determining θ_E, θ_C, and other parameters in Fig. 4 are given in Refs. 21 and 27.

EXAMPLE 2. SPICE [1].   The SPICE input format is very similar to that of SCEPTRE. The first letter in the name of an element specifies its nature. For instance, the circuit of Fig. 3*a* can be entered as follows:

    TWO STAGE COMMON COLLECTOR AMPLIFIER
    VIN 1-6 AC 1 PULSE 0. 100mV 0. 0. 0. 1.
    VB   6-0 DC 4
    VV   3-0 DC 12
    RL   5-0 650
    RS   1-2 15K
    Q1   3-2-4 BNPN
    Q2   3-4-5 BNPN
    ·OUT VRL 5-0 PRINT MA PLOT MA PRINT TR PLOT TR
    ·AC DEC 10 100HZ 100MEG HZ
    ·TR 10NS 500NS
    ·MODEL BNPN NPN BF= 220 BE = 0.5 RB = 75 VA = 100 CCS = 1.5PF
        CJE = 2PF CJC = 1PF
    ·END

The input voltage V1 is separated into a signal component VIN and a bias component VB with node 6 in between. Line 1 specifies the input voltage as connected to nodes 1 and 6. It has a value of 1 V during ac analysis, and is a rectangular pulse of 100 mV during transient analysis. Line 2 specifies the bias voltage as 4 V dc with its positive terminal connected to node 6. The next three lines are self-explanatory. Line 6 enters transistor Q1 (T1 in Fig. 3*a*) with its terminals C-B-E connected to nodes 3-2-4, respectively. The model for Q1 is BNPN. The next line enters Q2 as an identical transistor. However, as the operating points of Q1 and Q2 are different, the linearized models that are computed from the general model BNPN are different for the two transistors. Line 8 identifies the voltage across RL as the output variable and specifies that the ac magnitude and transient response are to be printed and plotted. The next two lines specify 10 points per decade for frequency response from 10^2 to 10^8 Hz, and 10 ns per point for transient response from 0 to 500 ns. The last line specifies the parameters BF, BR, RB, VA, CCS, CJE, and CJC in the BNPN model. There are 15 parameters to be specified in MODEL BNPN. The user has the choice of specifying any subset of the 15, and default values that are stored in the SPICE program will be used for the unspecified ones.

EXAMPLE 3. *Impulse Generator* (Contributed by S. E. Sussman-Fort).   The present example gives an analysis of an impulse generator with SPICE. Figure 4 illustrates the circuit of the impulse generator. The input voltage VIN is a high-frequency, sinusoidal voltage, and pulse shaping is performed by L1, D1, and R1. The diode D1 suppresses the phase-shifted positive peak and sharpens the negative peak. Consequently, the output voltage at terminal 2 is a series of negative pulses with a pulse rate equal to the frequency of VIN. The SPICE program is as follows:

    IMPULSE GENERATOR
    VIN 1 0 SIN(0 10 200MEG 0 0)
    L1 1 2 20NH
    R1 2 0 300
    D1 2 0 DIODE
    ·MODEL DIODE D(CJO = 10PF)
    ·TRAN .1NS 6.4NS
    ·PLOT TRAN V(1) V(2)
    ·PRINT TRAN V(1) V(2)
    END

The first four lines of the program define the circuit and circuit elements, as shown in Fig. 5. The next line selects diode model D with a junction capacitance of 10 pF at its built-in potential ψ. The selected model automatically gives a dc current and a junction capacitance versus voltage relationship

$$I_D = I_s(e^{qV/kT} - 1), \quad C_J = C_{JO}\left(1 - \frac{V}{\psi}\right)^{-1/2}$$

where $I_s = 10^{-14}$ A. The next three lines specify transient performance for a total time period of 6.4×10^{-9} s, to be plotted at 0.1×10^{-9}-s intervals. The result is shown in Fig. 6.

To summarize the above, there are three essential ingredients in a successful input language:

1. Simplicity and unambiguity.
2. Resemblance to traditional engineering terminology so that the input language can be easily understood, remembered, and used.

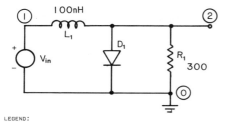

Fig. 5 Impulse generator.

```
LEGEND:

+: V(1)
*: V(2)

   TIME        V(1)

(+*)------------------  -1.000+001          -5.000+000          .000          5.000+000          1.000+001
                        - - - - - - - -                              X
    .000        .000        .                              X
  1.000-010   1.253+000     .                              *        +
  2.000-010   2.487+000     .                              *              +
  3.000-010   3.681+000     .                              .*                  +
  4.000-010   4.817+000     .                              .*                     +.
  5.000-010   5.878+000     .                              .*                        +
  6.000-010   6.845+000     .                              *                            +
  7.000-010   7.705+000     .                              *                               +
  8.000-010   8.443+000     .                              *                                  +
  9.000-010   9.048+000     .                              *                                    +
  1.000-009   9.510+000     .                              *                                      +.
  1.100-009   9.823+000     .                              *                                        +.
  1.200-009   9.980+000     .                              *                                         +
  1.300-009   9.980+000     .                              *                                         +
  1.400-009   9.823+000     .                              *                                        +.
  1.500-009   9.511+000     .                              *                                      +.
  1.600-009   9.048+000     .                              *                                    +
  1.700-009   8.443+000     .                              *                                  +
  1.800-009   7.705+000     .                              *                               +
  1.900-009   6.846+000     .                              *                            +
  2.000-009   5.878+000     .                              *                        +
  2.100-009   4.818+000     .                              .*                     +
  2.200-009   3.681+000     .                              .*                  +
  2.300-009   2.487+000     .                              *              +
  2.400-009   1.254+000     .                              *        +
  2.500-009   2.084-004     .                           +  *  +
  2.600-009  -1.253+000     .                              +   *
  2.700-009  -2.487+000     .                          +    *
  2.800-009  -3.681+000     .                  +    *
  2.900-009  -4.817+000     .                         .+
  3.000-009  -5.878+000     .                      +
  3.100-009  -6.845+000     .                  +
  3.200-009  -7.705+000     .          +.
  3.300-009  -8.443+000     .       +
  3.400-009  -9.048+000     .     +
  3.500-009  -9.510+000     . +
  3.600-009  -9.823+000     .+
  3.700-009  -9.980+000     +
  3.800-009  -9.980+000     +
  3.900-009  -9.823+000     .+
  4.000-009  -9.511+000     . +
  4.100-009  -9.048+000     .     +
  4.200-009  -8.443+000     .       +
  4.300-009  -7.705+000     .          +
  4.400-009  -6.846+000     .              +
  4.500-009  -5.878+000     .                  +
  4.600-009  -4.818+000     .                    .+
  4.700-009  -3.681+000     .                      .*        *
  4.800-009  -2.487+000     .               *           +
  4.900-009  -1.254+000     .        *                       +
  5.000-009  -2.084-004     .   *
  5.100-009   1.253+000     .  *
  5.200-009   2.487+000     .        *              +
  5.300-009   3.681+000     .                 .*
  5.400-009   4.817+000     .                      .*              +
  5.500-009   5.878+000     .                         *              +
  5.600-009   6.845+000     .                       *                +
  5.700-009   7.705+000     .                         *                   +
  5.800-009   8.443+000     .                         *                        +
  5.900-009   9.048+000     .                         *                           +
  6.000-009   9.510+000     .                         *                              +
  6.100-009   9.823+000     .                         *                                +.
  6.200-009   9.980+000     .                         *                                 +
  6.300-009   9.980+000     .                         *                                 +
  6.400-009   9.823+000     .                         *                                +.
```

Fig. 6 Transient response of impulse generator.

3. Allowing user freedom to specify in device models only the parameters that are pertinent to the specific analysis problem.

3.1.2 Modeling and Analysis

The set of *basic circuit elements* that are used as building blocks to represent the device models are the following:

1. Linear R, L, C elements and dependent sources
2. Nonlinear R, L, C elements and dependent sources
3. Transmission lines and time-delay elements

The nonlinear R, L, C elements and dependent sources are generalizations of the corresponding linear ones. For instance, a linear resistance R can be expressed in either voltage-controlled or current-controlled form, and their corresponding nonlinear generalizations are shown to the left:

$$\text{Voltage controlled:} \quad i = Gv \rightarrow \quad i = \hat{G}(v)$$
$$\text{Current controlled:} \quad v = Ri \rightarrow \quad v = \hat{R}(i)$$

Another example is a voltage-controlled current source:

$$i_{12} = g_m v_{xy} \rightarrow i_{12} = G_m(v_{xy})$$

On the left, the dependent current source i_{12} is equal to the voltage v_{xy} multiplied by a transconductance g_m. For the nonlinear case, i_{12} is a nonlinear function G_m of the voltage variable v_{xy}.

A capacitance relates the stored charge q to the voltage v across the capacitor, and can be expressed in two ways:

$$\text{Voltage controlled:} \quad q = Cv \rightarrow \quad q = \hat{C}(v)$$
$$\text{Charge controlled:} \quad v = C^{-1}q \rightarrow \quad v = \hat{C}^{-1}(q)$$

where C^{-1} is the inverse function of C. In either case the charging current i is related to q by $i = dq/dt$.

An inductance can be either current-controlled or flux controlled:

$$\lambda = Li \rightarrow \qquad \lambda = \hat{L}(i)$$
$$i = L^{-1}\lambda \rightarrow \qquad i = \hat{L}^{-1}(\lambda)$$

and the voltage drop v is expressed as $v = d\lambda/dt$.

The *hierarchy of models* is illustrated in the following:

$$\text{global model} \rightarrow \text{local model} \rightarrow \text{linearized model}$$

For instance, the Ebers–Moll model of a bipolar transistor in Fig. 4 is a global model. For large-signal analysis in the unsaturated region, $v_{CE} \geqslant 0.3$ V, the collector emission current i_{DC} can be ignored, and it becomes the local model of Fig. 7a. Figure 7b is an equivalent version of Fig. 7a. For small-signal analysis a linearized model (Fig. 7c) with constant branch parameters is used. The values of the branch parameters depend on the operating point. Detailed calculations for Figs. 4 and 7 and linearization are shown in Table 1.

For dc calculations, the inductances are replaced by short circuits, and the capacitances are replaced by open circuits. These replacements can be made in the model itself so that the number of nodes and branches are reduced, and the model is thereby simplified. A dc model is of lower hierarchy than its corresponding general version.

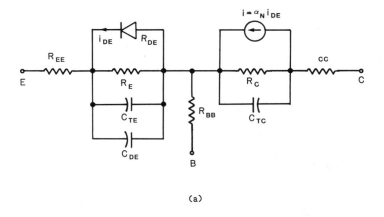

(a)

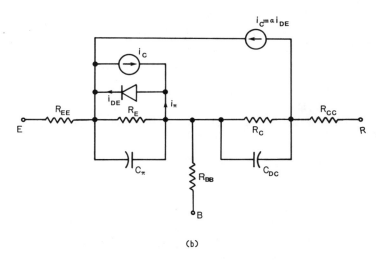

(b)

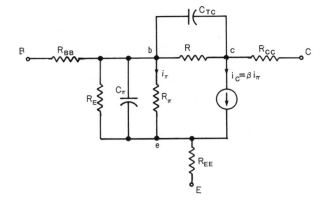

(c)

Fig. 7 Localized *npn* transistor model: (*a*) common base; (*b*) transition to common emitter; (*c*) common emitter.

371

Table 1

Ebers – Moll Model

1. R_{BB}, R_{CC}, and R_{EE} are the ohmic resistances of the base, collector, and emitter, respectively.
2. R_E = emitter–base leakage resistance ($>10^6\ \Omega$)
    R_C = collector–base leakage resistance ($>10^6\ \Omega$)
3. i_{DE} = base–emitter diode current

$$i_{DE} = \frac{I_{ES}}{1 - \alpha_N \alpha_I}\left[\exp\left(\frac{qV_{BE}}{M_E kT}\right) - 1\right] \qquad \text{(SPICE)}$$

where

I_{ES} = base–emitter diode saturation current, typically 10^{-9} to 10^{-14} A
α_N = common-base normal-mode current gain (≈ 0.99)
α_I = common-base inverted-mode current gain (≈ 0.5)
M_E = emission constant to be determined experimentally
$i_{DE} = I_{ES}[\exp(\theta_E V_{BE}) - 1]$ (SCEPTRE)

4. i_{DC} = base–collector diode current

$$i_{DC} = \frac{I_{CS}}{1 - \alpha_N \alpha_I}\left[\exp\left(\frac{qV_{BC}}{M_C kT}\right) - 1\right] \qquad \text{(SPICE)}$$

I_{CS} = base–collector diode saturation current $[I_{CS} = I_{ES}(\alpha_N/\alpha_I)]$
M_C = emission constant
$i_{DC} = I_{CS}[\exp(\theta_C V_{CE}) - 1]$ (SCEPTRE)
The constants I_{ES}, M_C, M_E, θ_E, and θ_C are determined experimentally.

5. C_{TE} = emitter–base junction transition capacitance

$$C_{TE} = \frac{C_{TEO}}{(1 - V_{BE}/V_{ZE})^{n_E}} \qquad (V_{BE} < V_{ZE})$$

V_{ZE} = emitter–base junction contact potential (0.4 V for germanium, 0.9 V for silicon)
n_E = grading constant (typically $0.3 < n_E \leqslant 0.5$)

6. $$C_{TC} = \frac{C_{TCO}}{(1 + V_{CB}/V_{ZC})^{n_C}}$$

7. $$C_{DE} = \frac{\tau_N q}{M_E kT}\left(i_{DE} + \frac{I_{ES}}{1 - \alpha_N \alpha_I}\right)$$

$$C_{DC} = \frac{\tau_I q}{M_C kT}\left(i_{DC} + \frac{I_{CS}}{1 - \alpha_N \alpha_I}\right)$$

where τ_N and τ_I are base transit times in the forward and reversed directions.

Forward Operation Models
Assuming that $i_{DC} \approx 0$, then $C_{DC} \approx 0$ and $i_E \approx 0$. The model of Fig. 5a is obtained. Figure 5b is the same as 5a, with the dependent current source i_C shown in an equivalent form. The new variable i_π is

$$i_\pi = i_{DE} - i_C = (1 - \alpha_N)i_{DE} = (1 - \alpha_N)\frac{i_C}{\alpha_N} = \frac{i_C}{\beta}$$

In Fig. 5c, C_π and i_π are specified by

$$C_\pi = C_{DE} + C_{TE}$$

$$i_\pi = \frac{(1 - \alpha_N)I_{ES}}{1 - \alpha_N \alpha_I}\left[\exp\left(\frac{qV_{be}}{M_E kT}\right) - 1\right]$$

The *linearized* R_π is given by

$$R_\pi[\text{linearized}] = \left(\frac{\partial i_\pi}{\partial V_{be}}\right)^{-1} = \frac{M_E kT}{q I_\pi}$$

where I_π is the zero-signal value of i_π.
   The *linearized* C_π and C_{TC} are obtained by using $I_\pi/(1 - \alpha_N)$ for i_{DE} in calculating C_{DE}, and zero-signal values of V_{BE} and V_{CB} in calculating C_{TE} and C_{TC}, respectively.

Thus a model of higher hierarchy (global model) can be used to generate lower-hierarchy (local and linearized) models but not the other way around. For any given computational program, the simplest model (lowest in hierarchy) that accurately represents the device is used.

The trend in computer-aided analysis is toward automation. In advanced programs, it is not necessary for the user to input a model of lower hierarchy. The program automatically computes the operating point of a device and generates a model of lowest hierarchy which is adequate for the required analysis program.

There are three basic analysis programs:

1. Dc nonlinear analysis
2. Ac–dc linear analysis
3. Transient analysis

Dc nonlinear analysis is used to determine the dc currents in various branches. One of its important applications is to determine the *operating point* of a device so that the parameter values in the linearized device model can be evaluated. The commonly used algorithms for nonlinear dc circuit calculations are the Newton–Raphson algorithm and the piecewise-linear method. These methods are discussed in Sec. 3.3.

Algorithms for linear analysis of ac and dc circuits are presented in Sec. 3.2. The formulation of circuit equations, solution by factorization into lower and upper triangular matrices, and sparse matrix methods are discussed.

The basic algorithm for transient analysis is numerical integration. At each instant of time a capacitor is equivalent to a dc voltage source and an inductor is equivalent to a dc current source. The branch currents and voltages are then obtained with either one of the dc nonlinear or linear algorithms. The average capacitor current (or inductor voltage) multiplied by the time interval gives the increment in capacitor charge (or inductor flux linkage). The capacitor voltage (or inductor current) is then obtained from the new value of charge (flux linkage). The new source voltage and current values are then used for the next round of computation.

An alternative method for linear transients is to use analytic solution, or e^{At}. Both methods are discussed in Sec. 3.4.

3.1.3 Optimization Problem

The first step in an optimization problem is to formulate a cost function, which is usually in summation form [28]:

$$F(\mathbf{x}) = \tfrac{1}{2} \sum_{k=1}^{k=N} |V_o(j\omega_k) - \hat{V}_o(j\omega_k)|^2 W_k \tag{1}$$

where $V_o(j\omega_k)$ is the actual output variable, and $\hat{V}_o(j\omega_k)$ is its desired value at frequency ω_k. The constants W_k are weighting factors at frequencies ω_k.

The vector $\mathbf{x}$ represents the design parameters $x_1, x_2, \ldots, x_n$ which are to be optimized. The dependence of F on x is *implicit* in the sense that the computed $V_o(j\omega_k)$ depends on the value of $\mathbf{x}$. An explicit expression of $F(\mathbf{x})$ in terms of $x_1, x_2, \ldots, x_n$ is usually unknown or nonexistent.

In addition to cost minimization, another significant problem is that of parameter uncertainty or tolerances. There are two known approaches to this problem:

1. *Minimizing sensitivity.* Let $\mathbf{y}$ and $\pm \Delta \mathbf{y}$ denote the nominal parameter values and their tolerances. In general, $\mathbf{y}$ represents a much larger set of parameters and includes the design parameters $\mathbf{x}$. The partial derivative of F with respect to y_i is its sensitivity to y_i:

$$\frac{\partial F}{\partial y_i} = \sum_{k=1}^{k=N} R\left\{ [V_o(j\omega_k) - \hat{V}_o(j\omega_k)]^* \frac{\partial V_o(j\omega_k)}{\partial y_i} \right\} W_k \tag{2}$$

where * denotes complex conjugate, and $R\{\cdot\}$ denotes the real component of the quantity inside $\{\cdot\}$.

The total variation of F is

$$\Delta F = \sum_i \frac{\partial F}{\partial y_i} \Delta y_i \tag{3}$$

If the variations Δy_i, $i = 1, 2, \ldots$, are independent of each other,

$$F_1 \triangleq \overline{(\Delta F)^2} = \sum_i \left(\frac{\partial F}{\partial y_i} \right)^2 \overline{(\Delta y_i)^2} \tag{4}$$

where an overbar indicates average or expected value.

The partial derivative $\partial V_o(j\omega_k)/\partial y_i$ can be evaluated with the aid of Tellegen's theorem (Sec. 3.6). Consequently, $\partial F/\partial y_i$ and F_1 can be calculated directly. Their values depend on the selected nominal value of $\mathbf{x}$ and can be regarded as implicit functions of $\mathbf{x}$. For a design with minimum sensitivity,

$$F_o(\mathbf{x}) = F + kF_1 = \text{minimum} \tag{5}$$

where $k > 0$. If k is small, the design emphasizes least nominal cost. If k is large, the design emphasizes least sensitivity to parameter variations.

2. *Minimizing the worst case.* It is generally valid that the worst case or maximum F occurs at a corner value of $\mathbf{y}$. However, even with this labor-saving assumption, the cost of a direct computation of maximum F can be prohibitive. If the number of parameters with tolerances is 20, the number of corner values of y is approximately $2^{20} \cong 10^6$!

The maximum value of ΔF can be calculated approximately with the aid of (3). Since Δy_i can be of either sign,

$$F_2 \triangleq (\Delta F)_{\max} = \sum_i \left| \frac{\partial F}{\partial y_i} \right| |\Delta y_i| \tag{6}$$

The worst case F is then

$$F_w(\mathbf{x}) = F + F_2 = \text{minimum} \tag{7}$$

The function $F_w(\mathbf{x})$ is also an implicit function of $\mathbf{x}$.

Equations (1), (5), and (7) are examples of cost functions to be minimized. Sometimes, the required time response is specified, and $F(x)$ is formulated as

$$F(\mathbf{x}) = \frac{1}{2} \sum_{k=1}^{k=N} [V_o(t_k) - V_o(t_k)]^2 W_k \tag{8}$$

Corresponding versions of (5) and (7) are obtained similarly.

The optimization algorithms are discussed in Sec. 3.5.

3.2   ANALYSIS OF LINEAR CIRCUITS

I. Hajj

3.2.1   Circuit-Equation Formulation

A circuit consists of an interconnection of elements where the interconnection can be represented by a graph. The graph consists of branches and nodes. Regardless of the types of elements, the set of currents and voltages associated with a graph obey linear constraints known as Kirchhoff's laws (KCL and KVL, respectively). These current and voltage laws equations are also known as topological equations and are stated as follows (see Sec. 3.1 of Vol. I):

$$\mathbf{A}\mathbf{i}_b = \mathbf{0} \qquad \text{(KCL)} \tag{1}$$

$$\mathbf{v}_b = \mathbf{A}^T \mathbf{v}_n \qquad \text{(KVL)} \tag{2}$$

where $\mathbf{i}_b$ is the set of currents in the b branches of the circuit, $\mathbf{v}_b$ is the set of voltages across the branches; $\mathbf{v}_n$ is the set of n node-to-datum voltages; and $\mathbf{A}$ is an $n \times b$ reduced incidence matrix which contains $+1$, -1, and 0 entries [6]. Note that (1) and (2) form a set of $(b+n)$ linear equations in $(2b+n)$ variables.

In addition to the topological constraints that define the element interconnections, the elements themselves are characterized by constitutive equations that relate the currents, voltages, fluxes, and charges in the branches. These constitutive relations may be in the form of algebraic, differential or integral equations. In this section these relations are considered to be purely algebraic and linear, with the following form (see Sec. 3.1.10 of Vol. I):

$$\mathbf{i}_1 = \mathbf{G}_1\mathbf{v}_1 + \mathbf{H}_1\mathbf{i}_2 + \mathbf{s}_1$$

$$\mathbf{v}_2 = \mathbf{H}_2\mathbf{v}_1 + \mathbf{Z}_2\mathbf{i}_2 + \mathbf{s}_2 \tag{3}$$

where $\mathbf{i}_b = [\mathbf{i}_1, \mathbf{i}_2]$, $\mathbf{v}_b = [\mathbf{v}_1, \mathbf{v}_2]$. Equation (3) forms a set of b equations and includes almost all types of linear circuits elements. Equations (1), (2) and (3) form a set of $2b+n$ equations in $2b+n$ unknowns.

These equations are referred to as the *tableau* equations and have been used in at least one computer program [2]. The tableau equations are usually large, even for small circuits, and sparse matrix techniques (discussed below) are used to solve the equations.

Another widely used formulation approach that is both general and easy to program is known as the *modified nodal* approach [7] (see Sec. 3.1.10 of Vol. I). In this approach the incidence matrix **A** in (1) and (2) is partitioned as follows:

$$[\mathbf{A}_1 \quad \mathbf{A}_2]\begin{bmatrix} \mathbf{i}_1 \\ \mathbf{i}_2 \end{bmatrix} = \mathbf{0} \tag{4}$$

$$\begin{bmatrix} \mathbf{v}_1 \\ \mathbf{v}_2 \end{bmatrix} = \begin{bmatrix} \mathbf{A}_1^T \\ \mathbf{A}_2^T \end{bmatrix} \mathbf{v}_n \tag{5}$$

Eliminating $\mathbf{v}_1$, $\mathbf{v}_2$, and $\mathbf{i}_1$ from (3), (4), and (5), one gets the modified nodal equations:

$$\left[\begin{array}{c|c} \mathbf{A}_1\mathbf{G}_1\mathbf{A}_1^T & \mathbf{A}_1\mathbf{H}_1+\mathbf{A}_2 \\ \hline \mathbf{A}_2^T-\mathbf{H}_2\mathbf{A}_1^T & -\mathbf{Z}_2 \end{array}\right]\begin{bmatrix} \mathbf{v}_n \\ \mathbf{i}_2 \end{bmatrix} = \begin{bmatrix} -\mathbf{A}_1\mathbf{s}_1 \\ \mathbf{s}_2 \end{bmatrix} \tag{6}$$

The first n rows in (6) represent the KCL equations at the nodes, other than the reference node, while the remaining rows consist of the constitutive relations of the elements through which $\mathbf{i}_2$ flows. Note that if there is no coupling in the circuit, the matrix in (6) would be symmetric. In assembling the equations in (6) it is unnecessary to formulate the incidence matrix and carry out matrix multiplications. Instead, the equations are formulated by reading one element at a time and using preprogrammed element "stamps" [7]. Table 1 shows the stamps of typical circuit elements in a frequency-domain analysis; for dc analysis put $\omega = 0$.

Table 1. Stamps of Typical Circuit Elements Used in Formulating the Modified Nodal Equations

Element	Constitutive Equation	Stamp
Resistor (or conductor)	i $i \longrightarrow\!\!\!\bigvee\!\!\!\bigvee\!\!\!\bigvee\!\!\!\longrightarrow j$ $+ \; V \; -$ $i = G(v_i - v_j)$	$\begin{array}{cc} & i \quad\; j \\ \begin{array}{c} i \\ j \end{array} & \left[\begin{array}{cc|c} +G & -G & \\ -G & +G & \\ \hline & & \end{array}\right] \end{array}$
Capacitor	C $i \longrightarrow\!\!\!-\!\!\mid\!\!(\!\!\longrightarrow j$ $i_C = j\omega C(v_i - v_j)$	$\begin{array}{cc} & i \qquad\; j \\ \begin{array}{c} i \\ j \end{array} & \left[\begin{array}{cc|c} j\omega C & -j\omega C & \\ -j\omega C & +j\omega C & \\ \hline & & \end{array}\right] \end{array}$
Inductor	L $i \longrightarrow\!\!\!\bigcirc\!\!\bigcirc\!\!\bigcirc\!\!\longrightarrow j$ $v_i - v_j - j\omega L i_L = 0$	$\begin{array}{cc} & i \quad j \quad\; i_L \\ \begin{array}{c} i \\ j \\ i_L \end{array} & \left[\begin{array}{cc|c} & & +1 \\ & & -1 \\ \hline +1 & -1 & -j\omega L \end{array}\right] \end{array}$
Independent current source	J $i \longrightarrow\!\!\!\bigcirc\!\!\longrightarrow j$ $i = J$	$\begin{array}{c} i \\ j \end{array} \begin{bmatrix} -J \\ +J \end{bmatrix}$ (RHS vector)
Independent voltage source	E $i \longrightarrow\!\!\!\bigcirc\!\!\longrightarrow j$ $\xrightarrow{\; i_v \;}$ $v_i - v_j - E = 0$	$\begin{array}{cc} & i \quad j \quad\; i_v \\ \begin{array}{c} i \\ j \\ i_v \end{array} & \left[\begin{array}{cc|c} & & +1 \\ & & -1 \\ \hline +1 & -1 & 0 \end{array}\right], \begin{bmatrix} \; \\ \; \\ E \end{bmatrix} \end{array}$

Table 1. Continued

Element	Constitutive Equation	Stamp
Voltage-controlled current source	$i_{ij} = g_m(v_k - v_l)$	$\begin{array}{c} \\ i \\ j \end{array}\begin{array}{cc} k & l \\ \left[\begin{array}{cc} +g_m & -g_m \\ -g_m & +g_m \end{array}\right. \end{array}$
Voltage-controlled voltage source	$v_i - v_j - \alpha(v_k - v_l) = 0$	$\begin{array}{c} \\ i \\ j \\ i_v \end{array}\begin{array}{ccccc} i & j & k & l & i_v \\ \left[\begin{array}{ccccc} & & & & +1 \\ & & & & -1 \\ +1 & -1 & -\alpha & +\alpha & 0 \end{array}\right] \end{array}$
Current-controlled current source	$i_{ij} = \beta i_x$	$\begin{array}{c} \\ i \\ j \\ i_x \end{array}\begin{array}{c} i_x \\ \left[\begin{array}{c} +\beta \\ -\beta \\ \end{array}\right] \end{array}$
Current-controlled voltage source	$v_i - v_j - r i_x = 0$	$\begin{array}{c} \\ i \\ j \\ i_v \end{array}\begin{array}{cccc} i & j & i_v & i_x \\ \left[\begin{array}{cccc} & & +1 & \\ & & -1 & \\ +1 & -1 & & -r \end{array}\right] \end{array}$

EXAMPLE 1. Consider the circuit in Fig. 1, which contains resistors, capacitors, inductors, controlled sources, and independent sources. Using the element stamps given in Table 1, the modified nodal equations in the frequency domain at $s = j\omega$ can be easily assembled as shown in (7). The circuit variables consist of the node-to-datum variables v_1 through v_5 together with the currents through the voltage sources i_E and i_α and through the inductor i_L.

$$
\begin{bmatrix}
G_1 & -G_1 & 0 & 0 & 0 & 1 & 0 & 0 \\
-G_1 & G_1+sC_1 & 0 & 0 & 0 & 0 & 0 & 1 \\
0 & 0 & G_2+G_3+sC_2 & -G_3-sC_2 & 0 & 0 & 0 & -1 \\
0 & 0 & -G_3-sC_2 & G_3+G_4+sC_2 & -G_4 & 0 & 1 & 0 \\
0 & 0 & 0 & -G_4 & G_5+G_4+sC_3 & 0 & 0 & 0 \\
1 & 0 & 0 & 0 & 0 & 0 & 0 & 0 \\
0 & 0 & -\alpha & 1 & 0 & 0 & 0 & 0 \\
0 & 1 & -1 & 0 & 0 & 0 & 0 & -sL
\end{bmatrix}
\begin{bmatrix}
v_1 \\ v_2 \\ v_3 \\ v_4 \\ v_5 \\ i_E \\ i_\alpha \\ i_L
\end{bmatrix}
=
\begin{bmatrix}
0 \\ 0 \\ 0 \\ 0 \\ I \\ E \\ 0 \\ 0
\end{bmatrix}
$$

$$(7)$$

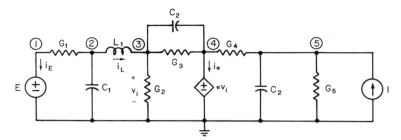

Fig. 1 Linear circuit.

Equation (7) can also be written as

$$
\left\{
\left[
\begin{array}{ccccc|ccc}
G_1 & -G_1 & 0 & 0 & 0 & 1 & 0 & 0 \\
-G_1 & G_1 & 0 & 0 & 0 & 0 & 0 & 1 \\
0 & 0 & G_2+G_3 & -G_3 & 0 & 0 & 0 & -1 \\
0 & 0 & -G_3 & G_3+G_4 & -G_4 & 0 & 1 & 0 \\
0 & 0 & 0 & -G_4 & G_4+G_5 & 0 & 0 & 0 \\
\hline
1 & 0 & 0 & 0 & 0 & 0 & 0 & 0 \\
0 & 0 & -\alpha & 1 & 0 & 0 & 0 & 0 \\
0 & 1 & -1 & 0 & 0 & 0 & 0 & 0
\end{array}
\right]
\right.
$$

$$
\left.
+s
\left[
\begin{array}{ccccc|ccc}
0 & & & & 0 & & & \\
& C_1 & & & & & & \\
& & C_2 & -C_2 & & 0 & & \\
0 & & -C_2 & C_2 & & & & \\
& & & & C_3 & & & \\
\hline
& & & & & 0 & & \\
& & 0 & & & & 0 & \\
& & & & & & & -L
\end{array}
\right]
\right\}
\left[
\begin{array}{c}
v_1 \\ v_2 \\ v_3 \\ v_4 \\ v_5 \\ \hline i_E \\ i_\alpha \\ i_L
\end{array}
\right]
=
\left[
\begin{array}{c}
0 \\ 0 \\ 0 \\ 0 \\ I \\ \hline E \\ 0 \\ 0
\end{array}
\right]
\qquad (8)
$$

which is of the form

$$\mathbf{Px} = [\mathbf{R} + s\mathbf{Q}]\mathbf{x} = \mathbf{y} \qquad (9)$$

where $\mathbf{R}$ consists of the resistive part of the circuit and $\mathbf{Q}$ contains the reactive part. In practice, $\mathbf{R}$ and $\mathbf{Q}$ can be constructed once from element values; then at each frequency ω, $\mathbf{Q}$ is multiplied by $j\omega$ to form the imaginary part of $\mathbf{P}$, while $\mathbf{R}$ forms the real part. This partitioning of $\mathbf{P}$ into two matrices $\mathbf{R}$ and $\mathbf{Q}$ saves computation time in frequency-domain analysis, where the circuit is solved at many different frequencies.

3.2.2 Solution of Linear Equations

The solution of a set of linear equations is an essential part of any circuit simulator. Frequency-domain analysis requires the repeated solution of linear equations at specified frequencies. As will be seen later, the dc and transient analyses involve solving linearized circuits at many iteration points.
  Consider a set of n linear algebraic equations of the form

$$\mathbf{Ax} = \mathbf{y} \qquad (10)$$

where $\mathbf{x}$ is an n-vector of unknown variables, $\mathbf{y}$ is a specified n-vector, and $\mathbf{A}$ is an $n \times n$ nonsingular real or complex matrix. Equation (10) can be solved by inverting $\mathbf{A}$ such that $\mathbf{x} = \mathbf{A}^{-1}\mathbf{y}$. However, matrix inversion is a computationally expensive procedure that requires about n^3 operations (multiplications and divisions). Thus, finding $\mathbf{x}$ by matrix inversion requires $n^3 + n^2$ operations. In addition, $\mathbf{A}^{-1}$ is usually dense even though $\mathbf{A}$ itself may be sparse (a matrix is considered to be sparse if only a small percentage, usually less than 30 percent, of its entries are nonzero). Instead, (10) can be solved more efficiently by first factorizing A into a product LU, where L is a lower triangular matrix and U an upper triangular matrix (if A is numerically symmetric, it can be factorized into the product LDL^T, where D is a diagonal matrix). Either L or U can have a diagonal of 1's. In the sequel it is assumed that U has a diagonal of 1's. The factorization is expressed as follows:

Factorization step:
$$A = LU \tag{11}$$

The unknown x is then computed in two substitution steps:

Forward substitution:
$$Lz = y \tag{12}$$

Backward substitution:
$$Ux = z \tag{13}$$

The factors of A, being upper and lower triangular, can be stored in one matrix B (i.e., $B = L+U-I$). In practice, B may be stored in place of A. The factors LU can be obtained by applying Gaussian elimination. Outlined below are two widely used procedures for factorizing a matrix A into the product LU. The symbol $\leftarrow$ means that the value on the left is replaced by the computed value on the right.

Doolittle's Algorithm. At the kth step in the factorization process:

1. Copy or keep column k as is.
2. Divide all nonzero elements $b_{kj}, j > k, j$ in row k by b_{kk}:
$$b_{kj} \leftarrow b_{kj}/b_{kk}.$$

3. For each element $b_{ij}, i > k, j > k$, subtract from it the product $b_{ik} \times b_{kj}$: $b_{ij} \leftarrow b_{ij} - b_{ik} \times b_{kj}$.
4. When $k = n$, stop.

Crout's Algorithm.

1. Put $b_{j1} \leftarrow a_{j1}, j = 1,2,\ldots,n$ (first column).
2. Put $b_{1j} \leftarrow a_{1j}/b_{11}, j = 2,\ldots,n$ (first row).
3. At the kth step, for column k, put
$$b_{jk} \leftarrow a_{jk} - b_{j1}b_{1k} - b_{j2}b_{2k} - \cdots - b_{j,k-1}b_{k-1,k}, j = k, k+1,\ldots,n.$$

4. For row k, put
$$b_{kj} \leftarrow \frac{1}{b_{kk}}\left(a_{kj} - b_{k1}b_{1j} - b_{k2}b_{2j} - \cdots - b_{k,k-1}b_{k-1,j}\right), j = k+1,\ldots,n.$$

5. When $k = n$, stop.

Note that in Crout's algorithm each element in the matrix is processed one at a time, while in step 3 of Doolittle's algorithm all the elements in the submatrix $b_{ij}, i > k, j > k$ are modified at the kth step. The substitution steps are performed as follows:

Forward Substitution: $Lz = y$. The components of z are calculated starting with z_1, then z_2 until z_n, according to the following formula:
$$z_k = \frac{y_k - \sum_{j=1}^{k-1} l_{kj}z_j}{l_{kk}} \tag{14}$$

Equation (14) can be executed as follows:
At the kth step,
$$z_k = y_k^{(k)} \leftarrow \frac{y_k^{(k-1)}}{l_{kk}}, \quad y_j^{(k)} \leftarrow y_j^{(k-1)} - l_{jk}y_k^{(k)}, \quad j = k+1,\ldots,n$$

Note that the kth step need be performed only when $y_k^{(k)} \neq 0$. The procedure above can be easily programmed when $\mathbf{L}$ is stored column by column.

Backward Substitution: $\mathbf{U}\mathbf{x} = \mathbf{z}$. The components of $\mathbf{x}$ are calculated starting with x_n, then x_{n-1} until z_1, according to the following formula:

$$x_k = z_k - \sum_{j=k+1}^{n} u_{kj}x_j, \qquad k = n, n-1, \ldots, 1 \tag{15}$$

This implementation is efficient when $\mathbf{U}$ is stored row by row. Another implementation of the backward substitution is as follows. At the kth step,

$$x_k = z_k^{(k)} \leftarrow z_k^{(k-1)}, \qquad z_j^{(k)} \leftarrow z_j^{(k-1)} - u_{jk}z_k^{(k)}, \qquad j = k-1, k-2, \ldots, 1$$

where the kth step is performed only when $x_k \neq 0$.

In all the above it is assumed that $l_{kk} \neq 0$ for all k. If during the factorization process $l_{kk} = 0$ at the kth step, it is then necessary to interchange rows and possibly columns to put a nonzero entry in the (k, k) position so that the factorization can proceed. This is known as *pivoting*. Pivoting is also carried out for numerical stability [8]. For example, at step k one would search for the entry with the maximum absolute value in column k below the diagonal and perform row interchange to put that element on the diagonal. This is called *partial pivoting*. *Complete pivoting* involves searching for the element with the maximum absolute value in the unfactorized part of the matrix and moving that particular element to the kth diagonal position by performing both row and column interchanges. Complete pivoting, however, is more complicated to program than partial pivoting.

The number of operations required in performing the factorization and the substitution procedures are now calculated. Let the symbol $|\cdot|$ denote the number of nonzero elements in a matrix or in a vector. Let $\mathbf{M}_{j\cdot}$ and $\mathbf{M}_{\cdot j}$ denote, respectively, the jth row and the jth column of a matrix $\mathbf{M}$. The number of operations required in factorizing $\mathbf{M}$ into the product $\mathbf{L}\mathbf{U}$ (assuming that $\mathbf{U}$ has a diagonal of 1's and $\mathbf{M}$ is numerically nonsymmetric) is

$$\alpha = \sum_{j=1}^{n} |\mathbf{L}_{\cdot j}|(|\mathbf{U}_{j\cdot}| - 1) \tag{16}$$

The number of operations required in the forward substitution is

$$\beta_f = \sum_{j=1}^{n} |\mathbf{L}_{\cdot j}||\mathbf{z}(j)| \tag{17}$$

and in the backward substitution

$$\beta_b = \sum_{j=1}^{n} (|\mathbf{U}_{\cdot j}| - 1)|\mathbf{x}(j)| \tag{18}$$

If $\mathbf{z}$ is full, the total number of operations required by the forward and the backward substitutions combined is

$$\beta = \beta_f + \beta_b = |\mathbf{L}| + |\mathbf{U}| - n \tag{19}$$

Note that β in (19) is also the amount of *storage* required for the factors $\mathbf{L}$ and $\mathbf{U}$. If $\mathbf{L}$ and $\mathbf{U}$ are full, then $\alpha = (n^3 - n)/3$ operations and $\beta = n^2$ operations. In general, α and β depend on the nonzero entries of $\mathbf{L}$ and $\mathbf{U}$, which in turn depend on the nonzero entries of the original matrix $\mathbf{A}$ and on the equation order in which Gaussian elimination has been applied to obtain the $\mathbf{L}\mathbf{U}$ factors. If $\mathbf{A}$ is sparse, it is usually possible to order the elimination steps so that much of its sparsity is preserved. This ordering concept forms the basis of sparse matrix solution techniques, which are discussed next.

3.2.3 Sparse Matrix Solution Techniques

The aim of sparse matrix solution techniques is to order the equations and the variables in solving $\mathbf{A}\mathbf{x} = \mathbf{y}$ by $\mathbf{L}\mathbf{U}$ factorization so that the values of α and β in (16) and in (19) are minimized as much as possible. This would tend to reduce both the number of operations ($\alpha + \beta$) and the amount of storage (β) required to solve for $\mathbf{x}$. Sparse matrix techniques become a necessity as the size of $\mathbf{A}$ increases. The following simple example illustrates the effect of ordering the equations on the sparsity of the factors $\mathbf{L}\mathbf{U}$, and consequently on the amount of storage and computation required to solve $\mathbf{A}\mathbf{x} = \mathbf{y}$.

Consider the circuit shown in Fig. 2. Suppose that the nodal formulation is used to write the network equations with the uncircled node numbers as shown. The structure of the circuit equations is shown in Fig. 3a. The x's denote the nonzero elements in the original matrix, and the F's denote entries that were zero in the original matrix and which became nonzero in the LU factors; these are called *fills*. It can be shown that 40 operations are necessary to carry out LU factorization and 25 operations are necessary to find the node voltage v; the amount of storage required for the LU factors is also 25. Figure 3b shows the structure of the circuit matrix created by renumbering the nodes to correspond to the circled numbers. In this case no fills are generated during the factorization process, which now requires only 8 operations. The number of operations required to find v is now 5, and the amount of storage required for the LU factors is 14.

The example above clearly shows the usefulness of using sparse matrix techniques to reduce both computation and storage. The reordering of the nodes is equivalent to off-diagonal pivoting. In general, off-diagonal pivoting may be more desirable from the sparsity point of view, or even necessary, especially if the diagonal contains zero entries. In the following, two schemes that are widely used for sparse matrix reordering techniques are outlined. These schemes operate on the structure of the matrix with no regard for the actual numerical value of the nonzero entries of the matrix. These schemes are applied once at the outset to reorder the variables and the equations of the circuit. During the solution process, the structure (i.e., the zero–nonzero pattern) of the equation matrix remains the same, whereas the numerical values of the entries change from one iteration to the other.

Scheme 1 (Markowitz criterion) [9]. At every step in the reordering process choose the pivot that would require the least number of *operations* when the factorization process is performed. If more than one pivot meets this criterion, any one of these pivots may be selected. Once a pivot is selected, a symbolic simulation of any fills that may be created by that pivot is carried out and the structure of the matrix is updated accordingly.

If the matrix is structurally symmetric and diagonal pivoting is chosen, scheme 1 implies that at every step one selects the pivot with the minimum number of off-diagonal elements in the portion of the matrix that has not been eliminated.

Scheme 2 (minimum fill scheme) [10]. At each step in the reordering process the pivot is chosen that produces the fewest number of fills. If more than one pivot meets the criterion, the one with the minimum number of off-diagonal elements is chosen. This scheme involves a trial simulation of every feasible alternative of the elimination process at each step; when a pivot is selected, the structure of the matrix is updated if any fills are created.

Note that the Markowitz scheme (scheme 1) attempts to minimize α in (16), whereas scheme 2 aims at minimizing β in (19). Both schemes use *local* criteria to decide which subsequent pivot to choose.

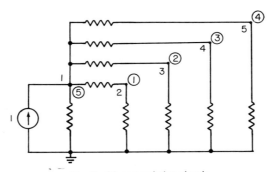

Fig. 2   Linear resistive circuit.

$$
\begin{bmatrix}
x & x & x & x & x \\
x & x & F & F & F \\
x & F & x & F & F \\
x & F & F & x & F \\
x & F & F & F & x
\end{bmatrix}
\begin{bmatrix}
v_1 \\ v_2 \\ v_3 \\ v_4 \\ v_5
\end{bmatrix}
=
\begin{bmatrix}
x \\ 0 \\ 0 \\ 0 \\ 0
\end{bmatrix}
\qquad\qquad
\begin{bmatrix}
x &   &   &   & x \\
  & x &   &   & x \\
  &   & x &   & x \\
  &   &   & x & x \\
x & x & x & x & x
\end{bmatrix}
\begin{bmatrix}
v_{(1)} \\ v_{(2)} \\ v_{(3)} \\ v_{(4)} \\ v_{(5)}
\end{bmatrix}
=
\begin{bmatrix}
0 \\ 0 \\ 0 \\ 0 \\ x
\end{bmatrix}
$$

(a)   (b)

Fig. 3   Structure of the factorized circuit equations for two different node voltage orderings.

Thus the obtained order may not necessarily be a globally optimal one. From the programming standpoint, scheme 1 is simpler to implement than scheme 2, since it does not require a trial simulation of every feasible pivot at every step. Both schemes in general produce the same ordering efficiency. As a result, scheme 1 is more widely used than scheme 2.

One of the steps in both schemes above is the determination of any fills that might occur after a pivot is selected. Let $a_{ij}^{(k-1)}$ and $a_{ij}^{(k)}$ represent, respectively, the ijth entry of the unfactorized part of the matrix $\mathbf{A}$ before and after the kth pivoting step is performed. A fill is created in the ijth position if $a_{ij}^{(k-1)} = 0$ but $a_{ij}^{(k)} \neq 0$. Since

$$a_{ij}^{(k)} = a_{ij}^{(k-1)} - \frac{a_{ik}^{(k-1)} \times a_{kj}^{(k-1)}}{a_{kk}^{(k)}}$$

a fill is created in the ijth position when $a_{ij}^{(k-1)} = 0$ and *both* $a_{ik}^{(k)} \neq 0$ and $a_{kj}^{(k)} \neq 0$. For structurally symmetric matrices with pivot selection restricted to the diagonal, $a_{ik}^{(k)} \neq 0$ indicates also that $a_{ki}^{(k)} \neq 0$; in this case, *two* fills are created in positions a_{ij} and a_{ji} by the kth pivot whenever $a_{ij}^{(k-1)} = 0$ and both $a_{ik}^{(k)} \neq 0$ and $a_{jk}^{(k)} \neq 0$.

Sparse matrix solution techniques are implemented by setting up integer pointer systems for equation reordering, storage, and for performing the factorization and the substitution steps. Only the nonzero entries of the LU factors are stored and only the essential nonzero operations are performed. Various schemes have been devised for implementing sparse matrix solution techniques; see, for example, Ref. 11. An easy-to-follow procedure suitable for reordering structurally symmetric systems using diagonal pivoting is given in Ref. 12.

3.3 DC ANALYSIS

I. Hajj

3.3.1 Solution of Nonlinear Algebraic Equations

In the dc analysis of electrical circuits the capacitors are treated as open circuits and the inductors as short circuits. The circuit thus becomes purely resistive. Dc solutions specify the operating points at which a nonlinear circuit is linearized for ac small-signal analysis; they also provide initial conditions for transient analysis, and indicate the possible equilibrium states that a circuit may attain.

The general form of the constitutive relations of nonlinear resistive elements can be written in the following form:

$$\mathbf{g}(\mathbf{i}_b, \mathbf{v}_b) = \mathbf{0} \tag{1}$$

Equation (20), together with the topological equations (3.2.1) and (3.2.2), form a set of nonlinear algebraic equations that describe the circuit. Note that the nonlinearities in the equations are due solely to the element constitutive equations. As will be seen below, the set of equations above can be reduced to a smaller set before being solved. These equations, however, can be written in the form

$$\mathbf{f}(\mathbf{x}) = \mathbf{y} \tag{2}$$

where $\mathbf{x}$ represents the circuit variables and $\mathbf{y}$ the independent sources in the circuit. Equation (2) represents a set of n nonlinear algebraic equations in n unknowns. The problem is basically as follows. For a given $\mathbf{y}$, find $\mathbf{x}$, if it exists. Nonlinear algebraic equations in general may have either one solution, a finite number of solutions, an infinite number of solutions, or no solution at all, depending on the value of $\mathbf{y}$ and the properties of the nonlinear function $\mathbf{f}$. For example, Fig. 1 shows the graph

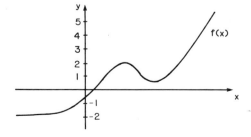

Fig. 1 Nonlinear function.

of a scalar function $f(x) = y$. If $y > 2$, one solution exists; if $y = 1$, three solutions are obtained; if $y = -2$, an infinite number of solutions exist; and if $y < -2$, no solution exists. In the following, it is assumed that a solution $\mathbf{x}^*$ exists for the specified $\mathbf{y}$, and our aim is to find this solution, using an *iterative* process. An iterative process consists of a procedure for generating a *sequence* $\{\mathbf{x}^k\}$ of vectors starting from given initial vectors, such that the sequence converges to the solution $\mathbf{x}^*$ as $k \to \infty$. A sequence $\{\mathbf{x}^k\}$ is *convergent* if for each $\epsilon > 0$ there is a positive integer N such that $\|\mathbf{x}^k - \mathbf{x}^m\| < \epsilon$ whenever $k, m > N$. The norm $\|\cdot\|$ can be interpreted as a measure of distance and can be defined as follows:

l_1-norm: $\|\mathbf{x}\|_1 = \sum_{i=1}^{n} |x_i|$

l_2-norm: $\|\mathbf{x}\|_2 = \left(\sum_{i=1}^{n} |x_i|^2 \right)^{1/2}$

l_p-norm: $\|\mathbf{x}\|_p = \left(\sum_{i=1}^{n} |x_i|^p \right)^{1/p}$, $1 \leqslant p < \infty$

l_∞-norm: $\|\mathbf{x}\|_\infty = \max_{1 \leqslant i \leqslant n} |x_i|$

Since in practice an iterative process is terminated after finite steps, any one of the norms above may be used to check when and if a sequence converges, depending on the application and the acceptable tolerance in the final solution approximation.

There are many methods for generating sequences for solving equations of form (2) (see, for example, Ref. 13). All of these methods are applicable to finding the dc solution of electronic circuits. In practice, however, Newton's method and its modifications have been found to be reliable and efficient, and hence have been used in almost all circuit analysis programs.

Newton's method is an iterative process that starts with an initial "guess" of the solution. Equation (2) is then linearized at the initial guess, say $\mathbf{x}^k$, using the first two terms of a Taylor series expansion as follows:

$$\mathbf{f}(\mathbf{x}) = \mathbf{f}(\mathbf{x}^k) + \left[\frac{\partial \mathbf{f}}{\partial \mathbf{x}} \right]_{\mathbf{x} = \mathbf{x}^k} (\mathbf{x} - \mathbf{x}^k) = \mathbf{y} \tag{3}$$

where

$$\left[\frac{\partial \mathbf{f}}{\partial \mathbf{x}} \right]_{\mathbf{x} = \mathbf{x}^k} \equiv \begin{bmatrix} \dfrac{\partial f_1}{\partial x_1} & \cdots & \dfrac{\partial f_1}{\partial x_n} \\ \vdots & & \vdots \\ \dfrac{\partial f_n}{\partial x_1} & & \dfrac{\partial f_n}{\partial x_n} \end{bmatrix}$$

evaluated at $\mathbf{x} = \mathbf{x}^k$ is a constant matrix also known as the *Jacobian* matrix. Equation (3) can be written as

$$\left[\frac{\partial \mathbf{f}}{\partial \mathbf{x}} \right]_{\mathbf{x} = \mathbf{x}^k} (\mathbf{x} - \mathbf{x}^k) = \mathbf{y} - \mathbf{f}(\mathbf{x}^k) \tag{4}$$

$$\mathbf{x}^{k+1} = \mathbf{x}^k + \left[\frac{\partial \mathbf{f}}{\partial \mathbf{x}} \right]_{\mathbf{x} = \mathbf{x}^k}^{-1} (\mathbf{y} - \mathbf{f}(\mathbf{x}^k)) \tag{5}$$

Note that (5) is an iterative formula that generates $\mathbf{x}^{k+1}$ in terms of $\mathbf{x}^k$. Formally, Newton's algorithm is as follows:

Newton's Algorithm for Solving $\mathbf{f}(\mathbf{x}) = \mathbf{y}$

1. Set $k = 0$.
2. Choose an initial guess $\mathbf{x}^k$ and find $\mathbf{f}(\mathbf{x}^k) = \mathbf{y}^k$.
3. Construct the Jacobian matrix $\mathbf{J}^k = \partial \mathbf{f} / \partial \mathbf{x}$ evaluated at $\mathbf{x} = \mathbf{x}^k$.
4. Solve $[\mathbf{J}^k]\mathbf{x}^{k+1} = \mathbf{y} - \mathbf{y}^k + [\mathbf{J}^k]\mathbf{x}^k$. (Alternatively, solve $[\mathbf{J}^k]\Delta\mathbf{x}^k = \Delta\mathbf{y}^k = \mathbf{y} - \mathbf{y}^k$, then put $\mathbf{x}^{k+1} = \mathbf{x}^k + \Delta\mathbf{x}^k$.)

5. Find $y^{k+1} = f(x^{k+1})$.
6. If $\|x^k - x^{k+1}\| \leqslant \epsilon$ and $\|y - y^{k+1}\| \leqslant \delta$, where ϵ and δ are some specified small numbers, a solution is found; otherwise (increment k by 1) return to step 3 and repeat.

A schematic example of the Newton iterative procedure is shown in Fig. 2 where the nonlinear function is a scalar in one variable. Note that the Jacobian in this case is the tangent line to the curve at the point x^k.

A Newton iterative process has quadratic convergence if the initial guess is close "enough" to the solution. However, there are situations when the process does not converge, even when a solution exists, as shown by the examples in Figs. 3 and 4.

To prevent divergence and to increase the chances for convergence, modified Newton methods have been developed and used. The general basis of these methods is the choice of a next iteration point x^{k+1} such that $\|y - y^{k+1}\| \leqslant \|y - y^k\|$. This modification prevents divergence, but still does not guarantee convergence.

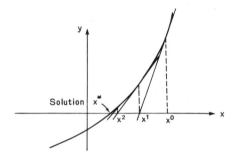

Fig. 2   Solution of $f(x) = 0$ by Newton's method; The solution is at $x = x^*$.

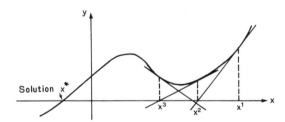

Fig. 3   Example illustrating a case where Newton's procedure gets stuck and does not converge to the solution.

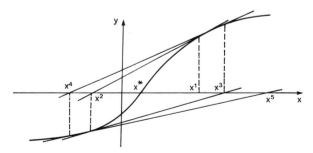

Fig. 4   Example illustrating a case where Newton's procedure diverges away from the solution.

Modified Newton Algorithm

1. Set $k = 0$.
2. Choose an initial guess $\mathbf{x}^k$ and find $\mathbf{f}(\mathbf{x}^k) = \mathbf{y}^k$.
3. Construct the Jacobian matrix $\mathbf{J}^k = [\partial\mathbf{f}/\partial\mathbf{x}]_{\mathbf{x}=\mathbf{x}^k}$ evaluated at $\mathbf{x} = \mathbf{x}^k$.
4. Solve $[\mathbf{J}^k]\Delta\mathbf{x}^k = \Delta\mathbf{y}^k = \mathbf{y} - \mathbf{y}^k$.
5. Put $\mathbf{x}^{k+1} = \mathbf{x}^k + \lambda\,\Delta\mathbf{x}^k$, where λ is a scalar which is chosen such that $\|\mathbf{y} - \mathbf{y}^{k+1}\| < \|\mathbf{y} - y^k\|$, and where $\mathbf{y}^{k+1} = \mathbf{f}(x^{k+1})$. Ideally, $\|\mathbf{y} - y^{k+1}\|$ should be minimized.
6. If $\|\Delta\mathbf{x}^k\| \leqslant \epsilon$ and $\|\mathbf{y} - \mathbf{y}^{k+1}\| \leqslant \delta$, a solution is found; otherwise, return to step 3 and repeat.

The main difference between modified and unmodified Newton algorithms lies in step 5. The choice of the step size λ, however, is not clear cut and generally requires some search techniques which might be computationally expensive. In practice, when the properties of the nonlinear functions in the system are known, λ may be chosen through empirical reasoning. In addition, λ need not be the same for all components of $\mathbf{x}$; a different value of λ may be selected for each component as long as $\|\mathbf{y} - y^{k+1}\|$ becomes less than $\|\mathbf{y} - \mathbf{y}^k\|$. This is elaborated upon below in more detail in connection with the dc solution of transistor and diode circuits.

Other modifications of Newton's method involve approximating the Jacobian matrix $\mathbf{J}^k$ by some other matrix rather than having to evaluate the partial derivatives of $\mathbf{f}$ with respect to $\mathbf{x}$ at every iteration point. However, in electronic circuits, the Jacobian matrix is readily available, and thus is usually constructed at every interation point.

3.3.2   Application to Electronic Circuits

As mentioned above, the nonlinearities in the circuit equations are due to the element characteristics. The linearization step in the Newton algorithm can thus be carried out at the element level. In other words, the element characteristics are linearized first and the circuit equations subsequently formulated. As an example, consider the dc characteristics of a junction diode that is described by an equation of the form

$$I_D = I_0[\exp(kv_D) - 1] \tag{6}$$

where k is a constant that depends on temperature. The plot of (6) is shown in Fig. 5.

The linearized equation at a point v^k is represented by a straight line tangent to the curve at v^k, as illustrated in the figure. The equation of the linearized model is

$$I_D = I_D(v^k) + \left[\frac{dI_D}{dv_D}\right]_{v_D = v^k} v_D$$

$$= I_0[\exp(kv_D) - 1] + (kv^k I_0 \exp(kv^k))v_D$$

$$= gv_D + b$$

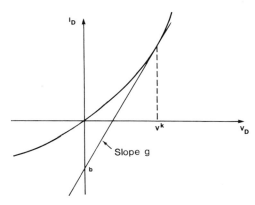

Fig. 5   Linearization of diode equation.

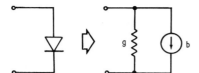

Fig. 6   Linearized equivalent model of a diode.

which may be represented by a linear resistor of conductance value equal to g in parallel with a current source as shown in Fig. 6.

Similarly, the characteristics of all nonlinear resistors in the circuit are approximated by linear resistors and sources which may be written exactly as in (5):

$$i_1 = G_1 v_1 + H_1 i_2 + s_1$$

$$v_2 = H_2 i_1 + Z_2 i_2 + s_2$$

Thus at every iteration point the circuit is modeled by an equivalent linear circuit and the same techniques used in Sec. 3.2 for solving linear resistive circuits can be applied to solve the equations at each iteration in Newton's method.

The use of Newton's method in the dc analysis of typical electronic circuits occasionally runs into problems. One of these problems is that of numerical overflow, which occurs during evaluation of the exponential term in the diode characteristic [see (6)], where the current value increases rapidly for relatively low positive voltage values. Another problem is that of nonconvergence, where the iteration process gets stuck at a given point or even diverges, as illustrated in Sec. 3.3.1. These problems may be overcome by using a modified Newton's method. Although in most cases a modified Newton's method works well, it may be relatively expensive to apply, particularly when searching for a proper step size λ that would minimize the error vector $\|y - y^{k+1}\|$ at each step. Various heuristic schemes have been proposed for finding step size with minimal computational effort. One such scheme, called the *current/voltage iteration scheme*, has been found to perform reasonably well for bipolar transistor circuits and junction diodes with exponential characteristics. In this scheme the step size λ is determined for each exponential function individually as follows. A critical value of the diode voltage v_{crit} is chosen. If $v_D^{k+1} > v_{crit}$ and $i_D^{k+1} > 0$, iteration on current is used to establish the next iterate, $\hat{v}_D^{k+1}$, as shown in Fig. 7, which in effect limits the step size λ to be less than 1. If $v_D^{k+1} < v_{crit}$, v_D^{k+1} is chosen as the next iterate.

If other types of nonlinearities exist in the circuit, different limiting schemes must be used. Various limiting schemes suitable for a wide class of nonlinearities that exist in electronic device models have been proposed in Refs. 14 and 15.

A flowchart of an algorithm for the analysis of nonlinear resistive circuits is given in Fig. 8.

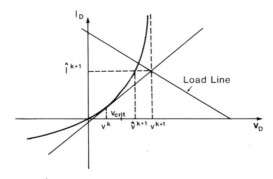

Fig. 7   Current/voltage iteration scheme:

$$V^{k+1} = \frac{1}{k} \ln\left(\frac{I^{k+1}}{I_o} + 1\right)$$

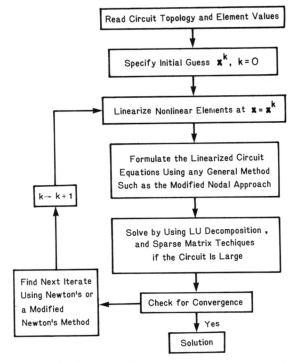

Fig. 8   Flowchart of an algorithm for the analysis of nonlinear resistive circuits.

3.3.3   Piecewise-Linear Method

In some applications the characteristics of the nonlinear elements in the circuit can be approximated by piecewise-linear (pwl) curves. In this case special iterative procedures have been developed which, under certain conditions, possess global convergence properties for finding the solutions.

A piecewise-linear one-dimensional (continuous) function $f(x) = y$ is a piecewise-linear curve which can be characterized by a set of *breakpoints* in the xy plane, as shown in Fig. 9. The set of breakpoints define *region boundaries* along the x axis. In each region the equation is of the form

$$y = a_i x + b_i \qquad\qquad (7)$$

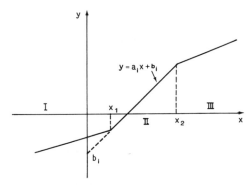

Fig. 9   Piecewise-linear continuous curve.

In n dimensions a piecewise-linear continuous function $\mathbf{f}(\mathbf{x}) = \mathbf{y}$ is a mapping $\mathbf{f}(\cdot): R^n \to R^n$, where the domain of $\mathbf{f}$ is divided into a finite number of convex n-dimensional polyhedrons called regions. A boundary between two regions is a subset of an $(n-1)$-dimensional hyperplane. In each region the function has the form

$$\mathbf{f}(x) = \mathbf{J}_i \mathbf{x} + \mathbf{w}_i = \mathbf{y} \tag{8}$$

where $\mathbf{J}_i$ is a constant (Jacobian) matrix and $\mathbf{w}_i$ is a constant vector. Both $\mathbf{J}_i$ and $\mathbf{x}_i$ are defined in each region R_i. In two *adjacent* regions the Jacobian matrices are related by a *dyad* [16] (a dyad is a matrix of rank 1); that is,

$$\mathbf{J}_{i+1} = \mathbf{J}_i + \mathbf{cr}^T \tag{9}$$

EXAMPLE 1. Consider the circuit in Fig. 10a, which contains two pwl resistors whose characteristics are shown in Figs. 10b and c. The breakpoints on the characteristics define boundaries and regions in the element variable space as shown in Fig. 11a. Supposing that node analysis is used to solve the circuit, the regions in the node voltage variable space are shown in Fig. 11b. In each region, each pwl element can be replaced by a linear element together with a current source in parallel with it (or a voltage source in series with it), as shown in Fig. 12. In region $(1, 1)$ the equations are

$$\underbrace{\begin{bmatrix} G + g_{11} & -g_{11} \\ -g_{11} & g_{11} + g_{21} \end{bmatrix}}_{\mathbf{J}_{11}} \underbrace{\begin{bmatrix} V_1 \\ V_2 \end{bmatrix}}_{\mathbf{x}} + \underbrace{\begin{bmatrix} I_{11} \\ I_{21} - I_{11} \end{bmatrix}}_{\mathbf{w}_{11}} = \underbrace{\begin{bmatrix} I \\ 0 \end{bmatrix}}_{\mathbf{y}}$$

In region $(2, 1)$, which is *adjacent* to region $(1, 1)$, the equations are

$$\underbrace{\begin{bmatrix} G + g_{12} & -g_{12} \\ -g_{12} & g_{12} + g_{21} \end{bmatrix}}_{\mathbf{J}_{21}} \begin{bmatrix} V_1 \\ V_2 \end{bmatrix} + \underbrace{\begin{bmatrix} I_{12} \\ I_{21} - I_{12} \end{bmatrix}}_{\mathbf{w}_{21}} = \begin{bmatrix} I \\ 0 \end{bmatrix}$$

Note that

$$\mathbf{J}_{21} = \begin{bmatrix} G + g_{11} & -g_{11} \\ -g_{11} & g_{11} + g_{21} \end{bmatrix} + \begin{bmatrix} \Delta g_{11} \\ -\Delta g_{11} \end{bmatrix} \begin{bmatrix} 1 & -1 \end{bmatrix} = \mathbf{J}_{11} + \mathbf{cr}^T$$

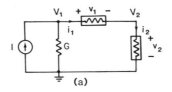

(a)

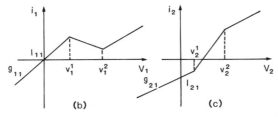

(b)   (c)

Fig. 10 (a) Circuit with two pw resistors. (b) and (c) Charachteristics of the pwl resistors.

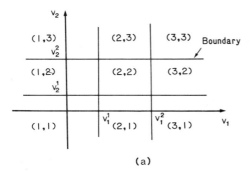

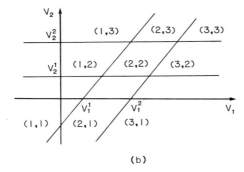

Fig. 11 (*a*) Regions in the element variable space. (*b*) Regions in the node voltage variable space.

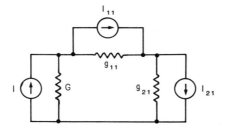

Fig. 12 Equivalent circuit in a region.

Newton's Method for Solving pwl Equations $f(x) = y$

1. Choose an initial guess x^k.
2. Find the corresponding region k.
3. Construct $[J_k]x^k + w_k = y^k$.
4. Solve $[J_k]\Delta x^k = y - y^k = \Delta y^k$.
5. Put $x^{k+1} = x^k + \Delta x^k$.
6. If x^{k+1} is in region k, a solution is found; otherwise, choose x^{k+1} as the next iterate and return to step 2.

Note that in step 6 no error criterion is used to determine when a solution is reached (i.e., the solution found is exact to within round-off errors). The error is due mainly to the pwl approximation of the original functions, not to the solution method. The algorithm above suffers the same nonconvergence problems as the general Newton's method, unless the initial guess is close enough to the solution. A modified algorithm that has good convergence properties is the following:

Katzenelson's Algorithm for Solving pwl Continuous Equation $f(x) = y$ [17]

1. Choose an initial guess x^k, $k = 0$.
2. Find the corresponding region and construct J^k and w^k.

3. Find $[\mathbf{J}^k]\mathbf{x}^k + \mathbf{w}^k = \mathbf{y}^k$.
4. Solve $[\mathbf{J}^k]\Delta\mathbf{x}^k = \mathbf{y} - \mathbf{y}^k = \Delta\mathbf{y}^k$.
5. Put $\mathbf{x}^{k+1} = \mathbf{x}^k + \Delta\mathbf{x}^k$.
6. If $\mathbf{x}^{k+1}$ is in region k, a solution is found; otherwise, choose $\mathbf{x}^{k+1} = \mathbf{x}^k + \lambda\Delta\mathbf{x}^k (0 < \lambda < 1)$ to be on the *boundary* of region k and cross into the adjacent region.
7. Put $\Delta\mathbf{y}^{k+1} = (1-\lambda)\Delta\mathbf{y}^k$ and update J^k to J^{k+1} using a dyad relationship and return to step 4.

A schematic description of the algorithm is shown in Fig. 13. Note that the iterates in $\mathbf{y}$ fall on the straight line joining $\mathbf{y}^0$ to the specified $\mathbf{y}$.

The key to the convergence properties of the algorithm above is in the choice of λ in step 6, which also results in the simplicity of step 7, which can be proved as follows. Because of continuity at the boundary:

$$\mathbf{J}^{k+1}\mathbf{x}^{k+1} + \mathbf{w}_{k+1} = \mathbf{J}^k\mathbf{x}^{k+1} + \mathbf{w}_k = \mathbf{y}^{k+1}$$

or

$$\mathbf{y}^{k+1} = \mathbf{J}^k(\mathbf{x}^k + \lambda\Delta\mathbf{x}^k) + \mathbf{w}_k = \mathbf{J}^k\mathbf{x}^k + \mathbf{w}_k + \lambda\mathbf{J}^k\Delta\mathbf{x}^k$$

$$= \mathbf{y}^k + \lambda\Delta\mathbf{y}^k$$

$$\Delta\mathbf{y}^{k+1} = \mathbf{y} - \mathbf{y}^{k+1} = \mathbf{y} - \mathbf{y}^k - \lambda(\mathbf{y} - \mathbf{y}^k) = (1-\lambda)(\mathbf{y} - \mathbf{y}^k) = (1-\lambda)\Delta\mathbf{y}^k$$

Since $0 < \lambda < 1$,

$$\|\mathbf{y} - \mathbf{y}^{k+1}\| = (1-\lambda)\|\mathbf{y} - \mathbf{y}^k\| < \|\mathbf{y} - \mathbf{y}^k\|$$

which shows that Katzenelson's algorithm is a modified Newton's method.

The value of λ can be determined at the element level as follows. Let v^k be the value of the voltage of a voltage-controlled element at iteration k, and $\hat{v}^{k+1}$ the value of the voltage obtained from the solution $\mathbf{x}^{k+1} = \mathbf{x}^k + \Delta\mathbf{x}^k$. Let v^k lie in the region determined by the breakpoints v_1 and v_2 as shown

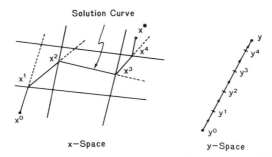

Fig. 13 Solution curve in Katzenelson's algorithm: (*a*) *x*-space; (*b*) *y* space.

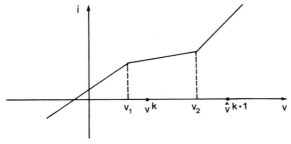

Fig. 14 Determination of λ at the element level.

in Fig. 14; then

$$
\lambda_j = \begin{cases} \dfrac{v_2 - v^k}{\hat{v}^{k+1} - v^k} & \text{if } \hat{v}^{k+1} > v^k \\[3mm] \dfrac{v_1 - v^k}{\hat{v}^{k+1} - v^k} & \text{if } \hat{v}^{k+1} < v^k \end{cases}
$$

If $\lambda_j \leqslant 1$ for all pwl elements, a solution is found; otherwise, $\lambda = \min_j \lambda_j$.

An important result concerning the convergence of Katzenelson's algorithm has been proven in Ref. 16. This result states that if $\det[J^k] > 0$ (or < 0) in all the regions, the pwl continuous function $f(x) = y$ has *at least* one solution for every y; furthermore, starting from any initial guess, Katzenelson's algorithm will converge to a solution in a finite number of steps.

The piecewise-linear approach has also been used to construct input/output characteristic curves and to solve systems with multiple solutions [18–21].

3.4 TRANSIENT ANALYSIS

I. Hajj

In the transient analysis of nonlinear and linear dynamic circuits and systems it is necessary to obtain certain output waveforms over a finite time interval $[0, T]$, given initial conditions at time $t = 0$, such as the dc solutions. Numerically, this is done by discretizing time over the interval $[0, T]$ and computing the corresponding output at the discretized time points. The interval between two adjacent time points is called a *time step* and is denoted by h. Ideally, h should vary automatically so that one could choose a small h when the response is changing fast and a large h when the response is relatively flat such that the approximate discretized solution is as close as possible to the exact solution (see Fig. 1).

A nonlinear dynamic circuit or system may be described by a set of first-order nonlinear differential equations of the following form:

$$
\dot{x} = f(x, t), \qquad x(0) = x_0 \tag{1}
$$

where x is referred to as a set of state variables. In general, a nonlinear dynamic circuit may be characterized by a set of nonlinear equations of the form

$$
f(\dot{x}, x, t) = 0, \qquad x(0) = x_0 \tag{2}
$$

In the following, we first consider methods of solving the initial-value problem (1); these methods can also be used to solve systems of form (2). The application of the methods to the transient analysis of nonlinear circuits is then explained.

There are basically two classes of numerical methods for generating a sequence of points x_n that approximates the actual solution $x(t)$ of (1). One class is based on a truncated Taylor series approximation in which the solution at the next time point is computed on the basis of the value of the present solution point and its derivatives (or approximations of these derivatives) at the present time point. These methods are one-step; that is, they use information computed at the latest time point and no information from previous points. Runge–Kutta formulas belong to this class of methods.

The second class is based on polynomial approximation where the values of the solution and its first derivative at both the present and previous points are used to generate the value of the solution at the

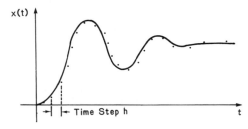

Fig. 1   Time-domain solution computed at discrete-time points.

next point. Methods based on polynomial approximation are more widely used in circuit simulation programs than are the first class of methods. Hence the derivation and properties of the methods based on polynomial approximation, namely, the linear multistep formulas, are explained below. Interested readers are referred to Ref. 22 for a more thorough treatment of both classes of methods.

3.4.1 Linear Multistep Methods

A general linear multistep formula can be written in one of the following equivalent forms:

$$x_n = \sum_{i=1}^{k} a_i x_{n-i} + h \sum_{i=1}^{k} b_i \dot{x}_{n-i} \tag{3}$$

or

$$x_n = \sum_{i=1}^{k} a_i x_{n-i} + h \sum_{i=1}^{k} b_i f(x_{n-i}, t_{n-i}) \tag{4}$$

or

$$\sum_{i=0}^{k} (a_i x_{n-i} + h b_i \dot{x}_{n-i}) = 0 \tag{5}$$

where h is the time step, $\dot{x} \equiv dx/dt$, x_n is the approximation of the solution $x(t)$ at time t_n, and $a_0 = -1$. If $b_0 = 0$, the formula is called *explicit* (i.e., x_n can be determined explicitly in terms of known quantities). If $b_0 \neq 0$, the formula is called *implicit* and x_n appears on both sides of (4) and interative solution techniques, such as the Newton's method, are used to solve for x_n at each time point.

The determination of the coefficients a_i and b_i for a k-step formula is carried out as follows:

1. Select a number $p \leq 2k$.
2. Select a set of polynomial basis functions

$$\{1, t, t^2, \ldots, t^p\}.$$

3. Compute the coefficients a_i and b_i of (3) such that the linear multistep method is exact for each of the basis functions. Equation (3) will then be exact for any polynomial of order p because of linearity. For $p < 2k$, some of the coefficients can be assigned arbitrary values.

The resultant formula is a k-step formula of order p.

EXAMPLE 1.   Consider the case where $k = 1$; the formula can then be written as

$$-x_n + a_1 x_{n-1} + h(b_0 \dot{x}_n + b_1 \dot{x}_{n-1}) = 0 \tag{6}$$

If one chooses $p = 2$ and fits the formula to the basis functions $\{1, t, t^2\}$, the following set of equations is obtained:

$$
\begin{aligned}
1\!: \qquad & -1 + a_1 = 0 \\
t\!: \qquad & -t_n + a_0 t_{n-1} + h b_0 + h b_1 = 0 \\
t^2\!: \qquad & -t_n^2 + a_0 t_{n-1}^2 + 2 h b_0 t_n + 2 h b_1 t_{n-1} = 0
\end{aligned}
$$

Putting $t_{n-1} = 0$, $t_n = h$, one gets

$$a_1 = 1, \qquad b_0 = \tfrac{1}{2}, \qquad b_1 = \tfrac{1}{2}$$

Therefore, the formula is

$$x_n = x_{n-1} + \frac{h}{2}(\dot{x}_n + \dot{x}_{n-1})$$

which is the *trapezoidal rule*. If one chooses $p = 1$ and uses the basis functions $\{1, t\}$, one gets

$$a_1 = 1, \qquad b_0 + b_1 = 1$$

If $b_0 = 0$ and $b_1 = 1$, the formula obtained is

$$x_n = x_{n-1} + h\dot{x}_{n-1}$$

which is the *forward Euler formula*. If $b_0 = 1$ and $b_1 = 0$, the formula becomes

$$x_n = x_{n-1} + h\dot{x}_n$$

which is the *backward Euler formula*.

3.4.2 Truncation Errors

In obtaining the solution numerically, there is always some error between the generated sequence of points and the actual solution. The difference between the actual solution $x(t_n)$ at time t_n and the computed solution point x_n is called the *global truncation error* at time t_n. The *local truncation error* (LTE) at time t_n, on the other hand, is defined as the difference between the computed solution point x_n and the "actual" solution, assuming all previously computed points up to x_{n-1} to be exact (i.e., LTE is the error committed in one step). These definitions assume infinite precision in obtaining x_n. In general, round-off error due to finite precision should also be taken into consideration. The global truncation error gives an indication of the convergence properties of the integration method; that is, ideally the global truncation error should be attenuated rather than amplified as t increases. The LTE, which depends in part on the time step h, is used to select the appropriate time step.

To find the expression for the LTE of a given formula the solution $x(t)$ is expanded at t_n into a Taylor series expansion as follows:

$$x(t_{n-k}) = x(t_n) - h^k \dot{x}(t_n) + \frac{(h^k)^2}{2!}\ddot{x}(t_n) - \frac{(h^k)^3}{3!}\dddot{x}(t_a) + \cdots \tag{7}$$

Substituting (7) in (5) and collecting terms, one gets

$$\text{LTE} = c_0 x(t_n) + c_1 h\dot{x}(t_n) + c_2 h^2 \ddot{x}(t_n) + \cdots$$

If the method is of order p, $c_0 = c_1 = c_2 = \cdots = c_p = 0$. If $c_{p+1} \neq 0$, then

$$\text{LTE} = c_{p+1} h^{p+1} x^{(p+1)}(\tau), \qquad t_{n-1} \leqslant \tau \leqslant t_n \tag{8}$$

where

$$x^{(p+1)}(\tau) \equiv \frac{d^{p+1}x}{dt^{p+1}}(\tau)$$

c_{p+1} is called the *error constant*.

EXAMPLE 2.   Consider the trapezoidal rule:

$$-x_n + x_{n-1} + \frac{h}{2}(\dot{x}_n + \dot{x}_{n-1}) = 0 \tag{9}$$

Using Taylor series expansion of $x(t)$ at t_n, one gets

$$x(t_{n-1}) = x(t_n) - hx(t_n) + \frac{h^2}{2}\ddot{x}(t_n) - \frac{h^3}{6}\dddot{x}(t_n) + O(H^4)*$$

$$\dot{x}(t_{n-1}) = \dot{x}(t_n) - h\ddot{x}(t_n) + \frac{h^2}{2}\dddot{x}(t_n) + O(h^3)$$

*$f(h) = O(h^r)$ means that for all $h < h_0$, there exists a $K > 0$ such that $|f(h)| \leqslant K|h|^r$.

Substituting the expression for $x(t_{n-1})$ and $\dot{x}(t_{n-1})$ and replacing x_n by $x(t_n)$ in (9), one gets

$$\text{LTE} = -\tfrac{1}{12}h^3\dddot{x}(\tau) \tag{10}$$

Similarly, the LTE of a backward Euler formula is found to be

$$\text{LTE (backward Euler formula)} = -\frac{h^2}{2}\ddot{x}(\tau)$$

3.4.3 Stability

Although the LTE may be small, the *global* truncation error may build up and increase indefinitely without bounds and hence the method may become unstable. Stability ensures that the global truncation error remains bounded and even decreases as $n \to \infty$. The stability properties of a formula are studied by applying the formula to a test function $\dot{x} = \lambda x$, which gives a linear difference equation of the form

$$\sum_{i=0}^{k} a_i x_{n-i} + h\lambda \sum_{i=0}^{k} b_i x_{n-i} = 0 \tag{11}$$

The characteristic polynomial of the difference equation in (11) is given as

$$P(z,h\lambda) = \rho(z) + h\lambda\sigma(z) = \sum_{i=0}^{k} a_i z^{k-i} + h\lambda \sum_{i=0}^{k} b_i z^{k-i} = 0 \tag{12}$$

For the method to be stable, the modulus of the roots of $P(z,h\lambda) = 0$ should be less than or equal to 1, with any root of modulus 1 being simple. In a given problem that is described by an equation of the form $\mathbf{x} = \mathbf{f}(\mathbf{x},t)$, there is usually a finite number of eigenvalues λ_i that may be spread out in the complex plane. These eigenvalues move in the plane as $\mathbf{x}$ travels along its trajectory and may enter the right-hand side of the complex plane temporarily, such as in the case of nonlinear oscillators. Thus it is necessary to study the stability properties of a given formula for a wide range of values of λ. Although in practice the time step itself may not be very small or very large, $h\lambda$ nevertheless may become very small, very large, negative, or positive. Thus it is important to investigate the stability of a formula for $h\lambda$ ranging from 0 to ∞.

For any given value of $h\lambda$, if the roots z_j of $P(z,h\lambda) = 0$ satisfy $|z_j| < 1$ for $j = 1,2,\ldots,k$, the formula is said to be *absolutely stable* for that particular value of $h\lambda$. The region of absolute stability of a formula is defined as the region in the complex $h\lambda$-plane where the zeros of the characteristic polynomial $P(z,h\lambda) = 0$ fulfill $|z_j| < 1$, $j = 1,2,\ldots,k$, for $h\lambda$ within the region. The boundary of the region of absolute stability is found from plotting the following equation:

$$h\lambda = -\frac{\rho(z)}{\sigma(z)}, \qquad |z| = 1$$

which can be written as

$$h\lambda = -\frac{\rho(\rho^{i\theta})}{\sigma(\rho^{i\theta})}, \qquad z = \rho^{i\theta}, \quad 0 \leqslant \theta \leqslant 2\pi$$

When $h\lambda = 0$, the characteristic polynomial becomes $P(z,0) = \rho(z) = 0$. If the formula satisfies the lowest-order basis function, namely $\{1\}$, it follows that $\rho(1) = 0$, and hence $z_1 = 1$ is a root of the characteristic polynomial when $h\lambda = 0$. This root is called the *principal root*. If all the roots of $\rho(z) = 0$ satisfy the condition $|z_j| \leqslant 1$, $j = 1,2,\ldots,k$, and any root of modulus 1 is simple, the linear multistep formula is said to be *zero-stable*.

When $h\lambda \neq 0$, the roots of the characteristic polynomial vary continuously with $h\lambda$. If for a given $h\lambda$, the roots of $P(z,h\lambda) = 0$ satisfy $|z_j| < |z_1|, j = 2,3,\ldots,k$, where z_1 is the principal root, the linear multistep formula is said to be *relatively stable*. Note that for a given $h\lambda$ a formula can be relatively stable but not absolutely stable, and vice versa. The region of relative stability defines the region where the formula is relatively accurate.

In practice, it is often desirable to have the region of stability of the numerical formula correspond to the region of stability of the differential equation. In this regard, a numerical method is said to be *A-stable* if its region of absolute stability contains the whole of the left-half plane, $\text{Re}\{h\lambda\} < 0$.

Examples of A-stable formulas include the backward Euler formula and the trapezoidal rule. The following results, which are called *Dalquist's theorem*, define the class of linear multistep formulas that are A-stable:

1. An *explicit* linear multistep formula cannot be A-stable.
2. The order of an A-stable implicit linear multistep method cannot exceed 2.
3. The second-order A-stable implicit linear multistep method with the smallest error constant is the trapezoidal rule.

It is obvious that although A-stability is desirable, it is restrictive in the sense that it does not include formulas of order more than 2. In practice, A-stability is not mandatory. In many cases system solutions contain both rapidly and slowly varying components. Mathematically, this means that the eigenvalues of the (linearized) system equations are widely spread in the complex plane. Such systems are called *stiff* systems. When the rapidly varying components which are caused by eigenvalues close to the imaginary axis are being computed, a small h is chosen in order to capture the change in the response, and thus $h\lambda$ is close to the origin. When the solution is relatively smooth, a large step size could be chosen without causing any numerical instability. Thus the step size $h\lambda$ is large. Formulas that are suitable for solving stiff systems are called *stiffly stable* formulas [23]. The desirable regions of stability of stiffly stable formulas are shown in Fig. 2. Note that when an eigenvalue λ is close to the imaginary axis, the response contains slowly decaying oscillatory components and a small step h should be chosen in order to capture the change in the response; hence $h\lambda$ is small. Similarly, when λ moves into the right-half plane, the system becomes unstable and again a small h should be chosen in order to track the unstable part of the response. Thus the formula should be accurate (relatively stable) when $h\lambda$ is small.

A class of formulas that are stiffly stable are Gear's formulas [23] which are written as

$$x_n = \sum_{i=1}^{k} a_i x_{n-1} + h b_0 \dot{x}_n \tag{13}$$

Note that (13) is obtained from (3) by putting $b_1 = b_2 = \cdots = b_k = 0$. The characteristic polynomial of

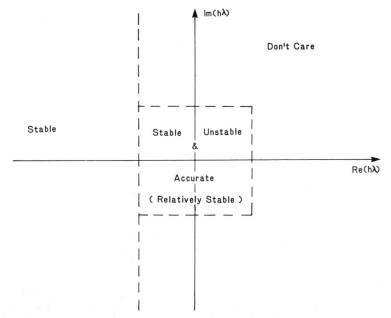

Fig. 2   Regions of stability of stiffly stable formulas.

Table 1.   Gear's Formulas of Order 1 to 6

Order	Formula	LTE
1	$x_n = x_{n-1} + h\dot{x}_n$	$-\dfrac{1}{2}\dfrac{d^2 x}{dt^2}(\tau)$
2	$x_n = \dfrac{4}{3}x_{n-1} - \dfrac{1}{3}x_{n-2} + \dfrac{2}{3}h\dot{x}_n$	$-\dfrac{2}{9}\dfrac{d^3 x}{dt^3}(\tau)$
3	$x_n = \dfrac{18}{11}x_n - \dfrac{9}{11}x_{n-1} + \dfrac{2}{11}x_{n-2} + \dfrac{6}{11}h\dot{x}_n$	$-\dfrac{3}{22}\dfrac{d^4 x}{dt^4}(\tau)$
4	$x_n = \dfrac{48}{25}x_{n-1} - \dfrac{36}{25}x_{n-2} + \dfrac{16}{25}x_{n-3} - \dfrac{3}{25}x_{n-3} + \dfrac{12}{25}h\dot{x}_n$	$-\dfrac{12}{125}\dfrac{d^5 x}{dt^5}(\tau)$
5	$x_n = \dfrac{300}{137}x_{n-1} - \dfrac{300}{137}x_{n-2} + \dfrac{200}{137}x_{n-3} - \dfrac{75}{137}x_{n-4} + \dfrac{12}{137}x_{n-5} + \dfrac{60}{137}h\dot{x}_n$	$-\dfrac{10}{137}\dfrac{d^6 x}{dt^6}(\tau)$
6	$x_n = \dfrac{360}{147}x_{n-1} - \dfrac{450}{147}x_{n-2} + \dfrac{400}{147}x_{n-2} - \dfrac{225}{147}x_{n-3} + \dfrac{72}{147}x_{n-4} - \dfrac{10}{147}x_{n-5}$ $+ \dfrac{60}{147}h\dot{x}_n$	$-\dfrac{60}{1029}\dfrac{d^7 x}{dt^7}(\tau)$

Gear's formulas is given as

$$P(z, h\lambda) = \left(\sum_{i=0}^{k} a_i z^{k-i} + h\lambda b_0 \right) = 0 \tag{14}$$

when $h\lambda \to \infty$. Gear's formulas of order 1 to 6, together with their local truncation errors, are given in Table 1 for *constant* time step h. For variable time steps, the coefficients will become functions of the step sizes.

Note that Gear's formula of order 1 is the backward Euler formula, and that although the trapezoidal rule is not included in Gear's formulas, it is stiffly stable. The regions of stability of Gear's formulas of order 1 to 6 with constant time steps are given in Fig. 3. Note that the formulas of order 1 and 2 are also A-stable.

Gear's formulas (13) can also be written in the following equivalent form:

$$\dot{x}_n = \frac{1}{hb_0} \sum_{i=0}^{k} a_i x_{n-i} \tag{15}$$

which is known as the *backward differentiation formula* [24].

3.4.4   Predictor–Corrector Methods

Consider the general nonlinear algebraic-differential system given by

$$f(x, \dot{x}, t) = 0, \qquad x(0) = x_0 \tag{16}$$

where it is necessary to compute $x(t)$ over the time interval $[0, T]$ using a linear multistep implicit formula. This formula can be written in the form

$$\dot{x}_n = \frac{1}{hb_0}x_n - \frac{1}{h} \sum_{i=1}^{k} (a_i x_{n-i} + b_i \dot{x}_{n-i}) = g(x_n) + s \tag{17}$$

where

$$s = -\frac{1}{h} \sum_{i=1}^{k} (a_i x_{n-i} + b_i \dot{x}_{n-i})$$

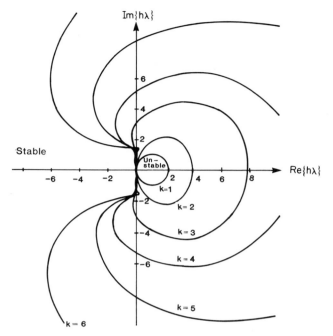

Fig. 3   Regions of stability of Gear's formulas.

is a known quantity. Substituting (17) into (16), one gets

$$f(x_n, g(x_n) + s, t) = 0 \tag{18}$$

a nonlinear algebraic equation that can be solved using a Newton iterative method to find x_n. To ensure and speed up convergence to the solution, a "good" initial guess is useful. This initial guess can be provided by using an *explicit* linear multistep formula of the following form:

$$x_n^p = \sum_{i=1}^{k+1} (\gamma_i x_{n-1} + \xi_i \dot{x}_{n-i}) \tag{19}$$

Equation (19) is usually referred to as a *predictor* formula and (17) is referred to as a *corrector* formula. When Gear's formulas are used to find the solution, the predictor formula has the following form:

$$x_n^p = \sum_{i=1}^{k+1} \gamma_i x_{n-i} \tag{20}$$

while the corrector formula is given in (15). From the computational point of view, it is advantageous to be able to vary the order k and the time step h as long as the solution stays within a prescribed error bound from the actual solution. The ability to change h and k during the solution process may significantly reduce the total number of time steps required to generate the numerical solution. At every time step one should be able to choose the order k which allows the *largest* step size h such that the LTE remains within a prescribed bound. Thus it is essential that a good estimate of the LTE can be easily obtained at each time step. One method of estimating the LTE is to use the predictor and corrector solutions; that is,

$$\text{LTE} \simeq c \|x_n^p - x_n\|$$

Another method is to approximate higher-order derivatives of $x(t)$ by *divided differences* as follows:

$$x[t_n] \equiv x_n$$

$$x[t_n, t_{n-1}] \equiv \frac{x_n - x_{n-1}}{t_n - t_{n-1}} \simeq \frac{dx_n}{dt}$$

$$x[t_n, t_{n-1}, t_{n-2}] \equiv \frac{\dfrac{x_n - x_{n-1}}{t_n - t_{n-2}} - \dfrac{x_{n-1} - x_{n-2}}{t_{n-1} - t_{n-2}}}{t_n - t_{n-2}} \simeq \frac{1}{2} \frac{d^2 x_n}{dt^2}$$

$$x[t_n, t_{n-1}, \ldots, t_{n-k}] \equiv \frac{x[t_n, t_{n-1}, \ldots, t_{n-k-1}] - x[t_{n-1}, t_{n-2}, \ldots, t_{n-k}]}{t_n - t_{n-k}} \simeq \frac{1}{k!} \frac{d^k x}{dt^k}$$

For various methods of implementing linear implicit backward differentiation formulas of variable step and order, the reader is referred to Refs. 23–26.

3.4.5 Application to Electrical Circuits

A general electrical circuit may be described by the following set of equations:

Topological constraints

KCL: $\mathbf{Ai} = 0$
KVL: $\mathbf{v} = \mathbf{A}^T \mathbf{v}_n$

Element constraints

Resistors: $\mathbf{f}_R(\mathbf{i}_R, v_R) = 0$

Capacitors: $\mathbf{q}_c = \mathbf{f}_c(\mathbf{v}_c), \; \mathbf{i}_c = \dfrac{d\mathbf{q}_c}{dt}$

Inductors: $\boldsymbol{\phi}_L = \mathbf{f}_L(\mathbf{i}_L), \; \mathbf{v}_L = \dfrac{d\boldsymbol{\phi}_L}{dt}$

In general, the element characteristics may be written as $\mathbf{f}(\mathbf{i}, \mathbf{v}, \mathbf{q}, \boldsymbol{\phi}) = 0$. For simplicity, the less general form above is assumed in the following. When using a linear implicit multistep formula in solving the equations above, the time derivatives are first approximated at time t_n using the implicit formula to get

$$i_{cn} = \dot{q}_{cn} = \frac{1}{hb_0} q_{cn} - \frac{1}{hb_0} \left[\sum_{i=1}^{k} (a_i q_{cn-i} + h b_i i_{cn-i}) \right] = \frac{1}{hb_0} f_c(v_{cn}) - s_c \qquad (21)$$

which represents an algebraic relation referred to Fig. 4.
Using the trapezoidal rule, one gets

$$\dot{q}_{cn} = \frac{2}{h} q_{cn} - \left(\frac{2}{h} q_{cn-1} + \dot{q}_{cn-1} \right)$$

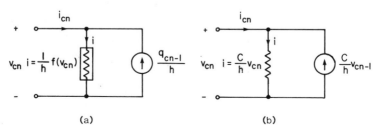

(a)   (b)

Fig. 4 Companion circuit model of a capacitor: (a) nonlinear model; (b) linear model.

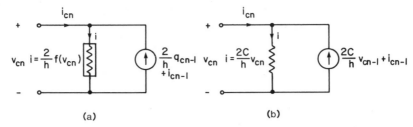

Fig. 5 Companion circuit model of a capacitor using the trapezoidal rule: (a) nonlinear model; (b) linear model.

which can be written as

$$i_{cn} = \frac{2}{h} f(v_{cn}) - \left(\frac{2}{h} q_{cn-1} + i_{cn-1} \right)$$

for a nonlinear capacitor or

$$i_{cn} = \frac{2C}{h} v_{cn} - \left(\frac{2C}{h} v_{cn-1} + i_{cn-1} \right)$$

for a linear capacitor. The corresponding companion circuit models are given in Fig. 5.
   Using a k th-order backward differentiation formula (BDF), one gets

$$\dot{q}_{cn} = \frac{1}{hb_0} q_{cn} - \frac{1}{h} \sum_{i=1}^{k} a_i q_{cn-i}$$

which can be written as

$$i_{cn} = \frac{i}{hb_0} f_c(v_{cn}) - \frac{1}{h} \sum_{i=1}^{k} a_i q_{cn-i}$$

for a nonlinear capacitor or

$$i_{cn} = \frac{C}{hb_0} v_{cn} - \frac{C}{h} \sum_{i=1}^{k} a_i v_{cn-i}$$

for a linear capacitor. The corresponding companion circuit models are shown in Fig. 6.
   Similar companion models can also be derived for inductors. For example, a k th-order BDF companion circuit model of an inductor characterized by

$$\phi_L = f(i_L), \qquad v_L = \frac{d\phi_L}{dt}$$

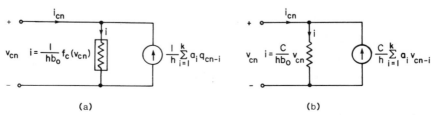

Fig. 6 Companion circuit model of a capacitor using a k th-order backward differentiation formula: (a) nonlinear model; (b) linear model.

can be derived as follows:

$$\dot{\phi}_{Ln} = \frac{1}{hb_0}\phi_{Ln} - \frac{1}{h}\sum_{i=1}^{k} a_i\phi_{Ln-i}$$

which can be written as

$$v_{Ln} = \frac{1}{hb_0}f(i_{Ln}) - \frac{1}{h}\sum_{i=1}^{k} a_i\phi_{Ln-i}$$

for a nonlinear inductor and

$$v_{Ln} = \frac{L}{hb_0}i_{Ln} - \frac{L}{h}\sum_{i=1}^{k} a_i i_{Ln-i}$$

for a linear inductor. The corresponding companion circuit models are shown in Fig. 7.

Thus at time t_n the capacitors and the inductors are replaced by companion models which are characterized by algebraic relationships. The circuit model then becomes purely resistive and dc analysis iterative techniques, such as the ones discussed in Sec. 3.3, can be used to solve for the circuit variables at time t_n. A typical transient analysis procedure can be outlined as follows:

1. Specify or determine initial conditions, namely the voltages across the capacitors and the currents through the inductors. This can be done, for example, using dc analysis.

2. Replace the capacitors and the inductors by corresponding companion models. For the initial time step, use a one-step formula; for the second time step, a two-step formula can be used. Thus a k-step formula can be used after k steps have been computed.

3. Find the solution of the companion resistive circuit using a modified Newton method. The initial guess for the Newton iterations could be the last computed time point or a predicted value. In solving the resistive circuit any general formulation method, such as the modified nodal approach could be used, in which case the currents in the inductors are chosen as part of the circuit variables. If the circuit is large, sparse matrix techniques could be used to solve the linearized circuit equations at each iteration point.

4. Compute an estimate of the LTE using the divided differences method or the predictor–corrector difference for each capacitor voltage and inductor current, and determine the time step h. If the LTE is found to be greater than a specified upper bound, the time step h is reduced and steps 2, 3, and 4 are repeated. If the LTE is smaller than a specified lower bound, the *next* time step is increased. If the LTE lies between the two bounds, the time step remains unchanged. In both these latter two cases, the time point is advanced one step and step 2 is reentered. If a variable-order variable-step method is being used, the LTE is also estimated for formulas one order greater and one order smaller than the current order and then the next order is chosen to be the one that allows the maximum time step h such that the LTE stays within its bounds.

5. Steps 2, 3, and 4 are repeated until the time interval of interest is completely covered.

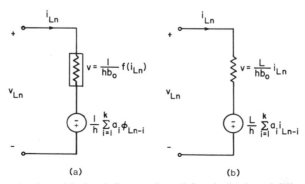

(a)   (b)

Fig. 7 Companion circuit model of an inductor using a kth-order backward differentiation formula: (*a*) nonlinear model; (*b*) linear model.

3.5   NUMERICAL OPTIMIZATION METHODS

S. S. L. Chang

Numerical optimization [28, 29] is very much a mixture of art and science. There are at least five commonly used methods and in each method there are one or more arbitrarily selected parameters. For any given problem, one or the other method may give the best result or least cost, but none is the universally best for all problems.

With rapidly rising computing power, a simple solution is to try out all five methods in a logical order. However, there remains the need of skillful user input. To narrow down the domain of search or to select a sufficiently close starting point can make substantial difference in computer cost and sometimes the ultimate result.

The problem can be formulated as follows: $F(x_1, x_2, \ldots, x_n) \triangleq F(\mathbf{x})$ is a scalar function of n parameters. The domain D is a closed set in parameter space. Determine x_0 such that

$$F(\mathbf{x}_0) = \min_{\mathbf{x} \in D} F(\mathbf{x}) \tag{1}$$

(1) means that $F(x_0)$ is minimum for all $\mathbf{x} \in D$. In the present article, five different methods for approximately accomplishing the above will be discussed:

1. Lattice mapping
2. Simplex
3. Steepest descent
4. Fletcher–Powell
5. Least-squares (or pth)

3.5.1   Lattice Mapping (Exhaustive Search)

Lattice mapping is the most straightforward method in numerical optimization. A lattice of points with spacings δx_i, $i = 1, 2, \ldots, n$, is selected to cover D, and $F(\mathbf{x})$ at the lattice points are computed. Let

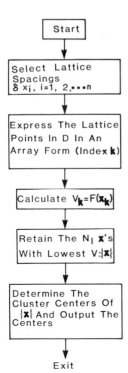

Fig. 1   Flow diagram of lattice mapping method.

N_1 be a small fraction of the total number of lattice points. The N_1 points with lowest $F(\mathbf{x})$ are selected and examined for cluster formation. A flow diagram of the lattice mapping algorithm is shown in Fig. 1. The cluster centers are then used as starting points in subsequent optimization procedures.

There are a few variations to the above:

1. Lattice mapping is the only optimization procedure used. Then $N_1 = 1$.
2. The points in $\{\mathbf{x}\}$ are scattered without cluster formation. Then $\delta \mathbf{x}_i$ is halved and the lattice mapping is repeated.
3. If (2) is impractical to do, a few points in $\{\mathbf{x}\}$ with lowest V are selected as starting points for subsequent optimization.

A variation from lattice mapping is the Monte Carlo method. The set of points $\mathbf{x}_k$ to be evaluated are selected at random. Otherwise, the two methods are identical. The Monte Carlo method can be used if lattice mapping is too costly.

3.5.2 Simplex Method

The simplex method can be described as a systematic way of searching for a downward slope with a minimum of computations. The steps are as follows:

1. Given a starting point $\mathbf{x}_0 = (x_1, x_2, \ldots, x_n), n$ other apex points are obtained as

$$\mathbf{x}_i = (x_1, x_2, \ldots, x_i + h_i, x_{i+1}, \ldots, x_n); \qquad i = 1, 2, \ldots, n \tag{2}$$

where h_i can be constants or functions of x. For example,

$$h_i = 0.1 x_i$$

$$h_i = 0.2$$

$$h_i = 0.1|x_i| + 0.2 \tag{3}$$

and so on, are possible forms of h_i.

2. Evaluate $F(\mathbf{x}_i)$, $i = 0, 1, 2, \ldots, n$.
3. The points with highest, next highest, and lowest values of F are denoted $\mathbf{x}_H$, $\mathbf{x}_{NH}$, and $\mathbf{x}_L$, respectively.
4. Calculate the centroid $\mathbf{x}_c$:

$$\mathbf{x}_c = \frac{1}{n} \sum_{\substack{i=0 \\ i \neq H}}^{n} \mathbf{x}_i \tag{4}$$

5. Reflection about $\mathbf{x}_c$:

$$\mathbf{x}_R = (1 + \alpha)\mathbf{x}_c - \alpha \mathbf{x}_H \tag{5}$$

where $0 < \alpha < 1$.

The meaning of the steps above for the special case of $n = 2$ is illustrated in Fig. 2. Let us assume that

$$F(\mathbf{x}_2) < F(\mathbf{x}_0) < F(\mathbf{x}_1)$$

Then

$$\mathbf{x}_H = \mathbf{x}_1$$

$$\mathbf{x}_{NH} = \mathbf{x}_0$$

$$\mathbf{x}_L = \mathbf{x}_2$$

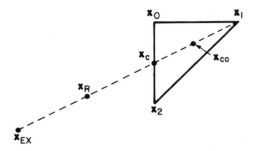

Fig. 2   Reflection, expansion, and contraction.

Equation (5) means that we choose x_R away from the high point x_H. There are three possible outcomes (i), (ii), and (iii):

   (i) If $F(x_L) < F(x_R) < F(x_{NH})$, x_H is replaced by x_R, and steps 3,4,..., are repeated with the new simplex (x_0, x_R, and x_2).
   (ii) If $F(x_R) < F(x_L)$, an *expansion* in the downhill direction is explored:

$$x_{EX} = (1 + \beta)x_R - \beta x_c \tag{6}$$

   where $\beta > 0$.
   (a) If $F(x_{EX}) > F(x_R)$, x_H is replaced by x_R. Go to step 3.
   (b) If $F(x_{EX}) < F(x_R)$, x_c and x_R are replaced by x_R, and x_{EX}, respectively, and (6) is repeated to move the new x_{EX} along the same downhill direction. Go to step (ii) (a).
   (iii)   If $F(x_R) > F(x_{NH})$, a *contraction* is tried:

$$x_{CO} = (1 - \gamma)x_c + \gamma x_H, \qquad 0 < \gamma < 1 \tag{7}$$

   (a) If $F(x_{CO}) < F(x_{NH})$, the contraction is successful, and x_H is replaced by x_{CO}. Go to step 3.
   (b) If $F(x_{CO}) > F(x_{NH})$, there is probably a ridge along the direction x_H, x_c. A new simplex will be formed near x_L by scaling.
   6.   Scaling:

$$x_i' = (1 - k)x_i + kx_L, \qquad i = 0, 1, 2, ..., n \tag{8}$$

We note that the point x_L is not changed by the scaling transform. The meaning of (8) is illustrated in Fig. 3. If $k < 1$, the simplex shrinks toward x_L. If $k > 1$, the simplex is reflected to the other side of x_L. In the following, we assume that $0 < k < 1$, and define x_i'' as

$$x_i'' = \left(1 - \frac{1}{k}\right)x_i - \frac{1}{k}x_L \tag{9}$$

and assign x_i' or x_i'', whichever gives *lower* F, to be the new value of x_i:

$$F(x_i) \leftarrow \min\{F(x_i'), F(x_i'')\} \tag{10}$$

   7.   If $F(x_i) < F(x_L)$ for some i, go to step 3.
   8.   If $F(x_i) > F(x_L)$, $i = 1, 2, ..., n$, we shall shrink the size of the simplex closer to x_L. However, first we shall test the value of k:
      If $k > 0.95$ or some other preset value close to 1, the program exits. Otherwise,

$$k \leftarrow \tfrac{1}{2}(1 + k)$$

   Go to step 6.

The various steps and branchings of the simplex algorithm are summarized in Fig. 4. In a system of many parameters, lattice mapping is usually too costly in terms of computer time. The simplex

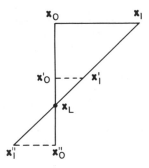

Fig. 3 Scaling ($k = \frac{2}{3}$).

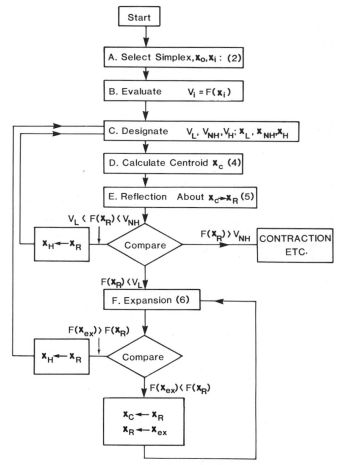

Fig. 4 Simplex algorithm.

algorithm can be used to improve an existing or proposed design, which is represented by the initial choice of parameters x_0. However, there is no way to tell whether the final parameters set represents a global or local optimum. Another drawback is that its convergence near the optimum point is very slow. The speed of convergence can be improved with one of the gradient search techniques.

3.5.3 Steepest Descent Method

The *idea* behind the steepest descent method is a very vivid one. First, we find the direction of maximum downward slope, and then estimate the distance to reach a valley or minimum point along the said direction. We shall describe the two steps and then discuss an essential shortcoming of this method.

1. *Determining the direction of maximum slope.* Given $F(x)$, the downward slope along the ith direction is

$$S_i = -\frac{\partial F(x)}{\partial x_i} \tag{11}$$

The steepest downward direction is given by the vector S. Therefore,

$$\delta x = \alpha S \tag{12}$$

where α is a scalar constant to be determined. The next point $x(k+1)$ is obtained from the present point $x(k)$ by

$$x(k+1) = x(k) + \alpha S \tag{13}$$

In practice, an analytic expression of $F(x)$ is not available, and S is *approximated* by

$$S_i = \frac{1}{h_i}[F(x_1, x_2, \ldots, x_i, \ldots, x_n) - F(x_1, x_2, \ldots, x_i + h_i, \ldots, x_n)] \tag{14}$$

2. *Determining the value of α.* The function $F(x + \alpha S)$ can be expanded into a Taylor series in α:

$$F(x + \alpha S) = F(x) + \alpha F'(x) + \frac{\alpha^2}{2}F''(x) + \cdots \tag{15}$$

where F' and F'' denote first and second partial derivatives with respect to α. As an approximation, we stop at the second term. If $F''(x) > 0$, the optimum value of α is

$$\hat{\alpha} = -\frac{F'(x)}{F''(x)} \tag{16}$$

Let F_0, F_1, and F_2 denote the values of $F(x + \alpha S)$ at $\alpha = 0$, α_1, and α_2, respectively. From (15), $F'(x)$ and $F''(x)$ can be solved in terms of α_1 and α_2:

$$F'(x) = -\frac{\alpha_2^2(F_0 - F_1) - \alpha_1^2(F_0 - F_2)}{\alpha_1 \alpha_2(\alpha_2 - \alpha_1)} \tag{17}$$

$$F''(x) = \frac{2\alpha_2(F_0 - F_1) - 2\alpha_1(F_0 - F_2)}{\alpha_1 \alpha_2(\alpha_2 - \alpha_1)} \tag{18}$$

Equation (16) gives

$$\hat{\alpha} = \frac{\alpha_2^2(F_0 - F_1) - \alpha_1^2(F_0 - F_2)}{2\alpha_2(F_0 - F_1) - 2\alpha_1(F_0 - F_2)} \tag{19}$$

Equation (19) gives the approximate optimum value of α only if the denominator is positive. A method that automatically satisfies this condition is as follows. A sufficiently small α_1 is selected so that $F_1 < F_0$. This is always possible because of (11) and (13). Then

$$\alpha_{i+1} = \alpha_i + a^i \alpha_1, \qquad i = 1, 2 \ldots \tag{20}$$

where $a \geq 1$, and (20) means that the distance between points increases exponentially. The function

$F(x + \alpha S)$ decreases as α increases until at some m

$$F(\mathbf{x} + \alpha_m \mathbf{S}) > F(\mathbf{x} + \alpha_{m-1} \mathbf{S})$$

In other words, m is the smallest integer for which the inequality above is satisfied. Then the following substitutions are made:

$$F_i \leftarrow F(\mathbf{x} + \alpha_{m-2+i} \mathbf{S}), \quad i = 0, 1, 2$$
$$\alpha_i \leftarrow \alpha_{m-2+i} - \alpha_{m-2}, \quad i = 1, 2$$

and $\hat{\alpha}$ is obtained from (19). Letting $\alpha = \alpha_{m-2} + \hat{\alpha}$ in (13) gives $\mathbf{x}(k+1)$.

A weakness of this method is that the direction of steepest descent is scale dependent. An improper choice of scale can lead to very slow convergence. The scale dependence is illustrated in the following example.

EXAMPLE 1. The overall cost of a system is given by

$$F(t, x) = t^2 + kx^2 \tag{21}$$

where t and x are in seconds and feet, respectively, and

$$k = 1 \text{ s}^2 \text{ ft}^{-2} \tag{22}$$

In terms of International Units, (21) can be written as

$$F(t, x) = t^2 + k'x^2 \tag{21a}$$

where x is in meters and

$$k' = 1 \text{ s}^2 (0.305 \text{ m})^{-2} = 10.75 \text{ s}^2/\text{m} \tag{22a}$$

With English units

$$S_1 = -\frac{\partial F}{\partial t} = -2t \tag{23}$$

$$S_2 = -\frac{\partial F}{\partial x} = -2x \tag{24}$$

With I.U., S_1 is the same, and

$$S_2 = -\frac{\partial F}{\partial x} = -21.5x \tag{24a}$$

We assume that we know nothing about (21), (21a), k, and k', and the direction of steepest descent is to be determined by test or computation, and that the tests are perfect. With E.U., it is

$$(\delta t, \delta x) = (-t, -x) \tag{25}$$

With I.U., it is

$$(\delta t, \delta x) = (-t, -10.75x) \tag{25a}$$

The two distinctly different results are illustrated in Fig. 5.

The difficulties with scaling can be there even if the parameters are of the same units. For instance, the collector resistor R_c of the input stage, and the emitter resistor R_E of a subsequent stage can be both involved as parameters in a given problem. The steepest descent method leads to overly large δR_E relative to δR_c if identical units are used for both resistors.

The scaling problem can be resolved as follows: Instead of (15), we expand $F(x)$ into a Taylor series of x_i, $i = 1, 2, \ldots, n$:

$$F(\mathbf{x}) = F(\mathbf{x}_0) + \sum_{i=1}^{i=n} \left(\frac{\delta F}{\delta x_i} \right)_0 \delta x_i + \frac{1}{2} \sum_{i,j=1}^{i,j=n} \left(\frac{\delta^2 F}{\delta x_i \delta x_j} \right)_0 \cdot \delta x_i \delta x_j + \cdots \tag{26}$$

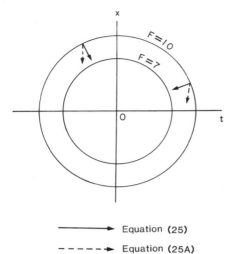

_____→ Equation (25)

– – – – – –→ Equation (25A)

Fig. 5 Scaale dependence of steepest decent directions. Solid arrows denote Eq. (25); dashed arrows denote Eq. (25a).

where $\delta x_i = x_i - x_{0i}$, $i = 1, 2, \ldots, n$, and the subscript 0 means that the partial derivatives are evaluated at x_0. Let G and H be row vector and matrix, respectively, defined by

$$G_i = \left(\frac{\partial F}{\partial x_i} \right)_0 \tag{27}$$

$$H_{ij} = \left(\frac{\partial^2 F}{\partial x_i \partial x_j} \right)_0 \tag{28}$$

Ignoring higher-order terms in δx, we can write (26) as

$$F(x) - F(x_0) = G\,\delta x + \tfrac{1}{2} \delta x^T H\,\delta x \tag{29}$$

If H has both positive and negative eigenvalues, x_0 is nearing a saddle point, and δx should be choosen along a direction in which both G and H are negative. If H is positive definite, x_0 is nearing at least a local minimum of F. Differentiation of (29) gives

$$G + \delta x^T H = 0 \tag{30}$$

$$\delta x = -H^{-1} G^T \tag{31}$$

It is easy to show that δx as determined by (31) is independent of scaling and is dimensionally correct. However, H^{-1} is difficult to determine experimentally or computationally. The Fletcher–Powell algorithm is a method of iteratively approaching H^{-1}.

3.5.4 Fletcher–Powell Algorithm

Let the matrix A denote an approximation of H^{-1}, and x be a point in parametric space in the vicinity of an optimum point x_{op}. The Fletcher–Powell algorithm aims at simultaneously moving $A \rightarrow H^{-1}$ and $x \rightarrow x_{op}$. The gradient G as defined by (27) is a function of x. It can be evaluated by direct computation as $-S$ in (14), or by some other method (Sec. 3.6). Initially, A can be set as

$$A = \alpha I \tag{32}$$

where I is an identity matrix and α is determined by the method of Sec. 3.5.3. The next point in x is given by

$$x' = x + \Delta \tag{33}$$

$$\Delta = -A G^T \tag{34}$$

We note that with **A** given by (32), (33) is identical with (12). The initial step of the Fletcher–Powell algorithm is a steepest descent algorithm.

Let **y** be a row vector defined by

$$\mathbf{y} = \mathbf{G}(\mathbf{x}') - \mathbf{G}(\mathbf{x}) \tag{35}$$

Then

$$\mathbf{A}' = \mathbf{A} + \frac{\Delta\Delta^T}{\mathbf{y}\Delta} - \frac{(\mathbf{yA})^T(\mathbf{yA})}{\mathbf{yA}\mathbf{y}^T} \tag{36}$$

In the next step **x** and **A** are replaced by **x'** and **A'**, respectively. Equations (33) to (36) are then repeated. The steps reiterate until $|\Delta|$ is sufficiently small.

Quite often **A** is *reinitialized* with (32) every few cycles while **x** continues to reiterate. The reinitialization frequently brings faster convergence or reduction in **F(x)**.

3.5.5 Least pth Method

The least pth method is a special case of (31). In some applications, $F(x)$ can be expressed as

$$F(\mathbf{x}) = \sum_{i=1}^{i=M} w_i[e_i(\mathbf{x})]^p \tag{37}$$

where p is an even integer, $w_i > 0$, and

$$e_i(\mathbf{x}) = v_i(\mathbf{x}) - c_i, \qquad i = 1, 2, \ldots, M \tag{38}$$

In (38), $v_i(\mathbf{x})$ is a variable depending on the parameters **x**, and c_i is a constant.

From (37),

$$G_i = \frac{\partial F(\mathbf{x})}{\partial x_i} = p \sum_{j=1}^{j=M} w_j[e_j(\mathbf{x})]^{p-1} \frac{\partial e_j}{\partial x_i} \tag{39}$$

$$H_{ij} = \frac{F(\mathbf{x})}{\partial \mathbf{x}_i \partial \mathbf{x}_j} = p(p-1) \sum_{k=1}^{k=M} w_k[e_k(\mathbf{x})]^{p-2} \frac{\partial e_k}{\partial x_i} \frac{\partial e_k}{\partial x_j}$$

$$+ p \sum_{k=1}^{k=M} w_k[e_k(\mathbf{x})]^{p-1} \frac{\partial^2 e_k}{\partial x_i \partial x_j}$$

At the vincinity of the optimum x_{op}, each error term e_k is expected to be very small. The second sum is proportional to e^{p-1} and becomes vanishingly small compared to the first term when x_{op} is approached. Therefore,

$$H_{ij} \cong p(p-1) \sum_{k=1}^{k=M} w_k[e_k(\mathbf{x})]^{p-2} \frac{\partial e_k}{\partial x_i} \frac{\partial e_k}{\partial x_j} \tag{40}$$

Let the matrices J, D, and C be defined by

$$J_{ij} = \frac{\partial e_i}{\partial x_j} = \frac{\partial v_i}{\partial x_j}, \qquad i = 1, 2, \ldots, M; \quad j = 1, 2, \ldots, n \tag{41}$$

$$D_{ij} = 0, \qquad\qquad i \neq j$$

$$D_{ii} = w_i[e_i(\mathbf{x})]^{p-2}, \qquad i = 1, 2, \ldots, M \tag{42}$$

$$C_i = w_i[e_i(\mathbf{x})]^{p-1}, \qquad i = 1, 2, \ldots, M \tag{43}$$

As defined, **J** is an $M \times n$ matrix, **D** is an $M \times M$ diagonal matrix, and **C** is a $1 \times M$ row vector. Equations (39) and (40) can be written as

$$\mathbf{G} = p\mathbf{CJ} \tag{44}$$

$$\mathbf{H} = p(p-1)\mathbf{J}^T\mathbf{DJ} \tag{45}$$

The terms of J are first partial derivatives which can be computed as *sensitivities* in a circuit analysis program, and H is a readily computed. Assuming that $e_i(\mathbf{x}) \neq 0$, $i = 1, 2, \ldots, M$, both $\mathbf{D}$ and $\mathbf{H}$ are positive definite. Equation (31) gives

$$\delta \mathbf{x} = -\mathbf{H}^{-1}\mathbf{G} = -\frac{1}{p-1}(\mathbf{J}^T\mathbf{D}\mathbf{J})^{-1}(\mathbf{C}\mathbf{J})^T \tag{46}$$

The optimizing parameters are then obtained as

$$\mathbf{x}_{op} = \mathbf{x} + \delta \mathbf{x} \tag{47}$$

3.6 SENSITIVITY ANALYSIS

S. S. L. Chang

Sensitivity analysis determines the change of a performance variable v with circuit parameters x's. For instance, v may stand for the output voltage, current, terminal, and transfer impedances (admittances, or H parameters) at and between ports; and x may stand for branch R, L, C values, transconductances, and so on. Sensitivity analysis is important in a design problem in two ways:

1. To determine the variations in circuit parameters that can be tolerated.
2. To determine the direction of change in a parameter optimization program (Sec. 3.5).

In general, the exact effects of a *finite variation* in circuit parameters can only be determined by straightforward performance computations with the changed circuit parameter values. However, the adjoint-network approach does offer a simple algorithm for computing $\partial v / \partial x_i$ for a *single* performance variable v, and *all* circuit parameters x_i, $i = 1, 2, \ldots$. Thus the effects of combinations of parameter changes can be estimated.

$$\Delta v \cong \sum_i \frac{\partial v}{\partial x_i} \Delta x_i \tag{1}$$

In the following, we approach the problem by analyzing a special case first: an *all-admittance network*. The results are then generalized.

3.6.1 An All-Admittance Network

Consider an all-admittance network with independent voltage sources $\mathbf{V}_s$. For convenience of analysis the voltage sources $\mathbf{V}_s$ are separated out as *port branches*. The remaining network branches which contain only passive elements and dependent sources are called *interior branches*. If a dependent source depends explicitly on a member of $\mathbf{V}_s$, say V_{s1}, an open-circuit interior branch is created across V_{s1} so that the dependent source depends on interior branch voltages only. Then

$$\mathbf{I}_b = \mathbf{Y}_b\mathbf{V}_b \tag{2}$$

where I_b and V_b represent interior branch currents and voltages, and Y_b is a branch impedance matrix. Since the network is linear, its input currents $\mathbf{I}_s$ at the ports are related to $\mathbf{V}_s$ by

$$\mathbf{I}_s = \mathbf{Y}_{in}\mathbf{V}_s \tag{3}$$

and $\mathbf{Y}_{in}$ is the input transadmittance matrix. Figure 1 shows the reference directions of $\mathbf{I}_s$, $\mathbf{V}_s$, and the reference directions $\mathbf{I}_b, \mathbf{V}_b$ of the internal branches. If we include port branches as parts of an overall network N, the port branch currents are

$$\mathbf{I}_p = -\mathbf{I}_s = -\mathbf{Y}_{in}\mathbf{V}_s \tag{4}$$

The branch currents and voltages of N are then

$$\mathbf{I} = \begin{pmatrix} \mathbf{I}_b \\ \mathbf{I}_p \end{pmatrix}, \quad \mathbf{V} = \begin{pmatrix} \mathbf{V}_b \\ \mathbf{V}_s \end{pmatrix} \tag{5}$$

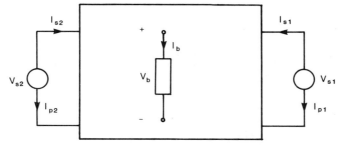

Fig. 1 Reference directions of branch currents.

Let $\hat{\mathbf{V}}$ denote the branch voltages of a network $\hat{N}$ with the same topology (incident matrix A) as N. From Tellegen's *theorem* (Vol. 1, Sec. 3.2.1)

$$\hat{\mathbf{V}}^T\mathbf{I} = \hat{\mathbf{V}}_b^T\mathbf{I}_b + \hat{\mathbf{V}}_s^T\mathbf{I}_p = 0 \tag{6}$$

Substituting (2) and (4) into (6) gives

$$\hat{\mathbf{V}}_b^T\mathbf{Y}_b\mathbf{V}_b = -\hat{\mathbf{V}}_s^T\mathbf{I}_p = \hat{\mathbf{V}}_s^T\mathbf{Y}_{in}\mathbf{V}_s \tag{7}$$

Consider a variation in $\mathbf{Y}_b$ defined by

$$\mathbf{Y}_b' = \mathbf{Y}_b + \Delta\mathbf{Y}_b \tag{8}$$

while the source voltages $\mathbf{V}_s$ remain unchanged. As both $\mathbf{V}_b$ and $\mathbf{Y}_{in}$ depend on $\mathbf{Y}_b$, they change correspondingly to

$$\mathbf{V}_b' = \mathbf{V}_b + \Delta\mathbf{V}_b \tag{9}$$

$$\mathbf{Y}_{in}' = \mathbf{Y}_{in} + \Delta\mathbf{Y}_{in} \tag{10}$$

The network topology remains the same, and (7) is satisfied also with the changed variables:

$$\hat{\mathbf{V}}_b^T\mathbf{Y}_b'\mathbf{V}_b' = -\hat{\mathbf{V}}_s^T\mathbf{I}_p' = \hat{\mathbf{V}}_s^T\mathbf{Y}_{in}'\mathbf{V}_s \tag{11}$$

Subtracting (7) from (11) and retaining only the first-order terms give

$$\hat{\mathbf{V}}_b^T(\Delta\mathbf{Y}_b)\mathbf{V}_b + \hat{\mathbf{V}}_b^T\mathbf{Y}_b\Delta\mathbf{V}_b = -\hat{\mathbf{V}}_s^T\Delta\mathbf{I}_p = \hat{\mathbf{V}}_s^T(\Delta\mathbf{Y}_{in})\mathbf{V}_s \tag{12}$$

Let $\Delta\mathbf{V}_n$ denote the changes in nodal voltages of N. The changes in branch voltages are also possible branch voltages for same topology:

$$\Delta\mathbf{V} = \begin{pmatrix} \Delta\mathbf{V}_b \\ 0 \end{pmatrix} = A^T\Delta\mathbf{V}_n \tag{13}$$

So far the network $\hat{N}$ is unspecified. If we require that

$$\hat{\mathbf{Y}}_b = \mathbf{Y}_b^T \tag{14}$$

then

$$\hat{\mathbf{V}}_b^T\mathbf{Y}_b = (\hat{\mathbf{Y}}_b\hat{\mathbf{V}}_b)^T = \hat{\mathbf{I}}_b^T \tag{15}$$

Since $\hat{N}$ and N have the same topology,

$$0 = \hat{\mathbf{I}}^T\Delta\mathbf{V} = \hat{\mathbf{I}}_b^T\Delta\mathbf{V}_b = \hat{\mathbf{V}}_b^T\mathbf{Y}_b\Delta\mathbf{V}_b \tag{16}$$

Substituting (16) into (12) gives

$$\hat{\mathbf{V}}_b^T(\Delta \mathbf{Y}_b)\mathbf{V}_b = -\hat{\mathbf{V}}_s^{T}\Delta \mathbf{I}_p = \hat{\mathbf{V}}_s^{T}\Delta \mathbf{Y}_{\text{in}}\mathbf{V}_s \tag{17}$$

Two admittance networks $\hat{N}$ and N satisfying (14) are called *adjoints* of each other. Suppose that the sensitivities of Y_{12} is to be calculated, where Y_{12} is the $(1,2)$ component of Y_{in}. Let

$$\hat{\mathbf{V}}_s = \begin{pmatrix} 1 \\ 0 \\ 0 \\ \vdots \\ 0 \end{pmatrix}, \qquad \mathbf{V}_s = \begin{pmatrix} 0 \\ 1 \\ 0 \\ \vdots \\ 0 \end{pmatrix} \tag{18}$$

and $\hat{\mathbf{V}}_b(1)$ and $\mathbf{V}_b(2)$ denote the calculated branch voltages of $\hat{N}$ and N, respectively. Then (17) gives

$$\Delta Y_{12} = \hat{\mathbf{V}}_b^T(1)(\Delta \mathbf{Y}_b)\mathbf{V}_b(2) = \sum_{i,j} \Delta Y_{bij}\hat{V}_{bi}(1)V_{bj}(2) \tag{19}$$

The summation is over all pertinent branch parameters Y_{bij}. The sensitivities are then

$$\frac{\partial Y_{12}}{\partial Y_{bij}} = \hat{V}_{bi}(1)V_{bj}(2) \tag{20}$$

Sometimes, the performance variable is the current I_L through a load impedance Z_L. An artificial port branch L in series with Z_L is created as shown in Fig. 2. Let $\hat{\mathbf{V}}_s = 0$ except for its Lth component:

$$\hat{V}_{sL} = 1$$

and $\hat{\mathbf{V}}_b$ is calculated accordingly. Then (17) gives

$$\Delta I_{pL} = -\sum_{i,j} \hat{V}_{bi}V_{bj}\Delta Y_{bij} \tag{21}$$

where V_{bj} represent branch voltages of N.

For an all-impedance network with independent current sources I_s, (14) and (17) are replaced by

$$\hat{\mathbf{Z}}_b = \mathbf{Z}_b^T \tag{22}$$

$$\hat{\mathbf{I}}_b^T(\Delta \mathbf{Z}_b)\mathbf{I}_b = \hat{\mathbf{I}}_s^T(\Delta \mathbf{Z}_{\text{in}})\mathbf{I}_s \tag{23}$$

3.6.2   Adjoint Network

Section 3.6.1 gives the rationale for defining an adjoint network as shown in (14). It leads to (16) and consequently the sensitivity equation (17) for the special case of an all-admittance network. We shall generalize the results above to networks with mixed parameters.

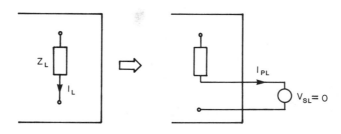

For Adjoint Network $\hat{V}_{SL} = 1$

Fig. 2   Creation of a short-circuited branch L.

As before, the independent voltage and current sources are separated out into port branches. Artificial internal branches are introduced so that the dependent sources depend on the internal branch voltages and currents only Referring to (3.2.3), the internal branch elements can be represented by

$$I_{b1} = Y_{b1}V_{b1} + H_{12}I_{b2} \tag{24}$$

$$V_{b2} = H_{21}V_{b1} + Z_{b2}I_{b2} \tag{25}$$

Equations (24) and (25) represent a generalization of (2). Similarly, (4) is generalized to

$$\begin{pmatrix} I_E \\ V_J \end{pmatrix} = - \begin{pmatrix} Y_E & H_{EJ} \\ H_{JE} & Z_J \end{pmatrix} \begin{pmatrix} V_E \\ I_J \end{pmatrix} \tag{26}$$

where the subscripts E and J denote port branches containing voltage and current sources, respectively; I_E represents currents entering the voltage sources V_E; and V_J represents voltages across the current sources I_J. The branch voltages and currents of the network N are then

$$V = \begin{pmatrix} V_{b1} \\ V_{b2} \\ V_E \\ V_J \end{pmatrix}, \quad I = \begin{pmatrix} I_{b1} \\ I_{b2} \\ I_E \\ I_J \end{pmatrix} \tag{27}$$

and similarly for the network $\hat{N}$. Tellegen's theorem can be expressed in an antisymmetrical form:

$$\hat{V}^T I - \hat{I}^T V = 0 \tag{28}$$

Substituting (27) into (28), and eliminating I_{b1}, V_{b2}, I_E, and V_J with (24) to (26) yields

$$\hat{V}_{b1}^T (Y_{b1} - \hat{Y}_{b1}^T) V_{b1} + \hat{V}_{b1}^T (H_{12} + \hat{H}_{21}^T) I_{b2} - \hat{I}_2^T (H_{21} + \hat{H}_{12}^T) V_{b1} - \hat{I}_{b2}^T (Z_{b2} - \hat{Z}_{b2}^T) I_{b2}$$

$$= \hat{V}_E^T (Y_E - \hat{Y}_E^T) V_E + \hat{V}_E^T (H_{EJ} + \hat{H}_{JE}^T) I_J - \hat{I}_J^T (H_{JE} + \hat{H}_{EJ}^T) V_E - \hat{I}_J^T (Z_J - \hat{Z}_J^T) I_J \tag{29}$$

The branch parameters of the adjoint network are defined to set the left-hand side of (29) to zero:

$$\begin{pmatrix} \hat{Y}_{b1} & \hat{H}_{12} \\ \hat{H}_{21} & \hat{Z}_{b2} \end{pmatrix} = \begin{pmatrix} Y_{b1} & -H_{12} \\ -H_{21} & Z_{b2} \end{pmatrix}^T \tag{30}$$

It follows that the right-hand side of (29) is identically zero for arbitrarily selected independent sources V_E, I_J, V_E, and I_J. Consequently, the quantities inside the parentheses are necessarily zero. We have

$$\begin{pmatrix} \hat{Y}_E & \hat{H}_{EJ} \\ \hat{H}_{JE} & \hat{Z}_J \end{pmatrix} = \begin{pmatrix} Y_E & -H_{EJ} \\ -H_{JE} & Z_J \end{pmatrix}^T \tag{31}$$

Equation (31) relates the input transmittances of the two mutually adjoint networks $\hat{N}$ and N.

3.6.3 Sensitivities of Networks with Mixed Parameters

Referring to (28), instead of I, V of N, we use I', V' of a network with perturbed internal branch parameters, while N is not changed. Equation (28) remains valid. The branch parameters in (29) are replaced as follows:

$$\left. \begin{array}{l} Y_{b1} \leftarrow Y_{b1} + \Delta Y_{b1} \\ H_{12} \leftarrow H_{12} + \Delta H_{12} \\ H_{21} \leftarrow H_{21} + \Delta H_{21} \\ Z_{b2} \leftarrow Z_{b2} + \Delta Z_{b2} \end{array} \right\} \tag{32}$$

Correspondingly, the input transmittances and internal branch voltages and currents of N are also changed:

$$
\left.
\begin{aligned}
\mathbf{Y}_E &\leftarrow \mathbf{Y}_E + \Delta\mathbf{Y}_E \\
\mathbf{H}_{EJ} &\leftarrow \mathbf{H}_{EJ} + \Delta\mathbf{H}_{EJ} \\
\mathbf{Z}_J &\leftarrow \mathbf{Z}_J + \Delta\mathbf{Z}_J \\
\mathbf{H}_{JE} &\leftarrow \mathbf{H}_{JE} + \Delta\mathbf{H}_{JE}
\end{aligned}
\right\}
\tag{33}
$$

$$
\left.
\begin{aligned}
\mathbf{V}_{b1} &\leftarrow \mathbf{V}_{b1} + \Delta\mathbf{V}_{b1} \\
\mathbf{I}_{b2} &\leftarrow \mathbf{I}_{b2} + \Delta\mathbf{I}_{b2}
\end{aligned}
\right\}
\tag{34}
$$

Substitution of (32), (33), and (34) into (29) and neglecting Δ^2 terms give

$$
\left(\hat{\mathbf{V}}_{b1}^T \quad -\hat{\mathbf{I}}_{b2}^T\right)
\begin{pmatrix} \Delta\mathbf{Y}_{b1} & \Delta\mathbf{H}_{12} \\ \Delta\mathbf{H}_{21} & \Delta\mathbf{Z}_{b2} \end{pmatrix}
\begin{pmatrix} \mathbf{V}_{b1} \\ \mathbf{I}_{b2} \end{pmatrix}
= \left(\hat{\mathbf{V}}_E^T \quad -\hat{\mathbf{I}}_J^T\right)
\begin{pmatrix} \Delta\mathbf{Y}_E & \Delta\mathbf{H}_{EJ} \\ \Delta\mathbf{H}_{JE} & \Delta\mathbf{Z}_J \end{pmatrix}
\begin{pmatrix} \mathbf{V}_E \\ \mathbf{I}_J \end{pmatrix}
\tag{35}
$$

Equation (35) is a generalization of (17) and (23) to networks with mixed branch parameters. Alternatively, (35) can be written as

$$
\left(\hat{\mathbf{V}}_{b1}^T \quad -\hat{\mathbf{I}}_{b2}^T\right)
\begin{pmatrix} \Delta\mathbf{Y}_{b1} & \Delta\mathbf{H}_{12} \\ \Delta\mathbf{H}_{21} & \Delta\mathbf{Z}_{b2} \end{pmatrix}
\begin{pmatrix} \mathbf{V}_{b1} \\ \mathbf{I}_{b2} \end{pmatrix}
= -\hat{\mathbf{V}}_E^T \Delta\mathbf{I}_E + \hat{\mathbf{I}}_J^T \Delta\mathbf{V}_J
\tag{36}
$$

The use of (35) and (36) to calculate the sensitivities of various output variables is similar to that shown in Sec. 3.6.1. Equation (35) is used to calculate the sensitivities of the terminal transmittance matrix, while (36) is used for output voltages and currents.

REFERENCES

1. L. N. NAGEL, "SPICE2: A Computer Program to Simulate Semiconductor Circuits," ERL Memo No. ERL-M520, University of California, Berkeley, May 1975.

2. G. D. HACHTEL, R. K. BRAYTON, and F. G. GUSTAVSON, "The Sparse Tableau Approach to Network Analysis and Design," *IEEE Trans. Circuit Theory*, **CT-18**(1), 101–113 (Jan. 1971).

3. P. R. BRYANT, I. N. HAJJ, S. SKELBOE, and M. VLACH, "WATAND Primer," University of Waterloo, Report 78-4, June 1978.

4. A. R. NEWTON and D. O. PEDERSON, "A Simulation Program with Large Scale Integrated Circuit Emphasis," *IEEE Int. Symp. Circuits Syst.*, New York, May 1978.

5. G. ARNOUT and H. J. DeMAN, "The Use of Threshold Functions and Boolean-Controlled Network Elements for Macromodeling of LSI Circuits," *IEEE J. Solid-Sate Circuits*, **SC-13**, 326–332 (June 1978).

6. C. A. DESOER and E. S. KUH, *Basic Circuit Theory*, McGraw-Hill, New York, 1969.

7. C. W. HO, A. E. RUEHLI, and P. A. BRENNAN, "The Modified Nodal Approach to Network Analysis," *IEEE Trans. Circuits Syst.*, **CAS-22**, 504–509 (June 1975).

8. J. WILKINSON, *The Algebraic Eigenvalue Problem*, Oxford Univ. Press (Clarendon), New York, 1965.

9. H. M. MARKOWITZ, "The Elimination Form of the Inverse and Its Application to Linear Programming," *Manage. Sci.*, **3**, 255–569 (1957).

10. W. F. TINNEY and J. W. WALKER, "Direct Solutions of Sparse Network Equations by Optimally Ordered Triangular Factorization," *Proc. IEEE*, **55**, 1801–1809 (Nov. 1967).

11. R. P. TEWARSON, *Sparse Matrices*, Academic Press, New York, 1973.

12. R. D. BERRY, "An Optimal Ordering of Electronic Circuit Equations for a Sparse Matrix Solution," *IEEE Trans. Circuit Theory*, **CT-18**(1), 40–50 (Jan. 1971).

13. J. M. ORTEGA and W. C. RHEINBOLDT, *Interactive Solution of Nonlinear Equations in Several Variables*, Academic Press, New York, 1970.

14. C. W. HO, S. A. ZEIN, A. R. RUEHLI, and P. A. BRENNAN, "An Algorithm for dc Solutions in an Experimental General Purpose Interactive Circuit Design Program," *IEEE Trans. Circuits Syst.*, **CAS-24**, 416–422 (Aug. 1977).

15. A. J. JIMENEZ and S. W. DIRECTOR, "New Families of Algorithms for Solving Nonlinear Circuit Equations," *IEEE Trans. Circuits Syst.*, **CAS-25**, 1–7 (Jan. 1978).

16. T. FUJISAWA, E. S. KUH, and T. OHTSUKI, "A Sparse Matrix Method for Analysis of Piecewise-Linear Resistive Networks," *IEEE Trans. Circuit Theory*, **CT-19**, 571–584 (Nov. 1972).

17. J. KATZENELSON, "An Algorithm for Solving Nonlinear Resistive Networks," *Bell Syst. Tech. J.*, **44**, 1605–1620 (Oct. 1965).

18. E. S. KUH and I. N. HAJJ, "Nonlinear Circuit Theory: Resistive Networks," *Proc. IEEE*, **59**, 340–355 (Mar. 1971).

19. M. J. CHIEN and E. S. KUH, "Solving Piecewise-Linear Equations for Resistive Networks," *Int. J. Circuit Theory Appl.*, **4**, 3–24 (1976).

20. T. OHTSUKI, T. FUJISAWA, and S. KUMAGI, "Existence Theorems and a Solution Algorithm for Piecewise-Linear Resistor Networks," *SIAM J. Math. Anal.*, **8**(1), 69–99 (Feb. 1977).

21. L. O. CHUA and P. M. LIN, *Computer-Aided Analysis of Electronic Circuits*, Prentice-Hall, Englewood, N. J., 1975.

22. J. D. LAMBERT, *Computational Methods in Ordinary Differential Equations*, Wiley, New York, 1973.

23. C. W. GEAR, "The Automatic Integration of Ordinary Differential Equations," *Commun. ACM*, **14**, 176–179 (Mar. 1971).

24. R. K. BRAYTON, F. G. GUSTAVSON, and G. D. HACHTEL, "A New Efficient Algorithm for Solving Differential-Algebraic Systems Using Implicit Backward Formulas," *Proc. IEEE*, **60**, 98–108 (Jan. 1972).

25. W. M. G. VAN BOKHOVEN, "Linear Implicit Differentiation Formulas of Variable Step and Order," *IEEE Trans. Circuits Syst.*, **CAS-22**, 109–115 (Feb. 1975).

26. S. SKELBOE, "The Control of Order and Steplength for Backward Differentiation Methods," *BIT*, **17**, 91–107 (1977).

27. J. C. BOWERS and S. R. SEDORE, *SCEPTRE: A Computer Program for Circuit and Systems Analysis*, Prentice Hall, Englewood Cliffs, N.J., 1971.

28. S. W. DIRECTOR, *Circuit Theory, A Computational Approach*, Wiley, New York, 1975.

29. R. W. DANIELS, *An Introduction to Numerical Methods and Optimization Techniques*, Elsevier, North-Holland, 1978.

30. S. W. DIRECTOR and G. D. HACHTEL, "The Simplicial Approximation Approach to Design Centering," *IEEE Trans. Circuits Syst.*, **CAS-24**(7), 363–372 (1977), and also Director, Hachtel, and Vidigal, **CAS-25**(3), 121–129 (1978).

SECTION 4

COMPUTER GRAPHICS

ROBERT F. SPROULL, EDITOR

Computer Science Department
Carnegie-Mellon University
Pittsburgh, Pennsylvania

GARY D. KNOTT

Division of Computer Research and Technology
National Institutes of Health
Bethesda, Maryland

CHARLES P. THACKER

Xerox Palo Alto Research Center
Palo Alto, California

CHARLES R. MINTER

Interactive Systems, Inc.
Santa Monica, California

Electrical engineers encounter computer graphics in two ways. Some design and build computer graphics equipment that becomes part of an application. Many more will find that graphics equipment and techniques are important tools to aid design and engineering tasks. Graphics is used extensively in computer-aided design to create, manipulate, and show pictures of logic diagrams, printed-circuit-board layouts, integrated circuit masks, signal waveforms, simulation results, and the like. An engineer can often improve the quality of a design by using computers and computer graphics to attack the numerous design problems that crop up in the course of a complex design project.

Parts of a Computer Graphics System.　Figure 1 illustrates the major components of an interactive computer graphics system and serves to define terms used throughout this section. The system's main role is to provide services to the *user*, who interacts with the system by observing pictures on a *display* and commanding the system by typing on a keyboard or by manipulating a *graphical input device* such as a joystick. The *imaging device* or *display* is a transducer that converts electrical signals into a visible image. It is the job of the *display controller* to generate these signals from information supplied by a computer. The computer is usually a conventional one, but its software may be specialized to support interactive graphics. The software usually consists of two parts: a *graphics package* that drives the display controller in the proper way, and an *application program* that provides the application functions invoked by the user. The illustration also shows other people involved in the design of a graphics system: the *digital system designer* who builds the display controller, a *system programmer* responsible for the graphics package, and an *application programmer* who designs the application program.

The proper design of a graphics system requires attention to all of its components and especially to the interfaces between them. The display designer is concerned with the properties of the image presented to the user: its brightness, its sharpness, its precision, its complexity, and many other factors that influence the user's perception of the image. The display presents an interface to the display controller: a small number of electrical signals

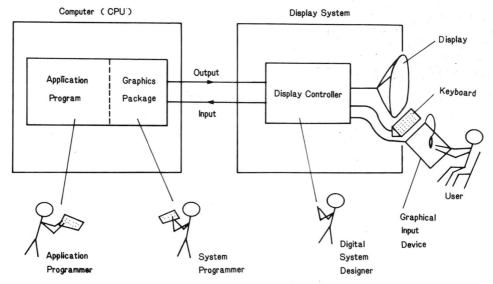

Fig. 1　Components of a graphics system and their designers.

that control image generation. The display controller designer defines an interface for the system programmer: a specification of the computer input/output commands and data structures in computer or display-processor memory that are used to control the display. In turn, the system programmer designs an interface for the application programmer; this usually takes the form of a set of subroutines in a graphics package, which the application program calls to construct the desired image.

The design of each of these interfaces exhibits a tension between high functionality and performance on the one hand, and simplicity and low cost on the other. A simple, low-cost interface may be suited to simple uses. An interface that provides a great deal of function is usually also costly to implement: a complex display controller architecture induces hardware complexity; a complex graphics package may be large and slow. High functionality and the resulting complexity may lead to confusion: a complex graphics package is hard for an application programmer to understand and use; a complex display station with multiple screens and countless knobs and gadgets may bewilder a user.

The following sections present an overview of the design of these interfaces and of the hardware and software techniques used to implement them. We shall concentrate on simple interfaces that offer sufficient functionality to address a wide range of graphics applications. Thus we shall describe techniques for building *general-purpose graphics systems*. Ideally, the internal interfaces leading from display to display controller to computer should be transparent, leaving a smooth interface between the user and the application program. If this ideal can be achieved, an application program can exploit the display's versatility to provide effective communication with the user.

General References   This section can only summarize the practice of computer graphics. A comprehensive text and reference is Newman and Sproull [16]. Information about displays and image-generation devices can be found in Refs. 4 and 17.

4.1   GRAPHICAL INPUT/OUTPUT DEVICES

R. F. Sproull

An important part of a computer graphics system is the output transducer that generates images from electrical signals and the input transducers that generate electrical signals from user responses. This section presents an overview of these input and output devices, emphasizing the characteristics of their interface to the user and to the display controller.

The most common image-generation devices for interactive graphics are the cathode-ray tube (CRT) and direct-view storage tube (DVST); applications that do not require pictures to change may use plotters to create images. In addition to a conventional keyboard, a computer graphics system often includes a *graphical input device* capable of measuring a two-dimensional position. Because stylus tablets and "mice" are the most common, we shall cover them briefly.

4.1.1   Cathode-Ray Tube

The CRT is the most popular and versatile output device for interactive graphics. Although new devices such as the plasma panel and liquid crystal displays occasionally emerge, the CRT remains attractive, in part because of its low cost and high quality resulting from decades of engineering and manufacturing. The details of CRT construction are discussed in Sec. 6.3 of Vol. I; here we mention those aspects of the CRT that are important for graphics displays.

A CRT is capable of producing a flash of light at a carefully controlled position on the screen. Each flash is controlled by three interface signals: x, y, and *intensity*. The separate horizontal (x) and vertical (y) addressing signals are used to condition the CRT's deflection system. Then the *intensity* signal, which controls a grid voltage, is altered to allow a burst of electrons to flow down the tube, changing direction due to the influence of the deflection system. During much of their travel, the electrons are subject to a high accelerating voltage, which increases their energy. Finally, they strike a phosphor coating on the back of the screen, which absorbs the electrons' energy. Some of this energy is radiated by the phosphor as visible light, thus producing a flash. Because each burst of electrons is very short (less than 0.5 μs), a complex image may be displayed by repeating the process rapidly, thus displaying many thousands of points.

Phosphor Characteristics.   When the electron beam strikes the phosphor, light is radiated by a *fluorescent* process, but even after electrons cease to arrive, light will be emitted due to *phosphorescence*. The light intensity decays exponentially, until the screen is once again dark. In order to produce

Table 1. Typical Phosphor Characteristics

Phosphor	Color	Persistence (ms)	Efficiency(%)
P1	Yellow-green	24.5	32
P4	White (typical television)	.06	43
P7	White (fluorescence)	400.	43
	Green (phosphorescence)		
P12	Orange	210.	—
P28	Yellow-green	600.	43
P31	Green	.038	100

the appearance of a stable image, therefore, the electron beam must be periodically aimed at the spot in order to reenergize the phosphor with a new burst of electron energy. This repetitive illumination of points to maintain a stable image is called *refreshing*, and is an important consideration in the design of display controllers for CRTs.

Table 1 lists some common phosphors and their properties. A phosphor cannot reradiate as light all the electron energy it absorbs; the *efficiency* of the phosphor is the ratio of the radiated to incident energies. The choice of phosphor will determine the color of the radiated light and will also determine its *persistence*, the length of time over which the spot continues to glow due to phosphorescence. If a long-persistence phosphor is used, the image will not need as frequent refreshing in order to appear stable. However, if the image is intended to appear to move, a long persistence phosphor produces disagreeable *after-images* or *ghosts*, faint phosphorescence at points where the image used to be.

Intensity. The intensity of a spot on the screen can be varied by controlling the beam current with the *intensity* control shown in Fig. 1. Intensity is varied by altering the number of electrons striking the phosphor per unit time. The energy of each electron is fixed, determined by the accelerating voltage.

Flicker. The rate at which an image must be refreshed is not determined by the phosphor persistence alone. The eye cannot discern extremely rapid fluctuations in intensity; above a certain flashing rate, it will *fuse* the flashes and perceive a stable image. The *flicker fusion rate* is the rate at which this fusion begins to occur, and depends on the brightness of the image. For very bright displays such as television (50 foot-lamberts) in a well-lighted room, a display must be refreshed 50 times a second (50-Hz refresh rate). For more modest brightnesses (20 ft-L), 30-Hz refresh is adequate. Long-persistence phosphors may reduce these frequencies somewhat. For line-drawing displays, it is unwise to fall below the 30-Hz refresh rate; 30 Hz is used for many raster displays and for U.S. television, although a 60-Hz image is perceptibly more stable than one refreshed at 30 Hz.

The *capacity* of a display is defined as the number of points or lines that can be displayed before the refresh rate drops below an acceptable level, causing flicker to appear.

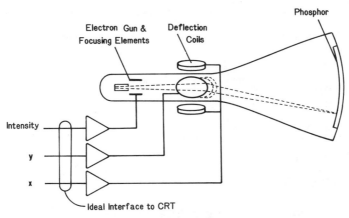

Fig. 1 Essential features of a cathode-ray tube (CRT) and its interface.

Spot Geometry.   The intensity profile of a spot can be approximated by a Gaussian distribution (Fig. 2). The *size* of the spot must be defined relative to this distribution. Isolated spots on a dark background usually appear to have width δ_1 (approximately 30 percent of maximum intensity), while closely spaced dots can be distinguished if they are separated by more than δ_2 (60 percent maximum). Typical spot sizes are 120 to 240 μm (0.005 to 0.010 in.).

There is a trade-off between spot size and brightness; the brighter the spot, the larger it will appear. However, a small spot size is desirable because the display will be able to show smaller details.

Resolution.   The *resolution* of a display measures the size of details that can be presented on it. Resolution is often expressed as a dot density: so many display dots per inch or centimeter. This dot spacing is usually related to the resolution of the deflection system and of the digital-to-analog converters used to drive it. A display measuring 10 in. square and addressed by 10-bit coordinate values has a resolution of 102.4 points/in.

The visual resolution of the display is usually not as high as the addressability of the deflection system, because the spot size is somewhat larger than the dot spacing. This size is chosen so that dots displayed along a line appear to form a smooth continuous line rather than a series of discrete points. However, the spot must not be so large that closely separated lines appear to fuse.

Deflection System.   The deflection system is one of the most demanding parts of a CRT system, because accurate deflection is required to avoid distortions in the desired image. Most computer-graphics and television displays use *magnetic* deflection coils to steer the beam. These have the advantage that excellent spot focus and brightness can be achieved, but have the disadvantage that they may be slow (about 35 μs for full-screen deflection, i.e., to change from steering the beam to one corner of the screen to steering it to the opposite corner). *Electrostatic* deflection systems deflect the beam by changing voltages applied to parallel deflection plates mounted inside the CRT tube. Electrostatic deflection is fast (about 3 μs for full-screen deflection), but large deflections may defocus the spot. This effect often requires *dynamic focus correction* to assure proper spot focus everywhere.

Both kinds of deflection system must be quite accurate and noise free. If a display is to resolve 1000 to 4000 points along each axis (x and y), the deflection system, including drive electronics, must be stable and linear to 1 part in 1000 or 4000. Noise that enters the deflection system may appear as objectionable *swimming* of the image. If a portion of the x deflection signal enters the y signal, distortions occur. Most familiar are the *pincushion* and *barrel* distortions due to geometries of the deflection structures, which make the edges of a square appear to bulge outward (barrel) or inward (pincushion). These distortions must be removed by suitable compensation in the drive electronics.

Timing.   An important feature of deflection systems is that they cannot respond immediately to changes in the drive signals x and y. To change the deflection, the drive electronics must increase or decrease the energy stored in the deflection plate capacitance (electrostatic) or deflection yoke inductance (magnetic)—this takes time. Moreover, large changes in deflection require more time than small changes. For example, a full-screen deflection change for a magnetic system may take 35 μs, while a change of $\frac{1}{1000}$ full-screen deflection may take only 0.5 μs. These speed differences suggest that the display will be able to show more points in the $\frac{1}{30}$-s refresh period if we arrange to show adjacent points one after another whenever possible, so that most deflection changes are small.

If the delays introduced by the limited frequency response of the drive circuitry are very carefully controlled, we can operate the CRT even faster. In this regime, we *sweep* the x and y input signals in a continuous fashion, and expect the beam to follow the sweep, perhaps with some delay. In this way, lines can be displayed by leaving the *intensity* signal on constantly as the deflection system sweeps along the line. Very careful engineering of the deflection system is required to achieve accurate positioning of lines of all lengths and orientations. The advantage of this approach, however, is a substantial increase in display capacity.

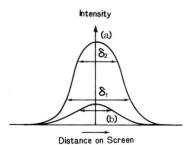

Fig. 2   Intensity profile of a spot on the screen.

Color. Several variations of the CRT are fabricated that can display color images. The *shadow mask* CRT, which is widely used for color television, employs three electron guns for red, green, and blue components, which produce beams that are jointly deflected to a small hole in a shadow mask near the screen. Electrons that penetrate the hole from each of the three guns do so at slightly different angles, and therefore strike the screen at three slightly different places. Each of these places has a small deposit of a different kind of phosphor: the blue beam will strike a phosphor that produces blue light, the red beam a red phosphor, and so forth. Nonprimary colors are obtained by mixing red, green, and blue colors of varying intensities.

The resolution of a shadow mask CRT is limited by the resolution of the mask, which can be quite coarse. Shadow masks used for television typically have holes spaced 0.6 mm apart on a tube face measuring 386 by 290 mm (19 in. diagonal). Thus there are about 480 horizontal "lines" of holes in the shadow mask. Recently, high-resolution shadow mask tubes with 0.3-mm hole spacing have been developed.

Another factor limiting the usable resolution of a shadow-mask CRT is the inability to *converge* the three electron beams precisely (i.e., to deflect all three beams by exactly the same amount). Convergence is usually worst near the edges of the screen, where an attempt to display a white point by using full beam current in the red, blue, and green electron guns shows up as three distinct dots, one red, one blue, and one green. The dots appear at different positions because the three beams have not been deflected identically. It is not unusual for electronics that drive a display to specify a convergence tolerance somewhat less than the hole spacing (e.g., 0.5 mm for a high-resolution tube).

The ideal interface to a CRT depicted in Fig. 1 appears to be very simple, but as the preceding discussion indicates, it becomes complicated when high performance must be achieved.

4.1.2 Direct-View Storage Tube

The major limitation of the CRT is the necessity to refresh an image in order for it to appear stable. This difficulty is remedied by the *storage tube*, but at a severe cost—persistent images are difficult to erase. The structure of the DVST resembles that of an electrostatically deflected CRT (Fig. 3), with the addition of a dielectric *storage surface*, near the surface of the screen, and a second source of electrons. Low-energy *flood electrons* arrive at the storage surface and penetrate it wherever the storage surface has sufficient positive charge, thus striking the screen phosphor. A high voltage applied to the screen imparts sufficient energy to the penetrating flood electrons to create a bright image. However, wherever the storage surface remains negatively charged, flood electrons are repelled and the screen remains dark.

The entire image may be erased by raising the potential of the storage grid briefly, which allows all flood electrons to reach the screen, causing an unpleasant "green flash." Soon, however, the flood electrons charge the storage surface negatively, so that when it is returned to its normal potential, flood electrons are repelled and the entire screen appears dark.

In order to write an image onto the storage surface, regions of positive charge must be created wherever the screen is to appear bright. The writing process depends on *secondary emission*: a writing beam of a certain energy will liberate more electrons from the dielectric than are absorbed from the beam, thus resulting in a net positive charging. These regions of positive charge will then allow flood electrons to penetrate and create an image on the screen.

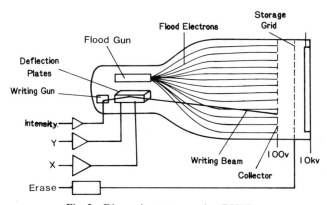

Fig. 3   Direct-view storage tube (DVST).

The DVST has played an important role in the spread of computer graphics because inexpensive display terminals can be built using this display. The cost is low because a display controller that does not need to refresh an image constantly is simple and inexpensive.

4.1.3 Pen Plotters

The mechanical pen plotter is illustrated schematically in Fig. 4. An arm and a pen armature are carefully positioned with stepping motors and cables or lead screws. In some designs, motion along one direction is provided by a rotating drum rather than a sliding arm. A pen can be raised or lowered by actuating a solenoid. Typically, the motor drive moves the pen in discrete steps of 0.025 mm at speeds of 400 mm/s. A typical pen will leave a trail of ink 0.5 mm wide.

The interface to a pen plotter is exactly like that to a CRT: x and y addressing signals that control the motors, and an *intensity* control that raises and lowers the pen. The pen plotter differs from the CRT principally in its slow writing rate.

4.1.4 Electrostatic Plotters and Laser Printers

An electrostatic plotter is illustrated schematically in Fig. 5. Specially prepared paper is passed under a row of electrodes, spaced very closely together (e.g., 200/in.). According to the *intensity* and x controls, these electrodes are at high potential wherever the image is to become black. The high potential transfers charge to the paper, which attracts black toner particles as the paper passes under the *toner station*. A variation of this technique uses photosensitive paper (e.g., coated with zinc oxide) that has been precharged and is discharged along a single line by a scanning laser beam that is turned on or off depending on the *intensity* signal.

These devices cannot accept arbitrary x and y signals, but insist that imaging proceed in a fixed sequence. For each y value (termed a "scan line"), intensities for each value of x must be provided before y can be incremented. This restriction arises because incrementing y advances the paper, whose direction of travel cannot be reversed. This addressing restriction is called a *raster scan*—all pairs of (x, y) coordinates are swept out, regardless of which points must be turned black in order to show the desired image.

4.1.5 Control of Output Devices

Two quite different control schemes are used to generate images on the output devices we have surveyed. The first, called variously *random-scan*, *calligraphic*, or *line-drawing* control, delivers an arbitrary sequence of (x, y) addresses to the display in the course of generating the image. The beam is deflected so as to trace out and illuminate the lines, characters, arcs, or other graphical shapes that comprise the image. The deflection signals for these shapes are calculated by the display controller and/or the computer. Random-scan control is typically used for the CRT, DVST, and pen plotter.

Another form of control, usually called *raster scan*, always visits all pairs of (x, y) addresses of the image, and modulates the *intensity* control of each point to create the desired image. The electrostatic plotter described above requires such a raster scan because of its physical construction. Raster-scan control is also frequently used for the CRT; television images are presented in this way. The deflection electronics for a raster-scan sequence are much simpler than fast random-scan deflection systems. This

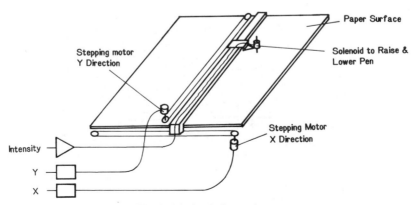

Fig. 4 Mechanical pen plotter.

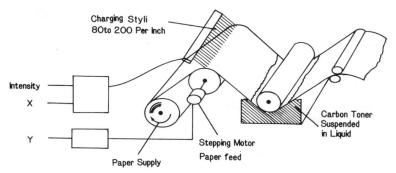

Fig. 5   Electrostatic raster-scan plotter.

is because the scanning sequence is chosen so that both horizontal and vertical deflection signals are sawtooth signals that repeat at a constant rate, and do not depend on the image being displayed (Fig. 6).

The control of a raster-scan device often uses an interface that differs from the $(x, y, intensity)$ interface because the values of x and y always follow a prescribed sequence. All the points (or *pixels*, an abbreviation for "picture elements") with the same y coordinate are displayed in order of increasing x; such a line of pixels is called a *scan line*. After one scan line has been displayed, the scan line with the next y coordinate will be displayed, and so forth until the entire image has been traced out. Thus the interface could be described with the following signals (Fig. 6):

Frame synchronization.   A pulse or signal transition that marks the start of the raster-scanning process for the image.

Scan-line synchronization.   A pulse or signal transition that marks the start of a scan line.

Pixel synchronization.   A pulse or "clock" signal that indicates the next pixel on the current scan line is being specified.

Video.   A signal that determines the intensity of the current pixel.

In some cases, the display mechanism itself must generate the synchronization signals because they are governed by slow physical motions (e.g., the paper transport of a laser printer). When driving a raster-scan CRT, there are usually timing restrictions on the way in which the synchronization signals must be presented. Moreover, the pixel synchronization signal is often given implicitly by presenting pixel video information at a specified *rate* once the scan-line sync signal is given.

Because a raster scan visits *every* point in the image, the rate at which video data must be delivered is often quite high. Table 2 shows typical characteristics of several devices. For a CRT being refreshed at frequency f, with y scan lines and x pixels on each scan line, a video value for each pixel must be generated in $p = 0.825/fxy$ seconds (the factor 0.825 is explained below). For a device such as a plotter that requires that the image be presented only once, we have $p = 1/r^2ws$, where r is the resolution, w is the width of each scan line, and s is the rate of paper motion. Of all the devices shown in the table, only the electrostatic plotter can be driven at a variable rate (i.e., the motor that moves the paper may be stopped); the other devices demand uninterrupted delivery of video data.

U.S. Video Standards.   Television monitors built to accept broadcast and closed-circuit video signals in the United States conform to a set of standard formats, RS-170 and RS-330 [5]. These same formats can be used to drive TV monitors for use in computer graphics. The formats are parametric, in that the number of scan lines, aspect ratio of the screen, and horizontal sweep frequency determine the details of the format. Define:

y to be the number of total scan lines per frame
a to be the aspect ratio of the screen (i.e., the length of a scan line divided by the other dimension)
H to be the length of time required to image one scan line

For broadcast video, $y = 525$, $a = \frac{4}{3}$, and $H = 1/15,750$ s. In the discussion below, example figures in brackets are computed from these parameters.

Of the y scan lines, only about $y - 42$ [483] are visible; the rest are normally "blanked" because they occur during the vertical retrace time (Fig. 6). For computer graphics applications, the number of

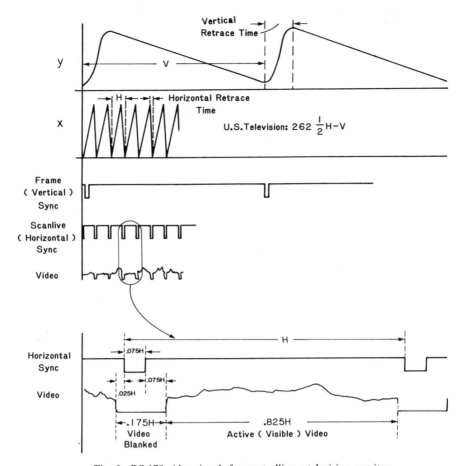

Fig. 6 RS-170 video signals for controlling a television monitor.

Table 2. Typical Raster-Scan-Device Characteristics

Refresh Device (CRT)	f (Hz)	y_{total}	$y_{visible}$	x	p (ns)	Number of Pixels/Frame
U.S. broadcast television	30	525	480	640	82	307200
Portrait, interlaced	30	875	808	606	51	489648
Portrait, non-interlaced	60	1024	981	736	18	722016

Image-Once Device	r (pixels/in.)	w (in.)	s (in./s)	p (ns)	Number of Pixels/Page
Xerographic printer	384	11	10	62	14×10^6
Phototypesetter	723	11	0.05	3400	49×10^6
Electrostatic plotter	200	11	1.5	1500	3.7×10^6

pixels per scan line is chosen so that the pixel coordinate system has a square aspect ratio (i.e., so that there are the same number of pixels per inch in both vertical and horizontal directions). Thus we require $(y-42)a$ pixels per scan line [644].

Within the period H devoted to each scan line, $0.175H$ is used for horizontal retrace and the remaining $0.825H$ for visible picture information. Thus the time p required for each pixel is $p = 0.825H/(y-42)a$. (For broadcast standards, note that to a very close approximation, $p = H/780$.)

The screen is scanned from top to bottom; when the scanning reaches the bottom of the screen, a vertical sync pulse lasting $9H$ is applied, followed by a period of $12H$ blanking; the vertical retrace period thus occupies $21H$. (In the RS-170 specification, the vertical sync pulse is encoded with equalization before and after to simplify broadcast decoding.)

The RS-170 specification requires *interlaced* scanning, in which the screen must be scanned twice to be fully displayed. The first scan presents all scan lines with even y coordinates (even field); the second scan presents scan lines with odd coordinates (odd field). Therefore, vertical sync pulses occur every $y/2$ [$262\frac{1}{2}$] scan lines.

4.1.6   Graphical Input Devices

Conceptually, graphical input devices are the dual of graphical output devices: they provide to the computer the two-dimensional coordinates of a point determined by a physical control that the user manipulates. Points must be reported to the computer quite frequently (at intervals of 5 to 30 ms) if it is necessary to sample adequately the motions generated by the user.

Tablets.   By far the most popular graphical input devices are two-dimensional tablets, manufactured using a variety of principles (Fig. 7). The user grasps a *pen* or *stylus* in his or her hand and steers it over the flat tablet surface. The control electronics are able to determine the location of the stylus at all times, usually to a precision of $1/100$ in. In addition, the stylus is usually fitted with a spring-loaded switch that closes whenever the user presses down firmly. The switch state is reported to the computer so that a program may determine whether the user is pressing. The overall effect is very much like that of pencil and paper.

One of the reasons for the tablet's popularity is its versatility. It can be used to digitize data from maps or drawings by placing the drawing on the tablet surface and pointing at or tracing parts of it with the stylus. Paper drawings of menus can be attached to the tablet surface; the user invokes a command by pointing the stylus at a menu item. The tablet is also useful without any drawings attached to its surface: the stylus position is used to control a *cursor* that is displayed on the screen.

There are many ways to implement tablets. The early RAND tablet contains 1024 horizontal wires and 1024 vertical ones, each transmitting a signal that encodes its x or y address. The stylus acts as a radio receiver, picking up the signal transmitted down the nearest two wires. The controller decodes the addresses and passes them to the computer.

Another tablet design creates high-frequency sound impulses with a spark inside the stylus tip. These signals are picked up by two strip microphones located at the left and top of the tablet. The time that elapses between the spark and the reception of the signal on the microphone at the left determines the x coordinate of the stylus position. The top microphone similarly determines the y position. Because the tablet depends on detecting sound signals in air, its operation may be disturbed by ambient noise or by strong air currents.

A very successful tablet design is based on magnetostrictive delay lines. Under a protecting sheet of plastic are laid down parallel strips of magnetostrictive material. At the tablet edge is a loop of wire that is pulsed with a large current to start a compression wave traveling down all the strips. The stylus tip is fitted with a small pickup coil that detects the passing magnetic disturbance. By measuring the time between the current pulse and detection, one coordinate is determined. A similar set of magnetostrictive strips is placed at right angles to the first set, and is used to determine the second coordinate.

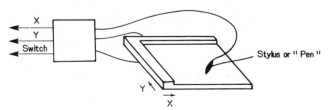

Fig. 7   Graphical input tablet.

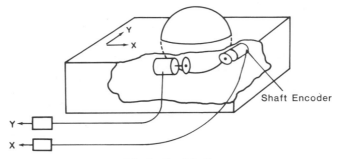

Fig. 8 Track ball.

Track Ball. A track ball is a spherical ball with two motion detectors in quadrature to measure motion in two orthogonal directions (Fig. 8). The detectors can be shaft encoders or potentiometers.

Mouse. The mouse (Fig. 9) can be thought of as a track-ball turned upside down so that the ball bears on the table. The top of the mouse contains three keys that can be easily pressed by the user. As the mouse is steered around, the motion of the ball is measured to determine the mouse's motion; coordinates are typically measured in units of $1/200$ in. The motion that is measured is relative to the mouse itself: forward, backward, left, right. Since the orientation of the mouse is unknown, it is not possible to determine the location of the mouse on the table surface. Moreover, if the user picks up the mouse and moves it to a new position, the ball will not rotate, and no motion will be detected by the computer.

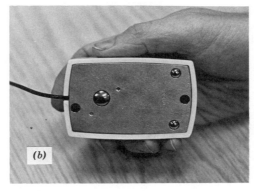

Fig. 9 The mouse, showing the rolling ball on its underside.

The mouse is very convenient for controlling a cursor to point to objects on the screen: lines, text characters, and so on [22]. It is awkward for freehand drawing because of its bulk. It is useless for digitizing data because its absolute position cannot be determined.

Light Pen. Historically, one of the first graphical input devices was the light pen. A stylus containing a very fast photodetector is pointed at the screen of a refresh CRT. If the stylus is pointed at a spot on the screen that is emitting light, the photodetector will detect the fluorescent emission when the electron beam strikes the phosphor. The discovery of light is reported to the display controller, which knows the coordinates of the point that was being displayed at that instant. This is an indirect way to determine the coordinates of the spot the user is indicating.

Without extra mechanisms, the light pen can be used only to identify information already displayed on the screen. To identify an arbitrary spot, we must *track* the light pen's position by displaying a pattern such as a cross on the screen, and arranging to move the cross so that it always stays in the light pen's field of view. Light-pen tracking thus requires maintaining a visible tracking target on the screen at all times.

The necessity for light-pen tracking makes this device very unattractive compared to others that report coordinate information directly. Although the light pen might appear to be ideal for identifying objects already displayed on the screen, the other devices can provide this function as well, with the aid of *comparators* in the display controller or software in the graphics package (see Sec. 4.4.4).

Other Devices. There is a tendency to provide a great many input devices to a user: tablet, track ball, joystick, function keys, and an alphanumeric keyboard. Generally, it is wise to avoid a proliferation of devices that becomes bewildering to a user. A standard keyboard and a single suitable graphical input device such as a mouse or tablet almost always suffice.

4.1.7 Connecting Input Devices to the Computer

The coordinates determined by a graphical input device have two uses: they are presented as inputs to the application program, and they are used to control a cursor or other form of direct feedback on the screen. Most often, the cursor displayed on the screen appears to follow the graphical input device directly; the feedback it provides helps the user to control the device and to see the relationship between the location of the input coordinates and other objects already on the screen.

Some sort of cursor is essential for the proper use of graphical input devices. The user does not look at his or her hand manipulating the graphical input device, but rather looks at the screen to see how the cursor is behaving. A human being's excellent hand–eye coordination is responsible for making the link between the desired cursor motion and hand movements that will achieve that motion. This coordination is similar to that used when driving an automobile: the driver watches the road and turns the steering wheel to correct the car's direction; the driver does not need to watch his or her hands to assess carefully how far to turn the steering wheel.

In some cases, the cursor position may not follow the motion of the graphical input device exactly. The precise form of feedback may be determined by the application program, which generates a feedback image using the same image-generation methods used for other parts of the image. For example, the application program might constrain the cursor to lie on a horizontal line, in effect ignoring the y coordinate returned by the input device. Or it may wish to display a nonstandard cursor shape, such as a circle with cross hairs. In some cases, the application program may choose to scale the input device coordinates to enlarge or reduce their effect on the cursor position.

To accommodate both of these needs, it is vitally important that the cursor position not be controlled *only* by the coordinates provided by a graphical input device. If a display controller provides a movable cursor, it is best if the cursor position can be set only by the computer. The cursor can be made to track the input device by programming the computer to sample the input device coordinates at frequent intervals (e.g., every $\frac{1}{60}$ s) and use these numbers to set the cursor position on the display. Alternatively, it is acceptable if the cursor position is set by the graphical input device directly, provided that this link can be overriden by the computer when nondirect cursor feedback is required.

4.2 DISPLAY CONTROLLERS

R. F. Sproull

Display controller hardware generates images on a display subject to commands from a computer. Display controllers can range from very simple devices to complex *display processors*, with many of the attributes of a general-purpose computer. The different requirements of random-scan and raster-scan devices lead to different kinds of display controllers. Before we examine the design of display controllers, we must present a model of how a computer program specifies an image on the screen.

4.2.1 Point-Plotting Techniques

Complex images on the screen are built up from simpler primitives, such as individual points, which a CRT can display directly. The creation of a complex display is therefore a matter of *synthesizing* it by combining its parts. The synthesis process is implemented by the display controller and the computer program that controls it.

Screen Coordinate System. One of the functions of a display controller is to establish a correspondence between digital coordinate values it receives from the computer and physical locations of points on the screen. This mapping defines a *screen coordinate system*, usually a Cartesian coordinate system with the origin in the lower left corner, the x axis extending to the right, and the y axis pointing up. The number of discrete addressable steps along each axis varies with the particular display: a high-precision display with a square screen might address 4096 points along each axis (coordinate values ranging from 0 to 4095 inclusive); a storage-tube display with a screen measuring 8.5 in. horizontally and 6.5 in. vertically might use x coordinates from 0 to 1023, and y coordinates from 0 to 780. In any case, it is helpful if the resolutions in x and y are identical (i.e., there are the same number of addressable points per inch along each axis).

Displaying Lines. Lines, or *vectors*, are presented by displaying a collection of dots that lie along the line. The line is specified by its endpoints in the screen coordinate system: (x_1, y_1) and (x_2, y_2). A *point-plotting line-generation algorithm* determines from the endpoints the coordinates of each point to be displayed along the line. Alternatively, more complex *sweep line-generation hardware* in a display controller can produce analog x and y deflection signals for sweeping out a continuous linear path on the screen, rather than displaying only addressable points.

A point-plotting line-generation algorithm can provide only an approximation to the line, because addressable points may not lie precisely on the line. The objectives of a good approximation are: the line must begin and end at the specified endpoints; must appear straight; must appear to have constant intensity independent of position, length, or slope; and must be generated rapidly if the display is to have sufficient capacity. The density objective is usually met by displaying exactly one dot for each coordinate position along the axis of maximum excursion of the line. That is, if a line has the property $|x_2 - x_1| \geqslant |y_2 - y_1|$, the axis of maximum excursion is the x axis, so a single point will be displayed at each x coordinate from x_1 to x_2 inclusive.

The following simple algorithm will generate a line with the required properties:

```
if |x₂ − x₁| ⩾ |y₂ − y₁| then begin
    m := (y₂ − y₁)/(x₂ − x₁);  b := − x₁*m;
    for x := x₁ to x₂ do begin
        y := m*x + b;
        Plot(x, y)
    end;
end else begin
    ...similar process for y axis, with roles
    ...of x and y interchanged
end;
```

The calculation of y uses the conventional line equation. The *Plot* function actually displays a point on the screen. Unfortunately, this algorithm requires a multiplication to generate each point and must moreover use a representation for m, b, and y that can accommodate nonintegral fractional values (e.g., a floating-point representation). Multiplication and floating-point operations will either reduce the speed of line generation or increase the cost of the display controller.

The Bresenham algorithm [1] generates exactly the same sequence of points, but is usually much more efficient because it requires neither multiplication nor fractional representations. A complete PASCAL procedure to draw a line with this algorithm follows:

```
procedure DrawLine (x1,y1,x2,y2: integer);
    var deltax,deltay,incrx,incry,e,einca,eincb,i: integer;
begin
    deltax := abs(x1 − x2);  deltay := abs(y1 − y2);
    incrx := 1;  if x2 < x1 then incrx := − 1;
    incry := 1;  if y2 < y1 then incry := − 1;
```

```
if deltax > deltay then begin (*x changes faster than y*)
    eincb := deltay + deltay;
    einca := eincb - (deltax + deltax);
    e := eincb - deltax;
    for i := 0 to deltax do begin
        Plot(x1,y1);
        if e > = 0 then begin
            y1 := y1 + incry;
            e := e + einca
        end else e := e + eincb;
        x1 := x1 + incrx
    end
end else begin (*y changes faster than x*)
    eincb := deltax + deltax;
    einca := eincb - (deltay + deltay);
    e := eincb - deltay;
    for i := 0 to deltay do begin
        Plot(x1,y1);
        if e > = 0 then begin
            x1 := x1 + incrx;
            e := e + einca
        end else e := e + eincb;
        y1 := y1 + incry
    end
end
end
```

This procedure requires only simple integer arithmetic. If the endpoint coordinates are n-bit positive integers, the variables in the algorithm take on values that lie between -2^{n+1} and 2^{n+1} (i.e., they can be implemented with $n+2$ bit 2's-complement arithmetic). (Note that the algorithm as given displays both endpoints of the line. If a series of line segments is chained together, this convention will cause the joints between lines to be displayed twice and appear too bright on a random-scan display. To avoid this, we can adopt the convention that the final endpoint of a line is not displayed. The algorithm given above can be easily modified to achieve this effect by replacing the two statements "**for** i := 0 **to** ..." with "**for** i := 1 **to** ....")

Character Display. If text characters are represented as a collection of line segments, a line-drawing method can be used to make images of them. This representation has the advantage that characters of different sizes and orientations can be obtained by applying geometrical transformations to the line endpoint coordinates. Unfortunately, the representation is not very compact.

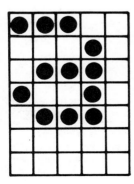

Fig. 1   A 5×7 character matrix.

A compact representation of a text character of a given size and orientation is a small *matrix*, or *raster*, describing the points that should be illuminated in order to portray the character (Fig. 1). A template such as this that is 5 dots wide and 7 high can be represented as a pattern of 35 0's and 1's that record the presence or absence of a dot at each point in the matrix. To display a character, the matrix is scanned; each 1 bit that is discovered causes a dot to be displayed on the screen, relocated to the proper position. The following procedure illustrates this idea schematically:

```
procedure DrawChar (x,y,charcode: integer);
    var i,j: integer;
begin
    for i:= 0 to 4 do
        for j:= 0 to 6 do
            if CharMatrix[charcode,i,j] = 1 then
                Plot(x+i,y+j)
end;
```

The array CharMatrix, which holds the representation of an entire character set, is indexed by a character code and the x and y coordinates within the template matrix.

4.2.2 Point-Plotting Display Controllers

The simplest display controller is capable of producing a single dot on the screen in response to commands from the computer. It consists of a small amount of control logic and two digital-to-analog converters (DACs), one that controls x deflection and one y. I/O instructions executed by the computer load the DACs with appropriate values and cause the *intensity* control of the CRT to be pulsed briefly, producing a single dot on the screen. Typical instructions might be:

LDXA	Load x value.
LDYA	Load y value.
LDXAP	Load x value and display a dot.
LDYAP	Load y value and display a dot.

The computer is programmed to pass to the controller as fast as possible all the points that should be illuminated on the screen. The line- and character-drawing algorithms illustrated above can be used to compute the points to be displayed: the procedure *Plot* is programmed to load the DACs and display a point. In order to keep the image refreshed, the computer must repeat this process about 30 times a second.

The major advantage of this technique is its simplicity and the small amount of hardware required to attach a display to a computer. Using this idea, a laboratory oscilloscope can become a useful display for a mini- or microcomputer.

This technique is not suitable for maintaining complex displays because most of the computer's execution capacity is devoted to the refresh process, leaving little capacity for other application computing. To reduce the load on the computer, a direct memory access (DMA) *channel* can be used to fetch coordinate information from computer memory and pass it to the display controller without interrupting the execution of computer instructions. The application program prepares a table in memory containing the coordinates of each point that is to be displayed; the refreshing process can thereafter be handled by DMA initiated by the display controller. With this refinement, the chief remaining drawback is the size of the table: a display of 30,000 points will require a table of 60,000 words if the representation of the coordinates of each point requires two computer words.

4.2.3 Line- and Character-Drawing Display Controllers

Since most of the points displayed on the screen are part of lines or characters, it is advisable to implement the line- and character-drawing algorithms within the display controller. In this way, the amount of information flowing from the computer to the display controller is reduced considerably. Each line is represented by its endpoints; each character by its character code and perhaps its position.

If several different functions are provided in the display controller, there must be a way for commands from the computer to invoke each one. In addition to coordinate data, the *function* must be encoded in the information sent from the computer to the display controller. Most encodings of data and function are variants of a simple model, which can be illustrated by four abstract functions; these functions use the concept of a *current point* (x_c, y_c) to simplify the encoding of data and function:

Move(x, y):   Set $x_c := x, y_c := y$.

Line(x, y):   Display a line from (x_c, y_c) to (x, y), and then set $x_c := x, y_c := y$.

Char(c):   Display the character whose code is c at coordinates (x_c, y_c), and then set $x_c := x_c + 5$ (or whatever the width of the character is).

Point(x, y):   Set $x_c := x, y_c := y$, and then display a single point at (x_c, y_c). Sometimes the *Point* function is omitted; in this case a line of zero length may be displayed as a single dot.

Figure 2 shows a displayed image that can be represented by the following functions:

Move(10,30); *Line*(40,30); *Move*(35,35); *Line*(40,30); *Line*(35,25);
Move(50,20); *Line*(50,40); *Line*(130,40); *Line*(130,20); *Line*(50,20);
Point(90,30);
Move(80,45); *Char*(66); *Char*(79); *Char*(88);

The following sections illustrate two different ways to encode these functions, one for display terminals connected to a computer using character-oriented transmission lines, and one for display controllers connected directly to the computer's memory.

Display Terminals

Perhaps the simplest way to connect a display to a computer is to use the same asynchronous telecommunication conventions used to connect character-oriented terminals to time-sharing computers. These connections and the operating-system functions that support them are designed to transmit character codes, for example from the ASCII set of 128 characters. To adapt this transmission mechanism to graphical information, we must encode the graphic functions and data as characters.

Although there are many ways to encode the graphical commands, the most popular scheme is that used in the Tektronix 4000 series storage-tube terminals. Under normal conditions, characters received by the display terminal are simply displayed on the screen as characters. Receipt of a special character (code 29) causes the terminal to "enter graphics mode," in which character codes are interpreted as graphical commands until another special character (code 31) causes it to "leave graphics mode," and revert to simply displaying characters. When in graphics mode, the terminal receives an encoded representation of coordinate pairs. The first coordinate pair received after entering graphics mode sets the *current position* to the specified coordinate; this is the *Move* function. Any coordinate pair received subsequently causes a line to be drawn from the current position to the specified spot, and then sets the current position to that spot; this is the *Line* function. If we wish to display a character, we leave graphics mode and transmit the character. It will be displayed with its lower left corner at the current position and the current x position will be incremented by the character width, usually a constant. Thus we have the following implementation of the *Move*, *Line*, and *Char* functions:

Move(x, y):   Transmit "enter graphics mode," followed by an encoding of the coordinate (x, y).

Line(x, y):   Transmit an encoding of the coordinate (x, y).

Char(c):   (a) If the terminal is in graphics mode, transmit the "leave graphics mode" character. (b) Transmit the character c.

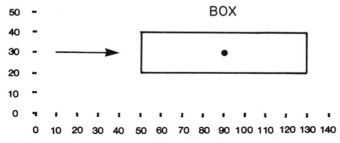

Fig. 2   Sample display image and the coordinate system used to measure it.

The encoding of a coordinate requires from one to four characters, depending on how the coordinate differs from the previous coordinate transmitted. A coordinate pair is divided into four 5-bit nibbles: Y_{high}, the five high-order bits of the y coordinate; Y_{low}, the five low-order bits of the y coordinate; X_{high}, the five high-order bits of the x coordinate; and X_{low}, the five low-order bits of the x coordinate. The encoding packs a 5-bit nibble into a single character, chosen so as to be in the alphabetic range of the ASCII character set (decimal 32 to 127), and tries to transmit only those nibbles that differ from the corresponding nibbles previously transmitted. The encoding is determined by the following steps:

1. If Y_{high} differs from the last Y_{high} transmitted, transmit the character whose code is $32 + Y_{high}$.
2. If Y_{low} differs from the last Y_{low} transmitted or if X_{high} differs from the last X_{high} transmitted, transmit the character whose code is $96 + Y_{low}$.
3. If X_{high} differs from the last X_{high} transmitted, transmit the character whose code is $32 + X_{high}$.
4. Transmit the character whose code is $64 + X_{low}$. The receipt of the X_{low} byte signals the end of the coordinate encoding.

Using this technique, we find that the encoding that will display Fig. 2 is: 29, 32, 126, 32, 74, 126, 33, 72, 29, 33, 99, 67, 32, 126, 72, 121, 67, 29, 116, 82, 33, 104, 82, 104, 36, 66, 32, 116, 66, 116, 33, 82, 29, 126, 34, 90, 91, 29, 33, 109, 80, 31, 66, 79, 88.

A storage-tube terminal also requires a function that erases the entire screen. The Tektronix protocol uses a two-character sequence ESCAPE FORM-FEED (codes 27 and 12) to cause erasure.

This encoding technique creates quite compact representations of pictures. Moreover, a graphics package can produce graphical output using character I/O functions already provided by the programming language and the operating system. Consequently, graphics can be introduced without altering either the programming language or operating system. Finally, the simplicity of the encoding technique argues strongly for its adoption whenever possible.

Refresh Display Controllers

Refresh displays must receive line- and character-drawing commands faster than can be transmitted on a conventional asynchronous communication line. These displays are usually attached directly to a computer, which passes full binary words to the display to control its function. To encode functions and data in these words, we define an *instruction set* for the display controller, which is similar in

Mnemonic	Meaning	15 . . . . 10 . . . . 5 . . . 1 0
$LD\left\{{X \atop Y}\right\}\left\{{R \atop A}\right\}$	LOAD	$1\ 1\ 1\ {x \atop y}\ {R \atop A}$ |← D: $x, y, \Delta x$ or Δy →|
$LD\left\{{X \atop Y}\right\}\left\{{R \atop A}\right\}M$	LOAD & MOVE	$1\ 1\ 0\ {x \atop y}\ {R \atop A}$ |← D: $x, y, \Delta x$, or Δy →|
$LD\left\{{X \atop Y}\right\}\left\{{R \atop A}\right\}L$	LOAD & LINE	$1\ 0\ 1\ {x \atop y}\ {R \atop A}$ |← D: $x, y, \Delta x$ or Δy →|
$LD\left\{{X \atop Y}\right\}\left\{{R \atop A}\right\}P$	LOAD & POINT	$1\ 0\ 0\ {x \atop y}\ {R \atop A}$ |← D: $x, y, \Delta x$ or Δy →|
SM	SHORT MOVE	$0\ 1\ 1\ 1$ |← Δx →|← Δy →|
SL	SHORT LINE	$0\ 1\ 1\ 0$ |← Δx →|← Δy →|
SP	SHORT POINT	$0\ 1\ 0\ 1$ |← δx →|← Δy →|
CHAR	CHARACTERS	$0\ 1\ 0\ 0$ |← F →|← char code 1 →|

\|← char code 2 →\|← char code 3 →\|

etc. until

char code $= 0$ (termination)

Fig. 3 Display processor instructions for showing lines, points, and characters. (Adapted by permission from J. Foley and A. van Dam, *Fundamentals of Interactive Computer Graphics*, Addison-Wesley, Reading, Mass., 1982.)

concept to the instruction set for a conventional computer, but is specialized for display generation. Figure 3 shows an example of an instruction set suitable for a 16-bit computer and a display with 10-bit coordinates. The high-order three bits of each instruction are an *op code*, which determines how the remaining bits are interpreted. The LOAD instructions contain an 11-bit value that is used directly in the interpretation of the instruction; in this respect, a display controller instruction set differs from computer instruction sets, which usually emphasize addressable rather than *immediate* data. The figure shows the exact interpretation of each instruction, using four registers x_c, y_c, x_n, and y_n that are contained in the display controller. The registers x_c and y_c hold the coordinates of the *current point*, converted by DACs into analog values to pass to the CRT deflection system. Registers x_n and y_n are auxiliary registers to hold the final endpoint of a line. The instruction set provides *relative* displacements to x_c and y_c, a feature that is useful in displaying symbols (see below).

Notes.

LOAD:	if $X/Y = 0$ then
	$\quad$ if $R/A = 0$ then $x_n := x_n + D$ else $x_n := D$
	else
	$\quad$ if $R/A = 0$ then $y_n := y_n + D$ else $y_n := D$
LOAD & MOVE:	do LOAD
	$x_c := x_n;\ y_c := y_n$
LOAD & LINE:	do LOAD
	draw line from (x_c, y_c) to (x_n, y_n)
	$x_c := x_n;\ y_c := y_n$
LOAD & POINT:	do LOAD
	$x_c := x_n;\ y_c := y_n$
	display dot at (x_c, y_c)
LOADSHORT:	$x_n := x_n + \Delta x;\ y_n := y_n + \Delta y$
SHORT MOVE:	do LOADSHORT
	$x_c := x_n;\ y_c := y_n$
SHORT LINE:	do LOADSHORT
	draw line from (x_c, y_c) to (x_n, y_n)
	$x_c := x_n;\ y_c := y_n$
SHORT POINT:	do LOADSHORT
	$x_c := x_n;\ y_c := y_n$
	display dot at (x_c, y_c)
CHARACTERS:	fetch character code
	while code $\langle\ \rangle$ 0 do begin
	$\quad$ display character in font F with lower left
	$\quad$ corner at (x_c, y_c); $x_c := x_n := x_c + $ width;
	$\quad$ fetch next character code
	end

The following instructions illustrate one possible encoding of the drawing in Fig. 2:

LDXA 10; LDYAM 30; SL 30,0; SM−5,5; SL 5,−5; SL −5,−5;
LDXA 50; LDYAM 20; LDYAL 40; LDXAL 130; LDYAL 20; LDXAL 50;
LDXA 90; LDYAP 30;
SM −10,15; CHAR 66; 79,88; 0,0

This sequence can be transmitted from computer memory to the display controller using an I/O channel (DMA). The channel must allow the display controller to fetch instructions at variable rates, because some instructions will require significant execution time (e.g., a full-screen line), while others may be executed almost instantaneously (e.g., a simple LDXA instruction). To maintain a stable image on the screen, the same set of instructions must be transmitted every $\frac{1}{30}$ s or so.

Display Processors

Although display controllers driven by channels are used occasionally, it is more common for the display controller to function as an independent processor, with its own *display program counter*, fetching instructions from memory independently of the CPU. To make the display processor truly independent, we must augment the instruction set shown in Fig. 3 with control instructions shown in Fig. 4. The most important use of the control instructions is to form an endless loop of display instructions so that the screen will be constantly refreshed. In the example sequence shown in the section "Refresh Display Controllers," we would place at the end of the sequence a JMP instruction to transfer the display controller back to the first instruction in the sequence. Generally, it is advisable to

Mnemonic	Meaning	$|$15 . . . . . 10 . . . . . 5 . . . . 1 0$|$
SJMP	SHORT JUMP	0 0 1 $\|$◄──── A: 13-bit address ────►$\|$
JMP$\left\{\frac{W}{-}\right\}\left\{\frac{I}{-}\right\}$	LONG JUMP $W = 1 \Rightarrow$ wait until next tick of $\frac{1}{30}$ sec. clock $I = 1 \Rightarrow$ interrupt CPU	0 0 0 1 1 - W I - - - - - - - -$\|$ $\|$◄──── A: 16-bit address ────►$\|$
PUSHJMP	Subroutine call	0 0 0 1 0 - - - - - - - - - -$\|$ $\|$◄──── A: 16-bit address ────►$\|$
POPJMP	Subroutine return	0 0 0 0 1 - - - - - - - - - -$\|$
NOOP	No-operation	0 0 0 0 0 0 - - - - - - - - -$\|$
INT	Set intensity	0 0 0 0 0 1 - - - - - - $\|$◄── I ──►$\|$

Fig. 4   Display processor control instructions.

refresh the image at a constant 30-Hz rate rather than at a rate that depends on the execution time of the instruction list. For this purpose, the JMP instruction is provided with a *frame wait* bit, which if set instructs the display controller to wait until a 30-Hz clock increments before executing the jump.

Notes.   Instruction execution rule:

           while true do begin
                INSTRUCTION := fetch(DPC);
                DPC := DPC + 1;
                interpret INSTRUCTION
           end

SHORT JUMP: DPC := A
LONG JUMP: DPC := A;
                   if W = 1, wait until next tick of 1/30 s clock;
                   if I = 1, interrupt CPU
PUSH JUMP: STACKPOINTER := STACKPOINTER + 1;
                   STACK[STACKPOINTER] := DPC;
                   DPC := A
                   Note: The subroutine stack is held in a small memory in the display controller. In this way, the display controller need not write into memory that is shared with the CPU.
POPJMP: DPC := STACK[STACKPOINTER];
                   STACKPOINTER := STACKPOINTER − 1;

Jump instructions have other uses besides making the instruction list into an endless loop. If the instruction list, or *display file*, cannot be allocated in a contiguous set of memory locations, jump instructions can link together the various pieces, so that the display processor traces through the proper instructions. Another important use is in providing *double buffering*. During the time that a new display file is being constructed in memory, the previous display file continues to be displayed to the user. When the new file is ready, a JMP instruction is switched so that the display processor begins interpreting the new instructions, and will no longer trace the previous display file. This technique maintains an image on the display at all times. The alternative, to erase the old display file and build the new one in its place, causes the screen to go blank for a moment as the new file is built, creating an annoying flash.

Symbols.   A *symbol* is a figure that is displayed several times on the screen, but at different positions. Each separate copy visible on the screen is called an *instance* of the symbol. The PUSHJMP and POPJMP instructions, together with the instructions that make *relative* changes to coordinates, help display instances. They allow us to build a display file that contains only one copy of the instructions for displaying a symbol, even though there may be many instances of the symbol visible on the screen. This technique is analogous to the use of subroutines, or procedures, in programming languages.

     The use of symbols is best illustrated with an example. Suppose that the arrow shown in Fig. 2 were to appear in several places on a display. We can make it into a symbol and define all its coordinates relative to a coordinate system that is local to the symbol, the *symbol coordinate system*. For our example, we shall assume that the origin is at the tip of the arrow. A display-file fragment to show the symbol can then be represented as:

```
Arrow:   LDXRM  −30
         SL 30,0
         SM −5,5
         SL 5,−5
         SL −5,−5
         SM 5,5
         POPJMP
```

This fragment assumes that the x_n and y_n registers in the display processor will contain the location of the origin of the instance when the instruction at Arrow is interpreted. Note that this symbol encoding returns the x_n and y_n registers to the symbol origin before finishing; thus any call to the symbol will leave these registers unchanged.

The POPJMP is similar to a "subroutine return" instruction—it returns control to the place in the display file from which the Arrow symbol was called. Such a display file might look as follows:

```
  0:   LDXA 40
  1:   LDYA 30
2,3:   PUSHJMP Arrow
  4:   LDYA 0
5,6:   PUSHJMP Arrow
7,8:   JMPW 0; Refresh after waiting
```

This display file will place two arrows on the screen, one with its origin at (40,30), and one at (40,0).

Text characters may be easily represented as symbols. Each character is represented as a separate routine using relative commands, and ending in a POPJMP. Unlike the example above, however, the symbol does not leave the x_n and y_n registers at the origin, but rather "spaces over" by the width of the symbol. For text that reads horizontally, this means x_n will be left incremented by the width of the character. This kind of representation is advantageous for character shapes that are not accommodated by a hardware character generator in the display processor. In fact, some display processors have no special hardware for character generation, but require instead that the display file define a symbol for each character displayed.

Design of Display-Processor Instruction Sets. Display processors must be designed very carefully to interact properly with the CPU; unfortunately, many commercial designs fall short in this respect. The problem is to ensure that the CPU can make rapid changes to the display file without disturbing the proper execution of instructions by the display processor. For example, consider the following simple program, shown with corresponding memory locations:

```
0,1:   JMPW 2; Wait to start refresh
  2:   LDXA 100
  3:   LDYAM 100
  4:   LDYAL 200
  5:   LDXAL 300
6,7:   JMP 0
```

How can the CPU alter this program to show another line from (300,200) to (300,100)? And how can the CPU alter the program to omit the line from (100,200) to (300,200)? These are examples of dynamic modifications to a display file that must be made often.

Illustration of the Problem. Suppose that we try to add the new line from (300,200) to (300,100) merely by inserting the instruction LDYAL 100 before the JMP instruction. To do this, we need to open up room for the new instruction at location 6 by moving the JMP instruction upward in memory. We try the following steps: (1) store 0 in location 8, (2) store a JMP instruction in location 7, and (3) store LDYAL 100 in location 6. Unfortunately, after step (2) but before step (3), the display file will not be legal. The display processor might fetch the JMP instruction that still resides in location 6, and then fetch the jump address from location 7, which now has the value 6144, the decimal equivalent of the JMP instruction. This sends the display processor off trying to interpret the contents of memory location 6144 as instructions; this is not part of the display file. As we can see, this sort of display file cannot be dynamically modified with ease.

Modifications by Changing Existing Code.   If we examine the example we used to illustrate the problem, we see that the trouble is caused by the fact that because the JMP instruction occupies two words, *two* modifications must be made to the original display file before it becomes legal again. Careful design of the display processor's instruction set can guarantee that the critical modifications can always be achieved with a single change to memory. Our example instruction set has two instructions that help: the SJMP short jump and the POPJMP return jump.

If the SJMP instruction had been used to terminate the original display file, we would have started with the following instructions:

```
0,1:   JMPW 2
  2:   LDXA 100
  3:   LDYAM 100
  4:   LDYAL 200
  5:   LDXAL 300
  6:   SJMP 0
```

Now adding an LDYAL 100 instruction can be performed in two steps: (1) place an SJMP 0 instruction in location 7, and then (2) place an LDYAL 100 instruction in location 6. Notice that after modification (1) the display file is legal, as well as after modification (2). Moreover, we could add any number of instructions in this way, as long as the last act is to replace the SJMP instruction in location 6 with its new contents.

In this instance, it is also easy to delete the last line from the display file, merely by placing an SJMP 0 instruction in location 5.

The only difficulty with this use of the SJMP instruction is that it has a small address field (13 bits in our design), which may not be sufficient to jump to arbitrary places in the display file. Of course, if we always build display files that are contiguous in memory, we only need a jump to the first instruction in the file.

The POPJMP instruction offers a slightly more versatile solution to this problem. We structure the display file as follows:

```
0,1:   JMPW 2
2,3:   PUSHJMP 10
  4:   SJMP 0

 10:   LDXA 100
 11:   LDYAM 100
 12:   LDYAL 200
 13:   LDXAL 300
 14:   POPJMP
```

In this example, we are not using the PUSHJMP and POPJMP instructions to call a symbol, but only to make the display file fragment beginning at location 10 easy to modify.

A slightly more complex problem is presented when adding text characters to a string of text that is already begun. However, because a character code of zero terminates a string and an instruction code of zero is a no-op, the instruction set allows incremental addition of characters. For example, suppose that the end of the display file looks like:

```
103:   LDXA 100
104:   LDYAM 240
105:   CHAR 65
106:   66,67 ; Interpreted as character codes
107:   65,0 ; 0 terminates character string
108:   SJMP 0
```

We can add a character with code 68 to this string as follows: (1) place SJMP 0 in location 109, (2) place 0 in location 108, and (3) place 65,68 in location 107. After modification (2), location 108 will be interpreted as a no-op if the display processor happens to fetch it. After modification (3), however, location 108 provides the zero that terminates the CHAR string.

Stopping the Display Processor.   If we cannot dynamically modify an existing display file, we might choose to stop the display processor whenever sensitive changes are made to the display file and to resume execution when the changes are complete. This technique is frequently used, but can be troublesome because the display must be stopped for almost any change to the display file on the chance that the display processor is executing instructions near the change. If the display processor is stopped frequently, the instruction execution rate is reduced, and the display may flicker objectionably.

For this technique to be usable, it is important that the display processor resume execution where it left off. Some displays make the mistake of requiring the display to be restarted at the beginning of the display file. Very frequent changes will cause only the first part of the display file to be visible—the display processor never reaches the end of the display file before it is stopped in order to make a change.

Modification by Changing Jump Addresses.   Clearly, a better solution to the problem of adding new instructions to the display file would avoid stopping the display processor. We can find some free memory, say at location 103, and build the new instructions there:

$$103: \quad \text{LDYAL } 100$$
$$104,5: \quad \text{JMP } 0$$

Then this new piece of display file can be "patched in" to the main loop of the original example in a single step: modify location 7 to have the value 103.

Changing JMP addresses is a common and powerful way to modify a display file. Its use requires preplanning to be sure JMP instructions are included at appropriate places when the display file is built, so that jump addresses can later be modified.

Segmented Display Files.   JMP address manipulation methods are particularly appropriate when the display file is segmented into large pieces (see Sec. 4.4.2). While a display file segment is being prepared by the CPU, it is not being interpreted by the display processor, and can therefore be modified at will. When the segment is complete, it is linked into the display file using pointer

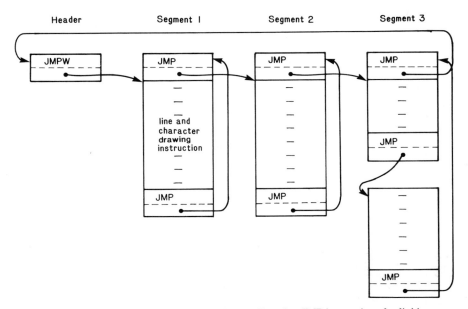

Fig. 5   Representation for a segmented display file using JMP instructions for linking.

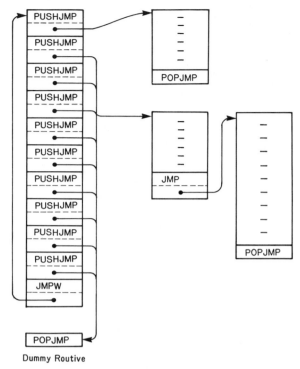

Dummy Routine

Fig. 6 Representation for a segmented display file using PUSHJMP instructions for calling segments.

manipulations. A segment being displayed can be removed from the display list by a similar change of JMP addresses. Figure 5 illustrates a format for segments that simplifies the linking operations because the JMP instructions are located in a fixed place in each segment; note that some segments use more than one contiguous block of memory.

Figure 6 illustrates another way to represent a segmented display file. Each segment is called with a PUSHJMP and finishes with a POPJMP. The list of segments to display is simply a table of PUSHJMP instructions, with a JMPW at the end to make an endless loop. Unused entries in the table are filled with PUSHJMP instructions to a dummy routine: this convention is chosen so that a segment can be inserted or removed from the display list by changing one word—an address of a PUSHJMP instruction.

The segmented display file provides a good example of the problem of *delayed reuse* of memory. Suppose that one of the segments illustrated in Fig. 5 or 6 is removed from the display list by changing an address of a JMP or PUSHJMP instruction. The display processor may for a brief period still execute instructions within that segment (e.g., suppose that it started interpreting the segment just before the address pointing to it was changed). As a consequence, the memory locations that hold instructions for that segment cannot be changed until we are sure that the display processor has finished execution of the segment: we must delay reusing this memory. It is sufficient to delay reuse for a length of time that exceeds the length of the display's refresh cycle, say $\frac{1}{20}$ s. Alternatively, we can arrange to have the display interrupt the CPU at the end of each refresh cycle, at which point we can be certain that any deleted segments may be reused.

Summary. The problems that arise in making dynamic modifications to a display file are caused by the fact that two independent processors are accessing a shared data structure—the display file. Although the memory hardware assures that the references to individual memory words are properly executed, it is up to the system programmer to be sure that a shared data structure composed of many words remains consistent at all times. There are two kinds of errors that can occur:

1. If the CPU modifies part of a display file that the display processor is executing, we must be sure that all intermediate states of the display file after each separate memory word is modified are legal. We cannot rely on simplistic and incorrect arguments such as: "The chances that the display processor will be fetching the instruction being modified are negligible" or "The display processor is

so slow compared to the CPU that the modifications can surely be completed before the display processor sees them."

2. If part of a display file is deactivated, we must delay reusing the memory used to represent it because the display processor may for a time still be executing the instructions that no longer form part of the display file.

4.2.4 Raster-Scan Display Controllers

Controllers for raster-scan displays have a very different structure than those for random-scan CRTs. This difference arises because the raster controller must furnish information to the CRT in a specific order, which may bear no relation to the order in which lines, points, and characters are specified in a display file for a random-scan CRT. The graphical information must be sorted into an order that matches the scanning sequence of the raster-scan display.

The most common solution to this problem is to insert a *frame buffer memory* between the raster display and the line- and character-drawing equipment (Fig. 7). The frame buffer is a large memory that records a digital value for the intensity of each pixel in the raster image. The video generator reads values from the memory in scan order to generate a video signal to refresh the display. Because pixel values must be extracted at quite high rates, the frame buffer memory must be organized with a highly parallel structure so that intensity values for many pixels along a scan line can be accessed at once.

The contents of the frame buffer memory precisely defines the image that will be displayed. The intensity of each pixel is represented by a fixed-size binary value. For example, if we record one bit per pixel, we can represent *bilevel* images consisting of two colors, usually black and white. Alternatively, the buffer might record 8-bit values for each pixel in order to represent 256 shades of gray; the 8-bit values are converted by a DAC to an analog video signal. To represent a color image, we might use three 8-bit values for each pixel to represent the red, green, and blue intensity components.

A *video lookup table*, or *color map*, is often used to map the representation used in the frame buffer into video values. Each entry in the frame buffer is viewed as a binary number, which is used to index a table of video values represented digitally. For example, a frame buffer with 4 bits per pixel would have a 16-entry map table. Entry i in the map holds a digital representation of the video signal that will be generated for pixels that have value i in the frame buffer. A table entry might specify an 8-bit value for gray-scale images, or three 8-bit values for full-color images. Only 16 of these colors will be available for any given image, but the colors can be chosen from the entire range that can be displayed. The main advantage of the map is that it saves memory: we can obtain very precise video values without having to record many bits for each pixel. Of course, the number of bits recorded per pixel still limits the number of different possible values within an image.

Mapping tables can be used to make certain changes to images very rapidly. For example, one of the 16 colors in the example above can be changed by altering a single table entry. More sophisticated methods can be used to make parts of the image appear or disappear rapidly. For example, suppose that each 4-bit pixel value is divided into two conceptual parts: a 3-bit value u, and a 1-bit value v. The value stored in the frame buffer for each pixel is $2u + v$, which requires 4 bits. These two parts can be viewed as separate images, or *planes*, on which different images may be written. An eight-color image is written into the u plane, and a bilevel *overlay* image is written into the v plane. The map table can control the way the images in the two planes are combined. Information in the overlay plane will not be visible if map entries i and $i+1$ are identical, for all even values of i. The overlay will appear to be written with white "on top of" the u image if all odd entries in the map contain the values for white, and the eight even values contain the eight colors for the u plane. This discussion merely illustrates some uses of the map; others are described in Ref. 18.

Writing the Frame Buffer.   The contents of the frame buffer are modified by commands issued by the CPU. Conceptually, the frame buffer memory serves as a two-dimensional array. Thus we might

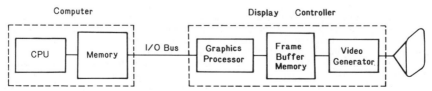

Fig. 7 Peripheral frame buffer.

use a programming-language notation to describe reading or writing the array:

$$val := FrameBuffer[x, y];$$

$$FrameBuffer[x, y] := val;$$

The convenient indices for the array are the pixel coordinates on the screen. Although some frame buffers locate the origin in the upper left corner of the screen and measure y coordinates increasing downward, a simple transformation on y values will allow us to use the more conventional system with origin at the lower left.

The process of converting geometric specifications of images into a corresponding representation in a frame buffer is called *scan conversion*. All of the point-plotting techniques outlined in Sec. 4.2.1 can be adapted for scan conversion. In effect, the calls to $Plot(x, y)$ are replaced by $FrameBuffer[x, y] := val$, where val is chosen freely to control the intensity or color of the line or character. In this way, the intensity of each pixel in a line or character is written into the frame buffer. Within $\frac{1}{30}$ s of the writing, the refresh process makes the change visible on the screen.

The frame buffer also allows information to be erased. A line or character is erased by scan-converting it again with a point-plotting algorithm, using an intensity that is identical to the *background* intensity of the display. Unfortunately, if two lines intersect and one is later erased, a one-pixel hole will appear in the remaining line. This hole can be filled in by redrawing any lines that are known to intersect a region in which objects have been deleted.

Unlike line-drawing CRTs, raster-scan displays can conveniently show *solid* or *filled* areas on the screen. For example, a filled rectangle of width w and height h with lower left corner at (x, y) will be displayed by modifying the frame buffer with the following simple procedure:

```
procedure DrawRectangle(x, y, w, h, intensity: integer);
    var i, j: integer;
begin
    for i: = 0 to w−1 do
        for j: = 0 to h−1 do
        FrameBuffer[x+i, y+j]: = intensity;
end;
```

More complex geometrical figures such as arbitrary polygons can be displayed and filled with more sophisticated scan-conversion algorithms [16].

The performance of scan-conversion algorithms is extremely important for interactive use of raster-scan displays. The problem is that the screen contains a great many pixels (see Table 2), many of which must be modified in order to achieve the appropriate change to the image. While adding another line-generation command to a display file for a random-scan display may take only a few CPU instructions, executing the line-drawing procedure outlined in Sec. 4.2.1 to write into the frame buffer a line that is 100 pixels long can take quite a long time. In addition to CPU execution time, we must also consider the time required by the CPU to modify a pixel in the frame buffer (i.e., to get the effect of the "$FrameBuffer[x, y] := val$" statement). The rectangle-drawing algorithm, when used to clear an entire screen of 480×640 pixels, performs this primitive operation 307,200 times.

Connecting the Frame Buffer to the CPU. The need for rapid changes to the frame buffer must be addressed by the controller that connects the frame buffer to the CPU.

The *peripheral frame buffer*, illustrated in Fig. 7, connects to the computer's I/O bus with what manufacturers call a "graphics processor." The graphics processor is capable of performing several different scan-conversion algorithms. It decodes commands that are sent via the I/O channel to govern scan-conversion algorithms for lines, characters, and rectangles. Commands are also provided for writing values into specified pixels and for reading pixel values from the frame buffer and returning them to the CPU via the channel.

The performance of the peripheral frame buffer is usually determined by the speed of scan-conversion algorithms, implemented in the graphics processor. Typical performances are 4.5 μs to write an arbitrary value in an arbitrary pixel, 15 μs to write a character, and $1.5 + 1.5 * length$ μs for a line, where *length* is the number of pixels that must be changed. But if the graphics processor does not contain a scan-conversion algorithm that is required (e.g., for displaying an arbitrary polygon), the CPU must execute it, and the rate of change to the frame buffer may drop dramatically. In estimating the performance of a peripheral frame buffer, it is also important to include the overhead for I/O channel transfers that may be introduced by the operating system.

The *integral frame buffer*, illustrated in Fig. 8, makes the frame buffer memory directly addressable by the CPU. This means that changing a pixel value by interpreting the "$FrameBuffer[x, y] := val$" statement will proceed very rapidly. Moreover, there is no limit on the range of scan-conversion algorithms that may be programmed directly in the CPU. To speed up the very common operations,

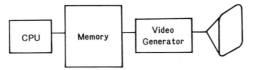

Fig. 8   Integral frame buffer.

special microcode may be provided for scan-converting lines or for other general-purpose operations such as RasterOp [16, 22]. For an example of a frame buffer design that allows CPU memory references to access the frame buffer memory, see Sec. 4.8.

Slow image-once raster-scan devices are often interfaced directly to the CPU, without using a frame buffer. This scheme requires the CPU to generate a digital representation of the video signal at the required rate and in the required sequence using software scan-conversion algorithms. For images with extremely large number of pixels, it is impractical for the CPU to simulate the effect of a frame buffer. Instead, the graphical information must be sorted into scan order and the scan-conversion algorithms must be executed incrementally so as to prepare the data for each scan line as it is required.

Evaluation.   Frame-buffer displays are rapidly becoming widespread because their construction depends on two technologies that have very high manufacturing volumes and therefore low price: television monitors and semiconductor memory chips. Moreover, they have several intrinsic advantages:

1. The frame buffer provides a system or application programmer with a simple, uniform model for controlling the image: the intensity of each pixel in a raster array.

2. Many programmers with no previous graphics experience find programming for frame buffers very easy. Controlling a raster display has none of the complexities of line-drawing display processors: gone are complex display files, display memory management, and synchronizing parallel processors.

3. The display is insensitive to the complexity of the picture being shown and to the type of image: text, line drawings, filled areas, and photographic images can be easily intermixed.

The only serious disadvantage of frame buffers is that rapid interactive response is hard to achieve because of the large number of pixels that must be changed. Even with very careful attention to scan-conversion performance, the displays cannot support many of the highly dynamic effects that are possible with line-drawing display processors.

4.2.5   Interface to the Display Controller

We have explored in the preceeding sections several different kinds of display controllers. Each presents a different kind of interface to the CPU, and therefore to a graphics package:

1. A sequence of image-generation commands controlling an image with storage. The Tektronix terminal protocol and the commands to a peripheral frame buffer are in this category, although the ability to draw with any intensity on a frame buffer to achieve partial erasure makes the details of these methods very different.

2. A shared display file. The random-scan display processor is the only example of this interface.

3. Access to memory to make direct changes to the picture. The integral frame buffer provides for reading and writing the *FrameBuffer* array directly.

In addition to these interface types, a myriad of other forms can be obtained by inserting another computer into our model (Fig. 9). This computer and the display are together viewed as a terminal, or a *graphics work station*, which is connected to the main CPU by a serial communication path or

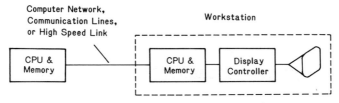

Fig. 9   Graphics workstation connected to a central computer.

computer network. A portion of the graphics package is usually implemented in the work station computer. The main CPU usually executes the application program and the remainder of the graphics package. This arrangement is sometimes called a *satellite graphics system* (see Ref. 20 for an example). In general, however, the work station and main CPUs may divide the effort in any suitable way: if the work station is a fully capable computer, it may execute the bulk of the application program, using the main CPU only for central file storage or printing. Generally, the interface protocol used for communication between the two CPUs is not the same as the interface to the display controller.

4.3 GEOMETRIC COMPUTATIONS

R. F. Sproull

The process of generating displays usually involves geometric computations performed by the application program and the graphics package. These computations aid in generating *views* of a geometric model, for example transforming a coordinate system that is convenient for expressing the model into the screen coordinate system required by a display controller, or transforming a three-dimensional image into a two-dimensional perspective projection to display. Geometric depth comparisons form the basis for *hidden-line elimination*, which removes from an image of a three-dimensional scene those lines that are hidden by opaque objects. Geometric computations are also used in *modeling* to represent the structure of symbols and instances in the model.

4.3.1 Coordinate Systems

The location of a point is measured with respect to a Cartesian coordinate system. We shall use a right-handed three-dimensional coordinate system with axes labeled x, y, and z (Fig. 1).

A representation of a two-dimensional point requires only measurements of the two coordinates x and y. We can view a two-dimensional system as being in a plane of constant z (say $z = 0$) in a three-dimensional system. In this section we generally develop three-dimensional techniques, with the understanding that they can be applied to two-dimensional problems by setting z to a constant. Usually when this is done, computational simplifications ensue.

Homogeneous Coordinates.   By converting three-dimensional coordinates into a homogeneous form, common operations such as linear transformations are simplified. To form the homogeneous coordinates of an ordinary point (x, y, z), we choose a scale factor $w \neq 0$ and obtain the homogeneous coordinates $[wx\ wy\ wz\ w]$. The homogeneous form is a four-element vector; we shall use bracket notation $[\cdot]$ for homogeneous coordinates while retaining parentheses $(\cdot)$ for ordinary coordinates. Given the homogeneous coordinates of a point $[a\ b\ c\ d]$, we find the corresponding ordinary coordinates by dividing by the scale factor: $(a/d, b/d, c/d)$. We shall often write the homogeneous coordinates of a point as $[x\ y\ z\ w]$, which corresponds to the ordinary point $(x/w, y/w, z/w)$. Note that corresponding to each ordinary point is an infinity of homogeneous points, each with a different value of the scale factor. Wherever possible, we shall choose $w = 1$ to form the homogeneous coordinates, so that the point (x, y, z) corresponds to $[x\ y\ z\ 1]$.

4.3.2 Linear Transformations

Arbitrary linear transformations can be expressed as a 4×4 matrix that transforms a homogeneous point. Usually, complex transformations are built up from three kinds of primitives: translation, rotation, and scaling. Expressed as transformation matrices, these primitives may be *concatenated*, or multiplied together, to form a single transformation.

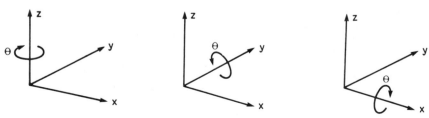

Fig. 1   The three primitive three-dimensional rotations.

Translation.   The translation of a point (x, y, z) to a new point (x', y', z') can be expressed as

$$[x'y'z'1] = [x \ y \ z \ 1] \begin{bmatrix} 1 & 0 & 0 & 0 \\ 0 & 1 & 0 & 0 \\ 0 & 0 & 1 & 0 \\ t_x & t_y & t_z & 1 \end{bmatrix}$$

The transformation matrix contains three parameters, t_x, t_y, and t_z, the three components of translation. The point (x, y, z) becomes the new point $(x + t_x, y + t_y, z + t_z)$. Note that although the examples above all use $w = 1$ to form the homogeneous coordinates, the transformation matrix will have the same effect on the ordinary three-space coordinates for an arbitrary nonzero value of w.

Rotation.   There are three primitive rotation transformations, corresponding to rotation about the three axes (Fig. 1). Rotation angles are measured clockwise when looking along the axis toward the origin. Rotation about the z axis can be expressed as

$$[x'y'z'1] = [x \ y \ z \ 1] \begin{bmatrix} \cos\theta & -\sin\theta & 0 & 0 \\ \sin\theta & \cos\theta & 0 & 0 \\ 0 & 0 & 1 & 0 \\ 0 & 0 & 0 & 1 \end{bmatrix}$$

This is also a primitive rotation in a clockwise direction about the origin of a two-dimensional (x, y) system.

The other rotation primitives can be obtained by permuting the coordinate axes. Rotation about the y axis is

$$[x'y'z'1] = [x \ y \ z \ 1] \begin{bmatrix} \cos\theta & 0 & \sin\theta & 0 \\ 0 & 1 & 0 & 0 \\ -\sin\theta & 0 & \cos\theta & 0 \\ 0 & 0 & 0 & 1 \end{bmatrix}$$

Rotation about the z axis is

$$[x'y'z'1] = [x \ y \ z \ 1] \begin{bmatrix} 1 & 0 & 0 & 0 \\ 0 & \cos\theta & -\sin\theta & 0 \\ 0 & \sin\theta & \cos\theta & 0 \\ 0 & 0 & 0 & 1 \end{bmatrix}$$

Scaling.   Points may be scaled (with respect to the origin) by the transformation

$$[x'y'z'1] = [x \ y \ z \ 1] \begin{bmatrix} s_x & 0 & 0 & 0 \\ 0 & s_y & 0 & 0 \\ 0 & 0 & s_z & 0 \\ 0 & 0 & 0 & 1 \end{bmatrix}$$

Other Transformations.   Some transformations are easily formed directly, rather than in terms of the primitives. For example, a transformation to interchange roles of x and y (which also turns the coordinate axes into a left-handed system) is obviously

$$[x'y'z'1] = [x \ y \ z \ 1] \begin{bmatrix} 0 & 1 & 0 & 0 \\ 1 & 0 & 0 & 0 \\ 0 & 0 & 1 & 0 \\ 0 & 0 & 0 & 1 \end{bmatrix}$$

Notation.   The three kinds of primitive transformations may each be expressed as a 4×4 matrix with certain parameters. We shall use shorthand notation to avoid writing out the matrices in full:

$T(t_x, t_y, t_z)$: Translate with parameters t_x, t_y, and t_z.
$R(z, \theta)$: Rotate about z axis through angle θ. $R(x, \theta)$ and $R(y, \theta)$ are the other primitives.
$S(s_x, s_y, s_z)$: Scale with scale factors s_x, s_y, and s_z.

Inverse Transformations.   Corresponding to each transformation is another that "undoes" the effect of the first; this is the *inverse transformation*. The inverses of the primitive transformations can be obtained by inspection: the inverse of $T(t_x, t_y, t_z)$ is $T(-t_x, -t_y, -t_z)$; the inverse of $R(j, \theta)$ is $R(j, -\theta)$ for j either x, y, or z; the inverse of $S(s_x, s_y, s_z)$ is $S(1/s_x, 1/s_y, 1/s_z)$ provided that all the s are nonzero.

The inverse transformation corresponding to a matrix M is the matrix inverse, M^{-1}. Although the inverses of primitive transformation matrices can be obtained by inspection, the inverse of a general transformation may need to be obtained by a numerical procedure that inverts arbitrary matrices [10].

Duality of Transformation.   Although we have thus far spoken of transforming *points* within a coordinate system, we can also speak of transforming the *coordinate system*, that is, changing the coordinate system used to measure the same points. These two kinds of transformations are duals of one another. If a point $Q = [x \ y \ z \ 1]$ is translated by $T(t_x, t_y, t_z)$, its new coordinates become $QT(t_x, t_y, t_z)$. If, however, the origin of the coordinate system used to measure the point Q is translated by $T(t_x, t_y, t_z)$, the new coordinates of point Q are $QT(-t_x, -t_y, -t_z)$. In general, a transformation M applied to points is equivalent to applying M^{-1} to the coordinate system used to measure the points. Equivalently, transforming the coordinate system by N requires transforming points by N^{-1}.

Concatenation.   Complex transformations can often be expressed by performing a sequence of primitive transformations. The complex transformation can be expressed by a single matrix, the matrix product of all the primitive matrices. For example, if we first transform a point (x, y, z) by the matrix M_1, we have

$$[x'y'z'1] = [x \ y \ z \ 1] M_1$$

If we next transform by M_2, we have

$$[x''y''z''1] = [x'y'z'1] M_2$$

Substituting the first equation into the second, we obtain

$$[x''y''z''1] = ([x \ y \ z \ 1] M_1) M_2 = [x \ y \ z \ 1] (M_1 M_2)$$

because matrix multiplication is associative. Repeated application of this idea allows us to multiply together an arbitrarily long sequence of transformations. The order in which transformations are applied is important; therefore, so is the order in which the matrices are multiplied together, because matrix multiplication is not commutative.

Because it is sometimes useful to compute the inverse of a concatenation of matrices, it is useful to remember that $(AB)^{-1} = B^{-1} A^{-1}$.

As an example of the use of concatenation, let us form a transformation that rotates through an angle θ about an axis parallel to the z axis passing through the point $(x_r, y_r, 0)$. In two dimensions, this is a rotation through an angle θ about the point (x_r, y_r). We derive the transformation in three steps:

1. Form a new coordinate system with origin at $(x_r, y_r, 0)$ by translating the origin of the present system to that point. The matrix will therefore be $T(-x_r, -y_r, 0)$.
2. Apply to all points a primitive rotation about the z axis through an angle θ. The matrix is $R(z, \theta)$.
3. Undo the effect of the first transformation, by returning the present origin to the point $(x_r, y_r, 0)$. The matrix is simply $T(x_r, y_r, 0)$.

The complete transformation is obtained by concatenating these three matrices: $T(-x_r, -y_r, 0) R(z, \theta) T(x_r, y_r, 0)$.

4.3.3   Perspective Transformation

A special kind of transformation is needed to map three-dimensional points onto a two-dimensional surface so that the image appears to have perspective. Figure 2a shows the *eye coordinate system* in which the coordinates of points must be measured. This system defines the viewpoint by placing the eye at the origin and the viewing direction by convention along the $-z_e$ axis. A square screen of size $2s$ by $2s$ is placed at $z_e = -n$; points are conceptually projected onto this surface, as illustrated by the points Q and Q'. This screen and the origin together define a *viewing pyramid*, shown in the figure, which encompasses all the information that will be projected onto the screen.

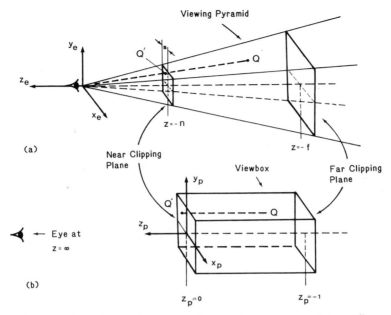

Fig. 2   Three-dimensional viewing: (a) eye coordinate system; (b) perspective coordinate system.

The perspective transformation maps the eye coordinate system into a special *perspective coordinate system*, shown in Fig. 2b. The portion of the viewing pyramid for which $-f \leqslant z_e \leqslant -n$ is transformed into a *viewbox*, with $-1 \leqslant x_p \leqslant 1$, $-1 \leqslant y_p \leqslant 1$, and $-1 \leqslant z_p \leqslant 0$. In the screen coordinate system, the eye is at $z_p = \infty$ along the z_p axis. Thus lines of sight emanating from the eye are parallel to the z_p axis. This means that the x_p and y_p coordinates of a point are its perspective projection, and can be transformed by scaling into two-dimensional screen coordinates for display. The z_p coordinate is ignored when making a simple line-drawing display, but is used to provide depth information for a hidden-line or hidden-surface elimination technique.

The perspective projection makes the same kind of image that is made by a camera lens on film. The *viewing angle* α, the half-angle at the vertex of the viewing pyramid, determines the kind of view we get. If $\alpha \approx 15°$, we obtain a "normal" perspective view; we can also obtain a "wide-angle" view ($\alpha > 20°$); or a "telephoto" picture ($\alpha < 10°$). Note that $\tan \alpha = s/n$.

The transformation from eye to perspective coordinate systems can be expressed as a matrix:

$$Q' = Q \begin{bmatrix} 1 & 0 & 0 & 0 \\ 0 & 1 & 0 & 0 \\ 0 & 0 & \dfrac{s}{n(1-n/f)} & -\dfrac{s}{n} \\ 0 & 0 & \dfrac{s}{1-n/f} & 0 \end{bmatrix}$$

Using the notation we introduced for primitive transformations, we denote this matrix as $P(s, n, f)$. If we let the far limit f approach ∞ and use the relation $\tan \alpha = s/n$, we obtain

$$Q' = Q \begin{bmatrix} 1 & 0 & 0 & 0 \\ 0 & 1 & 0 & 0 \\ 0 & 0 & \tan \alpha & -\tan \alpha \\ 0 & 0 & n \tan \alpha & 0 \end{bmatrix}$$

We can also let the near limit n approach zero, while holding $\tan \alpha$ constant.

It is important to notice that the fourth column of these matrices is not $[0 \ \ 0 \ \ 0 \ \ 1]^T$. Therefore, the scale factor in the homogeneous coordinates obtained for Q' will not be the same as the one used for Q. Thus even though we choose $w = 1$ to represent the point Q, the scale factor for Q' will not be

1. Therefore, a division will be required in order to compute the ordinary three-space coordinates x_p, y_p, and z_p of the point Q. *To create a true perspective view, it is necessary to divide by the depth of each point.*

Only those points that lie within the viewing pyramid, possibly restricted by n and f, will be visible on the screen. Points that lie behind the eye ($z_e > 0$) or off-screen cannot be seen. The conditions that a point Q' will be visible are

$$-w \leqslant x \leqslant w$$

$$-w \leqslant y \leqslant w$$

$$-w \leqslant z \leqslant 0$$

where the homogeneous coordinates of Q' are $[x\ y\ z\ w]$. In the case that we let f approach ∞, the third condition becomes simply $-w \leqslant 0$.

4.3.4 Lines and Planes

Although we have discussed only the transformation of individual points, the same techniques can be applied to lines and planes. Under all these transformations, lines transform into lines and planes into planes. Thus the transform of a line segment L between endpoints E_1 and E_2, is the line segment L' between endpoints E'_1 and E'_2, where $E'_1 = E_1 M$ and $E'_2 = E_2 M$. This observation has enormous importance: to make an image of a transformed line segment, we transform its two endpoints into the screen coordinate system, and then connect them using a line-drawing algorithm that operates in the screen coordinate system. Thus to display a line 100 points long requires that only two points be transformed.

A point Q on a line segment between two points E_1 and E_2 can be represented parametrically as $Q = (1-t)E_1 + tE_2$, for $0 \leqslant t \leqslant 1$. This equation applies to all coordinate components, so we can write, for example, $Q_x = (1-t)E_{1x} + tE_{2x}$.

An important way to summarize the locations of a collection of two-dimensional lines and points is the *bounding box*, a rectangular region aligned with the coordinate axes that just barely surrounds the points and lines. The box can be described by the coordinates of its edges: x_{left}, x_{right}, y_{bottom}, and y_{top}. The value of x_{left} is simply the minimum x coordinate of any point or line endpoint in the collection; x_{right} is the maximum of the x coordinates. Similar observations hold for y. In three dimensions, the bounding box will also have minimum and maximum z coordinates.

4.3.5 Clipping

A series of transformations that yields coordinates in the screen coordinate system may produce points or lines that lie wholly or partly off the screen. The conditions that the perspective projection of a point be visible were given in Sec. 4.3.3. For a two-dimensional point to be visible within a rectangular *clipping region* of the screen aligned with the screen's x and y axes, we must have

$$x_{left} \leqslant x \leqslant x_{right}$$

and

$$y_{bottom} \leqslant y \leqslant y_{top}$$

where the four parameters x_{left}, x_{right}, y_{bottom}, and y_{top} describe the edges of the rectangular region (Fig. 3). If this region comprises the entire screen, these parameters are simply the minimum and maximum values of legal coordinates that can be passed to the display controller.

The two inequalities given above will determine whether a point (x, y) is within the visible region (e.g., point E_2 in Fig. 3 is found to be visible). Determining the visibility of a line is more difficult, however. Some simple tests can be made: (1) If both endpoints are visible, the entire line must be visible, and is said to be *trivially accepted*. (2) If both endpoints lie on the invisible side of one of the four edges (e.g., if the x coordinates of both endpoints are greater than x_{right}), the entire line cannot be seen, and is said to be *trivially rejected*. If neither of these trivial cases applies, we must compute the intersection of the line with an edge of the clipping region that it is known to cross, discarding the part of the line that lies outside the clipping region, and then repeat the first set of tests. By noticing how the two endpoints are positioned with respect to the edges of the clipping region, we can determine which edge to intersect with the line. In Fig. 3, for example, E_1 and E_2 are determined to lie on opposite sides of the top edge by comparing their y coordinates with y_{top} —if the endpoints lie on opposite sides of the edge, the line between the endpoints must intersect the edge.

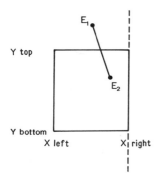

Y top

Y bottom

X left   X right

Fig. 3   Rectangular clipping region and a line that penetrates it.

The following Pascal algorithm captures these observations. Note that a set is used to summarize the position of an endpoint: the set will have the element *top* in it if the endpoint is above the top of the clipping region, *bottom* if it is below the bottom, and so forth. Set operations are then helpful in implementing the tests ($a*b$ is set intersection, and $[\cdot]$ is the empty set).

```
{Coordinates of the clipping region edges}
var Clipxl, Clipxr, Clipyb, Clipyt: real;

procedure Clip(x1, y1, x2, y2: real);
   label return;
   type edge = (left, right, bottom, top); outcode = set of edge;
   var c, c1, c2: outcode; x, y: real;

   {Code computes the set of edges that the point (x,y) is on
       the "outside" of, i.e., away from interior of clipping region}
   procedure Code(x, y: real; varc: outcode);
   begin
      c: = [ ];
      if x < Clipxl then c: = [left] else if x > Clipxr then c: = [right];
      if y < Clipyb then c: = c + [bottom] else
         if y > Clipyt then c: = c + [top];
   end;
begin
   Code(x1, y1, c1); Code(x2, y2, c2);
   while (c1 < >[ ]) or (c2 < >[ ]) do begin {While not trivial acceptance}
      if (c1*c2) < >[ ] then goto return; {Trivial rejection}
      {Find an endpoint that is outside clipping region and an edge
          that the line crosses. Compute point of intersection as (x,y).}
      c: = c1; if c = [ ] then c: = c2;
      if left in c then begin {Line crosses left boundary}
         y: = y1 + (y2 - y1)*(Clipxl - x1)/(x2 - x1);
         x: = Clipxl end else
      if right in c then begin {Edge crosses right boundary}
         y: = y1 + (y2 - y1)*(Clipxr - x1)/(x2 - x1);
         x: = Clipxr end else
      if bottom in c then begin {Edge crosses bottom boundary}
         x: = x1 + (x2 - x1)*(Clipyb - y1)/(y2 - y1);
         y: = Clipyb end else
```

if *top* **in** *c* **then begin** {Edge crosses top boundary}

   $x := x1 + (x2 - x1)*(Clipyt - y1)/(y2 - y1)$;

   $y := Clipyt$ **end**;

{If endpoint 1 was the "outside" point selected, results become new endpoint 1, else results become new endpoint 2.}

if $c = c1$ **then begin**

   $x1 := x; y1 := y; Code(x, y, c1)$

end else begin

   $x2 := x; y2 := y; Code(x, y, c2)$

end

end;

{If we reach here, the line from (x1,y1) to (x2,y2) is visible}

ShowLine($x1, y1, x2, y2$);

return: **end**;

[Clipping routine adapted by permission from W. M. Newman and R. F. Sproull, *Principles of Interactive Computer Graphics, 2nd ed., McGraw-Hill, New York, 1979.*]

Clipping Three-Dimensional Lines.   The visibility conditions for points within the viewing pyramid are more complex than those for the two-dimensional clipping region. There are more conditions and they depend on the homogeneous coordinates of the point. The inequalities represent the *planes* that limit the viewbox, which correspond to the planes that limit the viewing pyramid. The clipping algorithm given above can be adapted to clip lines in this system as well: (1) we will have six clipping planes, $x = w$, $x = -w$, $y = w$, $y = -w$, $z = 0$, and $z = -w$, where $[x \ y \ z \ w]$ are the homogeneous coordinates; (2) we shall need to intersect a line between two points expressed in homogeneous coordinates with one of these planes. Although the details of the geometric calculations change, the general form of the algorithm remains the same.

The clipping algorithm will guarantee that the three inequalities

$$-w \leqslant x \leqslant w$$

$$-w \leqslant y \leqslant w$$

$$-w \leqslant z \leqslant 0$$

are satisfied for both endpoints of the visible portion of the line. *It is essential that clipping be performed before the division by the homogeneous scale factor w.* The division will project points behind the eye ($z > 0$) into points that appear to be legal ($-1 \leqslant x_p, y_p \leqslant 1, z_p \leqslant 0$), even though these points should not be seen.

4.3.6   Modeling Transformations

A display on the screen originates as a geometrical model in the application program. The model may simply be a long list of points, lines, characters, or other geometrical figures. These are represented in a *world coordinate system*, chosen for convenience in the application. For example, a two-dimensional model of the geography of Manhattan might use a world coordinate system with x pointing East, y North, origin at 42nd Street and Fifth Avenue, with distances measured in meters. The map may be represented as a set of lines measured in this system.

Repetitive structure in a model can be captured as a set of *symbols* and *instances* of those symbols. A symbol is modeled in its own coordinate system, usually with an origin and axes chosen for convenience in describing the symbol. Each instance of the symbol is mapped into the world coordinate system by specifying a symbol-to-instance transformation. A simple example of this mapping was illustrated in Sec. 4.2.3, which describes the use of a translation transformation in mapping "arrow" symbols onto the display screen. In general, a symbol-to-instance mapping can be an arbitrary transformation. Moreover, the symbol–instance structure can be carried to an arbitrary depth.

The use of transformations in modeling is best illustrated with an example. Suppose that we wish to model a parking lot full of cars. The "top level" of the model consists of a set of lines corresponding to the borders of the parking lot, lines painted on the pavement, and so on, measured in the world coordinate system; and several "calls" for instances of the "car" symbol. Each call has an associated three-dimensional transformation that describes how the origin and axes of the car coordinate system are to be mapped into world coordinates. For example, one transformation might be M_{cw1}; the notation cw indicates this is a modeling transformation from the car coordinate system to the world coordinate system. A car 3 m to the right of that one might be called with a transformation $M_{cw2} = M_{cw1}T(3,0,0)$, and so forth. The car symbol is described in a local coordinate system with origin at the center of mass of the car, x axis pointing horizontally toward the right of the car, y axis pointing up, and z axis pointing toward the rear. The car is described as a set of lines that model the body, the windows, and so forth; and four calls to the "tire" symbol, each with a different transformation. The left front tire might be called with transformation $M_{tc1} = T(-1, -0.2, -2.5)$, the right front with $M_{tc2} = T(1, -0.2, -2.5)$, the left rear with $M_{tc3} = T(-1, -0.2, 2.5)$, and the right rear with $M_{tc4} = T(1, -0.2, 2.5)$. Note that a coordinate in the tire symbol, when called as part of the left front instance of the first car in the parking lot, would be transformed by M_{tc1} to obtain car coordinates and then by M_{cw1} to obtain world coordinates. These two transformations could of course be concatenated together, so that each coordinate need undergo at most one matrix multiplication.

A model structured such as this can be interpreted with a simple recursive rule. Assume that there is a *current modeling transformation* M that has been initialized to the identity matrix. The rule for interpreting a symbol is:

Interpret: Enumerate all geometric primitives (points, lines, characters, etc.) and symbol calls. For a:
Primitive: Transform coordinates by M to obtain world coordinates.
Symbol call: Push M onto a stack of transformations. Then replace M by $M_c M$, where M_c is the transformation specified in the call. Then *interpret* the called symbol using these same rules. When finished interpreting the symbol, pop the top of the transformation stack into M.

This interpretation rule is very similar to that for calling procedures in a programming language. The two notions have been elegantly combined as *display procedures*, a way to use procedures in a programming language to represent structured models [15].

Models structured with symbols and instances are often much more compact than flat, non-hierarchical models. In our map example, we could model each building in Manhattan as a cube, subject to an instance transformation that scales the cube in x, y and z separately to make a parallelipiped of arbitrary size. Moreover, the instance transformation could also place the parallelipiped in the proper position and orientation on the map. Thus a single transformation matrix (16 numbers) represents what would otherwise require eight points of three coordinates each (24 numbers). If we model more complex shapes than parallelipipeds, the savings are even more substantial.

4.3.7 Viewing Transformations

Transformations are useful for generating a view on a display screen of geometrical model. Generally, viewing transformations cope with three problems: establishing the viewing parameters, transforming coordinates into the screen coordinate system provided by the display hardware, and clipping out any portions of the model that are not visible. The viewing parameters govern what parts of a large geometric model may be seen on the screen; in three dimensions, the viewing parameters describe the location of the eye and the direction of view.

Two-Dimensional Viewing Transformations. A simple viewing transformation, called the *window-viewport transformation*, suffices for most two-dimensional viewing applications. The transformation is specified by two rectangular regions aligned with the axes: a *viewport*, which describes in screen coordinates the rectangular region of the screen in which the view should appear, and the *window*, which describes in world coordinates a rectangular region that should be mapped into the viewport (Fig. 4).

The window and viewport parameters together specify a scaling and translation that will convert world coordinates into screen coordinates. Let us denote the edges of the window by W_{xl}, W_{xr}, W_{yb}, and W_{yt}, and those of the viewport by V_{xl}, V_{xr}, V_{yb}, and V_{yt}. The transformation from world coordinates x_w and y_w to screen coordinates x_s and y_s can then be expressed as

$$[x_s\, y_s\, 0\, 1] = [x_w\, y_w\, 0\, 1]T(-W_{xl}, -W_{yb}, 0)S(s_x, s_y, 1)T(V_{xl}, V_{yb}, 0)$$

where $s_x = (V_{xr} - V_{xl})/(W_{xr} - W_{xl})$, and $s_y = (V_{yt} - V_{yb})/(W_{yt} - W_{yb})$. If these three matrices are concatenated, we obtain the matrix N:

$$N = \begin{bmatrix} s_x & 0 & 0 & 0 \\ 0 & s_y & 0 & 0 \\ 0 & 0 & 1 & 0 \\ V_{xl} - s_x W_{xl} & V_{yb} - s_y W_{yb} & 0 & 1 \end{bmatrix}$$

Note that the third row and third column are not necessary, since no z coordinates are being used.

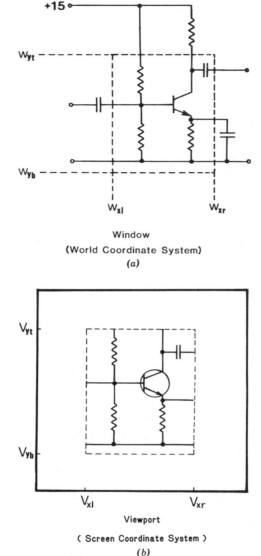

Window

(World Coordinate System)

(*a*)

Viewport

(Screen Coordinate System)

(*b*)

Fig. 4 Window–viewport transformation: (*a*) window (world coordinate system); (*b*) viewport (screen coordinate system).

Although this matrix transforms coordinates from the world system into a coordinate system suited for the display, we must still use a clipping step to eliminate portions of lines that lie outside the viewport. The clipping may be done in two ways: (1) we may transform line endpoints with matrix N, and then clip the resulting lines against the viewport edges; or (2) we may first clip lines against the window edges, and transform by N the endpoints of any lines found to be visible. These are equivalent computations. The second is slightly more efficient, because we transform only those lines that are found to be visible.

Very often it is convenient to precede the window–viewport transformation with other viewing transformations. For example, to see our model rotated 90°, we would like the entire transformation to be $R(z, 90)N$. If viewing transformations such as this are used, they may be concatenated with N to produce a single viewing transformation, provided that clipping is done after the window-to-viewport transformation (i.e., to the viewport edges). Thus even though clipping to the window is more efficient in some cases, the general viewing case suggests performing all viewing transformations with one matrix operation and then clipping against the viewport.

Three-Dimensional Viewing Transformations. Viewing transformations used for displaying projections of three-dimensional information are similar in spirit to those for two dimensions. The first step is to establish the viewpoint and viewing direction, which are used to compute a transformation from world to eye coordinates. (One way to control the viewing parameters is illustrated in Sec. 4.6.) The next step is to project points in the eye coordinate system into two dimensions. The perspective transformation given in Sec. 4.3.3 is one such projection; alternatively, an orthogonal projection can be obtained by mapping x_e and y_e directly to the screen, and ignoring z_e. The third step is a clipping step, which passes on only those lines that lie within the viewbox. Clipping is required for orthogonal projections as well; the viewbox is similar to that for the perspective projection. The fourth and final step is to convert coordinates into the screen coordinate system. This will require a transformation from the viewbox system $(-1 \leqslant x_p, y_p \leqslant 1)$ into a viewport on the screen. Moreover, the coordinates must be converted from homogeneous form to ordinary form by dividing by the scale factor.

These steps can be summarized:

1. Apply world-to-eye viewing transformation V.
2. Apply perspective transformation $P(s, n, f)$. Alternatively, an orthogonal projection can transform points into the same x and y regions of the viewbox; the transformation can be accomplished with a matrix $S(s, s, 1)$, where $s > 0$ establishes the overall scale of the projected image.
3. Clip a homogeneous point $[x \ \ y \ \ z \ \ w]$ against the boundaries:

$$-w \leqslant x \leqslant w$$

$$-w \leqslant y \leqslant w$$

and either

$$-w \leqslant z \leqslant 0 \text{ (general perspective case)}$$

or simply

$$-w \leqslant 0 \ (f \to \infty \text{ or orthogonal case})$$

Clip lines accordingly.

4. Apply a scaling and transformation to map the region $-1 \leqslant x, y) \leqslant 1$ to the viewport. The two transformations $N_v = S((V_{rx} - V_{lx})/2, (V_{ty} - V_{by})/2, 1)T((V_{lx} + V_{rx})/2, (V_{by} + V_{ty})/2, 0)$ will perform this mapping; the concatenation of these is equivalent to the N matrix illustrated earlier in this section, with $\mathrm{W}_{xl} = \mathrm{W}_{yb} = -1$ and $\mathrm{W}_{xr} = \mathrm{W}_{yt} = 1$.

The outcome of the last step is a point in homogeneous coordinates. The x and y components must be divided by the scale factor w to produce ordinary coordinates to pass to the display. The division is an essential part of any perspective projection. If a perspective projection is not used, the scale factor w should remain 1 throughout the transformation steps.

4.3.8 Transformation Systems

The transformation steps needed most frequently for modeling and viewing fit nicely into a single framework. This becomes the basis for a *transformation pipeline* that can be implemented in a graphics package or a display processor to convert geometry specified by an application program into a display image.

The complete transformation from a geometric primitive in the application model to the screen involves a sequence $M \quad V \quad P < \text{clip} > N_v < \text{divide} >$, where M is the concatenation of all modeling transformations, V is the concatenation of all viewing transformations, P is an optional projection transformation, $<\text{clip}>$ stands for a clipping process, N_v is the viewport transformation that produces screen coordinates, and $<\text{divide}>$ stands for the division that converts homogeneous to ordinary coordinates. To some extent, these steps can be reordered: for example, $M \quad V \quad P < \text{clip} > < \text{divide} > N_v$ works fine because the matrix N_v leaves the homogeneous scale factor unaltered.

This transformation sequence is directly applicable to three-dimensional viewing problems. For two-dimensional viewing, we replace the projection matrix P with a matrix N_w that maps the window into the viewbox limits, $-1 \leqslant x, y \leqslant 1$. Clearly, $N_w = T(-(W_{xl} + W_{xr})/2, -(W_{yb} + W_{yt})/2, 0)S(2/(W_{xr} - W_{xl}), 2/(W_{yt} - W_{yb}), 0)$. Note that the z scale is chosen to be 0 so that the clipper condition $-w \leqslant z \leqslant 0$ will always be true for two-dimensional cases.

These formulations allow a single transformation system to work for two- and three-dimensional applications, and to accommodate both modeling and viewing transformations. A coordinate pair (2D) or triple (3D) from the model is passed to the transformation pipeline. The first step is to convert the coordinates into homogeneous form, and to multiply by a single matrix, the concatenation $M \quad V \quad P$ for three-dimensional cases, or $M \quad V \quad N_w$ for two-dimensional cases. The second step is to clip lines to the viewbox limits, divide by the homogeneous scale factor, and scale by N_v to obtain screen coordinates. This second step is sometimes called a "clipping divide" [21]. The resulting line endpoints are then added to the display file.

This transformation scheme is a convenience to the application programmer, and is often included in a graphics package. Some display processors, such as the Picture System [8], provide a fast hardware implementation of the transformation pipeline to process line endpoint information before it is added to a display file memory. In other high-performance display processors, such as the LDS-1 [7], the transformation pipeline is part of the refresh process: the display processor is designed to extract information directly from the model data structure, apply the necessary transformations, and pass the results to a line generator for display. Display processors that offer transformation hardware cater for applications in which the transformations change rapidly (e.g., perspective images of several objects moving in space).

In software implementations of the transformation pipeline, it is sometimes important to improve performance by detecting simple cases. For example, unless a perspective transformation is used, the last column of the transformation matrix will be $[0 \quad 0 \quad 0 \quad 1]^T$, which means that the homogeneous scale factor will remain 1 and that no division will be necessary. If two-dimensional points are being transformed, there is no need to compute z values or to implement the two clipping conditions pertaining to z.

4.4   GRAPHICS PACKAGES

R. F. Sproull

A graphics package is a collection of subroutines that couple an application program to interactive display hardware. The application program creates a display image and accepts user inputs by calling procedures in the graphics package.

Graphics packages have several functions. At the very least, they shield the application programmer from intricacies of the display controller and from any messy details of the interaction with the operating system required to control the display. They must offer a *complete* set of image-generation functions; because the graphics package is the only way for the application program to generate images, image-generation functions that are omitted cannot generally be provided by the application program, which may not have suitable access to the display hardware.

Graphics packages may be customized for a particular application, but it is far more common to design a *general-purpose graphics package* that provides a set of functions appropriate for a wide range of applications. Many modern packages strive, in addition, to be *device independent*, that is, to be able to control a range of graphics devices using a single procedural interface between the application program and the graphics package. This technique allows an application program to be written so as to operate on a number of different displays.

Graphics packages also provide conveniences to the application programmer. Algorithms used frequently in graphics programs, such as transformation and clipping, are often included in the graphics package so that the application program can use them freely. These routines are really part of a *graphics subroutine library* provided to the application programmer.

Graphics packages are designed to help the application program achieve fast interactive response by allowing the application program to make *incremental changes* to the display. A small portion of the image may be added or deleted without recomputing or regenerating the remaining, unchanged, part of the image. The most common technique used to achieve incremental modifications is the *segmented display file*, explained in Sec. 4.4.2.

Designing a graphics package requires more than simply providing the functions outlined above. It must be simple, easy to use, and not easily misunderstood. It must not be so bulky or slow that it represents an impediment to the application. It must be robust in the presence of misuse or data-dependent errors. Robustness is an extremely important requirement for an interactive program: if a user spends several hours working on a project, it is unreasonable for a small user error or software error in the application program to cause the entire program to abort. Preventing catastrophes of this sort is a major requirement of a graphics package.

The remainder of this section is structured according to the facilities provided in a general-purpose graphics package. Sections 4.4.1 and 4.4.2 describe facilities for graphical output. Section 4.4.3 describes convenient functions for transformation and clipping. Finally, control of input devices is described in Sec. 4.4.4.

4.4.1 Simple Graphics Package

The simplest model of the image-generation process is that we start with a blank screen and repeatedly add to it *graphical primitives* such as dots, lines, and characters. Occasionally, we may erase the entire screen and begin afresh. A set of functions that could be used to generate images in this way closely parallels the abstract image-generation functions described in Sec. 4.2.3:

MoveScreen(x, y):   Moves the "current point" to (x, y) in screen coordinates.

LineScreen(x, y):   Draws a line from the current point to (x, y), and sets the current point to (x, y).

CharScreen(c):   Displays the character whose code is c at the current point, and increments the current point to account for the character's width.

PointScreen(x, y):   Displays a dot at (x, y) and sets the current point to (x, y).

EraseScreen: Erases the screen.

We have chosen to include the term "Screen" in the name of each of these functions to emphasize that they take arguments in the screen coordinate system. The set of primitive functions might be embellished with others to support extra facilities of the output device. For example, if the intensity of points, lines, and characters can be varied, we might include a function *IntensityScreen*(b) which sets the brightness modally (i.e., all subsequent graphical primitives specified by subroutine calls will have that brightness until the brightness is changed again). The alternative, to include a brightness argument for each primitive function, may be too inefficient. Another similar extension could specify the color of graphical primitives.

Good design of a subroutine package also requires that we be able to find out its internal state and any important parameters necessary for proper operation. Thus we include another function:

InquireScreen(r):   Stores into the record (or array) r several important parameters: the coordinates of the current position, the current brightness, the minimum and maximum values of legal x and y screen coordinates, the physical dimensions of the screen, the dimensions of text characters, and so on. The application program can use the values in r to control its image-generation computations.

Finally, we may need functions to initialize or finalize the operation of the display:

InitScreen: Prepare graphics package to accept other calls. For example, in a time-sharing system, this function might assign a display to the application job.

FinalizeScreen: Finish execution of the graphics package (e.g., release an assigned display).

The graphical output functions might be augmented with a set of library routines for common operations. For example, we could provide a routine to display an entire text string using the *CharScreen* function repeatedly; or a routine to draw circular arcs by approximating them with straight line segments and calling *MoveScreen* and *LineScreen*; or a function for drawing text characters not limited to the sizes and styles provided by the display controller. Note that these library functions do not depend on knowledge of the display hardware, but are written entirely in terms of the primitive functions such as *MoveScreen*, *LineScreen*, and *CharScreen*.

Implementation for a Refresh Display.   The major element of an implementation of these functions for a refresh display is a *display code generator* that creates instructions for the display processor from the arguments passed in the subroutine calls. The display-processor instructions can be added to a contiguous list of instructions. It is for this reason that the design of a display-processor instruction set must permit new instructions to be added at the end of a display file without stopping the display processor (Sec. 4.2.3). The *EraseScreen* function simply installs at the beginning of the region used for image-generation instructions the JMP or POPJMP instruction that terminates the display file. Note that after this is done, we must delay for one refresh cycle ($\frac{1}{30}$s) before we can begin adding new instructions again, because the display processor may still be executing the previous instructions.

This simple graphics package can be easily made robust. There are only two kinds of errors that must be anticipated. First, the application program could call functions with x and y arguments that are not legal screen coordinates. The graphics package defends against this error by building instructions using only the 10 low-order bits of the coordinate arguments. Although this may generate a strange-looking display (the result of errors in the application program), the display processor itself continues to function properly. The second problem is that the graphics package might exhaust the storage available for the display file. Again, a simple technique can cope with this error in a robust way: the graphics package ceases to add instructions to the display file and allows the application program to determine that because of this error the image on the screen does not match the image defined by calls to the primitive graphics functions. Such an error indication could be returned in the record created by the *InquireScreen* function. This solution illustrates a general property of graphics packages: the errors that arise may be of interest to the application programmer who understands the graphics package, but can almost never be understood by the user of the application. If each kind of error is reported to the application program, it may then decide what action to take. If informing the user is required, the error message may be phrased in terms that the user can understand.

Implementation for a Storage-Tube Terminal.   These functions are particularly well suited for implementation on a storage-tube terminal because the "erase, line, line…" paradigm is precisely that used by the terminal. Each of the primitive functions encodes its arguments and transmits them to the terminal, as described in Sec. 4.2.3.

Implementation for a Frame-Buffer Display.   The implementation for a frame-buffer display is conceptually very similar to that for a storage-tube terminal. The *EraseScreen* function clears the frame buffer to a background color, such as black. Each call to a graphical primitive function invokes an appropriate scan-conversion algorithm. For example, a call to *LineScreen* invokes the *DrawLine* algorithm given in Sec. 4.2.1. If the scan-conversion algorithms are implemented in a "graphics processor" (Fig. 4.3.7), the graphics package converts the arguments passed to a primitive function into the format appropriate for controlling the graphics processor.

Evaluation.   The simple graphics package fulfills almost all the objectives we have identified. It is general-purpose; it is simple and easily understood; it is device independent (the fact that the screen coordinate system is returned by the *InquireScreen* function and may be different for different devices is not an important breach of device independence, because it can be easily masked by a coordinate transformation); it can be augmented with library functions to add conveniences for the application program; and an implementation is compact and robust.

The single serious problem with the graphics package is that it does not accommodate incremental display changes. The only way to remove something from the display is to erase the entire screen and regenerate the image by calling the primitive functions again, leaving out the calls describing the item to be deleted. Moreover, on a refresh display, a small deletion causes a strange effect on the screen: the entire image disappears and is then rebuilt quickly. Even if the new image is built very quickly, we perceive an annoying flash as the display goes momentarily blank and is then rebuilt. The segmented display file is designed to rectify this problem.

4.4.2   Segmented Display Files

In order to make incremental changes to a display file, it is divided into units called *segments*, each of which may be changed separately. Each segment is independent of the others, and can be deleted or replaced without changing other segments. The segment thus becomes the unit of modification of a display file.

The graphics package gives the application program control over the manipulation of segments. The application program "opens" a particular segment, and adds display-processor instructions to it in response to calls to graphical primitives such as *MoveScreen*, *LineScreen*, *CharScreen*, and *PointScreen*. When all the primitives have been specified, the application "closes" the segment and it becomes part of the display file.

The following functions might be used for segment control:

OpenSegment(*n*):   Opens segment numbered *n*. Any calls to the graphical primitives *MoveScreen*, *LineScreen*, *CharScreen*, or *PointScreen* will add appropriate instructions to the segment that is open.

CloseSegment: Closes the segment that is currently open and adds it to the display file.

DeleteSegment(*n*):   Removes segment *n* from the display file and destroys it. Any storage used by segment *n* can be reused for subsequent segments.

UnpostSegment(*n*):   Removes segment *n* from the display list, but does not release its storage.

PostSegment(*n*):   Adds segment *n* to the display list. Usually, the segment was previously unposted.

Update: The application program calls this function whenever the displayed image must accurately reflect the state of the segmented display file. The need for this function is explained below.

All of these functions are designed to simplify incremental changes to the display file. When a segment is created, the application program specifies a *segment number* by which it can refer to the segment later. Posting and unposting allows often-used images such as menus or legends to be retained in display-file form so that they can be quickly added to the display list. *OpenSegment* provides double buffering: if segment n already exists and *OpenSegment*(n) is called, a new version of segment n is created and the existing version is not destroyed. Only when *CloseSegment* is called after the new version is complete is the new version added to the display list and the old one destroyed.

It is sometimes convenient to be able to add more graphical primitives to a segment that already exists. A sixth function can be provided for this purpose:

AppendToSegment(n): Like *OpenSegment*, in that subsequent graphical primitives will be added to segment n, but these new primitives are added to those already specified for segment n.

Additional functions may be added for convenience. For example, we might use the *EraseScreen* function to call *DestroySegment* on all segments that have been constructed, thereby resetting the graphics package to its initial state.

Like the simple graphics package, the segment-manipulation functions must be made robust. If the generation of a segment exhausts storage, we must stop adding instructions to the display file and provide an error indication to the application program. The several segment-control functions may be misused, often by specifying calls in absurd sequences; appropriate defaults and error indications to the application program must be provided. It is also useful for the application to be able to inquire into the state of the graphics package: what segments have been generated, which are posted, and so on.

Using a Segmented Display File. The segmented display file is a technique that can be exploited to improve the interactive response of a graphics application. Its effectiveness, however, depends on strategies used by the application program. Since the unit of image modification is the segment, the application program must place in separate segments those elements of the image that will be modified separately. For example, a curve-drawing system might place the axis lines and labels in one segment and each of several curves displayed in a separate segment. Thus if the user asks for another curve to be shown on the same axes, a brand new segment is created. Deleting a curve corresponds to deleting a segment. To redraw an existing curve with dashed lines, the segment corresponding to that curve is replaced. However, if the user requests that the scale of the axes and all curves be changed, all the segments must be replaced. Suppose further that each curve could have labels associated with it. We might choose to place the labels for each curve in a segment that is separate from the segment used for the curve. In this way, a user could ask to see the image with or without labels; the application program would respond by posting or unposting the segments that contain the labels.

The design of an interactive application program will specify what sorts of modifications can be effected by user commands. Once these modification patterns are known, the application programmer can exploit the segmentation facilities in the graphics package to help perform the modifications quickly.

Implementation for a Refresh Display. The segmented display file is well matched to the power of a display processor such as the one illustrated in Fig. 4.2.3 and 4.2.4. Section 4.2.3 sketches two different techniques for representing the display file. An important objective is to be able to add or remove a segment from the display list very quickly.

Implementation for a Storage-Tube Terminal. At first glance, it may appear that a segmented display file is not appropriate for controlling a storage-tube terminal. This is not so, however, because a graphics package using a segmented display file can save the recomputation done by the application program when rebuilding an image, even if it cannot selectively remove items from the screen. So the package holds in CPU memory a representation of the graphical primitives that comprise each segment. The subroutines for segmentation and for adding graphical primitives to the open segment operate on this representation. Whenever the graphics package is required to regenerate the image on the storage tube, it enumerates all posted segments and transmits to the terminal the appropriate encoding of the primitives in each segment. (In fact, the characters that must be transmitted to redraw a segment are a fine representation of that segment in the CPU.)

It is not wise to update the screen every time a segment currently displayed is removed by a call to *DestroySegment* or *UnpostSegment*, or because *CloseSegment* replaces an old version of a segment with a new one. Since an interactive program could remove several segments in response to a single user command, a long series of screen erasures and reconstructions might result. Instead, the changes are simply recorded in the CPU representation of the segments. When the application program calls the *Update* function, the graphics package decides what to transmit to make the screen image reflect what is recorded in the display file. If no deletions have occurred since the previous call to *Update*, no screen erasure is required. Even if a great many segment deletions have taken place, only one screen erasure will be required.

Implementation for a Frame-Buffer Display.   An implementation for a frame-buffer display is very similar to that for a storage-tube terminal. The updating process can be made somewhat more rapid because the frame-buffer display can selectively erase information by setting pixels to the background color. To erase a segment, we could scan-convert each of the graphical primitives in the segment, writing the background color into the frame buffer. Alternatively, we could erase all pixels within the bounding box of the segment. In either case, erasing the information created by one segment may also erase other information due to another segment that must be redrawn by appropriate scan conversion. To do this, we scan the list of posted segments, comparing their bounding boxes to the bounding box of the area on the screen that was erased. Whenever the two boxes overlap, we redraw the segment. (For an illustration of this technique, see Sec. 4.7.)

Evaluation.   Segmented display files form the basis for most modern general-purpose graphics packages. Although their implementation is more complex than that of the simple graphics package, the improved interaction justifies the cost.

Although the segmentation facilities are easily exploited by most applications, a *structured display file* provides a way to reflect the structure of the model more accurately in the display file [16, 23]. Changes to the model correspond easily to changes in the display file, and the displayed image changes accordingly. Although graphics packages with these facilities are more general, they are also much more bulky and complex than implementations of the segmented display file.

Graphics packages based on a segmented display file usually fall short of providing *dynamic* graphics, in which images change from frame to frame. Rotating a three-dimensional image in real time or simulating the image an aircraft pilot sees while maneuvering an airplane are effects that cannot be achieved by most computers and displays. The main limitation is the speed of transformation.

4.4.3 Transformation Functions

It is customary to include in a graphics package a *transformation pipeline*, as outlined in Sec. 4.3.8. The pipeline applies the most commonly used modeling and viewing transformations to points, lines, and characters specified in calls to graphical primitives. Unlike the calls described in Sec. 4.4.1, these describe graphical data in the *model* coordinate system. The results from the transformation functions provide parameters to the screen-coordinate graphical primitives to add information to the display; in this sense, the transformation pipeline is part of a graphics subroutine library.

Two dimensional geometrical information is presented to the transformation system by the functions $MoveModel2(x, y)$, $LineModel2(x, y)$, $CharModel2(c)$, and $PointModel2(x, y)$. The coordinates are transformed by the modeling transformation M, the viewing transformation V, and the window transformation N_w, all concatenated together to form a single matrix G. Then lines and points are clipped, and scaled and translated by N_v to obtain screen coordinates. The final result is to call $MoveScreen$, $LineScreen$, $CharScreen$, and $PointScreen$ appropriately to make the proper display. Characters can be handled in several ways:

1. The coordinates of the location of each character can be transformed as for points, clipped with a special test to be sure that the entire character will lie in the viewbox, and then displayed using $CharScreen$.
2. A character can be converted into a set of line segments, each of which is transformed as would be a normal line.

Three-dimensional information is passed to the transformation routines by the functions $MoveModel3(x, y, z)$, $LineModel3(x, y, z)$, $CharModel3(c)$, and $PointModel3(x, y, z)$. Coordinates are transformed by M, V, and P (the projection transformation), all concatenated together to form G, clipped, mapped by N_v into screen coordinates, and then displayed using screen-coordinate graphical primitives.

The behavior of the transformation pipeline is governed by two 4×4 matrices: G and N_v. The graphics package provides functions for setting these parameters:

$SetViewport(vxl, vyb, vxr, vyt)$:   Sets N_v from the parameters (see Sec. 4.3.7).
$SetG(matrix)$:   Sets the 4×4 matrix G.

These functions set state inside the transformation package that should be accessible via appropriate calls (e.g., $GetViewport$, $GetG$).

Transformation Utilities.   In order to construct the modeling and viewing transformations that are part of G, the application program will need to construct and manipulate matrices. The transformation package can provide functions to construct primitive translation, rotation, scaling, and perspective transformations. A function to multiply two matrices together is essential; one to invert a matrix is not as important. Functions that build *stacks* of transformation matrices are also useful: the operations on the stacks are initializing, pushing a matrix on a stack, and popping one off the stack.

Modeling Functions. If the application program uses a hierarchical model, the most common use of transformations will be to build the appropriate modeling transformations. Because the modeling transformation M is the first transformation in the concatenation G, symbol-instance transformations can be concatenated directly on the front of G. The following set of functions simplifies this task:

> *SaveG*: Pushes G onto a stack *GStack*.
> *RestoreG*: Pops a transformation off *GStack*, and places it in G.
> *Translate*(tx, ty, tz): Sets $G: = T(tx, ty, tz)G$.
> *Rotate*($axis, \theta$): Sets $G: = R(axis, \theta) G$.
> *Scale*(sx, sy, sz): Sets $G: = S(sx, sy, sz) G$.

These functions are used to implement the recursive symbol-interpretation rules given in Sec. 4.3.6. The individual functions *Translate*, *Rotate*, and *Scale* are used to compose M_c by concatentation. A typical use might be:

> *SaveG*;
> *Translate*(40, 50, 0);
> *Rotate*(z, 90);
> *Arrow*;{Call procedure to draw an arrow in its local coordinate system.}
> *RestoreG*;

Each coordinate specified in the *Arrow* procedure will be first rotated 90° about the z axis, then will have 40 added to each x coordinate, and 50 to each y coordinate. Then the modeling transformation in effect when the five-line fragment above was executed will be applied. *Note that the order of application of transformations to the symbol's coordinates is the reverse of the order in which the calls to Translate, Rotate, and Scale are specified.*

It often happens that an entire symbol need not be processed because it lies entirely outside the viewbox, and consequently cannot be seen. A small embellishment to the transformation system can help detect such cases:

> *Visible2*($xmin, ymin, xmax, ymax$): This function returns *true* if any part of the rectangular bounding box $xmin \leqslant x \leqslant xmax, ymin \leqslant y \leqslant ymax$, after transformation lies within the viewbox.
> *Visible3*($xmin, ymin, zmin, xmax, ymax, zmax$): Similar test for three-dimensional parallelepiped.

The use of this function can be illustrated with the *Arrow* procedure:

> **procedure** *Arrow*;
> **begin if** *Visible2*($-30, -5, 0, 5$) **then begin**
>   *MoveModel2*($-30, 0$); *LineModel2*($0, 0$);
>   *MoveModel2*($-5, -5$); *LineModel2*($0, 0$); *LineModel2*($-5, 0$)
> **end end**;

This simple example does not illustrate the power of the visibility test. The test is more effective for symbols that are more bulky or have further nested symbol calls.

Viewing Functions. The functions provided to facilitate modeling also help to construct the viewing transformation. The special transformations N_w and P are constructed with separate calls:

> *SetWindow*(wxl, wyb, wxr, wyt): Constructs N_w from the parameters (see Sec. 4.3.8) and sets $G: = N_w$.
> *SetPerspective*($alpha, n, f$): Builds the perspective transformation P (see Sec. 4.3.3) and sets $G: = P$.

We can now illustrate the use of the entire transformation package with a simple example:

{Set viewing transformation $V = R(z,90)N_w$}

$SetViewport(0,0,1023,1023)$;

$SetWindow(-100,-100,100,100)$; {$G = N_w$}

$Rotate(z,90)$; {$G = R(z,90)N_w = V$}

{Now trace model, manipulating M}

$SaveG$;

$Translate(40,50,0)$; {$G = T(40,50,0)R(z,90)N_w$}

$Rotate(z,90)$; {$G = R(z,90)T(40,50,0)R(z,90)N_w$}

$Arrow$; {Call procedure to draw an arrow in its local coordinate system.}

$RestoreG$; {$G = R(z,90)N_w$}

Orthogonality. Transformation functions are completely independent of the rest of the graphics package, and can be provided as part of a graphics subroutine library. They process geometric information and ultimately call the screen-coordinate functions *MoveScreen*, *LineScreen*, *CharScreen*, and *PointScreen* to create an image. Thus there is no link between viewports and segments, between windows and viewports, or the like. Windows, viewports, and transformation matrices are simply parameters to a coordinate transformation that is applied before calling the graphical primitives that add information to the display file.

4.4.4 Graphical Input Functions

A general-purpose graphics package is responsible for controlling a graphical input device. We noted in Sec. 4.1.7 that the graphics package must provide feedback by causing a cursor on the screen to track the current position of a graphical input device. It must also pass on to the application program information needed for its operation. Even though the graphics package (or operating system) must read the graphical input device position quite frequently to provide smooth feedback (e.g., once per refresh cycle, or $\frac{1}{30}$ s), only summary information needs to be delivered to the application program. Functions for reading this information are described in this section.

Positioning. Often, a graphical input device is used simply to indicate a position on the screen. The user moves the tablet stylus, watching the cursor position, until it reaches the desired position. Then the user presses down and releases, momentarily closing the pen switch. These actions have served to identify a particular point on the screen. The graphics package records that a *positioning interaction* took place.

Inking. Sometimes the input device may be used to trace out an arbitrary curve. The user steers the stylus to the beginning point, presses down, and traces the curve while the pen is pressed. When the entire curve is entered, the pen is released. As points along the curve are sampled by the graphics package, they are *thinned*, so that identical points or those lying very close to the last point sampled are discarded. The thinned points are recorded in an array as an *inking interaction*. The term "inking" arises because of the form of feedback that the graphics package must generate: a trace of the pen's position appears on the screen, resembling a trail of ink left by a pen. The display file for the ink is built like that for a segment, but the display processor must be showing the ink as it is being entered. Later, when the application program wishes to remove the ink trace from the screen, it may call a special function *DestroyInkTrace*. The graphics package can distinguish pointing from inking interactions by noticing whether the stylus position changes substantially while the pen is pressed down.

Keyboard. If a key is struck on a keyboard, the graphics package records the character code as a *keyboard interaction*.

The graphics package maintains a queue of input interactions in the order in which they occurred. The application program can interrogate the graphics package to determine the type of interaction at the head of the queue. Then it can extract the relevant information from the queue entry and delete it. The following functions illustrate one kind of interface:

type: $= GetInteraction(waitFlag)$: Returns the type of the first entry in the queue: positioning, inking, or keyboard. If the queue is empty and *waitFlag* is true, the function will wait for an interaction to take place. If the queue is empty and *waitFlag* is false, it returns the type *emptyQueue*.

ReadPosition(**var** *x, y*): Finds the first positioning interaction in the queue, waiting if necessary for it to occur. Sets the variables *x* and *y* to the coordinates pointed to by the user. Deletes all queue entries up to and including the positioning interaction.

ReadInk(**var** *inkArray, length*): Finds the first inking interaction in the queue, waiting if necessary. Fills the two-dimensional array *inkArray* with *x* and *y* coordinates of points along the inked trace, and sets *length* to the number of coordinate pairs returned. Deletes all queue entries up to and including the inking interaction.

ReadKeyboard(**var** *c*): Finds the first keyboard interaction in the queue, waiting if necessary. Fills the variable *c* with the character code for the key that was struck. Deletes all queue entries up to and including the keyboard interaction.

These functions are "high-level" input functions that are particularly convenient for the application program. The objective of the queue and the *GetInteraction* function is to allow input interactions to occur in any order on any device and to allow the application program to *parse* the input actions. This style allows considerable flexibility in the design of command languages. For example, suppose that we are building a program to draw simple graphs and charts, and the user is asked to specify some points along the graph. The user may be tracing an existing graph, and may prefer to use positioning interactions to specify the points. On the other hand, if the user has a table of numbers that are the source of data for the graph, he or she may prefer to enter numeric values on the keyboard. The application program can distinguish these inputs by examining the kinds of interactions that occur.

Another way to provide input functions is to eliminate the queue and just provide the *ReadPosition*, *ReadInk*, and *ReadKeyboard* functions. With these facilities, the application program must anticipate the kind of input that the user will provide, but the implementation of the graphics package becomes much simpler. In particular, the feedback necessary for the input interaction can be triggered by the call to the function (e.g., for inking).

Yet another method is to provide "low-level" access to *events* that occur on the input devices. Typical events for a tablet will be "pen going down," "pen has moved a small amount," and "pen coming up." The only event for a conventional encoded keyboard is "key struck." An unencoded keyboard may be able to distinguish motions of individual keys and thus provide separate "key going down" and "key coming up" events. These low-level events occur much more rapidly than do the high-level interactions. Consequently, the application program must be prepared to respond quickly to keep the event queue from filling (see Ref. 16, Chap. 13, for details on event queues).

The advantage of the event-based implementation is that almost arbitrary dynamic feedback techniques can be used. For example, the *rubber-band line* technique can be used to position lines carefully, as follows. The user first specifies one endpoint of a line with a conventional positioning interaction. Then he or she moves the stylus away from the first endpoint, toward the second. As this is happening, a line is drawn from the first endpoint to the current stylus position. As the stylus moves, the line is constantly changed so that the user can see how it would appear if the current stylus position were to become the second endpoint. When the user determines that the line is acceptable, he or she presses down on the stylus, causing another positioning interaction that specifies the second endpoint. At this point, the rubber-band line feedback is removed, but the application program presumably adds the line to its model, and then adds it to the display as well.

Pointing. Occasionally, it is desirable to use the input device to point to some object already displayed. This interaction is similar to a positioning sequence, but we are interested in the identity of the object displayed at (*x, y*) in addition to the coordinates. There are several methods that detect "hits" by comparing these coordinates with the geometry of objects visible on the display.

The simplest method is to require that the application program cope with this problem. It may be able to use a simple computation to determine what is being selected. For example, if the display contains only six horizontal lines of text, a simple calculation on the *y* coordinate of a positioning interaction will determine which line of text is closest to the pen position.

Another approach is to let the application program trace through its model again, but rather than generating a display, it calls versions of the *MoveScreen*, *LineScreen*, *CharScreen* and *PointScreen* functions that compute the distance from the pen position to the graphical object being specified. If the distance is less than some tolerance, we assume that is the object being identified.

Another approach is to provide a function in the graphics package that traces a specified segment of the display file and computes the closest distance between the point and any object in the segment: *distance*: = *HitDetect*(*segment, x, y*). Although this function may be somewhat slow, it may not be necessary to invoke it very often.

The *HitDetect* function is able to determine only which segment includes the object being selected. Some graphics packages provide the ability to name parts of a segment as it is being constructed. Then the *HitDetect* function is able to determine not only the distance to the closest object but the name of that object as well.

4.5   APPLICATION PROGRAMS

R. F. Sproull

The success of a graphics application depends as much on the design of the application program as on the design of the graphics components: the display and graphics package. Considerable skill is required to design a program that is effective in its application, convenient to use, forgiving of errors, and easy to learn. This skill at designing interactive programs has not been codified in a concise set of design rules or techniques. This section can only present an overview of the concerns in user-interface design.

4.5.1   User's Model

A user of an interactive program forms a mental model of how it operates and uses this model to figure out how to achieve the effects desired. A user's manual or training course tries to communicate the user's model to prospective users, but may fail. The user may develop quite a different model than the one intended, or may comprehend only the broad outlines of the model and ignore details. An infrequent user of a program is apt to forget some aspects of a complicated model, and struggle along on a simplified view of how the program works.

If a simple user's model can be devised by the application programmer, many of these problems can be avoided. A user is less likely to misunderstand the model and is less likely to forget it. The difficulty lies in designing simple models that are sufficiently effective.

By way of example, let us sketch a user's model for a simple interactive program to make illustrations:

1. An *illustration* consists of an arbitrary number of *lines* and *text strings*. We shall refer to lines and strings as *objects* on the display.
2. Objects can be *created* and added to an illustration, *moved* within an illustration, and *deleted* from an illustration. An illustration can be saved on a disk file or read in from a disk file.

The user's model says nothing about how the actions (create, move, delete, read, write) are invoked—that is a matter for command-language design. But it does explain the basic objects that the user can manipulate and lists the actions that can be performed. The user's model makes it clear that we cannot copy an object on the screen, or rotate or scale it.

This user's model may be so simple that it is ineffective for making illustrations and needs more capabilities. For example, we might wish to add a *grid* to ease positioning of objects:

3. Objects must be positioned on a $\frac{1}{4}$ in. grid (line endpoints, centers of text strings).

This decision simplifies the construction many illustrations such as organization charts, but rules out graphs.

User's models must be embellished cautiously. For example, suppose that we make the apparently innocuous modification to allow the grid spacing to vary. Is the grid spacing a property of the illustration or a momentary *mode* setting of the illustration program? The choice has far-reaching implications on how the program is used. Regardless of the choice, the user may forget what it is. We could design the command language so as to help the user remember, for example by inserting an item "change grid spacing" in a command menu that is constantly displayed on the screen.

Another dangerous embellishment might be to allow rotation of lines, but not of text strings. Now the user can no longer think of lines and strings in the same way: he or she has to remember which actions can be applied to which objects and must devise more intricate ways to construct the illustrations wanted with the varied set of actions and objects available.

The user's model presented in the example above is probably too weak to meet any significant illustration needs. It serves to illustrate the difficulties that arise when we attempt to design an interactive program.

4.5.2   Information Display

Part of the design of an interactive graphics program requires specifying what the user is going to see on the screen. This information includes the images generated by the application program—a visualization of the model the application program maintains—and the images generated to provide feedback to the user.

If the application is intrinsically geometric, the image displayed on the screen is usually some view of the geometric model. The simple illustrator mentioned in the preceding section would present on the screen the lines and text strings that comprise the illustration. The program might provide ways to select different views of the same data, such as expanding the scale of the display so that detailed relationships can be seen. For three-dimensional models, the user needs to control the view so that he or she can observe the features of the model that are of interest (see Sec. 4.6 for an example).

In nongeometric applications, we must design the graphical images to be presented. Sometimes there is a generally accepted style of presenting such information (e.g., graphs to show the behavior of mathematical functions). Sometimes there are a small number of alternatives: a short table of numbers can be visualized with a bar graph, a pie chart, or a table of numbers.

For an arbitrary nongeometric model, we need to design a *visualization* that effectively communicates to the user the properties of the model that concern him or her. This is generally a problem for a graphic designer, who understands how people perceive drawings and how to make the drawings emphatic and unambiguous. For example, a display of heat and coolant flow for a large building must define symbology for heat exchangers, pipes, valves, pumps, and so on. Perhaps measurements of the system status are visualized as gages on the display. The parts of the system must be laid out on the screen so that important status of the system can be determined in a glance; a jumble of crossed pipes might get too confusing. Perhaps equipment can be coded with color to indicate hot (red) or cold (blue) components. Such a visualization requires making a large number of decisions that will affect the quality of the final application.

Several simple guidelines can aid the design of visualizations. Visualizations that lead to ambiguities are to be avoided. Unfortunately, it is not always clear at the outset what ambiguities will arise or how important they will be. For example, a perspective projection of an ellipse can look just like a sphere, but maybe the user will select views in which the ambiguity is not troublesome. Perhaps the most important guideline for information display is to avoid cluttering the screen, but to display just enough information for the user to see what he or she needs. Sometimes this is not a simple matter—hidden-line elimination for displays of three-dimensional objects is designed to remove the clutter and confusion of hidden elements, but is a costly computation.

4.5.3   Command Language

Second to the user's model, the command language is the most difficult part of an interactive program to design. The temptation to "throw together" a set of commands should be resisted; instead, the commands must be designed in an orderly way, to be consistent, easily learned, and not easily misunderstood or misused. The only way to verify that a command-language design meets these objectives is to study carefully how users operate the program, to observe the kinds of tasks they undertake, their efficiency, their misunderstandings, their mistakes, and their successes.

One important issue in the design of command languages is that of *modes*. We often speak of a text editor being "in command mode" or "in text mode," to indicate that the interpretation of keystrokes will be different in these two different "modes." The typed sequence "ED" in text mode adds two characters to the file being edited, whereas in command mode, it means "Everything Delete." A user who is in the incorrect mode, either because he or she has not understood entirely how modes work or because he or she made an insignificant typing error, will be extremely annoyed by such catastrophic deletions. Whereas in the case of a text editor, it may be very difficult to avoid modes completely, many graphical command languages can be designed to avoid modes. Prior selection of objects is one technique that avoids modes: the user selects objects by pointing at them, and then points at (or types) a command, which is interpreted to apply to those objects. Section 4.7 describes an illustrator that uses selection to eliminate modes.

Another important issue in the design of command languages is that of handling errors, whether detected internally by the program or detected by the user. If a user detects an error in some command he or she is about to execute, he needs a simple way to abort the command. Alternatively, the program can demand that the user *confirm* each command before it is executed; this has the disadvantage that the confirmation must terminate each command, thereby requiring more user activity for each command. Another possibility is to have an UNDO command that *completely* undoes the effect of the immediately preceding command; if objects are deleted in error, they can be restored by UNDO. If a user issues an erroneous command, it must be detected and ignored by the application program. The most frustrating experience users can have is if a small mistake causes the entire program to abort (e.g., a typing error in a numeric value causes the language-dependent I/O run-time routines to abort).

A general method to defend against user, programming, and hardware errors is that of a *journal*. Each input transaction is recorded on a journal file, which is frequently written safely on a disk. If the program aborts, the computer crashes, or the user makes some drastic error, the journal can be used to "replay" the entire session, simply by taking input commands from it rather than from the actual input devices. Moreover, the replay can proceed only part way, and stop before the offending commands are interpreted. Although implementing journals can be tedious, they provide recovery from a wide range of errors.

4.5.4   Feedback

Three kinds of feedback images are generally necessary in interactive graphics applications: cursor feedback, which we have already discussed; selection feedback, used to show those objects on the screen that have been selected for some sort of modification that is not yet specified; and command feedback, which displays something for the user to verify the action he or she is about to take.

Selection of objects is a convenient way to designate those objects that will be modified in some way by a subsequent command. The example illustrator described in Sec. 4.5.1 allows objects to be moved and deleted. We could imagine MOVE and DELETE commands that operate on whatever objects have been selected. Thus we need a selection operation: perhaps just pointing at an object causes it to become selected if it is not already selected, or causes it to be de-selected if it is already selected. Although this is a natural design, it requires *selection feedback* — the display must somehow make it clear which objects are selected at any moment. This can be done by making selected objects brighter than others, or blinking them on and off (this may be distracting to the user) or changing their color, and so on. A common selection feedback technique on frame-buffer displays is to use *reverse video*, that is, change the selected object from bright lines on a dark background to dark lines on a bright background.

Command feedback may be identical to selection feedback if the application program is commanded with a *menu*, which displays on the screen a list of all commands available. The user may select a command from the menu in the same way any other object on the screen is selected; the selection feedback verifies which command is selected. The command is then confirmed in some other way (e.g., with a key, or by selecting a DOIT command). Before confirming a command, the user is free to select another command if the first selection is wrong or if the user changes her mind. An alternative form of command feedback is to alter the cursor shape to become a mnemonic illustration of the command's action. For applications that accept commands from conventional keyboards, the *echo* of typed characters on the display screen is usually sufficient for command feedback.

4.5.5   User Interface

The four topics we have presented in previous sections, the user's model, information display, command-language design, and feedback, comprise the user interface to an application program. The design of a user interface is simplified if these parts are recognized and designed coherently. Although our discussion of these issues falls short of specifying in detail how each of these parts should be designed, the issues help us recognize the good and bad features of potential designs.

Sections 4.6 and 4.7 contain concise descriptions of two successful interactive graphics applications. They are presented here both as examples of user-interface design and as examples of applications of graphics in engineering.

MLAB.   MLAB (Sec. 4.6) is a modeling system that helps a user build and investigate mathematical models of various sorts. MLAB models could be built to explore heat transport, electromagnetic wave propagation, filter transfer functions, and so forth. Graphics are used to show the user plots of solutions of the models and to generate publication-quality output if desired. The program is operated with a keyboard; no graphical input device is used. MLAB is implemented on a time-sharing computer using a device-independent graphics package that supports segmented display files.

SIL.   SIL (Sec. 4.7) is an "illustrator," a program for constructing illustrations. It presents a picture of the illustration on a high-resolution raster-scan display and uses a mouse as a graphical input device. An illustration can be saved on a disk file or printed on a raster-scan printer. Illustrations may also be combined with other text before they are printed, so that SIL may be used to prepare illustrations for technical papers.

SIL's most interesting application is in the computer-aided design of digital circuits. The engineer uses SIL to make a logic diagram, calling upon integrated circuits already defined as macros in SIL's library. The diagram is just a drawing—commands to SIL to construct it are designed to make drawings, not to manipulate wires, signal names, circuit packages, connectors, terminators, and the like. Instead, the drawing itself is analyzed to extract the meanings of the elements, and generate a wire list. This wire list drives subsequent steps in a CAD system: merging with wire lists from other drawings, wire routing, and semiautomatic wiring.

SIL's effectiveness in the CAD application stems in part from its simple user's model. The engineer need learn only how to make an illustration with SIL; the additional drawing conventions for the CAD application are natural. Moreover, SIL can then serve with equal ease to create much of the design documentation: logic diagrams, timing diagrams, explanatory diagrams, and so on. Only one smooth interactive program need be written to satisfy CAD needs, and it is a straightforward program.

4.6 GRAPHICS FACILITIES IN MLAB

Gary D. Knott

Computer graphics algorithms, like specialized algorithms generally, are tools to be employed to serve some external purpose. The variety and complexity of graphics algorithms makes it difficult to apply them easily without substantial preplanning.

Indeed, for more elaborate applications, so many conflicts arise, such as raster versus vector approaches, that the design effort requires special knowledge which is not easily acquired. One of the biggest problems is how to use algorithms that require a complex conceptual framework and special data structures without placing an undue burden on the final user, who is well within his or her rights to refuse to rise to the challenge thus imposed.

For some applications, of course, the input and output is well specified and limited enough in scope so that the design activity is less dependent on intangible skills of taste and judgment. For example, a ship or aircraft simulator, with the pilot's "scene" through the windows generated by a computer, is an extremely complex programming problem which requires concommitently elaborate graphics algorithms to achieve the desired results. The inputs and outputs, however, are so specific that the designer is not likely to build a defective system through misjudgment of the needs of the eventual user. An "open-ended" system intended for some general purpose such as architectural drawing or animation, however, stands in danger of failing, not primarily because of the lack of adequate algorithms, but because of a poor user interface.

An example of the use of graphics algorithms in a general purpose system is a mathematical modeling system [3, 11]. Graphics is a necessary adjunct to virtually any such system, and moreover, the graphics facilities must be flexible enough to meed diverse needs, yet be simple to invoke. We consider one such system here in some detail as an example of the application of modestly elaborate graphics software embedded in a relatively convenient manner in a general-purpose system.

The system we shall use as an illustration is an interactive mathematical modeling system called MLAB [12, 13]. The level of graphics services in MLAB is modest compared to "high-technology" display facilities with color, hidden surfaces, and motion; nevertheless, within the framework in which MLAB operates, its graphics facilities are adequately comprehensive and yet not unnecessarily complex.

MLAB imposes a conceptual framework of its own on graphics operations which is not very different from the underlying display routines [19], yet is rich enough to hide most unnecessary details. We shall describe the graphics objects and operations of MLAB below and then show an example of their use in a simple situation.

4.6.1 MLAB

MLAB is an interactive system whose name is an acronym for "modeling laboratory." It is a tool for experimentation with and evaluation of mathematical models (functions). The heart of the system is a curve-fitting program which will adjust the parameters of a model function to minimize the sum of the squared errors. A repertoire of mathematical operators and functions, a collection of routines for teletype and CRT plotting, and mechanisms for saving data between sessions provide a powerful and convenient environment for data manipulation, arithmetic calculations, and for building and testing models. MLAB was designed and programmed at the National Institutes of Health. It runs on a DECsystem-10 or DECsystem-20 time-sharing system and is available for public distribution.

The user communicates with MLAB by typing commands. Each command is executed at once. The graphics commands provide a means of rapidly examining data points or the results of a curve fit and, using a CRT display, preparing a graph for publication. A finished graph may be reproduced on a plotter.

Special facilities for drawing perspective views of three-dimensional surfaces or space curves are included. Various means of modifying the view are available. Again, plots may be easily obtained.

The most salient feature of MLAB is its civilized interface with human users. The statements are simple and direct and unnecessary details and trivia relating to programming have been suppressed. Functions are evaluated interpretively to avoid the necessity for user programming.

The data types of MLAB include scalars, matrices, real-valued functions, and various graphics data types, namely: plane-window-image triples (called windows), curves, three-dimensional windows, and surfaces. We discuss the graphics data types below.

4.6.2 Planes, Windows, and Images

All curves, text strings, and so forth, which are to be shown on a CRT display or eventually plotted must be drawn in a Cartesian plane. Many such planes may be in use simultaneously.

Each plane contains, at all times, exactly one rectangular region or "window" which may be displayed. Curves may be drawn anywhere in a plane but only those parts within the window of the plane can be seen.

One establishes a plane and its window (or changes the window of an established plane) by using the WINDOW statement. A name is given to a plane–window pair in the window statement, and that name is used henceforth to specify either the window or the plane.

The size and location of a window may be changed at any time.

Each window, W, always has associated with it a single "image," which is also called W. Thus the basic elements for graphics are plane–window–image triples. The image of a window is a rectangular region on the surface of the display CRT. The contents of the window W are seen on the CRT in the W image region. The notion of an "image" in MLAB is exactly the same as that of a viewport introduced in Sec. 4.3.7.

The image of a window is established or changed with the IMAGE statement. The images of various windows may overlap arbitrarily on the CRT. The size and location of an image may be changed at any time. The contents of a window as seen in its image are always scaled (stretched or compressed) linearly so as to fit the window rectangle into the image rectangle. This automatic application of a linear transformation can often be used to advantage.

The user may cause curves or text symbols which are independent of the contents of a window to be shown in the image (labeled axes may be obtained by this means). Thus an image can be thought of as a rectangle of glass upon which one may paint or inscribe things, as well as see through to view the contents of the window "underneath." Such plates of glass are infinitely thin and are laid, overlapping if desired, on the CRT surface where the final composite picture is seen.

One "inscribes" or paints on an image by first drawing in the associated plane and then using the INSCRIBE statement. The contents of the plane are transferred to the image and erased from the plane, and those parts that were in the window are now inscribed on the image. This process can be reversed by using the UNSCRIBE statement.

Finally, a connection of a certain sort can be maintained between the inscribed material on the image and the underlying plane. Namely, numeric point labels inscribed in an image can be declared to be *xfloating* or *yfloating*, which indicates that these numbers will change by the x or y increment involved whenever the underlying window is moved. This facility is required to maintain "location-independent" labeled axes. Inscription, together with xfloating and yfloating numeric labels, is the mechanism that allows one to create general axes in a plane–window–image for use with various sets of data.

4.6.3 Curves and Curve Strings

A curve in MLAB is an ordered set of zero or more points in the plane, connected by broken or solid lines. The points of a curve are always stored and manipulated by the user as a two-column matrix whose rows are the points (x, y) of the curve. The ordering of points is determined by the ordering of the rows in the curve matrix.

A curve is drawn in the plane of a plane–window–image triple by using the DRAW command. The points of a curve are plotted in the plane using various point symbols. Connecting lines of one of the several types provided are also drawn in the plane.

Points may be labeled by numeric values written in the plane.

A curve has a name which is assigned in the draw command that creates it. The curve name may be used in blanking, unblanking, redrawing, or deleting the curve.

A curve may have a single associated string of text written anywhere in the plane. Such a string is established with the CURVE STRING statement. Such strings may be used to label axes or to provide notes or comments.

The location of a string is given in window coordinates. However, a string that is located outside the window is still displayed unless it would be off of the screen. In this case any portion of the string that can be displayed is displayed.

4.6.4 Three-Dimensional Spaces, Images, and Surfaces

Perspective projections of three-dimensional objects can be produced by MLAB. To do this one establishes a three-dimensional space with an (x, y, z) Cartesian coordinate system and then draws a set of points in this three-dimensional space which may be connected by lines in various elaborate ways. Such graphs in space are called surfaces, since this is generally what is desired; however, an MLAB surface can be an arbitrary collection of points in space, including space curves, for example. Once one or more surfaces have been drawn, they may be rotated, scaled, or translated and then viewed as if photographed by a camera in space. The imaginary camera can be positioned at will and pointed in any desired direction, and the viewing angle can be set as desired.

A three-dimensional space is created by specifying a name for the space to be used in drawing a surface with the draw-3D command. Each three-dimensional space has an associated camera, which can be controlled by various forms of three-dimensional viewing control commands. The patch of the screen in which all scenes are displayed is set and reset by the IMAGE command, just as with two-dimensional windows.

A three-dimensional window is a named three-dimensional space with an embedded Cartesian coordinate system together with a fictitious camera which views some four-sided pyramidal region of the space called the clipping pyramid. The coordinate systems for three-dimensional windows are left-handed (as provided by the display routines [19]). If a right-handed coordinate system is desired, it suffices to scale z by -1 (i.e., execute [SPACE ZSCALE -1]) in the desired three-dimensional window.

A surface is a finite collection of zero or more points in space which are drawn and viewed in a three-dimensional window. Various line and/or point symbols may be used in graphing a surface. There may be many surfaces in a single three-dimensional window, and there may be many three-dimensional windows in existence simultaneously.

A surface is established and drawn in a three-dimensional window by means of the draw-3D statement. This statement will also create a three-dimensional window if the window mentioned in the draw-3D statement does not currently exist. A surface may be redrawn by drawing it again. Various parameters of a surface, including which window it is in, may be changed.

For each three-dimensional window, a two-dimensional projection line drawing of the visible parts of the surfaces defined by various three-column matrices is displayed. The combined set of surfaces is shown as though it were the result of a camera that recorded the scene from some point in space. The camera may be controlled by view control commands. The result is that the scene changes, thus reflecting the new state of the camera.

4.6.5 Graphics Statements

Window Statement.   The WINDOW statement is used to define a window or to change the size or location of an existing window. The statement WINDOW W, A BY B, AT C, D will cause window W to have width A, height B, and lower left-hand corner at (C, D).

Image Statement.   The IMAGE statement is used to specify or change the location of a picture on the display screen. The statement IMAGE W, A BY B, AT X, Y will cause the display of the two- or three-dimensional window W to be A inches wide, B inches high, starting at X inches from the left-hand side of the screen and at Y inches from the bottom of the screen.

For a three-dimensional window, the IMAGE statement is used to specify or change the location of the projected picture for W on the display screen.

If W does not exist, the image statement serves to create a two-dimensional window named W, however, if an empty two-dimensional window is used as a three-dimensional window, a conversion automatically occurs, so in practice one can say that an IMAGE statement creates a window whose type is yet to be determined.

Draw Statement.   The syntactic form of a draw statement is:
DRAW $<$ C $|$ [C $\leftarrow$]M $>$ [IN W][,LINETYPE A][,POINTTYPE B]
   [,[$<$ XFLOATING $|$ YFLOATING $>$]LABEL WITH $<$ N $|$ (N, E) $>$]
   [,AT X, Y][SIZE A][,INTENSITY B]
where constructs in square brackets are optional, and $<$ x $|$ y $>$ means a choice of only x or only y is to appear. C is a curve name or previously undefined name, M and N are matrix expressions, W is a window, and A, B, E, X, and Y are scalar expressions.

The DRAW command is used to display curves and associated information on a CRT display. A curve in MLAB is a finite set of points in two dimensions defined by the Cartesian coordinates specified by the matrix M. M must have exactly two columns; the first column is a list of the x coordinates, and the second column is a list of the corresponding y coordinates. M cannot be empty unless the curve C is being redrawn.

If the curve name, C, is omitted, a new unique name of the form TEMPCn is invented and used as the curve name.

A copy of the matrix M is retained with the curve information. M may thus be altered or deleted without affecting the curve C. The function CURVEMATRIX(C) will return a copy of the matrix associated with C.

When the curve name, C, does not name an already existing curve, then, if a window is not specified, a window called DEFAULTWINDOW will be used. Moreover, the size and location of DEFAULTWINDOW will be expanded (but never contracted) as necessary to accommodate the curve being drawn. Thus it is as if a window statement is executed before drawing to set the size and location of DEFAULTWINDOW according to the particular data and previous state of DEFAULTWINDOW.

Table 1.   Two-Dimensional Point and Line Types in MLAB

Point Type		LineType	
0	null	0	null line
1	vertical bar	1	solid line
2	cross (+ sign)	2	dashed line
3	triangle	3	long dashed line
4	square	4	mixed dashed line
5	horizontal bar	5	alternating solid–empty line
6	letter "Oh" oval	6	solid line with marker skipping
7	small dot	7	variable dashed line with marker skipping
8	circle		
"X"	the terminal-generated character X at the smallest size.		

If W is the name DEFAULTWINDOW explicitly, such automatic rewindowing does not occur, nor is DEFAULTWINDOW automatically accessed. If W is not specified and DEFAULTWINDOW has not been previously established, a special precomputed window will be used. Otherwise, whatever has been established as the window DEFAULTWINDOW is used. The image used for DEFAULTWINDOW is set relative to the display in use. All windows being used have their images established in the same way.

When the curve name, C, is explicitly given, and has been previously drawn, then the draw statement is taken as a request to redraw the curve C using any new parameters now specified. Parameters that are not given explicitly will retain their old values. This form of the draw command may thus be used to change line types, point types, windows, curve matrices, and so on, without disturbing other parameters of the curve. If W is given as an undefined symbol, a window 10 by 10 at 0, 0 called W will be established. If W is not given and C is drawn in DEFAULTWINDOW, the appropriate automatic rewindowing will occur.

The types of lines and points available are described in Table 1. If a nonzero line-type value is given, the points of the curve are connected by straight lines. If a nonzero point type is given, a symbol is placed at each point of the curve. The default values are 1 for the line-type value and 0 for the point-type value.

We will not describe here at AT, SIZE, and LABEL WITH clauses, which have to do with placing numeric labels. There are various other statements for two-dimensional graphics, notably the CURVE STRING statement, the INSCRIBE statement, and the UNSCRIBE statement mentioned above, which we shall not discuss here.

Draw-3D Statement.   The draw-3D command is used to display surfaces on a CRT display. Syntactically, it has the same form as an ordinary DRAW statement, namely: DRAW < s|[s ←]M > [IN W][,LINETYPE A][,POINTTYPE B], but the matrix M, if given, must have three columns, S must be a surface (or unknown), and W must be a three-dimensional window (or an empty two-dimensional window or unknown). Thus a draw-3D statement is recognized by the types of its constitiuents.

A surface in MLAB is a finite set of points in three dimensions defined by the Cartesian coordinate values specified by the matrix M. M must have exactly three columns; the first column is a list of the x coordinates, the second column is a list of the corresponding y coordinates, and the third column is a list of the corresponding z coordinates. M cannot be empty unless the surface S is being redrawn. An easy way to create a matrix to be drawn which holds points from the graph of some function of two arguments (i.e., a way to graph a given function) is to use the POINTS operator on the CROSS of two lists of coordinate values to obtain the desired matrix.

If the surface name, S, is omitted, a new unique name is invented and used as the surface name.

A copy of the matrix M is retained with the surface information. M may thus be altered or deleted without affecting the surface S. The function CURVEMATRIX(S) will return a copy of the matrix associated with S.

When the surface name, S, does not name an already existing surface, then, if a three-dimensional window is not specified, the symbol DEFAULT3DWINDOW will be used for W. In any case, if S is not an already existing surface, W will be established as a three-dimensional window and used only when W is an empty two-dimensional window or an unknown entity or an existing three-dimensional window. When a three-dimensional window is initially created, it will assume the default image on the screen which is appropriate for the current display, unless W is transformed from an empty two-dimensional window, in which case its image is maintained.

When the surface name, S, is explicitly given, and has been previously drawn, the draw-3D statement is taken as a request to redraw the surface S using the parameters now specified. Parameters

Table 2.   Three-Dimensional Point and Line Types

Point Type		Line Type	
0	null	0	null line
1	small dot	1	needles
2	small 3D-crosses	2	net
"X"	the terminal-generated	3	needles + net
	character X at the	4	sequence
	smallest size	5	half-sequence
		6	marker skipping sequence
		7	hidden-line net
		8	hidden-line bands
		9	upper-side hidden-line net
		10	upper-side hidden-line bands

that are not given explicitly will retain their old values. This form of the draw-3D command may thus be used to change windows, surface matrices, point types, or line types without disturbing other parameters of the curve.

Finally, using the interpretation above, the specified surface is drawn or redrawn in the left-handed three-dimensional coordinate system of the specified window. A surface is thus established in the specified window with the name S (or a name of the form TEMPCn if S is not given).

A surface may be drawn with symbols at each point on the surface, specified by a point-type code given in Table 1. Also, various lines may be drawn, including lines from the specified points to the floor plane (needles), direct connections from point to point (sequence), lines between every other pair of points (half-sequence), a rectangular network of lines connecting neighboring points in the x and y directions (net), and, with hidden lines only, bands of lines connecting neighboring points in the x-direction (hidden line bands). In the case where a net or bands are desired, the rows of the first two columns of the surface matrix must be in lexicographic order. That is, the surface matrix must be in sort by column one, and within that, in sort by column two. Moreover, nets may be drawn with hidden lines if desired. All of these options are specified by an appropriate line-type value as shown in Table 2. The default line type is 1, and the default point type is 0.

Hidden lines are best understood by considering the drawing of a set of lines, where there are two thresholds across the screen such that every line segment to be drawn has only the parts that extend above the high threshold and the parts that extend below the low threshold drawn. After each segment is drawn, the thresholds are suitably updated. When line segments are drawn in the proper order away from the point of view, a hidden-line effect is achieved. Upper-side means that only the high threshold is kept; the lower threshold is initially set at the bottom of the screen.

When the specified surface has been established in the appropriate three-dimensional window, all the surfaces, plus any auxiliary box, floor, or axes, are displayed in the appropriate image patch on the CRT screen. The combined set of surfaces is shown as though it were the result of a camera that recorded the scene from some point in space. The camera may be controlled by the view control commands.

The parameters of the camera are: (1) its location in space (the surface is transparent and the camera can be located "inside" an object looking out, if desired!), (2) the direction the lens is pointing, and (3) the angle of view (i.e., a narrow or wide angle lens may be simulated). Actually, changing the viewing angle is equivalent to scaling the object in the plane orthogonal to the viewing direction.

Initially, when the sole surface in a window is drawn, the camera is positioned heuristically looking at the surfaces with a viewing angle of 90° (i.e., $\alpha = 45°$; see Sec. 4.3.3). The bounding box of the surface determines the positioning of the camera so that the surfaces are seen more or less centered in the associated image region. Moreover, the surface is scaled to obtain pleasing proportions; if such scaling is not appropriate, the user can reset the scales using view control commands. Automatic scaling and camera positioning occurs only when a new three-dimensional window is established. The RESET command can be used to invoke such scaling and positioning manually.

Three-Dimensional View Control Statements.   A three-dimensional view control statement consists of a sequence of clauses that operate on a three-dimensional window to control (1) the camera; (2) the "structural format," involving scaling, the appearance of axes, boxes, floors, and so on; or (3) the orientation, positioning, and scaling of a particular surface in the window. These clauses may be intermingled as desired in one statement which applies to a common surface or set of surfaces in a common window.

The camera parameters controlled by the following clauses:

DOLLY K: The camera is moved K box units in the viewing direction.

TRUCK K: The camera is moved K box units horizontal to the viewing direction.

RAISE K: The camera is moved K box units vertical to the viewing direction.

PAN K: The viewing direction is rotated K degrees in the $x - z$ plane of the camera coordinate system. This is a left-hand screw rotation about the raise vector.

TILT K: The viewing direction is rotated K degrees in the $y - z$ plane of the camera coordinate system. This is a right-hand screw rotation about the truck vector.

TWIST K: The camera is right-hand-screw-rotated K degrees about the viewing direction.

TRACK AT A,B,C: The camera is rotated to point to the point (A,B,C). If no AT A,B,C clause is given, the camera is rotated to point to the box center of the box about the various surfaces.

TURN K: The camera is right-hand-screw-rotated K degrees about the box center of the box about the various surfaces in the plane containing the camera and the box center and normal to the raise vector. The camera's direction of view is modified to maintain the same deviation between the direction of view and the vector to the box center as existed before the turn operation.

ZOOM K: The viewing angle is set to K degrees. Photographers specify this angle in terms of its cotangent, but we use the actual angle.

ORIGIN: The camera is moved to (0,0,0) looking up the z axis with 0 degrees of twist.

RESET: The camera is automatically positioned so as to provide an overall view. Moreover, various individual surface scales, and the axes and floor parameters, are reset to pleasant default values.

The three-dimensional window W to which the camera belongs is specified by adding the final clause IN W, where W is the name of the window. If no such clause is given, DEFAULT3DWINDOW is assumed.

Except for the viewing angle, the various camera parameters are taken as incremental, so that DOLLY, TRUCK, RAISE, PAN, TILT, and TWIST arguments are added to the current values to obtain new quantities which determine the new picture to be displayed.

The arguments to DOLLY, TRUCK, and RAISE are in relative box units. The box surrounding all the surface objects has at any time an absolute size in scaled units of x_s by y_s by z_s. Then one unit of camera motion along the x-direction displaces the camera x_s scaled units, one unit of motion along the y-direction displaces the camera y_s scaled units, and one unit of motion along the z-direction displaces the camera z_s scaled units. One unit of transverse motion displaces the camera a certain combination of x_s, y_s, and z_s scaled units as determined by the Pythagorean theorem.

A real camera has additional degrees of freedom. In particular, one can control the height of the lens relative to the film and the angular position of the film plane relative to the direction of the lens-film vector. These parameters are used to control perspective. Moreover, an actual camera has a focus parameter which determines a plane or sphere of focus. All points on the plane of focus are seen as point images in the developed picture. Points that are off the plane of focus are seen as small disks whose radius is proportional to the distance they occur from the plane of focus. The intensity of light in such disks falls off from the center in a symmetric distribution. Thus a true camera causes more or less thick bands with fuzzy boundaries to occur where lines should be. For programming purposes it would suffice to map each point to a circle of appropriate radius. Actually, however, the infinite depth of field provided by the simple graphic simulation is preferable.

There are also clauses for modifying any particular three-dimensional window holding various surfaces.

SPACE XSCALE K: All x coordinates of space are scaled by K. The camera and all surfaces in the specified window are affected.

SPACE YSCALE K: All y coordinates of space are scaled by K. The camera and all surfaces in the specified window are affected.

SPACE ZSCALE K: All z coordinates of space are scaled by K. The camera and all surfaces in the specified window are affected.

FLOOR [AT K]:   A grid in the $x - y$ plane is drawn at $z = K$. If K is not given, K is taken as the previous floor value for the window involved.

NO FLOOR: The floor grid, if any, disappears from picture.

XNUMBER: The x axis is marked and numbered at four places.

YNUMBER: The y axis is marked and numbered at four places.

ZNUMBER: The z axis is marked and numbered at four places.

NO XNUMBER: x axis marks and numbers disappear from the picture.

NO YNUMBER: y axis marks and numbers disappear from the picture.

NO ZNUMBER: z axis marks and numbers disappear from the picture.

AXES AT A,B,C: Axes are drawn and labeled from the minimum to the maximum value of each coordinate variable, taken over all surfaces, and intersecting at (A,B,C). If no values for A, B, C are entered, $(0,0,0)$ is used.

NO AXES: The axes and labels disappear from picture.

BOX: Draws a box around the surface object.

NO BOX: The box disappears from picture.

The three-dimensional window to which the preceding clauses apply is specified by adding the final clause IN W, where W is the desired window. If no such clause is given, DEFAULT3DWINDOW is assumed.

When space is scaled, the apparent camera directions will be affected. When the camera is at the origin looking at the point $(1,0,0)$ and we have executed SPACE XSCALE 3, the command PAN 45 will cause the camera to look at the point $(1,1,0)$, but $(1,1,0)$ is not on the 45° radial from the origin! Thus scaling individual surfaces may be preferable to scaling space.

Finally, there are some clauses for modifying various surfaces individually, including moving them in space before looking through the camera at the entire scene. For any given surface, these clauses are as follows:

XSCALE A: The surface is scaled by A in its x coordinates.

YSCALE A: The surface is scaled by A in its y coordinates.

ZSCALE A: The surface is scaled by A in its z coordinates.

XTRANSLATE A: The surface is translated A units in the x direction.

YTRANSLATE A: The surface is translated A units in the y direction.

ZTRANSLATE A: The surface is translated A units in the z direction.

SYSTEM XROTATE A: The surface is right-hand-screw-rotated A degrees about the x axis of the underlying "system" coordinate system.

SYSTEM YROTATE A: The surface is right-hand-screw-rotated A degrees about the "system" y axis.

SYSTEM ZROTATE A: The surface is right-hand-screw-rotated A degrees about the "system" z axis.

AXES XROTATE A: The surface is right-hand-screw-rotated A degrees about the x axis of the user-specified coordinate system defined by the axes command.

AXES YROTATE A: The surface is right-hand-screw-rotated A degrees about the user-specified y axis.

AXES ZROTATE A: The surface is right-hand-screw-rotated A degrees about the user-specified z axis.

BOX XROTATE A: The surface is right-hand-screw rotated A degrees about the x axis of the coordinate system centered in the "box" enclosing the entire group of objects. This box always has its sides parallel to the system coordinate axes.

BOX YROTATE A: The surface is right-hand-screw-rotated A degrees about the box y axis.

BOX ZROTATE A: The surface is right-hand-screw-rotated A degrees about the box z axis.

SURFACE XROTATE A The surface is right-hand-screw-rotated A degrees about the x axis of the coordinate system, which is centered in the surface object itself, in the sense that the origin for this set of coordinates is the center of the smallest box that has its sides parallel to the system coordinate axes and encloses the surface object.

SURFACE YROTATE A: The surface is right-hand-screw-rotated A degrees about the individual surface y axis.

SURFACE ZROTATE A: The surface is right-hand-screw-rotated A degrees about the individual surface z axis.

The default rotation qualifier that is assumed when none is given is SYSTEM.

The particular surface to which the clauses above apply is specified by adding the final clause IN S, where S is the desired surface name. The clause IN W, where W is the name of a 3D-window, may be added instead, in which case the command applies iteratively to each surface in the specified window. If no such clause is given, IN DEFAULT3DWINDOW is assumed.

4.6.6 Example

Let us consider an oscillator with nonlinear damping. In particular, we consider an oscillator that is described by the Van der Pol equation,

$$y' + c(y^2 - 1)y' + ky = f(t)$$

where $f(t)$ is a forcing function, k is a spring constant, and $c(y^2 - 1)$ is the damping factor.

A circuit whose voltage function is approximately given by the Van der Pol equation can be constructed with a tunnel diode. The equation also arises as a neuron membrane model [9]. This equation is a favorite example in control theory and systems theory texts [2, 6].

Let us explore the properties of $y(t)$ with $f(t) = 0$, $k = 1$, and various values of c, so we have

$$y' = v(t), v' = -c(y^2 - 1)v + y$$

with initial conditions $y(0) = y_0$ and $v(0) = v_0$. Note that y is effectively a function of two variables, t and c.

Let us use MLAB to graph some curves of $y(t)$ versus t for various values of c. To start, we specify y' and $y' = v$ and all the auxiliary constants by using MLAB function statements, which define functions and differential equations, initial statements, which allow initial values to be specified, and assignment statements, which assign scalar or matrix values to variables.

> *function y diff t(t) = v(t)*
> *function v diff t(t) = − c*(y ↑ 2 − 1)*v − y*
> *initial y(0) = y0*
> *initial v(0) = v0*
> *y0 ← 1.04; v0 ← 0; c ← .2*

Now we may obtain $y(t)$ for $t = 0, 0.1, 0.2, \ldots, 29.9, 30$ by numerical integration as follows, using the MLAB integrate operator:

> *q ← integrate(y diff t, v diff t, 0:30:.1)*

The notation $a:b:c$ specifies a column vector of the values a through b in steps of c. The value of q is established as a matrix of five columns which is the result of the integrate operator applied to *y diff t*, *v diff t*, and the vector 0:30:.1. The first column of t is the time vector 0:30:.1. (Note the actual step sizes used in integration are chosen automatically and are not related to .1; the results are obtained by interpolation.) The second column is the computed values for y corresponding to 0:30:.1, and the third column is the computed values for y'. The fourth and fifth columns are the computed values for v and v'.

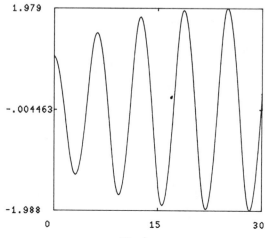

Fig. 1

Now we can draw a graph of y on the interval $[0, 30]$ as follows (Fig. 1):

> *display* $\leftarrow$ T4012
> *draw q col* 1:2

The particular device-dependent code for a Tektronix 4012 display terminal is loaded when the display assignment statement is entered, and then the set of points that are the rows of the first two columns of q are plotted, connected by solid lines. By default, the window DEFAULTWINDOW is used and automatically scaled to fit the data points. The figures that illustrate these operations were obtained by the MLAB dialogue shown with the addition of plot commands which allowed copies of these pictures to be obtained on paper.

Let us try a new value of c (Fig. 2):

> $c \leftarrow 2$
> $q \leftarrow$ *integrate(y diff t, v diff t,* $0{:}30{:}.1)$
> *delete defaultwindow*
> *draw q col* 1:2, *linetype* 3

We see that for both $c = 0.2$ and $c = 2$, we have an apparently steady-state oscillation, but the frequency and the waveform differ. We may explore further by looking at the surface $y(t; c)$ for (t, c) in some rectangle. Let us reset the initial conditions and choose t in $0{:}15.5{:}.5$ and c in $-0.2{:}.2{:}.1$. As you might expect, it took several attempts to determine the various ranges for t and c and the various values of $y0$ and $v0$ which are used throughout this example. Remember, however, the point of the example is not the systematic study of the Van der Pol equation, but rather the utility of MLAB graphics in performing such a study.

> $y0 \leftarrow 2.04;\ v0 \leftarrow 0;$
> $q \leftarrow 0{:}15.5{:}.5$
> *for* $c \leftarrow -.2{:}.2{:}.1$ *do* $(q \leftarrow q\&'(integrate(\ y\ diff\ t, v\ diff\ t, q\ col\ 1)col2))$
> $m \leftarrow cross(q\ col\ 1, -.2{:}.2{:}.1)$
> $m\ col2 \leftarrow list(q\ col\ 2{:}6)$

The operator &' denotes column concatenation, so that A&'B is a matrix of the columns of A followed by the columns of B. Row concatenation is denoted by the operator symbol &. The operator *col* selects

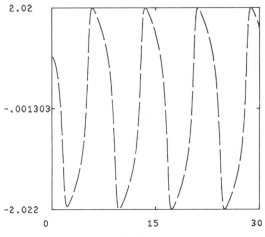

Fig. 2

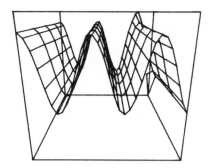

Fig. 3

a subset of the columns of a matrix as its result. The operator *list* applied to a matrix, A, results in a column vector of the elements of A, appearing in order row by row. The matrix *m* has been created so that the rows of *m* are the set of points $\{(t, c, y(t; c)) | t \epsilon 0:15.5:.5$ and $c \epsilon -.2:.2:.1\}$ appearing in lexicographic order. Such a three-column matrix is called a surface matrix, and may be drawn with the three-dimensional facilities of MLAB as follows (Fig. 3):

> *delete defaultwindow*
>
> *draw m, linetype* 7

By default, the window DEFAULT3DWINDOW was used. The linetype 7 clause selected the option of a net with hidden lines (mostly) eliminated.

We may see this surface from another view, with axes, by using two view control commands as follows (Fig. 4):

> *turn* 180 *raise* 1 *track zoom* 65
>
> *no box axes at* $0,0,-1$ *xnumber ynumber*

It appears that for $c = -0.2$, the oscillation is "blowing up." Let us go back to $y0 = 1.04$ and look

z

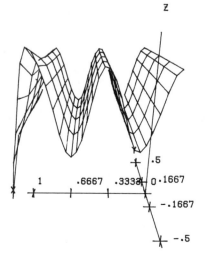

.5

1   .6667   .3333   0 .1667

−.1667

−.5   Fig. 4

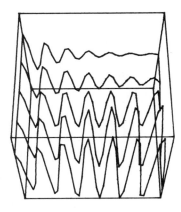

Fig. 5

at a similar surface (Fig. 5).

$$y0 \leftarrow 1.04$$
$$q \leftarrow 0:40$$
$$for\ c \leftarrow -.2:.2:.1\ do\ q \leftarrow q\&(integrate(\ y\ diff\ t, v\ diff\ t, q\ col\ 1)col2)$$
$$m \leftarrow cross(q\ col\ 1, -.2:.2:.1)\&list\ (q\ col\ 2:6)$$
$$delete\ default3dwindow$$
$$draw\ m, linetype\ 8$$
$$raise\ 4\ track\ zoom\ 30\ raise\ -2\ track$$

Here we see simple bands of the surface by specifying line type 8. Another device that may be employed to see a surface is a contour map. We can produce such a two-dimensional contour map drawing in MLAB as follows (Fig. 6):

$$h \leftarrow contour(m, -1.8\&(-1.6:1.6:.8)\&1.8)$$
$$delete\ default3dwindow$$
$$draw\ h, linetype\ 7$$

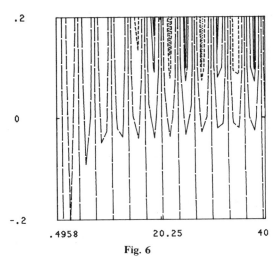

Fig. 6

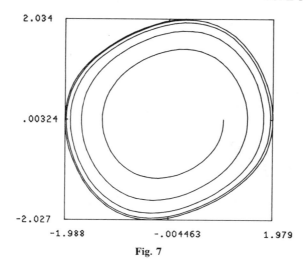

Fig. 7

For two-dimensional graphics, linetype 7 is a special line type for contour maps. We may note that, just as before, for $c = 0.2$ we have a steady oscillation, but for $c = -0.2$ the y curve is damped so that $y \to 0$.

The evidence suggests that for $c > 0$, we have a limit cycle; that is, $y(t)$ eventually settles down into an unchanging pattern of oscillation. This means that y and v oscillate and hence the point $(y(t), v(t))$ traces out a simple closed loop in the x, y plane as $t \to \infty$. This loop is called the limit cycle in phase space. (It is an easy exercise to prove this is the case.) The shape of the limit cycle depends on $|c|$. We may graph some limit cycles as follows (Fig. 7):

```
c ← .2
delete defaultwindow
draw integrate( y diff t, v diff t,0:30:.1)col2:3
```

This is the phase space plot for the first oscillation we examined. Other limit cycles are shown below. The shape differs, since we take $c = 2$ (Fig. 8).

```
c ← 2
delete defaultwindow
draw integrate( y diff t, v diff t,0:30:.1)col 2:3
y0 ← 2; v0 ← 2
draw integrate( y diff t, v diff t,0:30:.1)col 2:3
y0 ← −2; v0 ← 3.6
draw integrate( y diff t, v diff t,0:30:.1)col 2:3
```

For $c < 0$, we evidently have $y(t) \to 0$ as $t \to \infty$ or $y(t) \to \pm\infty$ as $t \to \infty$, depending upon $|c|$ and the initial values $y0$ and $v0$. Clearly if $(y0, v0)$ is close enough to $(0,0)$, we have $y \to 0$. The point $(0,0)$ in phase space is thus a stable point; when the system (y, v) enters the neighborhood of $(0,0)$, it remains there and approaches $(0,0)$ thereafter. The largest neighborhood, S, of $(0,0)$ for which $(y, v)\epsilon$S implies $y \to 0$ thereafter is called the region of stability for the stable point $(0,0)$. We can draw some phase

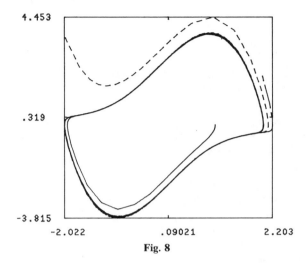

4.453

.319

-3.815

-2.022   .09021   2.203

Fig. 8

space trajectories which converge to $(0,0)$ by choosing intial values sufficiently close to $(0,0)$. For $c = -0.1$, it turns out that the region of stability is the disk of radius 2 about $(0,0)$ (Fig. 9).

$c \leftarrow -.1; \ y0 \leftarrow 1.04; \ v0 \leftarrow 0$

$q \leftarrow integrate(\ y \ diff \ t, \ v \ diff \ t, 0:20:.1)$

delete defaultwindow

draw q col 2:3

All such trajectories seem to spiral circularly toward $(0,0)$ in the same manner.

When $c < 0$ and $(\ y0, v0)$ is not sufficiently close to $(0,0)$, then $y(t) \rightarrow \pm \infty$ as $t \rightarrow \infty$. Thus $+\infty$ and $-\infty$ are points of stability and their joint region of stability is the region of unbounded stability, which for $c = -0.1$ is the region outside the disk of radius 2 about $(0,0)$. We can draw a trajectory

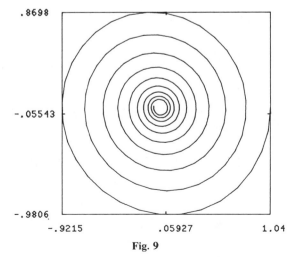

.8698

-.05543

-.9806

-.9215   .05927   1.04

Fig. 9

starting in this region below.

$y0 \leftarrow 2.04; v0 \leftarrow 0$

$q \leftarrow integrate(\, y \; diff \; t, v \; diff \; t, 0{:}60{:}.1)$

errfac: .001 (these lines are typed by MLAB)

TOLERANCE VIOLATED.

errfac: .002

TOLERANCE VIOLATED.

errfac: .004

TOLERANCE VIOLATED.

errfac: .025

POSSIBLE SINGULARITY NEAR 31.535

DERIVATIVES: 128545850.000 31443310000000.000

errfac: .063

POSSIBLE SINGULARITY NEAR 31.535 DERIVATIVES: 605465390.000

442314610000000.000

errfac: .398 T:31.535, # steps:278

The differential equation integration could not proceed past $t = 31.535$. The rest of the first column of q is zero. By using the compress operator, we can delete these unfilled rows, whereupon the remaining results can be plotted (Fig. 10).

$q \leftarrow compress(q)$

delete defaultwindow

draw q col 2:3

It is interesting to draw the "world line" of our system as a space curve of the points (t, y, v) which occur in the rows of the matrix q (Fig. 11).

delete defaultwindow

draw q col 1:3, linetype4

floor at 0

zscale .07 zoom 60 xscale .05 no box truck $-.1$ dolly $-.05$

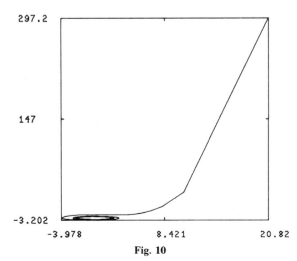

Fig. 10

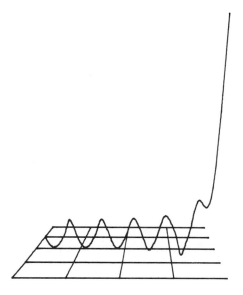

Fig. 11

We have used only the most elementary features of MLAB graphics in the example above. It is precisely the point that these elementary facilities are sufficient for many mathematical explorations. The construction of "custom" graphs with special axes and labels, or of particularly elaborate three-dimensional scenes, requires more effort; actually, more false starts, errors, and backtracking is what is required; the error-free process is still relatively short and simple. The problem of how to make complex drawings easily is one where a solution is not obvious. There undoubtedly will be many further advances toward such a solution in the future.

4.7 SIL—A SIMPLE ILLUSTRATOR FOR CAD

Charles P. Thacker

This section describes SIL, a Simple Ilustrator implemented on a minicomputer equipped with a raster-scanned display. SIL was originally built to produce high-quality logic diagrams for digital systems, as well as other specialized illustrations. Although it has a number of limitations, SIL has been applied to a wider variety of applications than originally anticipated.

Rather than simply being used to produce documentation, SIL is now used to generate input for a group of programs that aid in the implementation of digital hardware. The logic diagrams produced by SIL are the only input required by these programs; the SIL files are interpreted to provide the information required by the rest of the design system. SIL has also been used for a wide variety of general-purpose illustration tasks.

Section 4.7.1 discusses the hardware environment in which SIL was built and the main objectives of the program. Section 4.7.2 describes the user interface and editing functions provided by SIL, and Sec. 4.7.3 provides an overview of the implementation. In Sec. 4.7.4, the major applications of SIL are described.

4.7.1 Environment and Characteristics

The primary goal in the design of SIL was to replace manual drafting in the preparation of hardware logic diagrams. The intended user community consisted of approximately 20 engineers and scientists engaged in the design of experimental digital hardware at the Xerox Palo Alto Research Center.

SIL was designed to run on the Alto (Fig. 1), a personal computer described in detail in Ref. 22. The Alto is a small machine with 64K 16-bit words of main storage, and a microprogrammed CPU capable of executing a typical register load or add instruction in approximately 2 μs. Local storage on the Alto is provided by a 2.5-Mbyte cartridge disk drive.

The principal output device of the Alto is an 875-line monochrome television monitor, oriented with the long dimension of the tube vertical. The monitor shows a bilevel black-and-white image 600 pixels wide by 800 pixels high, refreshed at 30 Hz. The image is represented in an integral frame buffer that consumes slightly less than half of the Alto's main storage. The display hardware also supports a *cursor*, which is a 16 by 16 pixel bit map taken from a fixed area in memory. The cursor position can be set by a program, and the contents of the bit map are merged with the normal video at the indicated position. This implementation allows the contents and position of a small area of the screen to be ORed with the bit map rapidly without changing the contents of the main frame buffer.

Input is provided by a keyboard and a mouse, a pointing device that provides relative position information when rolled over a surface. In most Alto applications, including SIL, the mouse coordinates are clipped so that they lie within the boundaries of the display and are then used as the coordinates of the display cursor. The mouse also provides three buttons that allow the user to supply a small amount of information to a program without the necessity of moving his or her hand from the mouse to the keyboard.

A number of Altos are interconnected by an Ethernet network [14], a 3-Mbit/s packet-switched network that also provides access to remote file storage and printing services. The printer used for SIL output is a raster-scanned xerographic unit with a resolution of 384 lines/in., which produces 8.5 by 11 in. sheets.

Because of the characteristics of the printer, the contents of the SIL display correspond to a single hardcopy page. There are no provisions in SIL for using the display as a window onto a larger document, a feature often found in graphics systems. For applications involving figures for reports

Fig. 1   Alto personal computer display, keyboard and mouse.

and the like, this is not a limitation, since the normal format for these documents is an 8.5 by 11 in. page. Initially, there was concern that this format would be inconvenient for logic diagrams, since these diagrams are customarily prepared on 11 by 17 or 17 by 22 in. sheets. Experience has shown that this is not a problem, since a single page will usually contain a complete subsection of a design and fits conveniently in standard notebooks. A printed-circuit board containing 150 medium-scale integrated circuits, for example, can be shown in 15 to 20 SIL pages.

Objects. At its lowest level, SIL manipulates only two types of objects, *rectangles* and *text strings*. Rectangles are used for horizontal and vertical lines and for *backgrounds*, which are large areas that may be overlaid with other objects and printed in color on printers with color capability. Text strings may be specified in one of a number of fonts (typefaces) and may also be displayed in boldface or italic.

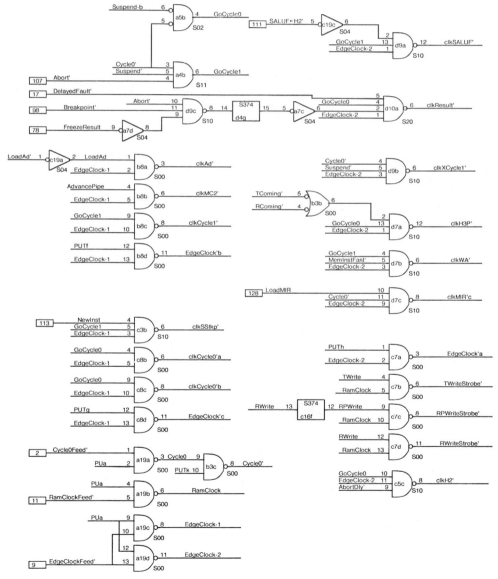

Fig. 2 Typical SIL logic diagram.

SIL also provides *display macros*, which allow an arbitrary collection of objects, including other macros, to be packaged together and subsequently referred to as a single character in one of five *macro fonts*.

Using only these primitives, a surprising range of illustrations may be created. For the logic drawing application, a font was designed that contains about 50 characters corresponding to the symbols on a logic designer's drafting template, and from this symbol set, several hundred display macros representing digital integrated circuits have been constructed. These macros are distributed as library files, and are used by all designers. Figure 2 shows a typical logic drawing produced with SIL using some of these macros.

One of the major apparent drawbacks of SIL is its inability to produce lines of arbitrary orientation. This disadvantage has been partially overcome by providing a font with characters consisting of line segments at various angles, and arcs of circles of various sizes. Using an operation that allows text to be placed at an arbitrary location with high precision, it is possible to produce complex figures using this font (see Fig. 3).

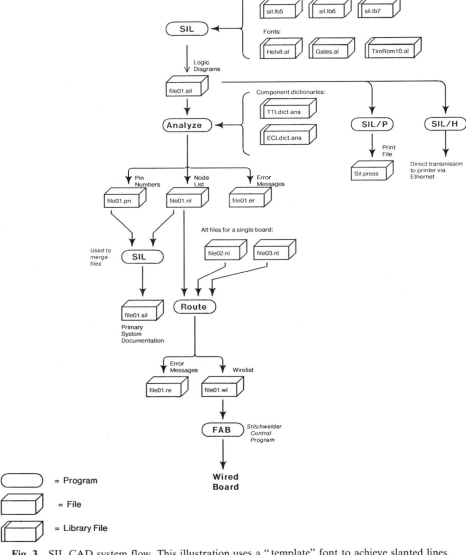

Fig. 3   SIL CAD system flow. This illustration uses a "template" font to achieve slanted lines.

SIL fonts are provided in two resolutions, a 75-pixel/in. version used with SIL itself, and a higher-resolution version suitable for the printer used for hardcopy output. SIL files contain the screen coordinates of the objects to be displayed, which are scaled appropriately for the particular printer used. The final output is thus a faithful rendition of the displayed image, but at high resolution. This makes the output much more readable than simply scaling the bit map to the resolution of the printer.

4.7.2 User Interface and Functions

The choice of a user interface is perhaps the most difficult part of the design of an interactive system, for once the functions the system is to provide have been selected, the user interface determines whether these functions can be accessed easily and naturally. The SIL user interface was designed with several primary ideas in mind:

1. The user should be able to develop a simple (although not necessarily correct) model of the operation of the program, and should be able to rapidly predict the result of a command, so that an appropriate operation can be selected easily.

2. The rate of interaction with the user should be high. Thus SIL commands are usually specified by a single keystroke or mouse button depression. This was done at the expense of a more easily learned command structure such as menu selection, since it was judged that speed of operation was more important than ease of learning. The office typewriter provided a precedent for this decision.

3. The amount of context that the user is required to remember should be small. The effects of a command should not depend on "modes" previously set by the user.

4. The user should not have to request status information from the program. Any status information required should be continually displayed, and the amount of such status should be minimal.

In this section, the functions provided by SIL and the commands used to evoke these functions are discussed. Also, the status display, which provides the user with information about the current state of SIL, is described.

Status Display. When SIL is started, the display screen is cleared with the exception of a single line of text, the *status line*, and three special indicators, the *cursor*, the *mark*, and the *origin*. Figure 4 shows the initial SIL screen. The cursor, the mark, and the origin serve to identify special locations on the screen. The cursor is a small arrow, displayed with the Alto's display cursor. Its position on the screen is changed by rolling the mouse over the work surface. The mark and the origin are short horizontal and vertical bars, respectively. They provide reference points for the commands described later, and are positioned using the mouse. To emphasize their positions, they blink approximately twice per second.

The status line displays the current values of a number of internal parameters, some of which may be changed by the user. It is updated by SIL whenever any of these quantities change. The significance of the entries in the status line shown in Fig. 4 is as follows:

GLFM: 4210 TFON Space: 10244 Selections: 0 X: 124 Y: 200

The Status Line

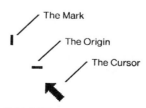
The Mark

The Origin

The Cursor

Fig. 4 Initial SIL screen.

COMPUTER GRAPHICS

GLMF: 4210b

G(4) is the current *grid*. The cursor and all objects added to the display will be constrained to start on points that are multiples of the grid spacing. The grid may be set by the user to any power-of-2 screen units (1,2,4,...). Use of a grid to constrain the placement of objects allows collections of objects with repetitive structure to be drawn easily.

L(2) is the current *line width*. The line width may be set by the user to any value between 1 and 9 screen units, and affects the width of any lines added to the display.

M(1) is the current *magnification*. SIL provides a facility (described later) to "zoom" a subsection of an image to allow precise placement of objects.

F(0b) is the current *font*. Any text characters added to the image will be displayed in this font. Four text fonts, one user macro font, and five library macro fonts are available. Boldface (**b**) and italic (**i**) attributes may be specified for text fonts. The correspondence between SIL font numbers and font file names is made by a group of entries in a *user profile* file. SIL and other applications programs read this file to obtain information user-specific parameters.

TF0N The first three of these indicators display internal state information that is usually useful only to SIL maintainers rather than to users. The fourth indicates the current color, Neutral (black) in this case. Any objects added to the picture will be printed in this color on printers with color capability.

Space: 10244 This entry indicates the number of unused words remaining in the storage pool for objects (i.e., how many more objects may be added to the display). A rectangle requires five words of storage; a string requires five words plus one word for every two characters in the string.

Selections: 0 This entry indicates the number of *selected* objects. Selection is a central idea in SIL, as most commands apply only to selected objects.

X: 124 Y: 200 These entries give the current coordinates of the mark. If a mouse button is depressed while the mouse is moved, the coordinates reported are those of the cursor. This facility allows the screen coordinates of objects to be determined rapidly by holding down a mouse button and pointing to the object.

In addition to the information above, the status line is used to display text used to prompt the user and to echo user input for some commands. For example, the names of input and output files are supplied by the user in this way.

Commands. The user provides commands to SIL using the keyboard and the mouse buttons. Keyboard commands are single *control characters*, generated by depressing the CONTROL key, then depressing the desired character key.

The most frequently used commands are specified with the three mouse buttons, sometimes modified by the CONTROL and SHIFT keyboard keys. The three mouse buttons are named MARK, DRAW, and SELECT, corresponding to their primary functions.

SIL commands use postfix syntax, in that the user specifies a location on the screen or an object or group of objects to be operated upon, then issues the command. All commands are carried as soon as the mouse button or key is depressed, and the only feedback usually given to the user is the command's effect on the contents of the display.

Selection. For commands that apply to existing objects, only the *selected* objects are affected. Selection of a single object is accomplished by moving the mouse so that the cursor lies over some portion of the object, and depressing SELECT. The selected object is displayed in gray (by changing alternate pixels in its bit-map representation white), and if any objects were previously selected, they are deselected and redrawn with solid lines and characters. CONTROL-SELECT is also used to select objects, but in this case, previously selected objects are *not* deselected. This allows the user to select a group of objects as the target of a command. It is also possible to select all objects within a rectangular area. One corner of the area is marked by moving the cursor to its location and depresssing MARK. The opposite corner is then located with the cursor and SHIFT-SELECT is depressed. SIL locates all objects lying completely within the area and selects them.

If an object is inadvertently selected, it may be deselected by pointing at it with the cursor and depressing CONTROL-SHIFT-SELECT. In all operations involving selection or deselection, when objects overlap, SIL chooses the object with the smallest perimeter as the target. When an object or group of objects is selected, the mark and the origin are moved to the upper left corner of the object, for use by later commands.

Adding Objects to the Display. Lines are added to the display by identifying the locations of the endpoints. First, the cursor is placed at one endpoint, and MARK is depressed. This places the mark at the indicated position. Then the cursor is moved to the other endpoint, and DRAW is depressed, drawing the line. Lines will be vertical if the difference of the endpoint x coordinates is less than the difference of the y coordinates, and horizontal otherwise. Lines are drawn at the current line width shown in the status line. The user may change the line width at any time by typing CONTROL-W followed by a single digit.

When a line is drawn, it becomes the selected object, so that it may be the target of a *move* or *copy* command. Also, when a line is drawn, the mark is moved to the endpoint last indicated by the user. This allows a path to be drawn by marking the starting point and depressing DRAW once for each line segment comprising the path.

Text strings are added to the display by positioning the mark (with MARK) and typing the string, terminated by RETURN, ESC, or by depressing any mouse button. Control characters are provided during text entry to backspace over characters, words, or the entire string. Text is added in the current font shown in the status line, and this font can be changed by the user by typing CONTROL-F followed by a digit or a single letter. A digit indicates the font; a letter indicates an attribute (bold or italic) or one of 16 colors indicated by a single letter.

When the string is terminated, the mark is moved down by the height of the particular font used. This amount may be changed to a constant value, allowing text strings to be placed with precise vertical spacing.

Since commands are control characters, the first character of a string can be identified as such. When the first character of a string is typed, SIL enters *Add Text Mode*, and the message "Add Text" is placed in the status line. While the string is being entered, SIL will accept only commands that terminate the string, so it is not possible to change the font during the input. Note that Add Text mode does not violate the principle of modelessness described earlier, since the user does not need to take explicit action to enter the mode.

Changing the Display. Experience with SIL has shown that users spend considerably more time modifying existing drawings than creating new ones. To facilitate rapid changes, SIL provides a number of commands that allow a group of selected objects to be moved, copied, or deleted.

With a frame buffer, moving a large area of the screen is a time-consuming operation, since a large number of words in storage must be moved, and the source and destination are not generally word-aligned. For this reason, SIL does not provide the ability to "drag" collections of objects. Instead, a group of objects are selected, causing the origin to be placed at the upper left corner of the rectangle that bounds the objects; then the user specifies the new position that the origin should occupy by pointing to it and depressing MARK; and finally, the *move* command (CONTROL-X) moves the objects so that their origin is coincident with the new position of the mark. The origin and the mark are then interchanged, so that if the user is not satisfied with the new position, an additional CONTROL-X restores the situation to its original state. This requires three keystrokes per move: one to select the object, one to indicate its destination, and one to do the move. Because moving is a frequent operation, an idiom has been supplied to optimize it. Once the desired selection has been made, the cursor is pointed at the destination, and CONTROL-MARK is depressed. This is equivalent to MARK followed by CONTROL-X. The only reason for retaining the CONTROL-X command is to provide the "undo" feature.

The use of a frame buffer for display refresh introduces a problem when it is necessary to move an object that overlaps another stationary object. The desired effect is that the object should disappear from its original position and reappear at its new position, and that any overlapping objects should not be modified during this process. Although it is possible in principle to achieve this effect, it is computationally expensive, since when the object is being removed from the display, the program must decide for each of its pixels whether the final value will be white or black, depending on whether it is also part of an overlapping stationary object. The strategy used in SIL is considerably simpler and less expensive: When an object is deleted, an area of the display corresponding to the object's bounding rectangle is cleared, deleting the object. The coordinates of the bounding rectangle are passed to a background process whose job is to rebuild the screen by redrawing any objects that lie within the rectangle. The object is then redrawn at its new position. Since the background process cannot run until the object has been redrawn, the user will see the object at its new position, and then the area around the old position of the object will be filled in as the rebuilding process runs.

When a group of objects is moved, each member of the group is deleted individually, and the bounding rectangle passed to the rebuilding process is incrementally expanded to cover the entire set of objects. When all objects have been removed from the display, they are redrawn at their new position and the rebuilder runs as described above. This strategy allows the user to see the objects at their new position rapidly, and keeps the screen consistent. Unless the total area of the object that is moved is large and there are a large number of overlapping objects, the rebuilding process is usually not noticeable.

In addition to moving the selected object, SIL will also stretch or shorten any horizontal or vertical lines attached to the object, provided that the object is moved only in x or y, respectively. This feature was provided to stretch and shorten lines connected to components in logic diagrams, and may be disabled using CONTROL-SHIFT-MARK rather than CONTROL-MARK to move the object.

Copying is similar to moving. The user selects one or more objects, then indicates the new position of the origin using MARK. The *copy* command (CONTROL-C) then draws the selected objects at the new position. An optimization, CONTROL-DRAW, is equivalent to MARK followed by CONTROL-C. After the copies are drawn, the original objects are deselected, the copy is selected, and the origin is moved to the upper left corner of the copy. This allows multiple copies to be made with one depression of CONTROL-DRAW per copy.

Since deletion is a common operation, two commands are provided for it. The first uses a keyboard command (CONTROL-D) to delete all selected objects. The second, SHIFT-DRAW, deletes the object at which the cursor is pointing, and is an abbreviation for SELECT followed by CONTROL-D. When an object is deleted, the origin is moved to the place it occupied, so that it may be replaced by another object using SELECT followed by CONTROL-X or CONTROL-C.

When objects are deleted, they are erased from the display but are not lost irrecoverably. Each deletion causes the selected objects to be placed on a last-in first-out stack, and this stack may be popped (and the objects restored to the display) by the CONTROL-U (undelete) command. The stack holds up to five groups of deleted objects; as more objects are deleted, the earlier ones are lost, and the storage space used by their representations is reclaimed.

Precise Positioning.   SIL provides two commands that allow objects to be placed on the display with high precision. The first provides a "zoom" capability, and is invoked by identifying two opposite corners of a rectangular area with two successive marks, then typing CONTROL-E (expand). SIL executes this command by clearing the screen, calculating the integral magnification that will cause the indicated area to most nearly fill the display, and redrawing the portions of the display that will fit at this magnification. The magnification chosen is reflected in the status line. A second CONTROL-E restores the original display. While magnification is in effect, all other commands continue to operate normally.

The second positioning command provides a limited form of "dragging." It is invoked by selecting an object, indicating a reference point within the object by moving the origin to the point and depressing SHIFT-MARK, then typing CONTROL-S. SIL responds by copying the area around the reference point into the bit map for the hardware cursor, replacing the normal arrow. This patch of the selected object can then be moved about the display rapidly, and if a move (CONTROL-MARK) or copy (CONTROL-DRAW) command is issued, the selected object will be moved or copied such that the reference area in the object exactly overlays the portion of the object in the cursor. The normal arrow is restored by invoking any command other than move or copy.

Macros.   The SIL macro facility allows a number of objects in a drawing to be encapsulated and subsequently treated as a single character. Macros may be user-defined and specific to a particular drawing, or they may be library macros. The definitions for user-defined macros are saved as part of the output file created for the drawing, but since the library macros are used for a number of drawings, their definitions are stored separately on specially named disk files. Font 4 is reserved for user-defined macros, and fonts 5 through 9 contain the definitions for library macros. When a particular library macro character is typed by the user for the first time in Add Text mode, the appropriate library file is read, and the definition is extracted from the file. Subsequent uses of the definition do not incur the disk delay.

To define a group of objects as the macro "M," the user selects the objects that are to make up the macro, and types "CONTROL-LM." SIL responds "Confirm with RETURN," or "Confirm with RETURN to overwrite" if there is already a macro with name "M." If the user issues the confirmation, the definition is created, and the original objects are replaced by an instance of the macro.

A macro definition may be modified by breaking an instance of it into its component objects, or *expanding* it, using the CONTROL-H command. The objects may then be modified individually, and the collection may then be redefined as the original macro. The CONTROL-V (view macro definitions) command puts the names of all existing font 4 macros into the status line, so that the user can determine which names have been used.

The main use of the SIL library facility is to provide a number of macros for digital integrated circuits. Library files are ordinary SIL files, distinguished only by their filenames, and the macro definitions they contain may be modified with SIL in the usual ways. To allow users to determine the contents of the libraries, a catalog is maintained with each library. This catalog consists of a number of SIL files showing the macros used for particular logic components, and the characteristics of the component. Designers keep a hardcopy version of the catalog at hand when using SIL for logic design.

4.7.3   Implementation

SIL is a *simple* illustrator primarily because of the simplicity of its implementation. Four aspects of SIL contributed to the simplicity of the implementation:

1. Since a SIL drawing represents a single 8.5 by 11 in. page, the number of objects will be small, usually between a few hundred and a few thousand. This means that the descriptions of all objects can be kept in main storage, and that simple linear search can be used to locate a particular object given its coordinates.

2. Since all SIL objects are rectangular, the routines to locate, clip, and draw objects on the screen are not complex. In particular, none of these routines require multiplication or division and are therefore quite fast.

3. By treating all complex objects as characters, it is possible to make use of an Alto machine instruction, *Convert*, that ORs the bit-map representation of a character into the display bit map. This increases the speed of these operations considerably over an implementation using load and store instructions.

4. Since SIL is interactive and runs on a personal machine as opposed to a shared system, there is a great deal of idle time available. This background idle time is used to simplify some of the operations required. Two examples are the reconstruction of the user display and reclamation and compaction of storage. Both of these operations are done in the background, and their implementation is simplified by not requiring that they be done rapidly.

In the balance of this section, the important features of the SIL implementation are discussed.

Representation of Objects. Each rectangle, background, and character string, whether a visible part of a drawing or part of a macro definition, is represented in memory by an *object descriptor*. The format of an object descriptor is shown in Fig. 5. It contains the coordinates of the object, its *type*, color, current *state*, and, if the object is a text string, the string itself. This information is sufficient to completely define each object, and is the only source of information about the object used by SIL. The bit map is reconstructed from the object descriptors when necessary.

The type field of an object descriptor determines whether an object is a rectangle or a string, and if it is a string, the font and type face to be used to display it. The I(italic) attribute in the object descriptor is applicable only to text fonts. The state field of the descriptor determines how the object is to be displayed. Objects with State = 0 are displayed normally. Selected objects have State = 1, and are shown in gray. Objects with $1 < State < 7$ are *deleted*. Deleted objects are not displayed, and each time a delete command is issued by the user, the state of all deleted objects is incremented. When the state becomes 7, the object becomes *dead*, and the storage it occupies will be reclaimed. When the user issues an undelete command, the state fields of all deleted objects are decremented, causing the most recently deleted set of objects to become selected. These objects are then displayed.

Each visible object has a single descriptor, and these descriptors are chained together in a singly linked list. A new object descriptor is created, added to the head of the list, and displayed each time the user issues a draw or copy command, or terminates a string in Add Text mode. In addition to descriptors for visible objects, there are also descriptors for components of macro definitions. Each macro definition is a separate list, the head of which is an element of an array (the *Macro Table*) indexed by the font and character that is the macro name. When a macro is defined by the user, the descriptors making up the macro are removed from the list of visible items, their coordinates are made relative to the origin of the macro, and they are chained together starting at the Macro Table entry corresponding to the font character specified by the user. A single descriptor for the macro is then added to the visible object list.

A single routine is used to scan convert an object into the bit map. This routine draws rectangles by ORing into the bit map at the locations determined by the coordinates of the object, converts strings using the machine's Convert instruction, and converts macros by calling itself recursively for each of the objects making up the macro definition.

The files produced by SIL are similar in format to the main storage representation. A SIL file consists of a one-word *password* that identifies the file as a SIL file, followed by a number of records, each one representing a single object. The format of the records is the same as that of an object descriptor, with the exception that the state field is always zero and the link field contains −1 if the record describes a visible object, and contains the (one byte) macro name if the record is part of a macro definition.

Rebuilding the Screen. When an object is initially added to the display, it is necessary only to scan convert it at its proper location, but when objects are moved, the situation is more complex. In this case, it is necessary to redraw any objects that lie within the bounding rectangle of the moved object, since this area is cleared as part of the move. This is done by a *rebuilder* routine that is invoked whenever there are no commands to be processed. The rebuilder is passed the bounding rectangle of the area to be redrawn, and it traverses the entire chain of visible objects, scan converting any objects that lie within this area. Each time an object is inspected, the rebuilder checks for new commands, and processes any that arrive. If a new command modifies the screen before the rebuilder is finished, the rebuilder is restarted at the head of the visible object list, and the size of the bounding rectangle is increased to be the smallest area that covers both the original and the new area. This simple technique works well only because the total number of objects is small and there are excess cycles available. If this were not the case, a more complex data structure that could rapidly locate all objects lying within a given area would be necessary.

Similar considerations apply to the problem of determining which objects are desired when the user makes a selection. SIL must examine the entire visible object list to find the one at the indicated

File:

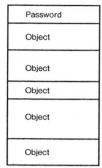

Password
Object
Object
Object
Object
Object

Object Format:

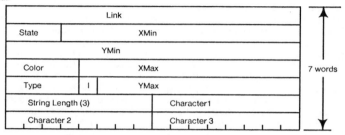

Link	
State	XMin
YMin	
Color	XMax
Type	I	YMax
String Length (3)	Character1
Character 2	Character 3

7 words

Storage:

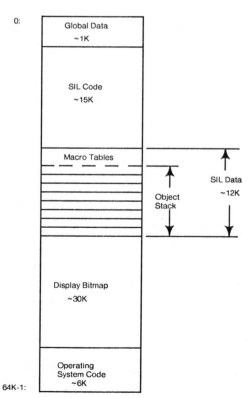

0:

Global Data ~1K
SIL Code ~15K
Macro Tables
Display Bitmap ~30K
Operating System Code ~6K

64K-1:

Object Stack

SIL Data
~12K

Fig. 5 SIL files, objects, and storage layout.

coordinates with the smallest perimeter (if a single item is selected), or to find the set of objects lying in a specified area (in the case of area selection). For a typical display, the time to do a selection is much less than a second, but this is only because the total number of objects is small.

Storage Management.   The amount of storage required for object descriptors expands and contracts as objects are added to and deleted from the display. Because of the small amount of main storage in the Alto, it is important that available space be used efficiently. SIL uses a simple technique that capitalizes on excess cycles to manage storage.

Storage for object descriptors is allocated from a stack. As objects are deleted, "holes" appear in the occupied region of the stack. A compacting routine, called only if there are no commands to be processed and if no screen rebuilding is required, is responsible for eliminating the holes by compacting storage. Like the screen rebuilder, the storage compactor is incremental. It continually traverses the occupied region of storage looking for dead descriptors. When it finds one (or more than one), it copies the first "live" descriptor it finds beyond the dead region down in memory, and readjusts the link field of the descriptor that points to the one that was moved. This causes the dead blocks to "bubble" to the top of the stack. Each time a descriptor is examined, a check for a new command is made so the process is invisible to the user.

4.7.4   SIL APPLICATIONS

The major application of SIL is to produce input for a digital logic design system. Figure 3 shows the information flow in this system, which is composed of several programs in addition to SIL.

The initial input to the system is a set of SIL drawings showing the desired logic, its interconnections, the types of all components, and their locations on a standard Stitchweld board. Each SIL file is processed by *Analyze*, a program that determines the interconnection of the components by interpreting the SIL files. Analyze produces three output files: The first is a "node list" file in text form containing a list of the integrated circuits used in the drawing and the pin numbers connected together by each signal path. The second is a SIL file containing any pin numbers not preassigned by the user. If the user assigns pin numbers in the original drawing, Analyze will check them for validity; otherwise, it will assign them from information in the *component library* file. The SIL file containing pin numbers is merged with the original drawing using SIL to produce the primary system documentation. The third file produced by Analyze is a text file describing any syntactic errors discovered during processing.

A set of node list files describing an entire board are then processed by the *Route* program. Route does further checking for unused or multiply used signal names and pins, and produces a wiring list for the board. Route uses a *board description* file that specifies the locations of all possible components on the type of board being used, and minimizes the overall length of the wiring. The wire list file generated by Route is used to drive a semiautomatic Stitchweld machine that does the actual wiring.

The major limitation of this system is that it does not do automatic component placement. It does eliminate most of the clerical work associated with logic design, and allows designers to produce all the documentation for a system with no support staff. Using this system, it has been possible to design, build, and test prototype boards containing approximately 100 integrated circuits in as little as 2 weeks.

The design system described here was built *after* SIL, when it was realized that the information in a SIL file could be interpreted to generate the interconnection information required by a routing program. SIL itself has no special knowledge of logic design, in contrast to the graphics components of most design automation systems.

SIL has also been used for a number of general-purpose illustration tasks, such as the preparation of the illustrations for this section. Many standard office forms have been prepared as SIL files, and are filled out by individuals using SIL. SIL is also used for preparing charts and tables for reports, and figures for technical publications. A program that merges several text files into a single file suitable for printing has been augmented to allow SIL drawings to be placed at arbitrary locations in these documents, further increasing SIL's utility.

Acknowledgments

A number of individuals have contributed to the success of SIL and the CAD system of which it is a part. Roger Bates implemented the color printing facility, as well as a number of extensions to the original SIL. Ron Pellar developed the font shapes used with SIL. Ed McCreight designed and implemented Route, and Butler Lampson made a number of helpful suggestions for improvements to the user interface.

4.8   COLOR BIT-MAP DISPLAY

Charles R. Minter

This section describes a simple color frame-buffer display designed to be used as a tool in the design of very large scale integrated circuits (VLSI) in a university environment. Some phases of the design of a VLSI circuit are done interactively. This requires that the designer be able to see the current design and to see design changes reflected quickly on the display. Because the function of an integrated circuit is determined by the geometric patterns used to fabricate different layers, the designer, in order to understand a circuit, must be able to see the layers overlapped as they are on the chip itself. A color display is probably the best way to represent this information, using a different color to show each layer.

At different phases of the work, the VLSI designer will want to see the circuit at different scales. At any scale each layer of the circuit is simply a collection of polygons, most of which are rectangles or are easily decomposed into rectangles. At times when large parts of the circuit are viewed at once, much of the low-level detail might be replaced by titled blocks. Nevertheless, the display must be able to display a small number of large rectangles or a large number of small rectangles. In some cases it is necessary to display a mixture of large and small rectangles.

Cost considerations are just as important as technical ones. The displays must be cheap enough so that a modest-size university department can afford several, so that a number of people can be working on designs concurrently.

Finally, the display must fit into the existing computing environment. No changes to the hardware of the central computer (DECsystem-20) or to the software running on it are acceptable. This implies that the display should appear to the central computer to be a terminal, albeit an unusual and very intelligent one. Furthermore, the terminal must communicate with the central computer over a standard RS232 communication line no faster than 9600 baud.

4.8.1   Display

The central feature of the design station is the choice of a color display technology (see Sec. 4.1.1). The need to display a large number of small rectangles suggests that a high-resolution shadow-mask display be used. We selected a raster-scan monitor fabricated by Hitachi that has a mask hole spacing of 0.3 mm over a 19-in. diagonal face, refreshed at 36 Hz. To exploit the usable resolution of this monitor, we require somewhere between 500 and 750 pixels along each axis.

4.8.2   Work Station Computer

The limited communication bandwidth available between the central computer and the display terminal suggests that the commands and data that are passed from the central computer to the display should be at as high a level as feasible. This in turn suggests that there be a computer with the display to interpret the high-level commands from the host, yielding the overall organization shown in Fig. 4.2.9. Once the display controller design is sketched, it is possible to estimate the power this local computer must have by computing the time required to perform a few common functions, such as clearing the screen or drawing a rectangle.

In this project the selection of a local computer was easy: the Digital Equipment Corporation LSI-11 microcomputer. It was clear that 8-bit microprocessors were not powerful enough and that a normal minicomputer was too expensive. The powerful 16-bit microprocessors that are available today would have been ideal, but they were not available at the time. A practical detail that was certainly the most important factor in the selection of a computer was that there were enough LSI-11's available within the department to use a few for displays.

4.8.3   Display Controller

The display controller, positioned between the computer and the raster-scan monitor, must be designed to match the interfaces to the computer and the display. Moreover, the needs of the application must also be kept in mind, for example to ensure that the computer can change the display image fast enough for smooth interaction.

There are two methods for generating raster-scan pictures. The first is to store in a frame buffer memory a digital value for each pixel's intensity and to have a simple processor fetch data from the memory and display it on the screen. The second is to store a display-list description of the screen and to have a complicated processor fetch the data and generate the display. The first technique is simple to implement but uses a lot of memory. The second technique is more complicated to implement but, depending on the length of the display list, could use substantially less memory. It would not be unusual for a VLSI designer to display thousands of rectangles. This would present a major challenge for a designer of a system using display lists.

For reasons of design simplicity we chose to use a frame buffer. As observed above, the resolution of the color tube should be somewhere between 500×500 and 750×750. However, more than twice as many bits are required to store a 750×750 image than are required to store a 500×500 image. Also, it is not clear that the full benefit of the higher resolution could be realized. It might turn out that the problems associated with shadow-mask CRTs result in a display that looks the same at a resolution of 500×500 as it does at a higher resolution. As a result, we chose a 500×500 format.

Pixel Representation.   For a color display it is also necessary to select the number of bits used to represent a pixel. The easiest choice is to use one bit for each of the three colors. This results in eight possible colors, one of which is white and another is black. The choice of colors is not flexible enough to represent overlapping layers of VLSI circuits as is required.

Our design uses a color map or a video lookup table. The frame buffer stores 4 bits for each pixel. The 4 bits that define a pixel's appearance are used as the address of a fast 16×12 random-access memory (RAM). The corresponding 12 bits are fetched and broken into three 4-bit fields. These fields are converted into analog voltages that control the intensity of each of the three colors.

The memory to store the screen image consists of about 250,000 4-bit pixels or about 128 Kbytes. The most economical way to provide this much storage in 1979 was to use 64 16K RAM chips.

Bandwidth Considerations.   As with any CRT image, the display must be repainted many times a second to avoid flicker. This refresh rate is normally 30 Hz, but we chose a display monitor with a 36-Hz refresh rate. To display 250,000 4-bit pixels 36 times each second requires an average data rate of about 4.5 Mbytes/s. In fact, only part of the path traced by the electron beams is used to display an image, so the instantaneous data rate is higher than the average figure given above. Because of the characteristics of the color monitor used with this display, the difference is unusually large. The instantaneous data rate for this display is about 8 Mbytes/s.

The most readily available 16K RAMs at the time of this design had a minimum cycle time of 410 ns. In order to get display information out of the RAMs at 8 Mbytes/s, at least 32 bits must be fetched at once. If 32 bits were fetched at once during the 30 to 40 μs in each scan line when data are needed at the full instantaneous rate, all the memory cycles would be used to fetch the data to be displayed.

The frame buffer must also allocate memory cycles to the computer. It would be possible to limit these accesses to the 15 to 20 μs periods in each scan line during horizontal retrace when no display data are needed or to provide enough buffering of the data to be displayed that update cycles could be inserted with no loss of display data. Both of these approaches have obvious disadvantages. Instead, the memory is arranged so that 64 bits can be fetched at once. The display then requires at most half the memory cycles to refresh the screen.

Accessing the Frame Buffer.   The LSI-11 changes the image on the screen by altering the contents of the frame buffer memory. We must design a mechanism for the computer to access the memory.

For the LSI-11 to address each byte of the 128K-byte display memory requires 17 bits of address. Since the LSI-11 has only 16 bits in its addresses, it cannot directly address the entire display memory. Two techniques were considered to provide access to the memory. The first uses four I/O control registers to cause reads and writes to the display memory. The second uses a mapping scheme to allow the LSI-11 to address directly a subset of the display memory.

Four registers are used in the first technique: a control register, a read address register, a write address register, and a data register. When the LSI-11 writes an address into the read address register, the data register is loaded with the contents of the byte in display memory specified by the read address. When an address is written into the write address register, the contents of the data register are written into the display memory byte specified by the write address. Because the address registers are both 16 bits long, an extra address bit for each of them is stored in the control register.

This technique has one advantage and two disadvantages. The advantage is that very little address space of the LSI-11 is used to provide access to all 128K bytes of the display memory. The first disadvantage is that byte access to the display memory is not as convenient and natural as it is with directly addressable memory. The other disadvantage is that logical operations on the data in the display are more round-about than they would be in a directly addressed memory.

The second access technique, selected for implementation, provides direct access to a selectable subset of the display memory through a memory map. The high-order 4 bits of the LSI-11 address are used as an address of a 16×8 high-speed RAM. Five of the output bits of this RAM replace the 4 high-order bits of the LSI-11 address, thus generating a 17-bit frame buffer memory address; the remaining bit tells whether or not memory references to that segment of LSI-11 address space are to be mapped to the display memory. This scheme allows the mapping of 4K-byte segments of LSI-11 address space into arbitrary 4K-byte pages of the display memory. Because the initial contents of the mapping RAM after power is applied is random, a master enable bit is provided in a control register to inhibit mapping of memory references until the mapping RAM is loaded with legal mapping information.

Memory Organization. There are two ways to organize the LSI-11's view of the frame buffer memory. One way is to allow the computer to access in one 16-bit word four horizontally adjacent 4-bit pixels. The addressing order of the words would be the same as the scan order used by the display. The other approach is to allow the computer to reference in a word the same bit from 16 horizontally adjacent pixels. The next word would be the same bit from the next 16 pixels in scan order, and so on. This has the effect that the low-order bits from all the pixels occupy the first 32K-byte section of display memory, all the next-to-low-order bits occupy the next 32K-byte section, and so on.

The different bits in each pixel are often used to represent different layers in a VLSI design, which are generally drawn one at a time. It is more convenient for the intended application of the display to use the second approach to organize the display memory. Moreover, by mapping only one bit at a time into the LSI-11 address space, the entire display (250,000 bits) can be addressed directly.

4.8.4   Detailed Design of the Display Controller

The display controller is divided into five parts: timing and control, the LSI-11 interface, TV sync and address generation, video shift registers and color map, and frame buffer memory. Its detailed design is shown in Fig. 1.

Timing and Control. The time base for the display is provided by a crystal oscillator running at about 15 MHz. This is the rate at which pixels are displayed (67 ns/pixel). All the timing and control signals for the rest of the display are derived from this clock. The output of the crystal oscillator is connected to the clock input of a 4-bit counter. This counter counts all the time and its outputs continuously cycle through 16 states. There are a number of signals in the display that are a function of these states only. These signals are derived by connecting the outputs of the counter to the address inputs of a PROM; the outputs of the PROM are in turn connected to the inputs of a set of flip-flops. These flip-flops are also clocked by the 15-MHz clock. Thus these control signals are synchronized with the master clock.

The control signals can be divided into three rough categories: LSI-11 interface control, video control, and memory control. Most of the signals generated by this section of logic are in the first category. Each of these sections will be discussed in detail later.

The timing PROM is programmed to divide the 16 timing states into two eight-state sequences. It is possible to execute a display memory cycle in each of these sequences. The first of the two sequences in every 16-state sequence is used to fetch 64 bits to be displayed and the second is used to read or write 16 bits for the LSI-11. The timing PROM used (74S288) has only five address inputs. Four of these are used for the timing counter. The other address input is used to indicate whether or not the LSI-11 is requesting a memory cycle. The PROM does not have enough information to determine whether data are needed for the display. So a memory cycle is always executed during the first eight-state sequence whether the data will be used or not.

These cycles are not entirely wasted. As will be described later, the cycles during horizontal retrace are used to refresh the dynamic RAMs. The cycles that take place during vertical retrace but not horizontal retrace are wasted. Their only cost, however, is to increase the power consumption in the RAMs by about 5 percent.

LSI-11 Interface. There is circuitry in the display to synchronize the asynchronous LSI-11 bus to the entirely synchronous display. This circuitry synchronizes every reference the LSI-11 makes to the display, whether it is strictly necessary or not. This technique results in simpler circuitry that may take longer than necessary to do some operations.

As described above, every other display memory cycle from a fixed pattern of possible cycles is potentially available to the LSI-11. Synchronization of LSI-11 operations on the display is based on when these LSI-11 display memory cycles can occur. About 260 ns before an LSI-11 display memory cycle could begin, the timing and control circuitry produces a pulse that clocks a type-D flip-flop. The data input to this flip-flop is a signal that is high if the LSI-11 is requesting any operation on the display, and low otherwise. Of course, this request signal can occur at any time with respect to the clock signal of the flip-flop. In particular the setup- or hold-time requirements of the flip-flop might be violated. It is possible for the flip-flop to enter a metastable state if the data input is changing when it is clocked. The probability that the flip-flop remains in this metastable state decays exponentially with time past the normal propagation delay of the flip-flop. About 60 ns before an LSI-11 memory cycle can begin, the output of the flip-flop is clocked into another type-D flip-flop by another pulse,

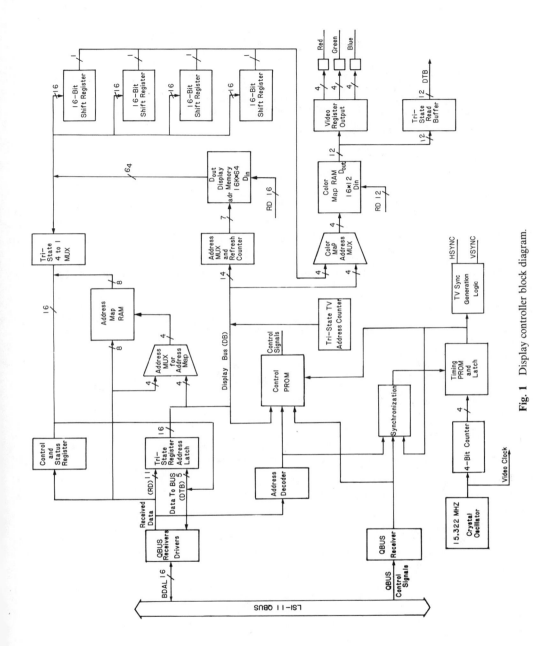

Fig. 1 Display controller block diagram.

produced by the timing and control section. Thus the output of the first flip-flop has about 200 ns to reach a stable state. The probability that the output of the first flip-flop is still in a metastable state at this time is exceedingly small.

The output of the second flip-flop is a signal synchronized with the master clock which indicates that the LSI-11 is requesting some operation on the display. This signal is used as the fifth address input to the timing PROM in the timing and control section described above. If this signal is asserted, then at the appropriate time in the 16-state timing cycle the PROM asserts signals that will cause a display memory cycle and that will enable the outputs of a control PROM that will cause any other actions that are appropriate.

The LSI-11 interface communicates with the rest of the display via three 16-bit buses. One of these buses always contains the outputs of the LSI-11 bus receivers and another is the bus driver register inputs. The third is the internal address bus for the display memory.

The LSI-11 uses a multiplexed address and data bus. The outputs of the bus receivers for the low-order 12 bits are latched while the address for the current bus cycle is on the bus. The bus receiver outputs for the high-order 4 bits go to the address inputs of the mapping RAM at this time; the outputs of this RAM are latched instead of the high-order 4 bits of the LSI-11 address. The bus receiver outputs also go to the data inputs of the mapping RAM, the display memory, the color-map RAM, and the control register.

The bus connected to the inputs of the bus drivers is driven by one of several tristate sources. The sources are the mapping RAM, the display memory output multiplexers, color-map RAM output buffers, and the control register. Which of these sources is driving the bus is determined by the outputs of the control PROM described above. The bus drivers used have a built-in register. This register is clocked at the end of the timing sequence in which an LSI-11 operation was actually performed. Both the display memory and the color-map RAM are used to refresh the CRT image, so they cannot hold their outputs indefinitely. On the other hand, the LSI-11 expects devices to hold data on the bus until the LSI-11 bus cycle is complete. The built-in bus register allows the display to keep the data on the LSI-11 bus as long as they are needed while the display memory and the color-map RAM continue to refresh the CRT.

The third bus is the internal address bus. It is a time-multiplexed bus driven by either the register that latched the LSI-11 address or the TV-address counters. Which of these two sources drives the bus is determined by the timing and control section. During the first half of the 16-state timing cycle, the TV-address counters drive the bus whether or not data are being fetched to be displayed, and the LSI-11 address register is driving the bus during the second half, whether or not an LSI-11 memory cycle is active.

TV Sync and Address Generation.   One of the signals from the timing and control section is connected to the sync generation logic. Because the color monitor used in the display is not RS-170 compatible, it was not possible to use any of the commercially available TV sync generation chips. The circuitry described below is flexible enough to have allowed the conversion of the interlaced color display described here into a noninterlaced high-resolution black-and-white display with very little work. Specifically, it is necessary to change two PROMs and to provide a different video clock frequency.

The sync signals and related internal control signals are generated by two finite-state machines—one for horizontal control and the other for vertical control. Each machine consists of two counters and a PROM. The first counter determines how long each state of the machine will last and the second contains the current state. When the first counter overflows, it increments the second counter and causes itself to be reloaded at the next clock pulse. The new contents of the first counter come from the outputs of the PROM. The PROM address is the output of the second counter. Another output of the PROM is a reset signal for the second counter. The remaining outputs of the PROM can be used as control signals. By appropriately loading the PROM it is possible to generate a complex repeating sequence of signals.

The horizontal machine uses two 4-bit counters and one 32×8 PROM. The first counter is enabled all the time, counting at 15 MHz. Only two of the outputs of the PROM are used to specify the duration of the next state. This means that there are only four possible durations. The possible ones are determined by the connection pattern and are 1, 2, 15, and 16 clock periods. One of the outputs of the horizontal PROM is an enable signal for the vertical state machine.

The vertical machine consists of two 4-bit counters for the first counter, one 4-bit counter for the second counter, and a 32×8 PROM. The enable signal from the horizontal counter occurs twice during each horizontal cycle. This allows the vertical machine to step at the end or in the middle of a horizontal cycle. This flexibility is necessary to generate interlaced sync signals. Six of the eight PROM outputs are used to load the duration counter. For this machine both the remaining two PROM outputs are used as machine outputs, so no signal is available to reset the state counter. This state machine cycles through all 16 possible states.

Control signals from these machines are used to enable the loading of the video shift registers and the incrementing of the TV address counters.

The TV address counters are included with the sync generation logic in the partition of the display controller because most of their control comes from that logic. These counters are incremented at the end of the first of the two eight-state sequences by the same clock signal that steps the sync state machines. The address counters are enabled to count only if they were used to fetch data that were to be displayed. The counters have tristate outputs that are connected to the bus that provides the address to the display memory. The outputs of these counters are enabled during the first half of the 16-state timing cycle.

The counters can be loaded with data from the display memory at the end of each scan line. This linked list display format has two advantages. First, it is possible to set up these links in such a way that peculiarities of addressing interlaced display memory are hidden from the LSI-11. Second, with a small amount of extra circuitry, it is possible to do very fast vertical scrolling with a single scan-line resolution. This mode is controlled by a bit that the LSI-11 can set or clear. When the bit is clear, the normal mode of operation, no extra memory is used and the counter is incremented after each display memory fetch. The counter is cleared when the vertical state counter overflows.

Video Shift Registers and Color Map. One of the control signals is used to control the video section. This signal provides a pulse for one of the 16 timing states. It is used to clock the sync generation logic and the TV address counters described above and to generate the signal to load the video shift registers. The 64 bits from the display memory are connected to the parallel inputs of eight 8-input parallel-in serial-out synchronous shift registers (74LS166). The clock input of the shift registers is the buffered output of the crystal oscillator. The shift registers are connected to make four independent 16-input parallel-in serial-out shift registers. The shift-in input of each of these registers is grounded so that when these registers are not loaded they will shift out zeros.

The shift registers are loaded at the end of each display memory cycle. The load input to the shift registers is a combination of a timing signal from the timing and control section and a control signal from the sync generation section. The pulse from the timing and control section comes at the end of the first eight-state sequence. This pulse is ANDED with a signal from the sync generation section that is present only when data are to be displayed.

The fact that the timing section cycles through 16 states means that the 16-bit-long shift registers will be displaying the last pixel loaded during the previous 16-state cycle when they receive the signal to load new data. On the next clock pulse they will begin displaying the first pixel of the new data. Thus there should be no discontinuity between 16-pixel groups.

As mentioned previously, the 4-bit pixel information passes through a color map before being displayed. The 4 bits from the shift registers pass through a quad two-to-one multiplexer and from there to the address inputs of three fast 16×4 RAMs. The outputs of these RAMs are loaded into flip-flops clocked by the master clock to resynchronize the video data with the clock. The outputs of these flip-flops go to a digital-to-analog converter implemented with a weighted resistor ladder. The outputs of the DACs are connected to the red, green, and blue inputs of the color monitor.

The LSI-11 can read and write the color-map RAM. The other inputs to the address multiplexer come from the internal address bus. At the time the color map is read or written by the LSI-11, the latched LSI-11 address will be on this bus. The select line of the multiplexer comes from the control PROM in the LSI-11 interface section. If the LSI-11 is trying to read or write the color-map RAM, the latched LSI-11 address will be applied to the address inputs of the RAM. The data inputs to the RAM come from the outputs of the LSI-11 bus receivers, so that when a write command is issued data from the LSI-11 are written into the color map. The output of the RAM is connected to a tristate buffer whose output is connected to the bus going to the input to the bus drivers. As described in the LSI-11 interface section, the data on this bus are latched at the end of the LSI-11 operation. This allows the color map to resume its normal function while the LSI-11 picks up the latched data some time later.

Although the RAMs used in the color map are fast enough so that it should be possible to squeeze a cycle for the LSI-11 between two successive video cycles, this is not done. About three or four extra components were necessary to implement this feature in a conservative way. It did not seem that such a feature was worth these extra components. When the LSI-11 reads or writes the color-map RAM, the LSI-11 address is passed through the multiplexer to the RAMs for two video clock periods. This causes the video outputs to go to an unpredictable state for these two clock periods. In the intended application, accesses of the color-map RAM by the LSI-11 are infrequent and are usually associated with gross changes in the display. As a consequence, these minor glitches have not been a problem.

Frame Buffer Memory. The image memory is provided by 64 16K RAMs that are organized as a 16K by 64-bit memory for the display and as a 64K by 16-bit memory for the LSI-11. As discussed in the section on timing and control, there are either one or two cycles of the memory every microsecond, depending on whether or not the LSI-11 has requested a cycle.

During a display cycle the low-order 14 bits of the 16-bit internal address bus are used to fetch one bit from the same location in each of the 64 RAMs. The timing and control section generates the row-address strobe (RAS) and column-address strobe (CAS) signals for the RAMs. It also produces the row enable signal to the address multiplexer. Write enable signals to the RAMs are inhibited during display cycles.

During an LSI-11 cycle the low-order 14 bits of the internal address bus are used to select one bit from each of 16 RAMs. The high-order 2 bits of the address bus that are ignored during a display cycle are used to select which set of 16 RAMs are accessed as described below. Again the timing and control generates all the required control signals for the RAMs and the address multiplexer.

There are four RAS and four CAS signals, each shared by 16 RAMs. These signals are provided by two one-of-four decoders with enable and polarity control. The controls on the decoders work such that when the decoders are disabled, the outputs are either all high or all low, depending on the state of the polarity signal. When the decoders are enabled, the selected one of the four outputs will be in the opposite state from the other three outputs. The display RAS and CAS signals are wired to the polarity control of the decoders and the LSI-11 RAS and CAS signals are wired to the enable control. The timing and control section ensures that only one set of these signals will be asserted in a memory cycle. Therefore, the display RAS and CAS signals activate all 64 RAMs, whereas the LSI-11 RAS and CAS signals activate only the selected 16. The address lines into the decoders come from the high-order 2 bits on the internal address bus, and at the time the decoders are enabled the address from the LSI-11 will be on that bus.

Because 64 bits are needed in parallel during display cycles, the outputs of the RAMs must be separate. Tristate four-to-one multiplexers are used to select which set of 16 bits the LSI-11 is reading. The multiplexers are enabled by a signal from the control PROM of the LSI-11 interface section. Just as with the color-map RAMs, the outputs of the multiplexer are latched in the bus driver register so that the display RAM can fetch data to display on the next cycle.

The 16-bit bus from the LSI-11 bus receivers is connected to the data inputs of the display RAMs so that each bit goes to its corresponding four RAMs. There are two write enable wires for the entire array. One is connected to the write-enable inputs of all the RAMs for high-order bytes, and the other is connected to all the low-order byte RAMs. The selection of which RAMs to write is done by the RAS and CAS signals. If the LSI-11 executes a write byte operation, the appropriate write enable signal will be asserted. If the LSI-11 executes a write word operation, both of the write enable signals will be asserted.

It is often the case that the ordered fetching of data to be displayed in a bit-map display will refresh the dynamic RAMs that contain the display image. The flexibility offered by the linked list mechanism in this display makes it possible for a programmer to alter the order in which words in the display RAMs are accessed so that the dynamic RAMs are not refreshed as required. For this reason the display hardware automatically refreshes the display RAMs. As mentioned before, the display cycles that take place during horizontal retrace are used to refresh the RAMs. The address multiplexer chip also contains a refresh counter. The contents of this counter are forced onto the address lines of the display RAMs during display cycles that occur during horizontal retrace. The display RAS and CAS signals occur normally. Although it is not necessary to assert CAS during refresh cycles, inhibiting these unnecessary signals would require extra components.

Packaging.   Packaging considerations played a major role in many of the decisions made during the course of the design of the display. We decided very early in the design to use the LSI-11 as the control computer. We hoped to be able to limit the number of components used in the implementation of the display so that the entire display could be laid out on a printed-circuit board that would fit in the LSI-11 mounting box. The benefits of this would be substantial—no extra box or power supply would be needed for the display.

About 135 integrated circuits are used in the display; 64 of these are the 16K memory chips that make up the display memory. Using current printed-circuit technology it should be possible to fit 135 integrated circuits on the 8×10 in. board space available. It would probably be difficult to fit many more chips on the board. For this reason we were extremely reluctant to include any feature that added components. As it turned out, however, not enough displays were made to make it worthwhile to design a printed-circuit board; all the displays were wire-wrapped.

REFERENCES

1. J. E. BRESENHAM, "Algorithm for Computer Control of a Digital Plotter," *IBM Syst. J.*, **4**(1), 25–30 (1965).

2. Y. CHU, *Digital Simulation of Continuous Systems*, McGraw-Hill, New York, 1969.

3. S. COHEN, "Speakeasy—A Window into a Computer," *1976 AFIPS Nat. Comput. Conf. Proc.*, **45**, 1039–1048 (1976).

4. S. DAVIS, *Computer Data Displays*, Prentice-Hall, Englewood Cliffs, N.J., 1969.

5. EIA, *EIA Standard RS-170*, "Electric Performance Standards—Monochrome Television Studio Facilities," Electronic Industries Association, New York, 1957.

6. O. I. ELGERD, *Control Systems Theory*, McGraw-Hill, New York, 1967.

7. Evans and Sutherland Computer Corporation, "Line Drawing System Model 1: System Reference Manual," Evans and Sutherland Computer Corp., Salt Lake City, Utah, 1971.

8. Evans and Sutherland Computer Corporation, "Picture System 2 User's Manual," Evans and Sutherland Computer Corp., Salt Lake City, Utah, May 1977.

9. R. FITZHUGH, "Mathematical Models of Excitation and Propagation in Nerve," in *Biological Engineering*, H. P. Schwan (ed.), McGraw-Hill, New York, 1965, pp. 1–86.

10. G. E. FORSYTHE, and C. B. MOLER, *Computer Solution of Linear Algebraic Systems*, Prentice-Hall, Englewood Cliffs, N.J., 1967.

11. G. F. GRONER ET AL., "BIOMOD: An Interactive Graphics Computer System for Modeling," Rand Corp. Report R-617-NIH, July 1971.

12. G. D. KNOTT, "Mlab—A Mathematical Modeling Tool," *Comput. Programs Biomed.*, **10**(3), 271–280 (Dec. 1979).

13. G. D. KNOTT and D. K. REECE, "Mlab: A Civilized Curve-Fitting System," *Proc. ONLINE '72 Int. Conf.*, Brunel University, England, Sept. 1972, Vol. 1, pp. 497–526.

14. R. M. METCALFE and D. R. BOGGS, "Ethernet: Distributed Packet Switching for Local Computer Networks," *Commun. ACM* **19**(7), 395–404 (July 1976).

15. W. M. NEWMAN, "Display Procedures," *Commun. Assoc. Comput. Mach.*, **14**(10), 651 (Oct. 1971).

16. W. M. NEWMAN and R. F. SPROULL, *Principles of Interactive Computer Graphics*, 2nd ed., McGraw-Hill, New York, 1979.

17. S. SHERR, *Fundamentals of Display System Design*, Wiley-Interscience, New York, 1970.

18. K. R. SLOAN and C. M. BROWN, "Color Map Techniques," *Comput. Graphics Image Process.*, **10**(4), 297–317 (Aug. 1977).

19. R. F. SPROULL, "Omnigraph: Simple Terminal-Independent Graphics Software," Xerox Palo Alto Research Center, CSL-73-4, 1973.

20. R. F. SPROULL, "Raster Graphics for Interactive Programming Environments," *Comput. Graphics*, **13**(2), 83–93 (Aug. 1979).

21. R. F. SPROULL and I. E. SUTHERLAND, "A Clipping Divider," *FJCC 1968*, Thompson Books, Washington, D.C., p. 765.

22. C. P. THACKER ET AL., "Alto: A Personal Computer," in *Computer Structures, Principles and Examples*, 2nd ed., D. P. Siewiorek, C. G. Bell, and A. Newell (eds.), McGraw-Hill, New York, 1981.

23. E. L. THOMAS, *Tenex E&S Display Software*, Bolt Beranek and Newman, Cambridge, Mass., Dec. 1971.

INDEX

497